CW01021103

The History of Government

VOLUME I

The
History of Government
From the Earliest Times

VOLUME I

ANCIENT MONARCHIES AND EMPIRES

S. E. Finer

OXFORD UNIVERSITY PRESS

1997

Oxford University Press, Great Clarendon Street, Oxford OX2 6DP

Oxford New York

Athens Auckland Bangkok Bogota Bombay Buenos Aires
Calcutta Cape Town Dar es Salaam Delhi
Florence Hong Kong Istanbul Karachi
Kuala Lumpur Madras Madrid Melbourne
Mexico City Nairobi Paris Singapore
Taipei Tokyo Toronto
and associated companies in
Berlin Ibadan

Oxford is a trade mark of Oxford University Press

Published in the United States
by Oxford University Press Inc. New York

© C. J. Finer 1997

All rights reserved. No part of this publication may be reproduced,
stored in a retrieval system, or transmitted, in any form or by any means,
without the prior permission in writing of Oxford University Press.
Within the UK, exceptions are allowed in respect of any fair dealing for the
purpose of research or private study, or criticism or review, as permitted
under the Copyright, Designs and Patents Act, 1988, or in the case of
reprographic reproduction in accordance with the terms of the licences
issued by the Copyright Licensing Agency. Enquiries concerning
reproduction outside these terms and in other countries should be
sent to the Rights Department, Oxford University Press,
at the address above

British Library Cataloguing in Publication Data
Data available

Library of Congress Cataloging in Publication Data
Data applied for

ISBN 0–19–820664–X

1 3 5 7 9 10 8 6 4 2

Typeset by J&L Composition Ltd, Filey, North Yorkshire
Printed in Great Britain
on acid-free paper by
Biddles Ltd., Guildford and King's Lynn

PREFACE

It was S. E. Finer's enduring wish that this, his most ambitious and encompassing work, would be published in one piece rather than as a 'mere' series of volumes. His feelings on the subject were understandable. For all its size and weight and number of years in preparation, the *History* is manifestly a single, sustained exercise in comparative analysis over time and space. It is the product, by the same token, of a single, magnificently sustained 'retirement' programme of research, consultation, and writing, for which he never lost zest and courage. Even so, Finer acknowledged towards the end that, for all his own repeated efforts to cut down on the length of the manuscript, it might prove physically impracticable to produce the *History* in one volume. This has indeed turned out to be the case, and it is for this reason, none other, that the present publication consists of three volumes to be brought out simultaneously.

A deteriorating heart condition progressively slowed him down and, at the last, prevented the work from being fully completed and the text finalized as he would have wished. Yet viewed from an opposite perspective—Finer's own perspective—he survived 'what should have been a fatal heart attack' in 1987 to be able to devote no less than six extra years to the pursuit *par excellence* of this, his last and greatest project. That he did not succeed in finishing the work has to be a matter for regret. But that he managed to complete no less than thirty-four out of the projected thirty-six chapters, in addition to introducing each 'Book'—including the final, unfinished Book V—with an overview forecasting and summing up its contents and import, should be cause for thanksgiving.

The *idea* of writing the History of Government as his retirement project had struck Finer—with typical aplomb—as a stroke of genius. Once settled on the idea (a matter of days rather than weeks), he could hardly wait to get started. As he saw it, and as has so emphatically turned out to be the case, it was to be the summation and culmination of all that he had worked at and stood for, throughout his long career as a political scientist and historian of seemingly tireless imagination, inventiveness, and sheer appetite for the mix of scholastic erudition with street-level realism he had made his own.

To be sure, this great idea did not necessarily strike others with the same force at the time. The then Social Science Research Council, for instance, was politely sceptical as to the entire project's viability, given its proposed 'combination of historical and analytic typologies' (the *essence* of Finer's approach in this consummate case), the dubiousness of the proposed periodization, and the insufficiency of the proposed selection of regimes from one period to the next.[1] Consequently his request for research grant funds was reluctantly turned down by this particular gathering of peer reviewers and it was left to the Nuffield Foundation generously to support Finer's endeavours thereafter, with a recurrent grant-in-aid of secretarial and manuscript production costs.

Inevitably, for all his meticulousness as scholar and author, the text Finer finally left behind was in an unfinished state. But this was a point—indeed likelihood—he had already anticipated and for which he had prepared. The 'Editorial Notes' left on the hard disk of his computer, continuously updated from 1987 for the benefit of whomsoever might be faced with the task of sorting out the unfinished manuscript, have themselves, lightly edited, furnished 'The Conceptual Prologue' to the entire work as now presented.

The range, depth, and complexity of the original enterprise, compounded by the varying state of completion of its different parts, meant that preparation of the final total manuscript for publication had very much to be a collective endeavour. All the experts that Finer himself had originally approached for advice and comment with regard to particular topics and/or periods were, so far as practicable, approached again—in addition to others variously suggested or deemed appropriate—for final points of correction with regard to facts, dates, and above all footnote references (one of the major practical problems being that Finer's own bibliography program had proved disastrously over-ambitious for his computer to cope with). The names of those thus consulted are listed at the end of this Preface. Their generosity of response is testimony to a continuing academic sense of community, with which Finer himself would have been as proud as he was happy to be associated. There has, of course, been no attempt to interfere with Finer's own interpretation of events and developments. Since specialists are prone to have their own views about particular episodes, if not entire epochs, in a country's or a continent's experience of government—not least when confronted by a comparativist on the grand scale at which Finer operated—their restraint on this occasion has been exemplary.

The British Academy, of whose Politics Section Finer was such a distinguished member, provided a grant of £2,500 towards the editorial costs of preparing the enormous manuscript for publication, for which we are most grateful. Special thanks are due to Vernon Bogdanor, who read through and offered detailed comments on the entire text, and to Jean Blondel, Ghiţa

---

[1] Correspondence 19. 11. 81—Catherine Jones Finer.

Ionescu, and Isabel de Madariaga for their careful reading of all of the unfinished Book Five. Humaira Ahmed has been in charge, literally from start to finish, of the book's processing, re-processing, and final preparation for publication, a case of 'beyond the call of duty' if ever there was one. Cesare Onestini chased up many of the 'computer lost' bibliographic loose-ends. Countless librarians across the universities of Oxford and Birmingham have in their turn responded with courteous patience, know-how, and inventiveness to requests for further (and further) bibliographic advice. Oxford University Press—in the persons of Tony Morris and copy-editor Jeff New in particular—has shown consideration, imagination, and enthusiasm in seeing this project through to completion. Of the actual editorial team, Jack Hayward has been responsible for orchestrating the collective effort and incorporating many, usually detailed, amendments suggested by our specialists, while Catherine Jones Finer has been responsible for the mammoth task of putting together the final version of the text.

A quite different order of thanks is due to members of staff of the John Radcliffe Hospital and of the 19 Beaumont Street Surgery, Oxford, who between them strove to keep S. E. Finer alive, alert, entertained and entertaining, able and eager to work for as long as he did. There is no way that one can put a value on such support, except to say that he counted himself, as did his wife, so very lucky to be in receipt of such care, concern, and friendship throughout.

Specialist Advisers

Professor J. R. Baines (Oriental Institute, Oxford), Dr Jeremy Black (Oriental Institute, Oxford), Professor P. Brunt (retired), Mr George Cawkwell (retired), Dr Patricia Crone (Gonville and Caius College, Cambridge), Professor Sir John Elliott (Oriel College, Oxford), Dr David Faure (St Antony's College, Oxford), Mr Peter Fraser (All Souls College, Oxford), Professor G. Holmes (retired), Dr J. Howard-Johnston (Modern History Faculty, Oxford), Mr Peter Lewis (All Souls College), Professor J. H. W. G. Liebeschuetz (retired), Professor D. L. McMullen (Oriental Institute, Cambridge), Professor F. G. B. Millar (Brasenose College, Oxford), Dr E. W. Nicholson (Provost, Oriel College, Oxford), Professor Tapan Raychaudhuri (retired), Dr John Robertson (St Hugh's College, Oxford), Dr Ann Waswo (St Antony's College, Oxford).

Catherine Jones Finer
Jack Hayward
Oxford, November 1995

CONTENTS

VOLUME II
The Intermediate Ages

BOOK III

PART I. EASTERN EUROPE AND THE MIDDLE EAST

VOLUME III
Empires, Monarchies, and the Modern State

BOOK IV. ANCIENT EMPIRES AND NEW MONARCHIES, 1500–1776

PART I. ASIA

The Conceptual Prologue

T he intention of this work is to provide a history of successive forms of government throughout the world from the earliest times to the present day. Not every form will be described. This would be quite unnecessary. The regimes discussed will be selected; and the criteria of selection remain exactly the same as I anticipated as early as 1983: 'first, the historically great and mighty polities, next the archetypal polities, thirdly innovators great or small; and, finally, the vivid variant.'[1]

This being so, this *History* will, *inter alia*, attempt to do the following things:

1. establish the space/time distribution of the selected forms of government, ground each one of these in its geographical/historical context, analyse each according to a standard format, and assess its general character, strengths, and weaknesses according to a standardized set of criteria;
2. identify similarities and differences between the forms of government described, according to a standardized TYPOLOGY; identify RECURRENT THEMES; and identify, with the aid of the Typology, those elements in these various forms of government that can be described as INVENTIONS.

For the purposes of this introductory discourse, we will take the Recurrent Themes first, before explaining and expounding the Typology; leaving the identification of Inventions to the last.

1. RECURRENT THEMES

This *History of Government* is a history of polities, which can be defined as 'the structures of government under which groups of men live, and its relationship towards them'.[2] This concept therefore subsumes tribes as well as states. Yet my concern is with states. Significantly, Easton and, for that matter, other functionalists like Almond dispensed with the word and the concept of the state; the word does not appear even once in the index to

---

[1] S. E. Finer, 'Perspectives in the World History of Government—A Prolegomenon', *Government and Opposition*, 18:1 (Winter, 1983). 8. [2] Ibid. 4.

Easton's *Systems Analysis of Political Life*.[3] It is heartening to know that in swimming against the functionalist tide of the 1960s, I was in fact riding the wave of the future. Everywhere today 'the state' is back in fashion, and the discussion of the polity and its evolution is everywhere conducted in terms of it.[4]

1.1. *State Building*

As the *History* makes clear, the state may have antedated writing, and, in my view, it certainly did. At all events it is coeval with the first written documents, whether these are located in Mesopotamia, or Egypt. It is therefore coeval with 'history' as we understand this term. Unquestionably tribes have government and are polities; and there have been times when the tribe conquered the state—for example, this happened many a time in China, when the northern tribesmen—be they Huns or Mongols or Tartars or Manchu—invaded and took over parts of the empire and, at times, seized the whole of it. But in all such cases the tribesmen either disintegrated if they tried to retain their tribal identity in the midst of the settled population, or alternatively they so adapted themselves to becoming its ruling class that they assimilated to its form of polity. As a form of polity, the tribe was, in Patricia Crone's expressive phrase, an 'evolutionary dead end'.[5]

How, then, define the state? Contemporary states possess five characteristics; but pre-modern ones usually possessed only the first three of them, and in many contemporary states the fourth and the fifth characteristics are still not present, or are present only to a slight degree. The characteristics are as follows:

1. They are territorially defined populations each recognizing a common paramount organ of government.
2. This organ is served by specialized personnel; a civil service, to carry out decisions and a military service to back these by force where necessary and to protect the association from similarly constituted associations.
3. The state so characterized is recognized by other similarly constituted states as independent in its action on its territorially defined—and hence

---

[3] See my critique of Almond in S. E. Finer, 'Almond's Concept of the "Political System"—A Textual Critique', *Government and Opposition*, 5:1 (Winter, 1970), 3–21.

[4] Cf. for instance, M. Mann, 'The Autonomous Power of the State', in J. A. Hall (ed.), *States in History* (Blackwell, Oxford, 1986); A. Giddens, *The Nation-State and Violence: Volume Two of A Contemporary Critique of Historical Materialism* (Polity, Cambridge, 1985; repr. 1987); R. M. MacIver, *The Web of Government* (Macmillan, New York, 1947; repr. 1965); K. Lowenstein, *Political Power of the Governmental Process*, 2nd edn. (University of Chicago Press, 1965), and so forth.

[5] P. Crone, 'The Tribe and the State', in Hall (ed.), *States In History*, 73.

confined—population, that is, on its subjects. This recognition constitutes what we would today call its international 'sovereignty'.

As we shall see, many pre-modern states merely approximated to these three conditions. For instance, many had fluid boundaries, in many the organs of government were but poorly differentiated, and the mutual recognition of each other's 'sovereignty' was irregular, intermittent, and served by very imperfect instruments.

The last two characteristics are more problematic. They are:

4. Ideally at least, but to a large extent in practice also, the population of the state forms a community of feeling—a *Gemeinschaft* based on self-consciousness of a common nationality.
5. Ideally at least, and again to a large extent in practice, the population forms a community in the sense that its members mutually participate in distributing and sharing duties and benefits.

With regard to characteristic (4), in antiquity, only a few populations can be said to have felt such a sense of separate identity. The ancient Egyptians certainly did and so did the Jews—'a nation apart'—as they called themselves. It is difficult to see how the earliest Chinese fit into the definitions of 'nationality'. 'Chinese-ness' was, originally, a matter of a superior civilization imposed by force by people whose origins we cannot identify but who recognized themselves as 'Chinese' by virtue of certain distinctive marks, which included, *inter alia*, dress, comportment, the ideographic script, and living in walled villages or towns. If we are contemplating only Europe, then there was no self-consciousness of nationality under the Roman Empire. By the fifth century AD its citizens were beginning to think of the Empire as 'Romania' and themselves as 'Romanians', but these were hazy concepts which recognized that they were members of a political community rather than that they had a common nationality; that is, it was the recognition of a *Gesellschaft*, not of a *Gemeinschaft*. In post-Roman Europe it took centuries for the sense of common nationality to emerge, and even then it began, earliest, in the peripheral regions—first in England in perhaps the thirteenth or fourteenth century; in France perhaps in the fifteenth and certainly by the sixteenth century. The sense of common Spanish nationality developed very late: the regional differences were far too great. Catalonia spoke a different tongue altogether from Castilian Spanish, and it straddled the Pyrenees in geography and sentiment. The same is true of the Basques—and so forth. Not till after 1713 did the kings of Spain refer to their kingdom as 'España'—previously they had called it 'las Españas'. The sentiment we call 'national' develops in the eighteenth century and then, widely, both in Europe and other continents after the great French Revolution.

The final characteristic is again a very recent phenomenon; a state could well have a sense of national identity, like eighteenth-century France, but nevertheless be governed in an authoritarian fashion by a ruling house, usually sanctified by a myth of divine election. Such dynastic states, or *Hausstaaten*, were regarded as in some sense the property of the ruler. The notion that the state's destinies are decided, in the last resort at least, by the politically significant members of its population, that is, that it belongs to the nation and not the ruler, arises distinctively late outside England, and for the explicit recognition that 'sovereignty resides in the nation' we must wait till the French Revolution and the enunciation of this doctrine in Sieyès's *Qu'est-ce que le Tiers État?*[6]

An important question of terminology arises here. Many authors use the term 'nation-state' although sovereignty does not reside in their population—their 'nation'. I think this very misleading. When I talk of four-teenth-century England and fifteenth-century France I shall call them 'national' states. When such national states are ruled by the members of the nation, that is, sovereignty is democratically exercised by the nation, then and then only shall I call it a nation-state.

So much for definitions of the state: the issue here is how these states came to be built. The reason for such interest is that the way in which they were built usually has most important consequences for the way they come to be governed. Now 'state-building', particularly in the 1960s, when so many new states were spawned as the great European colonial empires broke up, became an immensely fashionable research-topic for the numerous, mostly American, scholars who were interested in what they called 'devel-opment' or 'modernization' in these new states. In nearly all cases, these terms concealed the assumption that the new states ought—for their own good, of course—to develop into states on the European-Atlantic model. The 'modern European state', as it came to be called—the state that possessed in full measure all five of the characteristics mentioned above—became, implicitly or explicitly, the paradigm of a 'developed' or a 'modern' polity. And great attention came to be paid to the way in which the states of Western Europe had come into being after the collapse of the western Roman Empire, as they stumbled from feudalism to absolutism and from absolutism to democratic and national states, that is, nation-states.

This entire line of research was mistaken. It tacitly assumed that the state

---

[6] Finer, 'Perspectives in the World History'; and cf. id., 'The Role of the Military', in C. Tilly (ed.), *The Formation of National States in Western Europe* (Princeton UP, Princeton, 1975), 88.

had originated only in Europe and at the close of the Middle Ages. This is completely wrong. In fact the development of states in Europe is—in a world-historical perspective—highly idiosyncratic. Feudalism represented breakdown; a previously highly organized state being fragmented. Furthermore, even for post-Roman Europe it begs the main question. That question is the one of territoriality. As the chapter on 'Feudalism' (Book III, Chapter 5) demonstrates, the strikingly original characteristic of western feudalism is that political allegiance was divorced from territoriality: it was not a question of 'what country do you live in?' that determined whom you obeyed, but 'whose man are you?' Feudalism was trans-local. Such a phenomenon is found almost nowhere else, though it has been said to have existed in part under the Chou in China (*c.*1100–772 BC), and in some sense in Japan. However that may be, the formation of the 'modern European state' starts effectively with, and is built around, the erection of known frontiers. It is fashionable in many quarters today to mock the pre-modern states for the fuzziness of their frontiers, to point out that they usually consisted only of a *limes* or border, not a black line as they do today; and to make this one of the hard-and-fast criteria for the difference between the pre-modern and the modern state. It is true that the notion of territorial sovereignty as we know it in international law today was not finally defined till the Congress of Vienna in 1815.[7] Yet, however wavery their frontiers, these pre-modern states were states precisely because there was a core area whose boundaries did not fluctuate, whose people recognized a common superior. The notion that the emperors of China did not have a clear idea of what were their dominions and where individuals had to have the imperial passport is quite ridiculous. There was a multi-state system in China in the stage that begins with 722 BC and comprises the 'Spring and Autumn' period followed by the 'Period of the Warring States'. During the latter—by which time some 180 petty states had been reduced to just seven—a pattern of coalitions emerged based on the opposition of a 'horizontal' (East–West) coalition to a 'vertical' (North–South) one; and the principles that governed such interstate conduct were all described with a wealth of quasi-historical detail, in a treatise that bears the title *Chan kuo ts'e* ('The Intrigues of the Warring States').[8]

We ought, therefore, to bypass the European experience and generalize from the entire universe of past polities. We can also forget the preoccupations of the 1960s with development and modernization. Our interest in

[7] Cf. S. E. Finer, 'State-building, State Boundaries, and Border Control', *Social Science Information*, 13 (1974), 79–126.
[8] '*Chan Kuo Ts'e' or 'The Intrigues of the Warring States'*, trans. J. I. Crump, 2nd rev. edn. (Chinese Materials Centre, 1949)

state-building goes simply as far as it affects how a polity is governed. This requires us to distinguish between the (primarily) territorial format of different states. These fall into four main classes: city-states, 'generic' states, national states, and empires.

City-states are independent governing units consisting of a town or city with a narrow band of dependent territory around it. The earliest states in Mesopotamia are of this kind, as are, of course, the *poleis* of Greece and the medieval city republics of Europe. The term, as far as its use in English is concerned (its equivalent in European languages is but rarely found), seems to have first been used by Warde-Fowler, in his *The City-State of the Greeks and Romans*, published in 1893.[9] But Sidgwick was using the term freely in his *Development of European Polity*. Although this work was not published until 1903, the lectures on which it is based were delivered every year from 1885/6 to 1898/9; so perhaps he was the initiator.[10] Sometimes such a city-state extends its territory. The principal examples of this are Rome and Venice. The cities themselves are governed by their own, usually republican, constitution, but rule over the territories which they hold in subjection, as dependencies. They thus become empires as this term is defined below.

But what name to give to the much more common form of polity, rarely a republic, being nearly always governed by a king or prince who rules over an extensive tract of territory, usually contiguous territory? Various names have been volunteered. To call them 'kingdoms' or 'principalities' does away with the difficulty by begging the entire question as to what kind of state it is that the king or prince is ruling. Kingdoms and principalities are, in fact, sub-types of the states concerned here. Three names have been volunteered. One is to contrast them with the city-state as 'territorial state'. Just so did Peter Burke. He asks, 'When did Florence cease to be a city-state (which controlled a substantial amount of territory in Tuscany) and become a territorial state (in which the metropolis remained dominant in many respects)?'[11] There can be no sensible answer, because these two terms ride on quite different planes. Malta is a 'territorial' state, although its territory is not very big. The term 'territorial state' has nothing to do with the size of a territory—it is the contradictory of the non-territorial state, and the only type of this to be found in this *History* is the purest form of feudal state, which, as the chapter on the subject demonstrates, counts allegiance in terms of trans-local, man-to-man relationships, whereas in

---

[9] P. Burke, 'City-States', in Hall (ed.), *States in History*, 139.
[10] H. Sidgwick, *The Development of the European Polity* (Macmillan, London, 1903).
[11] P. Burke, 'City States', 143.

the territorial state the subject's allegiance arises from the fact that he resides or was born in that territory.

This leaves us with the only two remaining alternative terms to be widely used. Sidgwick uses 'the country-state'. Nowadays it is more common to use the term 'national state' or wrongly, as we have already shown, 'nation-state'. Sidgwick somewhat fudges the issue when he points out that the term 'country' as it is commonly used combines the notion of a specific territory with the notion of a specific kind of people inhabiting it. Effectively, though, we have only three alternatives: to call these states either 'country' states, 'national' states, 'ethnic' states. The last term would be a neologism, although it would exactly fit the ancient Egyptian and Hebrew states, where the territory and the *ethnos* are contiguous. The attractiveness of this term is that it would avoid using the word 'national', and hence 'nation', when, according to modern doctrine, nations and nationalism are a product only of the last two or three centuries, and even then only in Europe. Against it is to be set its novelty, and the argument that we can indeed speak of some *ethnoi* in the past as being nations in our present sense; but above all, the fact that many of the states we are considering were made up of a miscellany of *ethnoi*.

It would be possible to coin a word 'toponymous', so that a toponymous state would be one defined as it were by its place-name, that is, a state whose frontiers enclose a tract of territory that is specific enough to have a certain name, but without any implication that the people therein are of common ethnic, linguistic, or religious stock, and so on, or have any self-consciousness of being a single community, except in so far as all are subjected to the same ruler. A good example, because it is so exotic, is Transylvania, an area inhabited by a mixture of Magyar and Romanian elements. For a long period in the sixteenth and seventeenth centuries this was an independent principality. It was certainly not a national state, but can with justice be called a toponymous state.[12] But 'toponymous' is perhaps too bizarre an expression for common use in the text. The intention, after all, is to distinguish 'national' states, that is, those inhabited by a 'nation' (whatever that may be) from others which cannot be so called—a sort of residue. After much deliberation, therefore, I have settled on a nondescript term, to wit, 'generic'. When there is no reason to think that a communal self-consciousness exists among the inhabitants of a region, and there is reason to underline this fact, the state will be called generic, or a generic-type state.

---

[12] An even better example is 'Macedonia', cf. the French expression for a mixed fruit salad—*macedoine de fruits*. The 1990s struggle over Macedonia, following the breakup of Yugoslavia, underlines the importance of exclusive right to a historic name.

Where, on the other hand, there are elements of such self-consciousness, as in fourteenth-century England, that state will be called a national (not a nation-) state.

Finally we come to the much-abused term 'empire'. It connotes, first of all, bigness. An empire is a very large state. Yet to apply the term to any very large state would occasionally defy common usage; for instance, the United States is a very large and populous state, but we do not call it the American Empire. If we use that term at all—just as when some people talk of the Soviet Empire—it is not mere size we are talking about but the connotation of a second characteristic as well—domination.

The word derives from the Roman term *imperium*, which is difficult enough to translate in its specifically Roman context, but which always carries the connotation of domination. Empires are commonly thought of as having been brought into existence by conquest, and with good reason, for the term 'empire' carries the implication that an identifiable ethnic or communal group, and/or a core territorial unit (which might be a state-generic, national, or, indeed, a city-state) exert dominion over other ethnic, territorial, or communal groups.

A difficulty arises when we consider the Roman Empire after the Edict of Caracalla (AD 212) and Diocletian's reorganization (AD 284–305). First, when citizenship is applied to all free inhabitants of the empire, we can no longer talk of an identifiable ethnic group ruling the remainder; and next, once Diocletian treated Italy as simply one province among many, one cannot even consider this multi-ethnic state as being ruled by one privileged locality. The later Roman Empire was becoming a multi-ethnic state, exemplified by the introduction of the term 'Romania'. A similar puzzle arises with the Byzantine area; the issue here is whether it consisted of the Anatolian heartland ruling over the Balkans, or whether Anatolia and the Balkans together constitute a core area in themselves. Arguably the former interpretation should prevail, because the Asiatic part of the empire always enjoyed a status superior to the European part. We might get over this difficulty by adopting the suggestion that at this stage we have moved into an 'Empire Mark II' where, consequent upon the situation we have just described, there has evolved a common imperial culture which acts as the 'ticket of entry' for any who want to enter the ruling stratum. This extended definition would apply to Rome, Byzantium, and, as will be seen in the next paragraph, to China as well. Islamicists recognize, indeed stress, the difference between a large state founded on particularist domination, and the very same large state where a common Islamic culture predominates. They call the former the Arab 'Kingdom', and reserve the term 'Empire' for the Abbasid period, after 750. But we do not here have to follow this usage at all. We prefer to think of the Caliphal Empire Mark I (the four 'righteously guided' Caliphs and the Ummayads) and Mark II (under the Abbasids).

China is still considered as consisting of two parts—China Proper and Outer China (which includes, for example, Sinkiang, Tibet, and Mongolia). For most of its history China consisted only of China Proper. Yet this was called an empire. Originally this usage might be justified because the cultures south of the Yangtse were being colonized from the north. This would be the Chinese Empire Mark I. But by the Sung at the latest, China Proper was an Empire Mark II. The imperial culture was the passport to rulership. This is what successive waves of conquering northern nomads found—that unless they adopted Chinese imperial culture, they would not be able to legitimize and hence consolidate their rule.

We should note in passing that there is an entirely trivial usage of the term. The reason why some generic or national states are referred to as empires, for example, Bismarck's 'German Empire' (or even what used to call itself the 'Central African Empire'), is simply that their rulers chose to call themselves 'emperors'. These 'empires' are purely honorific.

This is a very long preliminary to the central question: how do states come to be what they are?—leaving aside the extremely obscure and contentious question of how states emerge from primeval and tribal societies.

The most obvious point is that states such as we know them today are the product either of aggregation from smaller territorial units or the disaggregation of large territorial units. Well over two-thirds of the states of today have been created since 1945, mostly since 1960, as a result of the liquidation of those vast multi-ethnic states which, rightly, were called the British, French, Belgian, Dutch, and Portuguese colonial empires. But this is only the latest manifestation of a very old and regularly recurring phenomenon. The states that emerged with the breakdown of the western Roman Empire, and which themselves disintegrated into hundreds of principalities and city-states, were the detritus of that large and multi-ethnic state. Likewise, the estimated 130–80 petty states of Northern China that emerged after 722 BC were the detritus of the Chou Empire. From the detritus of the breakup of the Arab Caliphate were (after a long interval, admittedly) to emerge a succession of states such as Iran, the Ottoman Empire, and the various states of the Maghreb.

On the other hand, many states which survive to this day—England, indeed the UK, is an example, as is France or Spain—were built up by the aggregation of smaller units. We do not know where this process started. If we simply took the Mesopotamian experience as the starting-point—and it is prior to the Egyptian one—then the process begins with the formation of city-states which then become aggregated, in ways to be discussed, into a larger political unit. But there is no evidence that this is how Pharaonic Egypt came into being. It was not urbanized, and for millennia it had no fixed capital. It was ruled from wherever the dynasty had decided to put their tombs. All that we know is that it gives every evidence of having been the product of the uniting of two territories, Upper and Lower Egypt; whether by conquest of the North by the South or vice versa is in dispute.

But in either case we assume there was an area from which the aggregation proceeded. It is usual to call these 'conquest centres', though in many cases the aggregation might well have been peaceful, and in many well-attested cases (Francia and the Regnum Francorum, or Wessex and the Kingdom of England, or Ch'in and the unification of China in 221 BC), the petty state that aggregated the remainder lay on the periphery, not at the centre. We could, I think, recognize two paths by which a 'centre' expands to form a larger territorial aggregate. The first case assumes a 'centre' with weak and fragile neighbours into which it can expand with relative ease. An example would be the Roman expansion into Iberia and Provence, and finally Gaul and Britain. The paradigm is a 'hard' centre and a 'soft' periphery. Here the limits to expansion are set, for the most part, by the sheer logistical problems of distances, sometimes compounded—as in the case of Varus' lost legions in respect of Augustus' Rome—by a defeat at the frontier (itself usually occasioned by these same logistical problems). The problem of maintaining Chinese garrisons beyond the Great Wall, or indeed, up at the Wall, provides another striking example. Sinkiang and Central Asia could be and were lost more easily than they had been gained. In these cases the tide of expansion stopped, not at an internationally agreed frontier—a product, really, of the last two centuries—but at a *limes*. (In Britain we call a hard line, which marks out sovereign territory, a frontier; we call a blurred, fluctuating, and debatable area a border (the Latin *limes*). The Americans use the terms in exactly the reverse sense.)

The *limes* was wherever the ruler decided to stop. Augustus, after the disaster of the Teutoburgian Forest, ordained that the Empire must not expand any more, and by and large it did not. It certainly never expanded into Germany proper. Likewise, the Chinese expansion into Turkestan and points west was stopped, partly by logistical problems but equally by Confucianist nagging about the uselessness and, indeed, the perniciousness of these caravan trails. In the eighteenth century the French invented the doctrine of 'natural frontiers', not in order to pursue further conquests to the east but, precisely, in order to put a limit at the Rhine.

Sometimes, however, the would-be aggregating 'centre' found its progress checked by another, similar, 'centre'. This was the case in ancient Mesopotamia and in classical Greece. Sometimes, as we have already pointed out, the large, multi-ethnic unit disintegrated to give rise to a large number of smaller political units roughly equal in power. In either case, this may be described as a 'balance of power situation': so it was among the various petty states of Italy after the disintegration of the Holy Roman Empire, or among the much larger national and country states that had emerged in Europe by the eighteenth century. In that event the result might be the perpetuation of a states-system as, notably, in Europe. Or, alternatively, it might end with one of the local states conquering the others. This is what happened in England, where Wessex gobbled up the other Saxon and the Danish king-doms, or in France where the Île de France region—Francia—acquired the rest of the provinces by a mixture of conquest, marriages, inheritances, and escheats.

There were three possible outcomes to such situations. In the first, the resources and mobilizing capacity of the would-be 'centre' were so much greater than those of the peripheric states that it could not only overrun them but also centralize its rule over them (that is, deprive the conquered units of discretion) and ultimately homogenize them culturally. This was what Ch'in did in 221 BC when it gobbled up the other six Chinese states; and the unifying work of its king, the 'First Emperor', Shih Huang-ti, was never to be undone. In the second case, the resources and potential for mobilization of the peripheric states and those of the would-be centre were roughly equal. Here the outcome was the perpetuation of a country-state system (as between the various country-states of Europe) or a very slow unification in which the regional particularism of the peripheric regions was never lost. In these cases a race was being run between the 'centre' and the periphery, and therefore the ultimate unification was a slow business. England was unified from Wessex long before the corresponding movement in France, and the unity so gained was only strengthened by the Danish conquest, to be finalized when the Norman conquest made the entire country the 'terra regis', corseted by 3,000 mail-clad Norman overlords. In France the unification process, emanating from Paris, did not begin till the beginning of the thirteenth century and was certainly not completed till perhaps the sixteenth or even seventeenth century; with the result that regional particularism and a sort of 'mosaic'-state was characteristic of the French monarchy until the Revolution. Finally, there is the case where the resources of the peripheric states are more powerful than those of the would-be centre. Here those states endure. No unification takes place.

So far we have considered the creation of a state by aggregation from smaller units or the disintegration of the larger units, and both presuppose unification from a special geographical area which we call a 'centre'. But historically there is another and radically different way in which states and empires have been formed; and this is by tribal conquest: the overrunning of existing states from the outside. The two principal examples of this are the Mongol Empire of Chinghiz Khan, and its successor-states; and the Arab conquests, resulting in the Caliphate which stretched from Spain to northern India. The latter example is, of course, of lasting and major historical importance. The Arabs are unique in history as the 'only tribal conquerors to have caused the cultural traditions of highly civilized peoples to be reshaped around their tribal heritage';[13] whereas the Mongols either took over the existing state structures and their values or, if they persisted in maintaining their original tribal customs and identity, fairly soon disintegrated and perished. What is so striking about the Mongol conquest of China is how soon the Mongol ruling group disintegrated, lost its military tradition, and was chased into the desert by a resurgent national Chinese revolt and never heard of again. The Toba Empire (c.440) provides a paradigm of what happened when northern nomads took over parts of China proper. In the event one group of Toba tribesmen assimilated themselves to Chinese and indeed Confucianist values; the others, however, wanted to retain the old tribal structure and values. The result was the breakup of the Toba Empire into the 'tribalistic' state of Chou and the Confucianist state of Ch'i. After decades of fighting, the former state was defeated, passed into pro-Chinese, then into Chinese hands, and its Toba tribesmen 'disappeared for all time'.[14] The fate of the original ethnic Arab conquerors was not dissimilar, in that their ruling status in a huge land empire disappeared after perhaps a century and other ethnic groups, usually of Turkic extraction, took their place; but—unlike the north Asiatic nomads—not before they had created a genuinely new civilization and a tradition which was common to all the lands they had conquered even when, bit by bit, these fell away from the central Caliphate and became effectively (and sometimes formally) independent.

We can summarize the diverse effects of these different modes of state-building on the form of government by considering two sets of summary variables. The first is whether and how far the rulers established a central and standardized administration throughout the state's territory; the second, how far in the course of that process they homogenized culture, language, and law. The various modes by which these outcomes were or were not effected must be left to the individual case studies. Here, all we are considering are the outcomes.

The two sets of summary variables yield four cells.

---

[13] Crone, 'The Tribe and the State', 74.
[14] W. Eberhard, *A History of China*, 4th edn. (Routledge & Kegan Paul, London, 1977), 152–4.

(a) Centralized and standardized administration; homogenized culture, language, and law. Examples would include the later Roman Empire, Byzantium, China, the kingdoms of England, and at a later remove, France.
(b) Central and standardized administration; little or no homogenized culture, language, and law. Examples: the Persian Empire; the Ottoman Empire.
(c) Absence of centralized and standardized administration; homogenized culture. Examples: medieval Germany and medieval Italy.
(d) Absence of centralized and standardized administration; absence of homogenized culture, language, and law. Examples: the Empire of Charlemagne; the Mongol Empire.

These crude divisions take no account of the subtle variations in each case: the absence of regional particularism in England as contrasted with its powerful presence in France, for instance, or the unique way in which the city of Rome knitted together a league of Italian tribes and cities in the first stages of its imperial expansion. This *History* brings out the nuances in each individual case.

There remains one final set of distinctions. It relates to the 'stability' of political systems. For instance, if we looked at the statistics for the turnover of Byzantine emperors, we might conclude that that state was very unstable indeed. But this is to fail to distinguish between three possible objects of our attention. The first of these, following Easton,[15] is what he calls the 'political community'. By this he does not mean a community in the sense of a *Gemeinschaft*, sharing common traditions; there need be no affect in the group at all. The political community is simply that aggregate of humans 'who are drawn together by the fact that they participate in a common structure and set of processes, however tight or loose the ties may be'.[16] Such a political community may well in fact be composed of groups with different cultures, traditions, or nationalities, for example, the Austro-Hungarian Empire. By the same token, that community can disappear. Sometimes it simply fragments into other smaller ones. Sometimes, as in the case of the Assyrians after the destruction of Nineveh, they simply disappear from history. The past is littered with the wreckage of political communities. After 722 BC the Chou Empire of China fragmented into some 130–80 separate political communities, which in turn were reduced by conquest to a mere seven, which in their own turn were reduced to one and one alone by Shih Huang-ti in 221 BC. There are reckoned to be some 300

---

[15] D. Easton, *The Political System: An Inquiry into the State of Political Science* (Knopf, New York, 1953), 172. [16] Ibid. 177.

separate political communities in Europe *c.*1500. Today they number about thirty.

However, the stability or collapse of a political community must be distinguished from that of the regime. By this is meant the constitutional order, the 'regularized method for ordering political relationships. It is much more than a mere "constitution", for the term implies also the notions of the goals and limits of tolerance, the norms and accepted procedures and the formal and informal structure of authority, all rolled up together'.[17] It is obvious that a political community may collapse and become three or four political communities, each of which, however, perpetuates the same regime or a similar regime to that of the original united community. We could say that this is what happened when the Thirteen Colonies split off from the larger political community of the British Empire in 1776. In the text I sometimes use this term 'regime' as synonymous with ' form of rule', 'form of polity', or even 'polity' itself; but the last is a dangerous identification since the regime is as much the way, the manner, the temper in which the policy is conducted as the polity itself. When used in this way, the context must decide.

Regimes may also change rapidly but not, perhaps, as rapidly as political communities do. The European experience is particularly misleading in this regard. Europe has been much, much more protean, changeful, and inno-vative than any other part of the globe. It has moved from Roman imperial autocracy and law, through a Dark Ages, into feudalism, thence into absolutist and territorial states, finally into representative democracy, and then, beyond that, into the socialist collective autocracies until 1989 of the eastern part of the continent. Compare this with China where, from perhaps the eighth century BC (or, if this is regarded as too early a starting-point for the tradition of the regime, than at least from 221 BC) the regime—an autocracy—remained essentially unchanged until this century. Chinese history is punctuated by innumerable peasant uprisings, sometimes on a national scale, and in some cases bringing about the fall of a dynasty; yet in no case—until we come to the Tai-Ping revolt of the nineteenth century—did the rebels want to change the regime. They simply wanted to change the authorities.

With the authorities we come to the third possible subject of 'political instability'. 'The authorities' are simply those who hold the authority-roles at any one time. We could in fact make further distinctions between the political, that is, policy-deciding authorities and the bureaucracies, but this is not worth doing; the latter are relatively permanent and unchanging and

---

[17] Cf. Easton, *The Political System,* 193.

are more usefully regarded as a fixture of the regime. But when we turn to
the political, that is, the decision-making authorities, we find that here the
turnover can be and often is very rapid indeed without in any way altering
the central characteristics of the regime. The toppling of kings, emperors,
and sultans in the Roman, Byzantine, and Mamluk polities is so frequent
that it gives the appearance of great instability. And instability there was—
in the top echelons of the government. But beneath the turbulence at the
palace level, the regimes themselves persisted unaltered for century on
century. China offers a contrast to these three examples in that there—
apart from its periodic periods of breakdown—the succession to the throne
was as regular as the regime was stable.

1.2. *Military Formats and Forms of Government*

I do not propose to deal with this important topic at any length here since I
have already written on the subject—in so far as it concerns Europe—and
the main concepts and themes in this *History* are ones elaborated in that
article.[18] The difficulty in being brief about this topic is that of having to
express sequentially a number of propositions which are simultaneously
interdependent. The best that can be done here is to state each proposition
briefly, give examples of its application, and pass on to the next one while
showing how they are interrelated.

That being understood, we might put forward the following propositions:

(a) The military organization is central to the establishment and perpetua-
    tion of the political community, the regime, and the ruling authorities.
(b) The way in which military power is distributed among the various
    sections or strata of society is decisive for the form that regime takes.
(c) The format of the military forces—*ad hoc* or permanent, unpaid or paid,
    and so on—criss-crosses with what is laid out in (b), and also has a
    critical bearing on the perpetuation, and/or the stability of the poli-
    tical community, regime, or ruling authorities.
(d) The format of the military forces decides whether or not, or how far,
    the rulers can extract resources from the population; but, equally, the
    other way round—the resources decide what kind of military format is
    adopted. The interdependency of the two is what I have elsewhere
    called the 'coercion–extraction' cycle.[19]
(e) Throughout the history of government, warfare, and hence the expen-

---

[18] Finer, 'State and Nation Building in Europe: The Role of the Military', in Tilly (ed.), *Formation
. . ., 84–163.*   [19] Ibid.

diture on the armed forces, has been—with the possible exception of the Old Empire in ancient Egypt[20]—the single most extravagant and continuous drain upon the fiscal and economic resources of the state.

(f) For this reason and the coercion–extraction cycle ((d) above), the raising and maintenance of military forces, particularly standing military forces, is the overwhelmingly most important reason for the emergence of the civil bureaucracy.

(g) Changing military technology is sometimes related to the domestic economy and society, but is sometimes an importation from outside, hence an independent variable. But some changes in that technology are decisive in (a), (b), and (c) above.

PROPOSITION A: The military guarantees the existence of the political community, in so far as only it can prevent secession from it, or its conquest and absorption from the outside. Likewise, it guarantees the form of the regime against subversion via rebellions or revolts. And, finally, the ruling authorities depend critically upon it for maintaining them in power in the face of even small-scale revolts. In the second and third of these cases, the military is in fact playing a policing role. It has been pointed out, quite rightly,[21] that that role was far more pronounced in pre-modern states than today, when the state has an extensive capability for the surveillance and the repression of the civil population. In pre-modern times—it is very noticeable in the Roman Empire, for instance—the military acted as a *gendarmerie*: to assist tax collectors, repress brigands, keep the roads open, and do a variety of jobs, including road-building, that today would be carried out by the police or the civil service. The same is true, for the most part, of Imperial China.

In addition, in the face of external attack the state can nowadays draw upon kinds of social solidarity unknown to the pre-modern world, notably nationalism

PROPOSITION B: The way military power is distributed among the social strata is closely connected with the nature of its technology (bronze weapons or iron, chariots or cavalry, and so on), and also with the pre-existent social stratification. The latter, indeed, forms a kind of 'stratification–domination' cycle; a nobility, for instance, will insist that only its members may ride a war-horse or carry a sword, and in so far as it succeeds in this will continue to dominate the rest of society.

[20] Exceptions made highly problematical in view of prodigal expenditure of manpower and material on pyramids and temples.   [21] e.g. Giddens, *The Nation-State and Violence*.

The nomadic horde starts off as highly democratic and egalitarian, until some war-leader can transform it into a state. The city-state, in its early phases at any rate, tends also towards republicanism for the same reason as in the nomadic horde—that the military force consists of all able-bodied men. But this does not entail an egalitarian distribution of power, that is, a democracy. For not everybody's weaponry is equally lethal, and the more lethal it is the more costly it tends to be; so that the distribution of political power tends to follow the distribution of wealth. Aristotle makes this absolutely explicit when he relates the pre-eminence of cavalry to an oligarchic republic, that of the hoplite to a sort of yeoman republic, while that of the navy corresponds to the democracy.[22] Rome was notoriously a *civitalii* Republic—the population being divided into so many strata according to their weaponry, with the cavalry at the top of the pile and the *proletarii*, who had only their proles or children to offer up to the Republic, at the bottom—and this distinction was reflected in their respective voting rights. The tendency to distribute political power in accordance with the possession of the most lethal, and hence costly, weapons is even more marked in feudal and feudalistic polities. The European Middle Ages provide the paradigm case. Here the mail-clad cavalry are militarily, and hence politically, dominant in the state. But the situation is quite different when the population—or even privileged sectors of it like the nobility—is disarmed, and military equipment is monopolized by the state. With a disarmed population on the one side and a permanent professionalized force on the other, the way is open for an absolutist regime; as in the Roman, the Byzantine, and the Chinese empires. But this very monopolization of weaponry in the hands of the state paradoxically threatens the ruling authorities' tenure of power; for the military forces may be more loyal to their own military leaders than their military leaders are to the ruling authorities. Hence the perennial problem of civil–military relations: such forces put the civil government under permanent threat of a 'take-over'. There are countless examples in antiquity where the troops substitute one ruler for another; the Praetorian Guard is particularly notorious but is really only one example among many. The way in which the fraught civil–military relationship has not disappeared but has simply been altered by the conditions in the modern as against the pre-modern state has been explored in my *Man on Horseback*.[23]

PROPOSITION C: The format of the military forces is not determined just by advances in technology, though it is influenced by them, nor just by pre-

[22] E. Barker (ed. and trans.) *The Politics of Aristotle* (Clarendon Press, Oxford, 1980), 1321a.
[23] 4th edn. (Praeger, Boulder, Col., 1988).

existing social stratification and the like, for it is also a matter of deliberate choice on the part of the authorities. As I have shown elsewhere,[24] rulers have to make a choice—or arrive at a combination—of three priorities: efficiency in battle, expense, and loyalty. Different kinds of armed forces correspond to each of these priorities. One sees this kind of calculus in Machiavelli's *Art of War*. By his time, the Italian city republics had abandoned their original civic militias for paid mercenaries—the *condottieri*. By general consent (though not by Machiavelli's, admittedly), they were more efficient; but they were untrustworthy and even actively disloyal. Hence Machiavelli's decided preference, as a republican, for the civic militia, and hence the *raison d'être* of his book.

On the whole, paid professional troops were the most efficient but also the most expensive. By the same token, popular militias or feudal levies were the least expensive but not the most efficient. And, finally, when it came to loyalty, the militia or the feudality or the paid army of nationals were likely to be more loyal than foreign mercenaries; yet that loyalty would be towards the political community or to the regime, not necessarily to the political authorities. On the contrary: a ruler might fancy himself more secure when surrounded by a band of foreign mercenaries who were entirely dependent on his pay and favour, like the Varangian Guard around a Byzantine emperor, than when he was dependent on the generals of his own native forces.

In some historical polities—the nomad states like those of the Mongols and the Arabs, or the republican states like those of Greece or the Roman Republic or the early Italian city republics—the army is almost entirely, or entirely, an *ad hoc* mass levy of the able-bodied adults. At the other extreme we find standing forces of paid professional volunteers, like those of the Roman Empire, Byzantium, or the armies of eighteenth-century Europe. These might be nationals but this was a pretty late development in Europe. Until the French Revolution they tended to be a mixed force of native and foreign mercenary troops, and Napoleon himself used large bodies of foreign troops to fight his battles. In the earlier stages, as Europe emerged from its Middle Ages, the preference of the authorities was 'rent-an-army'. It was simpler, in other words, to hire paid and highly trained foreign troops like the Swiss pikemen than to try to train your own.

However, as this *History* shows, it was rare for a state to use only one pure form of military format. Much more usual was a mixture, and the most common form of this was a kernel of standing regular troops who served both as a palace guard and the garrison for the imperial capital, and also

---

[24] Finer, 'State and Nation Building'.

served as the cadre for the mass army; plus a mass force made up of popular levies. This could be *ad hoc*, as in the case of the Persian army on its way to Marathon (so described by Herodotus); or it could be a permanent arrangement, as it was—under most dynasties, though not all—in China.

PROPOSITION D: The extraction–coercion cycle is so obvious it really requires no elaboration. Military forces call for men, materials, and—once monetization has set in—for money too. It has always proved difficult for the authorities to extract these from the population, especially in the agrarian economies, partly because their net tax base was very difficult to ascertain, partly because the techniques of tax-collection were primitive, and most important of all, because populations of peasants on the margin of subsistence were extremely recalcitrant. (It was relatively easy for city-states like Florence and Venice to tax their populations compared with the difficulties of the king of France or of the various 'Spains'.) Rulers had only two alternatives: they could try to coerce, or they could persuade. It was the ravenous need for money to fight the increasingly expensive wars of the fourteenth century and after in Europe that led rulers to convene assemblies of potential taxpayers and so to 'invent' the notion of representation.[25] But since these assemblies never gave the rulers as much money as they demanded, the latter also tried the alternative course—of coercion. The transition is marked by the struggle between the ruler and his Estates or parliament or whatever, in the course of which the rulers throughout most of Europe were able to neuter or to abolish the Estates and establish their own fiscal absolutism. But to do this they needed an armed force, the upkeep and pay of which was the original object of the entire exercise. In France, King Louis VII and his agents took to levying taxes without anybody's consent while in the throes of the Hundred Years War, and with the money so acquired he established the first standing army in post-Roman Europe, the *Compagnies d'Ordonnance*. From that time on French fiscal absolutism marched hand in hand with the repressive powers of the standing army. In Prussia the Great Elector began by using force to exact taxes despite the opposition of his Estates, expanded his army with the taxes, and then proceeded to make the Estates in Brandenburg compromise, while the rebellious Koenigsbergers were forcibly suppressed. From that time on (1669) the Hohenzollern forces continued to expand, establishing an administrative and fiscal grip on the country which was so great that wags remarked that Prussia was not a country with an army, but an army with a country.

[25] Cf. Bk. III, Ch. 8 on 'Representative Assemblies'.

These examples from Europe have parallels in antiquity and in other parts of the world. The ruler uses a military force to extract taxes, builds up that force, and with it extracts more taxes. There is a fixed connection between fiscal absolutism and standing armies. However, a change in the relationship occurred in the nineteenth century, first in Europe and then in many other parts of the globe. The reason was the rise of the novel ideology of nationalism. In the name of the nation, individuals were willing to fight and die on a scale quite unknown in the past. Individuals who were prepared to die for their country were equally prepared to pay taxes to sustain it. Wherever this ideology took root, the need for coercion diminished in proportion as popular consent, even enthusiasm, prevailed. The tacit consent to what in the past would have been regarded as massive extortion is one of the most striking features of the modern as contrasted with the pre-modern state. It goes hand in hand, we may remark parenthetically, with the improved surveillance and administrative techniques available to the authorities which makes detection of tax-evasion more easy, and progressive (hence more equitable) taxation possible.

PROPOSITIONS E AND F:

> Nam neque quies gentium sine armis neque arma sine stipendiis neque stipendia sine tributis haberi queunt
>
> (Tacitus)[26]

It is not argued here that civil bureaucracies originate with the need to maintain armed forces. This is clearly contradicted by the earliest known bureaucracies in the Sumerian cities and the Old Kingdom in Egypt. The great mass of these bureaucracies was concerned with redistributing wealth in a natural economy, that is, the counting, checking in, and checking out of countless and diverse commodities. These were what Weber calls *oikos* economies. In the redistributive process some of the commodities went to the temples, some went on the conspicuous expenditure of the palace— the pyramids are the most phenomenal example, but so are the grave goods in both cultures—and some went to pay the functionaries for their work. In the Sumerian cities, however, the great bulk of the goods collected went back to the peasant who produced them, as a form of stipend. In neither case are we able to estimate how much went to the armed forces, for we have no notion of how large these were. It is pretty clear, however, that most of the revenue went to satisfy other claims.

---

[26] *Hist.* IV. 74: '. . . for you can have neither peace among peoples without armies, nor armies without pay, nor armies' pay without taxes.'

But what can be argued is that once we have moved past the redistributive *oikos* economies of archaic times to the open economies that succeeded them, and particularly after about 800 BC when they started to become monetized, any movement away from the *ad hoc* mass levy of the armed citizenry towards standing regular forces necessitated a fiscal apparatus; in short, a bureaucracy. The cost of delivering justice was small, as indeed it is to this day. Public works were on a relatively small scale and in many societies—for example, in China or ancient Egypt—were carried out by corvée labour. Apart from the upkeep and glorification of the state cult, the other primordial function of the state was defence and this, for the reasons outlined, bulked larger and larger as warfare demanded larger forces, longer campaigns, and professional armies, including mercenaries. The result is that where we can put numbers to the bureaucracy—for instance, in the later Roman Empire or the Chinese Empire at various dates—by far the largest proportion of its members are to be found in the fiscal services. Consider, then, the administrative effort required in China *c.*140 BC in the reign of the warlike emperor Wu Ti when it is estimated that the 'conscript' army numbered anything between a quarter of a million and one-and-a-third millions for a population of some 60 millions (i.e. between $\frac{1}{2}$ per cent to 2 per cent of the population); or in the case of the later Roman Empire, where Jones[27] estimates the total armed forces at 600,000 for a population of some 60 millions.

On a much smaller scale—but with greater information—it is possible to trace the growth in the medieval European states of a central (and in some countries, such as France, of a local) bureaucracy, as feudal knight service was replaced by payment to *ad hoc bandes*, and then from the *bandes* to foreign mercenaries and native-born standing troops.

The bureaucracy spawned by such developments was by no means what we should today regard as fiscal only. In those states with highly organized standing forces like China, Rome, or Byzantium it included a highly developed logistical sector—which provided the arms and equipment, clothing, and the like from state-run armouries and magazines as well as rations in kind from state storehouses.

PROPOSITION G: This proposition concerns changes in military technology. I call it a 'wild card' because (until contemporary times) military innovations have more often than not been the consequences of serendipity (the bayonet) or reactions to enemy innovations (longbow or pike) than the result of conscious research and invention. Very often the technological

---

[27] A. H. M. Jones, *The Later Roman Empire, 284–602*, 2 vols. (Blackwell, Oxford, 1964).

innovation is of so simple a nature one might almost call it a gadget: the iron stirrup or the ring-bayonet are examples of such innovations, which completely transformed the art of war for centuries.

Such military innovations bear independently upon the subject-matters of propositions (a), (b), and (c). They have an obvious bearing, for instance, upon the state's capacity for defence and attack. Fourteenth-century England, a dwarf compared with France, was able to savage and indeed conquer that country by using the military format based on the longbow and dismounted armoured cavalry, against the heavily armoured cavalry charge.

More interesting is the effect of military technology on the second proposition, that is, on the social distribution of military power. The most extravagant example of this relationship is Lynn White's prodigious hypothesis about the consequences of the iron stirrup. It argues that the iron stirrup (as against leather stirrups) permitted mounted shock combat of very heavily armoured cavalry, a tactic so powerful that it dominated the battlefield until the fourteenth century. Mounted and armoured shock cavalry, in their turn, required men both rich enough to equip themselves in this expensive way, and trained from childhood in this mode of warfare. Hence the social and political dominance of the medieval knight, and the feudalism that went with it. All because the stirrup was made of iron and not leather![28] This hypothesis is hotly contested—it explains so much with so little; but there is absolutely no doubt that the superior effectiveness of the armoured shock cavalry over other arms guaranteed the social and political supremacy of the noblemen in the European Middle Ages.

Finally, military technology must clearly have an effect upon the subject of the third proposition, that is, upon the rulers' choice of military format. This is because one of the three considerations a ruler would have to bear in mind was, precisely, efficiency. Thus, in the fifteenth and sixteenth centuries it became usual for monarchs—particularly French ones—to rent pike-phalanxes from the Swiss cantons; these mercenary troops dominated the Continental battlefields for about a century-and-a-half. They were extremely efficient, but were they loyal? Only as long as the ruler paid them: *point d'argent, point de suisse*. Or, they might change sides if they got a better offer. Such switches of allegiance occurred during the French Fronde (1638–53). The Italian city-states which began to employ *condottieri* in the fourteenth century suffered similar experiences.[29]

This *History*, therefore, tries *inter alia* to demonstrate how the preservation,

---

[28] L. White, Jr., *Medieval Technology and Social Change* (OUP, Oxford, 1962).
[29] Cf. the treason of Venice's *condottiere*, Carmagnola, in 1432.

the internal order, the social distribution of power, the tenure of the authorities, the degree of bureaucratization, and the nature of the regime—popular or absolutist, for example—are all intertwined with the nature of a given state's military institutions.

1.3. *Religion and Religious Institutions*

Religions, however defined, are a subspecies of the main species, which is 'belief-systems'. This broader category will be dealt with in the next section.

In relating religion to political systems I have initially relied on the five-fold classification of Bellah.[30] The first of the stages that Bellah recognizes, and which he calls 'primitive religion', does not concern us here; it is the religion of very simple societies like the Bushmen and the Dinka. Then follow, respectively, the stages of Archaic religions and the Historic religions, which concern us very much in this section. Bellah's fourth stage, which he calls 'Early Modern', is based, as he himself acknowledges, on one (though major) case: the European Reformation. This is much more pertinent to the discussion of 'belief systems' than it is here, and is postponed accordingly. The fifth stage of 'Modern' religion is problematical and so I have declined to borrow it.

In Archaic religion, according to this scheme, the religious symbol system has moved beyond that of primitive religion, where the powers of nature are mythical, identified in some way with the living, and are not gods—though they may be, so to speak, demigods. Here, those mythical beings have been objectified. They are conceived of as actively controlling the world. Their interrelationships are formulated into what can become an elaborate hierarchy of control. A vast cosmology accompanies this, into which all things are fitted. Sometimes, where literacy prevails, the internal logic of all this can take the religion into speculations and themes that lead out of and beyond Archaic religion.

The characteristic action in Archaic religion is the cult. In this cult, man and the gods are distinguished from one another. Hence some interaction system is required. This interaction is served by the institutions of worship and of sacrifice. The organization which characterizes this type of religion is one of a proliferation of cults, the reason being that every group in archaic society has a cultic aspect—and such groups have multiplied as compared with the primitive stage of society. Moreover, the social systems to which Archaic religion responds are ones which may be deemed 'two-class', in so

---

[30] R. N. Bellah, 'Religious Evolution', in R. Robertson (ed.), *Sociology of Religion* (Penguin, Harmondsworth, 1969), 262–94.

far as the upper class which monopolizes military and political power also usually claims superior religious status. The extreme case is that of the divine king, like the Egyptian pharaoh, acting as the link between gods and man, the cosmos and the world. But kings never completely divest themselves of religious leadership. Although priesthoods develop, sometimes to marked degree, adherents do not. The temples provide for a transient clientele, one, moreover, that observes rather than participates, and is not organized as a collectivity.

Finally, Bellah describes the social and political implications of this stage of religion and reaches conclusions with which we can agree. He points out that here, society and the individual are both merged into a natural, divine cosmos. The traditional structures and social practices are all held to be grounded in this divine cosmic order. In this way social conformity is at every point reinforced with religious sanctions.

The next stage in religious evolution, the Historic religions, begins in the first millennium BC and endures for some 2,000 years. Bellah calls them Historic (he really means 'historical') because they are all relatively recent, having emerged in literate societies, so that they are studied by historians rather than by archaeologists and anthropologists. This kind of religion differs from the preceding, Archaic type in that it is always in some sense transcendental: the cosmological monism of Archaic religion is here replaced by a sharp dualism between this world and the supernatural world which is also the world of the hereafter. This involves the rejection of this world in favour of a more real one, beyond and above it.

Consequently the symbol systems are different. All the Historic religions are dualistic: like the Archaic religions, they arrange reality in a hierarchical order, but this has been reduced to the supernatural, which is above, and the natural, which is below. The central religious preoccupation of the masses is the world after death, hence salvation (whatever that may mean). The many gods of the Archaic religions are reduced to one, the supreme Creator; and at the same time, salvation is open to everybody. The religions are universalistic, not localized or sectionalized into cults.

Religious action is above all that which is necessary for salvation. The ideal of the religious life becomes separation from the world; and for the layman, piety is modelled on the behaviour of the religious. The dualism we have noted is reflected in the characteristic religious organization; that is, into two practically independent hierarchies—the political and the religious. The monarch can no longer monopolize religious leadership, hence the problem of legitimating power shifts into a new gear. This problem extends down into the masses of pious laymen, and consequently, the role of believer and of subject become distinct, even if *de facto* rather than *de jure*.

The implications are profound: a new kind of tension arises between the political and religious—the king versus the prophets, the *ulema* versus the *sultan*, the *pope* versus the emperor. Religion now provides the ideology and social cohesion for rebellion and reform movements at just the same time as it serves to legitimate and reinforce the social order, as of ancient times.

This last point is the one which is stressed in this *History*, but I put it in a somewhat different way. The 'historic' religions, of which the supreme examples are Judaism, Christianity, Islam, and Buddhism and (bringing up the rear for reasons that will be explained) Hinduism, are distinguished from the Archaic religions in that they are (1) Salvation religions which preach a definite code of conduct; (2) they are universalistic: they are held to apply to all humans as such; (3) they are dogmatic (but much less so in the case of Hinduism, which is why it 'trails' the others in socio-political consequences). By 'dogmatic' I mean that they hold that theirs is the only true way to salvation, and the best they will offer rival religions is a grudging toleration, at worst active persecution of the most horrible kinds. Finally—and this is the chief point, already made by Bellah but not strongly enough—they are what I call *kahal* religions. *Kahal* and *edah* are the two words which are used in the Old Testament to signify 'congregation'. In the New Testament this is translated as *ekklesia*—hence the Latin *ecclesia* and all its derivatives. In Islam the word that most nearly approximates to this idea is the *umma*—the (Muslim) community. In the Archaic religions there is no congregation; in the Egyptian and Middle Eastern variants, individuals were not permitted to pray in the temples, only the priests. The laity brought offerings to the shrine, yes, and they gathered and shrank in awe as the sacred model of the deity was brought out of the temple precinct to make a progress through the fields. But they did not participate. In Greek and Roman religion the layman might indeed enter a temple and pray; but as Bellah has justly observed, the laymen who did this were transients, not a collectivity. In the *kahal*, on the other hand, the individual participated in the worship of the single supreme deity *qua* individual with his own inalienable tie-line to that deity, and he was also part of an organized collectivity, a stable community of fellow-believers. In it, the ruler had no superior status. He was one with his fellow-believers, however humble and however politically subject, in having to obey the divine law. And this code was one he himself had had no part in enacting. On the contrary, it was divine, given from the outside, the product of religious revelation—ineluctable, unchangeable, necessary. This is what Bellah means when he says that the status of religious believer becomes distinct from that of political subject; and he is right again when he points out the tension that arose out of the conflict between the two opposing roles.

The point is that, for the first time in history, kings were not omnipotent but were confined by divine restraints. The Jews invented this doctrine; they thereby invented the notion of 'limited monarchy'. There were areas the king himself might not touch, might not amend. For he was there simply to administer the divine law, and since everybody was equally bound to this, so everybody might have an opinion on whether the ruler was interpreting it correctly or even abrogating it. In Jewish history this provoked famous tensions between the prophets and the kings, the *kahal* and the priestarchy, until, after the Dispersion, the religion fell into the hands of holy men who were recognized as teachers by a congregation (a *knesset*, or meeting, translated as 'synagogue' from the Greek, 'to bring together'). In Christianity the tensions weakened and helped to dissolve the Byzantine Empire, since the Egyptians were Monophysites who could not tolerate the Orthodoxy of Byzantium, any more than could the Nestorians of the Middle East. Later the rump of that empire was further disrupted by the Iconoclastic controversy. Only after this did the congregation and the ruling authorities come together in a more-or-less tension-free relationship. In the West, however, the struggle of the Papacy and the Church against the princes, kings, and the emperor himself is notorious. Similar tensions arose in Islam; the great split between the Shi'ites and the Sunni, the sectarian strife among both rival persuasions, permitted and legitimized revolt in the name of the Prophet as, for instance, the destruction of the Ummayads of Syria at the hands of the politico-religious rebellion of the Abbasids. In Buddhism the conflict was not necessarily as marked, because here the congregation was not as wide as in the former three religions. The true congregation was the monkhood, the *sangha*. They indeed did struggle with authority at times—in China, in Korea, and in Japan—but the wider community was not involved in the same intense way as in the other three religions. Hinduism did not have the same divisive effect. That religion was not exclusive in the way the others were, nor did it create a single *kahal* as they did. Hinduism was cultic; it consisted of groups clustered around a holy man, and it was also remarkably syncretic.

The more rigid the religious organization, the greater the potential for a clash with the political organization or state. Rokkan worked out a schema which is of value here.[31] It is entitled 'Secular–religious differentiation', and runs as follows:

---

[31] 'Cities, States and Nations', in S. N. Eisenstadt and S. Rokkan (eds.), *Building States and Nations* (Sage, London, 1973), i. 88.

1. MINIMAL = Local religions only. Traditional Tropical Africa.
2. INTERMEDIATE = local religion closely fused with political system.
   (a) No corporate church—Hindu India.
   (b) Weakly incorporated church—Moslem Empires.
3. MAXIMAL = Church differentiated and strongly incorporated.
   (a) Separate from society—Buddhist political systems.
   (b) Closely fused with political system, but supra-territorial
       —Greek Orthodox Church.
   (c) Supra-territorial organization, potentially in opposition to
       political authority—Medieval Catholic Church.
   (d) Nationally fused—Protestant state churches.
   (e) Separate from national political system—Protestant sects.

We are not bound by the examples that Rokkan gives. For one thing, he was not interested in the religions of antiquity, which largely pre-date what he calls 'churches' but which I call the *kahal*-religions. If we were to follow his classification, then, under the 'Minimal-differentiation' rubric I should place the religions of Egypt and Mesopotamia, which are essentially palace cults or palace-licensed cults; also the religions of Greece and Rome, which are likewise local cults. The *kahal* religions begin with Hinduism. Under the 'weakly incorporated' one might place Judaism at the time of the Hebrew kingdoms and, again, under the Second Commonwealth. But after this, when it becomes rabbinical-synagogal Judaism, uprooted from any native political system whatsoever, it would be classed in the same position as the Protestant sects in the schema above. The struggles between the Jewish religious institution and the state during the period of the kings was extremely fierce, despite the description of it here as being but 'weakly incorporated' (or, for that matter, classed as 'no corporate church', for this classification is very broad), and exactly the same remarks apply to the collision between the Moslem religious institution and the sultans and other local rulers. Because it was always a potential opposition, it restrained the ruler; but because its organization was non-existent or very feeble, it lacked anything like the compulsive and continuous directing power of the medieval Roman Catholic Church at the height of its influence in the thirteenth century. Here, as this *History* shows, the confrontation between the religious and the secular authorities was unique. The idea that a Supreme Pontiff should direct and regulate the secular rulers of mankind ought to astound us. The only reason it does not is because most of us have grown up with the story and take it for granted. Yet nowhere else at any time did anything else like this obtain.

One final word on religions concerns the highly peculiar status of

Confucianism. Confucianism in its pure state—uncontaminated by popular Buddhist and Taoist elements—sets no store by the supernatural. It is a moral code, a philosophy, and a cosmology, but it is not a religion in the sense that it requires a belief in a supernatural world beyond and better than our own. Furthermore, there was no single Confucian organization; only schools, academies, and private groups. Confucianism shaped the literati, and by virtue of that fact these were the statesmen and the civil servants. The Confucian Classics were something like the Bible in that they incorporated history, poetry, philosophy, cosmology, and a system of ethics. Rather than religion, it ought perhaps be called the Confucian 'persuasion'. In the earliest days of the empire it was confined to the governing circles. Even then, it often brought them into collision with the emperor. It enjoyed its great revival as Neo-Confucianism under the Sung (AD 976–1279). Under the Ch'ing (1644 onwards), it became the persuasion of the local gentry, while the central government prepared a sort of short catechism of Confucianist principles for the masses. The consequence was the permeation of the entire society by this philosophy. So, although it was not, ever, a religion, and never a church in any sense either, yet it was the functional equivalent of the Church in Western Europe. It suffused the entire society; China was Confucian in the way Europe was Christian. And one of the most amazing things about it is that, although it did not rest upon a belief in the after-life, zealous Confucianists were prepared to face the most insufferable tortures in opposing their principles to the wishes of the emperor, notably in the persecution of the Tung-lin Academy in the last days of the Ming dynasty.

1.4. Belief-Systems, Social Stratification, and Political Institutions

It seems to be common ground among scholars that the precondition for regime stability, possibly for the survival of the political community itself, is a certain congruence between social stratification and the political institutions. More problematical is the relationship of both these things to the belief-systems of the society. 'Belief-systems' goes wider than religion, usually, although some religions more or less encompass the totality of the belief systems; the medieval European Catholic Church could lay a fair claim to have done just this. But take Confucianism. We have already shown that this was not a religion, but there can be no doubt whatsoever that it was a belief-system as all-encompassing as that of medieval Roman Catholicism.

Yet it seems to me beyond a doubt that rulers cannot maintain their authority unless they are legitimated, and that they are legitimated by belief-systems. It would be completely useless for a British monarch today to claim absolute powers on the grounds that these had been conferred on him by God, but this was taken as read in Archaic Egypt and Mesopotamia. Where the claim of the ruler to authority is out of kilter with the prevalent belief-systems of the society, he must either 'change his plea', that is, make himself acceptable in terms of that belief-system, or else de-legitimize himself and fall. The belief-systems are stronger than the ruling authorities because it is by their virtue that rulers rule.

Much the same can be said of the relationship between the belief-systems and the social stratification of society. A belief-system which envisages the cosmos as arranged in a hierarchy, and humans as a part of that cosmos, will accept social inequality as natural. A belief-system which, *per contra*, starts with the unproven and unprovable axiom that 'all men are created equal, that they are endowed by their Creator with certain inalienable rights, etc. etc.', will not accept such inequality gladly, if at all.

There is, then, a three-way relationship between the belief-system, the social stratification, and the political institutions of a community. The hypothesis I advance here is that in some societies all three are tightly congruent and that, where this is so, though the authorities may be changed with some rapidity, the regime and the political community attain enormously long-lived stability. By contrast, where one or other of the elements is out of kilter with the others, change and political instability occur.

Two examples of the 'three-fold cord which is not easily broken' will make the point. The first is Archaic Egypt, and indeed the Middle East as a whole. Here the rulers are the link between the human and the cosmos; hence we never find a republic, only monarchies. The human order reflects that of the gods. They must be placated and so priests have to come in as intermediaries to offer the necessary sacrifices and perform the rituals. The monarch himself is above them, either as a god—the 'divine Horus, living for ever'—or as the *ishakku* or vicar of god. As to the common folk, they are not a *kahal*; they are observers and worshippers in the priests' cultic rituals. Thus the religion justifies and reinforces social conformity in every detail and by the same token every aspect of society: the kingship, the architecture, the art, the script, the mathematical formulae, the calendar were all invested with its same, quintessential sacredness. This is true of all and each of the diverse societies in Egypt and the Middle East down to the middle of the first millennium BC (excepting only the Jews, as already shown).

Confucianism offers another example. It justified the role of the emperor as the link between the cosmos and the sublunary world; but it also justified the elaborate social stratification that is to be seen in China from very earliest times, in so far as Confucianism is unabashedly a doctrine of inequality. The 'five relationships' which it preaches as the basis for all social interaction are all relationships of subordination: wife to husband, son to father, younger to older brother, and friend, and all to the emperor. The highly stratified and unequal society was legitimated by the Confucianist canon, and both together legitimated the absolutism of the emperor.

If we sought a contrast, we could find it in what Bellah called 'Early Modern religion' which, as he has rather ruefully to admit, is really the European Reformation by another name. The currents of social criticism that began to spring up from the fourteenth century were expressed in religious form, but the Church was remarkably adept at accommodating these. So, diversity was preserved in a new, albeit more protean unity, for in all this the central tenet of the Church was never questioned—that it and its priests mediated between man and God. But with Luther the heresy was pronounced that every man was his own priest. This was a political Pandora's box. For the logical consequence of every man being his own priest was that they could each interpret the Bible in their own way. Thus the unity of the prevalent Roman Catholic belief system collapsed. A gap opened between the now-protean belief-systems—we must use the plural—and the political institutions. The Reformation set in train an incongruence which has continued to this very day. The mobile thrustfulness and everlasting change in political institutions which is as characteristic of the West as it is absent in China and Islam, until their systems were in turn undermined by the western ideas one hundred years ago, is due to Europe's incongruence between its belief-systems and political institutions, and between both of these and its social stratification.

1.5. *Time-Spans*

We must always have in mind the time-spans over which the reported developments are occurring. To do otherwise will be grievously misleading. The greatest challenge here is to convey the sensation of a lapse of time. We need some unit which in the imagination will conjure up the feel of very, very long ago. To give some yardsticks against which to compare time-spans, let us consider the following.

The entire time-span of recorded history, hence the record of the developed polities, is from 3200 BC until let us say AD 2000: 5,200 years.

What we have described as the 'modern' state as against pre-modern ones commences from *c.*1776: 224 years.

Manhood suffrage, and hence mass democracy, commences *c.*1870: 130 years.

The First World War, 1914–1918: 82 years ago.

The Second World War, 1939–1945: 55 years ago.

In what follows I shall record two sorts of time-spans: (1) The life-span of whole political regimes until their extinction; (2) to give ourselves a proper sense of humility, of the fragility of human affairs, and a sense of discontinuity instead of cumulative progress, a list of the great breakdowns or Dark Ages in the life-spans of these regimes.

1.5.1. TOTAL LIFE-SPANS

The problem in calculating these is the definition of the political regime we are observing. Take the Roman 'regime' as an example: clearly, this was expanding almost continuously, from the core city of Rome until it encompassed the 'empire at its height', that is, under Trajan. How then define the regime?

I make the assumption that in all these cases of fluctuating boundaries there is a core area which remains irreduceable—except perhaps for very brief incursions, quickly shaken off or, alternatively, absorbed. It is this unfluctuating core area which I identify with the 'regime' in question. This is very rough and ready, but it serves quite well for purposes of comparison.

I said that the span of the historical (i.e. recorded) states to the present day is some 5,200 years. Consider first what a vast proportion of this vast span of time is taken up by three of four extremely long-lived political regimes:

Egypt. Conventional origin, 2850 BC; conventional end (incorporation into wider unit, i.e. Roman Empire), 30 BC: life-span 2,820 years.

China. From the Ch'in unification, 221 BC, to the Republic, 1912: life-span 2,133 years. (If we were measuring the age of this state from its very origins—say, in the Chou Empire (*c.*1100 BC) to the present day—the life-span would be enormously longer of course—3,087 years. But it is not only conventional but in my view correct to identify the beginnings of the Chinese Empire with the Ch'in unification.)

Rome. Not *ex urbe condita* in 753 BC but from the inception of the Republic in 509 BC, to the fall of the Western Empire, conventionally in AD 476 Hence: 985 years. (If we started with the conventional date for Romulus' founding of the city, i.e. 753 BC, the total life-span expands to 1,229 years. Even if we shrank the definition to the beginnings of the Empire—the seizure of Sicily in 241 BC—the life-span is still 717 years.)

Assyria. The beginnings of the Empire are conventionally put at 1356 BC, and after vicissitudes (see below) it was finally extinguished in 612 BC: life-span: 744 years.

Byzantine Empire. There is a choice of dates here, dependent on one's assumptions. It is possible to think of Byzantium as a linear continuation of the Roman Republic and Empire; or as such, but only from the foundation of Constantinople. Similarly, it is possible to think of it as terminating in 1204 with its capture by the Crusaders, or in 1453 with its capture by the Turks. According to these different assumptions the life-spans are as follows:

(a) From the Roman Republic (509 BC) to
    (i) its capture in AD 1204: life-span 1,713 years.
    (ii) its capture by the Turks, AD 1453: life-span 1,962 years.
(b) From the foundation of Constantinople 330 to its capture, 1204: life-span: 874 years.

Venetian Republic. From the election of its first Doge (687) to the extinction of the Republic by Napoleon in 1799: life-span 1,112 years.

Caliphate. From its foundation, 632, Buyid take-over, 943: life-span 312 years.

Ottoman Empire. From its foundation, *c.*1350, to its dissolution in 1918 (but still continuing as the Anatolian heartland thereafter): life-span 568 years.

Achæmenian Persian Empire. 550–330 BC: life-span 220 years.

Sassanian Persian Empire. AD 224–651: life-span 427 years.

British Empire in India. 1757–1947: life-span 190 years.

1.5.2. BREAKDOWNS AND DARK AGES

These are by no means the same things. A breakdown is the disintegration of a previously united state. It does not necessarily entail changes in technology, literacy, culture, or regime, though it may lead to a worsening and coarsening of these characteristics. Mostly it will entail a loss of military power against external foes, since the aggregate of wealth which the former central authority was able to accumulate is, *pro tanto*, smaller. Furthermore the succession-states are apt to make war among themselves, leading to further weakness against external enemies. A 'Dark Age', on the contrary, is one where the former civilization ceases to exist in recognizable form, and where the technology, culture, and form of rule has disappeared, and society is noticeably far poorer.

BREAKDOWNS

Egypt.
    From its origins to the end of the Old Kingdom (2850–2175 BC)   675 years
    1st Intermediate period (2175–1991 BC)   184
    Middle Kingdom (1991–1785 BC)   206

2nd Intermediate (1785–1570 BC)	215
New Kingdom to Alexander's (1570–332 BC)	1,238
China.	
Western Chou (1172–722 BC)	400
Break-up (722–221 BC)	500
Ch'in and Han (221 BC–AD 221)	442
Breakdown (AD 221–581)	360
Sui and T'ang (AD 581–907)	326
Breakdown (AD 907–76)	69
Sung, Mongols (Yuan) (AD 976–1912)	936
Assyria.	
Rise to empire (1356–1199 BC)	157
Breakdown (1199–1117 BC)	82
Empire (1117–1078 BC)	38
Breakdown (1078–935 BC)	143
New Empire (935–612 BC)	312

Dark Ages

Those which are most prominent in the history of government are as follows:

Greece

The Mycenaean civilization of Greece was destroyed c.1200 BC (what used to be called the 'descent of the Dorians'). There followed an age in which all traces of this great civilization and its characteristic palace-ruled petty kingdoms disappeared. Only about 800 BC do the signs of civilization appear again, and the onset is very rapid. Furthermore entirely new techniques are introduced, amongst them the alphabet and literacy, coined money, and the city-republic—the polis.

Europe

The Roman Empire in the West crumbled rather than 'fell', but if we date its fall at the conventional AD 476, a Dark Age set in soon after and was in full flood c.600. This age was one of barbarism, superstition, the almost complete loss of literacy, the virtual elimination of commerce and currency and, instead, a poverty-stricken rural natural economy, de-urbanization, invasion, plague, and continual wars and invasions. One has only to glance through Gregory of Tours's *History of the Franks* to see what a deprived and benighted period this was.[32]

---

[32] Gregory of Tours, *History of the Franks* (written between c. AD 576 and 591), trans. with an introduction by O. M. Dalton (Clarendon Press, Oxford, 1927).

It is a commonplace among historians that the peasants in the Western Roman Empire did not rise and fight against the barbarian intruders, because they were so oppressed by taxation that they no longer cared whether they lived under barbarian or Roman rule; indeed, that in many cases the transition was—in the short term—marked by a considerable reduction in taxation, since the huge regular Roman army no longer had to be maintained. All this is very fine and fair to a historian scribbling away in his comfortable room; but in my view—it is only a view, of course—if a peasant family in Gaul, or Spain, or northern Italy had been able to foresee the misery and exploitation that was to befall his grandchildren and their grandchildren, on and on and on for the next 500 years, he would have been singularly spiritless—and witless too—if he had not rushed to the aid of the empire. And even then the kingdoms that did finally emerge after the year 1000 were poverty-stricken dung-heaps compared with Rome. Not till the full Renaissance in the sixteenth century did Europeans begin to think of themselves as in any ways comparable to Rome, and not till the 'Augustan Age' of the eighteenth century did they regard their civilization as its equal.

2. THE TYPOLOGY OF REGIMES

This *History* is not meant to be a simple chronological account of the different ways in which men have been governed. It is an exercise in comparative government. This exercise is usually carried out synchronically, that is, by observing the similarities and the differences across different polities at one single point in time. This *History* carries it out diachronically, that is, identifies similarities and differences of various polities, across time.

Comparison requires classification; otherwise every unit of study is *sui generis*. The trick is somehow to find a middle way that reduces the number of units—but not too far. This caveat is necessary because as this Section proceeds it will be seen that the number of criteria of a polity can be multiplied almost indefinitely. Even as it stands, the number of the variables used in my typology may seem excessive.

The rudiments of that typology were first outlined by me in 1983.[33] Its essence is to class polities according to their predominant decision-making personnel, what some refer to as their 'political élites'. Since this yields only a few and consequently over-broad classes, it becomes necessary to introduce further distinctions. Generally speaking, the primary basis of the classification, that is, by the character of its ruling personnel, tells us the

[33] Finer, 'Perspectives in the World History', 16–17.

nature of the top decision-making process; while the further qualifications tell us more about the nature of what we might call their 'delivery systems', that is, the institutions by which they can make those decisions bite, that is, 'penetrate' the population.

2.1. *The Typology Summarized*

Territorial Dimension	1. City
	2. Generic or National
	3. Empire
Types of Polity	1. Decision-making personnel
	(a) The élite
	(b) The masses
	2. Decision-implementing personnel
	(a) Bureaucracies
	(b) Armed forces

Now let us proceed further. Let us start with the decision-making personnel and see how their broad types must be qualified. This yields the following:

2.1.1. THE DECISION-MAKING PERSONNEL: MAIN TYPES OF POLITY

The Characteristic Political Processes of these Types

There is a broad one-to-one relationship between the type of polity and its characteristic processes of arriving at decisions. These involve: the number of personnel involved; the procedures, including whether they are orderly or disorderly; and the tasks as perceived by the ruler(s).

The Legitimation of these Types

Here again, there are broad one-to-one relationships between the type of polity and its claims to legitimacy (what have been called its political formulae). These formulae sometimes serve more than one types of polity, so the correspondence is broader than in the previous case.

Together, these three sets of criteria serve to round out the description of the main types of polity, but still do not go far enough. For inside each 'family' of polities, members differ from one another in respect of the scope of their governmental activities, and the procedures they must follow in order to give authoritative effect to them. It is a question of how far the government is constrained, substantively or procedurally, or how far it is not. We may call this the dimensions of control. Hence:

The Dimensions of Control

(1) Level of relationships of control
    A. Central-government level ('horizontal' plane)
    B. Central-to-local level ('vertical' plane)
(2) Nature of relationships of control
    A. Scope of activities
        (1) Unconstrained
        (2) Constrained
    B. Procedure for exercising activities
        (1) Unconstrained
        (2) Constrained

This set of variables qualifies the main type of polity.

But so far we have analysed only in terms of the decision-making personnel. Polities are distinguished also by their decision-implementing personnel. This adds yet another criterion to the analysis of types of polity as categorized so far.

2.1.2. DECISION-IMPLEMENTING PERSONNEL

These are the civil bureaucracy and the armed forces. Their various types will be distinguished later. Their existence or non-existence and the various forms either of them may take will affect the 'penetration' capability of the authorities, and, particularly, their 'vertical' dimension, that is, their control over the local subdivisions and the fieldunits of the state.

Logically it is possible to envisage: (i) states without a bureaucracy and with a community-in-arms; (ii) states with a bureaucracy and, likewise, a community-in-arms; (iii) a bureaucracy and a standing army; and finally (iv) no bureaucracy, but a standing army. In practice—at least as far as I can ascertain empirically—the last does not exist. And there is an excellent reason for it—a standing army requires a bureaucracy in order to obtain the men, money, and materials it needs for its upkeep.[34] We shall not, therefore, consider this last logical case. Examination also shows that it is highly peculiar to find a bureaucracy but no standing army. As far as I know, this is confined to the early stages of Mesopotamian and Egyptian civilization. Hence the two standard forms are no (or little) bureaucracy and a community-in-arms; and a bureaucracy together with a standing army.

The normal relationship between the armed forces and the bureaucracy on the one side and the ruling authorities on the other is one of subordination. But this History, as well as contemporary experience, also attests a

[34] See p. 20 above.

pathological condition. In it, the bureaucracy, or the army, effectively take over the decision-making process from the authorities, who then play a nominal, though a necessary, legitimating role. This pathological relationship yields, in effect, two new types of regime: the bureaucratic and the military. But these will not be added to the main typology; they will be treated as perversions of the main types and the History deals with them *ad hoc.*

2.2. *The Main Types of Polity*

The main types of polity are identified and differentiated, in the first instance, by the nature of their ruling personnel. I recognize four pure kinds. These can be visually represented in a lozenge shape. At the apex comes what I shall call the Palace. At the base appears what I call the Forum. On the wings are, respectively, what I call the Church and the Nobility.

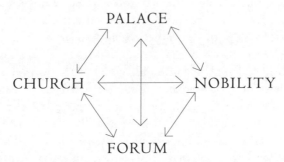

FIG. 1. *The main types of polity*

It is rare for any or each of these types of personnel to hold sway to the exclusion of the others, though it sometimes does occur. More often a polity is characterized by a mixed type of ruling personnel. The lines drawn across the lozenge show the major logical combinations of these, but this does not necessarily mean that they have existed in actuality. These logical combinations generate hybrid types of polity.

Hence the hybrid types can be formulated as:

> Palace/Church
> Palace/Nobility
> Palace/Forum
> Forum/Nobility
> Forum/Church
> Church/Nobility

Altogether, then, there are ten possible types of polity. But some of these are rarely if ever met with, while others are very common.

3. THE TYPES OF REGIME OUTLINED

3.1. *The Palace*

3.1.1. CONSTITUENTS OF 'THE PALACE'

'The Palace' is a metonym for the people who inhabit it. It is a very useful metonym, however, because it also describes the place in which they work. Sometimes we may refer to this not as Palace but as Court, and this again is a metonym for the courtiers who frequent it.

The Palace is, invariably, the seat of a monarch: what kind is immaterial—emperor, king, prince, tyrant, dictator—the important point here is that the Palace is a type wherein supreme decision-making rests with one individual. It is therefore, *inter alia*, autocratic and monocratic.

The Palace belongs to the monarch, and so, in a sense, do those who work in it. They are his servants. It is possible, and indeed it is very likely, that they will include priests and noblemen; but in this pure type of Palace-polity these have no independence. The priests will have been appointed or approved by the monarch and he can remove them; likewise for the court-nobility. It is quite possible that in the backlands there exist noblemen who live on their estates and are important in their own right, but these are not the ones who serve the monarch in his court. Indeed, very often there is an antagonism between the local and independent nobility and those who serve at court which provides the motor for governmental change.

Ancient Egypt, the Mesopotamian kingdoms or empires, the Persian, Roman, Byzantine, Chinese, and Islamic empires are all examples of the Palace-type polity. So too are some of the eighteenth-century European absolutisms—the court of Louis XIV, for instance.

3.1.2. THE BASE(S) OF ITS LEGITIMACY

Max Weber gives us a lot of help here and we can adapt some of his distinctions. Broadly speaking, we may divide the sources of the monarch's legitimacy into two, charisma and tradition. The first tends to slide into and become the second.

Charismatic Legitimation

'Charisma' is a theological term meaning the gift of grace; sociologically it refers to extraordinary, often superhuman powers and characteristics attributed to an individual. The powers may be military or religious or both. This charisma bespeaks a personality that breaks all norms. It is, literally, extraordinary. In its pristine state, charisma is personal. It is also highly unstable, for it can vanish as quickly as it came. In Shakespeare's *Antony and Cleopatra* (IV. iii), as Antony is lying in his tent at night, his guards hear a mysterious music. 'What should this mean?' asks one soldier and another replies:

> T'is the god Hercules, whom Antony lov'd,
> Now leaves him.

In the Bible, Saul is a charismatic king. 1 Samuel 11–6 tells how a divine madness came upon Saul as he was ploughing and drove him to convene the men of Israel against the Ammonites. After his victory Samuel anoints him king. But the same book, at chapters 15–26, tells how Saul transgresses, whereupon Samuel tells him: 'the Lord hath rejected thee from being king over Israel.' The divine gift has been taken as suddenly as it came.[35]

Legitimation by Tradition

Charisma is immediate and personal. As the gift begins to fade with time, this charisma starts to fuse with tradition. For who is to succeed the charismatic leader and how will he be found? So occurs what Weber called the 'routinization of charisma'. In some cases the ruler himself designates his successor. In others, a successor is acclaimed. This is sometimes expressed as 'elected'. But it is not an election in the sense we use it today. For this is not a choice; it is an epiphany. The ruler has been recognized, not made. In yet other cases the criterion of charisma is lineage-descent from the original charismatic leader. Thus the emperors of Japan have from the earliest times been credited with descent from the sun-goddess Amiterasu.

In the phase of routinized charisma the ruler's legitimacy rests on some divine, or at least supernatural, basis. It may be the claim that the king is himself a divinity, as in the case of the Egyptian pharaohs or the Aztec emperors. It may be—as in ancient Mesopotamia—the claim that the king is the vicar or *ishakku* of the gods, and that 'kingship descended from Heaven'.[36] This is a kind of vicarious divinity. The well-known European example, the 'Divine Right of Kings', exhibited itself in a wide variety of forms, but all of them reposed on the notion that monarchs derived their authority from God. The Chinese case is strange and interesting. The Chinese believed in a very shadowy kind of supernatural entity called *Ti'en*

---

[35] 1 Sam. 15: 26 (Authorized King James Version).
[36] 'The Myth of Etana', in J. B. Pritchard (ed.), *Ancient Near Eastern Texts*, 3rd edn. (Princeton, 1969), 114 (hereafter referred to as *ANET*).

or Heaven. One basis of the emperor's legitimacy was that he possessed the 'Mandate of Heaven' (a doctrine the Confucianists were to adopt and transmute into their own sanction for the emperor conducting himself along Confucian lines). But intertwined with this, and of more immediate salience, went the belief that the emperor was the link between humanity and the wider cosmos and that the indispensable harmony on earth and between earth and Heaven could be attained only if he pursued appropriate rituals of astonishing number and complexity.[37]

One final point about all foregoing varieties of legitimation. They are all, without exception, authoritarian. There is no question of popular sovereignty. The monarch's authority descends on him from a Higher Power and sets him above the people. This is what Ullmann has appropriately called the 'descdening theme of government'.[38]

Popular Legitimation

But it may be objected that some autocrats—nowadays a great many—are legitimated by popular election. True, but for reasons that will become clear later, these cases are best regarded as a most important mixed, not pure, type of polity. They are, in fact, Palace/Forum polities.[39]

For all that, there remain two seeming examples where the autocrat is apparently legitimated by popular election, and as these are the emperors of respectively the Roman and the Byzantine empires, they can hardly be shrugged off. Certainly these emperorships were supposedly the fruit of popular election, but this was entirely fictional, and moreover the notion lost any legitimating power it might have once had very early on.

In the Roman Empire the fiction grew from the Augustan settlement. Augustus pretended that the Senate and People of Rome had legally and duly conferred the highest magistracies upon him; hence the style in which he referred to himself—as the *princeps*. This fiction that the emperor was the outcome of election by the Senate was maintained till the very end of the Western Empire, but the succession was usually decided by an army acclaiming its general as *imperator*, or by the ruling emperor designating a co-emperor. In all cases the Senate simply ratified what had been decided elsewhere. When this pretence itself wore thin, as it had by the third century AD, it was succeeded by Ulpian's view that the emperors owed their legitimacy to a purported *lex regia*, by which (he alleged) the Senate and People of Rome had conferred their sovereignty upon the emperorship for

[37] See, in particular, M. Granet, *La pensée chinoise* (Albin Michel, Paris, 1934).
[38] W. Ullmann, *Law and Politics in the Middle Ages* (Hodder & Stoughton, London, 1975), 77, 92.
[39] Where the '+' sign indicates that the Palace is the predominant factor (see p. 55 below).

all time. This notion was to play an important role in the Middle Ages, when some jurists invoked it in the name of popular sovereignty, but in the Later Roman Empire it served only to legalize rather than legitimize the ruler. In practice emperors came increasingly to rely on religious legitimation. The imperial cult, attempted somewhat half-heartedly ever since the days of the first *divus*, Julius Caesar himself, was not really pressed until the early third century AD. By the time of Diocletian the emperor was routinely claiming divine descent; he was surrounded by the most elaborate oriental pomp and ceremony; he had to receive the obeisance; and he was referred to always as 'the sacred'. Once Christianity had become the empire's official religion, it did not weaken such religious legitimation, but made it an article of faith for the entire Christian *ecclesia*. The Sacred Christian Emperor was presented to the Christian community as ruling by Christ's grace for the purpose of sustaining his Church, and as *isapostolos*, the equal of the Holy Apostles themselves.

The 'popular election' of a Byzantine emperor was even more farcical because Constantinople had never had a Senate equivalent to Rome's. 'Election' by a duly constituted Senate was replaced in the empire's eastern capital by acclamation. Those who 'acclaimed', however, were the court-centred nobility and officials. Here again, it was the religious (Christian) legitimation that counted, symbolized by the coronation. To tell the truth, it was not a very powerful force. Most Byzantine emperors were not permitted to reign for long. The force of events, like the domestic controversy that attended Iconoclasm or failure in war, overrode it very easily.

3.1.3. THE CHARACTERISTIC POLITICAL PROCESS

The surviving histories of Palace-polities in, for instance, the pages of the Bible, Tacitus, or China's greatest historian Ssu-ma Ch'ien, are almost entirely concerned with personal relationships, with feud, faction, and intrigue. This is what makes them so entertaining, so dramatic. It also makes them very misleading. Rulers—or their surrogates, at least—were in the business of governing. How they did this appears in their archives, not in the 'histories', and what we know of it is the result of patient reconstruction by recent scholars. We have to distinguish, then, between the inter-personal relationships in the Palace—what we may call Palace-politics, and which are essentially pathological—and the orderly processes by which the palace carried on the business of government.

In either case, of course, the typical personnel of the Palace-polity remains, *mutatis mutandis*, much the same. They consist of the ruler and his family circle; his harem or gynecaeum; his courtiers, that is, persons who are either of noble birth or have had noble rank conferred on them; the higher clergy; the higher military commanders; and the ruler's personal staff which protects, counsels, informs, and acts for him and consists of such persons as ministers, clerks, slaves, eunuchs, guards, as the case may be. These are the main interest of the court historians we have mentioned. But, of course, only when they act in an interesting way, and that means when they act, so to speak, out of turn—in short, pathologically. This pathology basically consists in one or other of two things, or both things together. The first is the intrigue and conspiracy among the courtiers, the ruler's staff, the harem, and the like, to get privileged access to the ruler's ear and if possible to shut out all other voices—the 'gatekeeper' function. Or it can go much further; the same kinds of plots from the same quarters, but to remove the ruler and replace him with somebody else, or—as often occurs where the throne is left empty—to pre-empt the succession. The other variant of these last processes is where they are undertaken not by courtiers, but by the military. Here it is a prominent commander who takes the initiative in evicting the occupant of the throne, and either taking it for himself or choosing the successor. Often the civil and military personnel at the court coalesce to bring about such results. For English-speaking people the most vivid portrayals of the pathology of Palace-politics are to be found in Shakespeare's 'Histories'.

But there is a sober, systematized routine of government that goes on at the Palace, also. Where the polity is reasonably well bureaucratized—by which I mean that it has already thrown up specialized agencies for the main tasks of government—it is common to find something like the following. The ruler makes his decisions either alone or in council—or alone, after taking counsel. The decisions he takes are based upon informa-tion which has flowed in to be processed through the specialized agencies until it finally reaches ministers, who thereupon put it, together with the policy alternatives, to the ruler. But sometimes the ruler feels that he is being pressured by these ministers and advisers and sets up his own counter-intelligence agency: a personal staff of inner counsellors, usually of inferior birth and breeding to those who monopolize the great offices of state.

This process of sifting information, taking counsel, and then deciding can be done very well: witness Trajan or Hadrian or, in more recent Europe, Louis XIV or Frederick II. But it can go badly wrong. There is a pathology of this administrative process, also. Many are the cases where, with our historians' hindsight, we know that the information supplied to the ruler was suppressed or distorted; where the established official bureaucracy was at loggerheads with the ruler's personal staff; where his ultimate decision was bent by the influence of favourites or by the women of his harem; and, in the worst cases of all, by the defectiveness of the ruler. We find rulers who took no interest whatsoever in matters of state. There are others who did take an interest, but only to satisfy a momentary caprice. There are others who were mentally deficient or even mad.

There is one further point, I think, to be made about the political process in the Palace. It is the matter of ritual. Once again, this has to be reconstructed by modern historians, since the contemporaries took it for granted. The extent to which a ruler was committed to ritual varies with the kind of religion of his society. Where the ruler was the link between humanity and the cosmos, ritual bulked very large indeed and the ruler had to spend a vast amount of his time in it. Such was certainly the case in the archaic monarchies of Egypt and Mesopotamia, and in Imperial China. It was much less the case in, let us say, the Roman Empire, and even less so in its barbarian succession states.

3.2. The Forum

Another metonomy! Here the place where debate and voting takes place is used to stand for those who take part in this process. The pure type of this polity is the very antithesis of the previous one. The Palace system is a closed little world; the Forum system is open and wide. The Palace system is authoritarian—the right to govern has been conferred from on high; the Forum polity, though not necessarily democratic, is 'popular': that is, authority is conferred on the rulers from below. The Palace system is monocratic; the Forum is plural-headed.

One essential point must be emphasized here in the most explicit way (it will be used implicitly in all that follows), and it is this. To conform to the Forum type it is not enough that the government has been appointed by popular conferment. If this were all, then a government, once so appointed, could go on ruling indefinitely in the Palace fashion as explained above. Indeed, as will be seen, this is precisely what defines the at-first-sight paradoxical hybrid, the Palace/Forum polity.[40] To conform to the Forum type of polity, the government must be accountable to the people who have conferred on it the right to govern. In practice this means periodic renewal of its mandate by such processes as elections and the like.

It is here that the Forum polity differs essentially from the other three main types. The Palace, the Church, and the Nobility derive their authority from non-popular sources; accordingly, they are accountable to those sources—say, the Divinity—but they are not accountable to the people. One form of the Divine Right of Kings doctrine maintains that the

---

[40] See p. 56 ff. below.

monarch not only derives his authority from God but is responsible only to God. In short, all those three types of polity are authoritarian. The Forum is the only one of the four pure types that is not authoritarian. This distinction, which is obvious enough in most cases, is not so obvious in the Palace/Forum type, described below, where it is crucial. Hence this lengthy interpolation.

3.2.1. THE CONSTITUENTS OF THE FORUM POLITY

Definitionally these constituents are 'the people'. But who are 'the people'? What proportion of the population, and of what degree, must have the right to participate before we can say that a particular polity is of the 'Forum' variety? In Athens every adult male citizen had the right to vote and speak, but this franchise excluded all women, metics (foreign settlers), and slaves. In the more democratic of the Italian medieval city republics— Florence, for instance—the proportion of what the French Revolution was to style the 'active citizens' was only about 3–5 per cent of the total population, albeit perhaps 10–15 per cent of the adult male citizens. In some societies—the last named provide a good example—the active and the passive citizenry are distinguished by the amount of property they own. In others, residence qualifications are another discriminatory factor. In all societies, till the most recent times, women have been excluded. There have always been age limits on the right to participate, though such limits prescribe only a minimum age for participation and no society has yet, to my knowledge, disqualified citizens from participation because they are too old.

The problem of who are 'the people' is well illustrated by the history of the franchise in Britain. (The earlier figures given here are somewhat approximate but that does not matter in this context.) It is reckoned that in 1831 the total electorate (which consisted only of adult males) was about 2 per cent of the total population. The Reform Act of 1832 raised this to just over 3 per cent. This Act introduced a standardized property qualification and so, as the country grew richer, the number of electors increased until in 1866 they numbered some 5 per cent of the total population. The Reform Act of 1867 doubled this proportion to about 10 per cent. The further Reform Act of 1884 produced something approaching universal male suffrage, and raised the proportion of 'the people' to some 22 per cent of the total population. But when women were enfranchised in 1918 the proportion of electors to population soared to 78 per cent, and rose even further in 1928 after the voting age for women had been made identical with that for men: it was now 90 per cent of the adult population. Since the voting age was lowered from 21 to 18 years, the proportion has risen to 99 per cent of the total adult population.

This brief chronology indicates some of the variegated criteria which define 'the people'. The question is: what proportion of the population must be entitled to participate before we feel entitled to say that a polity is of the Forum variety? Whatever the answer, it must mean a large absolute number and a high proportion of those who actively desire to be part of the political process. Beyond that, simplistic quantitative formulae are of no use.

3.2.2. THE BASIS OF LEGITIMACY

The legitimizing principle—the political formula—is that the final say in all decisions inheres in the ruled and not the rulers. How this axiom is arrived at is another and altogether more complicated matter. In many simple societies it is a prescriptive right that inheres in the warriors precisely because they are warriors, and in a simple society most of the adult males are or have been warriors. This right can carry over into the succeeding and more advanced stage into which the simple society develops. We might call this the traditional basis of the legitimizing axiom. A second would be the rational basis, and is to be found in the numerous works of political theorists from Greek times to the present day. These give a philosophical grounding to what, in point of fact, is usually the expression of interests and/or passions. (This view is Paretian, but I believe it to be true.) These interests and passions can be expressed, and nowadays usually are, in an ideology, and the ideology provides a third legitimizing basis for the Forum-type polity. But the justification for the Forum-polity does not reside in whether it is true or false that the masses possess a superior wisdom or virtue. What is necessary is simply that these propositions, true or false as they may be, should be widely and deeply believed. This is Paretian doctrine, too: that given political actions do not depend on whether a proposition is true or false, but on what is believed about them.[41]

3.2.3. THE CHARACTERISTIC POLITICAL PROCESSES

The central political process consists, not of commanding—as in the Palace type—but of somehow persuading. Furthermore, information about public attitudes, desires, and reactions is much more openly accessible and abundant than in the Palace polity. Hence the institutional arrangements at the apex of the Forum polity are more complicated than in the Palace type. That is a monocracy and also an autocracy: in principle, all institutions are

---

[41] Cf. S. E. Finer (ed.), *Vilfredo Pareto: Sociological Writings* (Blackwell, Oxford, 1976).

embodied in the person of the solitary and supreme ruler. Such specialized organs as do develop tend to be of an administrative and judicial nature only, and depend upon the ruler. But the Forum has the more difficult task of 'collecting' the sense of the public, making arrangements for reconciling differences in its attitudes, and taking steps to ensure that the consequential decisions are in accord with the outcome. The ruling authority is plural and subject to procedural checks and balances: to use our previous terminology, it is procedurally limited on the 'horizontal' plane.[42]

These are mere abstractions. Their referents in the real world are factions, leagues, and parties; arrangements to gather choices and transmit them; decision-making procedures, assemblies, and the like. The political scientist finds this kind of system much more interesting to study than Palace polities because the political process consists of the interplay of a variety of intricately interlocking institutions: in contrast, the model Palace polity resembles a simple monolithic pyramid.

The central process of the system being the practice of persuasion, the well-ordered Forum polity assists this by a regular and wide distribution of information and options, and various sanctioned modes of bringing dissenting views into a conformity strong enough to ensure obedience to the laws. Forum polities do not presuppose literacy, although they are enormously improved by it. But the essence of persuading is, in the last resort, by speech; and hence one of the characteristics of the Forum polity is the cultivation of rhetoric. For in this system the people are not simply told from on high what they must do; they have to be won over. It is the Forum polity that generates the art and the science of rhetoric. It was discussed, analysed, and taught as a discipline in the Greek *poleis* and in the Roman Republic. The art of rhetoric has not disappeared from our contemporary Forum-type polities, it has merely changed its appearance. It consists, nowadays, in the command of the broadcast and the television appearance. These are the instruments which win elections. Today's functional equivalent of the Classical rhetorician is the PR firm.

The Forum polity is comparatively rare in the history of government, where the Palace polity and its variants are overwhelmingly the most common type. Only in the last two centuries has the Forum polity become widespread. Before then its appearance is, on the whole, limited to the Greek *poleis*, the Roman Republic, and the medieval European city-states. Furthermore, most of them for most of the time exhibited the worst pathological features of this kind of polity. For rhetoric read demagogy, for persuasion read corruption, pressure, intimidation, and falsification of

[42] See p. 36 above.

the vote. For meetings and assemblies, read tumult and riot. For mature deliberation through a set of revising institutions, read instead self-division, inconstancy, slowness, and legislative and administrative stultification. And for elections read factional plots and intrigues. These features were the ones characteristically associated with the Forum polity in Europe down to very recent times. They were what gave the term 'Republic' a bad name, but made 'Democracy' an object of sheer horror.

3.3. *The Nobility*

We need not spend very long on this type of polity. For one thing, it is very rare to find a nobility governing a polity entirely on its own, without any admixture of other ruling elements. Still, it is possible to find some examples. Poland in the late seventeenth and the eighteenth centuries would approximate to this type. It is true that Poland was a monarchy, but the monarch was elected for his lifetime by the assembled noblemen, and these, organized in two chambers, completely controlled his actions. One single nobleman could, by his individual voice, veto any proposal and at the same time bring about the dissolution of the Assembly (the *Sejm*).

3.3.1. THE CONSTITUENTS OF THE NOBILITY POLITY

It is essential to distinguish between two broad types of nobility. In one 'nobility' is ascriptive, in the other it is achieved. By and large, members of the former are recognized by their lineage, those of the latter acquire their status from serving the monarch and form a court nobility, often a service nobility. The former tend to possess their own personal and/or family power resources giving them independence or, at least, some autonomy. In contrast, the latter owe their resources to the monarch, and what he gave he can take away. In practice, the hereditary principle being what it is, the latter tend to acquire the autonomy of the former unless monarchs actively prevent them. When the time comes, a monarch may find that he can no longer insist on the contingency of the original grant of wealth or land to the recalcitrant aristocrat who claims it as his inheritance. In 1278 Edward I of England decided to challenge the right of his noblemen to hold what he suspected were originally Crown lands, and to do this issued the writ of *quo warranto*; it demanded by 'what warrant' did the lord hold that land. The Earl Warenne answered the King angrily by pointing to a rusting long-sword which hung over his great fireplace. For in natural economies it made sense for monarchs to pay for service by grants of the usufruct of land. While this grant of lands was contingent, the noble grantees would try in

48 CONCEPTUAL PROLOGUE

the course of time to elude the service obligation while retaining the land. This is what happened among practically all the feudal nobilities of Europe.

There has existed, however, a strange kind of half-way house between the ascriptive and the service nobility. Its most striking example is Egypt's Mamluks. 'Mamluk' means 'slave', and the slave-soldier was peculiar to Islamic societies and no others. The institution was to be found in the decaying Caliphate all the way from Central Asia to the banks of the Nile, and in every case the leaders of the slave troops usurped the throne from their masters, the legitimate sovereigns. Such military usurpation is in itself not at all uncommon, as the later paragraphs on the pathology of the decision-implementing personnel will show. What is so unusual in the Mamluk case is the way in which this new ruling class, this new nobility, perpetuated itself; for its leaders, the Emirs, continuously recruited more young slaves, who, after due military training, passed out as regulars, were duly freed by their Emir-owner, and henceforth became his faithful following.

In the present context, that of the Nobility polity, it is the ascriptive, autonomously resourced type of nobleman that is being referred to, not the court and/or service nobility. The fact that over time one kind might flow over into the other, and that, for instance, the ascriptive nobility might contain members who had become so poor as to be the venal servants of royalty, does not affect the analytical distinction; it merely complicates the historical account.

3.3.2. THE BASIS OF LEGITIMACY

What are the stigmata that mark out the ascriptive nobility ?

The usual criterion, as we have indicated, is lineage, but this only pushes the question back further. What is the justification for calling the ancestor noble? In eighteenth-century France the *noblesse d'epée* would have responded that their ancestors were the original Franks who had come in and conquered the population. A similar view is expressed in what in England came to be the theory of the 'Norman yoke'. The point is that lineage alone only masks the original stigmata which marked off some persons as of superior social status to others. In some simpler societies the important distinction was age, and where the aged are the ruling group we refer to them as a gerontocracy; but we are hardly concerned with that here except, possibly, in the cases of medieval Venice (or present-day China).

In most cases the basis of the superior status is wealth and/or military prowess. But in other cases this is replaced—or supplemented—by the ethnic or the cultural or the religious attributes of those persons. The Spanish conquistadores became grandees and noblemen in the New World because they were white and not brown, conquerors and not conquered, Christian and not pagan, and so forth; and on this basis they first acquired their wealth and then their noble status.

3.3.3. THE POLITICAL PROCESS

In a purely nobiliar polity each of its grander members thinks himself as good as his fellows and often much better. The essence of the situation is a continual and ongoing rivalry between the aristocratic houses, a striving for hegemony over the rest, the formation of factions, the recourse to blows and intrigue rather than orderly processes of choice, and finally, a central government that is plural, indeed conciliar. Until the fateful battlefield of Sekigashara in 1600, when Ieyasu Tokugawa imposed his personal rule over the feudality, all the above might stand as a succinct summary of one thousand years of Japanese government.

This type of polity usually has a characteristic 'vertical', that is to say, central–local dimension also, and this gives a peculiar 'texture' to the mode of government. A paradigm model of this nobiliar polity would reveal a number of equally powerful magnates each possessing his own power-resources—in lands, clientele, and wealth—in his own local territory. He controls the lives of the persons living in his area; sometimes *de jure*—as in some feudal polities—more often, though, *de facto*. The local peasants and the like are 'his' clientele, and he both exploits them and protects them from other lords. He also protects them from the central government's agents, and the way he does this is to take over that central government's local functions. In this way he inserts himself between the population and the central government so that the form of government is an intermediated one. It may also be regarded, visually, as a clustered one or one composed of so many cells. The greatest noblemen will, by a system of unequal exchange, control the destinies of an inferior stratum of nobles, and so on down to the common population itself. Thus the state will consist of a number of 'cells', each belonging to a greater cell, until at the apex we have the council of the greatest magnates, who form a sort of holding company of these inferior cells, constituting themselves as the greatest cell of all, one which is coterminous with the state itself. In the text this form of polity is frequently referred to as 'cellular'. It is to be found not just in formally nobiliar regimes but in others like those in nineteenth-century Latin America, where the 'nobles' were often local landowners who had built up their local clienteles—they had *gentes*. Such, for instance, were the *coroneis* of Brazil's backlands under the Republic till about 1930, and such again were the *jefes militares* in the Mexican Republic after Porfirio Diaz.

3.4. *The Church*

Yet another metonym; the word means the place of worship, from the Greek, *kuriakon doma* (the Lord's house), contracted to *kirche*, kirk, and church (via the Goths); also, the congregation of worshippers;[43] but finally, in the present context, also the structured organization, in so far as one exists, which serves that congregation. The last sense implies that there has been a fairly neat differentiation of roles between the ordinary worshipper and those leading his worship, that is, a priesthood; but also that these priests or holy men are articulated together and can be considered as a corporation, which is coterminous with the religious congregation itself. In certain cases—the Roman Catholic Church is the limiting one—this priesthood is sharply differentiated from the laity, and is organized on the strictest of hierarchical models. In other cases, like Islam, we are talking of pious and learned men, rabbis in fact, rather than priests, with little or no hierarchy existing among them. The degree of hierarchy and the way in which these churches are interrelated with government has already been dealt with.[44]

It must be said at once that the instances of a polity ruled exclusively by the Church with no admixture of other élite elements are rare in the extreme. Apart from the Vatican the nearest example is Tibet between 1642 and 1949. It is in admixture with other elements, notably the Palace and/or the Nobility, that the Church is significant in the history of government. Consequently we shall not spend much time on its constituents, legitimizing formula, and its characteristic political process.

As to the constituents, it is composed of individuals who, by a social and religious convention, are regarded as the leaders of the religious community. The nature of such persons and the marks by which they are conventionally recognized vary according to cases and will be described as each of these is discussed. On its legitimizing formula, again, there is little need to dally. It lies in the congregation's belief that this class of persons plays a specially defined role in bringing them to understand and placate the supernatural. It is the religion itself—'the Faith'—that provides the legitimation. And finally, as to the characteristic political process, it simply does not have one. If the only, or almost the only, case of a Church ruling society is to be found in Tibet, one is not justified in taking the internal political processes of the Lamas as characteristic of all Churches which might find themselves in that position. If, however, we are looking for the ways in which priests become priests, how they attain to positions of authority within their

---

[43] *Ekklesia, ecclesia, église, iglesia, chiesa,* as explained above, pp. 25–6.
[44] See pp. 24, 27 above.

Church, how their successors are designated, and so forth, then the answer is that these practices vary from one Church to another. What is said of the Roman Catholic priesthood bears absolutely no relationship to the Rabbinate or the *ulema* of Islam.

3.5. The Church/Nobility Polity

This is very rare, so much so that the only example that immediately springs to mind is that of the Teutonic Order in East Prussia and the Baltic. Here we have a religious Order, composed of noblemen, ruling a subjected population. The Order was founded in the Levant in 1198. With the collapse of the Crusader kingdoms, the Order had to transfer its activities and wound up, *c.*1225, on the eastern borders of Germany, in a barbarous and pagan land. Thence it conquered north and east to form and rule a territorial state.

The Order consisted of three classes of brethren: the priests, the serjeants, and the knights. These knights had to be both noble and of German blood. There is no mistaking the religious nature of the Order; no brother might hold private property or marry, and all had to follow a very harsh discipline and rule.

The government of the Order resided in the *Hochmeister*, who was elected in due form—as in all religious orders—by the General Chapter of the knights. He was assisted by the grand officers but in turn had to take counsel with them. The *Grosskomtur* was the Supreme Bailiff. The others were the battle-marshall, the hospitaller, the treasurer, and the quarter-master. Thus the central government resembled that of many of the other religious Orders—elective, limited, and conciliar.

But the vertical dimension of government was feudal. Below the *Grosskomtur* were grouped *Landmeisters*, and under them were grouped *Hauskomturs*. Each of the last-named ruled his *komturei*, which consisted of at least twelve knights. These were the lords or seigneurs of their peasants. Additionally, as the Order conquered the land it accepted local nobles to hold lands as its vassals.

This cursory outline of the Teutonic Order is intended merely to establish that it did indeed combine the elements of church and nobility in a governing body.[45]

---

[45] The great work on the Order is G. de Wal, *Histoire de l'ordre teutonique*, 8 vols. (Paris and Rheims, 1784–90).

3.6. *The Church/Forum Polity*

This type of government is also very rare. It has never been known to appear on a large territorial scale. To the contrary, it appears in very small communities. It is an extreme form of congregationalism, a denomination in which the pastors are chosen by their congregations much as synagogues choose their rabbis. Calvin's Geneva approximates to the type, for although Calvin's code regulated only the Church, that Church contained pastors and others who carried out worldly missions and also kept an eye upon the morals of the citizenry. But Calvin's Geneva is far more important in the history of religion than for the fact that it approximates to a Church/Forum polity. Other examples which in themselves are politically very unimportant do, nevertheless, provide much better models of the Church/Forum type. Such are the numerous and petty communities that emigrated to or burgeoned in America in the late eighteenth and early nineteenth centuries. Take Ephrata for instance (a name that must be all but forgotten). A Protestant—and highly congregationalist—sect, called Mennonites, had been formed by Dutchmen in 1536. Mennonites emigrated to America in the early eighteenth century. Some were joined in 1725 by a German called Beissel, a mystic with half-a-dozen followers, soon joined by many more, until in 1732 a regular communistic society was formed among them. This was Ephrata. The community flourished until Beissel's death in 1786, after which its membership slowly diminished. But there were many more, similar sects in which, so to speak, community, that is, Forum, and spiritual pastorship, that is, Church, were intermingled: Moravians, Dunkers, Rappites, and the like.[46]

3.7. *The Church/Palace Polity*

This is a much more significant type of polity than the previous two. It comes in three sizes, so to speak, depending on which pole of the hybrid is the more important: we could represent this as being either Church+/Palace, or Church/Palace+, or finally, an equilibrium, that is, Church/Palace. The first is often called a theocracy, but this is a very vague term. It was coined by Josephus, the Jewish historian, when he was trying to explain the polity of the Jews (in his *Contra Apion*); he meant by it that they regarded God as their ruler. That is not the same as what I want to convey in the present context. This requires the term 'hierocracy', that is, a polity in which the priesthood wholly or closely directs or controls the activities of a

---

[46] Cf. R. Strachey, *Religious Fanaticism* (Faber & Gwyer, London, 1928), esp. 30–65.

monarch. Examples are truly hard to find. Priest-kings are common enough; but these are either kings who are legitimated by the fact that they control the cult, or vice versa—whoever controls the cult is regarded as king. In either case we are dealing with a Palace-type polity, not a mixed type.

The second and third cases, however, are represented in the difference between medieval Western Europe and the Byzantine Empire. As the *History* shows, the Byzantine emperor was regarded as the head of the Church, its leader, protector, and definer (albeit not a priest). As we have said before, he was *isapostolos*, the equal of the Apostles. The predominance of the lay ruler over the Church, as here, is usually called caesaropapism, with Byzantium as its supreme example. But it is by no means the only one. In the traditional polity of Thailand, for instance, the king effectively controlled the monasteries, and thereby the *sangha*, that is, the organized Buddhist monkhood.[47] Again, during the European Reformation many Protestant monarchs took on themselves the role of head or supreme Moderator of their territorial Church. The title given such princes is 'Erastian', and Erastianism is being used for what is effectively caesaropapism.

The most interesting, and surely most significant, variant of the Church/ Palace relationship occurs, however, when these powers are in rough balance. The supreme example of this is, of course, during the European Middle Ages, from the Hildebrandine reforms of 1059 onwards, to the Palace's first effective check to the Papal claims of Boniface VIII (1294–1303). World history witnessed the astounding and unique sight of an organized and autocratically ruled priesthood, successfully challenging the right of monarchs to have a say in the appointment and control of the priestly hierarchy and then asserting that the Palace was, properly, the mere subject of the head of this Church, that is, the pope.

It is claimed that the tension this generated—the fact that the Church could support the baronage or other dissidents against the Palace—had 'democratizing' effects in the West as compared with the absolutism of caesaropapist Byzantium. This is surely true of England. It is less sustainable in the French case; the Papacy tended to depend on the French monarchy and therefore to take its side in civil conflict. But in Germany and Italy the counter-punching by the Church did not lead to any democratization of the political process but simply to territorial disintegration. The Church's ideology was authoritarian and remained so until well into the present century. It might plausibly be argued that its powerful organizational structure and enormous prestige made it able to limit monarchy; but a limited government is not the same as a democratic one, any more than

[47] Cf. H. G. Q. Wales, *Ancient Siamese Government and Administration* (London, 1934), 237–44.

liberalism is the same as democracy. They are different, and indeed in many cases quite antithetical.

3.8. *The Forum/Nobility Polity*

By this I mean a polity where a numerous class of active citizens—that is, those having the power to vote and to serve as magistrates—confides the leadership of affairs to the nobility. Such polities usually have a restricted suffrage. But although the proportion of active to total population is small, in absolute numbers it is large.

The definition of 'noble' varies. The Venetian aristocracy were merchants. The nobility, or as we tend to call them, the patriciate of the German medieval trading towns were very wealthy bourgeois. Who was 'noble' and who was not was a vexed question in the medieval Italian city-states. It was of the greatest significance there, since their political contests usually took the form of the *popolo* versus the nobility, who were defined by local criteria. In the Roman Republic the nobility were the original patricians to whom elements of the plebs attached themselves to form a new, socially superior class of ancient families.

The difference between such polities and the pure Forum type is that the latter are, by definition, polities of a wide if not universal franchise, whereas the former invariably exclude the bulk of their population by some device or another. In Rome the census graded the population into classes with differential voting strength—the wealthy having a vast superiority over the poor. In Venice the supreme overriding powers of the general assembly of the population was bit by bit whittled away in favour of the Great Council of some 3,000 wealthy families. Then these families 'closed' the doors on any further entrants to that Council and so became a hereditary ruling body. The expedients adopted in the medieval cities of Italy and Germany are too numerous and diverse to be recounted, but all had the effect of confining policy to the local nobility, as locally defined. The two supreme examples of the Forum/Nobiliar polity are the Roman Republic and the Republic of Venice, both of which are considered in detail in this *History*.

A point of terminology has to be noted here. From at least the time of Machiavelli to the beginning of the nineteenth century some theorists reserved the term 'republic' for any polities where supreme power did not rest in one supreme person but in several. Machiavelli did so at the beginning of *The Prince*. This usage puts the democracy of Athens and the Republic of Rome into the same category, as 'republican'. Other writers, however, distinguished between these two. For instance Hume, in his essay on 'The Populousness of Nations', talks of the Republics of Europe and goes on to say that 'Almost all of them are well-tempered aristocracies'.

In this *History* I take the view that both classes are certainly republics, as compared with monarchies or other forms of monocratic rule, but that it is useful to confine the meaning of 'democracy' to those with a very wide and equal franchise and competition for office (e.g. Athens), and the 'republic' to those where the franchise is restricted and applied in the interests of a narrow group of aristocratic families (Florence, Venice). Hence it is the former that qualify as pure Forum-type polities, while the latter fall under the present rubric, as Forum/Nobility ones.

3.9. *The Palace/Nobility Polity*

This type of polity comes in three—and possibly four—variants, so different that it is a shame we have to lump them all under the same title. The variations depend on which element preponderates in the combination. As before (in the case of the Church/Palace polity), I shall pursue the convention of writing, respectively, Palace+/Nobility, Palace/Nobility+, and the balanced type, Palace/Nobility.

Fortunately, we can largely ignore two of these variants. Take, for instance, the Palace+/Nobility type. Here the nobility are overshadowed by the monarch. They are his ancillaries. The court of Louis XIV provides an excellent example. Any monarchy with a tame nobility falls under this heading. Very often the reason why this nobility is tame is because it is a service nobility, deliberately created by the monarch as a reward for services rendered. As we said earlier, the danger is that a tame or service nobility may in various ways, for various reasons, acquire a hereditary hold upon the lands and the like conferred on it as 'pay' for the services rendered. In that event the nobility becomes more and more independent. The pole then tips to the other variant where the monarch is a cipher and the nobility run the state. The supreme example of this has already been mentioned—it is eighteenth-century Poland.[48] But it would not be too far-fetched to apply this to the British polity, 1714–60, when the Whig connection was supreme. This was the period Disraeli described as 'the Venetian Oligarchy'. The independent powers of the monarch were few, and in any case neither George I nor George II cared to assert those that they still held against the great Whig cousinhood which, using the king's name and his patronage, successfully controlled the electoral process and had itself duly returned to office again and again. But the king of Great Britain had much more going

[48] See p. 47 above.

for him than the unfortunate elected king of Poland, a 'transient and embarrassed phantom' if ever there was one. The executive in Britain was still a powerful and autonomous force which the parliament could control but not direct. In Poland, by contrast, the executive was non-existent.

The balanced Palace/Nobility type finds its supreme example in the European Middle Ages. The monarch rules but he is surrounded by a circle of semi-independent noblemen, jealous of their privileges and able, if necessary, to counterbalance the powers of the Crown. The result is limited monarchy and a conciliar form of polity: the king rules, but in council. By the seventeenth century, or the eighteenth at the latest, most monarchs on the European continent had managed to disarm and neuter their nobility, so becoming 'absolute'; in fact polities of the Palace+/Nobility type, as described already. The exception was, as we have to repeat, Poland, where the type swung to the opposite pole and became the Palace/Nobility+ type. The balance of Palace and Nobility maintained itself only in England, and it is from this unique state of affairs that there emerged constitutionally limited monarchy which was destined to have such a wide future.

But, I suggested, we might even distinguish a fourth variant here, and this would itself be a variant on the previous form, namely the 'balanced' Palace/Nobility type. In the previous example the result was an equilibrium, sometimes disturbed, but finding its centre-point of stability in the conciliar arrangements. In the present case the alternatives are either a pure Nobility type or a pure Palace type, and the polity oscillates violently between the two. The outward sign of this is the incessant struggle between rival noblemen or noble houses for the privilege of wielding the supreme power of the Palace. The result is a Palace-type polity punctuated by violent usurpations. The Mamluk regime in Egypt provides one example—the Sultan was the Emir who deployed at any one time a superior force to his rival Emirs. Japan provides a similar example up to Ieyasu's definitive victory in 1600. Until then, Japan's history appears to a European like a continuous, 800-year-long Wars of the Roses. For all that, the Mamluk regime and the pre–1600 Japanese regime must be characterized as stable Palace/Nobility type polities. For it was the rulers, the incumbents of office, who changed, while the general system of rule did not. We have already underlined the importance of distinguishing the two.

3.10. *The Palace/Forum Polity*

At first sight, this looks like a contradiction in terms. How, it must be asked, can the hermetic and authoritarian Palace coalesce with the wide franchise and the popularly conferred sovereignty of the Forum?

In principle the conditions would be met when a solitary executive, endowed with supreme and unrestricted powers, has to submit himself regularly to free and competitive election. After all, it could be said, are not the American and the French presidents elected in just such a way? This rescue-attempt just will not do. For the two presidents cited are not supreme and unrestricted. They have to work in conjunction with other elected authorities. The presidents are not sole rulers at all; they are part of what we have described as a conciliar form of government.

For all that, not only has the Palace/Forum polity indeed existed; it still does and is more widespread than ever before. It exists in a pathological form defined by Aristotle as the *tyrannos*. Here, a supreme ruler is authorized by popular acclaim to act according to how he sees fit. This variant of Palace/Forum differs from the pure Palace type in two ways—its characteristic political process, and its claim to legitimacy. As to the former; the Palace/Forum polity does not blend Palace and Forum but merely effects an amalgam between two discrete and separate processes. One is the appeal to populist sympathies, and to popular election or at least popular confirmation. The other is that, once this popular support is won, the ruler governs in pure Palace fashion—within a closed circle of dependents. Furthermore, in this polity the Palace is the predominant partner. Also, in most cases though not in all, the election or confirmation of the ruler by the people is achieved through the worst of those pathological excesses we described when examining the Forum type; the flattery, manipulation, falsification, and coercion of the appeal to the people.

This brings us to the second distinguishing mark. The ruler governs in true Palace fashion. But this does not make the polity the pure Palace type, because this *tyrannos* is legitimated from below: his authority is conferred on him by popular consent.

There is a long line of such Palace/Forum polities: the Greek tyrants, the 'perpetual dictatorship' conferred upon Sulla and Julius Caesar, and the so-called 'despotisms' that emerged among the medieval Italian city-states. In all these cases the *tyrannoi* arose out of Forum or Forum/Nobility polities. This is not a simple case of 'usurpation'. When some individual usurps the throne, the person of the monarch has altered but the regime remains exactly the same.[49] But in the present case the regime is quite altered; for to the plural rulership there succeeds monocracy. The Greek political theorists started a tradition which the medieval Europeans took up, to the effect that the tyranny was the inevitable outcome of democracy. In point of fact it was nearly always due to popular revulsion against a nobiliar

---

[49] See pp. 13–15 above for the discussion of this distinction.

oligarchy: most of the cases in Greece, all the Roman ones, and many of the Italian ones display precisely this character. It is hard to find instances where the tyrant rose on the back of a regularly functioning Forum-type polity like Athens. The tyranny of 'The Thirty' there was imposed by Sparta. But it is true, too, that individuals emerged and seized supreme power when constituted authority had vanished amidst civil tumult or anarchy. This was, precisely, what 'democracy' meant to the ancients and the Middle Ages. Hence the false notion that democracy must give rise to tyranny.

Napoleon was the individual who established our contemporary model of the seizure and subsequent legitimation of power. Having acquired office, he periodically validated it by popular plebiscite. In his case there is no reason to doubt that falsification was unnecessary, for he enjoyed massive and enthusiastic popular support. Napoleon was quite clear as to what he had done and why he did it. First, as he said: 'In no way did I usurp the Crown; I plucked it out of the gutter'. And again: 'Resorting to the People has the double advantage of legalizing the prolongation and purifying the origin of my power—otherwise it would always have appeared anomalous.'[50] This *ex post facto* legitimation of irregularly seized power has become the hallmark of the numerous so-called 'dictatorships' in nineteenth-century Latin America and, particularly since 1945, throughout the entire world.

What we nowadays call 'totalitarian' is an important sub-variety of the Palace/Forum polity. It differs from the ones mentioned so far in four main ways. In the first place, none of those assumed the right to control all aspects of society, including mental processes. The totalitarian ones are so called because this is precisely what they do claim. Secondly, they can make this claim partially effective because they dispose of the huge range of modern technological devices that have conquered time and distance. Thirdly, they are able to maintain their connection with the populace by means of a great political invention of the present century—the single, official, political party. And finally, that party is the bearer of a faith, a political religion, that is declared the official one, and to which all must subscribe. That kind of political faith is called an ideology.

In all cases, however, what we have is the shotgun marriage of two contradictory principles: the intrigues and the arbitrariness of the closed Palace world, and the corruption, falsification, and terrorization of popular opinion. The best way to understand the way Stalin worked is in no wise to go to the Webbs's egregious *Soviet Communism: A New Civilization*, but to reread Shakespeare's *Richard III*.

[50] Quoted, Napoleon I, Emperor of the French, *Vues politiques*, ed. and foreword by A. Dansette (Fayard, Paris, 1939).

4. DECISION-IMPLEMENTING PERSONNEL

Up to this point the classification has been governed by the character of the main decision-taking personnel in a given polity. The nature of that polity will also be influenced, however, perhaps decisively, by the sort of personnel who are there to carry out their instructions. These are the civil and the armed forces. So—in principle—each single one of the ten types of polity can be further qualified by whether they possess a bureaucracy and an army and, if so, of what types. So that, already, the ten main types of polity look likely to proliferate alarmingly.

In practice it is nothing like as bad as that. For one thing, the ten types of polity were reduced to five once the rare or marginal cases were eliminated. In principle, each one can operate in one of four different ways: with no bureaucracy and no standing army; or with both a bureaucracy and standing army; or with a bureaucracy but no standing army; or, finally, with a standing army but no civil bureaucracy. But the last possibility can be discounted. It hardly seems possible for a standing army to exist without a civil bureaucracy to raise men, money, and materials for it; and certainly, this *History* has found no examples. If some do indeed exist they must be highly exotic and quite marginal. In contrast, one does find instances of polities which have extensive bureaucracies but—as far as we know—do not have standing armies, or at least, ones of any material size. Such were the polities of the Sumerians and the Old Kingdom of Egypt; but they seem to be almost the only ones. In the *History*, therefore they can be set aside as *sui generis*. So that this leaves the major likelihoods as two: polities without either a bureaucracy or standing army and polities which have both. In point of fact this *History* suggests that the two features are interrelated: small or non-existent bureaucracies going along with small or non-existent standing armies, or the other way round.

At this stage, therefore, we could take the simple road and dichotomize the five main types of polity, thus yielding fifteen variants. But things are not as simple as this. There is bureaucracy and bureaucracy and there are armies and armies. It is necessary, therefore, to examine these more closely.

4.1. *The Armed Forces*

I have already discussed the relationship between the format of the army and the nature of the polity, and distinguished among various military formats in respect to the ruler's priorities—efficiency, expense, loyalty.

My point was that there is an ideal format for each. But I also made the point[51] that in practice nearly all armies were mixtures of these ideal formats. I propose to divide these mixed-format armies into three major types. They are what I shall call the community-in-arms; notables-and-followings; and the standing armies. It should be noticed at once that the first two kinds are *ad hoc*, unlike the third.

(i) We associate the 'community-in-arms' with the civic militias of the Greek city-states, with Rome till the time of Marius, and with medieval Italian republics. This type of army was also found, however, in the tribal or post-tribal polities of say, the German barbarian invaders of the Roman Empire. In these semi-tribal societies, all the adult males went into battle. Equally so in the nomadic tribal systems of northern East Asia—Huns and Mongols and Tartars and the like—or the Arabs in their first burst of military expansion. But armies of this kind were not incompatible with the existence of small, permanent bodyguards or palace-guards made up of professional fighters, like the Anglo-Saxon and Scandinavian housecarls.

(ii) The army of the notables? This, again, is consistent with a smallish, permanent armed force around the monarch. But the bulk of his army consists of followings brought into the field by local notables. These are not necessarily feudatories, but they do stand in some dependent relationship to the monarch. A European feudal army obviously corresponds to this type but so did very many in the ancient world. Herodotus has given us a marvellous description of the battle-order of Xerxes' army on its way to the Hellespont. Apart from the Great King's palace-guard of the Immortals, the army consists of contingents from all the varied territories of his vast domains, each led by their satrap or their native chiefs.

(iii) Finally, there are state-wide standing armies. This qualifying adjective, 'state-wide', holds a deep significance. For there are armies that constitute a permanent force but are made up of the permanent followings of notables who, themselves, are dependants of a common superior. Such was the army of the Mamluks, regular soldiers obeying and indeed belonging to the Emirs, who in their turn were dependants of the Sultan. So too, for that matter, was the Japanese samurai army: regulars, of aristocratic prestige, but completely subordinate to their daimyos who in turn were subordinate to the common superior (who held different offices, with distinctive titles, at different times).

State-wide standing armies come in two main varieties, with many intermediate ones of course. In the first subtype there is a smallish, long-term, professional force of 'regulars' plus a huge conscript component, to

---

[51] See p. 18 above.

which the regular forces serve as cadres. In the second subtype the entire force is paid, professional, and long-term, like the Mamluks, the Italian *condottieri*, and the armies of the Roman and the Byzantine empires.

There seems to be some broad correspondence between the types of army and types of polity.

4.1.1. THE COMMUNITY-IN-ARMS

This kind of army usually corresponds to the Forum or Forum/Nobility polity—Greece, the Roman republic, and the Italian city-states in their republican period. But it can coexist with quite absolute monarchies like the Merovingians, where the king is or is expected to be the war-leader. But because he was dependent on the support of his warriors, the absolutism of these kings was contingent—they held power only as long as they could retain the confidence of their warrior tribesmen. Much the same could be said of the pre-state polities of the Zulu, the Mongols, or the Ashanti. In such tribal or primitive states the vertical distance between the central authority and the community is much shallower than in the more complicated polities.

4.1.2. THE NOTABLES-IN-ARMS

In some polities the notables are prestigious and powerful hereditary chieftains in their native localities who, at some time and for many possible reasons, have yielded allegiance to a central authority—the King, the Great King, the King of Kings, and so forth. Elsewhere they are men who vow service to the ruler and thereby obtain a conditional title to the human and natural resources of lands. This is characteristic of a natural economy where such services cannot be paid for in cash. As we saw earlier, over time the notable often succeeds in shrugging off his service liabilities and begins to approximate to the previous type.

Similar, but not the same as the former, are notables who have accepted conditional land-grants but differ in that they have no residential, juridical, or hereditary rights over the inhabitants of the estates; they are entitled only to the produce they can wring out of them. This is the *iqta* which is found throughout Islam. Here again, some notables in the more distant corners of the Arab Empire were able to stay put and appropriate political control over the local inhabitants and so, again, approximate to the first of these three sub-varieties.

Armies consisting of such notables, each of whom brings his own following to the field, are found in feudal or feudalistic polities, usually natural economies, and they are part and parcel of the extensive fragmentation of power to be found therein. They are quarrelsome among themselves and ever striving to reduce their dependency on their monarch. For the latter's part, rulership consists in keeping them happy by conciliation, by success in war, and—if these fail—by bringing a winning coalition of faithful notables against the dissident ones. The essence of such rulership is what we might call 'baron-management'. It is to be found almost everywhere in this particular historical context. For instance, it characterizes both the Mamluk and the Japanese polities till modern times. In some European countries this survived long after military feudalism had vanished; in France, for example, up to the time of the Fronde (1648–53). The major effects of this kind of army are either to produce a polyarchic, decentralized, and conciliar form of government—the kind of polity we have called the Palace/Nobility type; or, as in medieval Japan, to create an unstable situation of latent civil war unless and until one clan-chief succeeded in subjugating his brethren and so brought about an autocracy, but of a brittle nature.

4.1.3. STANDING ARMIES

The first type of this kind of army consists of a huge force of conscripts who are constantly rotated, and which is spearheaded by a small force of regular garrison troops. This is characteristic of the Chinese Imperial armies for a greater part of her history. But the mass conscript armies of nineteenth- and twentieth-century Europe are not entirely dissimilar. In theory they consist of contingents of short-term conscripts who join the reserve when they fall out of active service. In practice many—usually over 50 per cent—are regular enlisted men on long service.

The second type of standing army, however, does consist exclusively of long-serving (often lifetime-serving) paid and professional regular troops. The Imperial Roman army was of this type. The armies of the absolute monarchies of eighteenth-century Europe were also of this kind, though their numbers were not nearly so large—in the order of perhaps 120,000–180,000, as against the 600,000 credited to Diocletian.

The standing army has been a prop to the absolutist regimes. It has been able to enforce the absolutism and assist vastly in its penetration of the population, particularly in the extraction of taxes. But it is not necessarily a prop to the incumbents in office. It strengthened the government because it could enforce the extraction of resources from the population (and in the process make itself stronger and larger). But it also weakened the monarchy in two ways. The first arose primarily in the context of conscript armies, as in China. Mountaineers or peoples from arid and poverty-stricken climates tend to be the ones who volunteer for battle, but the ordinary peasant hates war. So, in the effort to build up a large standing army by conscription, the authorities can alienate the very people that army is supposed to protect. The overthrow of the Ch'in dynasty in China was initiated by a handful of disgruntled conscripts on their way to the Great Wall.

The second way in which such armies might weaken the ruler arises from the potential conflict between their leaders and the monarch. In the monarchical regimes prior to the modern state, the conflict usually arose out of a contested succession. Other things being equal, the military decided this. But as the history of China shows, the struggle over the succession often degenerated into a situation where the countryside was controlled by 'war-lords', who fought ferociously to seize supreme power for themselves.

The main conclusions I draw are these. The community-in-arms, as defined above, is really suitable only for small and compact city-states. The army of the notables and their followings will, in a well-ordered monarchy, tend to decentralize and possibly provide a counterbalance to the powers of the Crown, and in an ill-ordered polity will pose a continual threat of disintegration. Finally the standing army, though it can provoke popular discontent and is a permanent threat to the incumbent of the royal or presidential palace, is nevertheless an instrument of high centralization and effective penetration by the central government.

4.2. *The Bureaucracy*

It seems as if big bureaucracies and big regular forces go hand in hand; that when we find no bureaucracy we tend to find only the community in arms; that when we find the notables-and-followers type of army we also find a low level of bureaucratization; but that when we find regular standing armies, even relatively small ones, we find a bureaucracy that is also strong and well organized.

'Penetration' by the bureaucracy is a function of two elements. The first is the range of the tasks it undertakes. The second is how far down the line, how far towards the village and city communities, does the chain of paid professional administrators reach.

Any discussion of 'bureaucracy' today is overhung by the looming shade of Max Weber. The trouble with Weber was that he took as essential criteria two of the more repulsive features of the Germany he grew up in. One was what is called 'Pandect law'. The other was the Prussian bureaucracy. As a result, he defines a so-called 'legal-rational' civil service in terms of whether its members are legally trained, and whether they fulfil the strict professonalized and hierarchical format of the Prussian civil service. So great is Weber's prestige that we tend to look on a bureaucracy as 'modern' or a 'proper' bureaucracy only when it fulfils these two conditions. In point of fact most modern bureaucracies do so. Starting from this standpoint, then, it is possible to discern what we might call an intermediate stage of bureaucracy and, beyond that, a rudimentary or even non-existent stage.

A modern bureaucracy is apt to have the following characteristics: it is hierarchical; permanently in function; specialized into its various fields; educationally and/or vocationally qualified; paid and full-time; rule-governed.

Many if not all of these characteristics could be found in ancient Egypt and Sumeria, the late Roman Empire, the Byzantine Empire, the Caliphate, and—most notably—in Imperial China. The two main respects in which they depart from Weber's own check-list is that they were not necessarily monocratic—China's elaborate bureaucracy was certainly not—and that the members, albeit qualified, were not qualified in law, let alone Pandect law. The first is of great administrative importance, the second is not. The British and the other common-law countries have thrown up excellent civil services without these consisting of lawyers.

But there is a large range of bureaucracies which lack other and important characteristics compared to those listed above. These are the ones which stand much closer to their origins in royal households. Like the 'modern' type, they are hierarchical in that the political heads—the ministers—are sharply distinguished from their clerical assistants. They are permanent, also. They are paid and full-time, although they are often paid in kind or by permission to charge fees for their services to the public. They differ from the advanced type described above in that first, at the higher levels, the ministers' fields of competence can be and usually are miscellaneous and interchanging, and the departments they are supposed to administer are not specialized along particularly rational lines. Secondly, the qualifications for entry can be minimal; in the case of the ministers, illiterates can be chosen because they are trusted—or because they have to be rewarded by the monarch—while at the clerks' level, the barest minimum qualifications of literacy and numeracy may be acceptable. Furthermore, these clerical staffs are recruited by the ministers themselves, whereas in a modern bureaucracy they are recruited by some kind of open examination by an impartial tribunal (as in Imperial China, which invented this system). Finally, these staffs—whether we are referring to the ministers or their minions—are not rule-governed. They are highly recent descendants of the household and the monarch often treats them as if they were still part of it; hence his arbitrary interference and caprice.[52]

---

[52] See, for instance, for England in the Middle Ages, T. F. Tout, 'The English Civil Service in the Fourteenth Century', in *The Collected Papers* (University of Manchester, Manchester 1934), iii. 192–213.

But finally, there are polities where the staff of the ruler does not go beyond the household officers: chamberlains, constables, butlers, and the like. These are rudimentary bureaucracies at the best, and in some polities we might not even call them bureaucracies at all.

We have, therefore, three major types of bureaucracies: the Developed, the Emergent, and the Rudimentary. These are the categories we shall be working with.

Unfortunately, yet one more complication must be added. So far we have been considering only centrally based staff. When we want to say how much impact the central government makes on the population—its penetrative power—we have to ask how far down the line do the paid and full-time servants of the rule stretch before they make an interface with unpaid, amateur, and often coerced local notables who carry on the administration and implementation from that point?

I do not propose to categorize these degrees of local penetration except to say that in some cases they are high by the standards of the time and in other cases pretty low. The individual instances are picked up in the appropriate chapters. But the matter is mentioned here because it is a most important dimension of the parameter of 'penetration'.

Let us simply give some examples. The Han Empire of China had four times as many civil servants per capita as the late Roman Empire. Yet even there the paid professional force of civil servants only went down as far as the sub-prefecture. Below that level the administration was taken over by the headmen and their colleagues in the little towns and villages. Under the Ch'ing the number of paid bureaucrats was held stable while the population underwent a prodigious increase. The local bureaucracy could only get obedience by reaching accommodations and compromises with the local notables and headmen.

The Roman Empire was not dissimilar. Here the local administrators were the local notables who made up the membership of the councils of the *civitates* into which the Empire was divided. In the beginnings these *curiales* not only administered gratis, but gave financial support to their towns. In time, the tasks became burdensone as the individual wealth of the notables became exiguous and they tried to escape this unpaid service. They were not permitted to. They were compelled to stay at their posts and administer the tax system, even to the point of making up any shortfall from their own pockets.

Two final examples exhibit the contrast between medieval England and France. When France started to become a united reality under Philippe-Auguste (1165–1223), he held it together by planting his own agents—the *gens du roi*—to enforce taxation and compel to justice. This path was followed by all subsequent kings, so that the field service of the bureaucracy became very swollen indeed compared with its headquarter staff in Paris. But in England the central, paid agents of the Crown only penetrated as far as the shire and there they entrusted the execution of the royal commands to the local notables sitting in the shire court. As time went on, Crown administration came to depend completely on this unpaid but ever-expanding service, carried out by the semi-judicial and semi-administrative lay administrators known as the Justices of the Peace. The victory of Parliament over the Crown in the seventeenth century guaranteed that this control of local administration by unpaid local notables was perpetuated into the middle of the nineteenth century before it began to be eroded by the planting of paid civil servants at local level.

4.3. 'Notables' and 'Despotism'

It seems that some scholars feel that if they establish that local notables existed, and that they influenced, or controlled, or actually acted as the local officials of the central government, they have thereby demonstrated that an empire was not really an empire or that a despotism was not a despotism, and so forth. In fact, all they have done is to draw attention to the fact that in pre-modern (indeed, one might often say pre-mid-twentieth-century) polities, the penetrative power of the central government fell far short of what it is today, and usually far short of what the then rulers would have liked. The plain truth is that central rule via the intermediation of notables in such polities is a commonplace, it is part of the scene. To judge by the reactions of some of the scholars mentioned above, it may be that it is so much a commonplace that it is often taken for granted in characterizations of pre-industrial or agrarian societies. The services of notables in the process of government; the obvious fact that the more a government relied on their services the more dependent it became on them, along with their interests and perceptions; that they were a major part of the very environment, the very atmosphere in which governmental decisions were taken and then executed—all these traits were intrinsic to the way what we called empires and despotisms and the like operated at the grass roots in practice. Sadly, in many of the polities dealt with in this *History* the data are lacking. This is true, for instance, of Egypt until well into the first millennium BC. It is true of Byzantium, true also of China until the post-Sung period. It is also true for the Caliphate until the tenth century, and even there the evidence is very patchy. In other cases, where the materials for a judgement are superabundant, they are often confined to one or two particular areas, making it hazardous to generalize for the entire polity: the Roman provinces provide the most obvious example.

Admitting the need to draw attention to the notables, then, in what ways, we must ask, did they relate to superior authority? Broadly speaking, they might act in symbiosis with it, in collision with it, or, at the ultimate limit, in complete disassociation from it—autonomously. The first of these three represents the normal and stable relationship, the one that the public authority knew it had to accept, and indeed, relied on to get its commands executed. It is a commonplace of political science that unless the authorities can win a measure of voluntary acquiescence, let alone active support, for what they are trying to do, so that they are not forced to use coercion and threats all the time to get their commands obeyed, they are engaged in a very expensive, time-consuming, and ultimately self-defeating enterprise. On the other hand, if they are assured by some means or another of acquiescence or even enthusiasm, the labour of administering and the numbers and expense involved in it are enormously reduced.

Now this has critical implications for the role of the government's field official. He must be able to assure his superiors that he can 'get on with' the local population—by which the government simply understands that he can get its wishes obeyed. A governor who provokes a tax revolt or a mayor who is always arousing riots is not much use to his superiors and they will remove him. If, on the other hand, such field officials can only get on with their local population by assimilating to their points of view, this also may be a reason for the government to remove them.

The obverse is equally true. If a governor (let us say) is left in place long enough he will, in order to control the population in his charge, tend to 'go native' and be in cahoots with the local bigwigs. This is the story of how the Louis XIV's *intendants* were transformed under later reigns from the docile servants of the king to particularist champions of their provinces' interests. Yet if the government tries to break such close assimilation—by rotating the governors or making sure that they are strangers to their province and so forth (as in Imperial China)—they will be so ignorant of the local social and power structures—often of the very language—that they too will be forced to depend on the local bigwigs and fixers.

Such are the developments implicit in the normal, the routine relationship between the locals and the public authority in their neighbourhood. But from time to time this breaks down, and instead the officials and the notables are at loggerheads. Antagonism can flare into riot or open revolt. The quarrels may arise over new taxation, or attempts to enforce some repugnant ritual or religion (one thinks of the frequent riots in Byzantine Alexandria in support of Monophysite bishops as against Arian ones).

When such antagonisms arise, the government official may decide to repress or intimidate the population, or alternatively, to go along with it. Either choice may be fatal to his career. He might have decided to repress and intimidate where his superiors would have preferred him to conciliate; and vice versa. In either case, he is likely to be replaced.

The limiting case of notables' influence is their partial or even complete autonomy. Such situations are much more likely to arise on the periphery than at the centre of the state, but the circumstances that give rise to the autonomy can be entirely unrelated to this. A common instance is a foreign invasion which destroys or at least drives away the native authorities, so that the city or region lies open and naked to the invaders. The population has to decide whether to stand and fight or make terms, and it is the local notables, its 'natural leaders', who take charge. Sometimes again, it is not invasion which paralyses or removes the agents of the government but a power-vacuum or a struggle for sovereignty at the centre. In such cases, the local notables will have to decide whether to recognize the new ruler, or the pretenders, or to continue in independence. Quite often the consequence is a continued fragmentation of authority. For instance, as wave after wave of invaders passed over the succession-kingdoms to the Roman Empire in the west, the conditions outlined above were repeated again and again until, in the end, power and authority resided exclusively in that notable who was able to impose his own local order on, and give his own protection to, the surrounding population: for example, the *castellanies* in eighth- and ninth-century France. Similarly in Eastern Iran in the last days of the Caliphate and later, when Turks and Mongols established short-lived Emirates on the ruins of the Caliphal provinces. A third example is to be seen in China in the protracted period of disunity that ensued after the breakdown of the Han dynasty.

The expression 'notables' is a generic one. Different historians give different names to the notables according to the country and the period with which they are concerned. Chinese historians talk of the 'gentry', medieval historians of England talk of knights of the shire and buzones, Roman historians note the *curiales* (or decurions). Who the notables were, and from what class, varies from country to country and period to period. The variance reflects the two analytically distinct modalities, of power-relationships on the one hand, and authority and status relationships on the other, which in practice usually merge and reinforce one another. The foundation of the notables' local strength may reside in lineage, or wealth, or military power, or the prestige and authority conferred by the local culture, which might be based on religion (Christianity and Islam stand out here), learning (the Chinese tradition), or caste (as in India).

The preceding section gave a few examples culled from some of these. To illustrate this just a little further, observe the changing nature of the local notable in China. In the Later Han period these notables are the heads of huge households—the Great Families—which own vast estates, have a multitude of armed retainers, and—this is a particularity—are literati or at least have literati in their family. But with the downfall of the Han and the four centuries of disunity these families were wiped out, and in the north of China the local notables came to be the descendants of the barbarian conquerors, whose local power rested on lineage and military prowess rather than on landed wealth, which they did indeed enjoy but thanks to the former two, not the other way round. As Confucianism took further hold under the Sung, acquaintance with the Classics became the precondition for any kind of social respect, let alone governmental authority, and in practice this meant accreditation through the system of state examinations which was then being perfected. Under the Ch'ing such accreditation became the essential passport to influence. As a consequence local influence was being wielded by a class of men who were only modestly well-to-do but who had won the necessary credentials as literati; similarly in the Caliphate, where at first the local notables were landed Arab nobility, disposing of land, wealth, and the military might of their tribal followings. By the eleventh century this was no longer so, and in ensuing centuries when Islam had become the majority religion it would seem that it was the *ulema* who enjoyed the greatest local influence, closely followed by those persons who had a military following, but not rich merchants and the like. *Autres pays, autres mœurs*: in Merovingian France the local notable with whom the king had to deal was often the bishop. Bishops and abbots and other high church dignitaries never ceased to be influential locally and were correspondingly courted by the monarchs; but as time went by they took second place to the great lay lords who had their followings of armed knights. The rule of the religious over the layfolk was nowhere near as exclusive and overwhelming in western Christendom as it was in Islam.

The consequence of all the foregoing is, basically, this. None of these earlier country-wide states, particularly those extensive and highly heterogeneous ones that we call empires, were under the full, firm, all-encompassing, and exclusive control of government officials. Control was patchy, and there was much wheeling-and-dealing at the interfaces where the officials and local populations met; and that was at the level of the local notables. If the governor was an outsider (and the same considerations apply to his sub-governors and so on, all down the line) he could only secure compliance by learning the ropes from the local notables, and by using them to pressure their dependants. By way of return he would accord them privileges, not the least being, perhaps, that of softening or cancelling the harsh demands of his superior authorities. Alternatively, the governor and/or other public officials might have been deliberately selected from among the local notables, so that they doubled as officials and as notables in their own right. In either case, their self-interests made themselves felt on the central authority.

The important and, indeed, often indispensable administrative role of local notables unquestionably acted as a substantive and sometimes a procedural brake on the power of a sovereign. But to infer that for this reason that sovereign was not a despot and his polity not a despotism is to fall into a confusion. It assumes that the freedom to act in any direction without restraint which we associate with the term 'despotism' is exercised all the time on all the population in all classes of matters. Such a government might well be termed 'totalitarian' or a 'totalitarian despotism'. But the material preconditions for this kind of polity did not exist until well into the present century. The source of the confusion has been very well put by Jean Dunbabin in her study of early medieval France. 'What distinguishes government from personal control', she writes there, 'is its unremitting character. To be governed is to be subjected to the regular pressure of an authority operating according to fixed rules. In the full sense of the word, it is arguable that nobody was governed before the later nineteenth century . . .'[53] Thus despotism refers to any autocracy pushed to the limits of personal discretion which is here defined as the despot's capacity, in practice and not just in theory, to take at his personal will the life, the limb, the liberty, and the property of any of his subjects without due process of law.

4.4. *The Pathology of the Decision-Making/Decision-Implementing Relationship*

We have seen above how from time to time the relationship of the bureaucracy and/or the armed forces to the duly constituted decision-makers becomes perverted. The decision-implementers are supposedly the instruments of those who take the decisions; but in certain cases their relationship is reversed and it is the former who take the place of the latter. We have a term for the bureaucracy's take-over of the task of decision-making; unfortunately it is, precisely, the same term—'bureaucracy', that is, the rule of governmental bureaux. In this sense bureaucracy does not refer to the agency, but to the form of rule—the regime. Two things only need be

---

[53] J. Dunbabin, *France in the Making, 843–1180* (OUP, Oxford, 1985), 277.

said about this. The first is that, unless it has a permanent set of specialized officials, even one that is very small and relatively unsophisticated, a polity will simply collapse in the absence of its personal ruler. The empire of Charlemagne was held together by his and his son's personal abilities. After that, even discounting the fact that it was partitioned into three, each component kingdom fell apart owing to the lack of a permanent body of officials. The Holy Roman Empire disintegrated for this reason too; it had no central treasury nor even a central chancery. Contrast this with the way the kingdom of England continued to run smoothly in the absences of Richard I or of Edward I.

The contrary situation, that is, the prepotency of the bureaucracy, obtains where the decision-maker(s) effaces himself or is effaced, leaving this bureaucracy to make the decisions, *faute de mieux*. The most striking illustrations come from various episodes in Chinese history. There, the civil service was the Mandarinate, a corporation trained in the morality and statecraft of Confucianism. Among its numerous variants an extremely potent one maintained that the sole duty of the emperor, apart from rituals, was to choose good counsellors (who would obviously be Confucians). As for him, he must stay within his palace, go through all traditional motions, but simply let the Mandarinate get on with making all the decisions. There was a perpetual see-saw between these two opposing notions of an active emperor and an active Mandarinate. Very often the latter got their way and reduced the emperor (or, through over-indulgence with his harem or his eunuchs he reduced himself) to a cipher and the Mandarinate took over.

The military take-over of the rulership differs from the above in two major particulars. The first is that, whereas the bureaucracy can attain power only by the default of the supreme decision-taker(s), the leaders of the military take power from them by force. The second is that, whereas in the former the legitimate authority(ies) is left intact and the bureaucracy remains vested with that legitimacy, this is not the case when the generals take over. They replace the hitherto legitimate authority. Hence they have to find a new legitimacy for themselves. There is a clear distinction between the ways this was done in pre-modern polities as compared with the modern ones. In the former, a favourite trick was for the generals to maintain and even exalt the status of the legitimate monarch, while effectively controlling all his decisions. This is the recurrent theme of all Japanese history right up to the Meiji Restoration of 1867. Another example comes from Mamluk Egypt. The Mamluk sultans established their native—and compliant— Caliph al-Islam as the figurehead ruler. In China, during the Spring and Autumn period, the period of the Warring States, and again in the very early period of the Three Kingdoms, the rival generals would drag the captive emperor round in their baggage train, to bring legitimacy to their actions.

This type of legitimation would cut no ice today, when the source of legitimacy is universally sought in popular mandate. Hence today's military take-overs are legitimized by plebiscites, faked elections, and the like in the manner already described under the heading of the Palace/Forum type of polity.

5. CONSTRAINTS: THE LIMITATION OF GOVERNMENT

No government has ever been all-powerful. For one thing, governments are all subject to natural constraints. Individuals simply cannot attend to everything. Compared with what is required there is nearly always an absence of manpower and of necessary information. There are natural limits, too, to the management of what resources and manpower are available. The problems were made that much worse when communication and transportation was so slow, as it was till the very recent past.

But governments can also be limited by man-made restrictions often referred to as 'constitutional' constraints, that is, by rules. These rules are of two kinds. The first delimit the range of a ruler's activities, the second subject him to following certain strict procedures. Such rules operate on the two different planes. To summarize:

Constraints are:
  A. Substantive.
  B. Procedural:
and are:
        (1) at 'horizontal' level (i.e. central government level)
        (2) at 'vertical' level (i.e. from central government downwards to
             locality).

5.1. *Procedural Constraints and the Central–Local Relationship*

It simplifies to confine analysis to two sets of variables: central and local, constrained as against unconstrained. The actual practice of states varies within these limits. Each polity is idiosyncratic. Furthermore, what is theoretically unlimited power over the scope and the procedure of local authorities always falls short in practice, owing to the natural and administrative restraints mentioned above. With these provisos in mind, the possible combinations are as follows.

5.1.1. CENTRAL GOVERNMENT CONSTRAINED. LOCAL GOVERNMENT WIDE DISCRETION

This combination gives rise to a highly decentralized form of polity. In the modern world the condition is best fulfilled by the United States. Its federal government is constrained by the separation of powers, and so are the fifty state governments, while the federal government does not in law possess any powers to tell the states how to carry out their functions nor to define what functions these must be. But the United States is rather a special case because it is a 'composite' state. Yet something like it appears in, let us say, the feudal monarchies of the European Middle Ages. In the tenth century the Regnum Francorum left almost no effective power in the hands of the (elected) Capetian kings, so that the great provinces were ruled in almost total independence by their counts and dukes. Their independence was curbed as time went on. By the fourteenth century the monarch—now no longer elected but hereditary—was the wealthiest and strongest ruler in the *regnum*, and his *gens du roi* were successfully encroaching on what had been the unfettered prerogatives of the magnates. Yet this still left huge swathes of local discretion to them, and not till the end of the seventeenth century had these been abrogated. The reverse development occurred in the Caliphate. The first caliphs wielded extensive powers over the localities, but as time went by these became effectively independent and the power of the caliph nominal.

5.1.2. CENTRAL GOVERNMENT UNCONSTRAINED. LOCAL GOVERNMENT NO DISCRETION

The government is absolute, both substantively and procedurally, and exercises total domination over the policies and the administrative procedures in the localities. The polity is completely centralized. Once again there was something approaching this in the modern world—the government of the USSR. It was supposedly federal, but in fact the Union Republics were modelled on and tightly controlled through the network of the Communist Party, which was directed from the Kremlin; while the local units inside each Republic were similarly controlled by that Republic's own central government. The Chinese People's Republic is a copy of this system, but a very poor one because the natural and administrative restraints on the central government are so very much greater.

Imperial China was supposedly run on similar lines, though the scope of the central government was, of course, very much narrower than in our own day. In principle the emperor knew no substantive or procedural limits to his authority, and the localities, down to the villages, were supposedly completely controlled and directed from his palace. One must repeat again that the size of the bureaucracy *vis-à-vis* the area and population of the country meant that in practice the localities did in fact enjoy a great deal of administrative and—at times—substantive discretion.

5.1.3. CENTRAL GOVERNMENT UNCONSTRAINED. LOCAL GOVERNMENT WIDE DISCRETION

While the central government wields absolute power, untrammelled by procedures and with indefinite scope of activity, the localities also enjoy discretion in both these respects; they decide on what to do and how to do it. The Persian Empire was of this type. The King of Kings was absolute but he governed the empire through his satraps. These were expected to execute the royal commands; but since these rarely went beyond raising forces for a campaign and collecting and forwarding the taxes, in practice the satrap was absolute in his province. Ancient Egypt tended to lapse into this condition whenever the power of the local nomarchs grew stronger than that of the pharaoh, for the royal power waxed and waned throughout Egypt's history. When it waned nomarchs became the almost sovereign rulers of their nomes. Indeed, at various points in the country's history they actually did assert independence. The times of troubles that ensued are the so-called 'Intermediate Periods'.[54] What is true of Persia and Egypt was true of all the empires of the Middle East in ancient and in classical times.

5.1.4. CENTRAL GOVERNMENT CONSTRAINED. LOCAL GOVERNMENT NO DISCRETION

This model would apply, in theory, to the absolute monarchies of eighteenth-century Europe. The monarchs were circumscribed substantively by the limitations of organized Christianity, but the localities were permitted no administrative discretion. Such at least was the theory. In practice the provinces enjoyed more latitude than this formula suggests, as in time the *intendants* came to collude with the local notables, and intermediate between them and the central power.

5.2. *Substantive Constraints on the Central Government*

This distinction is one that helps sort out the various members of the 'family' of autocracies—dictatorships, absolute monarchies, despotisms, and the like. Again and again it is pointed out that a Louis XIV, uncontrolled as he was by any other legal organ (i.e. 'procedurally unconstrained'), was

---

[54] See pp. 32–3 above.

nevertheless not free to do whatever he liked. He could not abrogate the ancient constitutional laws of the kingdom which laid it down, *inter alia*, that the king must not alienate the royal domain, and that the kingship must descend in the male line.

Such substantive limitations are of three main kinds, singly or in combination, and these stem from the principles by which the monarchy is legitimated. The three bases of legitimation are first, the religious; secondly, the tradition; and thirdly, the laws. An excellent example of the third, acting on its own at first, is the federal constitution of the USA, 1789. Examples of solely religious legitimation (and hence constraint) must, I think, be confined to primal charismatic rulership like that of Saul (and perhaps David), and Muhammad. Once such rulers die their charisma, as we saw,[55] is routinized and becomes tradition.

In practice most rulers are legitimated by a mixture of all three. To cut a long story short, consider Louis XIV of France. He is legitimated by religion—being anointed by the archbishop—and by the same token he is bound to observe the Roman Catholic faith and work within its limits. He is also legitimated by tradition—the line of the Capetians goes back to the tenth century. And he is legitimated by the laws—the Salic law which precludes descent in the female line, for instance.

Some rulers, however, suffer no such substantive constraints. The emperor of China was, in theory, free to act in whatever field he chose. So was the Athenian *ekklesia*, and equally the organs of the Roman Republic; for nothing in the Twelve Tables limited the kinds of things the Republic might do.

These observations touch on a most important point of principle. Absolutism signifies freedom from any procedural constraint.[56] What does not seem to have been widely recognized is that in certain polities the ruler can do as he likes and how he likes in one delimited area, but is completely shut out of another. As this *History* demonstrates, the initiators of this limited monarchy were the Jews. The Mosaic law was overriding. The king was merely administrator and judge under it. But that law did not provide the guide-lines for foreign policy, taxation, policing—in short all the matters that we seculars today would regard as the primary concerns of politics. The consequence is that if we read the Old Testament with even the slightest dispassion, we are forced to recognize that Solomon was a characteristic petty middle-eastern ruler in all matters except wherever the Mosaic Code operated.[57]

---

[55] See pp. 38–9 above.

[56] This is etymologically what 'absolutism' means—*ab legibus solutus*.

[57] Not even that, really—in his senility Solomon let his pagan wives worship their native idols. Solomon is one of the most overrated figures in history.

The same is true for both Christian and Islamic rulers and for the identical reason. Hence there is one generalization we can safely make: any of the hybrid types containing 'church' as a component is, definitionally, substantively constrained.

But quite apart from obeying the religious code, rulers were expected to revere tradition. Most of the apparently despotic autocracies respected private property and liberty of the person. True, they often breached these traditions in practice, but the compulsion to follow them was very strong. The story of Naboth's vineyard illustrates both sides of the coin. The king cannot simply expropriate the vineyard—that is against customary law. What he does do is to 'frame' Naboth on a false charge—that is, go through ' due process'—and get it out of him in this corrupt way.

Finally, when laws came to be written down they too were expected to limit the discretion of the ruler. This raised a difficult problem for the European Middle Ages. The king was clearly the source of law, but on the other hand, surely he was bound by it? Posed in these terms no answer is possible. But what emerged in the end was a practical compromise. The king was certainly bound by the laws in place. On the other hand he was entitled to suspend or dispense with the law in special cases, and by the same argument he was entitled to deprive an individual of his freedom in some deserving cause. Hence the 'suspending and dispensing power' of kings, abrogated in England by the Glorious Revolution of 1688. Similar extra-ordinary powers were granted to monarchs in other countries to be used in cases of public necessity. Even today the head of state can set aside penalties laid down by the courts, by exercising the traditional right of pardon.

5.3. *Procedural Constraints on the Central Government*

This is much easier to explain and illustrate than what has gone before. The reason is that any plural-headed form of government is *ipso facto* procedurally limited. For, being plural, in the highly likely event of a division of opinion it is necessary to set rules as to how the issue be concluded. It is a law that plural-headed government entails procedural rules. In effect this means that all conciliar forms of polity are procedurally limited. The list therefore includes: Forum, Nobility, Forum/Nobility, and Palace/Nobility. It would also include a Church if we were to consider pure hierocracies, but we can leave those aside. The Palace is procedurally unconstrained, by definition.

This leaves only one of the main types of government, the Palace/Forum type. Earlier we raised the possibility of treating the American presidency as Palace/Forum. We rejected that on the grounds that it is merely one component in a more extensive plural headship of the polity. As we pointed

TABLE 1. *Constraints on types of government*

Substantively	Procedurally	
	Unconstrained	Constrained
Unconstrained	Some Palace types; some Palace/Forum types.	Some Conciliar types: viz. Forum, Nobility, Forum/Nobility, Nobility/Palace.
Constrained	Some Palace types; some Palace/Forum types.	Some conciliar types (as above).

Note: Apart from the Church and those hybrid polities having a Church component, *any* one of the other main types may be either substantively constrained, or it may not be.

out[58] the Palace/Forum polity is the kind that stretches from the Greek tyrannies to the totalitarian regimes of today. Although legitimated—genuinely or falsely—by some show of popular support, these polities are all personal or collective autocracies. But they are not pluralistic. The difference between the authoritarian regimes (Napoleon, General Franco) and 'totalitarian' ones like the USSR and the other 'socialist' states is not a difference of type. It is a difference in respective scope and efficacy. The latter ascribe to themselves indefinite scope in what they do, as well as how they do it. The authoritarian regimes recognize certain substantive limits.

Hence we have:

(1) Neither procedurally nor substantively constrained.
   (a) Palace type: the Chinese emperor.
   (b) Some Palace/Forum types: these would include the Greek tyr-
       annies, some modern authoritarian dictatorships like that of
       Gomez of Venezuela or Dr Francia of Paraguay; and, finally
       all the 'totalitarian' states of the twentieth century.

(2) Both procedurally and substantively constrained.

All 'conciliar' types are necessarily procedurally constrained; some of them are also substantively constrained, for example, the medieval *regnum* where the king is constrained both by Christianity and by law and custom; the medieval Italian city-states—conciliar, but limited by Christianity; the 'liberal-democracies' of today, auto-limited by law and convention.

(3) Procedurally constrained, but substantively unconstrained.

[58] See pp. 57–8 above.

All conciliar types of polity were procedurally constrained (necessarily); but some of them were substantively unconstrained, for example, the Athenian *ekklesia*; the Roman republican institutions; the Japanese feudal polity.

(4) Procedurally unconstrained, substantively constrained.

This last produces what is generally accepted as the definition of 'absolutism', that is, the ruler can act without institutional constraints but is barred from certain areas of policy. This will be true of Palace and some Palace/Forum types of polity. It would be true of Louis XIV. He was bound by the traditional constitutional laws of the kingdom, by the conventions respecting property, and so on, and by the limitations of the Christian religion. The same might be said of King Solomon or the Caliph al-Mansur.

Some Palace/Forum polities also conform. The military or populist dictatorships of the nineteenth and twentieth centuries provide many examples. Napoleon, for instance—legitimated by plebiscite—made a Concordat with the Catholic Church. So did Mussolini.

5.5. *A Brief Recapitulation of the Major Variables*

1. There are four basic clusters of variables:
   (a) territory;
   (b) type;
   (c) the possession of army and/or bureaucracy;
   (d) limitations on activities.
2. Each cluster breaks down into sub-variables.
   (a) Territory breaks down into city, country, empire.
   (b) Type breaks down into ten types, of which five are major types and the principal subjects of the *History*. These types are in turn discriminated by the nature of their
      (i) dominant personnel,
      (ii) characteristic political processes, and
      (iii) legitimacy-basis.
   (c) Each of the five types, above, is served or not, as the case may be, by some kind of bureaucracy and some kind of army. These two services are each classified into three main kinds.
   (d) The final variable concerns how free the rulers are in each such polity to do what they choose and by any constitutional procedures they choose: that is, how far the rulers of the polity are substantively or procedurally constrained.

Together, the foregoing present the main features of any polities on a comparative basis.

6. THE CRITERIA OF APPRAISAL

My list of criteria begins with ones that are common ground and becomes progressively more controversial.

6.1. *Defence*

The ability of the polity to defend its population against invasions, plunder, or enslavement by outside enemies is primordial and a polity that cannot do this has, *pro tanto*, failed; the more so since, if the failure is drastic enough, the polity itself will be extinguished.

6.2. *Internal Law and Order*

6.2.1. 'ORDER'

This obviously embraces the repression and prevention of crimes of violence, but these are private acts. A polity should also be judged on how far its political arrangements conduce to civil wars, with all their attendant devastation and death. For instance, I should consider the Roman Empire's propensity to precipitate civil wars over the imperial succession to be a cardinal weakness.

6.2.2. THE ADMINISTRATION OF JUSTICE

There are two sets of issues here—the constitutive features of the judicial system, and the perversions of these features. The first may be bad, the second must be.

(i) To be considered as acceptable, the system of adjudication must be one that follows intelligible principles and procedures in a consistent way. This in no way entails that each individual shall be equal before the law. Very much the reverse. Where hierarchy is socially accepted, the principle of equality before the law is met by according equal treatment to individuals within the same social rank. There was no equality before the law in the Roman Empire, for instance. At first the law distinguished between citizens and non-citizens and then, when this distinction had been abolished, between the *honestiores* and the *humiliores*. Equality before the law in our modern sense is a fruit of the early-modern epoch of Europe.

(ii) 'Injustice' in the hierarchical society could be said to occur when the system fails to provide equal treatment for individuals in the same rank. This might occur through the absence or the defectiveness of a common code of law. 'Injustice' will also occur, however, when the law only purports to conform to the principle of the equality of all individuals, but in practice the courts favour one rank or class in society as against others. The latter was the practice—no matter what the law was supposed to be saying—in Tudor England or the France of Francis I, but not in contemporary Venice. There, research has shown, the nobility—despite their monopoly of political power—were treated in the courts on an exact equality with commoners. It was this impartiality that made Venetian justice so renowned.

To our minds, injustice must necessarily have been inherent in certain procedures and rules of evidence which used to prevail. However, whether we should indict polities on this account is disputable. It could be contended that such an attitude is unhistorical, because those curious and offensive procedures conformed to the mentality of the times. But from any objective standpoint it is obvious that the ordeals of fire or water or battle were utterly unsatisfactory—indeed ridiculous—ways of arriving at the truth. Again, the Roman inquisitorial method, though a vast improvement on the ordeal, commonly relied on a confession from the accused and permitted torture to secure it. The torture was required to be used only when the prima-facie case against the accused was overwhelming. In practice it was almost routine.

Up to very recent times political trials were almost always unjust. Where the interest of the ruler or the state was at stake—and the two were usually confounded—the accused was always treated as guilty unless he could prove otherwise, and the utmost pressures were brought on him and the court to bend the rules of evidence and predispose towards a 'guilty verdict'. By our standards a very high proportion of these state trials were simply judicial executions.

(iii) Even if the laws and the judicial procedures of justice were even-handed and rational, injustice could nevertheless be perpetrated, either by defective administration and/or by defective personnel. The most common instances of the former occur in the slowness and/or costliness of litigation. 'Justice delayed is justice denied.' In *The Later Roman Empire*, A. H. M. Jones pointedly remarks that the undoubted virtues of the Roman law meant little to most people for exactly these two reasons. The most common instances of the latter are the corruption and/or intimidation of judges and juries and—almost endemic throughout the ages in all polities till recent times— the venality of the judges.

6.3. *Taxation—Extortion*

Nearly every government has to organize the extraction of manpower, money, and *matériel* to carry out even its primordial functions of defence and keeping the peace, though some societies like Athens or early Rome managed this in the most rudimentary way. The general rule is that the more differentiated the polity, the more it needs to levy taxation.

Much primitive taxation is levied in kind. Indeed, this lay at the root of the *oikos* polities of Sumeria and the Old Kingdom of Egypt. It was an inflexible arrangement, which demanded big overheads in granaries and storehouses and, above all, an army of clerks to book the produce in and then book it out again. Wherever and whenever possible, governments have preferred to take the taxes in cash. But they may not be able to do this because the economic environment precludes it: for instance, the massive price inflation in the third century of the Roman Empire, or the reversion to the natural economy in the barbarian Dark Ages of Europe. It is noteworthy how early the feudal monarchs switched over to scutages and other commutations of knight-service for a cash payment. Nevertheless, one form of payment-in-kind persisted in many diverse polities and that was forced labour; what we tend to call the corvée, from the fact that it survived into eighteenth-century France. The Pyramids and the Great Wall of China were built with forced labour. Indeed, forced labour has always been part of the Chinese fiscal system and, lest it be thought that this simply reflected mindless despotism, we may say at once that this labour was absolutely necessary to handle the disastrously devastating floods which were so common. In the Han Empire, where military conscripts made up some 0.5–2 per cent of the total population, the proportion who had to give compulsory labour (a month per annum) was in the order of 20–5 per cent.[59]

Such matters must be borne in mind when assessing the effectiveness and/or fairness of a fiscal system. These two things are by no means the same. In Britain today the most effective form of direct taxation would be a flat rate of 15 per cent in the pound income tax. It would bring in about the same total as now but would cut out all the fancy footwork of allowances, and so on. But such a simplification would be opposed on the grounds of injustice. Why, for instance, should the family man pay the same as the single man? Why should the very rich and the very poor have to pay an equal proportion of their vastly disproportionate incomes?

[59] M. Loewe, 'The Campaigns of Han Wu-ti', in F. A. Kiernan and J. K. Fairbank (eds.), *Chinese Ways in Warfare* (Harvard UP, Cambridge, Mass., 1974), 81.

In establishing criteria for evaluating the fiscal system in any polity four things have to be considered.

6.3.1. THE MORAL RATIONALE OF THE SYSTEM

Once again it is vital to divest ourselves of the moral values of our own day. For instance, the notion that taxation should be progressive is not more than seventy years old in Britain. I do not know of any past polity which espoused this—to them—bizarre notion. On the other hand, a vague notion that taxes should be 'equitable' is to be found almost everywhere and at all times; but what this 'equity' meant in practice varied widely. The basic idea is that each should be taxed according to his means, and that therefore those of equal means should pay an equal amount of tax. It would, therefore, be fair to indict a fiscal system by showing that it failed in this respect, but this leads us to the next point.

6.3.2. THE TECHNICALITIES OF THE FISCAL SYSTEM

We must realize from the outset that, until very recent times, the assessment and collection of tax was bound to be crude and inequitable, however well-intentioned the government. The difficulties have been elaborately and intelligently described by Gabriel Ardant, to whose work reference should be made.[60] Briefly, he makes the following points. First, until modernity, all polities (outside a few city-states) had agrarian economies, where agriculture, moreover, yielded poor returns. Next, governments preferred to take their revenues in cash (or its currency-equivalent, like bolts of silk in ancient and medieval China), and therefore the producers had to find markets for their products, and this was not always easy. Thirdly, assessment per household was difficult because these agrarian economies were often ones of subsistence farming and always consisted of small farms. How, then, assess the peasant who was consuming his own produce, using family labour, and never keeping accounts?

Hence all fiscal methods were inefficient or inequitable or both. The tithe, that is, one-tenth in kind of the visible harvest, seems easy enough; in point of fact it was onerous to inventory the granaries, and in any case the harvest might be too early or too late for the taxmen to inventory it. So, very often, the matter was settled by a fixed payment agreed between the farmer and the taxmen. The assessment of capital was no more easy. It was virtually impossible to tax movables, which are easily concealed, so this left only fixed capital—usually land—to tax. But simply to tax acreage would

---

[60] G. Ardant, 'Financial Infrastructure of Modern States and Nations', in Tilly (ed.), *Formation*, 164–242; and Ardant's longer *Histoire de l'Impôt*, vol. 1 (Fayard, Paris, 1971).

have been grotesquely inefficient as well as inequitable. What was necessary was to assess the income the land brought in. This meant conducting that elaborate survey called a cadaster, and it is astonishing how early that method was used—in ancient Egypt for instance. But prices change, yields change, and the owners change, and it was always beyond the administrative capacity of governments to keep up with these events; the cadaster would have to be reviewed too frequently. What happened in Ming China happened everywhere else. The rolls on which the assessment were based became more and more out of date until the assessment-basis became almost a customary one. We have found exactly the same thing in Britain in the 1980s—when the revaluation of rateable property had been delayed so long that the assessment had become a quaintly notional one, while reassessment would create such different values as to pose a political threat to the government. The result was the politically disastrous experiment with a poll tax.

Indirect taxation was, therefore, a favoured option but even this ran into difficulties. Jones, in *The Later Roman Empire*, reckoned that at the height of its prosperity only 15 per cent of the Empire's revenue derived from taxes on commerce, and so on. Furthermore, even in urban communities it proved difficult to impose sales taxes until seventeenth-century Europe. The most favoured mode of collection was, consequently, to put taxes on the transit of the commodities, hence the value to medieval England of being an island, since the government could tax wool exports so easily at the ports.

6.3.3. BUT HOW MUCH TAXATION WAS REALLY NECESSARY?

Rome failed to repel the barbarians because this required a standing army larger, or at any rate costlier, than the Empire's agrarian tax base could support. It would be unjustifiable to condemn a fiscal system on grounds of this sort, which amount to saying, really, that a polity was too poor to carry out its essential tasks. But in fact, as Jones has pointed out, the later Roman Empire wasted fiscal resources it could have used for the armies by maintaining what he calls ' idle mouths'. He draws attention to the free rations given to the populations of Rome and Constantinople (and a few other cities); the under-taxation and fiscal privileges of the small but enormously wealthy Senatorial Order, which further enriched itself at state expense by making illicit profits from the offices it monopolized; by swelling the civil service; and, once the Empire became officially Christian, by the vast multiplication of the number of priests and other clergy, who were paid better than the civil service and in any case enjoyed tax-immunity on the ever-increasing estates they were endowed with.[61]

---

[61] Jones, *Later Roman Empire*, ii. 1045–6.

Unfortunately it is usually hazardous to proceed like this. It reflects our contemporary estimate of the priorities of a polity that existed in the past. Often, what might seem gross extravagance turns out be functional to the polity. The pomp and circumstance that bedecked the Byzantine court were necessary to impress the barbarian chiefs on whom the Empire was often forced to rely against its circle of enemies. Similarly, at various periods in the history of China huge amounts of tax were paid in silk, to be passed on to the nomads beyond the Wall in order to keep them quiet. So the costs of diplomacy have to be added to those of war in adjudging the fiscal needs of a polity. But when all this is said, it remains true that in the great majority of cases money was just frittered away on pointlessly conspicuous expenditure in needlessly large courts and their establishments; and in dynastic wars which served to aggrandize, enrich, and add to the self-importance of a ruler, but were of no tangible benefit to either his old subjects or his newly acquired ones. The only way to establish matters of this kind is to examine specific cases.

6.3.4. EVASION AND EXTORTION

Until quite recent times it is rare to find a tax system that was not distorted by systematic tax evasion on the one side and extortionate maladministration on the other, and in all such cases to the disadvantage of the many poor for the benefit of the powerful and rich. The latter, as the power-holders in all the regimes except the Forum type, always try and usually succeed in swinging the tax laws to their advantage. The most blatant examples of this are seen where an entire stratum or class of the population uses its political muscle to have itself exempted from taxes. In later medieval France, for instance (sharply contrasting here with England), the extensive nobility secured exemption from the *taille*. Since the Church was already exempt, this left the *Tiers État* to pick up the bill. The French example of exempting the nobles—and indeed regarding such exemption as the hallmark of the nobleman—was picked up by many imitators in late-medieval Europe. But all large landowners, whether noble or not, whether in Europe or in Asia, had extra-legal modes of evading tax. In the agrarian polities of any size, they were the local notables, with great followings of dependants and clients. In contrast, the government's local tax officials were small fry. It made their task easier, indeed in many cases it alone made it possible, to come to special accommodations with these local bigwigs. These paid proportionately less—meaning that the smallholders and fee peasantry had to pay correspondingly more.

Inequitable assessment, made inevitable for the technical reasons already mentioned, was made much worse by defective public administration. At the lowest echelon the assessment and collection passed from the government's professionals to the unpaid petty notables, village headmen, and the like.[62] Collusion between these persons and the government's own agents was a prime source of corrupt and extortionate taxation. This could be made worse by two common methods of tax collecting. In one, the government sets a tax target for each of its great provinces, but turns a blind eye to the local governor who took far more than the sum he had to pass on, and kept the rest for himself. This was the easier in that it was usual for the governor to retain a portion of the taxes to pay his own local staffs, and this confused the accounts. In another, the government 'privatized' tax collection; it offered the contract for raising such and such a sum in taxation to the highest bidder. This was the 'tax-farm'. The government was concerned only with the amount of tax it had set, not with the methods used by the tax-farmers to collect it.

6.4. *Public Works and Welfare*

Here we enter highly subjective territory. The positive services rendered the community by its government, like education, public buildings, and so forth, vary from time to time and place to place. One can only adjudge this aspect of the polity within the context of its time and geographical location. Two generalizations might be hazarded, however. The first is that the kind of things we nowadays think of as 'welfare' were mostly carried on by cities and not central governments, irrespective of whether those cities were independent or parts of a greater state, like the Roman *municipia*. As a sub-generalization to this it could be ventured that in such cities many of these activities were undertaken by private bodies and not the city council. For instance, the 'liturgies' of wealthy and patriotic Greeks and Romans endowed their cities with public buildings gratis. In the medieval city-states of Italy it was usually some clerical order or a fraternity or guild that cared for the poor, the foundling, and the sick. But cities could differ very much in their priorities. For instance, the municipality in Florence provided an extensive network of schools, which Venice did not; but Venice was the first polity in Europe to provide a state medical service—which Florence did not—yet left education to the great *Fratri*.

It would be wrong, however, to dismiss the role of central governments altogether. In Imperial China, for instance, it was the government that ordered the prefectures to set up schools. But the principal role of the central government was to provide 'public' goods like roads, locks, canals,

---

[62] See p. 66 ff. above.

and ports. In countries prone to flooding, drought, or famine, government might intervene very actively indeed. The Egyptians carefully watched the flood-level of the Nile and set up storehouses and magazines of food for distribution when famines occurred. The Chinese did this in a much more sophisticated way by establishing a system of state purchase of grains where these were in surplus, in order to sell them to those areas that were in famine. I have already referred to the intensive mobilization of forced labour to repair dikes and restore inundated areas in China; but in addition they cut the great network of navigable canals to link the Yellow and the Yangtse river basins, they built roads, and of course, they built the Wall.

But just as there were governments that took such tasks seriously so there were others that neglected them. And just as there were cities that tried to assist their less-advantaged citizens, so there were many others that did not. It would be absurd to condemn these past polities for not coming up to the exacting standards of the modern welfare state; but it is perfectly proper to do so for not conforming to the better standards practised in their era and region.

6.5. Rights and Citizenship

Because 'democracy' and 'participation' are today's buzzwords—no dictatorship can do without them—that is no reason for us to judge past polities by the absence or presence of these features. In fact, very much the reverse. It is natural for today's Europeans and their decendants overseas to look back to the Greeks as the forerunners of our present notions of civil liberties and civil rights. But is not at all cynical to point out that until the nineteenth century it was Sparta, not Athens, that was the model for the European avant-garde. The harsh fact is that the Greek democratic *poleis* form but a tiny spot, both spatially and temporally, on the five millennia of the world's forms of government. It was the Greeks who invented the notion of citizenship; and by this I mean (as the chapter on the *polis* in this History demonstrates) the notion that certain individuals formed a partnership in which they had the right to share in the making and the execution of public policy. A famous passage by Edmund Burke (it is in the *Reflections on the French Revolution*) reproaches Locke for having thought of the state as a joint-stock company. Burke replies that 'the state ought not to be considered as nothing better than a partnership agreement in a trade of pepper and coffee, calico or tobacco, or some other low concern'. But although Burke maintains that the state is more reverent and transcendent than this, he does not deny that it is a 'partnership agreement': he says it is that, plus something more noble. The originality of the Greek *polis* does not lie in its being a city-state—Ur,

Tyre, Sidon were all city-states; it is its being an association, a partnership, in which all ought to and had a right to play their part.

Athens's democratic concept of such citizenship and participation was rejected in Europe till 200 years ago and never even surfaced anywhere else. In the vast majority of cases, for almost all the time, the polity is based on some degree or other of dependency. In them the individual is not a citizen but a subject. What rights he has are what we call passive rights only: the customary rights to his property, to the enforcement of a contract, and so on. The government interferes with these at its peril; but it can interfere, for there is no constitutional mechanism to stop it. By active rights we mean those of sharing in the decision-making process; and these were entirely absent. What we confront instead are different degrees of dependency. These could range from sheer chattel slavery, to domestic slavery, through degrees of serfdom and the like, up to the legally free but in practice dependent peasant farmer. Even in the medieval towns where 'town air made you free', the great majority of artisans lived in dependence on the city's patriciate. The perspective we bring to the freedom or servitude of the individual in these societies must be orientated to the degree of dependency, the extent to which it disadvantaged the individual, and so forth, rather than to a latter-day democratic and egalitarian ideal that surfaced in one unique area of the world at one particular point in time. How anachronistic that would be can be demonstrated by the fact that chattel slavery persisted in the United States until 1865, and in Brazil till 1898.

7. TRAJECTORY WITHOUT TELEOLOGY: INVENTIONS AND DEAD-ENDS

Some practices in government originated in and have been transmitted from antecedent societies. The first attestations of such innovations are what we call here 'inventions', and the innovating society the 'inventor'. But similar practices sometimes spring up at a later time and different place quite independently of the former. Thus, if China be deemed the inventor of modern-style bureaucracy, then western Europe may plausibly be regarded as its re-inventor.

This *History* gives a special, a privileged, status to some of these inventions/re-inventions. They are listed below. They are the ones which are still in use in modern government. Others, discussed in the text but not included in this list, are obsolete. Looking at them from the standpoint of the world today, they are dead-ends.

This is not to deny originality to the societies that invented them. They could well have been every bit as original as those whose institutions, and so on, are being utilized today. It is simply to say that their innovations have proved to be time-bound in a way that the others have not. They were either outdone by better, simpler ways of tackling a particular problem, or alternatively, the problem that they were established to tackle is no longer a problem today.

To privilege those governmental innovations that are still relevant today is not teleological. It would only be teleological on the assumption that the modern state was the ultimate form of governmental organization, or that alternative forms could never have emerged—that sacral monarchy, for instance, was either 'doomed' to disappearance or that it could never return. 'Never' is too long a word to use in history. But it is perfectly reasonable to single out the first attestations of elements of modern governmental practice for the simple reason that by virtue of our inhabiting today's world they are of especial interest to us. But the phrase to stress here is 'of interest'. Being of special interest to us today does not confer on these particular inventions a superior moral or practical value to that of past ones which are no longer in use. What it does do is to confer on them the quite legitimate claim to be the objects of our special curiosity.

Nor is it ethnocentric to privilege those still-relevant governmental practices. It is true—on the ground, as it were—that the ones singled out are precisely those that are constituent parts of the modern European state—the form that originated in Europe round about the sixteenth century. But this is coincidental. It so happens that at the moment of writing, when the world is divided into some 180 independent states, every one of them has taken the modern European state as its model. This is now the global state-form. Events might have taken a different turn. The world-conquering model of the state might have been that of Imperial China. In that case the list of inventions and re-inventions would have been the first attestations of practices still in use in that particular form of polity, for example, the hierarchical ranking of society and autocracy, rather than citizenship, democracy, and representative government.

Some first attestations of a particular government practice are also the last attestations. They are singular. They have no history. But all the rest—and this includes both the inventions and re-inventions—do have a history and maybe an ecology too. This is as much as to say that all of them were or are transmitted to later societies and/or other places. That transmission is usually by direct material filiation over time. For instance, the Chinese Mandarinate was built up, dynasty after dynasty, its character maturing as it went along. But sometimes the transmission is ideational. The Greek *polis*, as I maintained above, invented the notion of citizenship. But the *polis*-type polity soon became extinct. Yet its idea of citizenship, like its idea of democracy, survived as a tradition which was picked up by later generations in different places and under different conditions. The same might be said of Roman law in western Europe—it was revived in the twelfth century, several hundred years after the polity which invented it had disappeared. But, what I would seek to avoid in the strongest possible fashion is giving the impression that when, say, I cite China as the 'inventor' of modern-style bureaucracy, this implies in any way that Europe derived it by transmission from China; or that, for instance, when we say that Achaemenian Persia invented the secular style of empire, it was by transmission from Persia that the Romans came to acquire that same form of polity.

By the same token, this list of inventions and re-inventions cannot be taken to imply a teleology in another sense, that is, that of a linear evolution towards the present. The mere selection itself should be enough to dispel that illusion. The Sumerian and Egyptian notions of kingship/godhead in no way led, in an evolutionary and ineluctable manner, to the Jewish theocracy, and none of any of these has any necessary connection with subsequent secular politics in Greece, or China, or Rome. The latter for its part did not derive its bureaucratic structures from China, and these emphatically did not 'lead' (except in the sequential sense) to feudal- ism—or for that matter to representation. The list does not and does not mean to represent an evolutionary scale. It is simply a selection of those inventions and re-inventions that happen to constitute the elements of the world's modal-state form of the present day.

7.1. Assyria

This unpleasant state invented Empire. Akkadian, Babylonian, and Egyptian monarchs had all ruled other peoples and polities through their native kings or chieftains. The Assyrians were the first to split their conquered lands into provinces governed by centrally appointed officials—the first empire in our modern sense.

7.2. The Persian Empire

The previous empires recognized the notion of the divinity or semi-divinity of the King of Kings, and the Assyrians began to go in for religious imperialism. The beauty of the Persian Empire was that it did not care at all who or how its subject peoples worshipped. It was the first secular- minded empire.

7.3. *The Jewish Kingdoms*

In these kingdoms the monarch is redundant. Only God is king. The secular monarch ought not transgress the (written) Law God had revealed to the congregation (the *kahal*). The king is not absolute because, although there is no constitutional machinery to constrain him, there are things which the religious sentiment of his people forbids him to do. This is the invention of limited monarchy. It did not die with the extinction of the ancient Jewish kingdoms or the Second Jewish Commonwealth. For, embodied in the Bible, it was transmitted ideationally, via Christianity, to become part of the tradition of barbarized western Europe.

7.4. *The Chinese Empire*

This great polity, the oldest in the world, did not directly or even ideationally contribute towards the development of the modern European state. But since its governmental tradition still persists in the People's Republic to this day, and since, too, that Republic contains one in every five of the world's population, it is not an inventor in the sense we have used but neither is it a dead-end. The rich variety and complexity of its Imperial government permits us to choose half-a-dozen great innovations. We can here confine ourselves to saying that this state is the very first that developed a rationally organized, professional, trained, and paid bureaucracy, along with a standing army with parallel characteristics. Both these institutional features were to be developed independently in Europe, but the Chinese were there first. They may be credited with the invention, then, even though the Europeans did, so to speak, 're-invent the wheel'.

7.5. *The Greek* poleis

The city-state polity was a dead-end. It could not expand, only replicate itself. It could not defend itself either. It was doomed to absorption. But—and this is a vast 'but'—as this *History* demonstrates and as we have already mentioned, the Greek *polis* was conceived as a partnership, a kind of super joint-stock concern, in which many citizens had active rights, and in some of which, like Athens, all of them did. The Greeks invented two of the most potent political features of our present age: they invented the very idea of citizen—as opposed to subject—and they invented democracy. The corollary of democracy is the accountability of the governors to the governed, and this the Athenians invented as well. True, their brand of direct democracy was consistent only with the small populations of city-states, but the notion was there and was ideationally transmitted to nineteenth-century Europe. The idea of citizenship was also ideationally transmitted, by its sister-development in early Rome. The boldness of the Greek inventions defies exaggeration.

7.6. *The Roman Republic*

The Roman Republic also developed a citizenship tradition like the Greek *polis*, but did not allocate rights and duties on the principle of the equality of all citizens but on the basis of their status- and property-qualifications. They created what, for want of an English word, we have to call a regime *censitaire*. Furthermore, whereas the *ekklesia* was the overriding and omni-competent body in the Greek democracy, authority in the Roman Republic was constrained by the invention of institutional 'checks and balances'. This immense invention is what differentiates the 'republican form', where government is procedurally limited, from the 'democratic' one, where it is not.

7.7. *The Roman Empire*

Its elaborate bureaucratic and military structures parallel those of the contemporary Han Empire, but, by that very token, are not inventions. The great novelty and enduring invention of the Roman Empire is the *Rechtstaat*. The individual was law-governed, in principle at any rate. The Empire took over from the Republic the notion of accountability and invented institutions to permit the governed to challenge the legality of the actions of the Imperial agents, whether these were provincial governors, or whether they were agencies like the fisc. The supremacy of law as against that of individuals—what Aristotle had adumbrated as the 'government of laws and not of men'—took on concrete shape in this Empire.

It is worth noting that until it succumbed to bigoted clericalism in the fourth century, this Empire, like the Persian and Chinese empires, was very this-worldly and secular, and above all indisposed to persecute its subjects on account of their religious beliefs. Christians were persecuted for the political effects of their outward activities, not for what went on in their minds. Persecution of individuals and groups for the latter reason is something we owe to St Augustine.

7.8. *Byzantium*

The Byzantine Empire made no significant inventions, except that, like the Arab Empire discussed below, it was a *kahal*-like polity. Although caesaropapist, the emperors' efforts to define the religion met political opposition when they went against the sentiments of their subjects. So the Byzantine Empire is a weak example of 'substantive constraint'.

This caesaropapist autocracy died when the Empire fell to the Turks (when it was succeeded by a Muslim caesaropapist autocracy!); but not before it had transmitted this main feature to the 'Byzantine Commonwealth', that is, the Balkans and, of major historical significance, Russia.

7.9. *The Caliphate*

The greatest achievement of the Arabian nomads was to meld a new civilization in the lands they had conquered. But the Al-Hambra is not our affair. In the history of government their contribution—we can hardly call it an invention—was, in Disraeli's words, 'Jews on Horseback'. As indicated above, the Jews invented the limitation of monarchy by a divine law beyond the power of rulers to invade or change. The Arabs—like the Christians—picked up this doctrine, but unlike the Jews, who were always a minority and whose very polity was ultimately wiped out, they were conquerors and could impose this view on the societies they conquered. Partly by the persuasiveness of Islam—it being strictly monotheistic and conversion being remarkably easy—and partly by discrimination against non-Muslims, this Arab ruling stratum was able to get the conquered peoples to adopt their religion and hence become part of the *umma*, which acted as a constraint upon the procedural absolutism of their rulers.

7.10. *Medieval Europe*

Medieval Europe is remarkably inventive. On the one side it revived certain past forms, and this revival was to have significance for the future. Notably, it revived the city-republic. Also, it revived the notion of the *Rechtstaat*, even to the point, on the Continent, of reviving Roman law itself. It also created a dead-end—feudalism. Feudalism was a makeshift for an organized, monetized, centrally controlled territorial polity. But the dead-end is an interesting one because it has analogies elsewhere at that time and even in the present day.

Medieval Europe invented two great things. The first is the hierarchically organized Church which both opposes and symbioses with the secular power, jealously staking out a sphere of authority into which it would not let the rulers enter. In no other part of the world was the substantive delimitation of autocracy institutionalized as it was here. There is nothing to compare with it in Islam, in the Confucian persuasion, or in the Buddhist *sangha*. Nowhere else was the religious institution so powerfully and ably organized. The second great invention is representation. It goes without saying that this lies at the very heart of the modern state which is today's world model.

7.11. *The Early-Modern State in Europe*

These European national states do not on the whole invent so much as re-invent or re-emphasize. The certain thing is that they re-invent for the West the notion of the territoriality of the state which had been erased in feudalism. They also re-invent caesaropapist tendencies, such as had been seen in Byzantium, with the Reformation and the founding of 'national' Churches. They do invent, however, the notion of the national state based on language and religious denomination and perpetuated by a balance of power.

One state, however, invented a form which was destined to become a distinctive and essential component of a form of the modern state, and that is England. Here, unlike on the Continent, where the monarchs and princes won their battle against the medieval representative assemblies, the national representative body, Parliament, was victorious. The English thus invented procedurally limited monarchy—to become known as 'constitutional monarchy'. In the course of doing this they also initiated the progressive development of an instrument that was essential to working this representative system: the competitive political party.

7.12. *The United States and France 1776–1789*

Enormous inventions! The French invent the modern ideology of nationalism and with it the idea of the nation-state, that is, the state belonging to the nation which is identified with the people, and not to a dynasty or a foreign power.

The Americans, for their part, invent four of the seminal features of today's state: the written constitution, the constitutional guarantee of civil rights, judicial review, and federalism. Many might wonder at the exclusion of the 'separation of powers' from this list, but that had already been invented (though in quite a different form, of course), by the Roman Republic.

7.13. *Full Modernity*

The entire material substructure changes, eliminating time and distance. Two great and unfortunate inventions haunt the period. Beyond the perfection of the competitive party system, there is invented something which is supposedly of the same kind but is in fact completely new and radically different. This is the official monopolistic political party, used by the government as its 'transmission belt to the masses'. The second invention is ideology, which increasingly usurps the place formerly held by religion, but retains and exaggerates its dogmatic and persecuting zeal. These two inventions, coupled with the now-pervasive power of the state, make the Palace/Forum type of polity into something new: the totalitarian state. This consists of an ideology (communism, nazism, fascism as the case may be); the organized and monopolistic support of a huge civic Church—the single-party; its control of the rest of the population by the new methods of surveillance; and the power of the rulers over that party and hence over surveillance, using the ideology as instrumental to their tenure of office.

On the other side appears a more benign invention. Just as the changes in the material substructure made intense surveillance possible, so it enormously increased wealth, while at the same time throwing up a work-force which was more organized and powerful than any in previous history. From this conjunction arose the invention of the welfare state.

In selecting this list of inventions, I repeat that I do not wish to give the impression that the history of government has followed a linear evolution. That, indeed, is the very last impression I would want this *History* to create. The dead-ends are so many, the breakdowns and reversions to barbarism so frequent and widespread, that it would be altogether misguided to think in terms of progressive evolution. What has happened is really this. In one particular part of the world, which was utterly barbarous when the first great polities began, ideas and institutions burgeoned which were then transmitted, materially or ideationally, to later generations until in the fullness of time they blossomed into the so-called modern European state. By that same time, this formerly undernourished and barbarous part of the globe had become so populous, rich, and militarily preponderant as to colonize or subject the rest of the world's polities. These, in turn, either in emulation and admiration, or to get revenge, copied the design of the states to which they were subjected. This is why the European modern state—the territorial nation-state that proclaims democratic and secular values—has become the model for the entire contemporary world. What I have done is to show the reader its antecedents. What I have not done is to construct a theodicy.

BIBLIOGRAPHY

ARDANT, G., 'Financial Infrastructure of Modern States and Nations', in Tilly (ed.), *Formation*, 164–242.

—— *Histoire de l'Impôt*, vol. 1 (Fayard, Paris, 1971).

BARKER, E. (ed. and trans.), *The Politics of Aristotle* (Clarendon Press, Oxford, 1980).

BELLAH, R. N., 'Religious Evolution', in R. Robertson (ed.), *Sociology of Religion* (Penguin, Harmondsworth, 1969), 262–94.

BURKE, P., 'City States', in Hall (ed.), *States in History*, 137–53.

'Chan Kuo Ts'e' or 'The Intrigues of the Warring States', trans. J. I. Crump, 2nd rev. edn. (Chinese Materials Centre, 1949).

CRONE, P., 'The Tribe and the State', in Hall (ed.), *States in History*, 48–77.

DUNBABIN, J., *France in the Making, 843–1180* (OUP, Oxford, 1985).

EASTON, D., *The Political System: An Inquiry into the State of Political Science* (Knopf, New York, 1953).

EBERHARD, W., *A History of China*, 4th edn. (Routledge & Kegan Paul, London, 1977).

EISENSTADT, S. N., and ROKKAN, S. (eds.), *Building States and Nations* (Sage, London, 1973).

FIGGIS, J. N., *The Divine Right of Kings*, 2nd edn. (CUP, Cambridge, 1922; 1st edn. 1914).

FINER, S. E., 'Almond's Concept of the "Political System"—A Textual Critique', *Government and Opposition*, 5:1 (Winter, 1970), 3–21.

—— 'State and Nation Building in Europe: The Role of the Military', in C. Tilly (ed.), *The Formation of National States in Western Europe*, 84–163.

—— (ed.), *Vilfredo Pareto: Sociological Writings* (Blackwell, Oxford, 1976).

—— 'Perspectives in the World History of Government—A Prolegomenon', *Government and Opposition*, 18:1 (Winter, 1983), 3–22.

—— *Man on Horseback*, 4th edn. (Praeger, Boulder, Col., 1988).

—— 'State-building, State Boundaries, and Border Control', *Social Science Information*, 13 (1974), 79–126.

GIDDENS, A., *The Nation-State and Violence: Volume Two of A Contemporary Critique of Historical Materialism* (Polity, Cambridge, 1985; repr. 1987).

GRANET, M., *La pensée chinoise* (Albin Michel, Paris, 1934).

GREGORY OF TOURS, *History of the Franks* (*c.*576–91), trans. with an introduction by O. M. Dalton (Clarendon Press, Oxford, 1927).

HALL, J. A. (ed.), *States in History* (Blackwell, Oxford, 1986).

JONES, A. H. M., *The Later Roman Empire, 284–602*, 2 vols. (Blackwell, Oxford, 1964).

LOEWE, M., ''The Campaigns of Han Wu-ti', in F. A. Kiernan and J. K. Fairbank, (eds.), *Chinese Ways in Warfare* (Harvard UP, Cambridge, Mass., 1974), 67–110.

LOWENSTEIN, K., *Political Power of the Governmental Process*, 2nd edn. (University of Chicago Press, 1965).

MACIVER, R. M., *The Web of Government* (Macmillan, New York, 1947)

MANN, M., 'The Autonomous Power of the State', in Hall (ed.), *States in History*, 109–36.

PRITCHARD, J. B. (ed.), *Ancient Near Eastern Texts* (= *ANET*), 3rd edn. (Princeton UP, Princeton, 1969).

SIDGWICK, H., *The Development of the European Polity* (Macmillan, London, 1903).

STRACHEY, R., *Religious Fanaticism* (Faber & Gwyer, London, 1928), esp. pp. 30–65.

TACITUS, *Historiarum Libri*, annotated and with a critical introduction by C. D. Fisher (Clarendon Press, Oxford; 1st pub. 1911).

TILLY, C. (ed.) *The Formation of National States in Western Europe* (Princeton UP, Princeton, 1975).

TOUT, T. F., 'The English Civil Service in the Fourteenth Century', in *Collected Papers of Thomas Frederick Tout* (University of Manchester Press, Manchester, 1934), iii. 192–213.

ULLMANN, W., *Law and Politics in the Middle Ages* (Hodder & Stoughton, London, 1975).

Vues Politiques, ed. and foreword by A. Dansette (Fayard, Paris, 1939).

WAL, G. DE, *Histoire de l'Ordre Teutonique*, 8 vols. (Paris and Rheims, 1784–90).

WALES, H. G. Q., *Ancient Siamese Government and Administration* (London, 1934).

WEBB, S., and WEBB, B., *Soviet Communism: A New Civilisation?* (Longmans, Green, London, 1935).

WHITE, L., Jr., *Medieval Technology and Social Change* (OUP, Oxford, 1962).

Book I

Context I

*T*he first unambiguously attested states yet known emerged round about 3200 BC in the Nile Valley and in southern Mesopotamia—'unambiguously', because writing had been invented in those two areas, and we have documents instead of merely archaeological records. There must certainly have been states before this: city-states, at least, since Jericho had massive walls and a temple shrine as early as *c*.6500 BC—but we know nothing of its social and political life. Likewise, there were important states after this which, if we could interpret their writing, might well disclose a political order to match the Egyptian or Sumerian: Minoan Crete, for example, that flourished between 2000 and 1450 BC. These states, however, all have another characteristic besides unfathomability: they were 'one-off' states, dead-end states. As they arose suddenly and in mystery, so they perished suddenly, in mysterious circumstances; and, dead, left no progeny. Their very existence was unknown until their ruins were exposed by the spade within the last hundred years.

This is emphatically not true of the Sumerian or Egyptian civilizations, which passed their tradition on through space and time. In a world-historical perspective, the Middle East is the cradle of organized government, and it was to retain its cultural, political, and military supremacy even under increasing pressure for over 2,000 years.

The 'Middle East' comprises the Nile Valley and, in Asia, the Fertile Crescent (Syria–Palestine), and Mesopotamia. Around 3500 the southern-most part of Mesopotamia, where the first states are attested, was inhabited by a folk who called themselves 'the black-headed people', and whom we call the Sumerians, intermixed with others who spoke a Semitic language. Who the Sumerians were and from whence they came is unknown. Their language has no affinity with any other. Semitic peoples lived among them and then also to the north and west throughout the Fertile Crescent and in Arabia. Further to the south-west, beyond the Sinai desert, the Nile Valley was populated by a mixture of the indigenous inhabitants and newcomers—from the east perhaps. The ancient Egyptian language is classified as Hamito-Semitic, since it has syntactical affinities with the Semitic tongues.

Both the Egyptian and the Sumerian societies were based on irrigation-agriculture, the ox-drawn plough and the wheeled cart, and the attendant arts of pottery and weaving, boats and sailing ships. Trade went on with distant lands: indeed Sumer, lacking stone, wood, and metals, had to import most of these from the north. The Sumerians were using bronze several centuries before this became common in Egypt. But for practical purposes bronze was so rare that we must think of these as *stone-age* societies. All agricultural and household tools were made of stone. This limitation must never be forgotten.

Both were 'two-class' societies. Power rested with a tiny group of court officials and priests around the monarch, supported by a corps of scribes and accountants, also a very narrow group, the scripts being so difficult to master. In both, the base of society was a massively dominated peasantry. Initially, at any rate, artisans and traders seem to have been the agents and servants of the rulers. Weights and measures and standards of value were in use, but no currency; both these societies were natural economies, but highly regulated, and of a type we might call 'storage redistributive': that is, the peasants' produce was checked in by the scribes and accountants to be paid out again or stored against hardship and famine. The form of government was absolute monarchy. Indeed, throughout the entire region we find only monarchies, never a republic; and likewise a religion of the kind scholars call 'Archaic'. It conceived of one great divine cosmos in which the human order reflected that of the gods, who, as all-powerful controllers of all natural processes, had to be propitiated by worship and sacrifice. Hence, there were priests as intermediaries—and above the priests, the monarch as the supreme intermediary—either the 'Vicar of the Gods', or, in Egypt, a god himself. The common folk did not constitute a '*kahal*'—a congregation, that is, they were not called on to exhibit or feel personal piety, but to conform as onlookers and worshippers in the cultic rituals undertaken by the priest king. The traditional social structure and practices formed part of the divine plan, so that religion fortified and reinforced social conformity in every detail. Every aspect of society—the kingship, architecture, art, script, mathematical formulae, calendar—was invested with sacredness, suffusing and inspiring every human activity as it did. Archaic religion made every aspect of their societies exactly cohere with one another, imparting a static uniformity to the entire civilization. Egypt and Mesopotamia are dissimilar, as will be seen, but nobody has failed to perceive in the societies of the Middle East down to the middle of the first millennium BC an underlying cultural unity in sharp contrast with subsequent civilizations, notably the Greek and Roman. It is the all-pervasiveness of the Archaic-type religion which gives it this unity.

Egypt, from its dynastic beginnings *c.*3200, was a centralized autocracy. This regime maintained itself until *c.*1700 (save for a century-long period of civil strife): an exhibition of stability and continuity unparalleled in the entire annals of human history.

The Mesopotamian experience was quite different. Sumer was a country of petty city-states, fiercely independent and always at war with one another. Its history is punctuated by these petty wars, by three successful but short-lived attempts to unite them in an empire, and by foreign invasions. In 2334 Sargon of Akkad—the Semitic-speaking region to Sumer's immediate north—created an extensive empire stretching from the Persian Gulf to the Mediterranean coast of Syria. It was brought to an end—characteristically for Mesopotamia—by an invasion of barbarous Gutian tribesmen from the Persian mountains in the area of present-day Suleimanya. In 2112 a second effort at unification was made by the third dynasty of Ur, marking the Sumerian revival. Supposedly its empire was an extension of Sargon's, but the details are lacking. It was shattered in 2004 when the tributary king of Elam revolted in the east, while nomadic wandering Semites, the Amorites, closed in from the west. Together they sacked Ur and destroyed it. The third unification was accomplished by the Semitic king, Hammurabi of Babylon. It lasted from his reign (1792–1750) until Babylon was sacked in an extraordinary raid launched by the Hittites, all the way from distant Anatolia, in 1595. When they withdrew the Sumerian cities were taken over by the barbarous highlanders from the Zagros—the Kassites.

The Hittites and the Kassites were new phenomena in the Middle East heartland. They were—or rather they were ruled and united by—a new type of people, who spoke a variety of Indo-European tongues.

Sumerian civilization moved steadily upstream into Assyria and the Fertile Crescent. Round about 1800 an Assyrian trading colony is found in southern Anatolia, passing on the cuneiform script and the Akkadian *lingua franca* to newly arrived Hittite princes who had established a kingdom there. Sumerian culture moved eastward, also—Elam adopted cuneiform in the middle of the second millennium BC.

By the beginning of the second millennium, a contemporary Aristotle, collecting constitutions, would have noticed the following. To the far east, in India, lay the city states of the Harappans; between it and Mesopotamia, the kingdom of Elam; then Mesopotamia itself, united at least as far as Syria, under the Sumerian Third dynasty of Ur; in Syria and Jezirah, powerful kingdoms like those of Mari, Ebla, and many lesser ones. Anatolia was a land of petty kingdoms, incessantly at war, some of them clearly powerful and wealthy, as the lavish grave furniture of the royal tombs at Alaca Huyuk and Troy II bear witness. From here metalworking techniques had been carried into tribal and barbaric Greece. There, if we turned south, however, lay another, and by now advancing, civilization: early Minoan Crete. It had been triggered by both Egyptian and Anatolian contacts, but evolved into something entirely original and idiosyncratic. Crete was an island of city-states, ruled by kings from great palaces, with storage–redistribution economies reminiscent of early Sumer. However, little is really known of the Minoan polity despite intense speculation. Finally, south-wards still lay Egypt, just about to receive its powerful XIIth dynasty.

Such was the world of states at the turn of the millennium. It was a very small world. It consisted of a few densely populated sites dotted about a huge landscape, which was wide open to nomadic wanderers or foraging highlanders. The sparsity of population, the almost total porousness of frontiers, and the incessant movement, infiltration, and finally implantation of the wandering peoples cannot be over-emphasized. That and that only makes the next development in the most ancient world intelligible. For from about 2000 two waves of new peoples were in motion. In the west of the Fertile Crescent, in the desert area that separates Jordan and Euphrates, nomadic Semitic-speaking tribesmen—Amurru (or 'westerners') infiltrated, settled, fought, and finally overthrew the rulers of the cities in Mesopotamia and north Syria, and established their own kingdoms. By 1800–1750, at the time of Hammurabi of Babylon, there was a 'vast community of Amorite states from the Mediterranean to the Persian Gulf'.[1] But the second set of peoples who were on the move spoke Indo-European languages, and their native institutions and outlook were completely alien to the Hamito-Semi-tic culture of the Middle East. Their wanderings began in the third millennium from, it is thought, a 'Pontic' epicentre north of the Black Sea. One great stream moved slowly westward across Europe—the 'battle-axe' folk. Some turned away south-westward, picking up the art of bronze-working on the way to invade northern Greece around 1800 BC. From the end of the third millennium, around 2300–2200, yet another group moved from the Pontic area down through the Caucasus into Armenia, where they assumed leadership of the native Hurrian tribes, and into the Zagros mountains, where they assumed the leadership of the Kassite tribesmen. The bulk of them continued southward, however, into Sindh and the Punjab.

These Indo-Europeans introduced into the Middle East a major inno-vation: the horse. (The Sumerians knew only the onager, the wild ass.) They did not ride the horse, but harnessed it to carts as the Sumerians had the onager from their earliest days. For purposes of warfare, however, the

[1] G. Roux, *Ancient Iraq*, 2nd. edn. (Penguin, Harmondsworth, 1980), 220.

Indo-European horsemen developed the 'horse-cart' into the elegant, swift, light-structured battle-chariot, manned by archers.

Between 1800 and 1700 the rim of Middle Eastern civilization was manned by outposts of these new peoples armed with their new weaponry. In Palestine, upset by the Amorite invasions, the local chiefs, *hyksos*, had made the battle-chariot their own. In Anatolia the first Indo-European kingdom—the Hittite—was established. In northern Mesopotamia were the Hurrians, ruled by Indo-European overlords (Mitanni). In the Zagros were the Kassite tribes, also ruled by Indo-European overlords. And on the frontier of the Harappa state were concentrated that Indo-European branch called the Aryans.

In 1725 the *hyksos* chieftains infiltrated Egypt and established principalities in the Delta. At about the same time, the Aryans—so one theory has it—fell upon the Harappan state and totally destroyed it. In 1595 the Hittites sacked Babylon, leaving it to be ruled by the invading Kassites; and in 1300 the Mitanni set up their empire in the north of Mesopotamia.

I

The Sumerian City-State

*T*his *History* begins with the Sumerian city-states because it has to: these city-states in the south of Mesopotamia are the first states we encounter in recorded history. They first appear *c*.3500 BC. By the time their form of writing had developed from pictograms to the true cuneiform script, *c*.2900–2800, the clay tablets on which it was impressed were numerous enough for Sumerologists to form an impression of the way these states were constituted and—in very broad outline—how they were governed.

But there are further reasons for beginning with these city-states. Not merely are they the first attestations of the state-form, but the polity we infer from the archaeology and the clay documents is no primitive emergent structure, like some of the African ones described by anthropologists. What is amazing is that here, at the very dawn of recorded history, we should find, not states with few functions and feeble means of execution, nor fragile and exiguous political structures, but the very opposite: states that are organized and administered, so it would seem, to the last degree. It is as if government as we conceive it today had already arrived, fully fledged, at the first moment the records begin to speak. The same miraculous parthenogenesis will be witnessed, not much later, on the banks of the Nile.

There are no better reasons for inclusion than these, but there are others, nevertheless. These city-states take their place among the great historic types of polity, as outlined earlier.[1] Accordingly, they present certain contrasts to other forms of polity as well as several parallels. Among the latter at least three stand out. The first is the sacral monarchy. The entire society—its politics, its economy, its art and culture, and its folkways and customs—was totally impregnated with the values, norms, and expectations of shared religion. This acted as a powerful social cement, bonding the inhabitants to one another to form a unity, and bonding this unity to the rulers, obedience to whom was part of the natural order of the universe. The king was the sacred point of interconnection between the divine heavenly part of the cosmos and its extension on earth. This conception of the monarchy and its central place in the scheme of things was to be found

[1] Conceptual Prologue, p. 6.

throughout the entire Middle Eastern area—and in its own form in Egypt also—until well into the first millennium BC.

Another parallel feature is the existence of a numerous bureaucracy. The state has a permanent administrative apparatus, which operates—as all such systems must do—on the basis of documentation, files, archives, and retrieval. The upper directing stratum of the bureaucracy consisted of scribes and accountants in the palace and in the temples. They are likely to be few compared with the menials—porters, carriers, labourers, and the like—since, as explained later on, the craft of writing took so long to learn. This is another characteristic of the Middle Eastern states of this period, and of Egypt also.

The third feature, again common to the entire region until the first millennium, is the monopoly of power held by the tiny group who alone possess the difficult mastery of letters and numbers. The absolute authority of the ruler over the population is strengthened by the absolute power which he had.

In what sense, if any, then, did the Sumerian city-state represent an innovation in the craft of government? In one sense clearly, it is *all* an innovation—but this is in the trivial sense that this is the first recognizable state that we encounter in history. But if the question be changed to ask, what is the significance of the Sumerian city-state to the history of government, the answer is threefold. First, its *oikos* character represents a distinctive sub-type of polity which, with variations, will be found elsewhere; in Egypt and pre-Columbian America, for example. Secondly, it acts as a yardstick for appraising other monarchical city-states in the Middle East at this period— Ebla and Mari, which we have mentioned briefly already,[2] differed very substantially indeed from the Sumerian model. Finally, it serves as a contrast to what the West has tended to consider as the archetypical city-state, that is, the Greek *polis*, since in every respect except that they are city-states the Greek *polis* and the Sumerian city-state are entirely antithetical.

1. THE SETTING

Mesopotamia is, strictly speaking, the land between the two rivers, the Euphrates and the Tigris. Here the expression will be used by an extended sense to cover the area enclosed in the triangle formed by Aleppo, Lake Urmia, and the Shatt Al-Arab.

The twin rivers form part of a great level plain which is ringed to north and east by mountains, the millennial home of barbarous highlanders, always

---

[2] Bk. I, Context I, p. 101, above.

ready and eager to descend on the wealthy cities below. On the west stretches a tawny gravel desert, flat as a table-top until it meets the mountains of Amman. The edges of the desert were home to Semitic nomads; Semites who infiltrated and squatted or raided and conquered. The 'land of the two rivers', then, was exposed on its borders, while its flat monotony enabled contending armies to sweep unchecked over great distances, but deprived them of natural features to help them hold their conquests.

The Tigris moves rapidly. The Euphrates bends and meanders in its course. But both are unpredictable, and because of the way they carry and throw up silt, they are apt to overflow and to change their course. That is why the sites of the Sumerian cities lie in what today is a waste of sand. But that too is one reason why irrigation canals and dykes to control floods (the Tigris being apt to flood) were then, as now, a prerequisite of farming.

Ancient Sumer lay between the two rivers, from the marshlands in the south to near the waist of the hourglass made by the two rivers just south of Babylon: that territory the Sumerians called Akkad, populated by folk indistinguishable from themselves except that they spoke a Semitic language, not Sumerian. Lacking rainfall, Sumer and Akkad could only support agriculture by means of perennial irrigation (not the 'basin irrigation' of the Nile). The sun's heat is so formidable, the soil so fertile, that irrigation generated immensely rich harvests. So it is that their cities sprang up along the courses of the two rivers as they were in that age. Each city and its satellite towns was, itself, separated from its neighbour by desert. Thus the cities were just as sealed off from their neighbours as the early Greek settlements were cut off from one another by sea and mountain. In both cases the consequence was a deep-seated, almost inextinguishable, local patriotism and, correspondingly, political particularism.

One final feature of the geography must be mentioned: Sumer has almost no stone or metal, nor any wood except the palm, tamarisk, willow, and poplar—not good building timber. So mud huts, mud walls, and baked brick walling characterized its architecture, and its scribes wrote by impressing a reed into rather hard clay. Bronze, stone, and building timber, if required in some quantity, could be obtained only by trading upriver to the far north.

Sumer was small—some 10,000 sq. miles, a little less than Belgium today, somewhat larger than Israel. For the early period before Sargon of Akkad's conquest (2444 BC) the number of major cities known to us is about fourteen. The earliest were Eridu, Uruk (the Erech of the Bible), Bad-Tibira, Nippur, and Kish. Ur, Lagash, Umma, Shuruppak, Sippar, and Isin (to name the most important) are thought to be later foundations but without firm evidence, and indeed, tradition had it that Shuruppak was antediluvian. Estimates of the cities' populations are quite conjectural and vary greatly. One estimate puts the population of Lagash at 30,000–35,000[3] inhabitants but another (Diakonoff) suggests 100,000.[4] Ur had only 10,000 inhabitants, c.2750–2375, its urban development coming later: Sir Leonard Woolley estimated its population in c.2000 (when it was the capital of an empire) at 360,000,[5] but we are advised to cut this figure in half.[6] Uruk, a very early city indeed, is thought to have contained 40,000–50,000 people in c.2900 and Umma the same.[7] However, not one of these quoted figures is evidenced, and techniques of deducing the size of population have so far been unproductive. These figures are completely unreliable, and the only thing that is clear is that the city-states were very small. This is cardinally important in accounting for their minutely controlled economic system.

CHRONOLOGY

BC

4300–3500	AL-UBAID period
3500–3100	URUK period
3100–3000	JEMDET NASR phase. Proto-literacy
2900–2750	*War Leaders emerge*
2900–2750	EARLY DYNASTIC I
2750–2600	EARLY DYNASTIC II
2550	*The royal tombs at Ur*
2400	*Palaces begin to appear*
2378–2371	Uruinimgina of Lagash, usurper and reformer
2334	Sargon of Akkad conquers Sumer
2193	Gutian tribesmen destroy Sargonic Empire
2123–2112?	*The Sumerian king-list; now thought to be much later (c.1800), but based on traditional materials*
2112–2095	Ur-Nammu, of Ur, issues legal code
2112–2004	IIIrd DYNASTY AND EMPIRE OF UR
2004	Ur razed by Elamites and Amorites
1793–1750	Hammurabi of Babylon conquers Sumer
1662	Kassites take Babylon

[3] Roux, *Ancient Iraq*, 125.
[4] I. M. Diakonoff, 'The Rise of the Despotic State in Ancient Mesopotamia: Ancient Mesopotamia: Socio-Economic History' (1956), repr. in I. M. Diakonoff (ed.), *Ancient Mesopotamia, Socio-Economic History: A Collection of Studies by Soviet Scholars* (Moscow, 1969), 173–203.
[5] *Journal of World History*, vol. 4 (1957), 246–7.
[6] S. K. Kramer, *The Sumerians—Their History, Culture, and Character* (University Press of Chicago, Chicago, 1963), 88–9.
[7] J.-P. Grégoire, 'L'Origine et le développement de la civilisation mesopotamienne du IIIème millenaire avant notre ère', in *Production, pouvoir, et parenté dans le monde méditerranéen de Sumer à nos jours* (Actes de colloque L'E.R.A., CNRS/EHESS, 1976, Paris, 1981).

2. HISTORY

The cities begin as village settlements. The archaeological record, such as it is (since no one site has been completely excavated), attests a continuous cultural development from at least the Al-Ubaid period, perhaps earlier. But although pictograms appear *c.*3100–3000, and later developed into the more flexible cuneiform writing, the corpus of inscriptions and the precision of the writing system are inadequate to supply any plausible historical account until about 2500. At that date we have a mass of inscriptions and archives that paint a history of the long-protracted war between Lagash and Umma. After that the documents permit reconstruction of the main events in Sumer as a whole.

That history is one of friction, rivalry, warfare, and conquests. Some cities, like Lagash, enlarged their borders to absorb other cities: in this Lagash example, the capital lay at Girsu, and the territory included Lagash, Nina, many villages, and even a port—Guabba. The contending rulers fought for hegemony over all Sumer. Later writings (*c.*1800) suggest there was but one high kingship for all Sumer and that it rested with one particular city at any one time, but this is probably only true for Ur III. The famous Sumerian king-list does indeed record the change of dynasties in terms of the city which held the kingship at any one time, but many Sumerologists maintain that it was compiled (using such traditional material) *c.*1800, in order to legitimate the notion of an all-Sumerian monarchy by saying that this is how it had always been from time immemorial. It was the practice for any hegemon to assume the kingship of Nippur, the sacred city of the great god Enlil, as title of his right. But these changes of hegemon are essentially barren, for later peoples inhabiting the same site inherited nothing from them. These states were absolutely undreamt of for over 4,000 years and, now that the spade has uncovered them, they are no more to any people on earth today than 'old unhappy far-off things and battles long ago'. The one really significant event is, in fact, the one that heralded the beginning of the end of the Sumerian city-state and its system. This was the conquest of Sumer by Sargon, a ruler of the Semitic-speakers who inhabited the 'waist' of the hourglass path of the two rivers.[8]

In these cities, immense and lofty ziggurats demonstrate a complete mastery of the practical problems of mensuration and the mechanics involved in erecting such large and exactly proportioned buildings. The sculpture too, carved as it often is from diorite, is as astounding for its technique as it is beautiful in its conception.

[8] See Context II below.

But just as there is a sharp contrast between the advanced state of arts and crafts and the relatively primitive techniques in agriculture, so is there a sharp contrast between this monumental architecture and the town itself. Temples—and in the high noon of Sumer, the palaces too—were large and imposing. But the town itself was a squat mass of mud houses packed up tight, one against the other, with lanes too narrow to admit even pack animals and, usually, no manner of disposing of domestic filth. Equally, there was a contrast between the mass of artisans and rural labourers, and the ruling élite which comprised the rulers and their courts, the temples and their priesthoods, the scribes and accountants. This élite was very narrow; the more so since the keys to power—literacy and numeracy—were so very difficult to acquire. Education in Sumer involved long and painful years of rote-learning and drill in the diffult cuneiform script—which consisted of some 800 basic signs—as well as in the various formulae for calculating and measuring.[9] These skills were transmitted by schools in temples and palace. But there were freelance schoolmasters also. As the former schools were open to pupils only by the grace and favour of the ruling élite and the latter (it is assumed) only to those who could afford the fees, the literate and numerate classes in society simply perpetuated themselves.

3. THE ECONOMIC AND SOCIAL BACKGROUND[10]

In 2500 BC a city-state usually consisted of three parts: the city proper, a walled area surrounding the palace, the temples, and the houses; then the suburbs, with fields, farms, and cattle-folds; and then the harbour and the quay (the *kar*), a trading area where foreign traders dwelt.

From early days the rulers imported bronze and precious metals, building timber and stone, down the rivers from the far north: the cedars of Lebanon were a thousand miles away. Traction power was supplied by oxen. Clumsy, heavy, wheeled wooden war-carts were dragged by onagers. Asses were used as pack animals. The horse is not attested till the Ur III period, and the camel, even if known, was not domesticated until an entire millennium later, so that the nomads of the Syrian desert could at this time move only by short, intermittent stages.

The basis of economy was cereal agriculture—chiefly barley. Date palms provided sugar-rich addition. Strong distilled barley-beer and palm- and grape-wine could be brewed from these plants. In addition, vegetables

[9] Kramer, *Sumerians—Their History*, ch. 6.
[10] For up-to-date information, see J. N. Postgate, *Early Mesopotamia: Society and Economy at the Dawn of History* (Routledge, London and New York, 1992).

abounded and so did fish, and the land, under irrigation, was extremely fertile. It was common to reap a snatch-harvest as well as the main crop, but equipment and techniques were primitive. Most tools and utensils were made of stone, for bronze was rare and expensive. The plough was light and did not carry a mould-board. The traction animals were harnessed by thongs passed around their necks—the horse-collar was undreamt of—so that the harder they pulled the more they choked. All the more surprising, perhaps, is the artistry and skill deployed by the Sumerian artisans and builders, for as the royal tombs of Ur attest (and they date from c.2550) their skill in metallurgy, metalwork, and jewelling was superlative.

The entire city-complex lay in an extended territory of gardens, palm groves, barley- and wheat-fields, and the land between the numerous irrigation canals served as pastures.[11] The total area comprised several districts, each with its own gods and temple but, arguably, the city-state as a whole was under the protection of the one particular deity who, in theory, 'owned' it. Thus Lagash belonged to Ningirsu, Umma to Shara, Ur to Nanna. The ruler governed the city on behalf of the god: and by the same token, at various periods in Sumerian history and at different localities, he represented the people or the city before the god and acted as the indisputable intermediary between man and the gods who controlled the wealth, power, and fortune of the city. However, this was not always the case—we have inscriptions which describe the temple rather than the kings as the 'Mooring-post of Heaven and Earth'. Often, too, the king is described as the 'chosen' of the god or the 'favourite' of the god, with no reference to his role as a conduit.

4. THE CENTRAL AUTHORITIES c.2600–2344 BC

4.1. Origins and Developments

We have already outlined the typical form of government—sacral monarchy, priesthood, bureaucracy, and oikos society—but though the general outline is reasonably plain, the details are not and many are unknown. A high proportion of what is known is often specific to one city or another at a given time. And even where the data are fairly uniform and widespread, they lend themselves to quite contradictory interpretation. Beyond the shadowy outline sketched above, almost everything else relating to the government of these cities is a matter of acute controversy.

It is just as well to be clear at the very outset, then, about how little is

[11] Roux, Ancient Iraq, 125; A. L. Oppenheim, Ancient Mesopotamia, rev. edn. (Chicago, 1977), 115–17.

known and how variously it can be interpreted. There are almost no written documents for the first 2,000 years of archeological evidence from southern Mesopotamia, and the votive inscriptions from the later periods come from a few sites only, so that they present a one-sided picture. On the other hand, for the third millennium there are tens of thousands of written tablets of all kinds, including administrative archives, economic documents, legal texts, law codes, and private letters. Indeed, for the famous IIIrd dynasty of Ur no less than 25,000 documents have actually been *published*; the trouble is, no team of scholars has got down to making a systematic examination of them.[12] Hence, although the two key institutions of the city-state are the palace and the temples, one leading authority frankly admits: 'we are rather poorly informed about the administration of the palace',[13] and 'very much in the dark' concerning the temple, 'knowing little' about the higher echelons of its organization and 'unclear' as to what cultic services it rendered to the community.[14]

Controversy is greatest over the prehistory of the city-states. The basic dispute arises from the theory that the cities were originally governed by the citizens in an *unkin* (= assembly) composed of a council of 'fathers' plus a general body of the younger men. According to the theory, the kings or *lugals* were temporary dictators appointed by the assembly as war-leaders in times of crisis, but whose rule was institutionalized as warfare became endemic (attested by city walls *c*.2700). The proponent of this theory was the famous Sumerologist T. Jacobsen. He did, admittedly, make some qualification; the assembly was 'provisional' and *ad hoc* and 'called upon to function in emergencies only'.[15] One of his followers is more rash,[16] and actually writes of 'a bicameral assembly consisting of an upper house of "elders" and a lower house of "men"'.[17]

Another, and quite different, view from among many that have since emerged, is that before the third millennium the cities were governed by a priestly hierarchy which took control of cereal production. Only as warfare became endemic were war-leaders appointed, this leading, as before, to the institutionalization of kingship.[18]

There are many objections to the former, 'primitive democracy' thesis. To begin with, it is not supported by the slightest shred of direct evidence. It is based upon religious and epical texts dating from *c*.1800 and later, though

[12] Grégoire, 'L'Origine et le développement', 87, n. 1.
[13] Oppenheim, *Ancient Mesopotamia*, 105. [14] Ibid. 106–7.
[15] T. Jacobsen, 'Early Political Development in Mesopotamia', *Zeitschrift für Assyriologie* (1957), 104.
[16] Cf. Oppenheim, *Ancient Mesopotamia*, 112; H. Frankfort, *Kingship and the Gods* (Chicago University Press, Chicago, 1948), 215–20. [17] In short, the US Congress dates back some 5,000 years!
[18] Grégoire, 'L'Origine et le développement', 67.

their substance may well go back to an earlier time; but the existence and functions of the 'assembly' are merely inferred from an *interpretation* of these texts.[19] Furthermore, not all Sumerologists infer the same thing: Falkenstein[20] takes them to mean that this assembly 'was hardly an organ of control, let alone of direction but . . . probably had consultative functions'. Finally, though the theory rests on these texts written *c*.1800, it contradicts a crucial passage in the Sumerian king-list, whose date is, today, plausibly put at around this same time. In its preamble, it says: 'When Kingship was (first) in Eridu.' Now, in Sumerian tradition Eridu was not only one of the cities that existed even before the Flood—that is, very, very ancient—but *the* city from which civilization spread to the rest of Sumer.[21] This tradition is reinforced by archaeology. The temple of Eridu goes back, through a series of eighteen consecutive rebuildings, to *c*.4000. This does not, of course, mean that kingship went back that far—only that the Sumerians regarded it as very, very ancient, going back as it were to a 'time whereof man's knowledge runneth not to the contrary'. Also, as this text says that 'kingship was lowered from heaven' or 'came down from on high', it is quite clearly affirming that kingship was *not* conferred from *below*. The 'primitive democracy' thesis can only be sustained, therefore, by asserting that these sentences are a late invention designed to give kingship an ideological sanction.[22]

Highly circumscribed archaeological evidence suggests (but no more than this) that from the earliest levels onwards, there is a always a shrine. Such shrines were built and rebuilt on the original site, becoming larger and more magnificent as time went on. Secondly, the very earliest written records uncovered in south Mesopotamia are pictographs from accounts mostly found within temple precincts. Written on clay tablets and incorporating a system of numeration, these show the temple of Eanna in Uruk acting as the redistributive centre of the society.[23] However, the first *palaces* discovered— at Kish and Eridu—date from *c*.2700. It is at this time too that the word usually translated as 'king', that is, *lugal*, is first encountered.[24]

Given such flimsy and dubitable evidence, is it possible to construct a plausible account of the evolution of the Sumerian city-polity?

A cultic centre, as is well-attested from other cultures (e.g. Egypt), is the

[19] Admittedly, evidence for an assembly is found for the period of the IIIrd dynasty of Ur, hence anterior to the date of these texts, but we are dealing here with the origins of kingship, emphatically *not* with what well-established kingship might or might not do in the way of consultation.

[20] Jacobsen, 'Early Political Development', 100–1, n. 11.

[21] For the myth of Innana and Euki, see Kramer, *Sumerians—Their History*, 116 and 160–2.

[22] Cf. Diakonoff, 'The Rise of the Despotic State', 195, where the Soviet Sumerologist places the theory of 'the divine primordial kingship' at the neo-Sumerian Empire, 2112–2004 BC.

[23] G. Clark, *World Pre-History in a New Perspective*, 3rd edn. (CUP, Cambridge, 1977), 79–80.

[24] But, for *lugal*, see below.

logical place for central storage for the community; for votive offerings, obviously, but also for warehousing against times of need. As the settlements grew, the temples also grew large, the sanctuary being surrounded by granaries and storehouses of all kinds. Checking the goods in and passing them out again demanded some system of docketing and counting; hence the early pictographic tablets with words for persons and objects, and with signs to number them (somewhat like the Linear B inscriptions in Crete); and hence, too, individuals to do the counting and labelling, that is, scribes and accountants. Thus the tiny shrine of the fourth millennium grows steadily into the temple complex of the third, and the primitive warehouse into the organizational centre of a storage–redistributing economy. At this stage, in the later fourth and early third millennium, these emergent cities were governed by a priestly hierarchy.[25]

The walls, the wars, and the first dynasts, which seem to appear at more or less the same time *c.*2900–2750, all suggest the emergence of war-leaders; possibly *ad hoc*, at first, but becoming permanencies as warfare became endemic. The first appearance of separate palaces, also at this time, and the use of *lugal* for 'king' and *egal* for his palace ('big-man' and 'big-house'), mark the institutional divisions between priests and kings. The ever-increasing bulk and elaboration of palaces, continuous from this time on, and the equally continuous aggrandizement of his status and function bear witness to the encroachment of the monarchical authority on that of the temples. That process could well be marked by friction: so much is evident from the famous 'reform' document of Uruinimgina (*c.*2378/2371).[26] The process culminated, however, in the ruler, the *lugal*, integrating the various temple households into or around his own palace-household, while at the same claiming to hold his kingship by favour of Enlil, the supreme Sumerian deity.[27]

Controversy does not end at the dynastic period, however. Kings—*lugals*—now rule in each city-state, agreed. But how does their rule relate to the great temple complexes still administering vast estates? Are these subordinate to the palace or autonomous, or indeed, pre-eminent? Next: since the documentary evidence still points to a closely regulated storage–redistributory society, how far does this extend? In brief, is there a 'private sector', and if so, of what kind and how important politically?

Not long ago it was commonly believed that all the land in the city-state

[25] Cf. Grégoire, 'L'Origine et le développement', 67, who so affirms, as does Roux, *Ancient Iraq*, 76.
[26] It is published in Kramer, *Sumerians—Their History*, 317–22.
[27] A vase of Lugalkigginedudu, King of Ur (*c.*2380), reads: 'When En-lil, the king of all the lands, directed a firm call to Lugalkigginedudu and gave them the en-ship together with the kingship . . .' (Kramer, *Sumerians—Their History*, 308).

was owned by the temples, and that all the inhabitants were either temple servants or, at least, dependants.[28] This might well have been true in pre-dynastic times, but the view that it held good for the dynastic era is now thoroughly discredited. There are numerous bills which relate to land purchase. From these it has been inferred that there existed an extensive private property in land. On closer examination, however, these bills of sale suggest that the purchasers were usually wealthy commercial agents belonging to the highest social stratum whose activities were linked to the palace and the temples on which, in most cases, they were directly dependent. This amounts, in effect, to saying that the large estates of the supposed private sector were really part of the official state establishment and that 'in south Mesopotamia private landed property plays no decisive economic rôle: it is virtually non-existent'.[29] It follows that the notion of the entire land being run by the temples is unsustainable.

4.2. Kingship

4.2.1. EN, ENSI, LUGAL

The earliest title of rulership in ancient Sumeria was *en*. Later this was used only as a purely priestly title or, Sumerologists concede, the sign that is read *en* may really be two different words. In the early period it seems to connote 'secular' rule of some kind, albeit with some sacral role also. Since we know nothing of the process by which ruler and priests came to be different people playing different roles, the meaning Sumerologists attach to the term *en* reflects the widely differing views they hold on this process.

The terms *ensi* and *lugal* do not make their appearance before *c.*2750–2600 BC (early Dynastic II). Scholars disagree over the relationship one term bears to the other. The word *lugal* is, simply, *lu-gal*, 'great man'. Significantly, however, 'this is the only term available in Sumerian to express a master's complete control over his slaves, or an owner's over his house'.[30] It seems to have escaped notice that this meaning is identical with the one Aristotle attaches to the Greek term 'despot'. The fact that (later, of course) all administrative officials are 'slaves' (Sumerian *ir*) of the kings (inscribed on their seals)[31] reinforces the point.

Some scholars believe that *lugal* referred to an independent ruler, while a dependent ruler was an *ensi*—but this does not seem to have been the invariable usage at all.[32] Some Sumerian cities never had a *lugal*, others never

[28] Cf. A. Falkenstein, 'La Cité-temple sumérienne', *Les Cahiers d'histoire mondiale/Journal of World History*, 1: 4 (1953), 784–814.   [29] Grégoire, 'L'Origine et le développement', 71.
[30] Jacobsen, 'Early Political Development', 119.   [31] Ibid., n. 54.
[32] Diakonoff, 'The Rise of the Despotic State', 182.

had an *ensi*; in Lagash there was at one period one, later the other; in some cities—or so it seems—the two existed simultaneously.[33]

4.2.2. SACRAL MONARCHY

'In no other antique society', says Roux, 'did religion occupy such a prominent position . . . the religious ideas promoted by the Sumerians played an extraordinary part in the public and private life of the Mesopotamians, modelling their institutions, colouring their works of art and literature, pervading every form of activity.'[34] To try to understand the Sumerian city-polity, some notion of its belief-system, however incomplete, is indispensable.

The Sumerians conceived of a divinely created cosmos of which the earth was but a part, and with which it interpenetrated at every point. Every object, every process on earth moved or acted in its appointed way by its own peculiar *vis animae*. The plough, the sickle, the kingship itself, were all animated and propelled by what they called *me*. These multifarious *me* were controlled by divinities; some minor, some major, some supreme. All divinities had human shapes, and it was in these shapes that they all had to be worshipped and propitiated. The human world, then, was populated by many and ubiquitous gods. So every house had its household gods, every village its village gods, every city quarter its local gods, and each city-state its ruling god or goddess to whom the city actually belonged. It was the god's property.

Earth reflected heaven. Since some gods were more important than others, so in heaven there was an assembly of fifty high gods, and over them seven great gods, and from among the seven, three who were supreme. One of these, An, was the great sky god. He was the king of all the gods but—like Brahma in Hinduism—in the course of time the role of An retreated in favour of the two gods, Enlil the creator of the earth and Enki (or Ea), god of the waters, of crafts and techniques, and of enterprise. Enlil, as the earth's creator, was the supreme god. He resided in Nippur, and just as Enlil was superior to all the other gods, so was his city superior to their cities. So, *c.*2400, Nippur and Enlil were recognized as the undisputable source of rule for 'the Land' as a whole, and the future 'kings of Sumer' were to derive their authority from being recognized in Nippur (rather than from their own cities and city gods.)

The great creation saga of the Mesopotamians describes why the gods decided to create man: 'Man shall be charged with the service of the gods that they might be at ease!'[35] The 'black-headed people' had been placed on

---

[33] Ibid. 181.   [34] Roux, *Ancient Iraq*, 91.   [35] *ANET*, 68.

earth to prepare food-offerings, tend the gods' sanctuaries, burn incense, improve their lands, and build their shrines.[36] Now these injunctions were *literal*. The idol of the god reposed in its *cella*. At morning it—or rather, he (or she)—was awakened by his priests. They roused him, cleansed him, dressed him, fed him, brought him forth in his divine litter, and so continued, with incantation and with sacrificial offerings throughout the day, till the time came to prepare him for the night. The simulation went further still, so that the distinction between human and divine faded. For in a large temple, serving a major deity, the city god—like humans—would have a great many *divine* servants. In Lagash, for instance, the city god Ningirsu had a lesser god (his son Igalima) as doorkeeper, another son as chief butler, and likewise an armourer, counsellor, chamberlain, and coachman. For his fields he had his god-steward, his god-bailiffs, his god-inspector of fishermen. Now the images of these divine attendants did not, of course, carry out these duties in dumb-show. They had to be carried out physically, which meant (according to one modern interpretation) by humans acting them out in these godlets' name. So much so, it has been claimed, that 'it was sometimes hardly clear whether men or gods were the acting parties'.[37]

And so pre-eminently, for the *king*. For when, finally, the gods had created the race of man to serve them, they found them 'befogged'—there was nobody to lead and organize them, in the manner the gods themselves were organized and led by their one supreme god. There was nobody to counsel the human race. Another version of the legend says that (presumably because they lacked a ruler) the people 'neglected the commands of the high gods'.[38] Kingship was of divine origin and its function was to make the race of men duly serve the gods. So, to actualize the role of the attendant gods towards their master, the city god was perhaps acted out by a human on his behalf. That human was the *ensi* or *lugal* of the city. He was more than the link between the human and the divine, since this way of putting the matter suggests two discrete spheres of being: he was the personification of the divine, and on the rituals he performed depended not only the security and wealth of the god's city but the very cycle of the crops itself. It used to be thought that this personification involved a 'sacred marriage' between Inanna and the shepherd-god Dumuzi. Dumuzi was the god associated with vegetation, cattle, and sheep. The story went that he coupled with Inanna and it used to be held that the Sumerians believed that the renewal of the

[36] *ANET*, 69.
[37] *Cambridge Ancient History*, eds. J. B. Bury, S. A. Cook, and F. E. Adcock, 5 vols. (CUP, Cambridge, 1927–39; 3rd edn., 1971), I. 2, p. 137 [hereafter referred to as *CAH*].   [38] *ANET*, 115.

crops and regular sequence of the seasons depended on this annual union. Logically, therefore, what the god Dumuzi did, his representative on earth must enact on his behalf. So (the theory goes on) every spring, the king and the high priestess of Inanna lay together. Only when this rite had taken place could the people breathe again with the assurance that fruitfulness would not come to a full stop.[39]

This interpretation is based on the work of J. G. Frazer and is nowadays considered obsolete. The only evidence to support it is literary, and only three kings are mentioned by name. Furthermore, there is no evidence of the king coupling with the high priestess. (Certainly, in distant Syria, in a much later period, i.e. the thirteenth and fourteenth centuries, a case is attested where the high priestess goes to the shrine and spends the night there.)

The king of a city, nevertheless, sat on his throne specifically to order the people's service to the gods and on him depended not only the routine business of the city, or even its safety and independence, but its well-being and the bounty of Nature itself. This immense responsibly of rulership implied an equally immense duty of obedience on the part of his subjects. The people had been created to serve the gods. The *ensi* or *lugal* was the surrogate of the gods. Hence the people had been created to serve the king.

4.2.3. THE LIMITS OF ROYAL POWER

Did this duty of obedience know any limits? Did it bear equally on all his subjects? Given the unequal value of our sources, and the fragmentary nature of the evidence on the ruler's relationship to his court circle and above all to the priesthood, these questions are hard to answer with any firm assurance. Certainly, every king was at risk from invading highlanders and/or Syrian desert nomads. The question here is whether there were any domestic constraints to his authority. It is quite certain that there were no constitutional and legal checks. The whole concept of the sacral monarchy was *monist*: one king over all the gods, so one king over all his subjects. We reiterate: the very word *lugal* signifies lord and master of a house, a field, a household (*oikos*) of slaves.

As subsequent chapters show, for all the legal and constitutional absolutism of a ruler there were usually practical constraints on his power, and these could come from one or more of five sources: the common people, the magnates, the priesthood, the army, or from inside his own palace.

To the best of my knowledge there is no evidence of popular revolt or even popular involvement in the government of the city. As for magnates, there were certainly wealthy subjects, but these seem to have been part of the

[39] Cf. Frankfort, *Kingship*, 295–9.

official circle, and wealthy for that reason; in short, not free-standing but part of the king's palace household. Of the composition of the armies we know very little. One tablet speaks of a corps of some 700 soldiers of the king of Shuruppak; it would seem that such armies consisted of a small standing force, supplemented by a popular levy. Nothing exists to make us suppose that kings were or felt threatened by army captains, the more so since they took the field in person.

This leaves only the palace circle and the priesthood as possible constraints on the *lugal*. As far as the former is concerned, the Sumerian monarchy was happily free of a dreadful weakness that beset most subsequent autocracies—the absence of a firm rule of succession. Unlike, say, the Roman emperorship or the Caliphate, it was not even theoretically elective, but hereditary, and unlike, say, the Chinese emperorship, polygamy did not confuse the issue of who was to succeed. The Sumerians were monogamous, albeit permissive of junior wives in certain circumstances and equally of concubines. Certainly kings had harems. But the principle was one of monogamy, hereditary succession, and as far as one can see, primogeniture. The dynastic lists show a clear prevalence of descent from father to son. However, we have evidence of usurpations. For instance, the throne of Lagash fell (*c.*2350) into the hands of two rulers who seem to have come from the priesthood and were not of the dynastic line—hence, usurpers. The second of these was dispossessed in his turn—but how?—by a much more famous figure, Uruinimgina. Again—but later (2123 and 2112)—there were two successful usurpations connected with Ur.

Throughout the history of government an organized priesthood has always been a possible and, more often than not, an actual source of constraint upon rulers. In the particular case of the Sumerian city-state, the rivalry of the priesthood seems, prima facie, all the more likely given the religion-saturated nature of the society and the unquestionably enormous managerial role the temples played in the economy. Again, we have no more than fragmentary indications. Little is known about the higher echelons of the temple organization; there is no clear evidence that a priestly hierarchy as it is usually understood existed, nor is it known whether heredity was a decisive qualification for appointment nor what the procedure for such appointments was.[40] The following points can be attested, however. First, rulers retained some priestly functions, though the general trend was to separate the function of ruler and high priest. (Thus, Entemena, the *ensi* of Lagash, was not its high priest in 2400. But wives and daughters of the rulers often officiated as priestesses.) It was the bounden duty of the ruler,

[40] Oppenheim, *Ancient Mesopotamia*, 106–7.

lavishly fulfilled, to maintain and beautify the temples and even build new ones while enjoying the use of the god's possessions. This was logical: he was, in a sense which is uncertain to us, the god. So the *ensi* of Lagash disposed of the carriage of the god with its team of splendid asses, and the temple organization took care of the needs of the royal family.[41]

Yet there is quite firm evidence that in Lagash this integration of the divine and the human, the Temple and the Palace, the priesthood and the ruler, did have conventional metes and bounds, and that failure to respect them could provoke serious friction. That evidence comes from the text of the reforms of Uruinimgina of Lagash (?2378–2371). Uruinimgina was the man who had deposed the previous *ensi* in some unknown fashion.[42] He then initiated sweeping reform measures on behalf of the common people who, according to him, were heavily overtaxed—often illegally. No less than three copies of his reform-text have come down to us.[43] Among other things, the document records as an abuse that the 'god's oxen' were used by the *ensi* to plough his own onion-fields and, moreover, that these fields and others were located among the best fields of the god.[44] The former *ensi*'s entourage was said also to have appropriated the head priests' barley and some of their clothing supplies. These encroachments Uruinimgina claims to have rectified. He also rectified clerical abuse of power: we learn that the *sanga* (steward) of the food (supplies) 'felled the trees in the garden of the indigent mother and bundled off the fruit'.[45]

For all that, despite Uruinimgina's concessions to the priesthood, his document does not of itself demonstrate that the priesthood was a constraint upon a ruler's power. Indeed, it tells us the very opposite. The abusive encroachment on the priesthood had been made by an *ensi*—and ended by an *ensi*. And it does not contain the slightest hint that Uruinimgina was constrained to make the reform. It would be pure speculation to suppose that his usurpation was prompted or supported by the priests, or that he felt obliged to court them in order to buttress his newly won office. All we can conclude safely is that in the last resort the *ensi* regulated the priesthood and his own relationship to it.

4.3. *The Agenda of Government*

The duties of the *ensi* or the *lugal* were first and foremost to maintain, and if possible improve, the service of the gods. In a sense, all that we would consider secular or material aspects of government were subsumed by this.

[41] *CAH*, I.2, pp. 128–9.   [42] See pp. 113 and 118 above.
[43] For a translation, see Kramer, *Sumerians—Their History*, 317–22.   [44] Ibid. 317.
[45] Ibid. 317, 319.

The service of the gods was not, as a twentieth-century agnostic might unheedingly think, irrational activity. It was highly purposeful. The very cycle of nature depended on ritual, worship, and propitiation.

Hence the ruler had the duty to maintain and build temples, support the priestly order, and participate in the frequent religious celebrations and cultic exercises. He had to defend the city from foreign enemies and, if possible by conquering them, exact and extend the glory of his city god, whose representative he was. In that capacity, as the god's steward for his city, he had to organize and control its economy, and—this was well understood—carry on works on dikes and canals. These rulers also played a great part in the dispensation of justice: in *c.*2112–2095 King Ur-Nammu of Ur was not only claiming to 'establish equity in the land and banish malediction, violence and strife', but actually promulgating a code of laws. We would, I think, be safe in assuming that the code was the culmination of royal involvement with justice and its administration over a long period.[46]

4.4. *The Polity as an* Oikos

At this point it is necessary to digress a moment, in order to introduce a concept which will recur in this history: the concept of the *oikos.*

Oikos is the Greek household.[47] According to Aristotle, its management is concerned with producing goods for the use of its own members and not for exchanging them with others. The household is *autarkic.* 'The members', he wrote, 'shared all things in common', 'no purpose is to be served by the art of exchange', nor, he adds, by the arts of acquisition.[48] Finally, this management resides in the household's *despot*—a single ruler. This description of the *oikos* was picked up in the nineteenth century by J. K. Rodbertus. According to him all antiquity was dominated by what he called 'an *oikos* economy' wherein production centred on the household, this being understood to consist of unfree workers: a slave household, in fact. In principle, these households were self-sufficient. Commerce was very secondary. It served merely to dispose of surpluses.

From Rodbertus, the idea found its way to Max Weber, who refined it further, and it is his definition that is current among sociologists today and the one that will be used throughout this book. Weber characterized the *oikos* thus:

---

[46] See, for text, *ANET,* 523–5.

[47] Hence *oikonomia,* economy, 'the management of the household'. Cf. Aristotle, *Economics,* dealing (more unsystematically, it may be said) with just this.

[48] Barker, *The Politics of Aristotle* (Clarendon Press, Oxford, 1946), 27 ff.

1. It is not just any household: it is 'the authoritarian household—of a prince, manorial lord, or patrician'.[49]
2. Its dominant motive is not capitalist acquisition but the lord's organized want-satisfaction, satisfied in kind. And this remains so if, in order to secure otherwise available goods, it has market-orientated enterprises attached to it.
3. In its pure state, however, it is completely autarkic.

Hence his description—in the pure case, that is, that of self-sufficiency, it is:

An apparatus of house-dependent labour which is often highly specialized, produces all the goods, personal services, economic, military and sacral, which the ruler requires. His own land provides the raw materials, his workshops with their personally unfree labour, supply all other materials. The remaining services are provided by servants, officials, house-priests, and warriors. Exchange takes place only if surplus is to be dumped or if goods simply cannot be procured by any other way.[50]

The Sumerian city-state was an *oikos* just like this. Supreme power vested in the ruler, and the *oikos* as a whole consisted of his palace as master-household and a number of others, arranged hierarchically in relation to it. These lesser households were the temples of the various gods, and their hierarchical position depended upon the position which its deity—the master of his own household—held in the local pantheon.[51] The Sumerian word *e* means, precisely, an *oikos*. But this was not the small, face-to-face community of Rodbertus, but a statist organization, authoritarian and highly bureaucratic, which, outside its social and religious function, existed to satisfy the wants of the lord and master, the *en* and *lugal*—*despots* to the Greeks. It was, therefore, a production unit, comprising domain—lands, villages, administrative centres, dwellings, workshops, storehouses, and granaries—and it was run by bodies of administrators, accountants, supervisors, and inspectors.

Not merely that. One of its principal characteristics, implicit in the concept of *oikos*, is that it was a storage–redistributive organization. Products were brought into storehouses and granaries and went out again in the form of rations, dues, and gifts.[52] Lands, particularly the cereal lands on which the entire *oikos* depended, were the god's—hence, in some sense, the ruler's. The temple's lands were cultivated by the temple's servants and administered by the chief priests in the name of the god, hence, the ruler.[53]

---

[49] *Max Weber: Selection in Translation*, ed. W. G. Runciman and trans. by E. Matthews (CUP, Cambridge, 1978), i. 381.   [50] Ibid.

[51] Grégoire, 'L'Origine et le développement', 73.   [52] See pp. 122, 124–5 below.

[53] Falkenstein ('The Sumerian Temple City') is the scholar largely responsible for the original idea.

The temple and the palace formed the town centre; the various neigh-bourhoods, each with their local temples, developed around them, encircled by the city wall. It has been argued that there was no market-place within the town.[54] There was indeed a special area at some distance from the centre which was called the *kar*. This was organized and controlled by the palace. *Kar* corresponds more or less to the medieval trading posts of the Italians or the Hanse in foreign parts, which we call 'the counter'. The *kar* was the counter, into which flowed manufactured goods and raw materials and goods for exchange (since these cities, as we saw, needed stone and metal and building wood). Coinage being non-existent, the process of exchange was assisted by sets of equivalencies. Such equivalencies were equally necessary in redistributing the domestic product between individuals. The goods sent in to the magazines and granaries of the various *oikoi* went out again to the labourers as rations, and the remainder to the 'staff' workers of the city, that is, the scribes, priests, soldiers, and of course the *lugal* himself. The entire, enormously complicated business of checking the natural products in, decid-ing remuneration to this, that, or the other individuals according to their due, called for quite an army of scribes, accountants, and inspectors.

On the temple domain the land fell into three parts: the god's land, which fed the priests and temple servants; the food-land which was allotted as their means of subsistence to the cultivators who worked the god's land; and the plough-land leased to tenants for one-seventh or one-eighth of the crop. Outside the temple domain which—in Lagash at all events—com-prised a third of the city's total acreage, lay the corn-lands and their cultivators. Their status is conjectural. The view taken here is that of Grégoire: the land was either leased to tenants by the authorities, or allotted to various classes of administrators and soldiers to serve as their subsis-tence.[55] Higher court officials did, indeed, enjoy the services of quite extensive holdings of these lands: but this was because they were officials, not because they were private investors. To be brief: all land-tenancies derived from the authority of the state, and all those who held them did so as part of the governing apparatus, or as subjects. Among these slavery was rare (confined to private houses), but extreme dependency was not rare—it was the rule. For seasonal agricultural work, for irrigation projects, or for other massive public works such as erecting the huge ziggurats, all available labour was mobilized by the institution of the corvée or forced labour.

---

[54] Cf. K. Polanyi, 'Trade and Market in the Early Empires', in K. Polanyi, C. M. Arensberg, and H. W. Pearson (eds.), *Economies in History and Theory* (Henry Regnery, Chicago, 1957), 16–17.

[55] Grégoire, 'L'Origine et le développement', 71.

4.5. *The Administration*

Palaces, as separate dwellings for the *lugal* and *ensi*, are attested *c*.24000 BC.
The earliest ones were comparatively small. In Kish, Eridu, and Mari (on
the upper Euphrates) they were only 270 × 140 feet, 135 × 200 feet, and
131 × 131 feet respectively. Even 300 years later under the IIIrd dynasty of Ur,
the royal palace was much smaller than the great temple of Nanna, whose
enclosure measured some 1,200 × 600 feet. The base of its immense ziggurat
alone was 200 × 150 feet—and it rose to 70 feet high. Yet the magnificence
and opulence of the city rulers can be in no doubt—the extravagant burial
goods in the early (*c*.2550) 'Royal Tombs' at Ur, with their gold and silver,
ivory and lapis, and the richly bejewelled court ladies and the attendant
spearmen who were buried alive, show the splendour they were surrounded
by and the greatness of their majesty.

But later, at the time of Hammurabi (*c*.1750), the palaces have become
vast.[56] Only at that point is it possible to infer how they were staffed and
administered, so that the way the master-*oikos* of the *oikos*-city functioned
remains unknown for the early period. But about how the temples functioned as so many storage–redistributive households we are better informed,
and it is from this evidence that we can infer the administrative system of
the city-state.

The temple of Bau, in Lagash, which was one of the lesser temples,
administered about 1 square mile of lands. These were worked exclusively by
its tenants and dependants, who numbered about 1,200 persons. Most of
them held some land and paid a fixed proportion of their crop to the
temple, or worked for daily doles of barley. In return the temples had to
maintain them all the year round, even in the seasons when agricultural
work was not possible, and supply them with seed-corn and implements. In
addition to these labourers, there were specialized teams for cattle-raising,
for freshwater and sea-fishing, and for craftwork like spinning and weaving.
All the produce was brought in and stored—in order to meet the outgoings.
Foremost among these was the care of the god: maintaining the temple
fabric, keeping up the canal-system, and providing the food, the drink, and
the clothing, and those coaches and teams of asses that we spoke of earlier.
And as the priests and other hierodules served, as we saw, as *locums* for the
lesser, attendant gods, quite large numbers of the city population found
their livelihood in this way.

All this was administered with a meticulousness that was truly pedantic.
In his *Excavations at Ur* (1954), Sir Leonard Woolley has left a vivid picture of

[56] Interestingly, the Ebla palace was quite enormous and that was much earlier—*c*.2350 BC.

a Mesopotamian temple organization of probably comparable complexity, from some 300 years later, in his descriptions of the temple of Nannar, patron god and owner of the city of Ur, at the time of the IIIrd dynasty (2112–2004).

Under the pavement of a Larsa annex to Dublal-makh we found a mass of clay tablets which had belonged to the business archives of Nannar's temple. They were of unbaked clay and were in very bad condition, reduced by infiltered moisture to the consistency of mud and impregnated with salts, and many had been broken or chipped when they fell from the shelves on which they had been stored; we had to lift them with the earth still about them and bake them in an extemporized furnace before any cleaning could be attempted, but in this way we did salvage several hundreds of interesting documents of the Third Dynasty.

It was no polite fiction that made Nannar the King of Ur. He controlled its destinies more effectually than did his mortal representative and he must therefore have his ministers and his court; he was a great landowner and therefore needed stewards to manage his estates; apart from the High Priest and his clerical associates we read of the Sacristan and the Choir-master, the Treasurer, the Ministers of War and of Justice, of Agriculture and of Housing, a Controller of the Household, a Master of the Harem, and Directors of Livestock, Dairy Work, Fishing and Donkey transport. All these carried on their duties in the temple precincts, and so the temple is not a single building like the self-contained temples of Greece and Rome, but a huge complex which is at once temple and palace, government offices and stores and factories. Something of this sort has already been assumed in our description of the ruins and is proved by the plans here published; fortunately just as our plans grow more complete and more complicated, the tablets turn up to throw light upon the use of those many courts and chambers.

As landowner the god received as well as tithes either rent or a part share in the produce of the soil, and since money was unknown, these were all paid in kind; and since the temple was also a fortress, enormous quantities of foodstuffs were stored within it, ready to meet the normal requirements of the temple staff but also to act as a reserve in case of war. For everything that was brought in a receipt was given, a small tablet carefully dated recording that so-and-so has paid in six pounds of the best butter, so much oil, sheep, cattle, or what not; and every month a full balance-sheet of all returns was drawn up in parallel columns showing each farmer's contribution under separate headings. While farmers and cowmen paid in country produce, the townsfolk used another currency; there are receipts for all sorts of hides, for gold and silver from the jewellers, for copper from the smiths; in one room we found a smelting-furnace, and in other rooms big jars full of scrap and copper and ingots of the metal presumably of some standard weight; evidence that this quarter of the building served a special department of the temple affairs.

But if the revenues are scrupulously recorded, the outgoings are not less carefully checked, and these are just as illuminating for the life of the time. Naturally the temple officials drew their rations from the stores, and the issue vouchers were all preserved in the registry; every man had his regular allowance of foodstuffs, flour and oil, etc., for which he or his servants had to sign, and special issues were authorized in case of sickness—thus a man may draw an extra quarter-pint of best oil as liniment for his headache. But the most interesting records deal with the industrial side of the establishment. Numbers of women devotees were attached to the temple, and these were employed in regular factories inside the precincts; there were slaves similarly employed, and piece-work was given out to private contractors who had small factories outside the temple area: all these had to be supplied with the raw materials which had been brought in as tithe, and with the food which was their wage. The main industry illustrated by the tablets found this season, was weaving. In the building E-karzida alone 165 women and girls were kept at work, and we have the accounts made out for the month, quarter, and year of the quantity of woollen thread supplied to each and of the amount of cloth produced, each sort distinguished by quality and weight, with due allowance for the wastage of thread in weaving. The rations are in proportion to the output, the older women receiving less than the young ones (who would have larger appetites but did more work)—no more in fact than did the youngest children; thus if four pints of oil a day was the standard allowance for adults, children of different ages got two pints, one and a half, or one, and the really old woman one also. For the sick there were special rates: if any one died, her name was kept on the books until the end of the financial year, but the date of her death was recorded and an entry made against the name to the effect that henceforth no rations were drawn, or were drawn only for an accredited substitute. The whole system was cold-bloodedly business-like. (pp. 143–6)

All this raises the question of how comfortable the common people found themselves under this system. There is no way of knowing; but we do know, quite definitely, that it could go dramatically wrong. The reform-tablets of Uruinimgina of Lagash already mentioned[57] vividly convey the shifting atmosphere of bureaucratic oppression and corruption. The officials in charge of the sheep and donkeys, and of the boats of the fisheries, were all stealing them. The king's paymasters were giving short rations. His officials were exacting illegal payments for shearing sheep. Artisans had to plead with them for their rations, their apprentices were fed on scraps and left-overs at the palace gate. And, it goes on, 'from the borders of Ningirso to the sea, there was the tax collector'.[58]

[57] See p. 119 above   [58] Kramer, Sumerians—Their History, 317–18.

5. SUMMARY AND APPRAISAL

Briefly, this kind of polity is a Palace-type city-state and not a Palace/Church variety. The king is more than a high priest, for in some way he is the carnal representation of the god and his legitimacy springs from this charismatic quality. He does not just control the cult, he is its epicentre. The tiny ruling élite stands immediately around him. It consists of his relatives, courtiers, priests, and their hierodules, a small army, and also the numerous accountants and scribes who serviced all the foregoing. Apart from this tight little circle, the entire population consists of a number of artisans and traders who are dependants on the palace and the temples, and—the vast majority—cultivators and fishermen. Both politically and religiously they form a supine mass, wholly subjected to the tiny group of rulers and their assistants. This group derives its legitimacy from its association with the *ishakku*, that is, the king as the 'vicar' of the city of god, and its power from its monopoly of armed force, literacy, and numeracy.

The monarch's tasks are to protect and if possible expand his borders. He must spend a great part of his working day in ritual activities, especially those relating to fertility, and to that end he must also direct the cult and maintain and embellish the temples. These rituals do not simply represent consummatory values; they are highly instrumental towards protecting the city and ensuring its subsistence. To the latter end, therefore, the king has to carry out the hydraulic works that are vital to agriculture, and ensure, through his scribes and accountants, that the redistributive–storage responsibilities of the *oikos* economy are fulfilled.

Royal authority derives from its quasi-divine—its sacral—status. The king embodies what Weber calls 'routinized charisma': he is the human representation of god on earth. The cult at whose centre he stands guarantees his own absolute power and the abject obedience of his subjects, since the Mesopotamian religion—one of the 'Archaic' type—teaches a role for the masses, to which they do in practice conform: it is that they are the labourers and servants of the gods. But since here on earth 'gods' translates as the king (chief god) and the high priests, it is they whom the masses obey, labour for, and serve. Like all Archaic religions, the cult is a routine of rituals and sacrifices carried out by the ruler and the priesthood, that is, the topmost ruling circle, on the people's behalf but without their participation; they are spectators, not officiants.

The absolutism of the king implies that there are no legal or constitutional or even conventional limits to his power unless it be the conventional duty of leading the cult, and there are certainly no procedural checks to it. The only practical constraints on his actions arise from the intrigue or even the rebellion of members of the court circle, or out of friction with the priesthood; but there is little evidence of the latter.

Not only is this polity ruled by the palace; its economy *is* the palace. The polity, the *oikos* economy, and the *oikos* society are simply facets of the same entity. In it the king's role is exactly the same as that of Aristotle's *despotes*: the head of a household of slaves. The economy is a natural agrarian one, where goods and services are paid for in kind through established or conventional equivalences and where freely alienable private property plays an insignificant part, if any at all. What trading activity there is exists only for purposes the ruler deems indispensable, and it is he who organizes and controls it. His palace is itself a factory, a storehouse, and an armoury interlocked with the temples which are also great economic enterprises, and all of these centres are so interlinked as to make the entire economy into the extended *oikos* of the king. Each individual *oikos* is minutely organized and controlled by a literate and numerate bureaucracy, and its activity is the organization of food production, and thereafter its collection, storage, and redistribution to the ruling élite, and back to the cultivators who produced it.

I do not know of any other polity in which all these features are found together. But some of the most striking can be found elsewhere. The *oikos*-type economy, for instance, finds parallels in Minoan Crete and Archaic Egypt. Its redistributive–storage character is likewise paralleled in Egypt, but also in Inca Peru. The sacral monarchy is, in some form or other, ubiquitous throughout the Middle East at this time. So, too, were city-states.

But in other respects the Sumerian city-states serve to point interesting and sometimes important contrasts with other forms of polity. Though they are city-states, they are politically, socially, and economically antithetical to the Greek type. Also, though they are city-states, Egypt, which is nearly coeval, was a country-state with few cities of any note. Another contrasts lies in their autarkic nature—they are polities of the *oikos* type, but few of their successors in the region were, and they disappear in the course of time.

Finally, these Sumerian states left a legacy. It was not one that came down directly to the modern world, but it was passed on immediately and powerfully to the immediate environment, where it moulded the culture, the religion, and the political theory and practice of monarchy and bureau-cracy for some 2,000 years to come.

6. THE PASSING OF THE SUMERIAN CITY-STATE

This Sumerian form of polity enjoyed a long span of healthy life. Some scholars would put its disappearance as early as Sargon's conquests *c.*2334; others after the destruction of Ur in 2004; others, not till Hammurabi, *c.*1750. Even the earliest of these dates implies that this distinctive state-form endured for perhaps some 800 years (it depends when it is thought to have begun in this form). This is a length of time which few forms of polity have rivalled. The first question to be asked, therefore, is not why the Sumerian city-state eventually disappeared but why it lasted so long? The short answer is that the Sumerians were superior to all of their neighbours, the barbarian tribes of highlander or desert nomads, in all relevant ways—militarily, culturally, and economically.

Nor was there any sign of internal decay during this (the third) millennium. On the contrary, it saw the perfection of the cuneiform script and the blossoming of a considerable literature, an equally sustained development in its art forms and its monumental architecture, and continuous elaboration of the bureaucratic apparatus of direction and control. During this entire millennium the city polity in Sumer was elaborating, refining, and completing the sketchy plan laid down at the very beginning, 3000–2750.

The passing of the Sumerian city-state began when it lost its military superiority. The reasons for this lie in the stormy vicissitudes *c.*2334–1600. The events were these. In approximately the year 2334 a usurper took power in Sumer and founded the Semite country of Agade, and within a short time had conquered all Mesopotamia and beyond from the Persian Gulf up to the shores of the Mediterranean in northern Syria. This was Sargon, whose name became a legend. The great conquest empire lasted less than a century-and-a-half, until in 2193 it and, indeed, nearly all Mesopotamia was overwhelmed by barbarians from the Zagros: the Guti. Gutian domination provoked a triumphant Sumerian reaction which gave rise to the glorious IIIrd dynasty of Ur. This succeeded in restoring most of Sargon's empire. But Ur's empire fell after no more than a century, under attack from the client-state of Elam in the east and, more significantly, the Semitic-speaking tribesmen from the Syrian desert in the west. These—the 'westerners' or *Martu* in the Sumerian tongue, *Amurrum* in their own, and Amorites in ours—filtered into the entire length of the river basins, from Sumer to the Jezirah. Although they quickly assimilated to the culture of Sumer and Akkad, they had different attitudes to certain features of the Sumerian *oikos*; notably—it seems—in respect to private property and exchange. For all that, the Sumerian city-state still persisted in some measure, to the south, in Isin and Larsa. However, a new Akkadian power was arising near the 'waist' of the two-river system: the city of Babylon. Hammurabi of Babylon (1792–1750) once more subjugated the Sumerian cities and then extended his empire northwards. Like its predecessors, this empire was short-lived. The Kassites, a mountain people, invaded in the wake of a Hittite raid on Babylon and established themselves there (1662). Kassite domination proved far more durable than any of their predecessors, for it lasted some 500 years.

The decline and ultimate disappearance of the city-state came about by the combination of three things: the socio-economic effects of the imposition of Akkadian rule over the Sumerians under the Sargonic kings and of Amorite rule in Sumerian cities after the destruction of Ur, some two-and-a-half centuries later; the related expansion of the kingly role *vis-à-vis* the temples as the territory to be administered grew; and the combined effects of war, destruction, spoliation, and salinization.

Though politically ephemeral, Sargon's conquests had a deep and lasting influence on Sumer. From his time onwards 'the land' was no longer Sumer, but Sumer-and-Akkad. Sumer thereupon became but one part of a wider culture. For Akkadians took from Sumer their cuneiform and indeed, reshaped it with a beauty hitherto unknown to spell out their own Semitic language, and they absorbed the entire literary and religious heritage of the Sumerians (to pass on, in their turn, further north, to Babylon and then, via Babylon, to Assyria). They expanded state-controlled trade widely with bronze, silver, stone, and timber flowing in from the north and north-west. This suddenly enlarged cultural and trade-area left the city-states as so many islands, and their autarky henceforward suffered steady erosion. Furthermore, the Sargonids seem to have evinced a certain preference for private ownership in land which sapped the *oikos* economy of the temples.[59] This development may be connected with the way the Sargonic kings rewarded followers by having land bought for and then conveyed to them in the conquered cities. At the same time, the prestige as well as the booty that came to these royal conquerors enormously increased their status *vis-à-vis* their subjects, the priesthood, and the gods themselves. From this time onwards the palaces grow to huge proportions, and in some of the bas-reliefs the gods, formerly portrayed giant-size *vis-à-vis* kings, shrink to being mere stars in the sky over the sovereign's head. This trend was to strengthen still further in the neo-Sumerian empire of Ur; its kings followed those of the Sargonic period in assuming divinity itself, and they had their own temples, with royal stewards in each subject-city. Both developments were carried further by Amorite leaders. Semitic semi-nomads, led by their sheikhs, these Amorites would squat on the empty spaces at the margin of the town. Since they could fetch and carry and be turned into soldiers, solid settlements were allowed to grow up. But other Amorite tribes remained nomads, and these began raiding the western approaches of the neo-Sumerian empire in the area of Babylon. In the welter that followed the

[59] Roux, *Ancient Iraq*, 153.

collapse of the empire of Ur in 2004 BC their chieftains took over the kingship of Larsa, then of Isin, and succeeded to the overlordship of the cities of Sumer, while other Amorite chiefs carved out kingdoms for themselves elsewhere. Shortly after the fall of Ur most Sumerian cities were being ruled by Amorites.

As newcomers and usurpers, these new kings magnified the royal power to the height. But they did not share the *oikos*-mentality of their predecessors, or perhaps it was simply because they had to reward their fellow tribesmen on whose support alone their power rested that they certainly gave away or gave indefinite leases on many royal or priestly parcels of land. They also seem to have lifted the corvée and numerous taxes in kind, replacing them with private rentals. The temples remained great landlords under *oikos* management, but increasingly they became islands in a society of other large estate-holders, free smallholders, and merchants.[60]

The traditional *oikos*-polity of the Sumerian cities was further eroded by yet other consequences of the invasions, the devastations of war and the exactions of conquest. Defeated cities lost their menfolk, who were massacred or led into slavery; their reserves of stone, timber, and above all metals were carried off, and their houses razed to the ground. This sequence occurred every time a city fell—and many cities were conquered and reconquered many times over. Furthermore, as mere units of a larger empire whose capital city lay elsewhere, the surplus which the *oikos* had redistributed locally was siphoned away to the benefit of the metropolis, in tribute and forced labour. True, some conquerors went out of their way to rebuild their temples: but on balance city wealth was drained away. To make matters worse, by this time the effects which over-irrigation has historically had on the entire southern part of Mesopotamia through the period of the Caliphate, namely the salinization of the arables, had made themselves felt in the southern cities, so that their harvest began to tail off just as tribute was being extracted.

The fall of Ur in 2004 marked the final end of Sumerian supremacy in Mesopotamia. From then on the ascendancy passed in due course, as we have seen, to Babylon and ultimately to Assyria. True, the peoples of these parts became acculturated, worshipped Sumer's gods, used its script, and copied and translated its myths and legends. But politically the city-state had reached its term. The Amorite chieftains, in dividing the country into personal kingdoms, finally erased all trace of them. Men, land, and livestock no longer belonged only to king or temples, let alone to the gods as in

[60] Cf. Roux, *Ancient Iraq*, 170; D. O. Edzard, 'Mesopotamia and Iraq', in *Encyclopaedia Britannica* (1979), xi. 977A.

proto-historic times but ever more to landed proprietors, peasants, and merchants. The temples were great landowners, yes, but among other and private landowners. Priests still cared for the gods, kings for their subjects, but the economic life of the city no longer belonged exclusively to them. When Hammurabi overran Sumer and made Babylon his capital, that city's obscure presiding deity, Marduk, was substituted for the Sumerian Enlil. Henceforth, the king who claimed lordship over 'the land' must 'take the hand of Marduk'. Later it would be the turn of Assur.

2

The Kingdom of Egypt to the Fall of the Middle Kingdom (1678 BC)

1. INTRODUCTION: 'AS THE TWIG IS BENT . . .'

'Tis education forms the common mind,
Just as the twig is bent, the tree's inclin'd;

(Alexander Pope, 'Epistle to Lord Cobham', 1734)

*U*ntil towards the end of the fourth millennium Egypt decidedly lagged behind Sumer in civilization. During the Late Uruk period in Mesopotamia (*c.*3300 BC), when cities like Erech and Eridu were arising, the peoples of Egypt were still tribal, living in small and primitive farming villages along the banks of the Nile. Then, near the end of the millennium, Egyptian culture makes a sudden leap. From a line of small villages dotted along the river-bank there emerged—so it would seem—statelets, possibly confederations, and then, *c.*3000, the unification of Upper and Lower Egypt under a single monarch. With this began the Archaic age, *c.*3000–2650, the period of the first two dynasties; and the succeeding dynasties III–VI, which we call the Old Kingdom, survived until *c.*2150 BC. Late-prehistoric Egypt had come under south Mesopotamian influence: art-motifs, the cylinder-seal, Sumerian-type boats, mud-bricks and brick buildings are all clearly attested. Yet before the beginning of the Old Kingdom all this had disappeared. In its place the Egyptians had developed their own individual style of writing—the hieroglyphs. Monumental architecture sprang up, and arts and crafts broke into flower. A pattern was set that was to last into the Hellenistic, indeed, the early Roman eras.

So began *three thousand years* of Egyptian civilization—its religion and its art, its social structure, its economic organization, and its form of government. Many scholars have chosen to stress its unchangingness over this enormously long tract of time. *Eternal Egypt*, for example, is the title a great Egyptologist has chosen to give his book.[1] It is a matter of perspective, however: from a distance the outline does indeed seem to be the same; but

---

[1] P. Montet, *Eternal Egypt* (Mentor, 1968 first published by Weidenfeld & Nicolson, London 1964).

close up, the details differ from one historical period to another. The course of Egyptian civilization over time is characterized by a set of variations on a few perennial themes, and what is true of the civilization as a whole is true of its peculiar form of government.

Our knowledge of it in these early times is exiguous, patchy, and problematical. For all that it is possible to sketch its main outline.

First and foremost comes the principle of the political unity of the Nile Valley and Delta from the first cataract to the sea. This principle was embodied in the royal styles—'Lord of the Two Lands', and so forth—symbolized by the dual crowns and commemorated, notably, in the great Sed festival.

Secondly, and impliedly here, unlike Sumer the form of polity is not the city-state. At this very early stage Egypt had mainly villages. This polity was the world's first centralized country-state whose core area was the Nile Valley from the Delta to the first cataract, a state with no autonomous units (except in times of governmental breakdown), only administrative divisions.

Thirdly, the ruler of this polity was an autocrat. He was the manifestation of a god (as will be explored below) and, in principle, the entire land was his.

Fourthly, he governed through a bureaucracy of scribes in his residence city and through district governors who, in their turn, had their own households of scribes.

Fifthly, the institutions of monarchy, the social structure, and the conformity to the laws were underpinned and legitimized by a religion of the Archaic type, but where the ruler was himself the chief priest of the cult in each and any of the temples of the principal gods. The resident priests were nothing but his deputies.

Sixthly, the social structure consisted of a tiny élite of nobles, scribes, and priests comprising around 5 per cent of the population, over and above a mass of illiterate peasants.[2]

Finally, the economy was an extended (and for that very reason, a not very well integrated) *oikos*. It was a money-less natural economy, where production-units, whether royal, nobiliar, or priestly, were all so many *oikoi*. In principle, the entire state formed the royal *oikos*, but in practice this was frustrated by administrative distance on the one hand and bureaucratic inadequacy on the other.

Mutatis mutandis, each and all of these major features except the fifth were to be found not only in the centuries when Egypt was independent, but also

---

[2] J. R. Baines, 'Egypt—History (up to the end of the First Intermediate Period)', *The New Encyclopaedia Britannica*, 15th edn., vol 18 (1989). He reckons that only 1% of the population was literate.

when she became a province of the Assyrians, the Persians, the Greeks, the Romans, the Byzantines, and the Arabs. The Sumerian city-state, as a distinctive form of polity, expired under conquest and economic stagnation. The Egyptian style of polity did not. It outlasted conquest. It outlasted its Archaic religion and, with that religion, the script, the art forms, and the world outlook that went with it; and ultimately it lost even the Egyptian tongue itself when Arabic finally replaced it around AD 1000. But where government is concerned, each new set of invaders took over the political and administrative structure of those it had replaced. It modified but it did not abolish the basic features.

Historical details constitute so many fluctuations around these principles. For example, the unity of the Nile valley was not always realized in practice. It broke up again and again, giving rise to what Egyptologists choose to call 'intermediate periods'. But the principle never died. The unificiation of the two kingdoms c.3000 BC was to Egypt what Shih Huang-ti's unification of China was to that country: however fractured into petty principalities, each kinglet nourished the ambition to recreate this unity of the state: all subscribed to the principle that it was one and indivisible.[3]

Similarly with the theology of sacral kingship. At one point the ruler was the manifestation of god; later the son of the god—indeed, of more than one god simultaneously. The way the ruler tried to sustain his autocracy fluctuated also. At one point rulers relied on members of their own family, at another on the older established administrative families, at another still on hand-picked meritocrats. Similarly the extent of his absolutism ranged from complete domination of the provinces by his own officers, to almost complete abdication to autonomous hereditary administrative élites, or—as in the early years of the Middle Kingdom—a *modus vivendi* with them. But throughout, the *principle* of absolute autocracy was upheld.

Always, whatever the fluctuation, it represented only divergence from a norm. To the norm itself—of a unitary, centralized country-state, ruled by the palace, as an *oikos* of a sacral monarch assisted and flanked by a scribal bureaucracy, priests, nobles, and armies—the polity always returned.

2. THE SETTING

Egypt is, effectively, the narrow ribbon of land bordering the Nile—never wider than twenty-four miles, sometimes as narrow as one—and its marshy, fan-shaped delta, 125 miles across at its widest point. Together they add up to some 13,000–14,000 square miles—the area of Belgium (or, as we saw, of

---

[3] Except in 8th–7th century BC.

Sumer). The rest is red desert: indeed, the ancient Egyptian called it 'the Red' (*Deshret*), as opposed to the riverine oasis which they called 'the Black' or *Kemet*. The surface of the entire state would have been 'red' but for the regular and perennial behaviour of the river. From the first cataract at Aswan it flows northwards to the Mediterranean for some 750 miles. No rain to speak of falls south of the Delta, and even in Cairo only one inch per annum can be expected. The river stands lowest in the month of May. Then rain in the Ethiopian highland sources increases its flow, which rises to a peak in September. So the ancient Egyptians divided the year into three seasons, not, like us, four. The first four-month season they called *akhet*, the inundation. The second was *peret*, the 'coming forth' of the land as the waters receded. The third was the dry summer season—*shomu*. The vast swollen torrent of inundation-time threw silt on the banks, depositing a thin layer of fertile mud. Also, the ancient Egyptians trapped the spreading flood-waters in rectangular earth-banked basins. As the waters receded these basins acted as storage tanks: and by breaking down a bit of the bank, the waters would flow out, via canals, into other, empty basins and so on, supplying water to the land to be sown. These operations sufficed for the main grain crops. But as a result of the annual deposits of silt, the banks of the river stand higher than land further away, and if water is to be brought to it, it has to be lifted. This toil was back-breaking, and even the introduction of the *shaduf*, *c.*1500 BC (a counterpoised wooden lever with a container at the end opposite the counterpoise) only partly relieved the labour, as one can see to this day in Egypt, where the *shaduf* is still in common use. But by these means the Egyptians were able to develop rich orchard- and garden-farming. Enormously fertile, and lying under a scorching sun, the Nile is the life-blood of Egypt: votive offerings were made to the inundation, and its regular and seemingly eternal rhythm was regarded as the gods' specific gift to their own country, Egypt.

The Nile served Egypt in yet another important way: as a highway. It is easily navigable below the cataracts and the Egyptians—who developed boats very early—could float downstream. It so happens that the prevailing wind is from the north, so all one had to do to proceed upstream was to hoist a sail. The river acted, therefore, as a broad arterial highway, the more effectual in that no part of the cultivated area was more than twenty miles away from it. Egypt's internal communication system was, consequently, the best in the entire ancient world, and accounts for the early territorial integration of its villages into a country-state and the preservation of this unity through the millennia. As a highway, it could and did transfer troops *and* their provisions and *impedimenta* rapidly from one province to another, and by the same token float bulk goods, like timbers and stone blocks, to any point desired.

Finally, this flood plain, this immensely long oasis in the midst of dry rock and sand, enjoyed on all sides what today we would call 'strategic space'. In the south the cataracts impeded forays from Nubia. In the north was 'the Great Green', the Mediterranean. The Egyptians did not take to the open sea but they did have inland ports and did conduct some overseas trade, notably to Byblos. On the west stretched nothing but desert with a few oases only, and eastwards to the Red Sea lay rock and mountain. Protecting the Delta from Asians lay the desert of Sinai. These arid spaces around the narrow valley-bottom gave the Egyptians the sense of being unique. Egypt was the norm; any other land the bizarre exception. The Nile flowed north, so that when Egyptians reached the Euphrates they described it as flowing upside down. Egypt was the land of the gods and the Egyptians their favoured people.

Yet, while the Kingdom did not have to fear invasion, it had to adjust somehow to infiltration; for a 750-mile-long narrow strip of land and waterway was very hard to police against nomads from the deserts, attracted by the riches and security of the riverine villages. The north-east border proved even more permeable by the Semitic nomads of Palestine who came down to graze their flocks and herds or to settle. But all these foes were far less formidable than those surrounding the Mesopotamian river-valley, though the cultural superiority and the enormous resources of Egypt were to hold them in check for over 1,500 years.

3. CHRONOLOGY

The inhabitants of the Nile Valley ceased to be nomads and hunters and turned to farming between 5500 and 4000 BC. They lived in small villages. It is surmised that they were tribal, and also that the areas they inhabited are comparable to those which were later organized around a head-settlement as the provinces encountered in the Old Kingdom. Some say that their provincial emblems go back to their original totem-god, others that they were ancient local symbols.

It is surmised that in the late fourth millennium BC a number of statelets had emerged, in the south and in the Delta. These were the precursors of the single, unitary state; but whereas it used to be thought that this unification took place rapidly, even in one swoop, current opinion tends to hold that it came about by conquest over a longish period of time, under one or more kings. It was made the easier when a cultural uniformity had pervaded the south—a necessary condition for political unification. It looks, too, as if the southern area—Upper Egypt (which is the Nile Valley proper)—was c.3200 brought under the control of one king, with Abydos (probably) as his capital. It is contested whether a similar consolidation occurred simultaneously in the Delta, as well. Paintings and sculptures identify the south with a white, mitre-shaped crown. The red diadem which also is portrayed on some objects was later, retrospectively, identified with the north. A carved mace-head in the Ashmolean Museum at Oxford suggests that a southern king called 'Scorpion' attacked and defeated Delta forces.[4] A carved palette of this time from Hierakonpolis shows a king, with his white crown, smiting an enemy who is elsewhere symbolized by reeds, while the king is symbolized by the falcon, the emblem of the god Horus. The obverse shows this king and his decapitated enemies; but here he is, significantly, wearing the *red* crown.

Scorpion is a pre-dynastic king. Some scholars think he is identical with a King Narmer whose sway must have been extensive, for he is attested all over Egypt and in Palestine. But he is seen, nowadays, as the last of a line of pre-dynastic kings, the kings of the so-called Dynasty O, which is thought to have reached back for a century or more. The first of the dynastic kings, c.2920, is a King Aha whom most scholars think is identical with that legendary King Menes who, Herodotus affirms, first united the 'Two Kingdoms' and so founded the historic state of Egypt.[5] This state was territorially the same as that which was to occupy the Nile Valley until quite recent times. It was not built up piecemeal and expanded from a conquest centre.

Certainly Aha/Menes founded a new capital town, 'the White Walls', which the Greeks were later to call Memphis. It stands roughly at the point where the Delta and river valley meet, not far south of modern Cairo. This event was crucial and remained stamped on the consciousness of more than one hundred generations of Egyptians until, with the advent of Christianity, the Pharaonic tradition was lost.

The consequent centralization of power precipitated an astonishing leap in the society's capabilities in every sphere: military, religious, artistic, economic. Egypt, after lagging Sumer for so long, springs suddenly well into the forefront. The 'Pharaonic culture',[6] compounded (to us) of vast pyramids and temples, obelisks and statues, its bizarre animal-headed iconography of the gods, and its sacred script, the hieroglyphs, had, quite abruptly, taken off.

[4] *CAH*, I.2, pp. 3, 6.   [5] Ibid. 11, 15.

[6] The term *pharaoh*, which means 'Great House' (i.e. Palace) but was applied to the ruler as a sign of respect, was not in fact in use until the New Kingdom (1540 BC).

Ancient Egyptian history is conventionally reckoned in terms of thirty-one dynasties, ending in 332 BC with the conquest of Egypt by Alexander the Great. An outline chronology runs thus:

CHRONOLOGY

EARLY DYNASTIC	Ist to IInd dynasties	*c.*3000–2650 BC
OLD KINGDOM	IIIrd to VIth dynasties	*c.*2650–2150
	1st Intermediate Period (VIIth–Xth dynasties)	*c.*2150–1980
MIDDLE KINGDOM	XIth–XIIth dynasties	*c.*1980–1640
	2nd Intermediate Period (XIIIth–XVIIth dynasties)	*c.*1640–1520
NEW KINGDOM	XVIIIth to XXth dynasties	*c.*1540–1070
	3rd Intermediate Period (XXIst–XXVth dynasties)	*c.*1069–664
LATE PERIOD	XXVIth to XXXIst dynasties	664–323

The first two dynasties set the pattern of the polity forever. Henceforth, the monarch was absolute, a divine king, a being set apart, the unique link between gods and men, the forces of nature and the world. He was served throughout the territory by officials of a central bureaucracy which monitored the irrigation of the Nile, carried out a biennial cadaster of cattle, collected taxes, and organized the polity.

The vast energy that the regime could tap and its quite remarkable organizational ability far outstripped the achievement of the Sumerian city-states. The IVth dynasty (2600–2475) typifies this. This is the dynasty that built the great pyramids of Giza and Dahshur. Their immense bulk compared with the lesser tombs of the courtiers which lie at their foot demonstrates the great gap between god-king and his most favoured subjects; and nothing serves better than those pyramids to demonstrate the formidable political power wielded by the government, its organizational ability, and the technical mastery of its servants. Cheops's (2589–2566) Great Pyramid is the largest stone edifice in the world. It is 756 feet square. Its original height was 480 feet. The cathedrals of Florence, Milan, St Peter's, St Paul's, and Westminster Abbey could all fit together into its base-area. It consists of 2,300,000 blocks of stone weighing on average 2.5 tons apiece. The sides of its base come within only 7 feet of forming a perfect square. Their orientation, north–south and east–west is perfect within one-tenth of a degree. Yet this gigantic edifice was built without benefit of pulley and wheel. Copper tools existed, but in effect all the blocks were quarried and carved with stone tools. The limestone of its casing had to be cut at Tura, ferried over the river and as far as possible to the site by canal. The granite was floated down the river all the way from distant Aswan. For the last part of their journey to the site the blocks were manhandled on to sleds, pushed up ramps running round the core of the pyramid by levels, and finally fitted with such exactitude that a knife-blade will hardly penetrate between them. It is reckoned that, over a twenty-year building period, the pyramid would have required 4,000 men working full-time at the site and 100,000 men, for three months in each of the twenty years, to drag the stone there.

The Great Pyramid is in every way the embodiment of [the] autocratic idea. The King, the living Horus, was Egypt; everyone else was subservient: everything was planned for the glory of the King: everything completely reflected his glory . . . the Great Pyramid . . . also offers the complete demonstration of what can be done when all resources are controlled by one man and directed solely for his purposes.[7]

The consolidation of the regime up to the gigantism of the IVth dynasty is one of the main themes of the period up to 1760, the end of the XIIth dynasty, with which we are here concerned. It has so impressed observers that some authors contrive to leave the impression of a polity as uniform, regular, solid, and indeed as pyramid-shaped as the monument itself—the god-king at the apex, and his subjects beneath him in strict 'courses' of hierarchical subordination. But every so often one may glimpse or perhaps infer episodes that suggest an irregular and untidier reality. We would do well to heed what the great pioneer Egyptologist, Erman, was saying nearly a century ago: 'the reader will have seen how frequently there occurred periods of political disorder: yet our knowledge is confined to those of long duration, we know scarcely anything of the short disputes about the succession to the throne.'[8]

This view, of the fragility and precariousness of the royal power, is one we share. But, as will now be seen, it contrasts with the ancient Egyptian conception of their ineffable and sublime divine kingship.

4. GOVERNMENT AND RELIGION

All or, at least, nearly all descriptions of the kingship in ancient Egypt used to begin with its supposedly *divine* character—that the king was actually a *god*.[9] But a succession of usurpations and the like suggest that the actual practice of kingship does not square with the theory. Some very eminent scholars have, in fact, expressed total disbelief that any ancient Egyptian

[7] Baines, 'Egypt', 466.
[8] A. Erman and H. Rank, *La civilisation égyptienne* (as revised 1922), trans. C. Mathien (Payot, Paris, 195?), 7?
[9] e.g. Frankfort, *Kingship and the Gods*.

(priests and theologians possibly excepted) could ever have believed such stuff, and have then passed on to the practicalities of rulership.[10]

This view, with which I have much sympathy, is not quite right, however. We often find an incongruity (sometimes total) between the *credenda* of government, that is, what we are taught to believe is its nature, source, and *raison d'être*, and what it actually is and does. A Chinese emperor, for instance (as we shall see), supposedly enjoyed the Mandate of Heaven. So, in principle, rebellion was rebellion against Heaven. Yet it often occurred. If it failed, that proved that the emperor did indeed hold such a mandate. If it succeeded, this proved that Heaven had decided to withdraw its mandate. The *credenda* may be irrational or self-contradictory or circular. That does not mean, however, that they served no purpose. On the contrary, such *credenda* are so many 'political formulae' and as such fulfil crucially important political and indeed social functions. To begin with, this Egyptian formula implicitly distinguished between a human and his office. Kingship had a sacral character; this was inherent in the office. So, whoever held the kingship, no matter what he did, or how he had obtained it, took on this sacral character.

Next, and even more importantly, formulae like these have a mollifying effect on conduct because they *moralize* the contest for power. They make it a matter of morals, of right and of religion, not a crude chronicle of human ambition, avarice, and revenge. Conventions like these are highly useful to both power-holders and their opponents alike, who maintain a sort of 'open conspiracy'. And finally, such formulae provide the grounds for popular obedience. The more acceptable the formula to the public, the firmer its allegiance. The more energetically the political élite and counter-élite propagate the formula—whether by word or deed, consciously or unconsciously—the more acceptable to the people the doctrine is likely to be.

In my view, the Egyptian doctrine of the king being a god was (after a relatively short time when it may have been taken literally) just such a political myth. This requires showing how the doctrine had its roots in Egyptian religious beliefs, and then demonstrating the inextricable tangles it got into in trying to accommodate untoward political events. This should show that the only plausible way of explaining its vigorous survival to the very end of Pharaonic Egypt is by taking it to be a political formula of the kind I have been describing.

---

[10] Erman and Rank, *Civilisation égyptienne*, 72–3; Montet, *Eternal Egypt*, 84–5; G. Posener, *De la divinité du Pharaon* (Imprimerie Nationale, Paris, 1960).

4.1. *The Nature of Egyptian Religion*

No aspect of Pharaonic Egypt can be studied in isolation from its religion. The earliest stone vessels were (as far as the record attests) for religious, not profane purposes. There is no secular art, only religious. Counting, measuring, observing the stars, chronometry derived from or contributed to religious purposes.

In its detail, Egyptian religion is deeply puzzling. For instance, Egypt recognized an immense number of gods, in human, animal, and material forms. But they were never grouped systematically for the country as a whole. Moreover, they were far from sharply defined; indeed, one was often equated with another on the basis of a single shared characteristic in power, sometimes even because of verbal punning.[11] Incongruity posed no intellectual problem. It was thoroughly acceptable.[12]

In its *generality*, however, Egyptian religion manifests all the distinctive traces of what (following Bellah) we have been calling the Archaic type of religion. Its symbol system is one wherein mythical beings, objectified, are conceived of as actively controlling the world: in short, they are gods. A vast cosmology, a hierarchy of gods is conceived—in the Egyptian instance, a number of such cosmologies and hierarchies, not just one. These gods are approached and activated by means of worship and sacrifices. As in Sumer, their images were kept in the holy of holies, to be roused, washed, perfumed and incensed, clothed and fed, brought out on a barque, taken back, and finally returned to their shrines. They were numerous; there were hundreds of temples.

The organization of religion also parallels Mesopotamia. There was a popular religion accessible to all, as against the 'official' religion whose cults were in the hands of the narrow official élite. There were no congregants. Only priests were allowed inside a temple. The believers' role was to admire and acclaim the idol as the priests brought it out on its barque bedecked for its sacred walk. The religion turned on ritual: personal piety, even when it appears, is never of primary importance, but ritual and spells are. And as in Mesopotamia, again, the monarch plays the central role in the communication between gods and men; but here in Egypt from the outset he manifests the god himself, so that he can move among the high gods in heaven, yet act as chief communicant, that is, chief priest in all the temples of all the gods throughout the Two Lands.

---

[11] R. Anthes, 'Mythology in Ancient Egypt', in S. N. Kramer (ed.), *Mythologies of the Ancient World* (Doubleday, New York, 1961), 35.

[12] Cf. Walt Whitman. 'Do I contradict myself? Very well I contradict myself. I am large. I contain multitudes' ('Song of Myself', 1865).

By these means both the individual and his society are merged into the natural divine cosmos. The order on earth mirrors that of the cosmos: it is guided by *ma'at*—the right, the appropriate order of things. Thus the traditional structure of society, its hierarchical nature, its division into a narrow ruling élite of possessors and the mass of illiterate peasants, is grounded in the divine order of things. So is social conformity—at every point it carries a religious sanction. More than 2,000 years after the period we are describing Herodotus noted that 'the Egyptians are religious to excess'[13] (although, to be fair, it does not follow that this was so in the earlier periods which are under present discussion). It is common ground that of all peoples, even including the Chinese, the ancient Egyptians were the most traditionalist. This is due to their attachment to a religion which pervaded every aspect of their social surroundings. When Christianity destroyed the religion, it destroyed the entire Pharaonic culture as well.

4.2. A God-king?

Egyptians found no difficulty in simultaneously believing statements which we, nowadays, would find contradictory. Equally they had a very vague idea of what exactly constituted a god—the divine and the human merged by such imperceptible degrees. The Egyptians displayed rather an uncritical syncretism. Instead of following the modern scholars' dictum 'when in doubt leave out', they seem to have pursued the opposite course—'when in doubt, leave in'. One fact, however, is of great importance in this regard: in the cosmic hierarchy, the king is not on a par with the high gods.[14]

The inscriptions talk of him as 'the perfect god', it is true, and use the same term for god—*netjer*—as for the high gods. But the epithet 'perfect god' is never used of actual gods; and the use of *netjer* for both king and god does not necessarily entail that the two were considered identical; that inference only follows if we assume the Egyptians had a special word for a being that was neither an actual god nor a simple human. In brief, they had no word corresponding to 'demigod' or some such notion.[15]

The *titularies*, on which so much reliance is placed, certainly affirm the king's divine descent and/or authority, whatever these terms might have meant in the historical context. And they give him more than one divine origin. Two are particularly prominent. He is Horus, the hawk god, the king of the gods. But later, in the IVth dynasty, which followed the cult of the sun god, Ra—who is king of the gods—the king is also the 'son of Ra'.

[13] See Herodotus, *The Histories*, trans. George Rawlinson, 2 vols. (Everyman edn.; Dent, London, 1940), ii. 37.   [14] Montet, *Eternal Egypt*, 58.
[15] Posener, *De la divinité*, 15–16.

The two lineages were henceforth put in parallel: the king was both the physical son of Ra, and the living god Horus, successor to the deceased king who was the god Osiris—and so on *in saecula saeculorum*. As the son of Ra, his death was but a re-unification with the sun-disc;[16] as Horus he was also every dead predecessor, who was Osiris.[17]

In all periods the king depended on the gods; he was not a 'god-king' who might dominate them, even if, because he was one and they were many, and he was present on earth, he might be more prominent than any one of them. His position is clearly stated in a 2nd millennium description of his role in the solar cult . . . which divides the beings of the cosmos into four categories: the gods, the king, the spirits of the dead and humanity. The king 'propitiates' the gods, 'gives mortuary offerings' to the spirits, and 'judges' humanity. These three actions convey the problematic of his position. He is marginal to the world of the gods, yet through him they rely on this world and on human efforts to sustain them and the cosmos. They must be propitiated because they are not predictable and they might at any time act capriciously and destructively . . .[18]

The king is inferior to the gods; from late pre-dynastic times he was shown receiving the gift of life from them. He can be the 'son' or be 'beloved' of any deity—both of these being relations of subordination and dependence.

Less confusing to us are the claims familiar in all Archaic religions. Through the rituals he performed, the Nile duly rose and fell, the sun shone, the crops matured. In the way the theologians phrased it, he established *ma'at*—the order of the universe and its defence against its imminent and immanent threat to disintegrate. *Ma'at* implies order, regularity, conformity to the way of things and, at the same time, all-encompassing morality and 'rightness' and, by this token, 'justice'. It is something like the Chinese Tao, but unlike it in that it is not neutral but, on the contrary, the vehicle and embodiment of supreme morality.[19]

[16] J. A. Wilson, *The Culture of Ancient Egypt* (Chicago UP, Chicago, 1951 Phoenix edn., 1956).

[17] On this confused and confusing issue see Wilson, *Culture of Ancient Egypt*, for an admirably compressed explication; Anthes, 'Mythology in Ancient Egypt', for an extended exploration. Frankfort, *Kingship* is a classic and formerly highly influential—but, I suspect, very misleading. A. Moret, *Du caractère religieux de la royauté pharaonique*, Ph.D. Thesis (Ernest Leroux, Paris, 1902)—is an exhaustive study of the cultic and ritualistic aspects of the divine kingship.

[18] J. R. Baines, 'Kingship, Definition of Culture and Legitimation of Rule', in D. O'Connor and D. P. Silvermann (eds.), *Ancient Egyptian Kingship* (Brill, Leiden, 1995), pp. 10–11.

[19] J. Assmann, *Ma'at, l'Egypte pharaonique et l'idée de la justice sociale* (Collège du France: Conférences, essais et leçons, Paris, 1989), and id., *Ma'at: Gerechtigkeit und Unsterblichkeit im alten Agypten* (C. H. Beck, Munich, 1990).

5. THE CENTRAL AUTHORITIES

5.1. *The Political Implication of Divine Kingship*

However hazy the nuances of theology, the political implications of the 'divine kingship' formulae are very clear indeed: as the manifestation of the god, as the 'son' of the god, the king was physically dangerous to touch and politically absolute. Here was the king, the 'perfect god' (one of his most frequent titles), and there were the masses and there was nothing in between. If one could use the expression one would like to say that in theory the king was not simply absolute but absolutely absolute.

In actual practice he very often was less than absolute, and sometimes he had no power at all. A contradiction emerged between the doctrine and the practice. It became complicated by the ambiguities inherent in *any* incarnation doctrine, and even more so by the rules relating to succession. As to the first, was the king of 'the same nature' as his admittedly divine father, Ra (and Horus) or a human, in special touch with them? Both views were held simultaneously.[20] It seems clear that (with the likely exception of the XIIIth dynasty) succession pertained to members of the royal *family* provided always that suitable candidates were available. But Egyptian kings maintained minor queens as well as the chief queen, and in some periods they also maintained harems. Such situations—as this history will repeat *ad nauseam*—put the rule of succession under permanent threat from pretenders. Moreover, what help could the theology give when, as happened very often given the high mortality rate in ancient Egypt, the royal line simply died out?

Simple! The usurper or the designated successor who was not the son of his predecessor's queen was, for all that, the son of the god. For whereas everybody can be certain about maternity, nobody can be sure who a child's father is. Egyptian theology recognized, indeed described in some detail, how the god descended, took the shape and form of the reigning monarch, and possessed his wife, so engendering a royal heir. But if the god could possess the queen, why not a minor queen, a concubine, why not indeed *any* woman whatever? Our credulity at such an excuse, and the Egyptians' credulity too, must *surely* have been strained beyond the limit by the succession in the XIIIth dynasty? For this was a line of quite ephemeral kings, whose average reign lasted a mere two years and a half, who left their government to a succession of all-powerful chief ministers, which included *inter alia* a son of a commoner and a general, and who, as far as is known, did

[20] P. Derchain, 'Le Rôle du roi d'Egypte dans le maintien de l'ordre cosmique', in *Le Pouvoir et le sacré* (Annales du Centre d'Étude des Religions, Brussels, 1962); Posener, *De la divinité*, ch. 3.

not acquire their title by hereditary descent but—in default of better knowledge—far more likely by way of a coup than by some kind of nomination or election. It passes all belief to suppose that the chief ministers, at least, who knew how and why these monarchs were made, thought that they were supernatural, or that their courtiers did, since many of these would have been candidates for the throne. And so, in widening circles, till the entire governing establishment was affected.

Yet the royal titulary, and the royal claims to divinity, persisted and indeed were revived with great *éclat* in the resplendent XVIIIth dynasty and survived the Third Intermediate Period and the subsequent times when Persians, Greeks, and Romans had supplanted native Egyptians as king. Indeed, the more the practice of kingship diverged from the ideal, the more elaborate and extravagant did the theology of the king's divinity become.[21] In the face of so manifest an incompatibility between theory and political practice, modern scholars have faced all ways.[22]

In my view, the answer is that, after a brief initial period when personal charisma was still highly active, the divine-king theory was turned, as it were, back to front. Originally, the king's person was a sacred person because, in accordance with certain rules or portents, he was, uniquely, indicated as the rightful possessor of the throne. His accession made this a sacred office; it was the projection of his 'personal' charisma. But later it was the throne that made the king; irrespective of a particular individual's personal history, or qualities, a divine power inhered in kingship as such: a 'routinized' charisma. Because *it* was sacred, so was the king, whether he was a commoner, a successful general, or whatever. What counted was that he was *there*, duly crowned with the emblem of the Two Lands, bearing the crook and flail and claiming divine descent.[23] There is powerful evidence to support this view. At certain times, notably the Graeco-Roman era, the personal information about a new king—his throne-name and the like—reached the temples of Upper Egypt so late that, perhaps, his reign had already ended (the same probably applied in the Second Intermediate Period). But the divine king was essential to the cult. Hence the priests, in default of the king's personal details, simply inscribed the two hieroglyphs for the word *pharaoh* in front of a cartouche that was left blank. 'By doing so the priests showed how little the real pharaoh mattered. The bas-

[21] Derchain, 'Le rôle du Roi'.

[22] Cf. Frankfort, *Kingship*; Derchain, 'Le rôle du Roi'; Posener, *De la divinité*; Erman and Rank, *Civilisation égyptienne*; Montet, *Eternal Egypt*; and E. Hornung, *Conceptions of God in Ancient Egypt*, trans. J. Baines (Cornell UP, Ithaca, NY, 1982).

[23] A broadly similar belief that the diadem made the emperor is found in Byzantium (see below, Bk. III, Ch. 1, Sect. 4.1).

reliefs no longer portrayed him in action, but the anonymous pharaoh, uncontingent, ideal, imaginary—almost an abstraction.'[24] Again after 664 BC, when Egypt was periodically ruled by foreign kings, the priests were prepared to accept them as legitimate, provided they acted like a pharaoh; that is to say, took on the titulary and the other forms, respected the cults, and assumed the priestly office. 'If someone acts like Pharaoh, he *is* Pharaoh.'[25]

If such an inversion proves difficult to comprehend, the papacy provides an analogy. The Chair of St Peter is a sacred one carrying supreme authority over the Church; and he who ascends it becomes, *ipso facto*, the pope, the *ex cathedra* infallible leader of the Catholic faith. But the Church did not cease to obey when a Borgia became pope, nor did the faithful cease to believe in the sacral role of the pope during the Great Schism in the fourteenth century when, at one point, three popes simultaneously claimed the sacred office.

5.2. *Kingship in Practice*

5.2.1. THE PALACE

In *authority* the king was absolute. The question is whether his *power* was equally so. The king was the sole ruler of the entire country, the Two Lands, irrevocably united in him. He was the highest authority in the land, unrestrained by any outside enforceable code of law, human or divine. He was the source of all legal decisions. He was the sole priest, all others being his deputies. He was the individual to whom war and peace appertained. He was head of the administration and appointed all ministers.

Putting aside the natural human limitations to the sovereign's power, what forces if any could constrain or control his absolutism? He was bound by rituals; without these he could hardly be considered the king. These were some kind of limitation. He was bound, no doubt, by custom and convention, but observance of these was a matter of prudence and could and did vary from one king to another. None of these restraints was enforceable. Any constraining forces could only be informal, that is to say, rest in the political *power* of certain individuals or groups of individuals to resist him, not a rival *authority*.

The populace did not count. Until the New Kingdom (*c*.1540 BC) neither the army nor the priesthood were politically significant either.[26] The scribes

[24] Derchain, 'Le Rôle du Roi', 63.

[25] B. G. Trigger, B. J. Kemp, D. O'Connor, and A. B. Lloyd, *Ancient Egypt—A Social History* (CUP, Cambridge, 1983), 297.   [26] Erman and Rank, *Civilisation égyptienne*, 370–4.

were certainly a self-conscious élite, but the famous 'Satire of the Trades' reflects only their satisfaction at having such a comfortable job.[27] Constraint, if it were to come from anywhere, could come only from the central administrative élite, which included the king's principal ministers; or from his territorial officials; or from those amongst them who at various periods had established a sort of hereditary claim on their posts and had struck local roots.

Was there an Egyptian 'nobility'? The term, in so far as it connotes 'blue-blood', is not popular among Egyptologists. Instead, they would use neutral terms like 'élite' or 'administrative élite'. However, there are groups in certain periods—and for that matter there are often individuals—whom it is difficult to think of as anything but, say, noble or aristocratic. The point is, though, that they are a *service* nobility, a *service* aristocracy.

This matter may be explicated as follows. It is necessary to distinguish between two types of 'nobility'. The first, a *service* or 'court' nobility, owes its social status and its wealth, initially, to the services its members render the monarch; usually, as officials. The second type of nobility is a class of individuals who hereditarily possess great landed estates and, as a consequence of their wealth, their economic hold over the common folk, and their influence with local and central officials enjoy enormous social esteem and considerable political power. In Egypt such 'nobles' as these are important only during the late Old Kingdom and early Middle Kingdom, as we shall see. As for a supposed superiority of 'blood' such as is characteristic of European nobilities, this is hardly encountered before the Late Period.

It was from these two quarters that restraints on the king originated.

5.2.2 CONSTRAINTS

The Court Circle

A king could not necessarily take his throne or his succession for granted. The evidence for usurpation or irregularities in the succession is convincing and has already been mentioned and may be taken as a constant feature dating from the Ist and IInd dynasties. Surviving literature, principally from the Middle Kingdom, leaves no doubt about the threat the royal officials posed to the monarch and the care he had to take to survive: the 'Instructions' which the powerful ruler Amenemhet I (1991–1962) supposedly addresses to his heir are eloquent in this. 'Beware of subjects who are nobodies, of whose plotting one is not aware. Trust not a brother, know

[27] M. Lichtheim, *Ancient Egyptian Literature: A Book of Readings*, 3 vols. (University of California Press, Berkeley and Los Angeles 1973). i. 184–92.

not a friend, make no intimates, it is worthless. When you lie down, guard your heart yourself, for no man has adherents on the day of woe.' And to make the point more vivid, the king recounts how, dozing after his evening meal, he was set upon by members of his own bodyguard.[28]

The throne, in fact, was 'a precarious institution'. The average length of a dynasty throughout the entire span of Pharaonic Egypt is only one century.[29] Ideally, the kingdom was owned and set in motion by one sacral king; in practice, as Erman noted, he was surrounded by counsellors, many of them long-established before his time, by priests and generals and the like, all of whom had to be conciliated. Many were potential usurpers and could provoke civil war.[30]

Different kings adopted different strategies to protect themselves. The kings of the IIIrd dynasty seem to have followed a policy of using 'new men', brilliant commoners like the great architect-cum-physician-cum-administrator Imhotep;[31] or at least, if they were royal kinsmen, they were at pains to conceal it. The great IVth dynasty (the builders of the great pyramids of Giza and Dahshur), however, concentrated all high administrative positions, including the head priests, in the royal family, but the Vth dynasty recruited commoners for the top posts. The VIth dynasty sees the florescence of a territorial nobility which came into its own in the troubles we call the First Intermediate Period. When the XIth and XIIth dynasties reunited Egypt, they established a kind of live-and-let-live accommodation with these provincial nobilities, while, as concerned the immediate palace circle, they adopted a device which was to be highly popular in several subsequent autocracies (such as the Roman and Byzantine empires and the Caliphate), that is, the *co-regency*. Amenemhet I associated with himself as king his eldest son Seostris I, and this practice was followed by three successors. At that point, however, for reasons unknown to us—perhaps the extinction of the royal line—the dynasty broke down.

The Territorial Magnates

While there is some archaeological evidence for provincial magnates in the Ist dynasty, maybe in the IInd and IIIrd, but definitely not in the IVth, we know nothing about them until, at the earliest, the Vth dynasty, and the VIth dynasty would be a surer date to choose; this means, for the first six-to-eight hundred years of the kingdom's history, an enormously long time! When they do emerge into written history it is clear that some do own land in their own right, legally distinct from what they hold from the king in

[28] Lichtheim, *Ancient Egyptian Literature*, i. 136. [29] Montet, *Eternal Egypt*, 83.
[30] Erman and Rank, *Civilisation égyptienne*, 70–3. [31] *CAH*, I.2, 159–60.

return for rendering him governmental service.[32] There is, however, evidence for the structure of provinces from as early as the IIIrd dynasty.

Similarly, their role in running the kingdom can, at the very best, be only surmised. It is pretty clear, however, that in the first four dynasties such magnates were not appointed as sole governors of a particular province or set of provinces. There was a difference between a *nomarch*, that is, one in general charge of a nome or province, and other posts such as 'ruler' or, very commonly, 'overseer of commissions' in a particular locality. Most of these Old Kingdom officials were buried at the capital, from which it might be inferred that they did not reside in the localities but roved between them on supervisory incursions. Since these places were too widely scattered and too numerous to permit continual supervision, we can say with confidence that local landed families did not at this stage act as the nomarch for their places of residence.

From the Vth and particularly the VIth dynasties we are on firmer ground: in the former a provincial élite began to attest itself, and in the latter it moved into high gear both socially and politically. In the latter part of the Vth dynasty local high officials—some of them nomarchs—began to be buried in their localities rather than at the capital and this practice became common in the VIth dynasty. The number of nomarchs increases, and instead of them controlling as many as three nomes apiece, each usually governs a single nome.[33] The expression 'great chief of a nome', which is the strict equivalent of the modern expression nomarch, is first attested at Edfu under King Teti (*c*.2350, at the beginning of the VIth dynasty).[34] In so far as some are appointed 'chief priest' in the local temples, they assert a manifest moral leadership also.[35] At the same time, the evidence that these local governors now formed dynasties, the office passing from father to son, is clear and positive.

Recent research suggests that the 'rise' of the provincial magnates/ nomarchs was part of a deliberate reorganization of government in the VIth dynasty: that they were firmly under royal control until the death of the aged King Piopi II (*c*.2150); that impoverishment by comparison with the pyramid-building IVth dynasty (though it should be noted that it is much less marked by comparison with the Vth dynasty) is reflected at local as well as central level and therefore cannot be due to the upstart land magnates holding on to the resources which they were previously channelling to the central government. None of the much canvassed 'explanations' of the

[32] Cf. Trigger *et al.*, *Ancient Egypt*, 57.
[33] N. Kanawati, *The Egyptian Administration in the Old Kingdom* (Aris and Phillips, Warminster, 1977), 73.   [34] Trigger *et al.*, *Ancient Egypt*, 108.
[35] Ibid. 109.

collapse of the VIth dynasty which link it with the supposed weakening of the central power and self-assertion of the local governors provides a sufficient explanation. The collapse remains unaccounted for.[36]

What is quite certain, though, is that once the dynasty had collapsed (in the period of Manetho's alleged 'seventy Kings for seventy days'), the local élite came into its own. As so frequently happens to service élites, they transform themselves into 'landed nobilities'. The conditionality of their lands disappears and they hold them and their official titles hereditarily and can live independently on the resources they have thus themselves (in Max Weber's term) 'appropriated'. As the governors in place, and wealthy magnates residing on their own estates, they cut their ties with the central government. There is even one instance of a nomarch of Dara who placed his name in a cartouche like any sovereign.[37]

From this time forward, to the later XIIth dynasty (*c*.1830)—some 500 years—there is a well-attested local aristocracy who play a significant political role. Certainly, they still used the idiom of state service in their titularies, but they behaved like great local princes; they dated events to their own terms of office, levied and maintained their own armies and fleets, quarried for their own monuments, and cut rock-tombs of immense splendour, which were surrounded by the tombs of their officials. On their funeral stelae they tell the people that they have ruled benevolently, stamped out violence, improved the irrigation system, restocked the herds, repaired the temples, and stored up grain against famine.[38] Aktoes (Khety) and his line held the nome of Asyut (Lycopolis, the thirteenth nome). At Beni Hasan lie the thirty-nine famous rock-tombs of which eight belonged to the 'Great Overlords' of the Oryx nome. The wall pictures testify to the immense scale of their manorial administration.

To say that such noblemen acted 'as a constraint' upon the king's absolutism would be a grotesque understatement. The kings had to nurse and manage them with as much care and anxiety as ever did a feudal monarch of Western Europe. Vivid testimony to this lies in the 'Instructions' which a king of Herakleopolis is presented as giving to his son, Merika-re: 'The hothead is an inciter of citizens. He creates factions among the young. If you find that citizens adhere to him, denounce him before the councillors, suppress him, he is a rebel.' 'Respect the nobles . . . sustain your people . . . Advance your officials.'[39] The advice which Amenemhet, founder of the great XIIth dynasty, offered to his son is similar.[40]

---

[36] Kanawati, *The Egyptian Administration*, 67–73   [37] Ibid. 67
[38] *CAH*, I.2, pp. 468 ff.
[39] Lichtheim, *Ancient Egyptian Literature*, i. 99–100. This text is nowadays thought to have been composed later than when it purports—possibly in the Middle Kingdom. But this does not seem to me to affect the thrust of the argument.   [40] Lichtheim, *Ancient Egyptian Literature*, i. 136–8.

The welter of local anarchs was ended by the XIIth dynasty, regarded as one of Egypt's most powerful; and few kings were more powerful than soldier-founder Amenemhet I. The traditional view of the XIth and XIIth dynasties of a now-reunited Egypt is of a feudalistic age, where the Middle-Egyptian nomarchy who had helped to defeat Herakleopolis were allowed immense licence. It is said that Amenemhet I relied on them in his bid for the throne and consequently rewarded them by restoring ancient rights and privileges, for example, the revival of the title 'great chief of the nome'. (This suggests that the XIth dynasty might have tried to suppress them.) They vied with the king himself in their wealth and display.[41] But then—it is said—Sesostris III suddenly suppressed them and their privileges alike. Their elaborate rock-tombs cease.

The truth is not necessarily as dramatic. For one thing, there is evidence that the XIth and XIIth dynasties made a far-going overhaul of the local administration. Amenemhet I firmly redrew their *nome* boundaries or perhaps he merely reconfirmed them. Certainly, the kings of this XIIth dynasty seem to have been able to get support from these nomarchs, even in major enterprises, whenever they demanded.

The new situation is best explained by social changes. There was far more governmental activity in this period (*c.*1950–1700) than during, say, the Vth dynasty, 400 years earlier. In that time the country had become more populous and society more complex and hence, one surmises, government with it. Two developments had come to work in the same sense: the enrichment and entrenchment of landed families in the First Intermediate Period (2130–1980), and the central government's decision, born of a felt need, to replace the old system of palace-based supervisory officials by one of locally resident and permanent governors each in charge of a delimited territory. The first development made it natural that these would be selected from the local magnates, and the second development made it unsurprising that they had to work to and with the central government and not independently. This entire arrangement, which seems to have been thoroughly successful at first, declined only gradually in the later XIIIth dynasty which was replaced, *c.*1630, by Hyksos rule in the northern parts of the country.

5.2.3. THE ROYAL AGENDA

That defence of the territory, the maintenance of order, and the dispensing of justice should form part of the agenda of government is only to be expected. These are the primordial functions of any government. Two

---

[41] *CAH*, I.2, 496.

activities figure, however, which by no means always occur in other forms of regime. The first is a ritual or cultic duty. The second is a degree of managing the economy.

The Egyptian monarch had no duty and—with the exception of the eccentric Akhnaton—felt no urge to enforce a particular religious belief on his subjects; on the other hand his ritual and cultic responsibilities were, without exaggeration, *central* to his office.

Although the doctrine of the king's divine nature accorded ill with the actual practice of politics, it never ceased, albeit in ever-changing variations, to retain its place in Egyptian theology.[42] It was indeed the very keystone of the theology: the king was the unique link and mediator between the gods and men. One scholar[43] has argued that precisely because the king had always been the central figure in cult and ritual from the earliest times, it was necessary *post hoc* to invent the theory that he was divine. Throughout the numerous temples in Egypt the cult reliefs always present the same basic scenes: they picture the king and the temple's god. Nobody else acts for the god; only the king. He supplicates the god who in return promises him those particular favours he has it in his special power to dispense—life duration, power, health, happiness, valour. In these pictures the king, through his ritual actions displayed there, is *actuating* the god to put forth his powers; but the god had already given *before* the king offered. What we have is a continuous cycle—the god has given, the king supplicates, the god has given, the king supplicates, and so on.[44] And although it was the temple priesthood that acted for him, the pictures do not show them. They show only the king.

This central activity of the kingship expressed itself in two main ways or—if we treat the mortuary cults as a separate item—in three. First, the king had to take part in frequent and numerous rituals. If we were to believe Diodorus Siculus (writing *c*.50 BC),[45] the daily life of the king began with state business. Next he attended the temple, then, for the entire day, he followed a timetable of ritual acts, as exactly prescribed as 'by a physician'. This has been seen as a vast exaggeration, but why? It was largely true of Chinese emperors.[46]

The king's second religious activity was to maintain the temples, arrange for the god's service there, and build new ones. The last of these is bound up with the royal funerary cult. In addition to the cults of their deceased person in their pyramid complexes, kings placed their statues in the various

[42] Cf. Derchain, 'Le Rôle du roi'.   [43] Moret, *Du caractère religieux*.

[44] Hornung, *Conceptions of God*, ch. 6.

[45] Diodorus Siculus, *Library of History*, trans. C. H. Oldfather (Loeb edn., London, 1935 repr. 1961), i. 203.   [46] Cf. Granet, *La Pensée chinoise*.

temples and set up what we would call a *chantry* bequest, that is, paid priests to carry out rites and prayers for the deceased monarch *in perpetuum*. Carving those statues, positioning them, providing the buildings to house them and the staff to service them, together constituted what has been aptly deemed 'the single largest industry running more or less continuously through the Old Kingdom and then after a break, and perhaps less so, through the Middle Kingdom'.[47]

The pyramids were a special case of such mortuary foundations. Whether we speak of the gigantic ones in Giza or the smaller ones that followed for a thousand years through the XIIth dynasty, pyramids had a dual function. The first was to make sure that the *ka* (soul) of the dead king was provided with everything it needed to make its successful journey to the afterworld, to join the divine essence of which it was a part, and thence continue to do good for the gods' own country, the land of Egypt. Just as vegetation dies to be reborn, so too can the king; if the efforts of man successfully bring this about, so all things would be reborn with him. The other function was to serve as a chantry for the cult of the dead king. The pyramid complex contained a mortuary temple where the priests intoned their prayers for the deified monarch. This practice was paralleled by pious sons of the aristocracy throughout Egypt also, albeit their expectations for the afterlife were modest compared to the king's. In this second function Kemp's suggestion about the funerary cult[48] strikes me as enormously illuminating, so that I quote directly:

Whilst it is common to emphasize the mortuary character of pyramids and to see them primarily as tombs with temples ancillary to them, the way in which they were in fact organized and referred to suggests that the emphasis should be reversed, and that they be regarded first and foremost as temples for the royal statues with a royal tomb attached to each, which, acting as a huge reliquary, gave enormous authority to what was, in essence, an ancestor cult, and an important factor in the stability of government. This was a phenomenon repeated on different scales throughout Egyptian society in the form of private funerary cults . . .[49]

In brief, these pyramids were not the whim of simple megalomania. They were expressions of a religion which made the king central to the well-functioning and continuance of life in Egypt. In that sense they were quite instrumental, one might almost say utilitarian.

The cultic and ritual agenda of the Egyptian monarch powerfully affected two other items of his agenda. The first of these is the duty to establish

---

[47] Trigger *et al.*, *Ancient Egypt*, 86.

[48] B. Kemp, *Ancient Egypt: Anatomy of a Civilisation* (Routledge, London, 1989), 85.

[49] For details on the professional administration of the funerary chapels, see ibid. 89–90.

justice. We have already mentioned the concept of *ma'at*. It is incumbent on the king to establish *ma'at*—the due order of things—because it is inherent in him that he brings earth and heaven, profane and sacred together into the cosmic balance. On earth, *ma'at* becomes 'justice' and the king is duty-bound to dispense this.[50] The good or ideal king, say the texts, which are the ancient Egyptian equivalent of later 'Mirrors of Princes', is one who dispenses *ma'at*. Such a statement does not, of course, mean that justice was necessarily well organized, accessible, or even-handed, still less that the king was anything less than absolute. *Ma'at* (whatever concrete that might mean) was in his or his servants' hands and no others'. But it does mean that the establishment of justice was regarded as a primal item of the royal agenda.

The cultic centrality of the king not only radiated into this duty to dispense justice, but also into what, as I said earlier, was one of the more distinctive items on the Egyptian agenda of government—public works; and this for the simple reason that the costliest component of public expenditure was undoubtedly the building and refurbishing of temples and the establishment of mortuary cults already mentioned.

It has long been fashionable, since Marx made scattered remarks on a so-called 'Asiatic mode of production' (expressed to its fullest extent in Wittfogel's 'hydraulic system' of government), to attribute Egyptian centralized autocracy to a supposed 'necessity' to carry out irrigation works. Quite aside from the objection that in their formulation Wittfogel's 'hydraulic' school make what may be a necessary condition for civilization and for statehood into a necessary and *sufficient* one, the example of Egypt would demonstrate the exact opposite of what is asserted. For with one major exception—the irrigation of the Fayyum by the XIIth dynasty kings—the central government's interest in irrigation was more or less confined to measuring the heights of the Nile so as to be able to predict the inundation and hence the harvest, *plus*—a significant consequence, as explained below—a *storage* system. Not that there were no public irrigation projects. Indeed there were—but they were carried out by the nomarchs, not the central government, as frequent biographical texts boast.[51] For the basin irrigation of Egypt does not require centralized control. It is essentially a local activity—or was, at least, until modern times when the high dam was built at Aswan.

But the central government, like the Han Empire of China, did accept

<hr/>

[50] Cf. Wilson, *Culture of Ancient Egypt*; H. Frankfort, *The Birth of Civilization in the Near East* (Williams and Norgate, 1951), 92–4. See also Assmann, *Ma'at*, and *Gerechtigkeit und Unsterblichkeit*.

[51] See above, pp. 149–50.

responsibility for countering, as far as possible, the effects of famine. It did this in conjunction with its local governors, the nomarchs. When these became independent in the First Intermediate Period, they continued to boast that they fed the starving out of their own stores of grain. The state-wide system, as it developed, called for grain deliveries to central government depots and to local ones also. These deliveries form part of the revenue system: for the taxes were levied in kind, stored, and then paid out to state beneficiaries and servants, or retained till famine arose. The quantities of grain stored against famine could be quite immense: in the New Kingdom the storage capacity of the Ramesseum, which was one of a large number of temple complexes in Thebes, was sufficient to feed a town of 17,000 for one whole year.[52]

In this way the economy, which in this period was entirely conducted through the separate *oikoi* (manors) of the king, the temples, and the local magnates, was brought into a rude unity as the statewide *oikos* of the king.

6. THE ADMINISTRATION

6.1. *The Territorial Framework*

Whereas the characteristic Sumerian form of polity was the city-state, the kingdom of Egypt is the first historical *country*-state. One of the most important, indeed, perhaps the most important implication of this is what we might call 'administrative distance'. The consideration applies to any state where a troop of soldiers is more than one or at most two days journey from the frontier. Above the critical distance, the central government begins to require outposts of its officials to take care of the localities. The slower and more imperfect the communications, the greater the discretion granted to these local officials, and the wider their range of powers. The most common outcome was to put local governors in full charge of all matters in the locality. The problem was to devise means of securing their continued loyalty and accountability. Both proved very hard to ensure, and in pre-industrial times few large country-states—let alone empires—ever found satisfactory long-term solutions.

Egypt's 'administrative distance' was peculiar in that, first, the country was long—some 750 miles—but very, very narrow; and secondly, that one travelled everywhere by water. It must have been very like getting round Venice today. We must imagine the central government's officials making

[52] Kemp. *Ancient Egypt*. 195.

their tour of inspection by getting in their galley, floating downstream or
hoisting sail upstream, and mooring at the village or town they had to visit
which would be situated on or near the water's edge.

We have already mentioned that until the Vth dynasty (c.2500–2350) the
Egyptian government relied on peregrinating central officials to control the
provinces, the resident local officials being, presumably, mayors or headmen
of the towns and villages, but that in the VIth dynasty the organization of
Upper Egypt into provinces, or nomes, was more locally effective and a
governor was placed in charge. There were normally twenty nomes of Upper
Egypt, though the number varied slightly from one year to another. Most
nomes were effectively delimited by their northern and southern borders,
while the deserts on the east and on the west defined those dimensions.
These nomes are numbered from south to north, the most southerly at
Elephantine (Aswan) being the First Nome, and the most northerly the
Twenty-Second, lying just south of the capital city of Memphis. Lower
Egypt, that is, the Delta and its apex, might still have been run from the
capital in the old-fashioned way until the XIth or XIIth dynasties, but we
cannot be sure. The distances from the capital are short, and it is probable
that the court was largely drawn from Lower Egypt and so had close
knowledge of the region and connections there. Furthermore we know
that some nomes existed there from the Old Kingdom and about fifteen
are attested for the Middle Kingdom. Their boundaries followed the
patterns which the main branches of the Nile make as they intersect with
one another, or are bounded by the Mediterranean.[53]

This arrangement into nomes was to remain in force throughout the rest
of ancient Egyptian history. From time to time, however, as will be noticed
below, the central government appointed one, or indeed as many as three or
four, high officials to superintend the work of a number of the nomes
together: a special governor for Upper Egypt was the most common but, as
will be seen, sometimes the viziership was divided, with one vizier being in
charge of this area.

6.2. The Central Administration

The Old Kingdom was governed by a central bureaucracy, but we have little
information about it apart from titles. Furthermore, they are titles without
job specification. In addition, we rarely know whether a particular individual
held these titles and discharged the duties of the offices simultaneously or

[53] For a map of the nomes, see J. Baines and J. Malek, *An Atlas of Ancient Egypt* (Phaidon, Oxford,
1980), 14–15.

sequentially. Far worse, the titles underwent inflation,[54] so that there are soon a very large number of 'Sole Companions of the Sovereign'. Governors of Upper Egypt are driven to describe themselves sometimes as 'the actual (or real) Governors of Upper Egypt', to distinguish themselves from the honorific ones. New titles proliferate like tadpoles from frog-spawn; and the general windiness of most of them is marvellously illustrated by one individual (the head of the Treasury) who calls himself 'the Governor of all that exists and does not exist'.[55] Next, even when we sort out the titles that are clearly functional, and so glean a crude idea of what departments were in existence, for example, a Treasury, a Vizierate, an Overseer of Fields or of the Granary, it is impossible to sketch an organization chart showing how they interconnected. There is little archival evidence (and this, mostly from the Abousir papyri).[56]

Some generalities may certainly be advanced: the first, that at top level the system was extravagantly *patrimonial*. Though ministries were specialized, ministers were not. An official like Metjen (IVth dynasty), for instance, acts in a variety of capacities: chief scribe of the provision magazines, overseer of all the king's flax, and 'ruler' of about a dozen towns and localities.[57] Another official is overseer of the baths of the Palace, and castellan of the Cow fortress.[58] Another is very much the palatine courtier; he doubles as high priest of Ptah, as the king' cup-bearer, and master of ceremonies.[59] The most variegated career is that of Weni, an official who served three successive kings of the VIth dynasty. Weni started at the bottom as a junior steward of the royal domain, became a judge, and then found promotion as director of the royal domains. From this position, he was called on to make a secret enquiry into a harem affair involving the queen. He led military expeditions into Sinai or southern Palestine on five occasions. Finally, he was promoted to the post of governor of the south and led expeditions to quarry stone for the king.[60]

[54] As in many later polities. See for instance the 'Han Empire' in Bk. II, Ch. 6, pp. 490–1 and the 'Later Roman Empire' in Bk. II, Ch. 8, p. 573 ff.

[55] A. Erman, *Life in Ancient Egypt*, trans. H. M. Tirard (1st English trans., Macmillan, London, 1894 repr. Dover Publications, New York, 1971), 96. To be fair, this glorious expression is the standard phrase for 'everything'. What else, indeed? The expression, along with the entire paragraph which encloses it, disappeared in the 1922 Erman-Rank edition. See Erman and Rank, *Civilisation égyptienne*, 128.

[56] P. Posener-Krieger, *Les Archives du temple funéraire de Néferirkare-Kakai: les papyrus d'Abousir; traduction et commentaire* (Cairo and Paris, 1976).

[57] J. H. Breasted, *Ancient Records of Egypt*, vol. I: *Texts* (University of Chicago Press, Chicago, 1906), 77–8. [58] Ibid. 87.

[59] Ibid. 132.

[60] A. Gardiner, *Egypt of the Pharaohs* (OUP, Oxford, 1961), 94–7, *passim*; Lichtheim, *Ancient Egyptian Literature*, i. 18–23.

Secondly, the administration may well have been a duplex one, with one organization 'The House of Upper' and another of 'Lower Egypt'. Certainly there is reference to the Two Treasurers and the Two Granaries and a number of other duplicated offices besides. But this may have been purely nominal: indeed, some think that the perennial harping on 'the Two Kingdoms' and 'Upper and Lower Egypt' did not reflect an organizational reality at all but simply carried on an inherent Egyptian tendency to visualize everything whatsoever in terms of a dualism.[61]

We are on firm ground in stating that from very early times the administration was monocratic: it was run by a chief executive, the *Tjaty*, a chief minister (but whom Egyptologists insist on calling a vizier). This title is in Egyptian *Taity-Zab-Tjaty*, which means 'he of the curtain' and 'judge' (no precise etymology can be given for the *Tjaty* element).[62] In the Vth dynasty he always carried two other titles,'Overseer of All the Works of the King', which relates to all the ramifications of building-policy, and 'Overseer of the Scribes of the Royal Documents'. This *must* refer to controlling the Chancery Office: for one thing, because there is no other specialized agency which can be identified as such, and secondly, because the Chancery—that is, the central registry without which no department would ever know what other departments were doing—should, logically, be under the direction of a chief minister. However, in the VIth dynasty there were sometimes two viziers at the capital. Sometimes one of them is specifically assigned to Upper Egypt.[63]

Finally there is evidence for a host of specialized departments. We hear, for instance, of the Treasury Department, a director of the scribes of the Treasury, and the said scribes. The overseer of the king's works we have already mentioned, in that it was usually but not always part of the vizier's duties. There is a director of the Fields and a director of the Granaries; there is also a Revenue Department, or rather a congeries of departments. The Treasury's function was to keep accounts and was associated with a division in charge of the income from the very extensive royal domain and

[61] Frankfort, *Kingship*, 19–23. I think this is most far-fetched (for all that it is valid on a religious level). For the contrary opinion, see Gardiner, *Egypt*, 102.

[62] The word *cancellus* means something akin to 'curtain', i.e. the railing or bar that divided the court from the outside. Officials stationed here were called *cancellarii*, hence our term 'chancellor'. They were effectively 'gatekeeper' controllers of ingress of those coming to judgement. But it might also be related to the 'bar' being the screen between the monarch and his subjects or foreign emissaries: in which case it is cognate with terms like 'Keeper of the Gate' and the like, which are common throughout the palace-regimes of Asia.

[63] K. Baer, *Rank and Title in the Old Kingdom* (University of Chicago, Chicago, 1960), and N. Strudwick, *The Administration of Egypt in the Old Kingdom: The Higher Titles and their Holders*, Studies in Egyptology (KPI, London, 1985).

with another, 'The Wardrobe', which looked after the king's personal store of vestments and valuables. One could multiple this list several times over but, as we do not know how it was articulated together, there is no point: the instances we have cited are simply to illustrate its differentiated character.

The Vizierate was capital. Over time, the vizier came to control the Treasury Departments and the Royal Domain Department, and in the Middle Kingdom this gave him a commanding role in managing the economy. In addition, however, he was the high judge; but this office went far beyond judicial duties. Mentuhotep, the supreme judge of Seostris I (XIIth dynasty) says it was his duty 'to give the laws, to promote men in their appointments, to adjust the places of the boundary-stones, and to settle the quarrels of officials . . . He made those to tremble who were disposed to be hostile to the king, he kept the barbarians in check and made the Bedouin to live in peace.'[64]

This dominance of the Vizierate is one of the two great trends in the way the administration developed between the VIth and the XIIth dynasties; and we may parenthetically remark that it is therefore not surprising to learn that the XIIIth dynasty saw a development similar to what occurred in Merovingian France: a line of *rois fainéants* who reigned, and all-powerful mayors of the palace—in Egypt's case viziers—who governed.[65]

The second trend is the increased specialization and hierarchization of the scribal bureaucracy. But first, something ought to be said about the ubiquitous scribes of Egypt who form almost an 'Estate' of the realm. *Qua* professional corporation, they had no political clout; but nobody could progress to official rank without first having been trained as a scribe, and some high officials compounded the word 'scribe' along with their titles.

First, it took long years of training to become a scribe. The pictographic hieroglyphic script was the one used for monumental texts. Side by side with it the scribes developed a cursive form which we call the hieratic script.[66]

The complicated nature of the written language and the existence of more than one script made the art of writing so very arduous to acquire that its practitioners had to become professionals. They were trained in special schools, satirized in model texts copied by pupils in the late New Kingdom. In the Old Kingdom there were such schools at court, but later, for example,

[64] Erman, *Life in Ancient Egypt*, 119. This passage has been omitted from the Erman-Ranke revision (1952), so that a more modern translation cannot be given here.
[65] Cf. J. Von Beckerath, 'Notes on the Viziers "Ankhu and Iymeru"', *Journal of Near Eastern Studies*, 17 (1958), 263–8.
[66] Used for administration till c.600 BC. Originally written vertically, then from right to left.

in the New Kingdom, the various government departments were running their own schools.[67] Lessons went on from daybreak to midday; food was sparing, beatings commonplace. After the first rudiments of orthography, the pupil went on to copy and re-copy extracts from well-known texts, then model letters, lists of places, and categories of words and set phrases. The entire emphasis was on rote-learning and the curriculum throughout all these schools was identical.

Scribes thought very well of themselves. In 'The Satire on Trades' the scribe-author smugly compares their sedentary life with the arduous, dirty, and smelly manual occupations of the peasant or metalworker or even army officer. But they knew they had more important reasons for self-satisfaction: they were exempt from the corvée, they paid no taxes, they did not have to do military service (though many did); but above all, the scribal profession was, as we have said, the path to office of all kinds: priest, administrator, military adjutant and the like. For in the higher levels of training, scribes learned arithmetic, mensuration, geography, and management skills. So much is clear from the late New Kingdom 'Satirical Letter', a purported correspondence between a tyro and his senior.[68]

In the Middle Kingdom, then, the bureaucracy had become more numerous and specialized. Thus, says Erman, 'The Treasury Department possesses . . . the Deputy-governor of the Treasuries, the Clerk to the Governor, the Clerk of the House of Silver, the Chief Clerk of the Treasury, the Custodian of the House of Silver, the Superintendant of the officials of the House of Silver and so forth.'[69]

6.3. *The Local Administration*

The central administration exercised supervisory and accountancy functions, execution being carried out locally, except for functions that only made sense if performed by one central agency, and certain special one-off activities. Among the general functions were Calendaring, measuring the height of the Nile inundation, and taking the biennial census. About the census we are poorly informed for the early period. It took place every two years. The Palermo Stone, which is inscribed with summary 'annals' of the first five dynasties, uses a formula mentioning a 'numbering of gold and lands'.[70] and we know also that it counted up flocks and herds, and many details peculiar to a particular estate such as wells, canals, trees, and so on.[71]

[67] Erman and Rank, *Civilisation égyptienne*, 421.
[68] *ANET*, 475–9 W. K. Simpson, *The Literature of Ancient Egypt*, 2nd edn. (Yale University Press, New Haven and London, 1973), 329–36.   [69] Erman and Rank, *Civilisation égyptienne*, 129.
[70] Breasted, *Ancient Records*, i. 64.   [71] Trigger *et al.*, *Ancient Egypt*, 82–3.

The 'one-off' activities include, for instance, the royal expeditions in the southland, Punt, the Sinai, and the eastern desert to collect such things as hard stones, building-stone, aromatic spices, even (in one case) a Nubian dwarf.

These executive operations in the localities were entrusted to a governor appointed by and, theoretically, revocable by the central government. Control was always a problem in every pre-industrial country-state or empire, but notably where landed magnates flourished. If a stranger were appointed over their heads, they could exercise their influence to frustrate him unless he accommodated himself to their pressures, in which case he was less than perfectly compliant with the central government's demands. Even the *intendants* of France in the eighteenth century responded to this centrifugal pull. If, on the other hand, the government appointed the most influential local landlord as its officer, it was—by parity of reasoning—no better off and, conceivably, worse. The problem was exacerbated in a natural economy such as Egypt, where the only way to pay the local governor was to assign the revenues of landed estates to him. This was standard in Egypt during this period, but analogous arrangements existed in the Byzantine Empire (the *pronoia*) and the Islamic states. This is not feudalism in the accepted sense, but a system of benefices or what Weber called 'prebendial feudalism'.[72] In such an arrangement the only way the central government could 'stop the pay' of the recalcitrant official was to dispossess him. This was often easier said than done, especially if the government, for various reasons, had made a habit of appointing sons to succeed their fathers, and this happened in the VIth and succeeding dynasties in Egypt down to the end of the period we are considering. Governments adopted all manner of expedients to make their resident local officials compliant: by rotating them from one area to another before they could strike local roots, by dividing local functions between two or more co-equal officers so that they would check and balance one another, by appointing kinsmen, or by *not* appointing kinsmen, by sending special commissioners to report or to interfere—and so forth. Each and every such device will be found again and again in the course of this *History*.

The simplest of all arrangements was for the government to leave all local execution to a single grand official. This pattern was followed in most of the ancient empires, for example, in the Persian Empire, the Han Empire, the Roman Imperial Republic and the Caliphate. The governments of such states relied on their authority and ultimately their powers of reprisal; but the frequency of revolts by satraps, governors, *strategoi*, *amirs*, and the like shows the unreliability of such recourses.

[72] See below, in our treatment of the Byzantine Empire and the Caliphate.

A common device to strengthen central control was to group a number of the more distant localities under the authority of a super-official. It reduced administrative distance, since the super-official was closer to the localities and the central government was nearer to him. The device of a governor of Upper Egypt who answered to a vizier of the central government was used frequently in the Old Kingdom because the capital, Memphis, was only 125 miles distant from the northern sea-border but some 600 miles away from the first nome in Elephantine in the south. In the XIth dynasty the capital was at the far southern town of Thebes, so the position was reversed; the king appointed a governor of Lower Egypt.[73] At times, however, a still further reduction of administrative distance was attempted. Most scholars think that Pepi II (*c*.2250–2180) divided Upper Egypt into the 'Deep South' and the Middle Provinces, with governors in charge of each. Others think there were three such governors of Upper Egypt and one thinks there were four—three in charge of groups of nomes and one other to supervise all three.[74] However this might be, the ruthless and efficient Sesostris III of the XIIth dynasty certainly divided Egypt into three sub-provinces: the North (perhaps subdivided into east and west halves), the South, and the Head of the South, and each was controlled by a special department in the capital. Each of these departments was headed by a reporter whose staff included a deputy, a council or court, and the supporting scribes. All three departments, like the departments of the Treasury, Agriculture, Justice, and Labour, came under the authority of the vizier.[75]

From their inception in the VIth dynasty perhaps to the late XIIth dynasty, the nomarch was a sole and all-purpose ruler in his nome. He was expected to respond to each and any extraordinary demand by the government as well as carry out the day-to-day administration. For instance, Ameny, son of Khnumhotep, of the Oryx nome (Beni-Hassan) made several special expeditions to fetch gold to the palace or to take ore to Coptos.

A nomarch was, to begin with, the commander-in-chief of the nome army which, inscriptions show us, was used to secure its borders during civil wars, to accompany expeditions like the ones mentioned, and to join the royal army when this was assembled to march on foes. Next, he collected the taxes and forwarded them to the government. He secured order and justice. He stored food and took other steps to ward off famine, such as extending the area of cultivation by irrigating more land.

His court was the pharaoh's court in miniature. It had its treasury,

[73] N. Kanawati, *Governmental Reforms in Old Kingdom Egypt* (Aris and Phillips, Warminster, 1980), 128–31; *CAH*, I.2, p. 483.   [74] Ibid. (Kanawati does not believe any of this), 66–73.
[75] *CAH*, I.2, p. 506.

responsible, *inter alia*, for all the artisans of the local government: its granaries, its military command, its desert-guard, its household officials, and so forth. A picture in the tomb of Ameny's father Khnumhotep illustrates the government offices at work.[76] On the left-hand panel the treasurer is shown sitting and watching an official who is weighing some object while a scribe sits, expectantly, to make a record. In the middle we are shown the revenue department. It is receiving taxes in kind—grain is being put into sacks, and their number is being noted by two scribes. The right hand panel shows what happens next: the sacks are carried up to the roof of the granary, and as they are poured out through an opening into the space below, yet another scribe sits noting the number.[77]

Ameny has left an account of the ideal nomarch. 'I spent the years as ruler of the Oryx nome with all dues for the king's house being in my charge. I gave gang-overseers to the domains of the herdsmen of the Oryx nome and 3000 oxen as their yoke-oxen. I was praised for it in the king's house in every year of the cattle tax. I delivered all their dues to the king's house, and there was no shortage against me in any bureau of his, for the entire Oryx nome labored for me in steady stride.' He goes on to claim that he never denied anybody justice, neither widow, peasant, nor shepherd, never employed corvée labour without paying, beat off famine by extending the area of cultivation, and saw that even the unprotected received subsistence.[78]

The final point concerns the payment of the nomarch by conveying to him the produce of certain estates. This is illustrated in a set of legal documents drawn up by the nomarch Hepdjefa[79] of Asyut. One contract allocates foodstuffs to the chief priest of Wepwawet (himself under another hat!) from his paternal estate (inherited) but *not* from what he calls 'the count's estate'—that is, the land with which the king endowed him—which, being conditional on services rendered, he could not of course bequeath.[80]

6.4. The Temples

The priesthood, in this period, was not nearly as economically salient as that of the Sumerian city-states. (In the New Kingdom it was to be different.) In the Old and Middle Kingdoms, most temples were relatively

[76] Whether of the province or his own personal estates cannot be determined, but the practices portrayed here would be the same in either case.
[77] Erman and Rank, *Civilisation égyptienne*, 126–7.
[78] M. Lichtheim, *Ancient Egyptian Autobiographies Chiefly of the Middle Kingdom: A Study and an Anthology*, Orbis Biblicus et Orientalis 84 (Universitätsverlag, Freiburg, 1988), 138–9.
[79] 'Hepdjefa', in Breasted, *Ancient Records*; see also Trigger *et al.*, *Ancient Egypt*, 106.
[80] Ibid. 258–71.

small mud-brick edifices, they did not manage very large estates, their priests were rather few, and these were not professional but lay priests. In fact, the temples were a branch of civil administration and their economic role, though not as yet overwhelming, was significant enough in Egypt's tiny towns such as Edfu or Abydos, and it was closely tied in with the *oikos* economy of the nome. A few brief notes on these matters must suffice to expand these points.

The priesthood 'proper' were the 'servants of the God', and were assisted by the *Wab* priests; only the former performed the main cult. In addition to their general ritual duties, they had other, more specialized ones; led by the high priest, the priests at the shrine of Osiris in Abydos, for instance, comprised one styled the Treasurer of the God and others called scribes of the God's House (i.e. the temple as a whole). In Asyut there were also overseers of the Storehouse, of the House of God, and of the Altar. Their incomes were very small[81] and so were their numbers—five in all at Abydos, ten at Asyut. The priesthood at this level was largely hereditary.

But the chief priests of the great sanctuaries stood quite apart in their religious—and political—importance. Some had special titles, very awesome, for example, the high priest of Ra at Heliopolis was the 'Chief of all the Secrets of Heaven', and 'Greatest of seers'.[82] These high priesthoods were the perquisite of men of rank holding secular positions, especially state officials, and the priesthoods tended to become hereditary in their families. In the VIth dynasty, when the nomarch was established in Upper Egypt and, as we have mentioned, usually became the chief priest, he often held several additional appointments as well; for example, the chief superintendant of the God's Oxen and of the Temple. Often too he was also 'chief superintendant of the prophets' (i.e. the priests) in minor temples. The point here is that these men were not just priests, like other priests, in the same full sense of the term.

In the VIth dynasty the growth of funerary cults for personages other than the king made for a closer integration of the temples into the economic life of the local communities. This came about because nomarchs and other officials arranged for their statues and those of their fathers to be placed in the temples, which they then endowed in order to pay for the appropriate prayers and rites. The produce which the temple received for this chantry service came from many different and scattered estates or foundations. The documents turned up for the mortuary services for King Neferirkara of the Vth dynasty—like those from Lahun for the XIIth dynasty—disclose a meticulously organized administrative organization, but

[81] Erman and Rank, *Civilisation égyptienne*, 372–3.   [82] Ibid. 372.

its magnitude may be due to its being a royal cult.[83] At all events, the documents contain lists of personnel and their duties, for example, guard duties, the collection of the 'offerings', or the performance of the various ceremonies. Also there are lists of equipment and details of breakages. There are also monthly accounts of the offerings—bread and beer, meat and fowl, grain and fruit, as well as who paid them in—the royal estates, members of the royal family, the palace, a nearby solar temple, two towns.

This interlocking of all local notables and of many and variegated estates and foundations with the priesthood made the temple a key component of the local economies and so, as suggested earlier, part of the integration of the many *oikoi* into a wider one. But, with the heavy infusion of otherwise secularly occupied notables, who were all the servants and officers of the government, the temples and priesthood occupied a dependent position in the politics and government of the country.[84]

6.5. *The Judiciary*

For this earlier period the exiguous evidence can be reduced to a few lines. First, *ma'at*, in its secular sense of *justice* and *order*, was always regarded as the central task of the monarch. It is not insignificant that the vizier possessed the metaphorical title of 'High Priest of the Goddess Ma'at'. The very numerous references to *ma'at* and the *obiter* we meet in sundry documents like the Middle Kingdom 'Instructions of the vizier Ptahhotep'[85] show that the Egyptians had a plain view that, *inter alia*, justice must not be denied, must be impartial, and that all complainants were equal in the eye of the judge. It is true that no code of laws, or even of precedents, such as are already found in Sumer (e.g. the fragmentary code of Ur-nammu, *c*.2112–2095), have come down to us and there is only one bit of evidence that suggests that any such code existed.[86] But this does not signify that the Egyptians may not have had something like a jurisprudence. For one thing, there may well have been codes which have not come down to us. Much more importantly, I think, the Mesopotamian codes, for instance, the especially celebrated one of Hammurabi, were proclamations of intent and not laws that could form the basis of a legal action in the courts. What we do know about the status of law in Egypt at this time is that, on the one hand, there are numerous references to law being 'in the mouth of the king', but, on the other, a king admonishes his vizier to stand strictly on precedent.

Thirdly, this argument from silence, such as it is, must not be taken to

[83] Posener-Krieger, *Les Archives du temple.*   [84] Cf. Trigger *et al.*, *Ancient Egypt*, 202.
[85] Lichtheim. *Ancient Egyptian Literature*. i. 62–76.   [86] Trigger *et al.*, *Ancient Egypt*, 84.

imply an absence of legal sophistication among these Egyptians. Earlier we mentioned a nomarch of the XIIth dynasty (Hepdjefa) who makes a contract between himself in his personal capacity and himself in his other, and official, capacity. And contracts and deeds of property transfers suggest an elaborate legalism where 'any transaction that was at all abnormal and was not duly notarized would not have effect'.

Finally, there was as yet no specialized judicial establishment. Those who dispensed justice were also general administrators—nomarchs, royal officers, and the like. Justice, order, and administration formed part of the same jurisdiction. This is, of course, very common, almost the standard, in most societies in history.

6.6. *The Army*

The records do not begin to speak until the VIth dynasty, when they tell of repeated military expeditions. Some are warlike—to repel the 'sand dwellers' of Palestine or push up the Nile beyond Aswan. Many, however, are quasi-economic: thus, troops are sent into Sinai for copper and precious minerals, or to the Wadi Hammamat to oversee the cutting of hard stones and presumably help lug them back. By and large, Egypt was not threatened by more than raiders, though its government took these very seriously, and not until the time of Sesostris I is there a sign of premeditated imperialism. Sesostris III, building on the annexation of Sesostris I, extended and consolidated Nubia up to the southern end of the second cataract.

There are indications of a royal bodyguard from the very beginnings but they become explicit in the Vth dynasty. Amenemhet I (XIIth dynasty) was attacked—possibly fatally—by his own bodyguard.

The nomes had their own militias, conscripted from villages by a 'scribe of soldiers'.[87] They were led by a full-time commandant, who presumably trained and exercised them, for in battle they were led by the nomarch himself. Kheti, nomarch of Asyut during the war between Hierakonpolis and Thebes, describes his campaign to the southlands, a characteristic example of internal war, for it relates how he fought running battles with his fleet of war-canoes on the Nile.[88] Ameny, nomarch of the Oryx nome in the reign of Oamenemhet I (as we have mentioned before) likewise moved his troops by boat; 400 in one expedition, 600 in another. We know precisely how they were equipped because the grave furniture from Beni Hasan contains model soldiers. They were swarthy Egyptians all, clad merely in

---

[87] Erman and Rank, *Civilisation égyptienne*, 702.   [88] Breasted, *Ancient Records*, i. 185.

the kilt, some of them bowmen and the others spearmen who carry large shields: in short, they were light infantry.

But the central government could call on other forces besides the nomarchs: the royal army, as such, was made up of contingents led by a highly mixed collection of officials, from a variety of sources, and commanded not by a professional career general by any means but by somebody who had the king's complete confidence. Peri I put Weni, his trusted official, in charge of a very large army, to overcome the 'Asiatics Who-are-upon-the-Sands'. Weni describes this force in his autobiography. It was recruited from every corner of the country and was made up of contingents under their local leaders. These included counts, royal seal-bearers, 'sole companions of the palace' (i.e. the court nobility); nomarchs and 'mayors'; chief priests; and a group called 'the chief district officials'. Each of these was at the head of a troop of soldiers of Upper and Lower Egypt, or of the villages and towns they might govern, or of Nubians from various 'foreign countries'.[89]

Such armies sufficed to keep the frontier and even permitted the XIIth dynasty to conquer Nubia, but they were no match at all for the Hyksos war-bands in the XIIIth dynasty. These incomers had bronze weapons and superior weaponry which may well have included horse-chariots.

7. AN APPRAISAL

7.1. *Egypt and Sumer: Similarities*

(a) In each society, the culture was homogeneous, as expressed through script, and religious and ethical ideas and ideals; more so for Egypt than for Mesopotamia, which was more diverse.

(b) In each, religious ritual and attitudes pervaded every level and every facet of human activity from agriculture and harvests, through science and medicine, the family mores and the rites of passage, through to the political structures themselves.

(c) The state, the social order, and the divine order are united, or at least, linked via the king who is the 'Perfect God' in Egypt and the 'Vicar of God' in Sumer.

(d) The structure of society is, essentially, two-class: a peasant-mass, wholly or almost wholly in a state of dependency on its immediate landlords, and a narrow governing élite and its supporting bureaucracy, comprising the palace and the priesthood.

(e) In both, the economy is a natural one, organized in *oikos* form; in both,

---

[89] Lichtheim, *Ancient Egyptian Literature*, 20.

the economy is state-controlled, foreign trade being a royal monopoly, and both are storage–distributive. So the surpluses from the tax-cum-distribution system are applied to monumental building for royal or religious purposes, a lavish life-style for kings, court-officials, and aristocrats, and, to some extent, to promote agriculture.

(f) Finally, the polities: they are unreservedly Palace-type royal autocracies, served by a large and ubiquitous bureaucracy. Their style is, alike, an authoritarian paternalism, although Mesopotamia was less despotic and centralized than Egypt.

7.2. *Differences*

The differences flow largely if not entirely from the consequences of scale. It is unlikely that any Sumerian city-state ever controlled more than 200,000 people at any one time, and most of the time these cities were no more than a half or a quarter of that size. But Old Kingdom Egypt is guessed to have had some million inhabitants and probably rising. And although the cultivable land area of both was roughly the same—about the area of Belgium today—there were some 750 miles between the Mediterranean coast and the Elephantine nome in Egypt. The Sumerian state was a city-state; Egypt was a unitary country-state.

The last characteristic had momentous consequences. To begin with, it concentrated an enormous surplus in the hands of an Egyptian government as compared to the Sumerian cities. The vast pyramids, temples, and tombs, the fabulous ornateness of the grave furniture, the extravagant *dolce vita* of the patrician beauties and the pomp and possessions of their menfolk should not be attributed to some inherent virtue of Egyptian civilization (whatever that may mean) over the Sumerian. It presupposed greater despotic control than a Sumerian ruler was wont to exercise, with an enormously larger catchment area of manpower and natural products over which to exercise it. It was as if the twelve or so cities of Sumer had all been rolled into one ball, and put into one royal hand, instead of being parcelled out and fought over.

The second consequence derives from the area of Egypt, accentuated by the very long, thin shape—like a ribbon development along a highway. We have drawn attention to the problem that this generates: the necessity to rely on local officials and to maintain their obedience. This is the first time the problem arises in the history of government, but from this point on, until the eighteenth century AD—and even then only in Europe—it could never go away.

7.3. *A Final Note on the Egyptian Polity*

One final note on the Egyptian polity at this stage: do not let us be deceived by the *Splendour that was Egypt* (the title of a modern popular book), its sculpture and monumental architecture, even the nobility of its ethical sentiments (according to many authors)—do not let us be deceived by any of them into thinking that its system of government was anything to match. It uses the most primordial device of government: an autocrat at the centre exercising his state-wide authority via sub-rulers in the localities. Furthermore, the only political actor apart from the monarch and his court circle was the provincial élite and the only times that this played a role were during the First and the Second Intermediate periods (particularly the former), really as successors to an autocracy that had, for reasons we know not, vanished and left a power vacuum. This is far different from the more complicated interplay of powerful new actors in the New Kingdom and the even more intricate ones in the Late period. From *c.*3000 to *c.*1540 BC, that is, for 1,400 years, Egypt was ruled from the centre by an autocrat, with great stability except in the two 'intermediate periods' each lasting about 150 years. To put it another way: this system of royal absolutism operated with no legal check or obstruction and limited only by its ritualistic and conventional restraints, for two discrete periods of respectively 800 and 300 years. In the scale of the 5,200 years of government history, the second is a rare achievement and the first almost unparalleled.

Context II

1. THE WORLD OF STATES AT THE TIME OF SARGON

*B*y the time of Sargon of Akkad (*c.*2360–2305 BC) other states besides Egypt and the Sumerian city-states had begun to form within the spaces between the two great political cultures of the Nile and the Mesopotamian valleys. East of Sumer lay the kingdom of Elam. To the north of Sumer Sargon built himself a new capital, Agade, whose site is still unknown, and founded the empire of Akkad, which briefly took in parts of Syria. Still further north, up the Mesopotamian plain, lay three small city-states—Assur, Irbil (Arbela), and Nineveh. Westwards across the Jezirah lay the city of Mari, drawing its wealth from the trade routes and from the rich agricultural region of the Khabur and Euphrates; and beyond that lay Syria. Archaeology has barely scratched at the lost cities of the interiors, but here lay, for instance, Ebla (see below) with Carchemish to its north and Hama to its south; and on the coast beyond them, the trading cities of Alakakh, Ugarit (Ras Shamra), and Byblos. To the south Canaan was later to become a land of petty city-states; and thus on to Gaza, and thence, Egypt. Crete was, as yet, bequeathing history no more than its carved stone vases and circular vaulted tombs; but by 2000 its princes had begun to build the first palaces and leave evidence of yet another set of palace-ruled city-states.

For most of these, evidence on political organization is scanty or non-existent. But all seem to share certain features. They are all monarchies; the royal palace, not the temple, is the centre of political and economic direction; a number derive their wealth and power from lying across trade routes, rather than from agricultural surpluses; and finally, although cultic practice and political power unite in the person of the ruler, congruence of social, political, and religious modes of thought and behaviour seems much less complete than in either Egypt or the Sumerian cities.

The differences in their political organization are, however, considerable. At one extreme lie cities ruled by a king with little adjacent territory under his control—a city-state proper, like Byblos. At the other, Elam, possessing its indigenous language, culture, and religion, was a large and authentic country-wide state. In between lay states like Mari or Ebla, where a great city had imposed its rule on a great deal of surrounding territory. The boundaries fluctuated with the fortunes of war, and neither the land nor its population had any particular identity. They are city-states writ large—or country-wide states of a primitive order. They are best described simply as *kingdoms*. The only common identity of the population and territory lies in that they are the subjects of one ruler rather than another.

Elam lay in what is now Khuzistan, in south-west Iran. Its population was probably autochthonous. In any event they spoke a distinctive language, now extinct, unrelated to any others, and which is still not clearly understood. It developed its own script, *c.*2500, and retained it till *c.*1600, when it was at last superseded by the dominant cuneiform of Mesopotamia. It had its own pantheon. Its territory embraced two very different regions: the mountains of the Zagros, and the coastal plain on which stood its capital town, Susa. The mountains contained timber, stone, gems and lead, tin, silver, and copper. These were coveted by the Mesopotamian farmers while the highlanders, for their part, wanted to plunder the farms. Warfare between Elam and the power which, at a given time, was exerting hegemony in the river-basin, was therefore unremitting.

Elam is first mentioned in 2700 when it was at war with the city of Kish. From then it was conquered and conqueror by turns.

Our knowledge of its political structure really relates only to the plain of Susa; of the highland area we know nothing. But what we do know is somewhat startling. The highly heterogeneous regions were politically united by a kinship network of overlords and the principal chiefs. At the head reigned the *sukkal-mah* as grand regent, from the capital, Susa. The related province of Shimashki, however, was ruled by his brother, who was the heir-presumptive to the throne: his title, the *sukkal*, or viceroy, of Elam and Simasliki. Finally, back again in the capital at Susa, there resided the grand regent's eldest son the *sharrum*—the king—of the province of Susa. In these provinces local government was conducted by governors (*ensi* or *ishakku*) controlled by an official who answered to the *sharrum* of Elam province. Apparently a recipe for usurpation and civil strife, this arrangement proved quite remarkably harmonious—and durable; for the state lasted a thousand years. The grand regent accorded the *sharrum*, his eldest son, wide discretion in the running of the province. On his death, the viceroy (his brother) succeeded—and there is no evidence of a *sharrum* ever disputing this claim. Additionally, when the grand regent died his brother, now the new grand regent, married his widow. Even more remarkably, she was usually his sister anyway; for in royal courts brother–sister marriage was the general rule! As Hinz remarks: 'nowhere could there ever have been anything like it'.[1]

---

[1] *CAH*, II 1, pp. 257–60. Walter Hinz is the author of ch. 7, 'Persia 1800–1550'.

At almost the opposite quarter of the Fertile Crescent area, to the far north-west, just south of Aleppo, lay the state of *Ebla*. Ebla was, quintessentially, a city-state, but by dint of annexing the surrounding territory and imposing fealty on an even more extensive area, it had turned itself into a large kingdom—indeed, a petty empire. First inhabited *c.*3500–3300, by *c.*2400–2250, 900 years later, it had become a large city. Sacked by Naram-Suen the Akkadian in *c.*2250, rebuilt, destroyed once more in *c.*2000, it experienced a second rebirth and became very prosperous and powerful. This is one period when it extended its territories. So it continued, a considerable power in the world of emergent states until, between 1700 and 1600, it was burned to the ground by the Hittites and sank into such a profound oblivion that its site (now known as Tell Mardikh) lay wholly unsuspected until a few years ago when the Italian team under Matthiae discovered it and exposed its greatness to the world.

Ebla was not a colony of the Mesopotamian world. Its peoples were neither Akkadian nor Amorite, but a north-western branch of Semites, speaking a distinctive dialect. It did not worship the Sumerian gods, but the characteristically West Semitic deities Dagon and Kamish. For all that, it was heavily penetrated by Sumerian culture. It borrowed Sumerian logograms so that, to write Eblaite, the scribe had to know Sumerian first. Indeed, as late as *c.*1800 the Eblaites were still teaching scribes Sumerian, and using word-lists and texts dating back to 3000, in order to write their own language.[2]

The boundaries of the state are not known,[3] but we can form a rough idea of how the territories outside the city walls were administered. The adjacent area was governed by an *ugula*, that is, a prefect, who was often a son of the king, but always a high dignitary.[4] Further afield the subjugated cities were placed in the hands of local dignitaries, who were accorded the title of the 'king'. Beyond these cities, again, lay a ring of client states or cities whose partial subordination was expressed by their payment of tribute.

It is the government of the city itself that merits attention, its striking features being its high monarchy, extensive bureaucracy, and meticulous municipal organization. Ebla was no small place: the population was large and the urban territory took up 140 acres.[5] Its ruler was styled *malikum*—king.[6] Whether the kingship was hereditary or not we do not know. A group of dignitaries, styled *abbu*, which means 'father' (cf. the Hebrew *abba*)

---

[2] P. Matthiae, *Ebla: An Empire Rediscovered* (Hodder & Stoughton, London, 1980), 220–2.
[3] Ibid. 182.   [4] Ibid. 185.
[5] C. Bermant and M. Weitzmann, *Ebla: An Archaeological Enigma* (Weidenfeld & Nicolson, 1979).
[6] Cf. the Hebrew, *Melech*.

co-operated with the king, wielding what one of the Italian epigraphists (Pettinato) calls 'numerous' powers.[7] The palace was the central and paramount ruling institution—very much so, in that it controlled a bureaucracy numbering 11,700 persons. The central administration in its 'Acropolis' was organized in sections of between 400 and 800 men, under thirteen court dignitaries. Other civil servants served in the city's four wards. Thus, the first ward was run by twenty superintendents and 100 subordinates; the fourth by twenty-one superintendents and fifty-one subordinates. These superintendents were grouped in colleges of five, and a number of such colleges came under the control of the court's superintendents, of whom there were two. Between them they respectively controlled all the superintendents of the first and second wards, and the third and fourth wards.

The apex of the administrative structure was the Acropolis which housed, not 'the palace' but *three* palaces. The first was the royal palace, with ten superintendents and sixty subordinates; the next was the Palace of the Elders with similar personnel. The third palace has proved difficult to interpret. Finally, the royal stables, separately organized, had its own superintendents and subordinate officials, also.[8]

Another great city that was able to conquer and hold great swathes of territory was the kingdom of Mari, on the Euphrates. Its wealth derived from its strategic position across the great riverine trade route of the Euphrates from the Persian Gulf to the 'High Country' of Amanus and the foothills of timber- and metal-rich Anatolia. It too was a very old foundation—no less then six temples lie one over the other, in the period between c.2700–2300. Though the rulers and the population have Semitic names, and worshipped Dagon (among other gods), they also worshipped Sumerian gods, for here—in contrast to Ebla—Sumerian influence in art, religion, and general culture was paramount. The city rose to a brief greatness, c.1800–1761, at which latter date it fell to its erstwhile ally, King Hammurabi of Babylon. Here again the palace was the nerve-centre of government, and the palace of Mari's greatest and last king, Zimri-Lim, was—with its six-acre site and its more than 260 chambers, corridors, and courtyards—the admiration of all the king's contemporaries. Under one of its kings, c.1800, it actually stretched to the Mediterranean coast and the high country of the cedar forests.[9] It was ruled despotically and with an ungentle hand. It was in his palace that the king both sat in judgement and watched his officials counting out their tax-collections, particularly when this was in gold specie. Hardly anything was too much for him, whether he

---

[7] Bermant and Weitzmann, *Ebla*, 155.   [8] Matthiae, *Ebla*, 182–4.
[9] A. Parrot, *Mari-capitale fabuleuse* (Payot, Paris, 1974), 182–5.

was conducting high diplomacy or having a canal dredged or sending a
doctor or a mason where one was urgently required. Subjects were pressed
into military service, and a protester might well be decapitated *pour encourager
les autres*.[10] Mari was a loose, gangling state, exposed on all sides to the
ravages of fierce bedouin, the rancour of subject cities, and the rapacity of its
great neighbours. Once the city had been sacked by Hammurabi it simply
disintegrated.[11]

Apart from such relatively short-lived kingdoms like Mari, Ebla, and
successor states such as Yamhad, Qatna, and Kadesh, Syria and Canaan were
studded with city-states proper: Byblos (Gebal) the ancient trading city, on
the Mediterranean coast, and Hazor, Megiddo, Jerusalem, and the like in
Canaan. Often—as at Jerusalem—the state was no more than a tiny city
perched on a crag, ruled by its king in independence from similar cities.
Such a king had wide power: he appointed military leaders, conscripted, and
imposed corvées on his subjects; taxed them by means of tithes and caravan-
dues; and generally assumed full charge of all military, economic, and—
importantly—religious and cult matters.

My intention in these brief notes was first of all to demonstrate how
statehood had become characteristic of political life in the great interstitial
area between the Mesopotamian and the Nile river valleys; secondly to
illustrate how various were the patterns of government they might evolve.
But there is also a third purpose. At this stage, *c.*2000–1700, we must
imagine these nascent states, subject as always to the perennial raiding
and squatting of desert nomads or highlanders, being also under mortal
threat from great swarmings of fierce warrior peoples with their own
barbaric cultures: folk like the Semitic Amorites who finally imposed their
rule on all Syria-Canaan and Mesopotamia, and the Hurrians who met the
eastward thrust of these Amorites with a westerly counterthrust of their
own; and later the Hittites, coming south from their Anatolian homeland;
and later still, *c.*1300–1200, the great wave of the Sea Peoples that dashed on
the Mediterranean coasts of Egypt and the Levant and totally destroyed the
Hittite Empire. In conditions that were at times so turbulent, it is unsurprising that the new states could not hold their frontiers long enough to
evolve from mere agglomerated kingdoms into something like a national
state—a state which had its distinctive 'political community' and not simply
a miscellany of subjects. Something analogous happened in Western Europe
between the fifth and the tenth centuries AD.

Nevertheless, from *c.*1700, after the shock of the Amorite invasions and

[10] Parrot, *Mari-capitale fabuleuse* 162.
[11] See e.g. S. M. Dalley, *Mari and Karana: Two Old Babylonian Cities* (Longman, London, 1984).

with the recovery of Egypt after the sixteenth century BC, some larger states consolidated themselves for long enough to constitute, for the first time in history, an international state system. Babylon, Assyria, Mitanni, the Hittites, the city 'alliances' of Syria-Canaan, and Egypt formed the chief elements in this system. From this point, then, we can briefly follow the chronology of the long period 1800–650.

1.1. *The Rise of Babylon, the Eclipse of Egypt—c.2000–1500 BC*

By *c.*1900–1800 Amorite dynasties were ruling from the waist of the Euphrates–Tigris 'hourglass' as far north as Assur. Other Amorites had overrun Syria and Canaan, destroying the flourishing cities, and turning the lands into little more than sheep-runs. Out of this chaos came the renascence of Ebla and Mari, as we have seen, while in Mesopotamia proper the town of Babylon, which had only begun to acquire importance *c.*1900, came into the hands of an Amorite dynasty. In 1792, under Hammurabi, the Babylonians subjugated southern Mesopotamia and then turned northwards, destroying Mari's empire and ruling from the Gulf to the Mediterranean.

The new empire was short-lived. From east and north new peoples, led perhaps by Indo-European warriors who somehow had imposed themselves as rulers, began to form new states. So was established the powerful, albeit inchoate, kingdom of Mitanni. Likewise, it is *c.*1740 that the Kassites make their first appearance in the Zagros mountains. Meanwhile, *c.*1800, war-bands of the Indo-European Hittites entered Anatolia and established their rule over the indigenous Hatti people. In 1750 their king Anitta conquered the city of Hattusas, in central-north Anatolia, and laid the foundations of a 500-year-long empire. We are now in the full age of horses, chariots, bronze weaponry, the composite bow. It was about this time, *c.*1720, that semitic war-bands called the Hyksos, also equipped in this way, entered the Nile Delta and established themselves. Now the Hittites began to threaten Mesopotamia. In 1620 a Hittite king, Mursilis I, took the capital of one of the Ebla successor states and later raided and sacked Babylon itself before withdrawing. In its weakened state Babylon was incapable of withstanding the encroachment of Kassite (Indo-European) war-bands. It succumbed in *c.*1570. Thenceforth, for some 500 years, that city led a not-unprosperous but an unaggressive life as a Kassite dependency.[12]

Around the time when Hammurabi was ascending the Babylonian throne and he and his heirs were pursuing their expansionist careers, Egypt fell into

---

[12] O. R. Gurney, *The Hittites* (Penguin, Harmondsworth, 1990).

decline and finally, c.1650, broke apart. Hyksos rulers dominated the Delta while Egyptian princes ruled Upper Egypt from Thebes. Then, just when the Hittites and the Kassites were ruining Babylon, these same Theban princes began their running battle to expel the Hyksos. In about 1520 one— Ahmose—finally succeeded. He founded the XVIIIth dynasty which, advancing south to Nubia and northwards into Syria itself, founded an Egyptian empire.

While Egypt broke down and revived stronger than ever; while Babylon moved into quietude; and while the Indo-European states of Mitanni and the Hittites began to spar for supremacy in the north of the Fertile Crescent; far away, more Indo-European war-bands in their war-chariots were slowly moving southwards from the Danube into Greece. By the time the Kassites took Babylon these people had entered the mainland and were establishing the Palace-type kingdoms we call Mycenaean. These would soon threaten the fabulous but undefended palace-states of Crete, which were now entering their high period.

2. THE INTER-STATE EQUILIBRIUM AND ITS COLLAPSE, c.1500–1200 BC

Around 1500 three greater states were in contention: they were Egypt, the Hittite Empire, and the kingdom of Mitanni. Later they were joined by the kingdoms of Assyria and Babylonia.

The Mitanni kingdom, comprising a Hurrian population and perhaps an Indo-European ruling structure, was located in the northern Jezireh, with its centre on the Khabur River. Its capital has not been discovered. Indigenous sources are almost non-existent. It is thought—but not at all clearly established—that, amongst other gods, their ruling stratum worshipped some of the same deities as the Indo-Aryans who had invaded and conquered north India, that they were a horse-culture, that they were masters of the war-chariot, and that, characteristically of the Indo-Aryans, their war-charioteers constituted a warrior aristocracy, called the Maryannu. They were obviously formidable fighters. As they conquered west of the Euphrates they came into armed conflict with the armies of Egypt which, reunified under the XVIIIth dynasty, took the war to Asia up to the Euphrates. From around 1580 the two powers fought inconclusively across that river.

The turning-point came around 1380. Following several dynastic murders, the power of Mitanni began to weaken. Assyria, though a vassal-state, began to interfere in its internal affairs. Around 1350 the new Hittite king,

Shuppiluliama, taking advantage of Egypt's paralysis, annexed Lebanon and then defeated Mitanni. That state simply disappeared from history.

While the Hittite king annexed all Syria up to the Euphrates, Assyria annexed all the Mitannian lands east of that river, so that the state system now comprised the three major powers of Egypt, the Hittite Empire, and Assyria. The latter was more interested in Kassite-ruled Babylon to its south, than Syria and Lebanon to the west, and it left these to the Hittites. Indeed, in 1249 the Assyrians temporarily captured Babylon and were engaged in hostilities against it thereafter.

This left only two powers in play—the rampaging Hittite Empire, masters of Syria, and the Kingdom of Egypt which, under its XIXth dynasty founded by Ramses I around 1290, shook off the last effects of Amenophis IV's (Akhnaton's) effete reign and resolved to reconquer Syria-Canaan. This brought the two powers into direct conflict. Seti I, in c.1290, confronted the Hittites at Kadesh but did not give battle. This was left to Ramses II, who has left us a vivid and detailed account of his great battle at Kadesh (1275). By his reckoning this was a brilliant and decisive victory. It was nothing of the kind, and it ended in stalemate. Both sides recognized this, and they effectively partitioned Syria-Canaan when they signed a peace treaty in 1259.

We must now, abruptly, shift the scene. So far our concern has been with land-powers to the east of an Alexandria–Istanbul line. Now attention shifts to sea-powers to the west of this line: at this point to mainland Greece, the Aegean, the coast of Asia Minor, and to Crete. All these were in the full era of bronze weapons and (Crete excepted) of war-chariotry. In mainland Greece, by 1530, Greek-speaking chiefs ruled plainsmen from their castles, in 'Mycenae rich in Gold', Tiryns, and the Argolid. Mycenaean civilization was at its height. So too were the palace-states in Crete. But in 1400, for reasons which we cannot fathom, the great Cretan capital of Knossos was sacked and destroyed. A Cretan civilization survived, but as we now know from the decipherment of the Cretan 'Linear B' script, it was ruled by the Mycenaean Greeks.

Then—suddenly—around the year 1200—a vast turbulence engulfed all the settled states of the Middle East. According to Egyptian accounts it was a great swarming of fierce seafaring peoples bearing outlandish names. Most modern scholars prefer to regard these 'Sea Peoples' as only a part of the great migrations; locating the homes of many, perhaps most, of the raiders in western Anatolia. However, that may be, the results were dramatic. Egypt, under Ramses III of the XXth dynasty, beat off a land-and-sea invasion around 1177, but this was Egypt's almost last gasp, and after his death, 1166, the dynasty went into decline. The Hittite Empire, too, collapsed under the Sea-Peoples' attacks. After 1190 its king-list terminates. In Syria the great cities of Ugarit and Alalakh were destroyed. Whether connected or not with these movements, a similar destruction occurred in Greece. The year 1200 is the one traditionally given for the 'descent of the Dorians'—a new wave of Greek war-bands who fought their way down the peninsula and destroyed the Mycenaean palace-states, so ushering in a Dark Age destined to endure for over 200 years.

Only one of the ancient powers remained intact: Assyria. The period 1200–650 is one of Assyrian (and later neo-Babylonian) domination of the Middle East; while almost unnoticed, on its flanks both to east and to west, built up an Indo-European presence that was eventually to put the eastern Mediterranean and the Fertile Crescent under new management.

3

The Egyptian Polity at Zenith:
The New Kingdom

I. INTRODUCTION: THE NEW KINGDOM

*T*he 'high' period of Egyptian government and administration really lasted 1520–*c*.1150 BC (the middle of the XXth dynasty). It was the era of the 'empire', the period when it had conquered Nubia in the south, exerted hegemony over and planted colonies in Syria-Palestine, and was engaged in full diplomatic intercourse with such powers as the Hittites, the Mitanni, and the Assyrians. For virtually all these 370 years the country was governed stably and well. There were only two brief intervals of indecision and dynastic confusion: in the aftermath of Akhnaton's Amarna experiment (1335–1315) and in the late XIXth dynasty (1204–1190). For any comparison we must turn to China, where the Han Empire lasted some four centuries with only a brief interval of usurpation and civil war between AD 9 and 23. Neither Persia nor Rome nor Byzantium could show such stability over so long a period.

After the Hyksos seized Memphis in *c*.1630 Egypt had fallen apart. The Hyksos ruled as suzerains over a number of principalities in the Delta, while in the Sudan beyond the third cataract lay the partially Egyptianized Kerma state which enjoyed its heyday in the Second Intermediate Period (i.e. 1640–1520). At Thebes, however, a line of Egyptian princes ruled Upper and most of Middle Egypt. For a long time in coexistence with the Hyksos north, these kings, having consolidated a tightly centralized riverine kingdom and equipped themselves Hyksos-fashion with chariots and advanced weaponry, defeated the Hyksos, drove them right out of Egypt, then turned south to crush the Kerma state. Thus they restored the unity of the whole Nile Valley and Delta, and more besides, for they now held Lower Nubia.

It was a *reconquista*. A 'new model' Egyptian army led by a novel kind of Egyptian king, to wit, a warrior who led his troops in person, had taken over Egypt by force of arms. The effects were far-reaching, although the framework was essentially the same as the Old and Middle Kingdoms, that is, a Palace-type government resting on an extensive bureaucracy in symbiosis with an all-pervading religion. But the kings' military occupation of the country created new emphases.

2. THE CENTRAL AUTHORITIES

2.1. *Kingship and the Gods*

The formula of the god-king[1] was reinvigorated, but with changes of emphasis. For one thing, Amon, who up to the XIIth dynasty had been an obscure local Theban deity, was now seen as the divine vindicator of Egyptian independence from the hated Asiatics. His priests at Thebes had long associated him with the ancient sun god, Ra, so that he was worshipped as Amon-Ra. A Theban cosmogony was evolved: Amon-Ra was the king of all the gods and the invisible omnipotent creator of gods and men. All other gods were but various forms of Amon-Ra, who could take their shapes at will. In time his high priests came to claim jurisdiction over 'all the gods', and his birthplace at Thebes was represented as the origin of the universe.[2] Throughout the New Kingdom the kings devoted the greater part of their treasures to Amon's priesthood, and this was to have a profound political effect in the 1100s.

The most common way the pharaohs expressed their divine nature now was in relation to Amon-Ra. So that for the most part (though not always) hymns, invocations, and inscriptions as well as visual art present the king in the son-to-father relationship, the latter being the 'great god' to the former's 'perfect god', the former imploring intercession and the latter working wonders in response.[3]

The connection between this and the realities of the succession was most characteristically made by the notion of a theogony: the god, Amon-Ra, has physically entered the favoured queen in the guise of her physical husband. Queen Hatshepsut (who was the aunt of Thutmose III) took the throne in his place as ruler and justified herself thus:

Amon took his form as the majesty of her [i.e. Queen Ahmose's] husband, the king [Thutmose I] . . . then he went to her immediately. Then he had intercourse with her . . . the words which Amon, Lord of the Thrones of the Two Lands, spoke in her presence 'Now Khenemet-Amon-Hatshepsut is the name of this my daughter whom I have placed in thy body . . . she is to exercise this beneficent kingship in this entire land . . .'[4]

---

[1] See p. 142 ff. above. [2] Cf. *ANET*, pp. 8, 365–7.
[3] Lichtheim, *Ancient Egyptian Literature*, ii. 35–8. [4] Quoted Frankfort, *Kingship*, 45.

On the whole such explanations were not violently contradicted by facts because the succession in both the XVIIIth and XIXth dynasties was, mostly, regular. But when any doubt arose it was easily brushed aside by virtue of a simple affirmation that the usurper was, in point of fact, of divine origin. Who could disprove this? How? In just this way the formula proved at least its social usefulness, by moralizing the seizure of power and legitimizing the subsequent dynasty. It also powerfully reinforced the royal absolutism. The proof of this is in the ability of the aberrant pharaoh, Ahmenhotep IV (Akhnaton) to enforce entirely by his royal authority a total subversion of the cult of Amon and all the lesser gods of Egypt. This could hardly have been welcome to his court: at the very least, courtiers must have been acutely worried at having to be buried away from their ancestral tombs in the new religious-administrative residence city at El-Amarna. 'Akhnaton and his family worshipped the Aton and everybody else worshipped Akhnaton as a god . . . he asserted he was the physical son of the Aton.'[5] (This is precisely why this cult collapsed on his death, the el-Amarna courtiers having contact with the Aton only through their worship of Akhnaton.) At home Akhnaton's rule was effective, the army obedient. He was able to carry through his revolution which not only (as noted) troubled his courtiers' concern for their life in the afterworld, but demoralized the populace by cancelling the traditional festivals, and threw the property rights and economic administration of the temples into doubt and confusion. Yet he was able to do all this without resistance of any kind as far as our information goes, though he was residing in an unwalled city on an exposed site![6]

The pharaohs thanked the gods—and themselves *qua* gods—by the immense riches they conferred on them, particularly on the Theban priesthood of Amon, by the gigantic stone temples they reared at Karnak and Luxor, and by the immense funerary temples they reared for themselves like Deir el-Bahri, along with colossal statues of themselves as part of their mortuary cult.

2.2. Kingship in Practice: Constraints and Strengths

In a Palace-type political system where rule is exercised by an autocrat, where everybody, whether his officials or his people, looks to him to motivate and to control, the ruler's personal authority, energy, and talents can and do make or break the polity. In the New Kingdom the succession was more regular than at many previous times, and with only a few

---

[5] Wilson, *Culture of Ancient Egypt*, 45.   [6] Cf. Trigger *et al.*, *Ancient Egypt*, 219–22.

exceptions the monarchs of the XVIIIth, XIXth, and the first two kings of
the XXth dynasties seem to have been men of exceptional personal prowess,
energy, and ability. Hence its brilliant success, its prosperity, and—as far as
we can judge—its good management.

2.3. *The Palace and Court*

2.3.1. THE SUCCESSION

The general practice was for the succession to pass from father to the son
of the chief queen, and failing that, of a lesser queen. But this convention
was fortified when one or possibly more kings followed the precedent set in
the XIIth dynasty and made the succession of the heirs-apparent the more
certain by adopting them as co-regents for the later part of their reigns. The
co-regency device also served to bring in new blood from outside the
dynasty when this offered no clear choice of heir-apparent. The co-regency
formula could be linked with another device—the outsider married the
daughter of the chief queen, so perpetuating the dynasty through its female
side.

Not only were the individual kings of the XVIIIth and XIXth dynasties
of considerable ability, so were the outsiders who, grasping the throne in the
years of confusion, restored stability and efficiency. Horemheb was a tough
general who instantly embarked on a sweeping review of the court and
military establishments, and had the good sense, being without an heir, to
co-opt as ruler another general, Ramses I, as his successor. This initiated
the glorious XIXth dynasty. When this ended in the dynastic confusion of
1204–1190 BC, it was another vigorous outsider—of obscure origin (Seth-
nakhte)—who took the throne, restored the authority of the central government, and was able, in bequeathing the succession to his son, Ramses III, to
found the XXth dynasty. And finally, it is noteworthy that so many
pharaohs from outside the dynastic blood-line were generals. Thutmose I
was probably a general, Horemheb certainly was, and so was his close
successor Ramses I.

2.3.2 CONSTRAINTS UPON THE MONARCH?

The Court

The pharaohs were so personally dominant during this period that they
imposed themselves on their court, not the other way round. The Akhnaton
case which we have already cited is a convincing demonstration. Only the
key members of the direct line of the dynasty—the heir-apparent and the
great queen who often became god's wife of Amon in the temple of

Amon—held appointments; collateral lines had been excluded since the Vth dynasty.[7] The court was made up of a *service* aristocracy, directly dependent on the king. Its servility to him is vividly attested in the matter of portraiture. Akhnaton had 'an overgrown face, receding forehead, prominent collar-bones, pendular breasts and paunch, inflated thighs and spindle shanks':[8] his courtiers permitted themselves to be portrayed as sharing identical characteristics.[9]

Any weakness in the royal position arose when the king was a minor or his succession disputable. For instance, Thutmose III was only 10 years old when he succeeded, and the regency was assumed—as was quite normal—by the dowager queen (*not* by his mother, who was a secondary wife named Isis). This was Queen Hatshepsut. Now, a few years later Hatshepsut assumed the crown of Egypt as pharaoh in her own right (1475) and she held this office, keeping Thutmose III on the sidelines, for more than fifteen years. This has been interpreted[10] as the result of a conspiracy between the high priest of Amon, the chancellor, the viceroy of Nubia, the treasurer, and the chief stewards, led by the chief steward Senenmut, which was brought to an end ultimately by a military coup mounted by Thutmose III.[11] Others discount this completely.[12] Whether this account is true or not is not material here: it is plausible and arguable that palace factions could form and dominate royal policy. The end of the XVIIIth and the inception of the XIXth dynasties certainly attests it. Tutankhamon was only 9 years old at his accession. The reversal of Akhnaton's Aton worship and the court's return to Thebes which took place at this moment could, therefore, only have happened at the instance of the leading official, Ay.

Quite unequivocal testimony to the presence of court factions and their threat to a king is the well-documented harem conspiracy to murder Ramses III. This was not a matter of policy preferences however. It seems to have been a matter of the personal ambition of one of Ramses's secondary wives, Tiy by name, who wanted to put her own son on the throne. This kind of story will become almost boringly familiar in the course of this history: in Persia, Rome, China, Byzantium, the Caliphate, the Ottoman Empire,

[7] Ibid. 207.   [8] *CAH*, II.2, p. 55.
[9] It has been suggested to me that this signifies no more than a change of artistic style—analogous to Modigliani models all having long oval faces. Maybe. But in that case why did this abrupt change in style begin and end only with the reign of Akhnaton? And would it have been possible without the direct support, possibly command, of the sovereign? As for the Modigliani analogy: it is one thing for a modernist painter to paint in a peculiarly individual style in an age when the accepted canons of portraiture are being consciously attacked and impugned, and quite another to breach the artistic canons of the last 1,500 years.
[10] H. Helck, *Zur Verwaltung des mittleren und neues Reiches* (Leiden–Cologne, 1958).
[11] *CAH*, II.1, p. 318.   [12] Cf. Trigger et al., *Ancient Egypt*, 218–19.

indeed, whenever the gynecaeum or the seraglio flourished, there flourished the palace conspiracy. The case of Tiy is characteristic in that the conspirators were not policy-makers or officials, but the staff who administered the women's quarters. Two officers were also involved, but neither of very high rank.[13]

Soldiers and Priests

The most troublesome outside pressure on a king under the Old and Middle Kingdoms was, it will be recalled, that of the territorial élites and the nomarchs. Under the XXth dynasty offices began to become hereditary and thus a new class of territorial magnates began to emerge: only the scarcest traces of either nomarchs or territorial magnates appear in the XVIIIth and XIXth dynasties. Likewise, the viceroy of Kush, with plenipotentiary powers as a 'Lord-Marcher', never exploited this potentially powerful position against the monarchy until this had become effete in the reign of Ramses XI.

It is generally agreed that the army or its high commanders did not play an autonomous role in constraining or opposing the monarchy: if anything, the reverse is true. It was a prop to the monarchy. Civil disorder was insignificant and easily dealt with by the *Medjay* constabulary. The impression one receives is that the new, professional officer corps was in symbiosis with the military monarchy who so often led it in person. These kings, for their part, treated it as a most valuable reserve of trained administrators. In Egypt anything 'expeditionary', whether war or trading, was a military matter; so, not unnaturally, they were used for royal trading or quarrying expeditions. The king would choose officers for intimate posts in the palace: as honorary fan-bearers, tutors of the royal children, administrators of the royal domain.[14] When Horemheb, himself a general, acceded to the throne and began to purge the administration, he significantly re-established the priesthoods (i.e. the administrative priests) whom Akhnaton had made away with, by recruiting them from 'the pick of the army'.[15] And we have already seen how a number of pharaohs, in default of a legitimate heir, chose military men as successors.

The political role of the priesthood, however, is wholly controversial. It is common ground that vast endowments flowed to the temples, that the bulk of it went to the Amon 'establishment', and that the bulk of that fell under the control of Amon's high priest at Thebes. By c.1153, in Ramses IV's reign,

[13] *CAH*, II.2, pp. 246–7.
[14] *CAH*, II.1, p. 372. Of course it may be that despite their lowly titles, they were persons of considerable importance—this too was common in the patrimonial cadres of the palace polity.
[15] Horemheb's Coronation Inscription, quoted *CAH*, II.2, p. 76.

temples owned about one-third of the country's cultivable land and about one-fifth of its population.[16] In grain, Amon's portion was 62 per cent; in all other income 86 per cent.[17] Though temple construction and refurbishment was always a royal expense, the endowments for running-costs came from the temples' own resources, and they demanded prodigious attention. Administering fields, mines, quarries, ships, not to speak of entire villages and towns, required an army of skilled administrators. In the Middle Kingdom major local temples had used selected members of their own priestly body to administer their endowments, but not so now. In Thebes, for instance, the temple of Amon was organized by a general headquarters staff. There were separate specialized divisions for precious objects, for the fields, for the granaries, and for the cattle. Each division was headed by a director, with his own staff of scribes. There was also a division of works and buildings and another for the intimate sacred contents of the inmost *cella* of the god. All these went along, of course, with all manner of workmen and artists. The temple possessed its own police force and prison.[18] Often, too, the high priest was entrusted with other secular powers, for instance, command of the local troops.

Clearly, here was a corporation of immense political potential. Did this potential materialize? It certainly did so in the reigns of Ramses IX–XI, but the question here is whether it did so in the XVIIIth and XIXth dynasties. Now, if inquiry is made as to whom the pharaohs appointed to high priesthoods, they turn out to be their own courtiers, often holding key positions in the civil administration. Ptahmose, high priest of Amon, was also vizier to Amenhotep III. And Queen Hatshepsut appointed her chief steward of the royal domain to be the chief steward of Amon with control over all the separate divisions of the temple administration enumerated above.[19] 'A strong Pharaoh normally controlled the priesthood as completely and by essentially the same methods as he did his household or his army.'[20] What is more, such contemporary iconography as bears on this matter suggests anything but primacy to the high priest of Amon. Two New Kingdom depictions of officials in procession show them headed by the crown prince, followed by the viziers, stewards of the domain and the palace, high-ranking civil and military officers, and—only then—important high priests (in turn followed, in one instance by a provincial officer, in the

[16] Trigger et al., *Ancient Egypt*, 202. And for land tenure generally, under the Ramessides, cf. S. L. D. Katary, *Land Tenure in the Ramesside Period* (Kegan Paul Int., London, 1989).

[17] Wilson, *Culture of Ancient Egypt*, 270.

[18] Erman and Rank, *Civilisation égyptienne*, 383–4.   [19] *CAH*, II.1, pp. 325–6.

[20] W. F. Edgerton, 'The Government and the Governed in the Egyptian Empire', *Journal of Near Eastern Studies*, 6:3 (1947), 152–60; quoted *CAH*, II.1, p. 328.

other by lesser clergy).[21] Again, though the concentration of economic power in the temples was immense, the prevalent opinion is that it was taxed. All in all there is no reason to dissent from the judgement that the administration of the religious establishments was 'essentially part of the civil government', and that 'the collection and control of [their] income appear to have been, at least partially, subject to the civil government'.[22] And if it still be doubted that the priesthood was subservient to the pharaoh at the time the monarchy was still in its heyday, how can it be explained that while Akhnaton was alive and carrying on his vendetta against the old gods, not a dog barked for Amon? From one end of the land to another those gods (and hence their priests) were deposed; there is scarcely a trace of resistance.

2.3.3. THE STRENGTH OF THE MONARCH

The royal absolutism then, unchecked as it was by any extraneous counter-forces, was free to exert all its inherent powers. The first of these was the *mystique* of divinity. Imagine the awe surrounding a monarch, reputedly with the powers of a god and crowned with the awesome fire-spitting Uraeus. His face was immobile, framed in the ceremonial black wig. He was wearing the ceremonial beard. His breast was adorned by a gold and lapis pectoral and in his crossed arms he carried the sceptre of Egypt and the flail. The king sat motionless on the throne, distanced from his most intimate courtiers. Or, if he travelled, he rode in a chariot, in glittering display amidst his fan-bearers and his richly caparisoned bodyguard. Furthermore, this mystique, this great symbolic pomp, was no longer mocked by the practical ineffectuality of transient puppets, as in the XIIth dynasty. It was fortified, indeed justified, by the godlike actions of hero-kings. Thirdly, and here they differed from most of their predecessors, they were the commanders-in-chief of a professional army whose officers were honoured by all manner of civil appointments, who not infrequently shared battle with the king and who, all evidence attests, were devoted to his person.

But finally, these pharaohs were rich—oh, so rich! It was a long tradition in Egypt that all trade, all tribute, and all booty had to pass first to the pharaoh. But never in its long history had booty flowed in on such a scale. This was the outcome of empire, for the pharaohs had learned what Joubert in the eighteenth century was to formulate as 'making the war feed on itself'.[23] They had discovered the 'coercion–extraction cycle', which sig-

---

[21] *CAH*, II.1, pp. 361–2. But we ought not discount the possibility that this procession followed a traditional *notitia dignitatum*, concealing the true power relationships.

[22] Trigger *et al.*, *Ancient Egypt*, 202.

[23] Barthelemy-Catherine Joubert, 1769–99, being a French general of period renown.

nifies simply that with an army you can extract manpower, material, and resources from the population to maintain the army which. . . and so on and so on. The New Kingdom pharaohs used the army to reinforce the collection of taxes at home, but they were also using it to take booty and tribute from foreigners.

But still more wealth derived from something new, the conquest of Nubia up beyond the fourth cataract. There, to the east of the Nile, lay the gold-bearing deposits of the ancient land of Wawat.[24] For those days, the amount of gold mined or washed was enormous. In the later years of Thutmose III it averaged 10,000 ounces each year from Nubia and Sudan (Kush) alone.[25] The income from this area was almost five times greater than from the ancient workings at Koptos, in the Old Kingdom.[26] An Assyrian monarch, soliciting gifts from pharaoh, reminds him that 'gold is accounted as dust in Egypt'.[27] Furthermore, because the Theban XVIIIth dynasty had come to power by a literal *reconquista*, it had acquired the lands of most if not all of the previous territorial magnates. Thus the king possessed a quite enormous personal domain—separately administered by a specialized branch of the administration—in addition to the bullion. And he used part of this to pay for extravagant rock-cut tombs and funerary temples in the Thebes–Luxor–Karnak area and for the vast colossi and temples erected there as well as for the proliferation of new shrines for Amon. Part of it went to further Egyptian diplomacy in the Levant, in the face of Mitanni, the Hittites, and the Mesopotamian powers in that region. But—and this is the point here—he used part of it to cement the loyalty of his chief soldiers and officials. Ordinary soldiers and lower officials were paid in rations, and senior officers and officials received the revenue of lands assigned to them. But the pharaoh would honour and flatter and also enrich them by making them gifts of the precious metals. This kind of gift—which was at the same time an honorific distinction—was called 'the gold'.[28]

'The gold of honour' and 'of favour' was conferred on soldiers for valour in the field, or on especially meritorious high officials. It was conferred publicly. It brought enormous esteem to the recipient, but it was also extremely valuable. 'The gold' that several kings conferred on the officer and treasurer Ahmose consisted of numerous golden bracelets, neck-clasps, lapis ointment-vases, and silver arm-clasps.[29] The personal bestowal of gifts links sovereign to subject by a powerful emotional bond. In the New Kingdom, however, this gift relationship was carried further in that it was

---

[24] Trigger *et al.*, *Ancient Egypt*, 253–66.   [25] See *CAH*, II.1. pp. 350–2.
[26] Ibid.; *contra*, J. J. Janssen, *Commodity Prices from the Ramessid Period* (Brill, Leiden, 1975). He thinks the Koptos mines were much the richer.   [27] *CAH*, II.2, p. 24
[28] Erman and Rank, *Civilisation égyptienne*, 156 ff.   [29] Ibid.

reciprocal. An old custom in Egypt decreed that each New Year's Day 'the House should give gifts to its lord', and Erman cites the New Year present given to Amenhotep II by a high (and very wealthy) official. It consisted of hundreds of shields, bronze daggers, swords, whip-handles, and coats of mail, numerous vases in the precious metals, carved ivory ornaments, and a centre-piece for the banqueting table wrought all in silver and gold.[30]

The Egyptian monarch ruled perhaps as many as about 4.5 million Egyptians, and we might estimate the population bearing tribute to him in the Levant and in Nubia–Kush at perhaps another million. He was the personal leader of a tightly centralized bureaucratic regime; and if we consider the XVIIIth dynasty—at least up to the accession of Amenhotep IV—it would be hard to find any absolutism more completely in command, more *ab legibus solutus*, in the history of government.

3. THE ADMINISTRATION OF THE NEW KINGDOM

3.1. *The Territorial Framework*

The central–local relationship was totally different from that prevailing from the Vth dynasty onwards. The 'Chinese Box' principle was abandoned. No longer did the central government work to a provincial plenipotentiary governor—except for the 'colony' of Nubia–Kush in the far south and extending northwards to just short of Thebes. Egypt proper was adminis-tered by two viziers at Memphis and Thebes, respectively in charge of Lower and Upper Egypt. Each vizier worked directly to the authorities in the cities, towns, and villages, namely, the mayors in these places, and the largely judicial *qenbet* councils. These mayors were responsible for carrying out what the government told them to do; for assisting any government official in their area; and for the rest, collecting and delivering the taxes which, bear in mind, were in kind—geese, oxen, grain, papyrus, baskets, and whatever.

The New Kingdom arrangement, compared with the pre-Hyksos ones, meant in effect *more* local officials with smaller districts and very restricted power which was, effectively, not over tax collection alone, but also, one surmises, over settling local disputes. Furthermore, since 'mayors' were responsible only for the tax collection, other services such as assessments, public order, and the like must have been carried out by central agents stationed in the localities, and scattered references in the inscriptions and papyri bear out this inference. We learn of a village of some 1,500 persons where the surveyors and assessors to the number of ten men were billeted

---

[30] Erman and Rank, *Civilisation égyptienne*, 156 ff.

all the year round. The police or *medjay* who came under the control of the central government's 'chief of *medjay* were organized into companies each under its captain in the chief towns.

The *qenbet* councils were mostly concerned with civil actions, principally over property, and the prosecution of lesser criminal offences. (Matters entailing a death penalty were for the king, but almost certainly handled by the vizier.) Their members were nominated by the government. All were personages of high local status, what in other polities are called 'notables' (Arab states), or 'gentry' (China). The *qenbet* pattern was replicated even in small communities, where of course the mayors would be quite lowly in national terms but 'bigwigs' in their own locality.

The great exception to this pattern of central–local relations was the province and colony of Nubia–Kush. This gold-rich area was, from the beginning, entrusted to a 'prince' (so-called, for he was not a prince of the blood) that is, a *viceroy* with plenipotentiary powers. His chief duties were to collect and deliver the taxes and tribute, to exploit the gold-mines, and to oversee agriculture and the civil government. In principle, the 'battalion-commander of Kush' commanded the army, but in practice the viceroy could assume supreme command whenever he thought fit. He was sufficiently important to bear the honorary title of 'king's son'.

3.2. *The Central Administration*

The royal palace comprised two areas; the pharaoh's own private apartments, housed in a separate building or group of buildings, and the quite separate administration area, where the vizier, treasurer, and others and their staff had their offices. To this topographical distinction corresponded a distinction in the senior officialdom, between the strictly palatine or household officers, and the bureaucracy proper (this pattern is repeated endlessly in most palace-polities; very rare are the cases when it was not). The significance of the topographical and functional distinction (to be strikingly illustrated in China) consists in the importance of access to the ruler. The household officers have more frequent and intimate access than the routine bureaucrats. Hence, they have a greater capacity for influencing the ruler's policy.

There are traces of collisions between the two groups in the New Kingdom, and it is highly probable there would be much more evidence than this if our records of the Egyptian court were as rich as the Han-Shou and Hou-Han-Shou are for the Han Empire. In fact, we know almost nothing about court factions in Egypt. For all that, however, we are pretty safe in affirming that on the whole the collisions were infrequent and not over major policy issues. This was due, first, to the overwhelming personal authority of so many of the pharaohs, and next to the fact that the top echelon of the bureaucracy was just as patrimonial as the royal households.

Let us start with the last. Access to the bureaucracy and the household officers was in principle open to those with ability and dedication regardless of birth, and some biographical mortuary inscriptions of important officials describe how lowly were their origins before the pharaoh promoted them. In practice, however, ability—and proof of dedication—reflected, as they do in the 'merit' systems of modern industrial societies, the pre-existing access to education which in turn reflects social stratification. Few, if any, of the subjected peasant labourers would ever have had such access; it would have been somewhat more open to the tiny class of wealthier peasant farmers, more so still among the professional soldiers or the skilled artisans, but for the most part it would have been confined to the children of the scribes, already literate and part of the bureaucracy. The widest access of all lay with the families of well-established officials and military officers. Thus, along with the funeral inscriptions of self-made men, we find many more of members of great official families. For instance, in the reign of Hatshepsut and Thutmose III, the viziership of Upper Egypt passed through three generations of the family of one Ahmose (also called Amotju).[31] This was also true of the household officers. Thus a general, Urhiya, became Ramses II's high steward. His son Yupa attained the same office half a century later, and Yupa's son became the (national) head of the police.[32]

A factor that mitigated collisions between the 'career service' and the household service was the frequent interchange between the two—underlining the overwhelmingly patrimonial nature of the bureaucracy. Paser, a son of the high priest of Amon, became a chamberlain in the household, then the vizier of Upper Egypt, until in his old age the king appointed him high priest of Amon.[33] His successor in the viziership, Khay, had also begun his career in the royal household. For all that, collisions occurred. On some occasion the friction between chief steward and vizier was so great that the pharaoh had to dismiss the former from office.[34]

The chief steward was more likely than other members of the household to clash with the bureaucracy because his office administered the vast

---

[31] *CAH*, II.1, p. 353.

[32] K. A. Kitchen, *Pharaoh Triumphant: The Life and Times of Ramesses II* (Aris & Phillips, Warminster, 1982), 139.   [33] Kitchen, *Pharaoh Triumphant*, 28, 36, 125–6.

[34] *CAH*, II.1, p. 360. Chief stewards tended to be the personal choices of monarchs and, usually their intimates—which makes sense, seeing that they controlled the household. The same phenomenon is found in the Caliphate—and, equally, the same collision between chamberlain and vizier. See Bk. III, Ch. 2, below.

personal domain of the pharaoh. His powers so increased that in the XXth dynasty he took over from the chancellor the supervision of the pharaoh's personal treasury and the palace storehouses. The chancellor was left with only the supervision of the royal harems which had to pay their own way as extensive factories for weaving cloth and milling flour.[35] (There were at least four such in Thebes, Memphis, and the Fayum, as well as an itinerant one. They were extensively used: Ramses II left 100 children). The court chamberlain was the general manager of the king's living quarters and his kitchen, wine-cellars, and the like. His extensive staff included the scribe of the table and the cupbearers. And there were numerous lesser officers such as private secretaries, spokesmen, attendants, fan-bearers, and so forth.

On the 'bureaucratic' side, the chief official remained as in the Middle Kingdom the *tjaty*, the vizier or, as we saw, a plural viziership. The vizier was responsible for *everything*. The official inscriptions record his working day.[36] He began it by reporting to the pharaoh and receiving any instructions, and then, on his way out, discussed matters with the household officer, the chancellor. He then proceeded to the administrative quarters and so to his own Hall of the Vizier. There he went through the reports of the local administrators, issued instructions to the various branches of the central government, confirmed or rescinded appointments, and took receipt of taxes. But his duties by no means stopped there. He was responsible for sealing and filing state documents, receiving foreign embassies and their tribute, and supervising the extensive[37] administration of the temple of Amon. Sometimes he took charge of launching quarry expeditions or of building operations. He levied troops and arranged for their inspection, supervised irrigation projects, and organized royal transport.[38] And, in addition to all such administrative duties, he was also the chief justice and regularly held his court in the capital (see below).

A great many of these administrative duties were formal or supervisory, to judge by the number of specialized departments below his office. The *Treasury*, with two overseers, handled the huge inflow of goods delivered as foreign tribute or domestic taxes, or made in government factories. The *Granary* supervised by an overseer for the entire country, controlled harvesting and recording and storing the cereal crops. Likewise, the state-wide *Cattle Bureau* supervised the local mayors in the administration of the state herds, and the accountants of cattle who took the annual census. The crucial task of measuring and assessing fields for tax purposes lay in the

[35] *CAH*, II.i, p. 360.
[36] Cf. C. P. F. van den Boorn, *The Duties of the Vizier: Civil Administration in the Early New Kingdom* (Kegan Paul Int., London, 1988).   [37] See p. 159 above.
[38] *CAH*, II.i, pp. 355–6.

hands of the scribe of the fields. There was an *Armed Forces* department for equipping and manning the army and navy. But building and architecture was not centrally organized. It fell within the tasks of the appropriate departments.[39] Finally, as we have noticed already, the administration of temple lands must be regarded as a branch of the civil administration.

This is what the written records tell us and there is no reason to dispute them. What they do not tell us is how well the departments interrelated with one another, the effectiveness of their working methods, their mentality. But even the written records show that the apparent symmetry outlined above was a sham and that what really existed was organized incoherence. To take the (central) example of royal expenditure: this arrived from three sources. The first was the immense royal domains. Second came those many individual institutions, usually temples, which the monarchy had licensed to collect taxes: they raised their own revenues by their own methods. The third was the general taxation on land and cattle and the lesser items already mentioned; and here, the point has been made, each district raised the resources in its own individual way. As if this were not enough, departments did not merely not co-operate but regarded others as potential stores of wealth to be raided and looted to make up for their own deficits. Consequently each department or institution defended itself by royal decrees that protected its revenues from seizure by officials of another department. There was no administrative 'code'; only a pile of separate royal decrees, issued *ad hoc* to endow some institutions and/or protect them from raids by their predatory fellow-administrators elsewhere.[40]

As to how efficiently the elaborate regime performed, we shall provide our own verdict later; but the tidiness, the apparent completeness, is illusory. Like almost all administrations in the distant past, Egyptian government was muddled, inefficient, and chaotic.

4. THE MAIN SERVICES

4.1. *Taxation*

Taxes were laid on almost everything and no person or institution was exempt unless by special royal decree—not even the temples, though it used to be thought they were. Taxes were laid on flax, wine, honey, textiles, incense, hides, eggs, fruits and vegetables, timber and metals. There were

---

[39] *CAH*, II.1, 359–60.
[40] Kemp, *Ancient Egypt*, 236. Similar raids were a feature of the 'command economy' of the USSR. A factory or a trust would pillage others in order to fulfil its part of the 'plan'.

also heavy custom dues on goods imported by non-governmental agencies (which must have been very few indeed).

The main taxes, however, were on land and cattle. The census of farm animals was as old as Egyptian history itself. The celebrated Palermo Stone (the annals of the first five dynasties between *c*.3000 and 2350 BC) records the cattle-count that took place every two years. Now it took place annually. The staff of the overseer of cattle counted the beasts, and a tax was levied on the year-on-year increase of each herd, and also on any draught animals from the state herds which had been hired by private farmers or institutions. Where animals were alleged to have died between each census, the branded hide had to be produced as evidence.

The harvest tax was mostly paid in produce. The standard rate was ten bushels per *aroura* (two-thirds of an acre), but was, quite subtly, adjusted for area and also productivity. The fields were surveyed every year to keep track of the boundaries, which often became effaced during the inundation, and to note any changes in condition. The great Wilbour Papyrus (XXth dynasty) has survived as part of the official measurement and assessment of a ninety-mile stretch of fields near the present el-Minya. Each field's location and measurements are noted, it is classified according to ownership, and the assessment is presented in two categories according to whether the owners or the cultivators were liable.[41]

Taxes were principally paid in kind, and this must have made the collection and the accountancy a jungle of administrative complexity. The following 'Record of the Report of the Deputy Amenemwiya' is the tax payment due from one Amenemwiya to the temple of Thoth (from Erman and Rank, *Civilisation égyptienne*).

To inform the officials of the things which were exacted from me between Year 31 and Year 3, making 4 years, by the hand of the messenger Sethmose of the temple of Khonsu:

skins, undressed	4	amounting to 8 *deben* of copper
skin, made into a corselet	1	amounting to 5 *deben* of copper
knobbed staff(?) of '*awn*-wood		
worked with '*aqu*	1	amounting to 4 *deben* of copper
staff of '*awn*-wood	1	amounting to 1 *deben* of copper
tunic of plain cloth	1	
shawl of plain cloth	1	
hoe	1	amounting to 2 *deben* of copper
barley	2 $\frac{5}{8}$ sacks	

---

[41] Gardiner, *Egypt*, 296–7.

emmer flour	$\frac{1}{4}$ sack	
shawl of plain cloth	1	by the hand of the servant Tjaroy
shawl of plain cloth	1	and one *sema*, ditto
Year	4:	ditto
tunic of plain cloth	3	
copper, *deben*	3	

And I was told to hand them over despite the fact that loaves are not being issued to the temple in which I am and rations are not being given, and I am not being given offerings (reverting from the cult).

When one reflects on the immense number of transactions, in miscellaneous items ranging from rolls of papyrus or hoes to sacks of grain or baskets of fruit and jars of honey, which were entailed in measuring, assessing, enumerating, collecting, moving, checking, and receipting in and storing; and further reflects that these items had to be checked out again to craftsmen, labourers, soldiers, scribes, sailors, and so forth, so entailing these innumerable separate activities all over again, but in reverse order; when one reflects on this, the parallel that must spring to mind can be only that of the Soviet economy in the 'war communism' period before national bank credits and accountancy brought some relief to the system, except that the Egyptian government did not yet set production targets for the economy (which was to come, in Ptolemaic times). New Kingdom Egypt was an almost wholly controlled economy, for, apart from agriculture, all significant international trade was a government monopoly, like manufacture and monumental building. Furthermore, even if cultivators were not set targets, they *were* compelled to cultivate and, accordingly, their produce would be taxed.

In one respect Egypt was even more of a command economy than the USSR under Stalin. His government could count on the forced labour of some 16 million prisoners in the labour camps of the Gulag; but the Egyptian government had been accustomed from time immemorial to the conscript labour of the entire population. The corvée was so much the primordial form of taxation that the Egyptian word for *tax* is the word for *labour*.[42]

4.2. *Forced Labour and the Command Economy*

As in the Old and Middle Kingdoms, Egypt was an *oikos*. There was virtually *no* private enterprise.[43] The smallholders who appear in papyrus records of court cases, or in stories and fables, the traders on their own account, and likewise artisans, formed a minute fraction of the total

[42] *CAH*, II.1, p. 381.   [43] Janssen, *Commodity Prices*; *contra*, Kemp, *Ancient Egypt*.

population. Egypt was still essentially a two-class society. The 'upper class' consisted of, first, the court, the high official army officers, and chief priests at the very top, and a relatively narrow class of scribes, professional soldiers, and lesser priests just below them. The small (though growing) sector of skilled artisans, organized in 'gangs' or 'companies' and employed in the state sector, were relatively privileged too. But the overwhelmingly great mass of the population worked on the land, as tied tenants or slaves, and the land they worked on was almost entirely in the hands of the Crown or the temples.

Not only was it, then, a state-*owned* economy: it was also run, on a command basis—a real *oikos*, a true 'household of slaves', and this in three different, albeit related, respects.

First, the status of most agricultural labourers on Crown and temple estates was servile in fact, even when not in law. Chattel-slavery had increased in the New Kingdom as a consequence of the Egyptian conquests in the Levant and Nubia. But the native peasantry were scarcely better off. Most of them worked on the royal or temple estates, receiving in return one day's reaping out of so many days of the harvest. In theory, they were free and had equal access to the protection of law. In practice, they were subjected to the owner or manager of the estate.

Secondly, one must not underrate the extent of state enterprise. It was by no means confined to the construction of pyramids, mortuary temples, and the like: the central administration laid out and built entire towns, and we have already mentioned the construction and redistributive role of grain silos and storage systems.

Thirdly, all public employees were paid in rations. This should not surprise us—the same was true of Sumer, and again of Assyria and Persia, and indeed the Roman Dominate when the state had reverted to a natural economy after the hyper-inflation of the third century AD. As we have said already, it was payment in rations due to the absence of currency that necessitated the host of scribal transactions in Egyptian administration and gave it its *oikos* character. Workmen were paid a standard ration of ten loaves of bread and a measure of beer which ranged from one-third to two jugs. An American scholar has estimated that a soldier received 3.75 kg of wheat and 2.25 kg of barley for a ten-day ration. This, it must be interpolated, is very meagre—so much so that it is scarcely credible: the calorific value would barely exceed 1,400 calories and a man on active service would require at least twice that.[44]

As one moved up the official hierarchy so the amount of the ration

[44] Ibid 174–8.

increased, so that a senior official could receive an allocation of 500 loaves. Of course he could not eat all these and we must assume that in some way or another these entitlements were treated as units of account and exchange-able into other commodities.

As mentioned earlier, the general population was liable to forced labour. There were exceptions, however. Officials (including scribes) were exempt, and the well-to-do hired substitutes so that the burden fell almost exclu-sively on the poor—mostly farm-labourers. Gangs could be assembled from all over Egypt like the ones that Amenhotep IV (Akhnaton) employed to quarry and drag stone for his solar temple of the Aton at Karnak. More commonly, corvée labour was used to repair dykes, dredge irrigation canals, test boundary marks, and generally keep the agricultural system in order. Another aspect of corvée, well attested in the documents, was the unpaid requisitioning of tools or boats by officials.

The likelihood of being forced to serve in the army was bitterly detested. It was a limited possibility but caused outspoken anguish. The most dreaded corvée of all was the quarrying expedition.

4.3. *The Army*

The standing army was radically reformed. For one thing, it was now a single unitary force for the entire state with one single command. The nome armies were no more. For the most part, until late in the XIXth and increasingly in the XXth dynasties, it was made up of native Egyptians; though there were also companies of Nubians, and from the time of Amenhotep III onwards, companies composed of prisoners-of-war, notably the Sherden, who were later to appear as redoubtable foes among the various Sea Peoples, c.1200. The army had always contained foreign formations from very early times, but this is true of almost all 'state' armies, everywhere, up to the nineteenth century. (The British Crown, for instance, was using German mercenaries in the American War of Independence.)[45] The bulk of the service, however, was composed of full-time regulars and reserves led by professional officers who received organized training in tactics and strategy. It was organized, equipped, and maintained by a full department of government and headed by a 'Grand General of the Army'. Replacements were mostly recruited from families of ex-servicemen. These families were quartered in military colonies throughout Egypt. Each received a smallhold-ing of two or three acres, on condition of supplying a recruit. In addition,

---

[45] Japan certainly stands out as an exception, but its ethnic homogeneity coupled with its acute insularity make it a very unusual polity. See below, Bk. IV, Pt. 1, Ch. 1.

however, the government from time to time conscripted men. Then, officials visited villages and registered the eligible youths. The ratio of men actually taken was not large—perhaps 1 per cent, possibly more—but very often the recruiting sergeants had to use force to get them away from their desperately unhappy families and fellow-villagers.

Recruitment, supply, equipment, and records lay in the hands of the vizier, assisted by the chief scribes of the army. The day-to-day administration rested with generals and adjutants. The peacetime army was divided into two corps, for Upper and Lower Egypt respectively, each one coming under the control of its own adjutant. The vizier presided over a sort of general staff composed of these senior officers. The peacetime army, or, if one likes, the home-based army, quartered in garrisons throughout the country, was fully integrated into the polity, the economy, and society. We have already seen that senior officers were selected to fill posts in the royal household and in the administration and the temples. In addition, however, the rank and file were always at hand to enforce order, to help in tax collection, and—a most essential part of their duties—to provide labour companies to and from the quarries.

The battle-army was very effective for those times: at all events it permitted Thutmose III to win a convincing victory at Megiddo, it forced the formidable Hittite army to a draw at Kadesh despite the rash, almost fatal, strategy of Ramses II, and later still was able to beat off repeated assaults from the Libyans and the Sea Peoples, whereas the Hittites and the Canaanite-Syrian states succumbed.

In weaponry it had learned from the Hyksos and now entered battle on equal terms. Its infantry consisted of spearmen and archers, equipped with heavy bronze spearheads and swords. The composite bow was an élite weapon. Each division was supported by some chariotry, but the main bulk of this formed a separate charioteer corps. It was the élite of the army and it was from them rather than from the infantry that the pharaohs picked their future administrators. The command-organization consisted of a number of divisions, named after Amon, Ra, Ptah, and Seth; each was commanded by a general, assisted by an Adjutant, in charge of high-ranking combat officers who took over frontier and fortress duties: and each such division contained some twenty-five companies of 200 men apiece, each made up of four fifty-man platoons. The charioteer corps was commanded by the 'Master of the Horse'. A chariot itself was manned by the driver and the fighter, unlike the Hittite practice where the chariot also carried a buckler-man to protect the other two. Chariots were as much prestige-objects as fighting resource: in diplomatic exchanges, a king's prestige was often reckoned by the size of his chariotry.

That the army posed no threat to civil society was chiefly due to the warrior-role of the pharaoh: the links between him and his officers were strong. But another reason was that for nearly four centuries there was no polarization in the political and civil society strong enough to force the officer corps into choices of king and (apart from, possibly, Akhnaton), kings were not dependent on the army for maintaining their thrones or even, for that matter, for maintaining domestic peace. There were no civil disturbances during the XVIIIth and XIXth dynasties that could not be handled by the police.

4.4. *The Judiciary*

We have already noted much talk of *ma'at*. Here, in the New Kingdom, we find attested 'Instructions' to the vizier, as chief justice, to be impartial, to deny justice to no man, and so on.

As far as can be seen, there were neither specialized judges nor a special judicial branch of government. If one can speak of a judicial system, then it consisted, at its apex, of the king himself: next, the equivalent of our High Courts, that is, two tribunals presided over by the viziers for Upper and for Lower Egypt respectively: and at local level, their equivalent in the *qenbet* councils. The most exceptional cases would be passed by the viziers to the king himself and these might include some capital cases, where, otherwise, one might expect the viziers' tribunals to pass sentence. These tribunals dealt only with serious offences. Most cases, especially those concerning property disputes, were handled at the local level. The viziers' tribunals did not have a fixed composition, and indeed the records speak of 'the court *of this* day'. The composition of one such court, in the reign of Ramses II, consisted of nine priests, the only layman being the clerk of the court. Another, under Ramses IX, contained the vizier, two priests, the city governor, the chief of the high priestess's establishment in the temple of Amon, the herald, and two notables.[46] The *qenbet* councils consisted of local notables who were nominated by the government.

In civil matters court procedure was in principle unexceptionable. Testimony was given under oath. There were strict rules of procedure. Rigid adherence to precedent underlay the judges' approach to their decision. In those cases that have survived, the diligence with which the evidence was checked out and assessed is really very impressive. The plaintiff made his case, the defendant replied, the witnesses were brought, and the court then rendered its verdict.[47] The entire procedure—and the way the cases were

---

[46] Erman and Rank, *Civilisation égyptienne*, 140, 183.

[47] A. G. McDowell, *Jurisdiction in the Workmen's Community of Beir el-Medina* (Nederlands Institut voor het Najige Oosten, Leiden, 1990).

docketed—is highly sophisticated and civilized and a far cry from the procedure in Anglo-Saxon and Norman England with its oath-bearers and barbarous ordeals, or from the procedure-constricted *sharia* courts of the Caliphate, for that matter. But, none the less, the courts were frequently prejudiced or corruptible.[48]

Criminal procedure, on the other hand, was rough. The preliminary investigation of not just the accused but relevant witnesses followed the identical pattern I myself observed as a duty liaison officer in the Central Caracol of Cairo in 1942, namely, a good beating.

There was brought the Scribe of the Army, Ankhefenamun, son of Ptahemhab. He was examined by beating with the stick, and fetters were placed upon his feet and hands, and an oath was administered to him, on pain of mutilation, not to speak falsehood. There was said to him 'tell the way in which you went to the places together with your brother'. He said, 'Let a witness be brought to accuse me'. He was examined again [beaten again?], and he said 'I saw nothing'. He was made a prisoner for further examination.[49]

The above extract comes from the famous case of the tomb robberies in the royal necropolis at Thebes. For all the brutality in examining the witnesses, the judges showed great ingenuity and perseverance in their investigation of the charge and leave a convincing picture at having arrived at the truth in a very complicated—and politically charged—case.[50]

5. ADMINISTRATIVE STYLE: THE 'UNWEEDED GARDEN'

Despite the appearance of meticulous organization and efficiency, the Egyptian administration was, in fact, a monument of laxity, procrastination, ineptitude, corruption, and petty brutality. This is an extenuation of the New Kingdom, not an indictment. It did endure, stably, for four centuries after all. It was handicapped by two things, neither of which are present today; a monocratic organization which made the accident of birth critical to the tone of the entire organization, and the absence of a market-economy which imposed an intractable handicap on the distributive system.

---

[48] Cf. R. D. Faulkner, 'The Installation of the Vizier', *Journal of Egyptian Archaeology* (1955), 18–29; cf. van den Boorn, *The Duties of the Vizier*. But corruption was so widespread throughout history, and indeed is still prevalent in most countries, that one should hardly marvel at this particular charge.

[49] Quoted in Gardiner, *Egypt*, 300. But—as subsquent chapters will show—this practice was so widespread as to be all but universal: one will find accounts of it for Imperial Rome, for the successive Chinese empires, and throughout the Islamic states.

[50] For a good account, often verbatim, of this case, see Erman and Rank, *Civilisation égyptienne*, 171–80. A more recent translation of the texts appears in T. E. Peet, *The Great Tomb Robberies of the Twentieth Egyptian Dynasty* (Hildesheim, Olms, 1930; repr. 1977).

The overwhelming first impression of the conduct of affairs is *paperasserie*, the accumulation and still further accumulation of masses of paperwork. We can do no better than to quote—extensively—the vivid account by Erman.

Numerous documents have come down to us, showing how the accounts were kept in the department of the 'house of silver', and in similar departments: the translation of these is however extremely difficult, owing to the number of unknown words and the abbreviations they contain. These documents show exactly how much was received, from whom and when it came in, and the details of how it was used. This minute care is not only taken in the case of large amounts, but even the smallest quantities of corn or dates are conscientiously entered. Nothing was done under the Egyptian government without documents: lists and protocols were indispensable even in the simplest matters of business.[51]

This mania for writing—there is no other way to describe it—is characteristic not just of later periods; it seems that just as much papyrus was consumed in the Old and Middle Kingdoms as in the New Kingdom. One need only glance at the paintings in Old Kingdom tombs to see that, whether grain is being measured or cattle led in, scribes are always on hand. They squat on the ground before the boxes of files and cases of papyrus rolls, a spare rush pen behind their ears, the papyrus roll or wooden board on which they are writing in their hand. Every estate has its own writing office and on occasion it is the incumbent's son himself who presides over it. The state administration is similarly organized, with every judge also holding the office of 'Chief Scribe', every chief judge is called the 'Overseer of the Writings of the King', and where one of the great men of Upper Egypt holds all the following titles:[52]

> Overseer of Scribes of Fields in the two Great Houses of Ten in Upper Egypt
> Controller of Scribes in the Office of Assignment of Provisions
> Controller of Scribes of Fields
> Supervisor of Scribes of Royal Documents.

In short, everything in the administration revolves around writing. In the Egyptian view, administration and writing documents are one and the same, and a 'scribe' is an official. Similarly, the administration of later times has its

---

[51] A. Erman, *Life in Ancient Egypt*, trans. H. M. Tizard, with a new introduction by J. Manchup-White (Dover Publications, New York, 1971), 112.

[52] It is now believed that these strings of titles represent careers and the offices were often held successively. In particular, the words rendered 'Controller', 'Supervisor', and 'Overseer' marked successive grades of office, 'Overseer' being the highest. (This note is kindly contributed by Professor J. G. Baines, who also also supplied the translation of the text.)

army of scribes—the 'Treasury' where Oageba and Ineni work has at least nine. Even the army is subject to the same under this bureaucracy, the 'Scribe of Élite Troops' being among its highest-ranking officers.

In addition, there are scribes who are personally assigned to the overseers of the individual administrative departments, for example to the vizier, to the 'mayor' of a city, or to the overseer of the treasury, and as representatives of their 'lords' these people no doubt often exercise considerable influence. Equally, the king has for his own use his personal scribe—the 'Scribe of Royal Documents' of the Old Kingdom, and the late New Kingdom 'Royal Butler and Scribe of Pharaoh'.

The well-known principle that what cannot be verified through documents does not exist applies also to the Egyptian administration. Because of this, business letters often include the observation, 'And you should keep my letter so that it can serve as evidence for us on another occasion'. Records are frequently copied so that both parties can produce appropriate evidence. Equally, nothing is prescribed from the treasury without an official transfer order, and even an official who wants to take his annual entitlement of firewood and charcoal from the stores cannot obtain them until the overseer of the treasury has given him 'a document'. Even a 'Commander of Police' tried in vain to obtain a number of men from the troop leaders: it was explained to him that not a single one would be given to him before he produced a 'list of names', and their superior fully supported their way of proceeding. This love of order embraces the most trivial things—a formal record is made even when a workman is given his quota of grain.

Below the record a scribe writes such office notes as: 'to be copied' or 'it is deposited in the archive'. The records are handed over for safe-keeping to the 'Chief Keeper of Documents' of the relevant administrative department, who then seals them in large jars and carefully catalogues them. An archivist of the XXth dynasty noted that in Year 6 of his king he checked two of the document jars. The first of these contained two 'silver (money) documents'—probably private debt bonds kept in the archive—a document concerning the audit of the 'wreaths' in the temple of Amun, and two large and four small papyrus rolls concerning the temple of Ramses II:

Total rolls which are in the document jar 9

In the other jar were stored records of one of the investigations of tomb robbers . . . This jar contained the following items:

Record of receipt of the gold, silver and copper which was found to have been stolen by the members of the work crew of the royal tomb: 1

The inspection of the pyramid tombs: 1

The inspection of the people who were found to have robbed tombs
on the West (Bank) of Thebes: 1
The inspection of the tomb of King Sekhem-Re Shedtawy: 1
The inspection of the tomb of the overseer of soldiers Wer, which was
carried out by the metalworker Wares: 1
Record concerning the copper and the objects which the robbers had
sold (?) from (?) this 'Place of Beauty':   1
The list of names of the robbers: 1
The examination of the foreigner Payqah <son> of Sethemhab: 1

It is worth noting that two papyrus rolls belonging to the Berlin Museum
are indeed said to have been found in a jar. This method of storing
documents is attested from Egypt in the Persian period and later.[53]

Most of this paperwork was due to the state's effort to direct the entire
distribution system, an effort whose infinite complexity we have already
pointed out. This exercise could never work as smoothly as the market.
Scholars have often wondered how it came about that at a time when
treasure was still coming into the state—even if in lesser quantities than
before—the artisans in the Theban necropolis were having to demonstrate
to get their rations. The case is famous among Egyptologists. These
workmen were paid monthly. Sometimes the rations were a day late, sometimes as much as several months. What was the explanation? On one
occasion they were told that the town granary was empty. This is almost
certain to be true, for whether a granary was full or empty was not a matter
of good or bad harvests but of whether or not some administrator had
failed to effect delivery. For instance, we learn from the Edict of Horemheb
of all kinds of obstruction to the physical transportation of tax-goods.
Officials requisition the boat in which a subject is about to deliver his taxes;
army units requisition hides from the taxpayer before the taxman has got to
him.[54] These offences were so widespread that Horemheb threatened the
offenders with mutilation of the nose followed by banishment to the
frontier fortress of Tjaru. It is easy to see how a multiplication of such
petty acts would disrupt the distribution system.

The system had another, no less serious effect, corruption, which in its
turn also dislocated the 'plan'. There is a long papyrus relating to the
misdeeds of a head-workman in charge of a company of artisans under Seti
II (1204–1198). Not only did he steal anything he fancied from the stores he
handled—for instance, cut stone to furnish his own tomb—but he lent out
the workmen to institutions for his private benefit and made a workman

---

[53] Erman and Rank, *Civilisation égyptienne*, 125–8.

[54] Jean-Marie Kruchten, *Le Décret d'Horemheb* (Universitaire Libre de Bruxelles, Faculté de Philosophie et Lettres 82, 1981). See also Wilson, *Culture of Ancient Egypt*, 238–9.

feed his oxen.[55] Another case concerns an official of the Royal Necropolis at Thebes, by name Thutmose. He sailed south to collect the tax dues and collected 343 sacks, but turned in only 314.[56] A far worse case is that of the priest of the Temple of Khnum at the first cataract. Grain-tax for this temple came from the Delta. It was carried by a ship's captain Khnumnakht. Over a period of nine years this man transported 6,300 sacks of grain but actually delivered only 576! The indictment against him shows that Khnumnakht was able to do this by entering into a conspiracy with the 'clerks, administrators and peasant-farmers' of the Temple.[57] In another case, the wife of a government storekeeper, left at home while her husband was seconded to another and distant post, coolly continued to frequent the storehouse and, acting in his name, ordered the transfer of goods to their private store. The amounts stolen were immense: 1,300 blocks of copper ore, 20,000 bushels of grain, thirty chariots (!), with harnesses to match, and much, much more![58]

One final impression of the administrative style—apart from its excessive paperwork, its delays, and its corruption—is its rather casual brutality. Punishments for criminal offences were often very cruel—mutilation of the nose and lips, amputation of hands or arms. Even worse, perhaps, was the living death of the Nubian gold-mines, where criminals alongside slaves were lashed each day into the caves and out again at night until they perished of overwork and malnutrition. The collection of taxes was brutal too. None of this cruelty is new, in the ancient world. The same rapacity is to be found in Rome, Byzantium, China, and the Caliphate, as will be seen. For that matter it is to be seen in the Iberian exploitation of the Amerindian populations or in the European slave trade.

6. THE NEW KINGDOM: AN APPRAISAL

This New Kingdom polity is altogether a quite remarkable achievement. It was incomparably in advance of any one of its contemporaries.[59]

[55] J. Cerny, 'Papirus Salt 124 (Brit. Mus. 10055)', *Journal of Egyptian Archaeology* (1929), 243–58.
[56] Wilson, *Culture of Ancient Egypt*, 279.   [57] Ibid. 279–80.
[58] Kitchen, *Pharaoh Triumphant*, 134–5.
[59] It has been suggested that the Hittite and the Assyrian kingdoms bear comparison. The former seems to have had a primitive feudalistic basis, the second, as the chapter on Assyria will show, had, *inter alia*, a tax structure that was immensely cruder than the Egyptian. But the most conclusive argument against equating these two polities and Egypt is that both the former were blotted out by their invaders (the Sea Peoples and the Medes, respectively) and thereafter perished so utterly that they retained no historic identity at all, but simply merged into the local landscapes. The Egyptian polity rode out all such storms over a period of some 3,000 years and when it succumbed, it was to Christianity. Even then, its territorial integrity and national identity were unimpaired.

As we have been relating, this state was a perfect autocracy, one might even say despotism; it was as totally centralized as human and natural resources permitted; in undertaking to manage the entire economy by command and from a central point, it set itself tasks the like of which occur only in the Sumerian *oikos*-type city-states, but far outranges them, in so far as it catered for a population of some 4 millions as against the city-states' 200,000. In undertaking this task of management it not only went far beyond any of its contemporaries, then, but beyond pretty well all states and empires that followed it with the possible exception of the Inca and the Aztec polities, which, however, in all other organizational aspects were much its inferior. And with all this, it was immensely stable for over 400 years.

It is very hard to estimate the way its services functioned in practice, because the documentation is lacking. We are treated merely to glimpses of the bureaucracy at work and to single cases of fraud and mismanagement. It is clear that its army was by far the most powerful in the region at that time. We know too little of the judicial system to comment on its customary private law, but what little we do know about a criminal trial shows that, though modes of interrogation were brutal, the sifting of evidence was carried out with skill and discernment. The taxation system seems too good to be true. These sophisticated cadasters, for instance, were to be used also in Han and T'ang China—but we know that these regimes were unable to meet the requirement of frequent reassessments, and we know from the tax systems of other pre-industrial states as well that the modes of collection laboured under inherent technical difficulties. What this means, though, is that to form any impression of how it might have worked in practice, we have to look at polities posterior to the New Kingdom. If we took late Rome, Han, T'ang, and Ming China, and the Caliphate as comparisons, we should expect to find that in Egypt the cadasters were thoroughly imperfect, that they were carried out irregularly so that assessments usually became traditional, that collection was terribly harsh, suffered from inescapable inherent technical difficulties, and was carried out fraudulently. And all this was the more complicated in the New Kingdom by the fact of the taxes being paid in kind. Yet the sheer sophistication and specialization and the skill of the scribal bureaucracy must compel admiration, even though the scribes did go overboard in carrying out their duties.

Two other considerations underline the magnitude of this Egyptian achievement. The first is that this was a natural economy, so that, apart from jewellery and bullion given and taken as gifts, all payments—taxes, wages, and salaries—were made in natural produce or the grant of land which would yield it. There was no circulating currency. And the second is that, although bronze was in use, it was so rare and costly that it could be used only for weaponry and especially important artefacts, but not for ordinary utensils. Agricultural implements were still made of stone. In short, the highly developed arrangements we have just sketched were created by what was effectively a stone-age society.

Against this background the achievements appear the more remarkable while, in comparative perspective, the blemishes seem less so. The brutal beatings in criminal trials were a commonplace in the ancient world, like-wise the mutilations and other cruel penalties and the corrupt practices of the bureaucracy, the tax collectors, and the law courts.[60] Again, when we suggested that the fiscal system probably worked badly in practice, we reached this judgement only by inference from polities that came after the New Kingdom. The latter is entitled to full credit for having at least elaborated a system designed to be both effective and equitable, and in these respects it is every bit as developed as anything to be found under the late Roman, Byzantine, Chinese, and Caliphal empires. Likewise, the over-complication and excessive reliance on paperwork that characterized the bureaucracy would be found, later, in China, Byzantium, and the Caliphate as well. All in all, my general conclusion would be that, in the light of its simplistic technology and wholly natural economy, the sheer intricacy—and ambition—of the New Kingdom polity compel admiration.

It still remains to be asked whether it benefited the great mass of the peasant population. We do not know the details of its condition. The most obvious reproach that might be made would be that Egypt was a two-class society where the peasantry were all, one way or another, in a servile condition. But here again, this polity is not altogether dissimilar from others. For at least a millennium China was a two-class society of this sort, although, admittedly, its peasants were mostly free. Vast tracts of the western Roman Empire approximated to this same two-class condition in the last two centuries of its existence. The point is that two-class societies were widespread in the Archaic age, both throughout the Middle East and in the far Orient. Nor was peasant dependency unique to Egypt. It crops up all the time in all manner of polities. Perhaps the most that one can really say about the condition of the people is that there is no evidence of civil disturbance or revolt until the demise of the New Kingdom under the XXth dynasty and thereafter.

[60] See also the *First, Second and Third Interim Reports of the Commission of Inquiry in Bribery and Corruption*, Accra, Ghana, 1972. The conclusion was that bribery and corruption were 'endemic'.

7. THE COLLAPSE OF THE NEW KINGDOM

Within a hundred years of Ramses III's death in 1153 Egypt became a broken-backed state and so remained, apart from short-lived sporadic intervals (e.g. under Sheshonk I, c.945–924), until the revival under the Saïtes (664–525). Even then, though reunited, it was a far cry from the tight, monocratic, and pyramidal structure of Ramses II.

Unified, wealthy, and militarily strong in the New Kingdom, Egypt became subdivided, poor, and militarily weak. The four centuries that witnessed this decline are known as the Third Intermediate Period. Its details are quite immensely complicated,[61] but over those 400 years the centralized unified state of the New Kingdom slowly fell apart.

Along with its territorial disintegration, the Egyptian state became impoverished, though one must be careful here; we are dealing in long, large periods and within them there are episodes of great economic strength as, for instance, in the fourth century BC. But obviously, the greater the subdivision of Egypt, and its territorial treasuries, the less revenue flowed into each of them in absolute terms. This is vividly illustrated in the tale of the bumbling emissary, Wenamon, sent almost penniless to Byblos to procure timbers for the bark of Amon at Thebes.[62] Previously, so the ruler of Byblos tells him, pharaoh sent six shiploads of trade-goods.

Furthermore, by the thirteenth century BC Egypt became relatively more vulnerable and this was, in its turn, a further factor in its disintegration. Unlike his defeat of the Sea Peoples, Ramses III's great victory over the Libyans was in no way definitive and Egypt faced a 'barbarian problem' similar to that of Rome and China, and met it in exactly the same fatal way: by incorporating the barbarians into its armies and settling them on Egyptian lands in order to give them the means of subsistence. So grew up the settlements of the Ma (short for Meshwesh). These colonies retained their tribal structure and their own chiefs. The latter rapidly Egyptianized themselves and soon came to colonize the Egyptian élite so that, for instance, by the end of the XXth dynasty the high priests of Thebes, who were military men, were 'Libyans'. At the same time, some of their military commanders became rulers of what were, in the end, effec-

---

[61] Cf. the comprehensive prosopography and chronology of K. A. Kitchen, *The Third Intermediate Period in Egypt* (Aris and Phillips, Warminster, 1973; 2nd edn. 1986).

[62] Lichtheim, *Ancient Egyptian Literature*, ii. 224–30. 'Wenamon' is a work of fiction and some claim it is really a parable to show that Amon is more important than people or kings. Maybe. But why would one invent a wildly improbable scenario to illustrate this? Clearly the events are founded on a certain reality.

tively fiefdoms, in the Delta. The presence of these principalities spelt a degree of disintegration in itself.

In addition, however, Egypt's age-long penetration of the upper reaches of the Nile was at last having the effects that cultural imperialism and continuous military harassment has upon tribal peoples: the emergence of proto-states as a form of self-defence. The Egyptian kings had withdrawn from upper Nubia at the end of the XXth dynasty, leaving it totally impoverished. Two hundred and fifty years later, however, the state of Napata arose from an indigenous post-New Kingdom culture. Its kings worshipped Amon and followed his prescriptions with a puritanism akin to the Wahabis in Islam. In the eighth century BC they reversed history by claiming that they were the true pharaohs and, advancing victoriously up the Nile, founding the XXVth or Nubian dynasty.

Meanwhile a new order of states had emerged in Canaan, while further north lay the various Syrian principalities and the Phoenician thalassocracy. Beyond them and about to engulf them all was the powerful militaristic state of Assyria.

But while such military pressures were mounting, internal conditions made Egypt less and less able to cope with them. Disunity, poverty, and military weakness were all interconnected and reinforced one another. For instance, the loss of Nubia reduced the gold flow to the court, which in turn cut off military expenditure, leading to further disintegration and further impoverishment. In the tightly knit New Kingdom, in short, a failure in one sector of the system—in the collection of taxes or the flow of tribute, for instance—weakened another, and in turn another. The system fell apart, bit by bit and sector by sector, until the state reached a nadir of fragmentation just at the time the Assyrian advance from the north coincided with the Nubian invasion from the south.

The common denominator in each sector-failure was, however, the king. The kingship was—and was designed to be—the hub of which the spokes were the military establishment, the temple priesthoods, the local officials, the central court bureaucracy, and the managers of the economy. Under a Thutmose III or Ramses II, even perhaps a Ramses III, as later under a Sheshonk, these 'spokes' were held in their respective fixed positions by the controlling clamp of the hub. Under the Ramessids of the XXth dynasty the hubs, so to speak, came loose, the spokes lost their relationship to one another, and the wheel collapsed.

Ramses III's mostly short-lived successors lost personal control of the army. Within two or three generations—by the XXIst to the XXIVth dynasties—the generals could—and did—supplant the dynast. In no position and, very likely, with little inclination to re-establish control over the military commanders by force, kings fell back on arranging dynastic marriages for them, or alternatively, giving commands to their kinsmen. The Egyptian administrative élite began to present the picture of a great network of family connections, holding military, priestly, and financial posts throughout Egypt. Such a policy did not restore royal supremacy but scattered it. For where collateral lines were placated in this way they threatened the succession, and where generals were intermarried with the pharaoh's family their control of their forces was simply legitimized.

Given the personal and (now) institutional weakness of the king, most military and priestly posts became hereditary. Thus the old centralized bureaucracy working from vizier down to mayors and councils in the towns was replaced by a return to the even older Middle Kingdom relationship of a central court working to a local potentate, who controlled the economic and military resources in this area. These resources were, as often as not, priesthoods. The temples were, as ever, economic corporations. One way of 'paying a salary' or 'granting a pension' was to make somebody a first or second or third priest and so forth, in a particular temple or a number of different temples. To become high priest of Amon was to become the director of vast estates, amounting to perhaps one-fifth of all Egypt and to become Amon's second or third priest was to share in managing the corporation and participating in its income. What was true of the Amon cult was true, on a lesser scale, of the other cults.

As the political control of the kingdom disintegrated in this way, with military power, priesthoods, and tax collection becoming hereditary in local families, so the central direction of the economy broke up too. The last years of the fully centralized economy have left us a number of vivid examples of its defects: under Ramses IX (1126–1108) the robberies in the royal tombs and the 'pilfered grain' case;[63] under Smendes (c.1075–1050) the tomb robberies still continue, Wenamon[64] is presented as having no resources to buy timber in Byblos; and so forth. I have suggested earlier that economic dislocation, local shortages, and corruption were inherent in the Egyptian redistribution-controlled economy.[65] A minor, or apathetic king would make bad worse. Such systems only work at all when each echelon in the hierarchy from king to village tax collection picks energetic and able subordinates and disciplines them for the slightest infraction. How far this was ever done, even in the New Kingdom, is problematical. It was far less likely under the XXth dynasty and subsequently, with feeble monarchs and a bureaucracy that had lost its position to the priesthood and the military.

[63] See p. 203 above.   [64] See p. 206 above.   [65] See p. 202 above.

The dismemberment of the economy and its decentralization to local hereditary princes was disastrous to the monarchy. Its revenues were being tapped and diverted at source and so were its sources of labour-power—the corvée. This further enfeebled the kingship. Such was the vicious circle in which the state was trapped and such the reason that its dilapidation and dismemberment went from bad to worse after the Ramessids. True, despite the Third Intermediate Period, with its at times considerable internal violence, the country revived very quickly in the XXVth and XXVIth and again in the XXIX and XXXth dynasties. This suggests—as the later, Ptolemaic regime would bear out—that the agricultural base was unaffected, and that the administrative structure persisted, so that prolonged periods of revival interrupted the secular decline.

4

The Assyrian Empire, 745–612 BC

1. THE RELEVANCE OF THE ASSYRIAN EMPIRE

Why should the Assyrian Empire deserve a place in the history of government? It was never free from revolts and secessions, and when it collapsed after the sack of Nineveh in 612 its ruler and its statehood disappeared. Yet a history of government would be very pedantic to ignore a power which in its time was the scourge and master of the entire Middle East. And in fact, there is a better case for including it. It is that the Assyrian Empire represents a new type of state formation.

So far we have encountered in Sumer the city-state and in Egypt we met with the country-state. Here for the first time in history we encounter Empire.

Conventionally speaking [writes Garelli], 'imperial' domination connotes a political and often, a spiritual hegemony exercised over a significant portion of the known world at a given moment. We next introduce the criteria of territorial extent and of ethnic, linguistic and religious diversity. From this standpoint the Assyrian 'empire' can be contrasted with the former 'kingdoms' which comprised only small areas and thin populations.

It is also relevant to note that efforts at hegemony manifested themselves very early on, from the era of Sargon of Akkad—who was, perhaps doing no more than replying to the similar efforts of the Kings of Ebla. But not one of these former vast political formations was marked by the permanent occupation of the soil.

(Here, I interrupt to say that this was true of the Egyptian domination of the southern Levant, under the New Kingdoms: that area remained under the rule of client or allied kings, watched over by scattered Egyptian garrisons.)

The first empire involving a methodical and permanent occupation of conquered territory, with the implantation of military garrisons and its division into provinces directed by governors who were strictly subjected to the authority of the central government was that founded by the King of Assyria, Tiglath-Pilaser III, from 745 BC.[1]

---

[1] P. Garelli, 'L'État et la légitimité royale sous l'empire assyrien', in M. T. Larsen (ed.), *Power and Propaganda: A Symposium on Ancient Empires* (Akademisk Verlaag, Copenhagen, 1979), 319. Similar criteria apply to the so-called 'Empire' of the Shang and Chou dynasties in China, from *c.*12th(?) to the 8th centuries BC. Both were 'hegemonic' dominations; not until Shih Huang-ti (221 BC) was there a Chinese 'empire' in the Assyrian mode. Even so, there are reasons other than this to deny it the title of 'empire'. See below.

2. A BASIC CHRONOLOGY

The Assyrian heartland was the triangle between the towns of Nineveh, near modern Mosul: Assur, some sixty miles south, near the confluence of the Tigris and Lesser Zab; and Erbil, roughly midway between both, some fifty miles south-east of Nineveh and seventy miles north-east of Assur. All this territory lies on the southernmost line of the rain-belt: the winter rains are more abundant and regular than in the south; harvests grow in the valleys without it always being necessary to bring water to them. The highlands supply abundant pasture for horse-rearing. The vine flourishes.

It is very exposed to attack. The mountains lie only thirty miles north of Nineveh, perhaps fifty miles to the east of it. On the west, however, stretched the cornlands of the Jezirah, divided north and south by the Sinjar ridge, but, this apart, forming a vast flat and unbroken plain watered by the Khabur River and meeting no rising ground until, some 260 miles due west of Nineveh, it reaches the great bend of the Euphrates.

All these cities were very old indeed, going back far beyond 2800 BC. Assur was a major religious centre with monumental buildings in mud-brick. Despite a large Hurrian element in its population, Assyria's culture had strong affinities with Sumer's. Cuneiform appears in 2500. By that time all these cities were speaking Assyrian, a dialect of Akkadian.

The history of Assyria, as such, begins when an Amorite adventurer, a contemporary of Hammurabi of Babylon, seized the throne of Assur in *c*.1813. From then on, the three cities, hitherto separate, formed part of a single kingdom with Assur as the capital. This was the kingdom of Assyria.

This history, from Shamshi-Adad I onwards, is one of almost unceasing wars. Some were fought from necessity to prevent the highland barbarians on the north and east or nomad barbarians from the west seizing the fields and villages of the heartland. Some were fought for plunder—the wealthy cities of the Euphrates and Syria offered rich prizes.

And, as time went on, and the Assyrian army experienced a run of successes, the wars were also fought as a holy duty in the name of Ashur, father of the gods, who commanded his early vicar at his coronation as Assyria's king to extend his borders. When the neighbouring states were strong the kingdom was reduced to its heartland. When their pressure relaxed, the borders extended again.

This occurred in a number of great waves. There is little point in recounting it in any detail, but a bald chronological summary is necessary, if only to introduce some of the names and dates that will crop up in the following pages.

CHRONOLOGY

1813 BC	SHAMSHI-ADAD I. *First expansion.* Falls tributary to Mitanni, 1450 BC
1366	ASHUR UBALLIT I. *Empire* includes Babylon. Collapses 1209
1116	TIGLATH-PILESER I. Restores Empire until this is brought down by Aramaeans and Chaldaeans, 935
859	SHALMANESER III. Expansion resumes, but soon pushed back by Kingdom of Urartu to c.738
745	TIGLATH-PILESER III. Defeats Urartu, 735. *Creation of the true Assyrian Empire* under the following:

Tiglath-Pileser III	745–728
Shalmaneser V	728–722
Sargon II	722–705
Sennacherib	705–682
Esarhaddon	681–670
Assurbanipal	669–627

Then succession disputes and short reigns, until:

612	Destruction of Nineveh by Medes and Babylonians.

Here, a few points of commentary must be made. First, until Tiglath-Pileser III, conquered territory was left under its native dynasties. The true empire, that is, a system of annexed provinces, begins with him.

Next, while some conquered territories accepted Assyrian rule (and were well treated) and others did not even wait to be conquered to submit, many territories refused to accept their fate for long, and rose in revolt. In extenuation of the Assyrians, it is argued that this was due to manipulation and incitement by other powers such as Egypt, Elam, or Urartu; but this does not show *why* they wanted to revolt, only that they thought they could get away with it. A very crude, abbreviated tally of the Assyrian campaigns indicates this. In the north-eastern region, there were fifteen campaigns between 911 and 653, of which five apiece were against the Medes and the Mannai. In the north-western region, there were five campaigns into Nairi. In the south, towards and into Babylonia, there were at least six campaigns between 814 and 681 In the west as far as Euphrates, there were at least nine campaigns between 911 and 743. In the west *beyond* Euphrates, in Syria, there were at least twenty-five campaigns between 883 and 722. And in Judah, Philistia, and Egypt, there were six campaigns between 705 and 653.[2]

Thirdly, the Assyrians terminated each of these renewed revolts by impaling, flaying, mutilating, and decapitating warriors and leaders, carrying off the total contents of the countries' exchequers, and deporting huge numbers of their people.

[2] Figures derived from A. T. Olmstead, *History of Assyria* (University of Chicago Press, Chicago, 1923; repr. Midway, 1975).

3. BASIC BELIEFS OF THE ASSYRIANS

It has been a common error to treat Assyrian and Babylonian beliefs as identical, but it would be totally perverse and misconceived to go to the opposite extreme and consider them as significantly different. They were not. Assyria adopted the cuneiform script, accepted Akkadian as the official language, and received Babylonian literature just as, in its own turn, Babylon had received this from Sumer. Sumerian had long since ceased to be a spoken language: it was by now the 'Latin' of Mesopotamia, the sacred religious language, and the Sumerian texts survived side by side with Akkadian translations in the Babylonian archives and temples. The Assyrians accorded similar respect to these texts. Sargon II collected a great library of 1,200 works. There were other great libraries, too—Sennacherib and Assurbanipal each had one housed in a different palace.

The Sumerian myths, legends, and cultic practices were very largely separate and distinct from Babylonian and Assyrian ones, but the basic religion of these three peoples was akin. The differences were minor: different emphases placed, at different epochs, on different gods and goddesses in the pantheon; the non-observance of some festivals, the observance of others; certain differences in rites—and so forth. The only major difference was the status in the pantheon of Assyria's patron god, Ashur. Among the Sumerians, Enlil had been accepted as father and king of the gods. When the power of Babylon eclipsed ancient Sumer, its local god Marduk was identified with and thereby took the place of Enlil in the pantheon. Such was the vast fame—and dread—of this Babylonian *Bêl* that he was almost equally revered in Assyria. In 689, however, Sennacherib, blind with fury at the revolt of subject Babylon, destroyed the city and wrote out Marduk as father and king of all the gods.

Ashur was, originally, the obscure local deity in the capital city of Assur. He was by no means worshipped exclusively: he was effectively the god of the palace and the dynasty, and so the patron god, the object of the official cult. In his name was the king crowned. As his earthly vicar did the king reign. And at his express command at the coronation did the king set out to enlarge the borders of the kingdom and establish his symbol and cult through conquered territory. In this cult the king was the high priest of Ashur: the image of Ashur and the link that mediated earth and heaven, sacred and profane. And—a fact of great political importance—the Assyrian monarchy never allowed itself to be separated from the high priesthood as its counterpart in Babylonia did.

As in Sumer and Babylonia, religion—a web of ritualistic practices, serving perhaps as many as 3,000 gods, great and small, local or state-wide (many replicating names and attributes, admittedly)—permeated society. It legitimated the monarch, and, more, the entire social order whose practices it channelled and enforced by its supernatural sanction. The cult of the high gods was not for the common people. But all Assyrians, high and low, inhabited a world of fearsome malignancies to be bought or driven off by appropriate sacrifices, spells, and incantations, and the high gods were gods of fear. They were 'powers', and it was fear not piety that kings expressed in the often very moving prayers they addressed to their protective deities.[3]

This terror of the gods had important political consequences. For one thing an Assyrian monarch was tightly cocooned in a tissue of daily, weekly, monthly, and annual rituals, fasts, and invocations. He had to wear special garments, eat or not eat special foods on specified occasions: he had to plan his activities to avoid inauspicious days. And no Assyrian king, any more than any Assyrian general, would make an important decision without consulting the gods in various ways: by divination and, in the late period, by astrology. The Assyrians had taken over from Babylon the pseudo-science of hepatoscopy: divination through inspecting sheep's livers. Its methods were highly 'scientific'. All that was unscientific about it was its basic hypothesis, that is, that the liver of a sheep could give information about anything other than the condition of the sheep. What happened was this. A sheep was sacrificed to a god. Thereafter the priests removed its liver and inspected the markings on it. All such markings met with previously, along with the events that had accompanied or ensued from the questions posed to the god, had been meticulously collected, collated, and filed; similarly with the events attending various astronomical and astrological conjunctions. On the basis of this extensive exercise in induction did the priests finally produce the answer to the royal questions. We possess an entire file on the questions addressed to the sun god Shemesh, and the answers given.[4] Of the Babylonians, the late C. J. Gadd wrote of the astonishing coexistence, in military campaigns, between practical mensuration and field trigonometry on the one hand, and the consultation of omens on the other. What he writes about Babylonia is exactly true of Assyria also: 'The . . . military academies may be imagined, without extravagance, as divided into the faculties of applied mathematics and of divination, and the general in the field might hesitate whether to time his operation by computing the mass of his ramp and the number of his hands, or by meticulously scrutinizing the blemishes upon a sheep's liver.'[5]

[3] Cf. Ashurnasirpal I's (1052–1032 BC) moving supplication to Ishtar of Nineveh, to relieve him of the boils, pestilence, and blindness that was afflicting him. Olmstead, *History of Assyria*, 73–4.
[4] Cf. ibid. 358–73.   [5] *CAH*, II.1, p. 200.

4. THE CENTRAL AUTHORITIES

4.1. *The Nature of the Assyrian Polity*

Here we have an economy of ploughman and shepherd. Virtually the entire working population, including the tiny artisan and merchant strata, is of dependent status and all owe military or labour service to the state. This is another Palace polity governed by an absolute monarch and his narrow circle of chief priests and service-noblemen through a scribal bureaucracy and a regular army. The religious and the secular are fused, once again, in the person of the monarch. But this state differs from Sumer and Egypt in not being a storage–distributive economy. For instance: the taxes of a district, paid over in straw/hay, were not sent to a distant depository and then distributed. Instead, they were sent straight to the nearby army or administrative unit which required it. Hence the bureaucracy is not, like those of Egypt or Ur III, engaged in much more than bookkeeping the public income and expenditure. Since the physical movement of the taxes-in-kind is, as a rule, direct from point of production to point of consumption, this bureaucracy is less numerous, looser-knit, and less specialized than in Sumer and Egypt.

Assyria was not a city-state or a country-wide state like Egypt, although she had passed through each of these two stages. From 745 she was an *empire*. This is the first, the prototypical historic empire and hence a new format in our catalogue of polities. Its core area was surrounded by conquered kingdoms, which now were annexed and ruled by centrally appointed plenipotentiaries. This area was itself surrounded by tributary states still governed by their own kings, and outside this area lay still others, in treaty relationships. The central innovation is the incorporation of conquered territory via the royal governorships on a long-term institutionalized basis. But two observations ought to be made here and now. First, the imperial rule was unstable. Aramaic and Phoenician inscriptions of vassal rulers in Syria and Turkey indicate that many kings were glad to serve under the Assyrians. But the record shows that a good many were, manifestly, not. Secondly, where a loyal ally had suffered some or another kind of damage, the Assyrian monarchs were certainly quick to help, but in the rest of the empire their rule seems to have been wholly and exclusively exploitative.

4.2. *The Kingship*

4.2.1. THE LEGITIMATION OF THE MONARCH

The kingship was the strength of the Assyrian state in that the total concentration of power in the monarch's hands facilitated instant and ruthless decision, but it was also the weakness because this very power opened up ferocious ambitions when the throne became vacant. Not every king, by any means, lived up to the full potentiality of the office, but the Assyrian state was lucky in enjoying, at various critical moments in its career, long sequences of forceful monarchs who not only turned the adverse tide, but enlarged upon their predecessor's successes.

The monarch's authority derived from his religious status, from his lineage, and from the acclamation and oath of fidelity of the notables. In Assyrian (and Babylonian) belief, the true owner of a locality, any locality, was its god. However, the god exercised his local power only through a local man; but not any man, only one predestined and pre-formed for this very task. An Assurbanipal would claim to stem from an 'eternally royal seed'.[6] Shalmaneser I claims to be the 'faithful shepherd whose name Anu and Enlil have pronounced for eternity'.[7] Kings frequently claimed to be of divine parentage, though, unlike their Egyptian counterparts, they couched this in very general, vague terms.[8] We possess the actual ritual of the coronation. It took place in the temple of Ashur. To cries of 'Ashur is King, Ashur is King', the ruler himself (acting in his capacity as high priest) made the initial sacrifice. From that point *he* became the object of the ritual. The chief priest crowned him and, so crowned, duly installed, he was regarded as the link between the human and the supernatural. As such and by carrying out the required rituals, he guaranteed the prosperity of the kingdom and the fertility of the land.[9] One recognizes the common traits of 'Archaic' religion.[10]

The choice of monarch was concentrated in a particular family, the self-styled 'royal seed'. Esarhaddon (who had to defeat his brother's army before acceding to the throne) claimed to be the god's only choice as 'faithful shepherd', but made it plain, nevertheless, that he was not his father's eldest son. The rule of primogeniture was never inflexible in Assyria, more a norm of reference. In early Assyrian history there are many examples of younger brothers succeeding instead of the late king's sons, and under the empire the rule was superseded by the reigning king selecting any one of his sons as crown prince and making him co-regent.[11] This device was no more

[6] R. Labat, *Le Caractère religieux de la royauté assyro-babylonienne* (Paris, 1939), 41.
[7] Ibid. 47.   [8] Ibid. 56–7.   [9] Ibid. 295.
[10] See p. 23 ff., p. 115 ff., p. 141 ff. above.
[11] Cf. Garelli, 'L'État et la légitimité royale', 321.

successful than the previous 'norm' of primogeniture in preventing attempts—sometimes successful—at usurpation. Significantly, however, such successful usurpers always appear to claim to be of the blood-royal, for example, Tiglath-Pileser III (acceded 745). In brief, though the precedence in the order of succession was frequently in dispute, royal lineage was always respected as conferring legitimacy.

But descent in the 'royal seed' was only the necessary, not the sufficient, condition for mounting the throne. The king had to be accepted by the notables of the kingdom also. From Sargon's time it became normal practice for the reigning king to nominate his heir apparent and to present him as such to the magnates and other leaders. Esarhaddon related how his father put his name before Shamash and Adad and received their approval, and then 'he brought together the people of Assyria, great and small, as well as those my brothers born in my father's house'. (His son Assurbanipal uses almost the same words.)[12] Those assembled had to swear to the gods of Assyria—Ashur, Sin, Shamash, Nabu, Marduk, and others—to 'respect his precedence' or 'status as heir-apparent'.[13] Thereafter he was inducted into the *bet redutti*, 'the house of succession', and began his co-regency.

Not only that. Once he succeeded, the new king exacted an oath of loyalty from his subjects. This was the *adu*. It was taken on days chiefly during the New Year festival by the priesthood in the presence of the statues of the gods so that whoever broke it incurred their wrath. Often, so the documents reveal, the oath was administered by vocational groups, such as the scribes, diviners, exorcists, doctors, augurs on the palace staff not living in the city, or else 'the soldiers, their sons, wives and gods'. Sometimes, however, on very important occasions, all members of these categories were brought to the capital; for instance, when Queen Zakutu, the widow of Esarhaddon, took steps to guarantee the succession of Assurbanipal.[14] This oath was far-reaching. It obliged the swearer to recognize the king, provide him with information, keep his peace, obey his instructions, and break all relationship with his enemy and assist him in all his campaigns.

4.2.2. ABSOLUTISM

The king was legally absolute.[15] He was also not just nominally, but effectively the head of two of the central institutions in the state: the army and priesthood. The generalissimo was called the *turtanu*. He was the greatest of the great magnates and came first after the king in the *limmu*

---

[12] Labat, *Le Caractère religieux*, 71.   [13] Ibid. 71–2.

[14] P. Garelli, *Le Proche-Orient asiatique*, 2 vols. (Presses Universitaires Françaises, 1974), 132.

[15] J. N. Postgate, 'Royal Exercise of Justice under the Assyrian Empire', in *Le Palais et la royauté*, ed. P. Garelli (Paris, 1974).

list, the roster of officials who gave their names, in turn, to the Assyrian year. These generalissimos sometimes overshadowed the king: the great Dayyan-Ashur, *turtanu* of Shalmaneser III, went on campaigning long after the monarch himself had grown too old, and another *turtanu*, Shamsi-ilu, served under four weak monarchs to become king-maker when the direct line died out in 754. For all that, there is no gainsaying the military character of the Assyrian monarchy. Their stone reliefs and statues regularly portray war, campaigns, and violent physical activities such as lion-hunting. An Assyrian king was supposed to be a war leader, and conspicuous failure in campaigning was the most common single reason for deposing the reigning monarch. A king was the commander-in-chief and the regular forces, the *kisir sharri*, were 'the royal army'. It was he who made the great decisions in foreign policy and as to where, every year, the campaigns were to be fought. The annals show him personally in the field: Sargon II died on campaign in Cilicia, and Esarhadden while marching against Egypt. Although Assurbanipal left the campaigns to his generals, he personally directed their strategy and even tactics from the palace. The letters prove abundantly how closely the king controlled them.[16]

The king was *sangu*, the priest, of Ashur. This was no nominal office. He himself, each day, made the sacrifice and recited the prayer before the statue of the god. He did the like on many other occasions also, such as at special feast-days, or on a triumphant return, or inaugurating a temple or palace. In addition, the king had other priestly titles, for example, 'purifier of the god's statues', showing that he played a number of different roles in the complex of rituals.

The king was also the builder and restorer of the temples, and indeed, this was one of his chief religious preoccupations. Built of mud-brick, the temples crumbled very rapidly and many, too, were sacked by invaders. Not the king but the god decided a temple must be rebuilt, and the king was so informed by a vision, a dream, or an omen. Before the reconstruction he proclaimed a period of penitence and mourning. The oracles were, as usual, consulted. When the gods had been consulted and had consented, the king himself measured out the dimensions of the location. Many omens were required before the foundations were laid. The king himself opened the construction by carrying a basket of bricks. After the temple was finished the king came to purify and sanctify it. Finally came the rites of consecration, with the king once more at the centre of the ceremony.

Lastly, the king was head of the priestly orders and the highest religious authority in the land. It was he who appointed and included the high priests

---

[16] F. Malbran-Labat, *L'Armée et l'organisation militaire de l'Assyrie* (Droz, Geneva/Paris, 1982), 162–3.

of the various divinities, often choosing relatives. He it was, also, who fixed the quantities and quality of the sacrifices the priests made. He prescribed that certain rites were to be performed. One of his vital functions was to fix the calendar, for example, the beginning of each month and when the intercalary month (for it was a lunar calendar) should be inserted. These duties were of capital importance because each day had its own particular rites.

4.2.3. KINGSHIP IN PRACTICE: CONSTRAINTS AND STRENGTHS

For all the concentration of power, wealth, and patronage in the person of the monarch, few Assyrian kings had an easy reign. The death of Sargon on a distant campaign provoked a revolt put down by his heir-designate, Sennacherib. The latter was murdered by his sons. Esarhaddon had difficulty in succeeding him and had to carry out extensive purges. His choice of Assurbanipal as his heir provoked a revolt of that prince's brother, and when he died he left no less than three competitors in the field all claiming the throne.

The oracle-texts we possess are full of references to 'usurpers'. A usurper was by definition a *failed* pretender. Good religious and dynastic reasons were found to show that the defeated king had sinned against the gods; or, if he were a brother or another relative of the successful pretender, that he was a *junior* or otherwise ineligible. As usual, the legitimating formulae were circular. Success itself legitimated, since it proved the gods were with the victor.

Assyrian kingship was stronger than that of Babylonia, and a comparison helps indicate its strengths. First, Assyrian kings enjoyed long reigns: in the period 735–688 BC the average reign in Babylon was only three years—in Assyria it was nearly twenty. Secondly, Babylonia, unlike Assyria, had been thoroughly overrun by wandering Aramaean and Chaldaean tribes to north and south respectively. Thirdly, in Babylonia the great religious centres like Sippar, Nippur, and Borsippa were 'free cities'. This status was conferred for a reign and reconfirmed by the next king. We do not yet know precisely what was involved, but it would seem this included the right of inhabitants to appeal to the king in person in court cases, and freedom from taxation, imprisonment, military service, and forced labour. So, what with the tribal areas and these free cities, the authority of the Babylonian monarch was often exiguous, the enormous power of a Nebuchadnezzar II notwithstanding. Finally, the Babylonian priesthood was more independent of the king than the Assyrian.

In Assyria, on the other hand, the constraints on the monarch might come from four possible quarters: certain cities, the priests and augurs, the service nobility, and the royal princes. And alongside any or all of these went the past and present constraint of possible intervention by foreign monarchs.

Among the cities, Assur was particularly volatile. It was the home of the county's patron god, it was the first capital, and its citizens enjoyed immunities. It was sensitive to any threat to all or any of these privileges. The great warrior-king Tukulti-Ninurta (1244–1205) affronted it when he built a new capital on the west bank opposite. The chronicler says, 'his son Ashur-Nadin-Apal and *the nobles of Ashur* [my italics] rebelled against him, removed him from the throne, imprisoned him in a building in Kar Tukulti Urta [i.e. the new capital] and killed him with a weapon'.[17] The city was just as affronted when Ashur Nasir-pal (885–860) built Calah as his capital, so it is not surprising to find it figuring among the twenty-seven cities that joined in the rebellion against the heir-apparent, Shamsi Adad V, in 827. Indeed, almost all the cities of the heartland, notably Nineveh, Ashur, Arraphan, and Arbela joined in. Significantly, Calah, the capital, stood by the prince and his father, King Shalmaneser III. Perhaps, the least obscure of these examples is Sargon II's usurpation, often deemed a usurpation from the reigning king, Shalmaneser V (727–722). The latter, for reasons we do not know, had withdrawn the privileges of the great city of Harran on the Euphrates and of Assur itself. Sargon II, who seized his throne, reconfirmed their immunities: the citizens of these cities were freed of all dues, taxes, military service, and forced labour. This helped his efforts to legitimate himself against a host of rivals and promote his claim that the god Ashur had become angry at the sacrilegious king who disdained to fear him, and therefore overthrew him and called Sargon in his place.[18]

The constraints imposed by religion were of quite another order. Some scholars do indeed maintain that the priests manipulated the omens and oracles to press political points, but I find this hard to believe and impossible to prove. However, the very supremacy which the king exercised over the priesthood by his capacity of *sangu* to Ashur acted also as an extraordinary constraint on his personal activity; for it made him a prisoner of the gods. As the representative of his people to the gods he was 'manipulated almost like a talisman—or he became the scapegoat charged before the gods with all the sins of the community'.[19] Consequently, much of his time was taken up with rituals of penitence, like fasting and ritual shaving. One specific omen was singularly inauspicious: the occurrence of an eclipse in a particular part of the sky. In that event a 'substitute king' was

---

[17] H. W. F. Saggs, *The Might That Was Assyria* (Sidgwick and Jackson, London, 1984), 55.
[18] Olmstead, *History of Assyria*, 206–7.   [19] Frankfort, *Kingship*, 259.

appointed and stayed on the throne for 100 days, to ensure that the threatened doom did not fall upon the king, but upon this unfortunate 'whipping-boy' figure who, on the expiry of the prescribed time, was put to death.[20]

The political constraints on a king, however, came from his great officials—the service nobility—and the royal princes. In the early empire and before, the constraint had come mostly from the former. After Sargon, and especially as primogeniture was dropped in favour of the king nominating the heir-apparent, it came from the latter's disappointed relatives.

These great officials, as will be explained more fully later, were *palatine* officials who still bore the old patrimonial titles of the royal household— the 'herald', the 'cup-bearers', and so forth—but whose functions were now to act as governors of huge provinces. The *turtanu* who took precedence over all these others was not only a governor but the generalissimo. These officials mostly resided at court, making only periodic visits to the provinces, but it was their word which had to be obeyed there. In addition to this control over their province's resources, they possessed lands given them as life-benefices by the monarch, with which to maintain their estate, as well as private estates which they owned by right of inheritance or purchase. Altogether, the resources of any one of these officials at any time were formidable: huge wealth, the local taxes, their own bodyguards, and the authority to call out the militia. Let the cases of Dayyan-Ashur and Shamsi-Ilu illustrate their power in the earlier period.

Dayyan-Ashur came to be the *turtanu* in some obscure palace reshuffle in the fifth year of Shalmaneser III (858–824), and became the dominant figure in the government, re-selecting the great palatine officials-cum-governors and, from 832, in sole charge of all military operations. His province was Harran, that is, the entire west of the Jezirah. Olmstead describes him— possibly with exaggeration—as one who 'for a quarter of a century . . . ruled the empire in the name of his nominal master'.[21] In 827 the crown prince rebelled, but the old king and his son Shamsi Adad held out successfully—by reason of the firm support of Dayyan-Ashur and his ministerial colleagues. Modern Assyriologists see this revolt as an attempt of the intermediate service-nobles to dispossess the grandees who had ruled the roost for so long and were clearly never going to abdicate voluntarily. They failed and it was Shamsi Adad, defender of the *status quo*, who succeeded as the fifth king of that name (823–811)—and maintained the grandees in their posts.[22] Indeed, some of these were permitted to hold several offices, so

---

[20] Roux, *Ancient Iraq*, 31.   [21] Olmstead, *History of Assyria*, 153.
[22] Garelli, *Le Proche-Orient asiatique*, 95.

concentrating vast power in one single person: for instance, one Bel-Balat was, in 814, *turtanu*, herald, administrator of the temples and chief of hosts, as well as being the governor of six towns near Harran.[23] Shamsi-Ilu, a former governor of Assur, and *turtanu* in 782, likewise combined the functions listed above. He kept regal state, immortalizing his victories over Urartu without ever mentioning the name of his king. He was by no means the only nobleman to act in disdain of the sovereign. One governor ruled the huge province of Rasappa, in the eastern Jezirah from the Khabur to the Tigris, for twenty-eight years (804–776). His authority extended over 331 towns and villages.[24] One could cite many similar instances.

With Sargon II and the Sargonids the political constraints on the monarch alter. The era of grandee independence and rebellion wanes, and there is a stealthy but steady growth in royal absolutism. This is attested by the changes made in the eponymate. (From time immemorial, each year was marked by the name of the king, followed by the great palatine ministers— the *turtanu*, chief herald, cupbearer, chamberlain, steward, and so on.) At first the order of precedence had been decided by lot, then a strict order of rotation was established. From Sargon's reign the honour of the eponymate no longer depended on fixed tradition, as formerly, but solely on the decision of the monarch. Also, to undercut the powers of the service-nobility, and eliminate interregna and dynastic disputes, Sargon adopted the practice of nominating the heir-apparent as his co-regent. This did not serve. The oath of allegiance sworn to that heir-apparent by the magnates[25] may well have precluded nobiliar rebellion, but it provoked the bitter envy of the princes whose claims the kin had set aside. Henceforth, to the end of the empire, the death of a king was the signal for a civil war between the heir-apparent and his rivals, like the protracted three-way civil war after Assurbanipal's death in 631.

4.2.4. GRANDEUR AND WRETCHEDNESS OF THE ASSYRIAN KINGSHIP

'*Esarhaddon*, Great King, Legitimate King, King of the World, King of Assyria, Regent of Babylon, King of Sumer and Akkad, King of the Four Rims of the World, the True Shepherd, Favourite of the Great Gods . . .'[26] His empire stretched from the Persian Gulf to Lake Van and from Susa and Ecbatana in Persia and Elam to the Mediterranean, the entire Levant and the Nile Delta. So vast an assemblage of territories had never before been gathered under one hand. His armies were ever victorious. At his word

---

[23] Garelli, *Le Proche-Orient asiatique*, 95.   [24] Ibid. 99.   [25] See p. 217 above.
[26] *ANET*, 289.

communities were uprooted and transported 1,500 miles' march away. Vast piles of booty, trains of captives, vanquished kings were paraded before him. In his palace, guarded by the great winged-bulls, in the audience chamber lined with the huge bas-reliefs that showed him hunting lions, storming cities, and impaling, flaying, mutilating his prisoners-of-war, the king was surrounded by adulators. Thousands of princes, grandees, priests, diviners, scribes, courtiers, servants, eunuchs, concubines, generals, soldiers looked to him alone. The Prism Stele inscriptions all attest his might and his resoluteness, his military successes,[27] thus: 'I also (had) made this stela (bearing) my name-inscriptions, and had written thereupon the praise of the valour of my lord Ashur, my own mighty deeds—as well as my triumphal personal achievements . . .'[28] In most very ancient history, official documents are the only ones we have, and it is usually impossible to see behind this great display and penetrate the actor's true state of mind. But in the Assyrian case we can, and the reason is that we possess a file of the questions the king put to the oracle. We often have the oracle's reply as well, but this is rarely as revealing as the questions. These authentically reveal the mind of the 'King of All'. In what follows, it must be remembered, first, that the king was taking omens all the time, so that these cited queries to the oracle are a only a one-sided and highly concentrated selection. Next, since these queries were put over a long period of time, but appear here as though concentrated at one particular point of time, it must not be supposed that they represent the king as in a state of blind panic, rushing to the oracle and discharging all these fears together.

Here, then, are some of the innermost thoughts of Esarhaddon's chosen successor, the crown prince Assurbanipal. This prince has received the allegiance of the convocation of notables. He sits in the *bet redutti* as co-regent. But he has his anxieties.

Is danger to be anticipated from the bearded chiefs, the King's Companions, his own brother and the brothers of his father, the members of the royal family? He doubts the loyalty of his charioteer and of his chariot attendant, of the night-watch, of his royal messengers and of his body-guard, of the officers in the palace and those on the frontier, of his cellarer and baker. He fears for what he eats and what he drinks, he fears by day and by night; in the city and without, there is danger that a revolt against him will be undertaken.[29]

Now, here is a selection of the doubts and fears of the King Esarhaddon himself, he of 'the mighty deeds . . . [the] triumphal personal achievements'

[27] *ANET,* 289–94.   [28] Ibid. 292.   [29] Olmstead, *History of Assyria,* 396.

cited above. Here he is, for instance, faced by the Scythian incursion in the north, and the sort of questions he asks are like this:

Will they emerge from the pass of the city of Hubuskhia and fall upon the cities of Harrania and Anisus? Will they ravage the Assyrian border and carry off much spoil? If an ambassador is sent to Hubushkia, will the Mannai slay him? Will the expedition against the Mannai be successful? Will the general enter the pass of the city of Sandu and aid the city of Kilman in May? Will they take the cities of Karibti and Suba in Saparda in the same month? The city of Dur Bel, the fortress of Esarhadden, has been taken by the Mannai; will it be recovered? Will the expedition against the land of Sirish be fortunate? Will the Mannai or the Rimai fall upon it? Shall the general named upon the tablet go against the land of Kukkuma, the cities of Udpani and Ramadani, or will the Medes and the Mannai take them? Shall the commander-in-chief, Sha Nabu-shu, go against Amul and will he take it? What of Ahsheri, who has united with the Cimmerians? Will the city of Sharru-iqbi be taken by engines, hunger, or want, through fear or the defeat of the Assyrian troops?[30]

There is much, much more of this, but enough has been cited, perhaps, to make the point.

5. THE ADMINISTRATION OF THE EMPIRE

5.1. *The Territorial Framework*

The accession of Tiglath-Pileser III in 745 marks the beginnings of organized empire, as opposed to hegemony. His fierce personality and military victories were enough to control the great governors; and the device of the co-regency after the accession of Sargon II (722) permitted the succession of able and strong-willed monarchs in Sennacherib, Esarhaddon, and Assurbanipal, so that the frontiers went on expanding. Tiglath-Pileser III made the decisive innovation of treating conquered territory as 'heartland' Assyrian territory. That is to say, he no longer left the local kings in possession and contented himself with indirect rule as in the past and as Hittites and Egyptians had also done. Henceforth, this was only the initial stage; soon afterwards—how soon depending on circumstances—the territory was treated as though it were heartland. In short, the local dynasty was abolished and in its place the Assyrian local-government system was introduced, reporting to and acting on (very detailed) instructions from the king.

   A vast tract of territory stretching into the Levant from Cilicia in the north to Judah in the south, as well as the entire Jezirah, became part and

---

[30] Olmstead, *History of Assyria*, 361. Here Olmstead is paraphrasing the texts in E. G. Klauber, *Politische-religiöse Texte aus die Sargonenzeit* (Leipzig, 1913).

parcel of the Assyrian heartland. It was divided into provinces, each ruled by an Assyrian governor, who in his turn controlled his own staff who governed and collected taxes in the towns and villages. The people in these provinces were treated on a par with the 'old' Assyrians. They were not discriminated against on the grounds of origins and antecedents; the administration was not interested in this, or in their juridical status. They were *nishé*, 'people'; and as such they were the servants of the king to whom they owed total obedience. All were *urdu*—'slaves'—of the monarch, and like the 'old' Assyrians shared the common Assyrian obligation—*ilku*—to perform military and/or forced labour-service, as well as pay the various imposts and taxes. This process of amalgamation was paralleled by a programme—equally effective—of assimilation. The latter was achieved by the mass deportations. It is reckoned that some 4.5 million persons were uprooted and sent to diverse parts of the empire, and that 80 per cent of these were deported from the days of Tiglath-Pileser III onward.[31] These people, too, were treated in their new homes just like the 'native Assyrians'—no distinction was made.[32] Simultaneously, great bodies of 'native' Assyrians were transported to various frontier posts, sensitive areas, or simply to replace deportees. Thus a huge mixing of the population took place over the century-and-a-quarter, with a corresponding erosion of particularist sentiments and cultural and political identities. Everyone was now, in an even more realistic sense, the 'slave' of the king.

The Assyrian power was of course felt outside the provinces, and in this zone the system of tributary states was maintained. The local monarch continued to keep his court, but under the supervision of a *qepu*, an Assyrian resident governor.

For all the mass of cuneiform tables we possess today, we can draw only an outline sketch of the way this empire was administered. For one thing, the tablets come overwhelmingly from the palaces, such as those at Nineveh and Calah, that is, from the central government. We have little corresponding detail for any of the provinces. Even the Babylonian material is limited, and Babylon was a most exceptional province anyway. In the second place, the material offers no possibility of quantitative studies and is unlikely ever to do so.[33] Thirdly, even after the most patient collation of texts, many of the key terms are still obscure.[34]

Before attempting to describe the territorial and hierarchical structures, however, it is worthwhile noting some general features of the system. The

---

[31] B. Oded, *Mass Deportations and Deportees in the Neo-Assyrian Empire* (Ludwig Reichert Verlag, Wiesbaden, 1979), 20.   [32] Ibid. 79–87.

[33] J. N. Postgate, 'The Economic Structure of the Assyrian Empire', in Larsen (ed.), *Power and Propaganda*, 196–7.   [34] Ibid., *passim*.

available evidence does not suffice to show whether it was sophisticated or in what ways. It followed the common features of virtually all antique societies—including for that matter the Roman Empire—in that provincial governors were 'omnibus' officials, with civil as well as military duties, just as the common peoples' *ilku* was, indifferently, military service as well as forced labour. The governors were responsible for justice as well as public order. We know little more about how it was dispensed other than that the cases were based on witnesses' evidence; and, as to arbitrariness, it must be remembered that Mesopotamia had a long tradition of law-codes stretching back to the earliest times. About the governor's staff we know nothing except that some subordinate staff, such as the grain-tax officials or the *iskaru* officials, only carried out their duties seasonally, or as an adjunct to other duties.[35]

Next, it was highly patrimonial. The nomination and removal of the governors was at the pleasure of the king. These governors were as much *urdu*—slaves—to the king as anybody else and for their part whenever they had to write to the king they were very anxious to tell him that they knew it—'I am a dead dog'[36] is one not uncommon expression.

Correspondingly, the centre as well as the peak of the administration is the king in person. We forget, nowadays, when government is so vast, that up to the days of Frederick II the great, absolute monarchs in Europe seriously aspired to run their states in person—one thinks of Philip II of Spain, Louis XIV of France, Joseph II of Austria—and did effectively do so. Their affairs were much more complicated than the Assyrian Empire's, which were almost exclusively concerned with three things: taxation, worship, and war. One interesting feature of Assyrian history is the—apparent—absence of 'do-nothing' kings: we do not find kings reproached—as Roman, Byzantine, Chinese, and Arab emperors are so frequently—with idling away their time in their harems, or in hunting, or some other frivolous pursuit while their kingdoms sink in disorder. Most Assyrian kings were indefatigably assiduous and poked their noses into the most trivial of provincial details.

The same pattern of patrimonial interference and concern with trivial details was characteristic of the lower levels also. Just as the king directed the activities of his governors, so did these direct their local subordinates. The Assyrian Empire operated on the Chinese box principle of all-purpose governors looking after their provinces.

We should also note the organization of *intelligence*. It served civil purposes as well as military ones. Indeed, it was the neural network that kept the empire together. Assyria was surrounded to the north, east, and south by

---

[35] Postgate, 'Royal Exercise of Justice'.   [36] Olmstead, *History of Assyria*, 461.

enemies always ready to strike; and again, unlike Egypt, its ecology was not some enormous 'ribbon-development' with the Nile as an arterial road. It was a land empire where the fastest horse-relays could not cover more than about fifty miles in the day, while an army made only twenty. Without intelligence gathering it would rapidly have fallen to pieces. Today we live in societies where 'intelligence', even in the most rudimentary sense, is taken for granted: newspapers daily report on whatever is going on up and down the country, let alone specialized periodicals; foreign affairs are reported, changes in potentially enemy states are analysed by local correspondents. Radio and television broadcasts bring these same matters into our living room. Imagine every one of these sources drying up and the rail and road systems non-existent. The only information one would receive would be odd scraps of information about, perhaps, a fire, a rape, a robbery, perhaps an epidemic, passed on in the street or market by strangers: in short, *bazaar* gossip, a confused murmur of trivia *except* to the man who knows what he is looking for. Such was the condition of the Assyrian Empire, and its rulers made up for the absence of press and radio and special correspondents' reports by, so to speak, organizing bazaar-gossip on an immense scale and providing for its analysis. Everybody, high and low, had an absolute obligation to report everything, however trivial, that touched the king, and the superabundance of royal exhortations on this matter shows the importance attached to it. The local officials of all ranks had to give priority to passing intelligence upwards without delay. Intelligence about the enemy was obtained by informers, spy-networks, and special units of scouts and secret agents who hid in enemy country. We find crown princes like Sennacherib acting from time to time like a central intelligence agency—collating the bits of information, systematizing them, and passing them up to the king.

This information had to be transmitted from its sources as fast as possible, so certain royal routes were established, with relay and guard posts. Along these there passed simple messengers, mounted messengers, and the *kalliu* or 'express couriers'. Although intelligence gathering is attested from the time of Hammurabi, the Assyrians may well have developed it further than their predecessors.

Between the palace and the provinces there also passed from time to time the *qurbutu*—direct representatives of the king, that is, a 'guard-royal'—whose authority to receive messages of prime importance was overriding. In this connection we might mention the offices of the *rab sukallu*, usually translated as vizier but best, I think, as comptroller-general. He seems to have headed a corpus of *sukallus* who visited the governors and were able to check and control their activities, but of further detail we are ignorant.[37]

[37] Malabran-Labat, *L'Armée et l'organisation militaire de l'Assyrie* (Droz, Geneva/Paris 1982), 13 20, 41 54.

We can now turn to the structure itself. This operated at three levels: provincial governors, district governors, mayors.

Governors went under two names and there is unresolved argument about the precise significance of this. Usually the terms, *shaknu* and *Bêl pihati* are thought to be interchangeable. But the *Bêl pihati* were appointed chiefly from officials called *sha reshi*, and this means 'he of the head'. Because of this and because texts also speak of the *shaknu* as appointed from a category called *rabani*, which means, effectively, something like 'big men', hence, chiefs or nobles, Kinnier-Wilson thinks that there were *two* governors in each province: the *shaknu* would be the military governor, the *Bêl pihati* the governor subordinate to him. Possibly, but the reasoning seems shaky.

Along with the *shaknu* and the *Bêl pihati* there is evidence of deputy-governors. This member of the province's rulers was *rab alani*, the district governor, in charge of a group of towns and villages. We do not know how many such were appointed in a province. In the towns and villages themselves, the chief official—the headman or mayor—was *the hazanu*. He was particularly active in the law-courts and in notarizing all arrivals and departures in his town. He had a deputy and the third of the city triumvirate was the scribe of the city, a very senior appointment. These formed the executive. Side by side with them there existed the council of elders—*the shibuti*—made up of heads of upper-class families,[38] an institution that had existed at least since the time of Hammurabi.

A governor's chief duties were to raise the taxes, collect and forward tribute, collect provisions for the royal army, and call up his provincial militia as and when necessary. He had at all times to collect and forward intelligence. And, frequently, he would be in charge of the military operations in his province.

Governors paid the central government only the surplus over their own administrative expenses. (This was almost the rule in all taxation systems up to the nineteenth century.) Tax consisted primarily of straw and grain. Much of this was stored locally for the use of the royal armies. Similarly, the corvée which the governor was entitled to levy was used partly for his own administration's purposes, partly to assist the route-march of the royal army, and—sometimes—to prepare for the settlement of deportees in the area.

Although they were subject to continual interventions, commands, queries, and complaints by the king, these governors were very powerful and, sometimes, when the province was in crisis, were effectively viceroys. They had their own palaces, courts, and officials. So the question arises as to why they never tried to secede. For although they took sides in dynastic

---

[38] J. V. Kinnear-Wilson, *The Nimrud Wine Lists* (British School of Archaeology in Iraq, 1972), 8.

disputes—and it is hard to see how they could have avoided this when royal princes were in competition for the throne—they do not ever appear either to wish to set up their own independent kingdoms or to seek the throne themselves. In this they differed very signally from some of the Persian satraps, from Roman generals, from some Byzantine *strategoi*, and from governors in the Caliphate. One restraining factor might well have been the *adu*, the oath of allegiance they had sworn to sustain the king. Another would have been the gifts of precious metals or land assignments from a grateful monarch. A third, we may suspect, was the acceptance that the kingship resided in a certain 'royal seed'; they could and did participate in civil wars to decide which member of this stock should be king, but knew that they themselves stood no chance, as commoners, of breaking in. Finally, I suspect that most of them—in the empire period—were just too scared. Sargon and his successors were formidable characters who led formidable armies in person. At all events, whether for all or any one of these reasons, provincial governors did not ever attempt to break away and set up on their own. When after 130 years the empire did collapse, it was by invasion after it had been undermined by dynastic civil wars and, quite possibly, by the over-extension of the local administrative system just described. This is a quite different sort of demise from that of say, the Caliphate, where first one and then another outlying province asserted its independence.

5.2. *The Central Administration*

It was not possible to construct a very coherent picture of the central administration of Egypt, but for Assyria we are somewhat better off. The archive found at the capital city of Calah provides a list of the officials in the palace and it enables us to form a quite vivid impression of an oriental court. It will not be the last we shall encounter, for the same pattern of kings, harem, nobles, and palace staff, including possibly eunuchs, will be found with local variation in, for instance, Persia, the later Roman and the Byzantine empires, in the Arab Caliphate and its successor states in India, and in China.

Yet, for all the formidable scholarship which Kinnear-Wilson has lavished on the archive of the Nimrud Wine Lists[39] the picture is very incomplete. We learn of the existence of the court craftsmen, doctors, diviners and augurs, of musicians, cooks, table and household servants. We learn there were two harems. But, to take the last as an example, we know nothing of the harem organization or its size, whereas for Han China

[39] Ibid.

we know all these details and more besides. Next, we are told nothing of the relationship between the royal palace and the *bet redutti*, 'the house of succession', which the crown prince occupied as co-regent. Finally, we are given no information on the interrelationships between the various officials and departments that are named. The result is a very hazy impression of the kind of work carried out from the palace and the titles of the officials responsible for it. It is very unsatisfactory.

We have already encountered the great officials, the two *turtanus* or commanders-in-chief; the *rab shaqi*, the cup-bearer; the *nagir ekalli*, or palace herald; and the *abarakku*, variously translated as 'steward' or 'treasurer'. These were originally household offices, as their names indicate, but under the empire—or indeed some time before—their function had become the civil and military control of four great provinces, three of them partitioning up the entire Jezirah area and the fourth lying on the northern frontier.[40] The *turtanu* spent most of his time in his own capital on the Euphrates and on campaign, and the *rab shaqi* was also often away, campaigning. The *nagir ekallu*, 'herald', responsible for proclaiming the royal call-up of the levy, seems to have had special responsibility for home defence.[41] The *abarakku* appears to have been the treasurer, and head of commissariat: receiving *ilku* payments and other imposts (*namurtu*), storing them, and paying them out again.[42] These four magnates, along with the comptroller-general, and probably the king's scribe also, were especially intimate with the king and dined with him or his men.[43] One point may be added: the *rab shaqi* or cup-bearer, possibly owing to his intimacy with the king, was highly influential and his rank prestigious.

The palace compound contained two courts, as would be the case in Achaemenian Persia, the Caliphate, the Ottoman Empire, and the Chinese Empire. The *bitanu* or inner court included the private quarters. Here was the harem, here too the salons and bedrooms of the monarch. The outer court, or *babanu* (from the root *bab*, meaning gate, which in the ancient Orient had originally been, and often continued to be, a complex building containing guard-rooms, places where judgements were given, and the corresponding offices), was the area where the council rooms were situated as well as the offices to be described.

We do not know whether the Assyrian court used eunuchs. The earliest reference to eunuchs being used systematically has been traced to the Hittite Empire, where they appear as a particularly trusted retinue, charged with informing the king of any threats directed at him and with protecting him

---

[40] J. V. Kinnear-Wilson, *The Nimrud Wine Lists* (British School of Archaeology in Iraq, 1972), 14.
[41] Ibid. 36.   [42] Ibid.   [43] Ibid. 35–7.

and his family.[44] But this identification turns on the meaning ascribed to the word *sha-reshi*. If (as Kinnear-Wilson does) we translate it as 'eunuchs', then the proposition is certainly right; but if, as more recent scholarship maintains, the term should be translated as simply 'officials', we are no better off than when we started.

The second great group of officials was called the *rabani*: Kinnear-Wilson names twenty-two of these as provincial governors and others are found manning the household cavalry and chariotry. In short, their functions overlap with the *sha-reshi*. Kinnear-Wilson regards these two terms as designating two different types of officials. But there is no more reason to suppose this than to suppose that the two terms imply today that 'officer' and 'sergeant' represent different and mutually exclusive kinds of policemen.

We can turn now to such central ministries as the Calah archives happen to disclose. They consist of a number of commissariat departments and of three others. The commissariat departments numbered eight—for grain, bread, beer, fruits, wine, honey and dates, fodder, and oils. Each had its chief accountant, and was headed by one of the *rabani*. If, as Kinnear-Wilson seems to think, the hallmark of the latter was their warrior status, one wonders at this very civilian type of function.

The first of the three major ministries was the 'treasury'—to accept Kinnear-Wilson's term for the *abarakku*. Its functions have been described.[45] The next is the highly problematical office of the *sukallu*. This has usually been translated as vizier, an implicit suggestion of an identity between the Islamic states and Assyria which, in this case, Kinnear-Wilson himself rejects. The fact is, there is not a shred of evidence that the *sukallu* supervised the rest of the departments, which was the cardinal function of the Arab vizier.[46] The *sukallu* seems rather to have acted as an independent control on the operation of the other departments. Even more problematical is whether, as is sometimes alleged, he had a staff of inferior *sukallus* who controlled the activities of the provincial governments.[47] *Sukallu* meant, generically, personal—indeed ambassadorial—messengers, and there are mentions of such throughout the Assyrian texts, differing according to their place in the hierarchy and with powers differing according to the time and the place.[48] While it is certain that the *sukallu rabu* (i.e. the grand *sukallu*) *had* subordinate *sukallu*, the texts 'hardly permit definition of their functions'.[49] It is worth noting that this lack of precision may not be just due to our linguistic inadequacies. It may be that the Assyrians did not use precise

---

[44] J. V. Kinnear-Wilson, *The Nimrud Wine Lists* (British School of Archaeology in Iraq, 1972), 47.
[45] See previous page.   [46] See p. 191 above.
[47] Garelli, *Le Proche-Orient asiatique*; Malbran-Labat, *L'Armée et l'organisation*, 157.
[48] Ibid. 156.   [49] Ibid. 157.

administrative terms because the duties of the administrators were imprecise. Most officials performed a number of functions. This *sukallu rabu*, for
instance, had military as well as civil responsibilities. There is a letter which
shows one of them as the commander of 200 cavalry and another as military
adviser to the king. A *sukallu rabu* might also, if need arose, take over the
governorship of a province.[50]

Finally comes the *bab ekallu*, the 'palace gate'. This was the *chancery*. As we
have said earlier, *all* departmentalized bureaucracies *must* have a central
recording—and filing—office—a chancery. This office, probably headed
by the king's scribe (*tupsar ekallu*), comprised two sections. The first contained specialized scholar-scribes, teachers, master craftsmen, and probably,
the librarian. The second was the secretariat proper. Its clerks maintained
written records, and wrote and copied and filed the king's correspondence.

This woefully inadequate picture of the central administration can be
marginally improved by looking at some of the administrative services,
notably taxation—although it should be borne in mind that the taxes
here described pre-dated the Assyrian Empire, perhaps by more than a
thousand years.

5.3. *Central Services*

5.3.1. SOME TERMS RELATING TO TAXATION[51]

ILKU: 'Either the performance of military or civilian service for the state, or
the payment of contributions as a commuted version of that service.'[52] It
was associated with owning land, but most city-dwellers did not do so and
instead of paying by giving their services, they paid in kind.[53]

ISKARU: meant *either* the raw materials (including animals) issued to an
employee or the payment the latter made in return (usually in silver in the
late period). Originally, a craftsman or as it might be a shepherd received his
raw materials and after processing these returned the product in full. The
'added value' was the way he paid his tax. Under the empire he retained
some of the produce for his own use and, selling the remainder, paid the
purchase price over to the government in silver. On the royal estates the
system was organized by a steward (*abarakku*), a subordinate of the provincial
governor, who controlled a large staff. This organized the distribution of
the *iskaru* assignments, and then, later, collected the contributions, through
state-collectors or alternatively tax-farmers.[54]

---

[50] Garelli, *Le Proche-Orient asiatique*; Malbran-Labat, *L'Armée et l'organisation*, 156–8.
[51] This follows Postgate, 'Royal Exercise of Justice'.   [52] Ibid.   [53] Ibid.
[54] Ibid.

MUSHARKISI: Like the Chinese, the Assyrians, never had enough horses for their military needs, and the *musharkisi service*, which involved horse-studs, collecting-points, and the like, was very extensive. The *musharkisi* were high-ranking officials, immediately below the governor, and communicating directly with the king.

SIRSHU: This was the corn and straw tax. Straw was in high demand and always in short supply, for it was essential in brick-making. The collection, obviously, was seasonal and there was no special term for the collectors, who were simply officials temporarily taken off their regular jobs. Every government department collected the tax on the lands under its control.[55] For private lands, the responsible official was the governor or his deputy. So, at harvest time the governor would second his staff to the villages—accompanied by a troop of soldiers; partly to intimidate the farmers and partly to escort and transport the proceeds of the collection. Certainly the lands were assessed—there still exists a sort of 'Domesday Book' for some Crown land in Harran—but the assessment was probably made on the spot at the time of collection.[56] Postgate thinks an 'ideal' crop was assumed for each village and the tax actually paid was a fraction of that 'ideal sum'.

The chief object of the tax system was to finance the *army*. Strangely—for it is so prominent in the Assyrian annals—once again we know no more than the bare outlines.

5.3.2. THE ARMY

It clearly was extremely efficient, for it managed to maintain and then extend its original frontiers in the face of immense pressure from highlanders, desert nomads, and the warrior states of Mitanni and Urartu, for some six centuries up to the formation of the empire in 745, and to conquer the entire Middle-East in the subsequent 130 years. Yet we know nothing of its training or code of discipline.

Originally, it was a peasant militia army. It was Tiglath-Pileser III who formed the *kisir sharutti*, the 'Royal Forces', a full-time professional force. The recruits came largely from the outlying provinces. Certain tribes, notably the Ituai, were taken into regular service in return for tax-exemption. To this hard core was added the regular conscript contingent, the *shabe sham*. For exceptional campaigns—and always for home defence—the militia would also be called out. By the end of the empire this army was made up of many different *ethnoi*, rather like Achaemenian armies were to be.

The numbers of troops recorded must be treated with great caution.

---

[55] This follows Postgate, 'Royal Exercise of Justice'.   [56] Ibid.

Shalmaneser says he put 120,000 men into battle against the enemy's 70,000 at Qarqar (854); Assurbanipal speaks of an army of 50,000 and Sennacherib boasted of no less than 208,000 men.[57] The tactical organization appears to have been along the following lines. The basic unit consisted of ten men, led by the *rab esirte.* These tens were grouped into a unit of fifty men, led by a *rab hansu;* this was the most widespread and important of the tactical units, although 'seventeens' are also found and so are 'centuries'. But above the fifty, the main tactical unit was the thousand.

The main groups of the army were the light and the heavy infantry; the chariotry; the cavalry; and the engineers and siege-train.

Among the infantry figure first the heavy archers, wearing a calf-length tunic of armour of overlapping scales, a hauberk of the same kind, and a pointed metal helmet. They carried the composite bow and a sword, and always went protected by a buckler-man, who carried the quiver and was armed with a sword. Medium archers—also accompanied by a buckler-man—wore just the scale-armour corselet. Light archers wore no armour. Slingers, however, were equipped like the heavy archers. The other infantry arm consisted of spearmen. They wore helmet and corselet, and carried sword and long shield. There were also light spearmen with helmets but no corselets.

The chariotry had developed over almost two millennia. At first—*c.*2500—the chariot was a ceremonial car, pulled by onagers or some other equine species, but certainly not by horses. By about 1400 the chariots had become battle-carts pulled by horses. Horses were also used independently of chariots, ridden in the very clumsy way one rides a donkey and used to carry messages. By the time of, say, Sargon II, the chariot had become highly developed, while a true cavalry had emerged. The chariotry was still very much an élite corps. The chariots themselves had much heavier wheels than the Egyptian ones, and carried a crew of three, not two. Later still, some chariots even carried four persons—the driver, the archer, and two buckler-men. As to cavalry—mounted archers and lancers—other peoples had also used it, but the Assyrians were the first to do so systematically and on a large scale.

---

[57] These figures, particularly Sennacherib's, are barely credible. They would be immense by any historical yardstick—Louis XIV's armies, *c.*1710, or Frederick the Great's, for instance—but relatively more so at this time considering the likely size of the population. C. McEvedy and R. Jones, *Atlas of World Population History* (Penguin, Harmondsworth, 1978), estimate the total population of all Mesopotamia at about 1.25 million. These authors go on to say that there is no reason to suppose that medieval Iraq could support more than 5 million people, and that the number who actually lived there ever exceeded half this figure. When Louis XIV put some 200,000 men in the line, *c.*1710, the population from which it was drawn was some 20 million.

Assyria had used an engineer corps from very early times. It was highly efficient. It could float troops across rivers on inflatable rafts, and hack out roads with iron hatchets. To carry city walls it perfected battering-rams, movable towers, earth-ramps, and the skills of mining and sapping.

This discussion of the army brings us fittingly to considering, as its *raison d'être*, the empire as a whole.

6. AN APPRAISAL

As a governmental structure, the Assyrian state was less differentiated and less sophisticated than the kingdom of Egypt. One principal reason was that it was not a redistribution–storage economy—an *oikos* economy—so that it did not need the extensive bureaucracy this entailed. It was an economy of farmers, with considerably more trading abroad than was the case with Egypt. Also, unlike the southern part of Mesopotamia, it lay astride the rain-belt so it did not rely entirely on irrigation. As we stated at the beginning, it is the first attestation of empire properly so called, that is, the direct rule of the subjected territories via agents of the imperial power. However, such is the opprobrium that has attended this particular empire that it is desirable to say a few words on this topic. It is chiefly reproached for its unceasing aggressions, its cruelties, and its murderousness. To such charges its defenders, Olmstead or Saggs, retort that it was no worse in these respects than other empires in the past and that it played a positive role in that it defended 'civilization' against barbarians and, also, saved a great deal of bloodshed by imposing its *pax Assyriana.* In my view the charges and the defence ought both to be treated with caution.

There is absolutely no doubt that the Assyrian armies and their kings carried out exquisite tortures and extensive atrocities. Defeated enemies were flayed alive, impaled on pillars or stakes, walled up alive, castrated, decapitated. After the defeat of Elam its king was decapitated and his head slung round the neck of a captured courtier; three rebellious chieftains had their tongues pulled out by the roots and were then flayed alive; three other noble rebels were slaughtered and their flesh distributed around the surrounding lands. Two more were forced to crush the bones of their father.[58]

Nor is there any doubt that the empire was a predator. The piles of booty carried off at each successful expedition were prodigious—Carchemish: 20 talents of silver, 100 of bronze, 250 of iron; couches, buckles, rings, and swords of gold; beds, thrones, and tables of ivory. Musasir (a town on the northern frontier): 6,100 captives, 380 asses, 525 cattle, 1,235 sheep in

[58] Olmstead, *History of Assyria*, 439.

addition to 34 talents of gold, 167 talents of silver, bronze, lead, cornelian, lapis lazuli, vases, daggers, and the like.[59] The empire preyed on humans as well as on precious metals and valuable ornaments. From the time of Tiglath-Pileser III the deportation of the conquered peoples was institutionalized—some 4 million people in 530 years to the end of the empire. The reasons were various—to punish, to weaken the rival power, to enlarge the Assyrian manpower base, to import skilled craftsmen, to populate urban centres and strategic cities and re-cultivate abandoned lands.

It is true that this empire was no more bloody or cruel than others in the subsequent past. This must be admitted. One thinks, for instance, of Chinghiz Khan, but one can go back to empires that are thought to be more noble, such as the Roman, only to find atrocities like those committed in the 'pacification' of Iberia, mass crucifixions and deportations (e.g. from Judaea), and slave-trading on a vast scale like that of Julius Caesar in Gaul. Yet the charge that still rests against the Assyrians is that they gave such a prominent place to recording these acts of sadism in their bas-reliefs and in their chronicles. Many (myself included), would attribute this to sheer bloodthirstiness. One apologia is that they did it to remind potential 'trouble-makers' that acquiescence was in their interest, a reply that begs the question as to why there were such 'trouble-makers'.

> Und willst du nicht mein Bruder sein
> So schlag ich dir den Schädel ein.[60]

Next is the claim that the Assyrians were the 'shepherd-dogs of civilization'.[61] Olmstead's case is that most of its wars were fought to hold back the 'savages from the Arabian wastes or the equally backward Indo-Europeans from the northern grass-lands'. This claim might be justified in respect of the immediately neighbouring mountain states, although even here archaeology has shown that the kingdom of Urartu was much more civilized than Olmstead could have known over sixty years ago. On the other hand the apologia is totally unjustifiable in respect to the conquest of states like Elam, Babylon, and Egypt. It would be absurd to maintain that any of these were less civilized than Assyria, and indeed they were more so.

The *pax Assyriana* argument is highly questionable, also. The Assyrian rulers would certainly have *liked* to impose such a peace, permanently, on their conquered subjects; the facts were that too many of these obstinately

---

[59] Olmstead, *History of Assyria*, 239.
[60] Approximate translation: 'And if you will not be my brother, I'll beat your head in!'
[61] Olmstead, *History of Assyria*, 654.

refused to accept it. Babylon tried to break away four times,[62] the Assyrian conquest of Egypt was contested,[63] Elam revolted along with Babylon in 652/648 and fell when its capital, Susa, was sacked in 639.

The mass deportation of subject populations is one of the Assyrian policies to have attracted the greatest odium; yet in the context of that time and later it is, perhaps, the most justifiable. We have already stated that the resettled populations were treated exactly on a par with the native Assyrians. Similar population-transfers were to be carried out in many other empires, for example, Han China and Byzantium, and for the same kind of reasons already mentioned. In those days and for long afterwards, unless the imperial power had good reason to believe that the conquered people would lay down their arms and not take to the field again as soon as it had departed, it had only three alternatives. It could enslave the enemy soldiers, or a large part of their population. This is what Julius Caesar did in Gaul. But the Assyrians did not go in for chattel-slavery on a mass scale. The second alternative was to massacre all the enemy combatants, and this sometimes occurred but it could not be applied to entire populations. The third, and in this case the preferred alternative was to move the conquered people away from their homes, a policy that broke the local resistance and at the same time augmented the material resources of the empire.

The final charge relates to the predatory character of the Assyrian Empire. All empires are predatory: it is the first and often the last reason for their existence. All imperial conquerors have made off with huge quantities of spoil. In this respect the Assyrians were no different at all from any other empires, including Napoleon's. That is not the question. The real issue concerns the 'duty of care'. Although all empires were exploitative, some were exclusively so whereas others brought—whether intentionally or not—residual or incidental benefits to the subject peoples. This *History* will argue that the Persians did so, and, emphatically, so did the Romans and the Chinese. The case against the Assyrians is that they were predators and nothing else. To use an old-fashioned phrase, they had no 'sense of empire'. They did not feel they had any 'duty of care', and they gave their subject peoples nothing whatsoever in return for their massive exploitation and oppression.

---

[62] 731 BC, 705 BC, 652–48 BC, 626 BC.

[63] Esarhaddon had defeated the Egyptians and entered Egypt, 671 BC, but died in the course of the campaign. The attack was resumed and the Assyrians defeated the Egyptians in heavy fighting, 667–663, and established puppet kings and docile princes in the Delta.

5

The Jewish Kingdoms, 1025–587 BC

Small, poor, ill-managed, divided, and short-lived: the Kingdoms of Israel and Judah were two of the petty monarchies extinguished by the Assyrians and their Babylonian successors. But these states, and Judah in particular, represent, however, a revolutionary breakthrough in the tradition of government traced so far. After a span of 2,000 years—since 3200 BC—there appeared, briefly, a form of government with a wholly original and totally different characteristic. After AD 132 the political community itself was uprooted, driven out, and dispersed. Yet the memory of its peculiar polity was preserved as part of the sacred writings of the late-Roman world. As such, it served as an exemplar for the new, barbarian peoples of Western Europe. In this way it entered into the Western state tradition and, through that, into the governmental norms of our entire contemporary world.

Every polity in the ancient Middle East was, as we have seen, monarchical. The institution of monarchy was seen as part of the natural order. It was never contested, though individual incumbents might be toppled. Its powers were absolute: it was the source of all law. The only restraints upon it were the natural limits of any human's capabilities, the extra-constitutional obstruction in court, camp, or locality, and the obligation arising from its role as cult-leader. All these operated likewise on the Jewish monarchy. The difference lies in the third, the religious role, and this stems from a different concept of God and the relationship between Him and the community.

For the Jewish monarchy was not part of the natural order at all. It was a factitious man-made institution, grafted on to the community in historical times in circumstances vividly recounted in the records. The Jewish monarch was neither divine nor semi-divine: God was . . . God; the Creator of all things, the Almighty, the Ineffable, the one sole God, the Lord of the Universe. And the Jewish monarch was not the intermediary between the community and God, either: the entire community had covenanted itself to God at Mount Sinai. This is the central event in Jewish history. Everything else was elaboration and commentary. At Sinai God gave out his law: it was written down and the people covenanted to obey it. So, each individual, and the community as a whole, was in direct communion with God. An intermediary was superfluous—indeed, he would have been noxious.

It does not matter for our enquiry whether the Jews were right about the nature of God, or whether the events at Sinai occurred as the tradition had it, or indeed whether they occurred at all. Nor does it matter whether the biblical account is contemporary with the events or interpolated later. The vast corpus of source-criticism, form-criticism, and the even more recent forms of the higher criticism are totally irrelevant here, because the Christianized German barbarians who founded the medieval European states did not have the benefits of it. For them the Bible account was wholly and perfectly true.

This Jewish religion is the first of the world's so-called 'Historic' (as opposed to the 'Archaic') religions,[1] and it is one I characterize as a *kahal* religion. For the first time the people form a *congregation* (Hebrew: *kahal*; Greek: *ekklesia*). The cult is not royal, not official, not priestly. It is *popular* and its essence is *participation*. The entire population not only may but must participate, and as individuals, not as a mass, even if it is the king or the priests who perform the rites in front of them. Again, for the first time the religion is not just a cult confined to rituals. It is a code of moral behaviour which is coextensive with the everyday behaviour of everybody. Moreover, this code, increasingly elaborated as time goes on, is full and highly explicit. In the end, after the Return (537 BC), it was to govern the entire life of the community. Thirdly, this God-given code applies with equal force to everybody in the congregation and hence to the king equally with the commoner.

Some significant *political* corollaries follow. In the first place: the monarch is bound by an explicit and written law code imposed on him, coequally with his subjects, *from the outside*. The code does not consist simply of rituals he must perform: it is a set of explicit rules in criminal, civil, family, and property jurisdiction. Secondly, this code is the possession of the entire congregation. It is possible for any member to note that what the king does and what the code prescribes are not the same and, since it is his possession as much as the king's, to denounce the behaviour of the king. Hence the prophets. The king was not absolute. He was not a law-giver. He was bound to administer a law which he had not created but which he had received, and must himself observe. He is history's first *limited monarch*.[2]

The weakness in this entirely new conception of the state is that there is no institutional mechanism for 'correcting' the king, for making the limita-

---

[1] See pp. 23 ff., 115 ff., 141–2 above for definition, discussion, and instances of archaic religions.

[2] This point is made by Lord Acton in his essay 'The History of Freedom in Antiquity', in G. Himmelfarb (ed.), *Essays on Freedom and Power* (Meridian Books, New York, 1955). This contains an extended passage on the matter. What is of particular interest here is that Acton employs the very same term used in the text above: 'That early example of limited monarchy and the supremacy of law.' Ibid. 56 7.

tion effective. Any such action had to be extra-constitutional and it depended on the intrepidity of certain individuals. Yet the royal authority was, in fact, frequently challenged by such persons and this was often to effect. One underlying pre-condition of this effectiveness was that the Jews possessed the *alphabet*. Indeed, they had had an alphabet for so long that some modern Bible scholars have even surmised that the Ten Commandments (*c.*1230 BC) were, as the Bible says they were, really inscribed on stone. In any event, by the final years of the kingdom of Judah its people were literate. So the Law, written, lay open to all. Moreover, so was its interpretation: for, under the Covenant everyone had his personal part in it. The 'spirit of the Lord' could and did descend on anybody. A holy man, who might be a very humble individual, could harness popular feeling. So, beyond the formal rituals carried out by the priest and the interpretation of the law carried out by the king in his capacity of judge, there was *challenge* backed up in the last resort by popular support. Nothing at all like this had been witnessed in the Middle East before. Unlike the empires, where social structure, religious values, and the political institutions reinforced one another to provide a massive stability, the Jewish kingdoms vibrated with tension. Their society was much more egalitarian: a free peasantry, literacy, a popular militia side-by-side with the royal mercenary army.

The religion was one where each was equal to each other. Even more, it was one that did not really have any place for a monarch. The king of 'the land' was God—'Our Father and King'—and the laws of the land were God's laws. The monarchy was in principle redundant, except 'to judge us and go out before us and fight our battles' (1 Samuel 8: 20)—that is, purely secular and instrumental concerns—and, as the later prophets like Isaiah and Jeremiah argued, entirely subordinate to the purpose of the Jewish people, which was to keep the Covenant by obeying the Law. The moment the king seemed to be breaching the Law—not just its formal prescriptions but its ethical spirit—the prophets denounced him. Thus the wholly novel, revolutionary concept of a *limited monarchy*, limited not as in the rest of the Middle East by cultic or ritual obligations, but in ever more elaborate social and ethical detail, by extraneous and immutable law.

At its worst, the Jewish polity was a cheap, run-me-down autocracy tempered by religious challenge. The Old Testament, *qua* 'history', is written entirely from the standpoint of how far, why, and through whom the autocrat did or was made to conform to the Law. At its ideal best, it should have been a nomocracy where the *nomos* was God's, hence a theocracy, where the Law was supreme and the king was just its administrator. In practice it could not be so. It necessarily left much to the king: defence and security, and hence conscription, taxation, regulation. In this sphere a monarch could and did act quite despotically; witness the court excesses and the unpopular corvées of Solomon. That is why so much of the history of Israel and Judah is so distastefully similar to that of its neighbouring kingdoms, and its dynastic history, court intrigues, assassinations, and massacres so intellectually unpleasant. The distinguishing feature of the polity, however, was precisely that it was under constraint; the ethical and religious challenge from the prophets.

The dichotomy between the despotism of the monarch in secular matters and the Law as the regulator of personal morals and everyday conduct was never resolved until the land became a sub-province of the Persian Empire; for then defence and foreign affairs ceased to be a preoccupation and the Jewish people could practise their everyday lives according to the Law, which by Persian edict was made the enforceable law of the land, under the guidance of their religious leaders. The polity had reverted to its original form: theocracy.

That dichotomy of monarchical despotism *vis-à-vis* the role of religious law in everyday life was not unique to ancient Israel. It resurfaced in the Christian empire of Byzantium and again in the Caliphate.[3] The cause was the same. The religion made ultimate demands on the population and reasons of state made ultimate demands on the ruler. Where these converged, the new popular religions brought the rulers popular self-sacrifice and dedication in a fashion unknown in the ancient Middle Eastern states. Where they diverged, however, they put monarchy and people on a collision course. A new force had come into the world—religious fanaticism and with it intolerance and persecution. These popular religions of personal salvation were political dynamite, as the rest of this history will attest.

I. THE PEOPLE OF THE LAND

Writers differ on what to call the people and the land they inhabited. 'Jew' is a late expression. Earlier terms were 'Hebrews' and 'Israelites', or 'Children of Israel'. For all that, it is the same people who are being referred to and nobody would deny that a history of the Jews starts with the Patriarchs, Exodus, and the conquest of the land. So it seems clearest if the ancient term of Hebrew and Israelite are subsumed under the later generic term by which the people is known today—as Jews.

The name of the land they occupied is equally arbitrary. To the Jews of the Exodus it was Canaan. When they occupied it they called it *eretz israel*, the 'land of Israel', or, simply, *ha-eretz*—'the land'. 'Palestine' was the Greek

---

[3] See Bk. III, Ch. 1 below, 'The Byzantine Empire' and Ch. 2, 'The Caliphate'.

name for the corner occupied by the Philistines.[4] It was the last name the Jews would choose to give to their own country and indeed, the name was deliberately revived and imposed on the territory by the Emperor Hadrian after he had crushed the Bar Kochba revolt of AD 132–5, in order forever to erase the name Judaea and its association with his contumacious subjects, the Jews. Arabs used 'Jund Falastin' to denote the southern part of the land, and the Crusaders followed suit. But the name was never used officially again until the British received their Mandate in 1920. That Mandate and its partition between 'Palestine' and Trans-Jordan in 1922 has given a factitiously defined border to the land (i.e. the Jordan River) which historically it never had. The term 'Land of Israel', by contrast is appropriately vague.

Its north–south limits correspond closely to the popular understanding of the term 'Palestine' today, but not so the east–west dimension. The western boundary is, obviously, the Mediterranean coast, but the eastern boundary was *not* the Jordan River: it was the arid zone of the Syrian desert. The historic Land of Israel—it is important to emphasize this—was the country lying *athwart* the Jordan. The land, therefore, was very small: some 250 miles long from Dan to the Gulf of Aqaba and about 60 miles across at its widest bulge: not much more than 15,000 square miles, about the size of today's Denmark, at its full extent, but often considerably smaller.

Geography underlies certain persistent historical traits. First: this land of Israel lies across the Road of the Sea, the military highway par excellence, still the most heavily used north–south route in modern Israel, running from Gaza through the valley of Megiddo whose fortress was the key to the north. The Land of Israel, then, was of great strategic importance throughout history, always contested between the African and the Asian landpowers of the day: Egyptian and Hittite, Egyptian and Assyrian, Ptolemaic and Seleucid, Roman and Parthian, Byzantine and Persian.

The climate and topography of the Land of Israel conditioned its economy, its size of population, and indeed, to some extent, its social structure. Unlike Egypt and Mesopotamia, it is not a land of irrigation but depends on seasonal rainfall. It was a country of pastoralists and farmers, therefore, with almost no mineral resources. Though described as 'flowing with milk and honey', the country was not rich. The standard of living was never more than modest. Its staples were bread, dairy produce, and fruits. Nor was the country very populous: at the very height of its prosperity in the eighth century BC the total population of the two kingdoms did not exceed 1 million—some 800,000 in Israel and only 200,000 in the kingdom of Judah.[5] The so-called 'towns' were tiny. Most, says de Vaux,

[4] Herodotus, i. 105.
[5] R. de Vaux, *Ancient Israel: Its Life and Institutions* (Darton, Longman and Todd, London, 1961 2nd edn. 1965, pbk. edn. 1973), 66–7.

could have been fitted quite easily into Trafalgar Square: some, he adds, would scarcely have filled the courtyard of the National Gallery![6] Samaria, the capital of Israel, had only 30,000 inhabitants at its height and Jerusalem, even at the time of Jesus Christ, held only 25,000–35,000 people.[7]

The social structure—at the time of the monarchy (eleventh–seventh centuries BC)—was fairly egalitarian. Certainly it was nothing like the highly and sharply stratified two-class societies of Egypt or the Mesopotamia-based empires. It was led by men of rank and influence, certainly: the administrators and the heads of important families. These were the *sarim* (chiefs) or *gedolim* (the great ones), but they were in no wise a nobility in the sense of a privileged hereditary class which owned the largest portion of the land. Most of the population were free smallholders. Wage-earners increased alongside the growing inequality denounced by the prophets and, despite the protection of the Law, were often exploited by unjust masters. The number of craftsmen also increased over time and, as in most of the Middle East, the trades tended to become hereditary as, for that matter, did the priesthood. There were no great merchants. Large-scale commerce was either a royal monopoly—as under Solomon—or, later, was handled by the Phoenicians.[8] Slaves were not very numerous: the census of the returned exiles[9] counts 7,337 slaves to 42,360 freemen. They consisted of debt-slaves and prisoners of war, and were mostly domestic slaves. They were heavily protected by Mosaic law, because for one thing the condition of slavery had a legal limit of six years only.[10]

As conditions grew settled and the country grew richer, inequality of incomes increased. A slow social revolution had occurred, where officials and others had made profits from the land: hence the denunciations of Micah and Isaiah.[11] Again, the sufferers were heavily protected by the Mosaic law. For instance, in law debts were to be cancelled after seven years but, as usual, the law was often evaded. For all that, 'the poor' were not a social class, merely a number of the less-well-off individuals.[12]

In the days of the Judges (i.e. prior to *c.*1000 BC), there was no distinction between army and the able-bodied male population. The Jews at that time were ferocious hillsmen, unlike their Philistine and Canaanite enemies who relied on bodies of mercenary professionals. It was David who introduced

---

[6] Ibid. 66.   [7] Ibid.
[8] Ibid. 76–9.
[9] Ezra 2: 64–5, Neh. 7: 66. Biblical quotations are taken from the Authorized King James Bible unless otherwise indicated.
[10] According to Jer. 34: 14. However, the law was evaded.
[11] Isa. 5: 8, Mic. 2: 2; Amos 4: 1, 3, 12; 8: 4, 5, 6.   [12] de Vaux, *Ancient Israel*, 73.

this latter pattern, and thereafter all the kings of Judah and Israel had their own picked corps of guardsmen. But the popular militia persisted by its side and was called in to reinforce the professionals in the grand campaigns. In short, the population was armed and this, too, added to the egalitarianism of society.

Finally, this population was literate. Certainly—as in other societies—there existed a class of trained 'craft-literate' scribes—the *soferim*—but both David and Solomon could write.[13] By Deuteronomic times (not later than the seventh century, and arguably much earlier) every Jewish householder was supposed to be capable of writing the words of the Law,[14] and Habbakuk (*c.*600 BC) is told to write his vision on a tablet so that those who pass by can read it.[15]

Clearly, we are not dealing here with the servile and illiterate dependent agricultural masses of Egypt or Mesopotamia, but with an egalitarian society of independent, semi-literate small-holders—all warriors if need be—each having his own individual share in the Covenant with his community's god.

2. FROM ABRAHAM TO DIASPORA

CHRONOLOGY

*c.*1800 BC	The legendary date of the settlement of Abraham in Canaan
*c.*1750–1650	Possible dating for the legendary Joseph and the subsequent settlement of the Jews in Egypt
*c.*1280	Possible date of the EXODUS under Ramses II
*c.*1280–1220	The revelation on Mount Sinai; the Ten Commandments; the people of Israel enter into their Covenant (*brith*) with God
	This is followed by the 'forty years wandering' in the wilderness
*c.*1220–1050	The twelve Jewish tribes (so it is said) enter and conquer Canaan, led by their *shofetim* or 'Judges'
*c.*1080/50–1011/10	Threatened by Ammonites and Philistines the tribesmen institute the KINGSHIP under Saul
1011–1010/970	King David. Smashes Philistines, founds an empire with Jerusalem as its capital
970–930	Solomon and the FIRST TEMPLE at Jerusalem
930	Solomon's empire breaks into the northern Kingdom of Israel (ten tribes) and the southern Kingdom of Judah (two tribes, Benjamin and Judah)

---

[13] 2 Sam. 11: 14; 35: 4.   [14] Deut.: 6: 9; 11: 20.   [15] Hab. 2: 2.

722	Kingdom of Israel destroyed by Assyria, its ten tribes carried off and 'lost'
621	King Josiah of Judah 'discovers' the Book of the Law we call DEUTERONOMY
587	Babylonians conquer Judah and carry its great men into captivity in Babylon
583	Cyrus the Persian conquers Babylon, returns exiles to Jerusalem. The SECOND TEMPLE (536, rebuilt 520–515)
458	(Or, controversially, 444): Ezra sent from Persia with rescript making Mosaic law the law of the land
331–323	Alexander of Macedon conquers Persia
323–198	Land of Israel a Province of Ptolemaic Egypt.
198–167	Land of Egypt a Province of the Seleucid Empire.
168–165	Antiochus IV persecutes the Jewish religion. Revolt of the Maccabees. Jerusalem retaken. The SECOND COMMON-WEALTH under the Hasmonean dynasty
63	Pompey establishes a Roman protectorate over Judaea
AD 66	Jewish Revolt against the Romans
70	Romans take Jerusalem
73	The last Jewish fighters commit mass suicide at Masada
132–5	The Bar Kochba revolt against the Romans. Final suppression of the Jews. The community dispersed. The DIASPORA

3. THE COVENANT PEOPLE

When Israel out of Egypt came
Safe in the sea they trod;
By day in cloud, by night in flame
Went on before them God.
He brought them with a stretched out hand
Dry-footed through the foam
Past sword and famine, rock and sand,
Lust and rebellion, home.[16]

God's annunciation to his chosen people, through the mouth of Moses; His deliverance of them from 'the land of Egypt, the house of bondage'; His Covenant with them at Mount Sinai and His delivery of the Law—together these form the cardinal event in the history of the Jews. This is the origin of the Jewish religion. It is likewise the beginning of the Jews as a nation. The connection between the two is indissoluble, even to this our own day. It is unique. As J. A. Bright rightly says, their conquest of the Land of Israel is in

[16] A. E. Housman, *More Poems* (Jonathan Cape, London, 1936).

no way a unique occurrence: nor, without the religion, would history have paid it much regard. But, 'it was this [the religion] alone that set Israel off from her environment and made her the distinctive and creative phenomenon that she was. Apart from it [Bright concludes] Israel's history neither is explicable nor, one might add, would it be especially significant.'[17]

What is said to have happened at Mount Sinai? What is the nature of this Covenant the fleeing tribesmen are said to have concluded there?

The Bible relates that after they have travelled for three months in the wilderness, they approach Mount Sinai. There God calls Moses and commands him to speak to the tribesmen as follows:

Ye have seen what I did unto the Egyptians and how I bare thee on eagles' wings and brought you unto myself.

Now, therefore, if ye will obey my voice indeed, and keep my covenant, then ye shall be a peculiar treasure unto me above all people: for all the earth is mine.

And ye shall be unto me a kingdom of priests, and an holy nation'.[18]

Moses reports these words to the people who unanimously answer 'All that the Lord hath spoken we will do'.[19] Thereafter they are told to make themselves ritually clean over the next three days and on no account to approach the mountain on pain of death. On the appointed day thick cloud descends on the mountain, with thunder and lightning and the sound of the *shofar* (ram's horn) exceeding loud: they are now allowed to come to the lower slopes, whereupon smoke and fire envelop the mountain, which quakes as God calls Moses to ascend it. There God tells him to return and pronounces the Ten Commandments. Moses draws near and God continues with a much longer set of rules and pronouncements, which the text later sums up as 'the Book of the Covenant', and concludes with a promise that they will possess Canaan.

The narrative becomes highly complex: Moses ascends and returns from the mountain a number of times. First, he comes down and reports what God has told him and again the people respond 'all the words which the Lord hath said will we do'.[20] He writes all the words down, reads out the 'Book of the Covenant', and seals the people's assent by a blood sacrifice. From the mountain he brings two inscribed stone tablets but breaks them when he discovers the people worshipping a golden calf. God forgives the people and tells Moses to make a second set of tablets and to write the Commandments upon them, and God says 'After the tenor of these words, I have made a covenant with thee, and with Israel'.[21]

---

[17] J. A. Bright, *A History of Israel*, 3rd edn. (Westminster Press, Philadelphia, 1981), 144.
[18] Exod. 19: 4–6.   [19] Exod. 19: 8.   [20] Exod. 24: 3.
[21] Exod. 34: 27.

There has been endless controversy over this story, but there is a broad consensus nowadays that Moses was indeed a historical figure; that something prodigious happened at Sinai (or Horeb); that from this day the people thought of themselves as covenanted in a special relationship with God; and that the Decalogue itself does indeed date from this time (and some scholars are prepared to affirm it was indeed written down). Whatever be legendary in the story as we have it, it is very ancient, and goes back beyond the Conquest. And whatever theologically motivated critics may claim to demonstrate, it is, if a myth, the *constitutive* myth of the Jewish people. For practical purposes it might just as well be completely true, for the event is presupposed by the prophets from the eighth century onward.[22] Moreover, the Covenant was formally re-enacted. Joshua recounts the wondrous works of God and, recalling the Covenant, demands that the people choose between Him and the gods of the Amorites, and they reply 'Nay, but we will serve the Lord', on which 'Joshua made a covenant with the people that day and set them a statute and an ordinance in Shechem'.[23] Likewise, King Josiah, some six centuries later, having found the ancient Book of the Law (usually taken to be Deuteronomy) and realizing how far worship had departed from it, reads aloud 'all the words of the Book of the Covenant', and covenants himself to the Lord to obey them, whereupon 'all the people stood to the Covenant'.[24]

Though the Covenant applies to the children of Israel, this is not due to any especial merit on their part. Furthermore, it is not a contract between two equal parties. On the contrary, as archaeology has shown, it takes the form of a Hittite 'suzerainty' treaty: in this the overlord *imposes* conditions on his vassal, requiring obedience and promising support only if it is forthcoming. Here, the overlord is God Himself. God is King.[25] The Ark of the Covenant is the symbol of His throne, Moses's rod his sceptre. God is like no other God—indeed there *is* no other. The name (which is formed of the consonants YHWH, the pronunciation of the vowels being lost to us) may be some form of the Hebrew verb 'to be': perhaps, 'who causes to be' might reach the meaning.[26] When He commands the people to have 'no god before me', the implication is that He neither needs nor has intermediaries as assistants; He has no Pantheon, no consort, no progeny.

There are no Jewish myths about God. He is ineffable and incorporeal—hence images of him are prohibited. And he is alone and unique: for though the earlier texts of the Bible assume the existence of other gods, the sense

---

[22] Cf. Amos 3: 1–2.   [23] Josh. 24.   [24] 2 Kgs. 23: 2–3.
[25] Cf. Exod. 15: 18; Num. 23: 21; Deut. 33: 5.
[26] Cf. Bright, *A History of Israel*, 157 n. 36.

seems to be that in which we might talk of the gods of the Chinese, that is, though these deities were around they were not *gods*. Only one god was God!²⁷ Finally: unlike any of the gods of the neighbouring countries, His exclusive concern with mankind was *moral conduct*. His purpose was that people should live good lives. Hence, *inter alia*, the execration of the fertility-rites, the nature-worship, and the sexual perversities of the Canaanite religious cults. The rules of moral conduct are laid down as part of the Covenant and the obligation of the Jews is to observe them. That is how the Covenant is fulfilled.

Hence the form the story of the Covenant takes and the nature of God which it presupposes imply a *code of laws*. 'The Law' and *torah* (lit. 'instructions') are the embodiment of the Covenant relationship. This is where the religion moves directly into and over the sphere of government and politics. 'God is supreme' is read as 'God's *laws* are supreme'. These laws are not something vague like *ma'at* in Egyptian thinking. They are explicit, numerous, and written down. They are exterior to any earthly power. And they are overriding.

The Pentateuch represents this corpus as having been delivered all at the same time, by the mediation of Moses at Mount Sinai. This is very unlikely.²⁸ It would be true to say, however, that by the demise of the kingdom of Judah—from Josiah's reign—the entire corpus was believed to be God's law delivered by the hand of Moses. For practical purposes this was the divine law by obeying which they fulfilled their part in the Covenant.

We have already noted that the Covenant at Sinai is couched like a Hittite treaty of vassalage. Both begin with historical introductions recalling the events leading to the treaty. Both end with curses and blessings as sanctions. Both are inscribed, on tablets or a *stele*, and placed in a sanctuary in the presence of the gods. Several Hittite treaties, moreover, were ordered to be read periodically before the vassal king and his people: compare Deut. 31: 10–13, where the Law is to be read out every seven years.

The differences are more startling. To begin with, there is the very nature of 'laws' as such. Egypt, as we saw, left no code of laws at all; there is no record of any pharaoh having been a lawgiver; and the language has no word for 'law' as such. In Babylonia, however, the Code of Hammurabi, which once created such a sensation, turns out to have been anticipated several times in Mesopotamia: the codes of Ur-Nammu (*c.*2050), Lipit-Ishtar of Isin (1850), and of Eshnunna (perhaps earlier), for example. But these codes are

---
²⁷ Cf. Bright, *A History of Israel*, 160.
²⁸ e.g. ibid. 173; W. Eichrodt, *Theology of the Old Testament*, 6th edn. (SCM Press, London, 1961), i. 72.

neither binding texts nor texts to which the judge had to defer: judges still acted by 'justice' or custom. The legal tradition was put into writing in Mesopotamia more, it seems, for the benefit of the people than the judges. The Assyrian code, c.1100 BC, is a manual of jurisprudence, but covers only certain fields and is not a code of the state's law; while the Hittite laws (c.1300) are based on customary law, do not form a code, and are an even looser collection than the Assyrian laws. As for Syria and Canaan, no similar collections have so far been found at all.[29]

Mosaic law is in fact *radically* different from all such legal collections. In the first place it is a *religious* law: here God is not the guarantor of the laws (as in Hammurabi's code, for instance); he is its *author*. Next, since the law is 'the charter of the Covenant with God', its prescriptions (unlike other Middle Eastern texts) are often supported by a justifying motive.[30] There is, moreover, a definite connection of the moral precepts with the basic religious commands.[31] The substance differs, too. Since the legislation is designed to safeguard the Covenant, the penalties are especially severe for all the crimes against God: idolatry, blasphemy, and those affecting the purity of the elect people, for example, bestiality and sodomy. But for the rest—except in the lower status it affords to women compared with Babylonian law—it is markedly more humane. There is no death-penalty for property offences, for instance, whereas these are dispensed unsparingly in the Hammurabi code. The slave was protected against his master's abuse. The children—explicitly—must not be punished for the sins of their fathers (compare the quite barbarous opposite in China!). Mutilation, much practised in horrible forms in the Hammurabi and Assyrian laws, is totally absent in the Mosaic code except in one unique (and rather bizarre) circumstance. Flogging is limited. The 'eye-for-an-eye' principle—the *lex talionis*—was itself a limitation to blood-feud, and in any case, lost force.[32] Finally, quite unlike the Hammurabi code which provides different satisfactions and different penalties according to the social condition of the parties (notably the privileged, the commoners, and the slaves), the Mosaic code assumes equality before the law. There was no special status for priesthood or aristocracy, and even slaves had the protection of the law.[33]

[29] de Vaux, *Ancient Israel*, 145.　[30] For examples, see ibid. 149.
[31] Eichrodt, *Theology*, i. 76.　[32] de Vaux, *Ancient Israel*, 149.
[33] Eichrodt, *Theology*, i. 79–80.

4. THE MAKING OF THE JEWISH KINGSHIP

The Bible suggests that the conquest of Canaan took place simply as a single operation, after which each of the Twelve Tribes took its appointed portions, some east and some west of the Jordan River. In fact, both biblical tradition and the extensive findings of archaeology concur to show that the conquest was piecemeal, protracted, difficult, and incomplete. The invaders, having forced a passage across Jordan into the highlands of Samaria and Judaea, confronted numerous Canaanite city-states in the lowlands. Their material culture was advanced in contrast to the Jewish tribesmen's—the second generation of a serf-population, without any professional and aristocratic leadership. The Jewish settlements and their pottery are crude, almost primitive. The Canaanite cities were walled; some were fortresses. Each was ruled by its king—often of foreign birth—with a bodyguard of trained mercenaries and a militia in support: they fought from chariots and with iron weapons. While warring with them, the new, Jewish occupants of the highlands were also confronted by new enemies. Even on their way into Canaan they had had to fight and outflank recently created kingdoms in Edom, Moab, and Ammon on the east of Jordan. Beyond them to the east lay the desert confederacy of the camel-riding Medianites, always ready to pounce on Jews or Canaanites indifferently. To the south-west the Philistines had established themselves in a league of five cities. The Book of Judges reflects the situation: the stories are authentically contemporary, but they have been collated and edited later.

During this long period the tribes persisted side by side, each regulating its affairs in the territory it had conquered, sometimes allying with its neighbours against a common enemy, sometimes feuding with them. Yet there was an overriding coherence based on ethnic ties, joint interest, but above all on the cult of YHWH and the common memory of the flight from Egypt and the Covenant.

The invaders, as they settled down, adopted many Canaanite cults.[34] But this was the 'popular' religion, the religion of locality and of the household: there was no national apostasy from YHWH or his cult. Never was Baal adopted as the god of the tribes. On the contrary, YHWH had no rival and his worship was shared by all the tribes. His palladium was the venerable Ark of the Covenant, portable, and housed in its tabernacle. Sometimes this reposed at one holy site—as it might be Shechem or Bethel or Gilgal—sometimes at another. In the end it came to rest at Shiloh.

So much was the religion of YHWH, of 'the Lord', the unifying factor

---

[34] Judg. 6: 25–6, cf. Judg. 17: 3–5.

among the dispersed tribes, that one school of historians thinks that the tribes made a formal confederacy, each of the twelve assuming responsibility for the upkeep of the shrine in a monthly roster There is no direct evidence at all to support this hypothesis.[35] More plausibly, it has been argued that the account of the re-dedication to the Covenant which Joshua led at Shechem[36] was in fact a solemn pact sealing the religious unity of the invading tribes. By it they acknowledged their common god, a common sanctuary (the Ark), and with these, the common statute and the common law that went with it.[37] This was the pan-Israelite law in contrast to individual tribal law and custom; and it would have consisted of the Book of the Covenant.[38]

But central direction there was none. Some scholars do, admittedly, think that on major matters an all-tribal council was held. That certainly happened when the other tribes decided to punish the tribe of Benjamin.[39] Others go further and think that for lesser infractions of the Law matters were decided by the 'minor judges' mentioned in Judges. It seems that matters were less systematic than even this: as though all the 'judges' mentioned in the text, 'minor' or 'major', dispensed judgement or led in battle as the case arose.[40]

The lack of any central organization was nowhere more obvious than in warfare, and the book of Judges is, basically, an account of how the tribes coped with their enemies. Its 'major' judges are all heroes—in Deborah's case a heroine—who in time of defeat emerged to rescue the situation. Here are the great hero names: Deborah and Barak, Samson, Gideon, Jephthah, and the like, with their military exploits. Deborah and Barak defeat the Canaanites near Megiddo and so open a land bridge between the tribe of Dan or Danites in the north and the tribes of Ephraim and Manasseh south of the vale. Gideon defeats the raiding Midianites from the Arabian desert. Jephthah defeats the Ammonites. Samson, the last of the twelve judges, fights a new foe—the Philistines.

The Hebrew word translated as 'judge' is *shofet*. Archaeology has helped us to interpret this term. The Mari texts (*c*.1700 BC) already use the term and mean by it a prominent tribal leader whose authority went much wider

[35] M. North, *The History of Israel* (Black, London, 1960); cf. K. W. Whitelam, 'The Just King: Monarchical Judicial Authority in Ancient Israel', *Journal for the Study of Old Testament*, ser. 12, Supplement (1979), 47–8.   [36] See p. 247 above.

[37] Cf. Josh. 24: 25; de Vaux, *Ancient Israel*, 93.

[38] Exod. 21–3; North, *History of Israel*, 103–4, de Vaux, *Ancient Israel*, 143.

[39] Judg. 19–21.

[40] A. Malamat, 'Origins and the Formative Period', in H. H. Ben-Sasson (ed.), *A History of the Jewish People* (Weidenfeld & Nicolson, London, 1976), 68–9.

than mere legal judgement. It was used in the Phoenician cities and in Ugarit: it has come down through Latin sources as *suffetes*, meaning 'magistrate'.[41] They came from the most variegated backgrounds: Deborah was a seer, a prophetess; Gideon the son of a poor country family; Jephthah a bandit leader. Their common characteristic is the spontaneous, uninstitutionalized, *ad hoc* nature of their leadership. It is *charismatic* leadership; every one of them is believed to have been designated by God to deliver the people from their oppressors. Of Othniel: 'The spirit of the Lord came upon him: and he judged Israel, and he went out to war.'[42] Deborah reports the Lord's command (Judges 4: 6); God's messenger tells Gideon to 'Go in this thy might and thou shalt save Israel from the hand of Midian' (Judges, 6: 14); Samson is predestined by God to save Israel from the Philistines.[43] These beliefs are not the pious frauds of a later redactor. They belong to a land where it was a commonplace to encounter bands of *nebiim*, holy men, ecstatics who went dressed in skins,[44] raving, and playing musical instruments.[45] The divine soul, the divine spirit (*ruach elohim*) was in them, hence their appellation *ish ha-ruach*—men possessed by the spirit—or *ish elohim*— men of God.[46] The early Jewish culture was saturated with the idea of divine possession: it could only be called *Gott-betrunken.* Perhaps the supreme description of how a commoner could be seized by the spirit of God and go forth to work great deeds is in the story of Saul.

Saul is the first of the kings; but he is also the last of the judges. With him we reach a watershed in ancient Jewish government: the transition from tribal confederacy to kingship, which is to say, from tribe to state. The occasion for the transition to monarchy was the Philistine's occupation of Samaria. They had defeated the tribal levies at Aphek, capturing the Ark itself, and sacked the central shrine at Shiloh. Thereafter their garrisons occupied the strong-points in the hill country. The tribal confederacy seemed to have collapsed, with only Benjamin and Judah still independent.[47] At this point another natural saviour-hero seemed to have arrived. One account of how he came to prominence is instructive about the charismatic nature of leadership at this time. The son of a humble family of the tiny tribe of Benjamin, Saul is ploughing with his oxen when messengers arrive from the town of Jabesh-Gilead. They say their city is besieged by the king of Ammon, who will only accept their surrender on condition that he shall put out all their right eyes. 'The spirit of God came

[41] A. Malamat, 'Origins and the Formative Period', in H. H. Ben-Sasson (ed.), *A History of the Jewish People* (Weidenfeld & Nicolson, London, 1976), 68.

[42] Judg. 3: 100.   [43] Judg. 13: 5.   [44] 2 Kgs. 1: 8.   [45] 1 Sam. 10: 5.

[46] Judg. 13: 8; 1 Sam. 2: 27; 9: 6.

[47] Though 1 Samuel does talk of a Jewish rally at Eben-ezer, and the return of the strong-points.

upon Saul' at these words: and he cuts up two of the oxen into pieces and sends them through the tribes summoning them to battle. If they fail, they will be cut up like the oxen. All come and he marches against Ammon next day and utterly routs the enemy.[48] The exploit makes him famous. He is hailed as *nagid*—'charismatic leader'.[49]

The point, however, is that then Saul *does* become *melek*, that is, king. And here we have two accounts of the manner of his kingship, one hostile and one favourable. These two contradictory accounts are the forerunners of what was to be the perennial debate among the Jews down to the Dispersion: of theocracy versus monarchy.

The favourable account[50] ascribes Saul's accession to the initiative of God, who chooses him as the liberator.[51] 'I have looked upon my people because their cry is come unto me', the Lord tells Samuel, 'and thou shall anoint him to be captain [*nagid*] over my people Israel, that he may save my people out of the hands of the Philistines'.[52] Saul summons the tribes—as related above—and defeats the Ammonites. The doubters are silenced and Samuel summons the people to Gilgal and there 'made Saul king [*melek*] before the Lord'.[53] Thereafter he does mighty deeds against the Philistines and the enemy on the east bank of the Jordan.[54]

The other version puts a very different light on the matter.[55] Here the 'elders' (the *zekkenim*, i.e. the 'bearded ones')—the heads of the influential families who participate in decisions from the earliest days of the Exodus,[56] form a deputation to Samuel and demand that he 'make us a king [*melek*] to judge us like all the nations'. Samuel—who has himself been judging the tribes for the whole of his life—feels rejected and prays to God. Then occurs the critical passage: God tells Samuel to acquiesce and consoles him by saying that this is all of a piece with Israel's long record of backsliding and worshipping strange gods: 'For', God says, 'they have not rejected thee but they have rejected me, that I should not reign over them.'[57]

Samuel then addresses the assembly of elders. He repeats the divine reproach, and he goes on to foretell 'the manner of the king that shall reign over you': his military conscriptions, his drafts of forced labour, his taxation, his confiscations. (Some scholars find this so exact a description of Solomon's reign that they claim it is a later interpolation. Why? Samuel had ample examples in contemporary Egypt and the adjacent Syrian and trans-Jordanian kingdoms.) The elders are not convinced: 'Nay', they cry, 'but we

[48] 1 Sam. 11.
[49] 1 Sam. 9: 16; 10: 11 *not* king (*melek*) but *nagid* (translated in RV as 'prince').
[50] 1 Sam. 9: 1–10, 16; 11: 1–11; 13, 14.   [51] 1 Sam. 9: 16.   [52] Ibid.
[53] 1 Sam. 11: 14–15.   [54] 1 Sam. 13, 14.   [55] 1 Sam. 8: 1–22; 10: 18–25; 12; 13.
[56] Exod. 3: 16.   [57] 1 Sam. 8: 7.

will have a king over us: that we also may be like all the nations: and that
our king may judge us, and go out before us, and fight our battles.'[58] This
narrative goes on to present the accession of Saul as taking place, not at
Gilgal, but at Mizpah. Here, Samuel again reproaches the assembled people
with 'rejecting your God'.[59] In 1. Samuel 12 he again reproaches them and he
justifies his own administration of affairs. Though the people now repent of
their sin in demanding a king, Samuel declines to undo what he has done.
Instead he tells them that all can still be well: provided that they and the
king 'do not rebel against the commandment of the Lord then shall both ye
and also the king . . . continue following the Lord your God'.[60]

From this moment two traditions interweave in the history of the Jews:
the tradition of the monarchy, ever strengthening itself during the period of
the First Temple; and the counter-tradition, harking back to theocracy. For
if the Law had already been laid down by God, and as such is immutable,
what need was there for a king? To judge disputed cases, perhaps: to
organize defence, certainly. But, these traditionalists were to argue, this
could be done in the old way, by trusting in God who would in his due
time see that the saviour-hero would appear. The tension between the two
positions was never resolved under the monarchy. The compromise position
was the one Samuel finally laid down: that the people *and the king* must obey
God's law: in short, a monarchy whose powers were simply administrative
and instrumental to the Law: a *limited monarchy.*

5. THE JEWISH STATE AND THE MONARCHY

In comparative and historical perspective there is little originality in the way
the Jewish states were organized. By contrast, the nature and role of the king
is unique. What one discerns in the Bible, however, is an oscillation,
between an expanding exaltation of kingship drawing it ever nearer the
old Middle Eastern norm, and traditionalist insistence on the supremacy of
the Covenant and the Law. And this was how Jewish history was to be
portrayed to what was to be the Christian world.

Not Saul (who seems to have created no institutions) but David and
Solomon were the founders of the state. David created a central administration of palace officials, took a census—which suggests conscription and
possibly taxation too—and created a palace guard, a *corps d'élite* of picked
professional mercenaries of all and any nationalities. He conquered far and
wide, incorporating as far north as Hamath and as far east as the Syrian
desert. This gave him control of the two north–south routes, the Road of

<hr>

[58] 1 Sam. 8: 19–20.   [59] 1 Sam. 10: 19.   [60] 1 Sam. 12: 13–14.

the Sea and the King's Road, so permitting Solomon to go in for the lucrative caravan trade on the Anatolia–Egypt–Red Sea routes. Solomon divided the kingdom—a small empire by now—into administrative districts governed by his prefects for tax and labour-service purposes, and launched a crash building programme: the Temple at Jerusalem, the adjacent palace, and the fortification of strategic towns. Unlike his father David, Solomon also organized his army around a large fleet of chariots, the most advanced military arm of the day. His exactions and forced labour provoked the northern tribes—Ephraim and Manasseh—into rebellion at the accession of his son, and from that time Israel and Judah formed two separate states.

We know only the outlines of the administrative system: patrimonial household officials at the palace, twelve administrative districts each governed by a royal prefect, local affairs regulated, as of old, by the *zekennim*, the 'elders'. The principal palace officials were the 'Master of the Palace', the royal secretary, and the royal herald. The first originated as the steward of the palace and the royal estates but developed into the chief minister, the equivalent of the Egyptian vizier.[61] The secretary was responsible for all internal and external correspondence and, also, for the Temple collection. His was a small-scale replica of the Egyptian office. The herald, or *mazkir*, also similar to an office in Egypt, kept the king informed on anything affecting the state and its inhabitants and passed the monarch's commands on to the people.[62] In addition, the king appointed the priest of the Temple (he also exercised control over the priestly tribe of Levites throughout the kingdom); the army commander; and a chief of the forced labour service (for as long as this endured).[63]

There was also (under Solomon) a head of prefects. The latter numbered twelve, one per district in the north, and another twelve in Judah. Later Hezekiah (715–687) regrouped the latter into four. These districts served for collecting revenue and, one supposes, for militia and corvée services. Little is known of the tax system. There was no distinction between the royal and the public treasuries, and by the same token the king bore all expenditures. There was likewise only a nominal distinction between the public treasury and the religious ones; the Temple treasures were frequently used to buy off foreign invaders. The taxes were supplemented by the produce of the royal estates, the profits of the king's commercial activities, and tolls, and transit dues from the caravan trade. Exceptional emergencies were met by exceptional taxation: thus King Menachem of Israel (745–736) bought off the Assyrians by a levy of 50 silver shekels per head on his 'mighty men of wealth',[64] and Jehoiakim

[61] de Vaux, *Ancient Israel*, 132.   [62] Ibid. 132.   [63] Ibid. 125.
[64] 2 Kgs. 15: 20.

of Judah taxed his people according to their means to buy off the pharaoh
Necho.[65] Regular taxation was paid in kind. According to 1 Kings 4: 7 each
of the twelve districts had to provide one month's upkeep of the royal
household.[66]

In addition, Solomon impressed labour to cut timber for the Temple and
the palace, and to fortify the frontier towns.[67] The scale was very heavy:
30,000 men working on a shift of one month every quarter to cut the logs,
another force of 150,000 engaged in quarrying and powdering stone in the
Land of Israel.[68] The population of Ephraim simply refused to carry on at
this rate when Rehoboam succeeded Solomon, and when the master of the
levy (Adaram) came to remonstrate with them they murdered him. It seems
unlikely that forced labour was ever reinstated as a regular feature; I infer
this because later references are rare and the circumstances exceptional.
Examples are Asa calling up the entire male population to fortify Geba and
Mizpah to thwart the invasion of Baasha, king of Israel.[69]

Outside the capital, local affairs were left to the elders—as in most of
Israel's neighbour states. They formed a kind of village or town council.
They dispensed justice, also, sitting 'in the gate'. Jehosophat (873–849)
seems to have been the first king to reorganize this arrangement. He
appointed his own judge in every fortified town. At Jerusalem there was a
law-court consisting of priests, Levites, and heads of families; its jurisdiction is not very clear. For matters concerning the Lord, the court was
presided by the high priest, but for the 'king's matters' by the 'chief of the
House of Judah'.[70] Priests were certainly involved in adjudication but we do
not know their precise competence. It seems as if they had jurisdiction in all
religious cases but also intervened in those civil cases where some religious
law or procedure was involved.[71]

In short: the state was a copy of adjoining palace-regimes: a patrimonial
set of household officials, a priestly establishment, a royal mercenary guard,
an extensive harem, a primitive taxation system. There is nothing here to
catch the eye. But when one turns to the role and status of the king, it is a
different matter. For in principle, at any rate, kingship is, as we have been
emphasizing, *limited* not *absolute*. It is confined within the bounds of the
Mosaic laws. But these laws do not—not at this early period—cover all
eventualities by any means. Above all, they do not cover the principles of
foreign policy and the means to effect it; that is, the recruitment of an army

---

[65] 2 Kgs. 23: 34–5.
[66] Whether this exhausted the extent of regular taxes in kind is impossible to say. Cf. de Vaux,
Ancient Israel, 140–1.   [67] 1 Kgs. 5.
[68] 1 Kgs. 5: 17–18.   [69] 1 Kgs. 15: 22.   [70] de Vaux, *Ancient Israel*, 153–4.
[71] Ibid. 155.

and the raising of taxation to pay for it. Where then did the royal prerogative stop?

This is not all. The Law is also religion, so a crime against the Law is a crime against God. This was obvious to all from the earliest days in the matter of the second commandment: 'Thou shalt have no other gods but Me.' It was Solomon himself who permitted his Egyptian wife a temple for her own gods and, so the Bible says, was himself seduced into worshipping alien deities towards the end of his reign. From that point on many kings in both Judah and Israel did the same. Here the *popular* nature of the Jewish religion created a wholly novel constraint upon the monarch. The religion was not a royal cult, as everywhere else in Egypt and the Middle East. It was the faith of the *edah* or *kahal*—the *congregation* of Israel. Neither the king nor for that matter priests supporting the king could command the people's devotions. So, the latter had every right to insist on the fulfilment of the second commandment and, for that matter, had an interest in it. Hence the perennial struggle for the allegiance of the populace between lay-preachers from all walks of life who clung to the Covenant and the backsliding monarch and court circles. No incident illustrates this so vividly as the contest between Elijah and the prophets of Baal. Elijah had no official status whatsoever. He is a haunting figure who appears from nowhere, clad in haircloth. The people, having been led astray by King Ahab and his Tyrian queen, Jezebel, are beginning to worship, as she does, the deity Baal-Melcarth. In the presence of the multitude Elijah challenges the 450 'prophets of Baal' to a contest between the power they impute to him and that of the Lord. The point is that he puts the issue squarely to the *people*. It is for *the people* to decide: 'How long halt ye between two opinions? If the Lord be God, follow him: but if Baal, then follow him.'[72]

By comparison with everywhere else in the Middle East, Jewish kingship was a very diminished institution. What were regarded as its essential characteristics elsewhere were entirely lacking here. To begin with, the king was not a legislator—like Hammurabi, for instance. The Law had been made already, and in the tradition nothing might be added to or subtracted from it.[73] The king had extensive administration authority, yes: he organized the kingdom, appointed officials, made decrees. But he did not enact *law*. What he commanded, therefore, was what today we would call 'subordinate legislation'—it had to be within the authority of the 'parent act', and this 'parent act' was Mosaic law. There exist in the Old Testament two passages which scholars call 'the laws of the king': these prescribe what

[72] 1 Kgs. 18: 21.   [73] Deut. 4: 2.

he may or may not do.[74] Strikingly, they make no allusion whatsoever to any
power of the king to lay down laws! On the contrary! The former reference
has Samuel warning the people against his arbitrary acts. The latter concludes by ordering him to make a copy of the Law, consult it daily, and keep
all the words of this law and these statutes—note!—'that his heart be not
lifted up above his brethren'.[75] The king's function was to be a judge. The
Hebrew word used, the root *shofet*, is the same as that used for the judges in
the book of Judges. To judge connotes something more than merely
adjudicating a *lis inter partes*, though it certainly included that, as in the
famous case of King Solomon and the disputed parentage of the child. It
connoted 'governing' in its etymologically Greek sense of 'steering' the
state—but within the prescribed limits. Absalom desperately aspired to
the throne of David his father, but what he cries out is: 'Oh that I were
made judge in the land!'[76]

The king was not a *priest*, either. Certainly he regulated the cult and the
priesthood. Throughout the adjacent lands the priesthood was usually
hereditary, and here among the Jews it was strictly confined to the priestly
tribe of Levi. One branch of this tribe, the Aaronites, had achieved the
status of a perpetual priesthood; the remaining Levites were relegated to the
less important functions of the cult. Among the Aaronites, two lineages
contested the chief priesthood: the line of Zadok and that of Abiathar. The
latter having conspired against David, Solomon rusticated him to a minor
shrine—a demonstration of the scope of royal power in the cult. A much
more conspicuous example, of course, is David and Solomon's establishment
of Jerusalem as the cult centre. David brought the Ark, which had lain
obscurely at the village of Kiriath-Jearim, back to Jerusalem; and Solomon
built the First Temple (1. Kings 6–7 and 2 Chronicles 3–4), to house it. He
also instituted the way the priesthood would officiate there, and the upkeep
of the Temple and the ordering of its ceremonies became a central preoccupation of all his descendants. But the king of Judah was not himself a
priest. King Uzziah was stricken with leprosy when he insisted on burning
incense on the altar in defiance of the chief priest and eighty of the minor
priests, who objected that only the sons of Aaron were consecrated to burn
incense and told him to get out of the sanctuary.[77] There were indeed
occasions where the king did perform a priestly rite, but they are all special
and exceptional: such as the transference of the Ark, the dedication of a
sanctuary, the great annual festivals; in short, in solemn circumstances he

---

[74] 1 Sam. 8: 11–18; Deut. 17: 14–20.   [75] Deut. 17: 20.
[76] 2 Sam. 15: 4.   [77] de Vaux, *Ancient Israel*, 113.

could act as the religious head of the people, but ordinarily the conduct of worship pertained to the priesthood alone.

But the most important difference of all between the Jewish kings and their local counterparts was that they were not, as elsewhere, the unique and exclusive conduit between God and the people, or the world of nature and the world of man. From Solomon's time, the investiture of the kings of Judah was surrounded by the most solemn religious ritual and ceremony, and some phrases used about him—'saviour', 'son of God', and the like— might seem to elevate him to superhuman status. These phrases do not appear often, and reflect a deliberate attempt in court circles, often includ- ing the court priesthood, to exalt the monarch to a status nearer to God than the ordinary run of humanity. We shall return to this, but the hard fact is that *never* in official religion or the popular religion was the monarch deified or considered equal to God: and as de Vaux says, 'the Prophets [who] accuse the kings of many crimes . . . *never* [accuse them] of claiming divinity. Israel never had, never could have had, any idea of a king who was a god.'[78]

The king did not interpret God's will. Priests did that in early days by casting lots. Furthermore, anybody, however humble, might become the mouthpiece of the Lord, that is, a prophet. And finally, no Jewish king could attain to the sacral role of all the neighbouring monarchs—the integration of human society and nature—because Jewish religion totally excluded it. In this religion God is transcendent. He is the one and only cause of all existence. Nature itself is devoid of divinity. It is simply his creation, and only obedience to the Creator Himself can bring goodness of life. The king stood under God's judgement as every other Jew did.[79]

The kingship, we may say, was *accessory*. And it was a *secular* institution, despite the court-circles' attempts in Judah to move it nearer the conven- tional sacral monarchies of the region.[80] The court circles, as we shall see, postulated a second and special Covenant between God and the House of David: but this was made to David, not to the people. It only runs parallel to the Sinaitic Covenant, it does not coincide with it, and in this it is unique in the ancient Middle East. On the one side then, the war-leader; on the other the people covenanted directly with God. It was a distinction between the profane and the sacred, only imperfectly blurred by the monarch's duty to protect the cult.[81]

But once the kingship had become institutionalized, with the accession of David, there turned out to be no lack of people prepared to make these

[78] de Vaux, *Ancient Israel*, 113.   [79] Cf. Frankfort, *Kingship*, 342–4.
[80] North, *History of Israel*, 223   [81] Cf. Frankfort, *Kingship*, 341–2.

two parallel lines coalesce. It must be remembered that a king was very rich, comparatively and in absolute terms. Jerusalem, for instance, was the personal possession of King David. Also his extensive conquests brought him vast estates, many of which remained the private possession of himself and his line. Solomon and, later, the house of Omri of Israel drew great profits from trading expeditions and from transit fees. The 'Ivory House' of Ahab in Samaria became legendary (archaeology bears out its reputation). Although Judah had only 200,000 or so inhabitants, its king, Josiah, was able to donate no less than 30,000 sheep and 300 bullocks for personal offerings.[82] Kings paid their ministers by endowing them with estates, they regulated the priesthood, they had regular mercenary palace-guards who formed a circle of dependants looking to the king for office and wealth. Such were the circles that exalted the monarchy.

When the northern tribes refused to accept Rehoboam, son of Solomon, as their king, they thereby served notice that they did not accept the rule of dynastic succession in the line of David. In Judah, however, the dynasty was underpinned by the so-called Davidic Covenant. This 'Covenant', and what we know of the accession ceremonies, were the two contrivances which the court adulators used to exalt the status of monarchy.

The former was the commitment God gave to David through the prophet Nathan: 'I will establish the throne of his kingdom for ever.'[83] Not merely the throne: its dwelling-place, Jerusalem, also. Over the centuries, this Covenant outdid the Mosaic Covenant in popular belief: the existence of the state and the security of its shrine and capital was seen in terms of God's *unconditional* promise to David, not in the highly conditional response to the Sinaitic Covenant. Isaiah did not accept that the state could be saved by mere lip-service—and even less than that—to the Mosaic Covenant, but even he believed to the end that the dynasty and Zion would be preserved.[84]

The accession rituals coalesced with this Davidic Covenant. The coronations took place in the Temple, where the high priest invested the king-to-be with the diadem (*netzer*) and the *eduth* (the protocol), and then solemnly anointed him. From Saul onwards all the kings of Judah (probably all those of Israel also) were anointed. This anointment conferred a grace. After it the king shared some of the holiness of God, his person became inviolable. At this point the new king was acclaimed by the people or those

---

[82] 2 Chron. 35: 7.   [83] 2 Sam. 7: 13.

[84] Because of this belief in the perpetuity of the state and dynasty, the fall of both to the Babylonians in 586 BC produced a national trauma: this is why, in exile, Jeremiah, Ezekiel, and the 2nd Isaiah fundamentally reinterpreted the mission of the Jews among the nations, and how the religion was so regenerated that most scholars date the beginning of Judaism, as now understood, from this time.

(the elders) representing them: this was not election but recognition. It was an epiphany. The king took the throne, which was the 'throne of the kingdom of the Lord over Israel'.[85]

From these two roots—the Davidic Covenant and the anointing—there sprang up a vigorous cult of the monarchy. It is observable in the so-called 'Royal Psalms', and it is from expressions found in these that some scholars were rash enough to affirm that the monarchy was a semi-divine, or even a divine, institution. In Psalm 2 the king is called 'the son of God'.[86] But this is a formula of *adoption*, comparable to Hammurabi's Code where someone adopting a child says 'You are my son'.[87] It did not mean that the king had been deified, which would, as we said earlier, have been nonsense to these early Jews. In Psalm 72 he is the 'saviour' of the child of the needy; but so were the judges.[88]

In the highly flattering Psalm 45, in verse 6 one line runs which the AV translates as 'thy throne, O God [*Elohim*] is for ever and ever'. From this it has been inferred that the singers are hailing the king as God. But this passage can also be rendered as in the RV alternative, 'thy throne is the Throne of God'.[89] Others translate it as 'Thy throne is like God—forever'. Some consider it a mere parenthesis. In any case, as de Vaux points out, *elohim* is also used of exceptional men.[90] But although these expressions cannot mean that any Jews regarded their king as divine or even semi-divine, they are undoubtedly grossly flattering. They are probably the work of the so-called 'court prophets',[91] a professional class which was beginning to form even in Elijah's time, as court and priesthood began to mingle and fuse. Temple prophecy became incorporated into the regular cult, a liturgically prescribed message at a particular point in the service.[92]

The exercise of kingship was subject to human as well as the divine constraints. The succession was a chancy business, rebellion and usurpation common. The northern throne was particularly insecure, since the dynastic principle—accepted in Judah—had been rejected there. Kings and Chronicles paint a terrible picture of murder, intrigues, and assassinations. Baasha usurps the throne from the son of Jeroboam and murders the entire Jeroboam family; his own son, Elah, is murdered in his cups along with his entire family, by Zimri, a cavalry officer; Zimri is overthrown within the week by another military commander, Omri, and perishes in the flames of his palace; Omri's offspring reign for only some thirty years before they are wiped out by a chariotry captain called Jehu—and so on. In Judah the

[85] 1 Chron. 28: 5.   [86] Ps. 2: 7.   [87] Cf. de Vaux, *Ancient Israel*, 112.
[88] Judg. 3: 9–15.
[89] The *New English Bible* (*NEB*) translates as: 'Your throne is like God's throne, eternal.'
[90] de Vaux, *Ancient Israel*, 112.   [91] Cf. p. 264 ff. below.   [92] Eichrodt, *Theology*, i 333

murder and intrigues take place inside the ruling family—but Joram kills all his brothers, Queen Athaliah usurps the throne by killing all her late husband's male heirs save one, who was hidden away. She is herself over-thrown by a priest-led palace coup which puts this sole surviving boy on the throne . . .

As we have seen, it is the same story throughout the Middle East (and indeed, as we shall see, in *all* Asian Palace-type polities), but in the Jewish kingdoms other constraints existed also. For one thing, the older tribalistic institutions of the elders, and the gatherings of elders called *edah* or *kahal* (translated as 'assembly', or 'all Israel', or the 'congregation') had not entirely lost their force. The elders were the local judges.[93] Ahab consults the elders as to whether to resist Ben-Hadad of Syria, Josiah convenes them to hear the newly discovered 'Lawbook' recited to them.[94] The elders are involved in the choice of David as king, their advice is fatefully disregarded by Rehoboam. Their armed intervention ensures the enthronement of the child Josiah.[95]

Far more exceptional, and probably unique, was the deep-seated respect for law. The monarchy could pervert this but not disregard it. The familiar stories of Uriah the Hittite[96] and Naboth's vineyard[97] perfectly illustrate the point. The Jewish king was not the master of his subjects' lives or their property. He could not pronounce *sic volo, sic jubeo* to take them. David has to make Uriah's death look like an accident. In the story of Naboth, King Ahab of Israel is asked by Jezebel his queen, who is well-used to Canaanite practices in such matters, 'Are you or are you not king in Israel?'[98] For all that, the vineyard is not forcibly acquired. Instead Naboth is accused of a crime, judged, found guilty, and executed. The case was fabricated and the judges suborned: the point, however, is that the affair had to observe the forms of law.

Of all the constraints, however, the most enduring and far-reaching in its consequences was the persistence of the Sinaitic Covenant tradition and the corpus of Mosaic law which it sanctified. In this respect, as we have repeatedly stressed, ancient Israel was unique. The Law was threatened by the ever-growing cult of monarchy to which we have referred, and the attractive power of the Canaanite cults with their 'high places', sacred groves, and orgiastic festivals, but each advance was met by a Mosaic reaction on the part—as it might be—of the king, or the population, or prophets, or a combination of these. Elijah represents the combination of

---

[93] 1 Kgs. 21: 8; Deut. 19: 12.   [94] 1 Kgs. 20: 7; 2 Kgs. 23: 1.
[95] 2 Sam. 5: 3; 1 Kgs. 12: 1, 6; 2 Kgs. 21: 23; cf. also 2 Kgs. 23: 30.
[96] 2 Sam. 11.   [97] 1 Kgs. 21.   [98] 1 Kings 21: 7 (*NEB*).

prophet and population against Ahab; Elisha is a prophet who, by anointing Jehu and inciting him to mutiny, brings about the destruction of Jezebel and the entire house of Omri, and the wholesale (albeit short-lived) extermination of the cult of Baal. In Judah, the usurpation of the throne by the Baal-worshipping Queen Athaliah was terminated by a revolt led by the priests of the Temple. The historical books of the Old Testament portray violent swings from idolatry back to Covenantal worship under Asa,[99] Jehoso-phat,[100] Jehoash,[101] Jotham,[102] and especially under Hezekiah[103] and Josiah.[104] And after the passing of Elijah and Elisha, there surges up that line of visionaries that the scholars call 'the writing prophets': their searing, excoriating messages—Hosea, Isaiah, Jeremiah—all invoke the Covenant. The Covenant tradition must have run deeper than Kings and Chronicles suggest. Otherwise the sudden surfacing of the Book we call Deuteronomy is hard to understand.

For Deuteronomy is a retelling of the Exodus and the Covenant and Commandments at Mount Sinai, along with the entire Mosaic code. (Later, after the Return, when it was put into force in the now Persian sub-province of Judah, the Persian court referred to it as 'the constitution of the Jews'.) St Jerome was the first to identify Deuteronomy with the 'Book of the Law' which the Bible says was discovered by the high priest in the Temple in 621 BC, in the reign of Josiah, and this identification is accepted by most scholars today. When the scroll was read to Josiah, he realized how egregiously even he (a reformer), let alone the common people, had strayed from the code of the Covenant. He convened the elders and with them re-consecrated the people to the Covenant, and the strictest adherence to the provisions of the code. In one central respect his sweeping religious reforms mark an innovation rather than a restoration. According to the scroll, there must be one and only one ritual centre for the worship of the Lord: the rustic altars where sacrifices had been made from the earliest times were all to be destroyed. The reason is implicit but clear enough: these spots—mountains, hills, groves—were the sites of former Canaanite nature-cults.[105] It requires little imagination to see that this was regarded as the source of the people's perennial and ubiquitous backsliding, for as the following verse makes explicit,[106] the Canaanite altars, pillars, asherim, and idols remained in use there. The scroll ordered all of them to be burned and smashed to pieces, and the sites made desolate. From that time on, the

---

[99] 1 Kgs. 15: 11–14.   [100] 1 Kgs. 22: 43.   [101] 2 Kgs. 12: 2–16.
[102] 2 Kgs. 15: 34.   [103] 2 Kgs. 18: 3–5.   [104] 2 Kgs. 22, 23.
[105] Deut. 12: 2.   [106] Deut. 12: 3.

reform party formed a school devoted to this new orthodoxy, and it was this school that moulded the perceptions of the Jews in the Babylonian captivity.

The discovery of Deuteronomy was therefore a most momentous event for the future of the Jewish religion. But it is also remarkable for what it reveals of its past. For where did the document come from? Some scholars (W. Staerk, Y. Kaufman, S. Yeivin, and E. Robertson) claim it was written during or shortly after Solomon's reign.[107] Most believe, however, that though it indubitably contains material going back even to Mosaic times, it was brought together in the northern kingdom (Israel) some time in the seventh century BC, and brought to Jerusalem after the fall of Samaria in 721, that is, a full century before its rediscovery.[108] But even if the book was composed in Josiah's reign and the 'discovery' was simply a pretence, as some still maintain, the massive fact remains: a magisterial reconsolidation of religion and state law comes at almost the *very close* of the independent kingdom. This Law tradition, then, had not just survived the efforts to hype up the monarchy via the Davidic Covenant and the continual pressures to make it conform to the pattern of the neighbouring pagan monarchies; it had resurfaced triumphantly to deny the exaltation of monarchy above the Law.[109]

It has been suggested[110] that the fervency with which Josiah and the reformers embraced the new-found book and strove to carry out its provisions was in part due to another, parallel development in the history of the two kingdoms: the prophets. Their activities signal a final and supreme difference between the Jewish states and that of all the others in the region. It was not unknown for the latter's priesthoods to oppose the monarch in defence of the cult, for instance, the priests of Dagan and Hadah at Mari demanding the king's abdication, the priests of Marduk in Babylon conspiring against Nabonious. So that the Jewish prophets' condemnation of royal idolatry is not unprecedented elsewhere. But their denunciations went far beyond that. In a society where Law is divine, a breach of the Law is a sin against God. In a society where the laws and rules of conduct are the word of God, those who speak and interpret the word of God are in opposition to those who break that word. The prophets were persons called—nay compelled—to speak this word, even against their will. The persons who had broken that word were the backsliders, but that included kings. Religion and politics became one and the same thing. The prophets denounced the apostasy of the entire people. They denounced empty

[107] G. Cornfield, *Pictorial Biblical Encyclopaedia* (Macmillan, London, 1964), 262.
[108] Bright, *A History of Israel*, 318–19.   [109] Cf. Eichrodt., *Theology*, i. 90.
[110] Bright, *A History of Israel*, 320–1.

observance of cultic rituals and called for true belief and for deeds to follow words. They denounced, in burning words that resonate even today, the injustices, corruption, and oppressions of the poor at the hands of the rich. Their oracles are the subject of universal admiration, and equally, of a mountain of commentary and exegesis.

It is everywhere agreed that the Jewish prophetic movement has neither precedent nor parallel. What concerns us here, however, is the political aspect of their activities. Where in that region and up to that time could a nobody denounce a mighty king like Ahab to his face (Elijah) or inspire insurrection against the royal house (Elisha)? The great line of fearless 'writing prophets' that opens with Amos and Hosea, and denounces social oppression and religious apostasy, are utter and uncompromising political agitators, and their targets were sometimes individual monarchs but sometimes the very institution of monarchy itself. Hosea denounces kingship in the northern state by referring to its vice of origin, Saul's disobedience at Gilgal,[111] and again where God says to him 'I have given thee a king in mine anger and have taken him away in my wrath'.[112] Jeremiah and Ezekiel both, in their ways, look forward to a quite new order. Jeremiah denounces the 'shepherds' that have destroyed God's flock: he foretells that one day, when they have been destroyed in their turn as punishment for their faithlessness, a new, a real king will come—a 'righteous branch' of the stem of David who will execute 'judgement and justice'. And what will his name be? His name will be *Yhwh 'z'idkanu*—'The Lord our righteousness'![113] Ezekiel foresees a new, an everlasting covenant, with a sinless people united under one monarch—God's own servant, David.[114]

The prophets, even those of wealthy families like Isaiah, Zephaniah, and Ezekiel, all inveigh against the rich. They were not democrats. Their most sympathetic support came from the elders. Much more worrying to the kings were the prophets' views on foreign policy, and nowhere does the clash between a secular kingship and a theocratic religion emerge more starkly. If the kingship had any function at all it was for defence. But the prophets had absolutely no interest in the royal army, or chariotry, or fortifications, or foreign policy. They were offences to God. If God wanted to help Israel, urged Isaiah, help Israel he would. In the case of the approaching Babylonian forces Jeremiah promised grace and life to those who would surrender! God was using the entire scenario of the Middle East simply to reach Israel: hence 'Assyria, the rod of Mine anger!' The underlying presumption was always the same and it took the Jews back to their very origin as a nation— the Exodus and the Covenant. The people were apostates. They had

---

[111] Hos. 9: 15–17.   [112] Hos. 13: 11.   [113] Jer. 23: 5–7.   [114] Ezek. 37: 24.

deserted the Covenant. The curses would be invoked upon them. Fighting and entangling alliances were vain: the only hope lay in a true return to the Covenant and its Law. Just as God had saved them from Pharaoh and brought them safely to the Promised Land, so, then, he would see them safe among their formidable enemies.

Weber correctly portrays them in their political role as 'political demagogues and, on occasion, pamphleteers'.[115] They addressed their audiences in public—impossible even to imagine in Egypt, Assyria, or Babylon! He describes their 'curses, threats, personal invective, desperation, wrath and thirst for revenge'.[116] They were indeed frightening, and they intended to frighten. Jeremiah publicly smashes a jug: he buries a leather belt and digs it up again when it is rotten; he walks the streets with a yoke around his neck. Other prophets donned iron horns. Isaiah for a long time went around naked—a terribly shaming thing to this people. The prophets heard sounds, saw visions, stammered out and blurted aloud. They were feared by the people. They were also mocked by them. Some paid a terrible price for their prophesying. Isaiah was scoffed at,[117] Jeremiah was maltreated and ended his life in exile. He speaks, too, of a bloody persecution of former prophets.[118]

When in 621 Josiah found the scroll we call Deuteronomy, he recited it to the elders and they covenanted to observe it: and he himself made his own covenant with God, 'to walk after the Lord and to keep his commandments and his testimonies and his statutes'.[119] Thus the king placed himself squarely under the Law. That law-book announced that 'if you [the people] will obey the Lord your God by diligently observing all His commandments which I lay on you this day, then the Lord your God will raise you high above all the nations of the earth'.[120] But it also warned 'But if you do *not* obey . . . then all these maledictions shall come to you and light upon you',[121] and there follows a quite horrendous list of the most fearsome maledictions—death and disease to individuals, and captivity and exile to the community.[122]

In this same dread, apocalyptic spirit did Isaiah and Jeremiah and Ezekiel preach national repentance, the return to the Covenant, and the worship of God to the exclusion of all secular hopes and fears. And it was in the midst of these clamours of doom from the Deuteronomist and from the prophets that the kingdom of Judah collapsed, its royal line was carried off, the Temple destroyed, and its people exiled to Babylon. The state had foun-

---

[115] M. Weber, *Ancient Judaism*, trans. and ed. H. H. Gerth and D. Martindale (Collier-Macmillan, Free Press, London, 1952), 267.   [116] Ibid. 272.
[117] Isa. 28: 18.   [118] Jer. 2: 30.   [119] 2 Kgs. 23: 3.   [120] Deut. 28: 1 (*NEB*).
[121] Deut. 28: 15 (*NEB*).   [122] Deut. 28: 15–68.

dered amidst the very same doctrine that it had sprung from: theocracy. 'Israel is Yahweh's people and has no other master but him . . . the human rulers . . . are chosen, accepted, or tolerated by God, but they remain subordinate to him and they are judged by the degree of their fidelity to the indissoluble covenant between Yahweh and his people . . . the State in practice, the Monarchy—is merely an accessory element.'[123]

6. THE TRANSMISSION

The destruction of the Temple, the fall of the House of David, and the deportation to Babylon of all Judah's leading citizens came as a thunderbolt to all those—the vast majority—who had clung to the Davidic Covenant as an unconditional guarantee that the kingship and Jerusalem were inviolable. In this form the Davidic Covenant was dead, and with it died the cult of monarchy at the expense of the Mosaic Covenant. To be sure, the Davidic Covenant did not vanish, but it was reinterpreted; it became the basis for a Messianic expectation of a regenerate Israel under a monarch of the stem of Jesse.

When the northern capital, Samaria, had fallen in 722 to the Assyrians and its people were deported, that spelt total politicide. State, community, and virtually all their history sank without trace. That might have been the fate of Judah too, but it was not. Here, although the state had been destroyed, the political community persisted; for the Exile turned out to be only a brief hiatus and the Jewish people and their national cult were to be reunited on their own soil for another 600 years.

The Exile is a watershed in Jewish history second only to the Exodus and the revelation at Mount Sinai. Deuteronomic law at last became the life-style of the common people, while the historical traditions and documents relating to the First Commonwealth were collated together and edited to point a Deuteronomic moral. Consequently there are two possible endings to this chapter. One would pursue the subsequent history of the period of the Second Temple until its destruction in AD 70. The other would examine the way the traditions of the First Temple period were transmitted to, and the effects it had on, subsequent polities. As students of government, our interest in the former lies in the continuing—and unresolved—tension inherent in theocracy. Our interest in the latter is how something of that tension was carried, via the Bible, into the nascent states of medieval Western Europe, let alone the Caliphate. In the perspective of the history of government, the latter is much more significant than the former and it is

[123] de Vaux, *Ancient Israel*, 99.

this that the rest of the chapter will address. But it seems desirable to make a brief excursus on the first topic, partly because it throws light on the problems inherent in the Jewish kingship and, more importantly, because of its analogy with what happened in a subsequent and much more grandiose experiment with a theocratic state—the Caliphate of Islam. When Benjamin Disraeli describe the Arabs as 'Jews on horseback', the remark was far more shrewd than the sense in which he intended it.

I have tried to show in my account of the Jewish kingdoms the collision between the imperatives of state/monarchy on the one side, and religion/law on the other, and how by tilting to one side we arrive at a *theocracy* (or possibly we should call it a hierocracy)—rule according to divine precepts under religious leaders—or else *caesaropapism*, the subordination of religion to *raisons d'état* under a secular ruler who is also head of the cult. This collision formed the recurring theme of Jewish history after the Exile as it did before it.

Under the influence of Deuteronomy, the Jewish exiles were led to believe that the disaster that had befallen the state was a just visitation for their apostasy. They preserved their identity by making *torah*—the Law—the rule of their daily lives. Scribes—the *soferim*—through schools and ceremonies—expounded the Law, and within the fifty years of Exile the Deuteronomic religion had become the religion of the mass. The identity of the people was no longer rooted in the Temple ritual, the native soil, or the state. It was a distinctive *ethnos* now because it practised a distinctive religion. It had become the People of the Book.

Its subsequent history down to the destruction of the Second Temple in AD 70 continued to exhibit the inherent oscillation between theocracy on the one side and secular monarchy on the other. Under Cyrus the Persian (559–529) the exiles were permitted to return to Jerusalem and they rebuilt the temple in 516, just seventy years after the exile began. In 458 (or 444?) Ezra the scribe came armed with an imperial prescript that gave the 'Law of God' the same legal status as the law of the Persian King-of-Kings, while the assembled people publicly covenanted themselves to the Law as recited to them by Ezra. Henceforth the community conducted itself strictly according to the Mosaic law, which its 'scribes' 'fenced about' with numerous additional injunctions and prohibitions. This detailed code was widely inculcated in school and through ceremonies, daily worship, and readings. Under the *soferim*—'the Men of the Great Assembly'—the Jews at last formed a true theocracy and they could do this precisely because they no longer constituted a sovereign state. They were an *ethnos* in a vast, polyglot empire that tolerated all religions, and *it was the Empire, not the Jews, which took on itself the secular functions of the former Jewish monarchy.*

But under the rule of the Greek Ptolemies and Seleucids, the wealthier landowners and the temple hierarchy succumbed to the seduction of Hellenism. An abyss opened between them and the scribes and *hasidim* among the people, horrified at the desecration of the Sabbath, the neglect of circumcision, and the reappearance of idolatry. When Antiochus IV (175–169), a crazed Seleucid who fancied himself God made manifest (*theos epiphanes*) prohibited the practice of the Jewish religion and desecrated the Temple, Jewish patriots and *hasidim* joined forces under the leadership of the Hasmon family, known as Maccabee ('the Hammer'). Within twenty years the revolt had won independence and initiated the Second Commonwealth, a sovereign Jewish state ruled by a Hasmonean as *nasi* ('prince'), *but* who also took over the office of high priest. His powers, however, were controlled by the Sanhedrin, a Council of elders. So, once again, the scene was set for the contest between theocracy and caesaropapism. The Hasmonean dynasty and court circle itself began to compromise with Hellenism, but were opposed by the spiritual descendants of the *soferim* and *hasidim* known to us as the Pharisees. These kept the state in turmoil.

Now Rome intervened. In 63 BC the state became a Roman protectorate: first under satellite kings (the Idumenan dynasty of the Antipater family), then a Roman sub-province ruled directly by procurators. Superficially this seems a return to the 'Persian solution', a Jewish theocracy inside a religiously tolerant world empire. But these were not Persian times. The orthodox Jews were uncompromising and the Jewish patriots fanatical at having their independence snatched from them, while the Romans were more interfering than the Persians had been. A collision course opened between the proponents of theocracy and the Jewish Temple-establishment which was compromising with the imperial authorities. In AD 64 that collision occurred: the Jews rose in revolt. In 70 the Temple perished in flames and in 73 the last Jewish fighters committed mass suicide at Masada. State and Temple-cult were both finished. After the last abortive effort to cast off the Roman yoke in 132–5 (Bar Kochba's revolt) the Jews became simply a network of religious minorities scattered over distant lands, and the problem of how a theocracy could coexist with a secular sovereign became an irrelevancy.

But, by a most curious paradox, the earlier experiment with monarchy did not! On the face of it this sounds absurd, but it can be understood in the light of two considerations. The first concerns the way in which governmental forms may be transmitted, the second what—in this particular instance—was being transmitted.

For the most part transmission takes place within a continuing political community and the same territory in which the governmental form first emerged. It is, so to speak, anchored there, and is modified through successive generations. It is what one might style a *physical* transmission, almost a 'laying-on of hands'. But this is not the only mode of transmission. It is possible, though it rarely occurs, for a governmental form to be dissociated from its original source, and its time also, and yet be transmitted elsewhere. In this way a society could be the innovating agency for other societies that were not its physical sequels. This is what one might style *ideational* transmission: and this was the mode in which the ancient Jewish monarchical experience was transmitted.

'Transmission' implies two things—the object or the message carried— and the carrier. What and who, in this present instance, were they? To find the message that was transmitted we must return to our earlier discussion of the Babylonian Captivity. The exiles, as we have noted, were profoundly under the influence of the Book of Deuteronomy with its recitation of the *magnalia dei*, its detailed exposition of Israel's duties under the Mosaic Covenant, its insistence on the centralization of the cult in what nobody doubted had to be Jerusalem, and its terrible threats against those who rejected the Law. During their exile, the scribes and learned men, thrown back now on nothing but their national traditions and their religious precepts, began to bring these into systematic order. The 'historical books' of the Bible, from Joshua through Kings, were already being compiled in the last days of Judah from the ancient sagas, court records, genealogies, and the like, by scribes already under the influence of Deuteronomy. The final editing took place in Babylon, where all the accounts were brought into line with one another and with Deuteronomic theology. That, substantially, is the form we have received them in today.

These books are *not* history in any modern, scientific sense. They provide historical information, but selected—and slanted—to illustrate Deutero- nomic doctrine. The editor(s) judge a king's reign not by his military successes, or wealth, or the general prosperity, but by one unwavering criterion: his fidelity to God's Law. It is through archaeology, not the Bible, that we know how powerful Ahab was: the Bible is concerned only with his contests with Elijah and his tolerance of idolatry. Fidelity to God's Law meant two things particularly: that only the Lord must be worshipped and consequently all idolatrous practices must be rooted out; and that the hill- shrines too must be wiped out and worship offered only at Jerusalem. This is why so little is told us of the events in the northern kingdom of Israel. Their kings are regularly condemned for following the practices of Jero- boam (who, it will be remembered, set up rival sanctuaries to Jerusalem and so 'caused Israel to sin'). Even Jehu, who persecuted the Baal worshippers and restored the cult of the Lord, is censured since he too maintained the rival sanctuaries. The kings of Judah are judged by the degree to which they tolerated Canaanite cult practices, and only Hezekiah and Josiah receive unqualified praise. The theological syllogism, as it were, is completed by the finding that those faithful to the Lord prosper and the ungodly do not, and the historical narrative is edited to this effect. For instance, Solomon's loss of territory is relegated to the end of his biography so that it can appear in the same place as the account of his polygamy and idolatry at the close of his reign.[124]

The events of Kings are told over again in Chronicles. Chronicles was composed much later—from internal evidence, around 300 BC. Here the compiler's viewpoint is somewhat different, and to present it he distorts true history even more than Kings.

All historical success or failure are the direct product of Divine reward for loyalty to the Torah, or punishment for apostasy. Those great institutions of post-exilic Judaism, the ritual and religious practices, the Temple, the organization of the Priestly and Levitical courses, the celebration of the feasts, notably Passover, the role of the messianic prince, all receive full and detailed treatment: and the understanding of these, characteristic of post-exilic Judaism, is traced back to pre-exilic days: the history of the People of God is presented so as to demonstrate the insight of the Levitical teachers of the Torah.[125]

Thus the whole monarchical experience of ancient Israel is portrayed as good kings and bad kings. Good kings like David, Hezekiah, and Josiah realized that they were below the Law and obeyed it. They were rewarded. The bad kings set themselves above the Law. They were punished. The denunciations of the prophets carried the same message.

Such was the message. Why did it survive? Who carried it? Why was it influential?

The message survived and was influential because of Christianity. Christianity began as a Jewish sect. The earliest Christians turned to the Old Testament for proof-texts for their claims and they interpreted its events and stories in a new, a Christological way. The Gospels were unintelligible and indefensible without the Old Testament. Thus the Old Testament became part of the sacred books of the Christian Church. That answers 'how the message survived'. As the Christian Church waxed larger and more influential, and finally became the official and then the orthodox religion of the Roman Empire, so the message was spread far and wide by the priests of the new religion. This answers 'Who carried it?'

---

[124] 1 Kgs. 11: 4.
[125] A. S. Herbert, 'I and II Chronicles', in M. Black and H. H. Rowley (eds.), *Peake's Commentary on the Bible* (Nelson, London, 1962), 358.

Why was it influential? The collapse of the imperial authority in the West left the Church the mentor of the barbarian monarchs and peoples who succeeded; and the Bible was their handbook. Translated into Latin by St Jerome at the turn of the fourth and fifth centuries, the Vulgate 'was the most influential source of governmental ideas in the Middle Ages'.[126] 'Human law could not contradict divine law as demonstrated in the Bible, and in some respects became, when once issued, part of the world order itself. In the last resort this is the explanation of why law in the Middle Ages assumed so crucial and overriding a role and was viewed with a respect which it has never since enjoyed.'[127] This idea of law 'led to the maxim of the rule of law, the idea of the Rechtstat'.[128] Not only that. 'When a Carolingian wanted a picture of how a God-directed king should behave, his attention was directed to the Old Testament and particularly to the two books of Samuel, and the two books of Kings.'[129] To be sure, they were more impressed by the sinfulness of revolt than by the contingent nature of Jewish kingships, but for all that Charles the Great's exemplars were Moses, David, Josiah, and Solomon.[130]

It would be quite wrong to leave this chapter with the suggestion that the only message that the Old Testament conveyed was the Deuteronomic one of the king's subjection to the Law, or that the more equivocal attitudes towards the secular power in the New Testament can be ignored. The Bible, Old Testament and New, was 'the most studied book of the Middle Ages',[131] and because of its divine authority it was the veritable thesaurus for *any* disputes over the nature of kingship, its limitation or otherwise, the right of disobedience or the duty of passive obedience, and the like. That the king was properly high priest as well could be demonstrated by plucking from its context the reference to the obscure figure of Melchizedek[132] in

---

[126] W. Ullmann, *Law and Politics in the Middle Ages* (Hodder and Stoughton, London, 1975), 41. Cf. among a voluminous literature, F. Kern, *Kingship and Law in the Middle Ages* (Blackwell, Oxford, 1939), esp: 'Magistracy, according to the Church Fathers did not derive its lawful sanction from itself but from something higher than the State, from the law of nature, from divine law' (p. 28) and the quotation from Clement of Alexandria: 'He is king who rules according to law.' For the medieval knowledge of and interest in the Bible, see E. H. Kantorowicz, *The King's Two Bodies* (Princeton UP, Princeton, 1957)—note the Old Testament references under 'Bible' in the index. See, too, A. J. Carlyle, *A History of Medieval Political Thought* (William Blackwood Press, Edinburgh and London, 1950), vol. 3, chs. 3 and 4 ('The Source of Law'; 'The Maintenance of Law'), and Part II on 'Political Theory in the Eleventh and Twelfth Centuries', and vol. 5, chs. 4 ('The Nature of Law'), 5, 6 ('The Source of the Law of the State'), and 7 ('The Source, Nature and Limitations of the Authority of The Ruler').
[127] Ullmann, *Law and Politics*, 46.   [128] Ibid. 47.
[129] M. Wallace-Hadrill, 'The Via Regia of the Carolingian Age', in B. Smalley (ed.), *Trends in Medieval Political Thought* (Blackwell, Oxford, 1965), 25.   [130] Ibid. 26.
[131] B. Smalley, *The Study of the Bible in the Middle Ages* (Hodder & Stoughton, London, 1952), p. xxvii.
[132] Gen. 14: 18 ff.

Psalm 110; inviolability could be demonstrated by the accounts of the anointment of the kings; and super-sanctity by the 'Royal Psalms' with their fulsome adulation of the monarchy. 'The Devil himself can cite a text', as everyone knows, and *a fortiori* the clerics and theologians who wrote for or against the unlimited supremacy of the monarch.

In Western Europe, however, as opposed to Byzantium and the Grand Duchy of Muscovy, the supremacy of law over the king, the belief that he was *non sub nomine sed sub Deo et Lege*, as Bracton put it, was assisted by special features. Among these were the Roman (Stoic) tradition of the Law of Nature and the Roman legal concept of the *ius gentium*; the way law as binding custom was understood among the Germanic peoples; and the political configuration of the age whereby kings were confronted by the hierarchy of the very Church that carried the sacred scriptures, and at the same time by vassals whose feudal loyalty to them was conditional. Significantly, it is not until the end of the Middle Ages, in the sixteenth or seventeenth centuries, when the power of the monarchy began to wax and that of the Church to decline, that anointment, the Royal Psalms, and the Divine Right of Kings were invoked to justify the *absolutism* of the monarch. But this set of developments will be picked up in detail when we come to discuss the feudal regimes of medieval Europe. Here I have been concerned only to sketch in outline why the Old Testament message of *limited monarchy* became what—to put the claim at its lowest—was one of the most predominant and potent components in the corpus that went to establish that position.

BIBLIOGRAPHY

ACTON, J. E. E. (Lord), 'The History of Freedom in Antiquity', in *Essays on Freedom and Power*, with an introduction by G. Himmelfarb (Meridian Books, New York, 1955), 53–81.

—— 'The History of Freedom in Antiquity', in *Essays on the Liberal Interpretation of History* (University of Chicago, Chicago, 1967), 243–70.

ANTHES, R., 'Mythology in Ancient Egypt', in Kramer (ed.), *Mythologies of the Ancient World*, 15–92.

ASSMANN, J., *Ma'at, l'Egypte pharaonique et l'idée de la justice sociale* (Collège de France: Conférences, essais et leçons, Paris, 1989).

—— *Ma'at: Gerechtigkeit und Unsterblichkeit im alten Agypten* (C. H. Beck, Munich, 1990).

BAER, K., *Rank and Title in the Old Kingdom* (University of Chicago, Chicago, 1960).

BAINES, J. R., 'Egypt—History' (up to the end of the First Intermediate Period), *Encyclopaedia Britannica* (15th edn. 1989), xviii. 145–56.

—— 'Kingship, Definition of Culture and Legitimation of Rule', in O'Connor and Silvermann (eds.), *Ancient Egyptian Kingship*, 3–47.

—— and Malek, J., *An Atlas of Ancient Egypt* (Phaidon, Oxford, 1980).

BARKER, E. (ed./trans.), *The Politics of Aristotle* (Clarendon Press,Oxford, 1946).

BERMANT, C., and WEITZMANN, M., *Ebla: An Archaeological Enigma* (Weidenfeld & Nicolson, 1979).

BLACK, M., and ROWLEY, H. H. (eds.), *Peake's Commentary on the Bible* (Nelson, London, 1962)

BREASTED, J. H., *Ancient Records of Egypt*, vol. 1: *Texts* (University of Chicago Press, Chicago, 1906).

BRIGHT, J. A., *A History of Israel*, 3rd edn. (Westminster Press, Philadelphia, 1981).

BURY, J. B, COOK, S. A., and ADCOCK, F. E., *Cambridge Ancient History*, 5 vols. (CUP, Cambridge, 1927–39; 3rd edn. 1970–94).

CARLYLE, A. J., *A History of Medieval Political Thought* (William Blackwood Press, Edinburgh and London, 1950).

CERNY, J., 'Papirus Salt 124 (Brit. Mus. 10055)', *Journal of Egyptian Archaeology* (1929), 243–58.

CLARK, G., *World Pre-History in a New Perspective*, 3rd edn. (CUP, Cambridge, 1977).

CORNFIELD, G., *Pictorial Biblical Encyclopaedia* (Macmillan, London, 1964).

DALLEY, S. M., *Mari and Karana: Two Old Babylonian Cities* (Longman, London, 1984).

DERCHAIN, P., 'Le Rôle du roi d'Egypte dans le maintien de l'ordre cosmique', in *Le Pouvoir et le sacré* (Annales du Centre d'Étude des Religions, Brussels, 1962).

DE VAUX, R., *Ancient Israel: Its Life and Institutions* (Darton, Longman and Todd, London, 1961; 2nd edn. 1965; pbk. edn. 1973).

DIAKONOFF, I. M., 'The Rise of the Despotic State in Ancient Mesopotamia: Ancient Mesopotamia: Socio-Economic History' (1956), repr. in I. M. Diakonoff (ed.), *Ancient Mesopotamia, Socio-Economic History: A Collection of Studies by Soviet Scholars* (Nauka Publishing House, Moscow, 1969), 173–203.

DIODORUS SICULUS, *Library of History*, trans. C. H. Oldfather (Loeb Classical Library, London, 1935; repr. 1961).

EDGERTON, W. F., 'The Government and the Governed in the Egyptian Empire', *Journal of Near Eastern Studies*, 6: 3 (1947), 152–68.

EDZARD, D. O., 'Mesopotamia and Iraq, History of' (up to *c.*1600 BC) in *Encyclopaedia Britannica* (15th edn. 1974), xi. 963–79.

EICHRODT, W., *Theology of the Old Testament*, 6th edn. (SCM Press, London, 1961).

ERMAN, A., *Life in Ancient Egypt*, trans. H. M. Tirard (1st English trans., Macmillan, London, 1894; reprinted Dover Publications, New York, 1971).

—— and Rank, H., *La Civilisation égyptienne* (as revised 1922), trans. C. Mathien (Payot, Paris, 1952).

FALKENSTEIN, A., 'La Cité-temple sumérienne', *Les Cahiers d'histoire mondiale/Journal of World History*, 1: 4 (1953), 784–814.

FAULKNER, R. D., 'The Installation of the Vizier', *Journal of Egyptian Archæology*, 41 (1955), 18–29.

First, Second and Third Interim Reports of the Commission of Inquiry in Bribery and Corruption, Accra, Ghana, 1972.

FRANKFORT, H, *Kingship and the Gods* (Chicago University Press, Chicago, 1948).

—— *The Birth of Civilization in the Near East* (Williams & Norgate, 1951)

GARDINER, A., *Egypt of the Pharaohs* (OUP, Oxford, 1961).

GARELLI, P., *Le Proche-Orient asiatique: Les Empires mesopotamiens: Israel*, 2 vols. (Presses Universitaires Française, Vendome, 1974).

—— 'L'État et la legitimité royale sous l'empire assyrien', in M. T. Larsen (ed.), *Power and Propaganda: A Symposium on Ancient Empires* (Akademisk Forlag, Copenhagen 1979), 319–28.

—— (ed.), *Le Palais et la royauté: archéologie et civilisation: Compt rendu* (D. Geuthner, Paris, 1974).

GRÉGOIRE, J.-P., 'L'Origine et le développement de la civilisation mesopotamienne du IIIème millenaire avant notre ère', in *Production, pouvoir, et parenté dans le monde méditerraneen de Sumer à nos jours* (Actes du colloque L'ERA, CNRS/GHESS, 1976, Paris, 1981).

GURNEY, O. R., *The Hittites* (Penguin, Harmondsworth, 1990).

HELCK, H., *Zur Verwaltung des mittleren und neues Reiches* (Series: *Probleme der Aegyptologie*, E. J. Brill, Leiden, Netherlands, 1975).

HERBERT, A. S., 'I and II Chronicles', in Black and Rowley (eds.), *Peake's Commentary*, 357–69.

HERODOTUS, *The Histories*, trans. George Rawlinson, 2 vols. (Everyman edn.; Dent, London, 1940).

HORNUNG, E., *Conceptions of God in Ancient Egypt*, trans. J. Baines (Cornell UP, Ithaca, NY, 1982).

HOUSMAN, A. E., *More Poems* (Jonathan Cape, London, 1936).

JACOBSEN, T., 'Early Political Development in Mesopotamia', *Zeitschrift für Assyriologie*, 18 (Aug. 1957), 91–140.

JANSSEN, J. J., *Commodity Prices from the Ramessid Period* (Brill, Leiden, 1975).

KANAWATI, N., *The Egyptian Administration in the Old Kingdom* (Aris & Phillips, Warminster, 1977).

—— *Governmental Reforms in Old Kingdom Egypt* (Aris & Phillips, Warminster, 1980).

KANTOROWICZ, E. H., *The King's Two Bodies* (Princeton UP, Princeton, 1957).

KATARY, S. L. D., *Land Tenure in the Ramesside Period* (Kegan Paul International, London, 1989).

KEMP, B., *Ancient Egypt: Anatomy of a Civilisation* (Routledge, London, 1989).

KERN, F., *Kingship and Law in the Middle Ages* (Blackwell, Oxford, 1939).

KINNEAR-WILSON, J. V., *The Nimrud Wine Lists* (British School of Archaeology in Iraq, 1972).

KITCHEN, K. A., *Pharaoh Triumphant: The Life and Times of Ramesses II* (Aris & Phillips, Warminster, 1982).

—— *The Third Intermediate Period in Egypt* (Aris & Phillips, Warminster, 1973; 2nd edn. 1986).

KLAUBER, E. G., *Politische-religiöse Texte aus die Sargonenzeit* (Leipzig, 1913).

KRAMER, S. N. (ed.), *Mythologies of the Ancient World* (Doubleday, New York, 1961).

—— *The Sumerians—Their History, Culture, and Character* (University Press of Chicago, Chicago, 1963).

KRUCHTEN, J.-M., *Le Décret d'Horemheb* (Universitaire Libre de Bruxelles, Faculté de Philosophie et Lettres 82, 1981).

LABAT, R., *Le Caractère religieux de la royauté assyro-babylonienne* (Paris, 1939).

LARSEN, M. T. (ed.), *Power and Propaganda: A Symposium on Ancient Empires* (Akademisk Verlaag, Copenhagen, 1979).

LICHTHEIM, M., *Ancient Egyptian Literature: A Book of Readings*, 3 vols. (University of California Press, 1973).

—— *Ancient Egyptian Autobiographies Chiefly of the Middle Kingdom: A Study and an Anthology* (Orbis Biblicus et Orientalis 84, Universitätsverlag, Freiburg, 1988).

McDOWELL, A. G., *Jurisdiction in the Workmen's Community of Beir el-Medina* (Nederlands Institut voor het Najige Oosten, Leiden, 1990).

McEVEDY, C., and JONES, R., *Atlas of World Population History* (Penguin, Harmondsworth, 1978).

MALAMAT, A., 'Origins and the Formative Period', in H. H. Ben-Sasson (ed.), *A History of the Jewish People*, (Weidenfeld & Nicolson, London, 1976), pt. I, 1–87.

MALBRAN-LABAT, F., *L'Armée et l'organisation militaire de l'Assyrie* (Droz, Geneva–Paris, 1982).

MATTHIAE, P., *Ebla: An Empire Rediscovered* (Hodder and Stoughton, London, 1980).

MONTET, P., *Eternal Egypt* (Mentor edn. 1968; first published Weidenfeld & Nicolson, London 1964).

MORET, A., *Du caractère religieux de la royauté pharaonique* (Ernest Leroux, Paris, 1902).

NORTH, M., *The History of Israel* (Black, London, 1960).

O'CONNOR, D., and SILVERMANN, D. P. (eds.), *Ancient Egyptian Kingship* (Brill, Leiden, 1995).

ODED, B., *Mass Deportations and Deportees in the Neo-Assyrian Empire* (Ludwig Reichert Verlag, Wiesbaden, 1979).

OLMSTEAD, A. T., *History of Assyria* (University of Chicago Press, Chicago, 1923; repr. Midway, 1975).

OPPENHEIM, A. L., *Ancient Mesopotamia*, rev. edn. (Chicago, 1977).

PARROT, A., *Mari: Capitale fabuleuse* (Payot, Paris 1974).

PEET, T. E., *The Great Tomb Robberies of the Twentieth Egyptian Dynasty* (Hildesheim, Olms, 1930; repr. 1977).

POLANYI, K., 'Trade and Market in the Early Empires', in K. Polanyi, C. M. Arensberg, and H. W. Pearson (eds.), *Economies in History and Theory* (Glencoe, 1957).

POSENER, G., *De la divinité du Pharaon* (Imprimerie Nationale, Paris, 1960).

POSENER-KRIEGER, P., *Les Archives du temple funéraire de Néferirkare-Kakai: les papyrus d'Abousir* (Cairo and Paris, 1976).

POSTGATE, J. N., 'Royal Exercise of Justice under the Assyrian Empire', in P. Garelli (ed.), *Le Palais et la royauté*.

—— 'The Economic Structure of the Assyrian Empire', in Larsen (ed.), *Power and Propaganda*, 193–221.

—— *Early Mesopotamia: Society and Economy at the Dawn of History* (Routledge, London and New York, 1992).

PRITCHARD, J. B. (ed), *Ancient Near Eastern Texts (ANET)*, 3rd edn. (Princeton UP, Princeton, 1969).

ROUX, G., *Ancient Iraq*, 2nd edn. (Penguin, Harmondsworth, 1980).

SAGGS, H. W. F., *The Might That Was Assyria* (Sidgwick & Jackson, London, 1984).

SIMPSON, W. K., *The Literature of Ancient Egypt*, 2nd edn. (Yale UP, New Haven and London, 1973).

SMALLEY, B. (ed.), *Trends in Medieval Political Thought* (Blackwell, Oxford, 1965).

—— *The Study of the Bible in the Middle Ages* (Hodder & Stoughton, London, 1952).

STRUDWICK, N., *The Administration of Egypt in the Old Kingdom: The Higher Titles and their Holders* (Studies in Egyptology, KPI, London, 1985).

TRIGGER, B. G., KEMP, B. J., O'CONNOR, D., and LLOYD, A. B., *Ancient Egypt—A Social History* (CUP, Cambridge, 1983).

ULLMANN, W., *Law and Politics in the Middle Ages* (Hodder and Stoughton, London, 1975).

VAN DEN BOORN, C. P. F., *The Duties of the Vizier: Civil Administration in the Early New Kingdom* (Kegan Paul International, London, 1988).

VON BECKERATH, J., 'Notes on the Viziers "Ankhu and Iymeru"', *Journal of Near Eastern Studies*, 17 (1958), 263–8.

WALLACE-HADRILL, M. A., 'The Via Regia of the Carolingian Age', in Smalley (ed.) *Trends in Medieval Political Thought*, 22–41.

WEBER, M., *Ancient Judaism*, trans. and ed. H. H. Gerth and D. Martindale (Collier-Macmillan, Free Press, London, 1952).

—— *Max Weber: Selection in Translation*, ed. W. G. Runciman and trans. E. Matthews (CUP, Cambridge, 1978), i. 381.

WHITELAM, K. W., *The Just King: Monarchical Judicial Authority in Ancient Israel, Journal for the Study of Old Testament*, Supplement Ser. 12, (1979).

WILSON, J. A., *The Culture of Ancient Egypt* (Chicago UP, Chicago, 1951; Phoenix edn. 1956).

WOOLLEY, Sir L., *Excavations at Ur* (Ernest Benn, London, 1954).

—— 'The Urbanization of Society', *Journal of World History*, 4: 1 (1957), 236–72.

XENOPHON, *The Cyropaedia*, trans. W. Miller (Heinemann, London, 1914).

Book II

Context

Cyrus the Persian's capture of Babylon in 539 BC was a dramatic sign that a new historical era had arrived. For no less than two-and-a-half thousand years a single dominant pattern of government had remained fixed in the valleys of the Nile and Mesopotamia. Its fantastic stability and longevity were due to the tight fit between the the belief system, the social structure, and the political institution. Now all three were to change, and moreover, to change independently. Hence an unprecedented flux in political forms occurred.

Three huge technological advances underlay the changes in social structure. Iron was coming into common use from about 800 BC , and so was the alphabet, based on the Jewish/Phoenician models of c.1000 (though the prototypes go back to at least 1500). Coined money was invented in Lydia in the late seventh century. All held democratic potentialities. Coined money encouraged an interstitial class of private traders. The alphabet ended craft-literacy's monopoly of law, learning, and religious leadership. Cheaper and plentiful iron—as compared with costly bronze—permitted larger numbers to bear arms. The age of charioteers faded, the heavily armed infantrymen and the mounted fighter came into their own.

These iron weapons also enabled new peoples to conquer the ancient centres of civilization: the Persian conquest of Babylonia and Egypt is but one example. Many of these newcomers were peoples speaking some form of Indo-European language. They seem to have originated from an area north of the Black and the Caspian seas. In the Bronze Age some branched eastwards and descended into northern India—the Aryans. Others moved westwards to the Balkans into Anatolia and yet others down into Greece—the Achaeans—where they founded the Mycenaean culture. Later waves moved eastward and down into Iran—the Medes and then, on their heels, the Persians: and another group of Greek speakers, the Dorians, descended upon the Mycenaean kingdom and destroyed it utterly. Yet another wave moved westward into central Europe, or turned south at the Alps—these last being the Latins. It was to these peoples that the immediate future belonged.

These tribal semi-nomads of the steppes knew nothing of sacral kingships. They were warrior peoples whose kings were, above all else, war-leaders. The warriors were free followers, self-equipped, neither slaves nor dependents. In the Bronze Age they were the restricted, hence semi-aristocratic, circle of those rich enough to bear the enormous expense of chariots, horses, arms, and armour; in the Iron Age they were a less noble, more numerous gathering. In my own view the polities these peoples established in the conquered lands stemmed from just such tribal institutions. Thus, the polities of the ones that migrated in the Bronze Age were aristocratic monarchies. In India, for instance, the Aryans expanded their indigenous three-caste system of priests, warriors, and cultivators into a four-caste one where their new subjects were the servant caste, the *shudras*. The Hittites, as we saw, instituted a monarchy which was supported and *pro tanto* controlled by a warrior nobility, and the Achaeans in the Peloponnese set up small states where the king ruled from a castle stronghold in the manner recalled (albeit inaccurately) by Homer.

The Iron Age polities were more democratic. They are best exemplified in Greece and in Italy. In the former, a first wave of Iron Age warriors destroyed Mycenaean civilization and inaugurated a 200-year-long Dark Age, so that when succeeding waves came down they found no strong political structures to take over as rulers. Instead, they settled piecemeal in the pockets of arable land between mountain and sea and there, cut off from their neighbours, founded their *poleis*, their cities, and the tribal threefold basis of king, elders, and warriors, to be developed over time into magistrates, *boulé*, and *agora*. The Latins who descended into Italy much later found only small—Etruscan—states, and they too, settling in the interstices, developed a city-state form. But the Medes and Persians who moved into western Iran from about the twelfth or eleventh centuries and thence conquered the Babylonian Empire became the rulers of an immense, wealthy, and highly bureaucratized political organization. Residuary legatees of its former rulers, their tribal democracy was dissolved by their sudden change of status, though traces of the egalitarian relationship between the Great King and the 'Seven great families' was to persist for long years to come.

These new peoples carried new belief systems, and one characteristic common to them was the view that kingship was instrumental, highly secular, rather than being divine or semi-divine. In so far as Hittites or for that matter the Hellenistic monarchs of Egypt and the Middle East claimed to be gods or demigods, it was through borrowing the attributes of their Semitic neighbours or predecessors. The Hellenistic empires and their Roman successor are markedly secular: religion was, so to speak, unhitched from the machinery of government. In imperial Persia this secular outlook had to accommodate itself, however, to the new religion of Zoroaster. In Judaea it clashed openly with the reformulated and now universalistic Judaism of the Hellenistic period; and later still, out of a fusion between

Judaistic and Hellenistic elements, the new religion of Christianity was born. This, too, clashed with Rome's secularism. When Constantine made Christianity the orthodoxy of the empire, it signalled the end of an age. A new one, an age of faith, was about to commence. Indian religion was cut off from such developments, elaborating Hinduism at much the same time that Zoroaster was preaching to the Persians, Josiah was finding the Book of the Law in Jerusalem, and Gautama began his preaching and so founded yet another world religion, Buddhism.

Thus, in their various ways in these different places, social structures and belief systems altered in different directions. Literacy, iron implements, and coined money loosened the tight two-class structure of the precedent societies, while new belief systems—especially Greek intellectualism—challenged, corroded, or replaced the old ones; and the ancient centres of civilization in Egypt and throughout the Middle East passed into the hands of new master. As all three elements altered in themselves and against one another, new political forms emerged. The exception was the great Persian Empire, a grander and more magnanimous reconstitution of the neo-Babylonian one. North India was the home of some sixteen petty kingdoms and ten ephemeral tribal republics, until in 321 BC they were conquered and united in the Mauryan empire, itself shortly to be succeeded by the empire of one of the world's most benign and remarkable rulers, the Buddhist Asoka. These tribal republics in India were an innovation, but too short-lived to pass its tradition on.

It was to the far west, in Greece and then Italy, that there emerged a form of government that was not merely innovative but quite revolutionary in its nature. Here for the first time in the world's history sprang up states which contradicted the major characteristics of all preceding ones. Instead of being saturated by religious values, they were worldly and secular. Instead of being monarchical they were republican. Instead of being palace-states, where dependent or servile populations submitted to the uncontested rule of a tiny circle of kings, courtiers, and priests, they were forum-states—full or partial democracies. Instead of being the products of immemorial tradition, their political institutions were the product of deliberate intellectual planning. The city-states of Greece and the republican form of Rome's government were a phenomenon. They represent, after what we have said about the Jewish kingship, a revolutionary turn in the theory and the practice of government.

By world-historical standards both forms were highly durable, but in the end they both collapsed and for opposite reasons. The city-states succumbed because they were too small to resist external attack. The Roman Republic fell because of its gigantism: it could no longer cope with the governance of a huge empire. Both reverted to the precedent type of government, the archetypal form, monarchy. But the *tradition* they had created did not die. It, too, like that of the Jewish kingships, was to survive in disembodied form, until, in the fullness of time, it was reincarnated in institutions.

This does not, however, complete the outline of this present epoch in the history of government. It will be noticed in the course of what has been related so far that the locus of governmental forms has expanded. Now, with the Persian and the Hellenistic empires, it has moved far east into Central Asia and joined there with the new states and early empires of northern India. At the same time it has moved far west into Greece, Italy, and—on the back of Phoenician colonization—into the southern and northern shores of the western basin of the Mediterranean sea.

All these areas are contiguous and therefore it is only to be expected that ideas, techniques, and modes of government should be carried from one to another, either by imitation, immigration, or tides of conquest. But at about the same time as the Indo-European peoples were moving southwards into the Balkans, Anatolia, and India, *c.*1700, a wholly unrelated people were establishing a state 3,000 miles of trackless steppe and desert eastwards of Babylon. Around 1400, at their capital An-Yang (in modern Shansi province), was the fullness of a brilliant but barbaric culture: huge tombs, magnificent bronzes, an ideogrammatic script, chariots and weapons in bronze—all of superior and highly finished quality. The society was highly organized, with a king at its head, an elaborated class system, walled towns, and an agricultural basin. Its religion, such as we know of it, was a form of ancestor-worship. Some of its techniques probably filtered across the steppes from the Mesopotamian area: it seems unlikely that the chariot had been invented twice, and although the Shang technique of bronze-casting is entirely different from that of the west, it is likely that the notion of using bronze and the way to obtain it were also learned *via* the steppes. But most of the cultural features were entirely indigenous and from this point developed with astonishing precociousness independently of everywhere we have described so far. The Shang were constituted as a loose empire. They were conquered by another Sinic people, the Chou, in the eleventh century BC, when a more firmly articulated empire was established on feudalistic lines. This empire disintegrated into a congeries of rival states which were ferociously fighting one another right though the wars of the Greeks and Persians and the campaign of Alexander until all succumbed to the state of Ch'in in 221 BC. This unification was the immediate precursor of the empire of the Han (206 BC–AD 220).

The historical epoch ended in the presence of two triumphant reconstitutions of the centralized and absolute monarchical role, with strikingly different characteristics, however, and standing at the opposite ends of the vast Eurasian land mass. And just as in Europe the Roman legacies of law and Christianity were to mould all subsequent political forms, so the bureaucratic system of the Han and the teachings of the sage Confucius (551–479 BC) were to inform all subsequent Chinese government until only a half-century or so ago.

In the part of the book that follows I propose to turn first to the Persian Empire, then to the Greek city-states, and then to the Roman Republic. After this I shall turn away to distant China to explain the origins of classical Chinese government up to the Ch'in conquest. The next chapter will continue with an account of the Han Empire. Then, finally, I shall conclude by turning back to the west with a comparison and contrast of the empires of the Han and of Rome.

I

The Persian Empire

We do not know the details of how the Persian Empire was governed. What we do know is mostly derived from literary sources, and most of these are Greek, that is, an enemy account. Recently two Persian archives, the Treasury Tablets and the Persepolis Fortification Tablets have somewhat increased our understanding.

Nor is very much claimed for its mode and techniques of government. The Persian Empire is mainly seen by historians as a stepping-stone to some later order: to an increased syncretism of religion and fusion of culture, or to the spread of Hellenistic civilization, or to the creation of the subsequent Iranian states. As to the effects of its rule, most opinions are favourable. It is claimed that most areas of the vast empire enjoyed some two-and-a-quarter centuries of peace under the Achaemenid dynasty, that it treated its subjects' religious and social institutions with respect, that it was no more repressive than the suppression of open rebellion required it to be, that apart from perhaps the provinces of Babylonia, Egypt, and Phoenicia, the burden of taxation was tolerable, and that, providing the subject population kept the king's peace and paid their taxes, the Persian yoke was positively benign. It is conveniently contrasted with the unmitigated ferocity and exploitativeness of Assyrian over-rule and the rapacity and extortion of the subsequent Hellenistic monarchies.

The question, therefore, inevitably poses itself: why should we study a state like this when we possess so few hard facts about its mode of government and when what little we do know points to its being of a somewhat simplistic character? The short answer is simply that a history of government finds it hard to ignore a state of such territorial immensity which was able, moreover, to maintain itself for some 220 years and which succumbed only by reason of military defeat. The longer answer might be as follows. To begin with: this is not the first case of backward tribesmen suddenly having to run the advanced political system they have conquered (the Arab Caliphate and repeated conquests of north China by steppe nomads provide others): but it is the first where we have some evidence of how they set about doing it. Secondly, as an absolute and centralized monarchy the empire clearly qualifies as a 'Palace-type system', but it differs sharply from the Sumerian and Egyptian forms. There, government is a matter for kings, bureaucracy, and priests. Then the Assyrian monarchy suggests that the bureaucracy and priests are flanked and their relative weight reduced by a territorial aristocracy. In the Persian state this process has visibly gone much further: government is a matter for the king (and his family) and a powerful territorial nobility buttressed by a numerous central bureaucracy, but where the political role of the Persian clerisy was negligible. Also, and in line with this, the tight congruence of belief system, social stratification, and the monarchical institutions so characteristic of Sumeria and Egypt has dissolved. There is no all-pervasive religion or even a state cult. The structure of society is no longer the simple two-class one: the empire was so large it embraced a wide variety of social structures. The central political institution—the monarchy—was, therefore, no longer closely related to either. It sustained itself by appeal to an idiosyncratic set of values and played a different role from the sacral monarchies that had preceded it. Finally, this empire was immensely bigger than anything that had ever gone before and wildly heterogenous.

These observations raise more questions than they answer. How, for instance, could perhaps a million Persian tribesmen keep some 50 million natives of the empire together and for so long? What kind of institutions enabled them to do it? Could these institutions have continued to hold the empire together if there had been no Greek conquest?

1. THE LAND AND THE PEOPLE

The Medes and Persians were two of the Indo-European peoples who called themselves Arya (Aryans) and occupied the vast area between modern Afghanistan to the east and the Zagros Mountains to the west at some time during the second millennium BC. Other of their peoples were the Hyrcanians (east of the Caspian Sea), the Parthians of Khurasan, the Bactrians around modern Balkh, the Chorasmians (around modern Khiva), and so forth. All were illiterate tribesmen: sedentary, semi-sedentary, or, like the Sagartians, nomadic horsemen. Of these peoples, the Medes and the Persians were the westernmost. The Medes, famous already for their horses, are mentioned (as enemies) by the Assyrians in 836 BC. They inhabited the Zagros Mountain area. The Assyrians also mention the Parsua, as dwelling south of Lake Urmia at that time. Whether or not these were 'Persians' is controversial, because when the Persians do clearly appear on the historical scene in the sixth century BC they are living far to the south-east, in the part of Iran we now called Khuzistan. Xenophon[1] says that in his time (the

---

[1] Xenophon, *The Cyropaedia*, trans. W. Miller (Heinemann, London, 1914), 12, 15

fourth century) they numbered 120,000 adult males (less than the Medes), and this estimate is regarded as reasonable.[2]

These Persians consisted of ten great tribes which lived in considerable diversity. Three clans headed the rest, three were sedentary cultivators, and the other four pastoralists.[3] Their life was hardy and simple. They worshipped the moon, the streams, the winds, but above all the sun and fire. Their principal gods were Mitra, the sungod, and Anaïtis, a goddess of running water and of fertility. They made no idols. Their temples were simple constructions to house fire-altars. Their social structure conformed to the threefold divisions of warriors, priests, and cultivators found in Aryan India (where they later congealed into castes); for the Persians (we know) acknowledged a hereditary tribe or caste of priests, the Magi, without whose presence no sacrifice might be offered. Also they seem to have had some kind of aristocracy, probably a warrior aristocracy, from the very beginning.

Passages from Herodotus suggest an appealing simplicity in their earliest institutions. The Medes, he tells us (i.96) first lived 'in scattered villages without any central authority'. They established kingship in a fashion remarkably similar to the accounts of its institution in ancient Israel.[4] The account goes as follows: anarchy and lawlessness were so bad that they would 'all be forced to leave their own country'; a certain Deioces had earned a reputation as a just judge; his friends, therefore, urged the people to 'get a king over us so that the land may be well governed'. (Naturally, they suggested Deioces.)[5] This for the Medes. Of the Persians of his own day Herodotus says that 'the most disgraceful thing in the world, they think, is to tell a lie; the next worse, to owe a debt'.[6] 'Their sons are carefully instructed from their fifth to their twentieth year in these things alone—to ride, to draw the bow, and to speak the truth'.[7] These observations need not be taken *au pied de la lettre*; but the general drift is clear enough and wholly credible.

2. THE CREATION OF THE EMPIRE

For some 200 years—836 to 626 BC—Assyria held the world stage and the Medes alternately feuded with or made submission to her. In the ascendant, the Assyrians made the Mede kings their vassals, in adversity they had perforce to recognize their independence. With the death of the last

---

[2] J. M. Cook, *The Persian Empire* (Dent, London, 1983), 38. M. A. Dandamaev and V. G. Lukonin, *The Culture and Social Institutions of Ancient Iran*, trans. P. L. Kohl and D. J. Dadson (CUP, Cambridge, 1989), 223.   [3] Herodotus, i. 125.
[4] See p. 252 ff. above.   [5] Herodotus, i. 97.   [6] Ibid. i. 139.   [7] Ibid. i. 136.

Assyrian world-conqueror, Assurbanipal (669–627), the Assyrian throne changed hands rapidly, while Babylon once more rebelled. Its king, Nabopalassar, formed an alliance with Cyaxares, the king of the Medes. Together they fell upon Assyria. In 612 Nineveh was taken and in 609 the last Assyrian resistance collapsed at Harran. Cyaxares annexed Assyria, and pushed on via Armenia to annex Anatolia up to the Halys River, where he was checked by King Alyattes of Lydia. This state, rich in precious metals, had been formed by Indo-European invaders in the seventh century BC, and currently exercised hegemony over Asia Minor. After five years of inconclusive warfare culminating in a battle that was broken off in terror at a solar eclipse, both sides accepted the Halys as their boundary. Thus was formed the Median Empire: the eastern half of Anatolia, the former Assyria, all western Iran, and a goodly part of eastern Iran also, as far, some say, as modern Tehran.

Cyaxares ruled as a Great King, or 'King of Kings', in the old primitive fashion and Cambyses I, the king of Persia, was his vassal. The two Iranian tribes of Medes and Persians had close affinities. They were linked closer when Cyaxares' successor, Astyages, married his daughter to Cambyses' son Cyrus II of Persia. Cyrus was highly exceptional. He welded his conglomerate peoples together and, rebelling against his father-in-law, overthrew him in 550, and so founded the first Persian Empire. His next move was against Lydia, which he conquered and annexed in perhaps 546, and followed this up by forcing the Ionian Greek cities of the Anatolian sea-coast to accept his suzerainty. Babylonia was his next target: its disaffected citizens opened the gates of Babylon to him in 539. Egypt remained independent, since Cyrus was distracted by troubles on the far eastern borders of Iran. He spent his last ten years campaigning there and it was there that he lost his life. But he had made the Persian rule recognized as far as the distant Oxus and Jaxartes rivers (Transoxania), between the Aral Sea and modern Afghanistan. In 525 Egypt was added to the empire by his successor Cambyses. Darius I, who succeeded him, expanded his suzerainty over Macedonia and Thrace in the north-west of the empire and conquered much of India up to the Indus to round off the south-east. It was the largest state the world had yet seen, and it had taken only thirty years or so to complete.

3. CHRONOLOGY

Darius I (521–486 BC) was the first to organize the empire into provinces and establish its administrative arrangements systematically. Darius belonged to a cadet line of the Achaemenes family. Cyrus the Great had been succeeded by his son, Cambyses (530–522). When he died on his return from his protracted campaign in Egypt the throne was seized by a man called Bardiya who either really was his brother, or (the official version) a usurper posing as that brother (who was allegedly dead). The leaders of seven great aristocratic families, 'the Seven'—of whom Darius was one—conspired and murdered this Bardiya at a castle in Media and, by agreement, set Darius on the throne. But revolts had broken out all over the empire as usurpers with large armies also claimed to be of the royal line, while in the former kingdoms of Elam, Babylon, and Media pretenders to the local throne rebelled in the name of independence. Darius fought nineteen battles and took captive 'nine kings' before emerging as uncontested ruler of a firmly reunited empire.[8]

At the end of his reign, some of the Ionian cities of the Anatolian coast rebelled, assisted by Athens and Eretria. The rebellion failed and Darius sent on troops into Greece. This force was defeated by the Athenians at Marathon (490). Henceforth, Persia would never be free from trouble in the eastern Mediterranean, not only in Greece but in Cyprus and Egypt as well. Darius was succeeded by his son Xerxes I (486–465) whose first act was to suppress an Egyptian revolt and likewise, two successive revolts in Babylon (484; 479)—provoked by his abolition of its status as 'Kingdom of Babel' and his refusal to 'take the hand of Bel' as all rulers had had to do. His great enterprise, however, was to mount the expedition destined to conquer Hellas. It was a disastrous failure: his forces were beaten by sea at Salamis (480), and by land at Plataea, and then in Asia Minor itself, at Mycale (479). Figures for the size of Xerxes' army and the losses he sustained are quite unreliable, but the failure of his expedition was decisive. The Greek campaign marked a turning-point in the empire's history. Henceforth, its successes in the Aegean were owed to its skilful exploitation of the fratricidal wars of the Greek states, not to military prowess.

In 465 Xerxes was murdered by the commander of his bodyguard and, probably, vizier (the 'chiliarch'), with whose support Artaxerxes I 'Long-imanus' acceded (465–423). Another Egyptian revolt was suppressed (460–454), and likewise two satrapal revolts, one in Bactria and the other by the conqueror of Egypt, the satrap Megebyzus. But hostilities between Persia and Athens came to an end by the 'Peace of Callias' in 449.

From the year of Artaxerxes' death (423) the elements of weakness in the empire, that is, disputed successions, civil wars, and rebellions, became more

---

[8] R. G. Kent (ed.), *Old Persian: Texts* (Yale UP: New Haven, Conn., 1950), 119–30, where a translation of the famous Behistun inscription will be found. It recounts the suppression of the widespread rebellions in the year of Darius' accession.

and more pronounced. Xerxes II (425–424), the son of Artaxerxes II, was murdered by his brother, who was himself murdered by his half-brother, the illegitimate Ochus, satrap of Hyrcania. He took the throne as Darius II (424–404). With him Persia, allied to Sparta, reopened an offensive against Athens. Darius sent one of his two sons, Cyrus, to Asia Minor to prosecute the war and after his death his elder son, Artaxerxes, succeeded. Cyrus had contested the throne and collected together a formidable army of Greek mercenaries, only to be killed at the Battle of Cunaxa (401). This is the famous expedition of the Ten Thousand, and the ability of the Greeks to fight their way back out of Persia encouraged all Hellas to believe the empire was wide open to conquest. Nevertheless, much gold and skilful diplomacy enabled Artaxerxes II to impose the 'King's Peace' (387–386) by which the Greeks gave up any claim to Asia Minor, so once again abandoning the Ionian cities to the Persians. Apart from that, however, his reign was racked by continual revolts. Egypt had revolted successfully and an expedition to recover it (373) failed. Hard on the heels of this, in 366 all the satraps of Asia Minor rose in rebellion, but the self-divisions among them brought about their downfall and by the year of Artaxerxes II's death (359) the central authority was fully restored. He was succeeded by the ferocious Artaxerxes III 'Ochus', again amid a welter of harem intrigues. To make his position secure Ochus murdered nearly all his relatives, forced all satraps to dismiss their mercenaries, and suppressed the satraps of Phrygia who dared to disobey. His first efforts to reconquer Egypt (351–350) failed and led to a most serious revolt by Sidon and the other Phoenician cities. After it was with great difficulty put down, Ochus led yet another attack on Egypt and this time it succeeded (343). So ended Egypt's *last* native dynasty—the XXXth.

One of the two generals who conducted this war was a eunuch called Bagoas. He was put in charge of the upper satrapies, amassed great riches, and became Artaxerxes III's supreme counsellor at court. But in 338 he poisoned Artaxerxes and put his son Arses on the throne (338–336). Arses tried the same trick on Bagoas, but was detected and likwise murdered. With so many of the direct line of Artaxerxes II now dead or murdered, Bagoas turned to the cadet branch of the family of Darius II. Calling himself Darius III, the new king forced poison on Bagoas. In that very year Philip of Macedon had sent his troops into Asia Minor. In 334 his son Alexander took up the campaign. By 330 Darius was dead and the Persian Empire was no more.

As recounted above, this is a tale of 'rebellions, murders, weak kings trapped in the harem, missed chances and foolish policies'; but, as has been justly remarked, 'this cannot be the whole story. The sources, mostly Greek, are often prejudiced against the Persians and tend to view events from but a single point of view. No government could have lasted so long, found its way somehow through so many difficulties, and in the end fought so hard against the conqueror without having much virtue with which to balance its vices.'[9] Perhaps some glimpse of these balancing virtues will shine through from what follows.

4. KINGSHIP AND ARISTOCRACY

The Persian Empire was run by a network of enormously rich Persian territorial aristocrats with Persian and, possibly, Mede commoners in support. This network was articulated and directed by its supreme head, the Great King, or *Shah-in-Shah*—the King of Kings.

What were the credentials of such a Great King? We are given an insight by the great trilingual rock inscriptions that King Darius I put up at Behistun after making good his seizure of the throne. He claims that the kingship had 'from long ago' belonged in his family: he had but reclaimed it from the usurping pseudo-Bardiya.[10] He traces this family claim through eight generations to a certain Achaemenes: 'For this reason we are called Achaemeneans . . . Eight of our family there were who were kings afore: I am the ninth.'[11] The very first paragraph of the inscription ascribes his kingship to the 'Great God Ahura-Mazda', but the second paragraph runs: 'I am Darius the Great King—son of Hytaspes an Achaemenian, a Persian, son of a Persian, an Aryan, having Aryan lineage.' In short: the Iranian people is a favoured people, the tribe of Persians is especially favoured among the Iranians, and the Achaemenid family is especially favoured of all the Persians. Under Ahura-Mazda, Iranian kingship rests in a special royal family. The notion suggests that each ruler was to be succeeded by his son, but as may have been noticed[12] that expectation was frequently disappointed. But being Aryan-Persian-Achaemenian was so basic to the title to reign that kings and their offspring were forbidden to marry foreigners and indeed, by the 'compact' of 522 BC, might intermarry only with the six (later five) great families which had helped Darius attain the throne.

Religion, or the cult, played an insignificant role in legitimating the monarch, so marking a sharp, almost complete, break with the preceding monarchies in the Middle East and in Egypt. True, initially the Persian kings 'took the hand of Bel' in Babylon, and played the role of pharaoh in

---

[9] T. Culyer Young, Jr., 'The Persian Empire', *Encyclopaedia Britannica* (15th edn. 1979), ix. 836.
[10] Kent (ed.), *Old Persian*, 120.   [11] Ibid.   [12] See pp. 290–1 above.

Egypt, but this was to placate local tradition, not the Persians' own; and in any case the practice was abandoned from the time of Darius.

We know very little about the religious beliefs of the Persians. Who were the Magi, for instance? What was their relationship to the court, and to the worship of Ahura-Mazda? Was Darius a Zoroastrian? What might Zoroastrianism have meant in this age? We have no firm date for Zoroaster, and it seems doubtful whether he was a near-contemporary of Darius; his basic notion of a cosmic struggle between the forces of Mazda and Ahriman— light versus Darkness, Truth versus the Lie—are to be imputed to Achaemenid times only by inference from the *Zend Avesta*, which is itself of later date. The Magi are said to have been Medes, not Persians, a special class or tribe whose chief duties were to lead the ceremonies and attend sacrifices connected with fire, fire being central in the cult of the ancient Iranian gods. Certainly the Magi attended the royal court. But Herodotus' account of the succession to Cambyses has it that the alleged usurper, the pseudo-Bardiya, was really a Magus named Gaumata: if true, this might imply that the Magi opposed the cult of Ahura-Mazda and hence made a bid for the throne, only to make their peace when Darius imposed himself. But all this is pure speculation.

Only two facts stand out clearly; but they suffice. First of all, the Magi were not an organized priesthood and, from Darius onwards at any rate, play no political role *vis-à-vis* the king. Secondly, Darius and his son Xerxes regarded Ahura-Mazda as the supreme god but not, however, the only god. He created heaven and earth and he created mankind; those who worshipped him would be blessed with many children and a long life: Darius worshipped him and the god had bestowed the kingship upon him. Darius does not mention the other two Persian deities, Mitra and Anahita; it was Artaxerxes II who first mentioned these in his royal inscriptions.

Though Darius claims Ahura-Mazda as the bestower of his kingship, this is about as far as any specifically divine authorization or mission is claimed. Ancient Iranian religion conceived of the *hvarena*, 'the awful kingly glory' created by Ahura-Mazda and conferred on the heroes and the chiefs (*kavi*) of Iranian myth; and hence also, of course, on the king. This *hvarena* was the concrete and shining apparition of light and sometimes it appears in sculptures as a nimbus[13] hovering over the person of the king as the figure of Ahura-Mazda, enclosed in a winged sphere. On his public processions the king was preceded by the chariot of Ahura-Mazda drawn by white horses, with two following chariots for Mitra and Anahita. Behind these

[13] F. Dvornik, *Early Christian and Byzantine Political Philosophy: Origins and Background*, 2 vols. (Washington DC, 1966), i. 84–7.

came men—Magi?—carrying fire for the altar, a symbol of the royal hearth. The monarch himself was a magnificent sight. On his head sat the royal tiara. His upper body was clothed in the tunic of purple shot with white, which only the king might wear: his trousers were scarlet, his mantle, purple. As he passed by, all prostrated themselves.[14]

It had not always been so. Ever since Darius's day the king was crowned at Pasargardae in the original humble capital of Cyrus, and there the new sovereign still ate the poor peasant meal of fig-cake, terebinth, and sow milk; a far cry from the rare wines, the special flasks of distant spring waters, the 15,000 guests who sat down at the king's tables. After Darius the king drew himself apart, increasingly inaccessible; only the six great nobleman might approach him directly. He dwelt in immense palaces fabulously rich in cedar-woods and precious stones, richly embellished with coloured ceramic reliefs depicting the nations that paid tribute and scenes of victory, surrounded by the thousand spearmen and bowmen of his bodyguard. His throne was made all of gold, and elaborate indeed was the ritual encompassing his sitting on it and descending from it.[15] We have a vivid description of royal audiences where all perform *proskynesis* or prostration; of his golden sceptre, of the jewelry that bedecked him, worth (according to Plutarch) 3 million sterling (in 1982 prices).[16] Also of feasts where the king presided over his guests and the small private parties afterwards; of the 300 or so concubines in his harem and the thousand-strong bodyguard under the *chiliarch* that guarded him. Similar pomp had, of course, surrounded pharaohs, and the kings of Babylonia and Assyria and China, as it would attend the Roman, Byzantine, and Arab sovereigns also. The point is that all this inaccessibility, mystery, and circumstance made it clear that the king, whether he was divine or vicar of god or none of these, was nevertheless not at all as other men: he was—somehow and for some perhaps inexplicable reason—superior: he was there to be obeyed. The visual symbols of royal power—the *miranda* of power—are, for all we know, arguably much more powerful than the *credenda* (the rationale of his legitimacy, of his claim to be obeyed). 'It would take a very refined reason indeed to regard the Grand Turk as you would any other man as he sits in the midst of his magnificent seraglio surrounded by forty thousand Janissaries.'[17] And indeed, this overwhelming visual impression of the monarch's difference from ordinary mortals was necessary to reconcile the ordinary mortal to the quite extraordinary powers of the king. For his authority was absolute. No corpus of

[14] F. Dvornik, *Early Christian and Byzantine Political Philosophy: Origins and Background*, 2 vols. (Washington DC, 1966), i. 114.   [15] Ibid. 120.
[16] Cook, *Persian Empire*, 138.   [17] Pascal, *Pensées* (Dent, London, 1932), iii. 3.

traditional conventions limited him (except the ones forbidding the royal family to marry foreigners). No religious precepts, nor any organized priesthood constrained him. He was the unique source of 'the king's law'. He was the very fountain of justice and so could do no wrong. In principle he owned all property, his subjects were his *douloi* (*bandaka* in Persian), which translates as his subjects, servants, or slaves—in short, he had the power of life and death.

In practice this absolute power was limited in three ways. The first was by natural limits: this could be somewhat expanded or contracted according to his access to information, and I shall return to this. The second was by court intrigue. There was plenty of this, as the murder of reigning monarchs and the fratricidal struggles for succession well demonstrate. But these only affected the identity of who was to be king; it in no way affected the absolutist nature of monarchy as an institution. The third limitation was the effective one—the territorial nobility.

The empire was ruled, as we said at the outset, by a Persian aristocracy under the leadership of the king. A large part of this ruling aristocracy consisted of members of the royal lineage itself.[18] Who were the others? To judge from other pastoral peoples, such as the horse-riding Sinic and Turkic invaders of China over the centuries, to say nothing about the Indo-European tribes as implied in the *Vedas*, *lineages* are of enormous importance: the heads of clans and families outside the royal one are aristocrats, who originally were much on a par with it. Such an aristocratic component would have been expanded during the reign of Cyrus the Great, for we are told that he incorporated Persian (as well as other) clans into his own kingdom and their leaders would certainly have retained their aristocratic status *vis-à-vis* their own people. Altogether, these aristocrats were the *eugeneis*, the 'well-born'. They brought their fellow tribesmen into Cyrus' wars against the Medes and then across the Middle East and shared the spoils of the conquest in the shape of landed estates and governorships. Among them, six families were of much greater political importance than the others—the families whose heads conspired with Darius to murder the pseudo-Bardiya and help him to the throne. One of these men was subsequently done away with for an act of *lèse-majesté*; but what is known of the others shows them indeed as enjoying high favour throughout the empire.[19]

The royal family and the other nobles provided the king with his provincial governors—the satraps—whom we shall dwell on later. This being so, the Great King's problem was similar to that of the kings of medieval Europe, what we might call 'baron-management'. He could give

[18] See p. 296 below.   [19] Cf. Cook, *Persian Empire*, 167–71.

effect to his orders only through them. This is the cardinal feature of the polity. Therefore they must be induced to give enthusiastic support (the best outcome) or acceptance (the next best) and discouraged from foot-dragging or, at the very worst, open resistance. This called for a kind of distributive justice, a calculus of rewards and deterrents, for the vast extent of the empire made inspections and control mechanisms of little avail. Hence satisfy—with honours, power, and wealth; and also divide—so that in doubtful cases the satraps' mutual rivalries would nullify a threat to the royal authority. The classic case-study of this divide-and-rule policy is the way the great Satraps' Revolt of 366–360 BC was extinguished by Artaxerxes III.[20]

On the whole, the satrapal nobility were loyal and served the king with diligence, so there must have been more to their allegiance than just material or honorific satisfaction. And indeed there was. They had carried over from their Iranian tribal beginnings the tradition of personal loyalty to one's legitimate overlord. This tribal trait was also self-serving since they demanded—and got—similar personal loyalty from their own retainers and dependants. Notice how, even in the ever-worsening adversity, the aristocracy remained loyal to the clearly miscast Darius III as he fled—fled not once but three times—before Alexander. That at the very end he was abandoned and left to die by Bessus is not surprising; what is remarkable is that it took his noblemen so long to desert him. Personal allegiance counted very high, then; but beyond that, these aristocrats—paupers turned princes!—realized that they were the ruling class, tied together by inter-marriages, speaking together a language unknown to their subjects, sharing the same manners and customs, worshipping their own peculiar gods, and made multi-millionaires by sharing in the spoliation of their conquered subjects. The satrapal nobility's self-conscious pride and solidarity made them see themselves at one with the Great King in their self-appointed (and self-serving) mission of governing the empire.

5. CENTRAL AND LOCAL GOVERNMENT

The world has seen a number of vast empires which fell to pieces on the death of their founder or his immediate successors—the 'conquest empires' of Chinghiz Khan and Tamerlaine spring to mind immediately; and so, for that matter, does Alexander the Great's empire which was, of course, the late, the ex-Persian, empire itself. The Persian Empire that Cyrus founded survived, however, for more than two centuries. How?

[20] Cf. Olmstead, *History of Assyria*, 417–22.

Here, on the one side, were the 120,000 adult male Persians, illiterate, and so far quite unused to statecraft and administration. On the other lay the most immense territory and the most heterogeneous collection of peoples that had ever been brought together in a single unit. It comprised the territory which is nowadays divided into the following sovereign states (or parts of them): Thrace and Macedonia (in modern Greece), Egypt up to at least the Libyan frontier, Turkey, Syria, Lebanon, Israel, Jordan, Iraq, Iran, Afghanistan, Pakistan, and the following republics of the former USSR— Georgia, Azerbaijan, Armenia, Turkmenistan, and Tadjikstan. The total area was, therefore, approximately 2,503,838 square miles! The Assyrian Empire had totalled only 638,368 square miles at its largest extent; the land surface of the Roman Empire measured only 1,600,000 square miles. The Persian Empire would have covered 70 per cent of the land-surface of the present-day USA. From north-west to south-east, and from south-west to north-east it measured some 3,000 miles in either direction. Its administrative capital lay roughly equally between Macedonia and Gandhara—1,600 miles from each. Darius made a 'Royal Road' between Susa and Sardis in westernmost Asia Minor—some 1,600 miles. Special couriers posting night and day continuously could perforce deliver a message between the two towns in seven days.[21] Ordinarily, travellers took 67.5 days to cover that journey; an army, 90 days.[22]

Not only that: the social, political and religious conditions of the 50 million people who lived within this huge area were vastly dissimilar. According to Herodotus it contained seventy different peoples and tribes.[23] These might be governed in bureaucratically centralized units like Babylonia and Egypt, or the city states of Phoenicia and Ionia, or by chieftains or sheikhs in Arabia, Zagros, Mysia, Paphlagonia, and Bithynia. The empire contained, indeed, great tracts of tribal lands where the Great King's writ ran but intermittently or not at all. Here the cult was that of Marduk, and there that of Ammon. In Syria it was the cult of Baal and Astarte while in Judah the ancient Jewish religion was shortly to be restored. These peoples had nothing in common—certainly not a language—except a common destiny: subjection to Persian over-rule.

The formula the Persians applied for governing this empire was as simple as it proved successful. It was to set themselves the most limited objectives possible, short of losing control: in brief, to provide an overarching struc-

[21] Cf. the time taken by an Arab courier to cover the distance Meru–Teheran, in the ninth century AD: 750 miles in three days.

[22] Herodotus, v. 52 and viii. 98. Cook, *Persian Empire*, 108; Dandamaev and Lukonin, *Culture and Social Institutions*, 233.

[23] Cf. Dandamaev and Lukonin, *Culture and Social Institutions*, 98.

ture of authority throughout the entire territory which confined itself to two aims only: tribute and obedience. Otherwise *nothing*. There was no interference with local cults, local legal tradition and processes, social or political structures. Darius coined his own money—Darics—but allowed other currencies to circulate. He had cuneiform script adapted for the Persian tongue and used it in his inscription, but alongside Akkadian and Elamite. Not Persian but Aramaic was used as the common official language of the empire, alongside Greek and Elamite where necessary. There was *no standardization*, that is the point. The Persian Empire came as close as any state could to being the fabled 'night-watchman state' of Humboldt. In a way, one could say that the formula for running the empire was to let it run itself, providing only that it paid up and kept the peace. So, government effectively resolved itself into a two-way set of relationships: between the king and his noblemen, administrators, and temple-priesthoods together forming the ruling class; and between this ruling class and the subject population.

All the Greek writers concur that the Great King made decisions on his own responsibility,[24] but we have only the most fragmentary information about the context he made them in. Despite the evidence of the treasury and fortification tablets which will be adduced later, we still know almost nothing about the way the court and palace were organized. We learn about certain officials, such as the royal 'spear-bearer', 'bow-bearer', 'cup-bearer'. Nehemiah was the king's cup-bearer, and since he was allowed to go to Jerusalem as its local governor it is clear that this office was one of trust and influence. From this, and what we know of how quite humble household or palatine offices retain the lowliness of their title, but in practice discharge highly confidential and important duties (which incidentally may have become quite unrelated to the original office),[25] we can infer that the offices mentioned were of high consequence.

One such is the man the Greeks called the *chiliarch* because he was the commander of the thousand-strong royal bodyguard. Edward Meyer thought—and most scholars follow him—that the *chiliarch* had become a first minister, a vizier, and the head of the entire court and imperial administration.[26] The *chiliarch* was assuredly the officer who controlled access to the king, and for this reason alone was of supreme importance. Furthermore, since it was he who brought in all messages, he played a pre-eminent role in foreign negotiations. From these two—attested—roles it is

[24] Cook, *Persian Empire*, 145.
[25] Cf. *Byzantium, infra*, pp. 693 ff.; also *T'ang, Ming, infra* p. 826.
[26] E. Meyer, 'Persia', *Encyclopaedia Britannica* (11th edn. 1911), xxi. 208B.

logical to infer back that he was the head of the chancellery. This inference is nowadays widely accepted.[27]

Nor is it certain that there existed a royal Council of Seven, despite the reference in Ezra.[28] This might have been a panel of seven jurists,[29] but when Herodotus mentions 'councils'—and he does so only three times—they are all special occasions and the most important Persians attend them. 'Ministers' in a specialized sense simply did not exist. The court was patrimonial, that is, a set of household officers, their duties defined—and changed—according to what the king wanted done (surely attested by the 'anonymity' of Pharnakes mentioned in n. 27 below) and his degree of confidence in them. It looks as though the king took counsel when and with whom he wanted. This is not to say that he lacked sources of outside information. The large and growing class of royal princes who held commands in the provinces could supply one pool of advice. There seem to have been specialists in the affairs of, say, Greece or Egypt who were summoned to court especially for their opinions. Then the Great King would receive information from the satraps, the castellans, and—it appears—from the imperial secretariats that maintained an independent status, responsible only to the centre, at the satrapal courts.[30] And we must not forget the intelligence network known as the 'king's eyes and ears', though how and to whom they reported and in what packaged form the information reached the monarch, we simply know not of.

Though we are ignorant of the inner organization of the chancellery and of the imperial household, both clearly existed. We can infer the former from the circulation of the texts of inscribed stones and tablets and Aramaic documents throughout the empire, not to speak of the circumstantial account in the Bible of how the decree of Cyrus (relating to the rebuilding of the Jewish Temple) was challenged, until a copy was duly found in the royal archives.[31]

As to the second, a palace with a harem of 300 women and where 15,000

---

[27] Cf. Cook, *Persian Empire*, 144. Dandamaev and Lukonin, *Culture and Social Institutions* are quite categorically of this opinion, 111–12. In the fortification tablets there appears a certain Pharnakes, clearly a very important man, chiefly concerned (in these tablets) in economic management. But the tablets do not attribute any title to Pharnakes, so that some have seen him as the head of the imperial household, others as the *chiliarch*. What is very clear is that he has a large number of scribes, writing in all the important languages of the empire, under his control; as well as the scribal staff of his immediate subordinate official, one Zissawis. Cf. D. M. Lewis, *Sparta and Persia* (Brill, Leiden, 1977), 7–11, who speaks of this as 'his' chancellery. But whether it was the central imperial chancellery is another question.

[28] Ezra 7: 14.

[29] Cook, *Persian Empire*, 145.   [30] Lewis, *Sparta and Persia*, 24–5.

[31] Ezra 2–6. The account should be read. It gives a rare glimpse of the administration in action. Since the rescript was ultimately found in an out-of-the-way archive (at Ecbatana), filing and preservation of documents were reliable but the retrieval system was obviously pretty poor.

guests fed at the royal tables could not possibly have functioned without its own bureaucracy. (This is attested universally where similar circumstances existed—Imperial Rome, Byzantium, the Caliphate, Imperial China, and so forth.) This is where the Persepolis and Treasury tablets are so valuable: for whatever else they tell us about the important official they name as Pharnakes, they show him as directing the allocation of rations to various members of the imperial house as well as to officials, and controlling via his subordinates a staff of overseers who form and lead work-details, and others who allocate the rations due to these.[32] This has led at least one commentator to believe that Pharnakes was the *Hofmarschall*, a court-marshal, that is, a comptroller of the household.[33] What *is* quite certain from these documents is that the Household bureaucracy was very numerous and highly organized, and that its officials and workers were paid in rations.[34] The imperial household was, in fact, a huge *oikos*.

One sure sign of a palace bureaucracy is the existence of eunuchs, and these are amply attested in the Persian court. Most palace eunuchs, wherever we find them—in the late Roman and the Byzantine empires, in the Caliphate and Ottoman Empire, and in Imperial China—are humble menials, but some, more educated and talented than the rest, rise to positions of influence.[35] This is what happened in the Persian case, and from the time of Artaxerxes I such eunuchs formed one of the power factors at the court, along with the imperial bodyguard and the great Persian noblemen. We only catch glimpses of their activity, so that it is not possible to situate or define their political role with the same precision as we can that of their Roman, Byzantine, and above all Chinese counterparts. Nevertheless, it is worth dwelling on them for a moment because here, for the first time—and in its most succinct form—we find a *theory* as to why eunuchs were utilized to such an extent. This theory is to be found in Xenophon's *Cyropaedia*.

As we have shown, the Assyrian monarchs may have employed eunuchs extensively,[36] so it is possible that the Persians inherited the institution from them. But they must have used them in huge numbers, if Herodotus is to be believed, since he tells us that Babylonia and Assyria (alone) had to supply the court with 500 boy-eunuchs a year.[37] At first the ones mentioned by

---

[32] Cf. *Cambridge History of Iran* (Cambridge, 1985), ii. 588–609 [hereafter *CHI*] ('The Evidence of the Persepolis Tablets' by the late R. T. Hallock). Also Lewis, *Sparta and Persia*, ch. I.

[33] So Hinz, 'Achämendische Hofverwaltung', *Zeitschrift für Assyriologie*, 61 (1971), 260–311; *contra* Lewis, *Sparta and Persia*, 8.

[34] As one might expect in a natural economy. In this respect the Persian court resembles those of Assyria and Egypt.   [35] See p. 495 below.

[36] See pp. 230–1 above.   [37] Herodotus, iii. 92.

name are confidential emissaries, but from the time of Artaxerxes I the eunuchs appear in highly influential positions: Artoxares, for instance, who played the king-maker on Ataxerxes I's death, and later Bagoas who was commander of the bodyguard (i.e. the *chiliarch*), general in the Egyptian campaigns, and finally the king-maker who placed Darius III on the throne.[38]

Why and how eunuchs could attain such importance is explained by Xenophon: and what he has to say is exactly applicable to the later palace-systems in late Rome, the Byzantine Empire, and Imperial China.[39] Xenophon cautions against the facile belief that eunuchs were weaklings: 'they are not made any less efficient horsemen or any less skilful lancers or less ambitious men . . . rather the contrary, and even if physically weaker [which he doubts] in battle, steel makes the weak equal to the strong'. But they were (he says) more *faithful* than most men. Men would put children, wives, and sweethearts first—not so the eunuchs, whose chief affection would go to those who could make them rich, protect them, and give them high office. Furthermore, eunuchs were despised by the rest of mankind, hence they were dependent on a patron for protection.[40]

We are left with intimations of a characteristic 'oriental' court: its pomp, its protocol, its banquets, audiences, palace ladies, slaves and eunuchs, and a group of household officers who bear insignificant titles but serve really as the all-purpose high officials of the king. We have, in short, the ornamental aspects of the court. About the inner organization of its efficient part—chancellery, bureaucracy, and treasury—we know little except what has already been related. Nor do we know much about the taxation system. It seems that Cyrus laid tributes on an *ad hoc* basis and for this reason won the reputation of being open-handed. Darius on the other hand was accounted mean and avaricious because he imposed system on the empire. It was he who divided it into the provinces we call satrapies[41] and imposed on each of these a fixed tribute. It is said that he also carried out a cadaster survey to graduate the tribute to the wealth of each province; but if he did, it must have been pretty rough-and-ready, and in my view he simply told the bureaucracies in post in Egypt, Babylonia, and other long-bureaucratized parts of the Empire to update their registers.

The tribute for each satrapy[42] represented only what each province had to pay the imperial treasury; the local satrap raised as much as he wanted and kept the surplus for his own local requirements. It was a cheap and easy

---

[38] Olmstead, *History of Assyria*, 312, 344, 355 ff., 363–4; and 437–8, 440, 488–92, 508, 512.

[39] See p. 574 ff., 641 ff., 787 ff. below.   [40] Xenophon, *Cyropaedia*, vii. v. 60 f.

[41] See pp. 192–3, 574 ff below.   [42] Cf Herodotus, iii 89–94 for a list

system for the court to administer and wholly consistent with the general
sense of Persian imperial administration, which was to tell the satraps what
the king required and let them get on with it. But it was not necessarily
cheap for the populations, who were obviously liable to unlimited extortion.[43] Taxation was reckoned in silver but was largely paid in kind, except
in the west where metallic currencies were now circulating. The Persian
kings were avid and avaricious hoarders of gold and silver, which they kept
(as we know from the hoards Alexander discovered) in palace treasuries at
Susa and Persepolis. Outside the fixed tributes in cash or kind which are
listed by Herodotus, the authorities could call on forced labour service and,
in times of war, for food and equipment. These could and indeed did fall
very heavily on the areas that were the sites of repeated campaigns. Thus the
great revolt of Sidon in 352 BC was provoked by too many calls on it to
provide the wherewithal for one Egyptian campaign after another.

Locally the taxation arrangements must have gone on much as before the
Median and Persian conquest so that in some areas, notably Egypt, but
possibly Babylonia also, they would have retained the redistributive character of former times. On the imperial plane, however, the fiscal system had
now entirely ceased to be redistributive. There is no trace of even the
primitive Assyrian system of directing supplies to specified reception areas
(though this might well have continued locally). The taxes were a one-way
flow to the centre, to provide for its overheads: palace-building, officials,
and the hire of mercenaries. Almost the only remnants of the old Assyrian
system seems to be the requirement that the satrapy of Babylon provide the
needs of the palace for four months in the year,[44] and the arrangement in
Persis (modern Fars). Persis was different from the other satrapies in that it
was the imperial province and hence not subject, so that it did not pay
monetary tribute though it paid tax in kind.[45] It seems to have been run
bureaucratically. At its head stood a comptroller-general who lived in great
state. He controlled the provincial household, administrative services, and
the central treasury; the last of these controlled in its turn a network of
regional treasuries and workshops. These delivered grain, cattle, fruit and
vegetables, and the like to various departments, which in their turn issued
rations to the high officials entitled to indent on it. These include the king's
bow-bearer and spear-bearer and of course the comptroller-general
himself.[46]

Persis apart, the empire was administered on the very simplest basis: by

[43] Cf. Conceptual Prologue, p. 81 ff. above.   [44] Herodotus, i. 192
[45] Dandamaev and Lukonin, *Culture and Social Institutions*, 179.
[46] Cook, *Persian Empire*, 89–90.

extreme decentralization to local governors. These were the satraps. The word itself is the way the Greeks chose to write and pronounce *khshahthrap-avan*—accentuating the *Shahthrap* component and swallowing the rest—and it means 'Protector of the Realm'.[47] There were almost certainly satraps before Darius, but Darius was the first systematically to divide up the empire into provinces and put a satrap in charge of them, henceforward called the satrapies. Herodotus lists twenty by name and description. Some scholars have claimed that his satrapies are really taxation-districts, and that the true satrapies were army-commands and so forth,[48] but this must imply that satraps and tax-collectors were different and separate. Likewise, many scholars, following the great Edward Meyer (whose views can be painlessly consulted under 'Persia' in the 1911 edition of the *Encyclopaedia Britannica*), thought the empire was much more strictly ordered than recent historians do. On the basis of a solitary and parenthetical phrase of Herodotus (iii. 128), he inferred that the satrap was checked by an imperial secretary reporting directly to the king; that military authority rested with a commander directly responsible to the king; that royal 'king's eyes' made unpredictable descents on the satraps to check their administration.[49]

Recent scholarship qualifies this. It agrees that Herodotus was broadly correct in his list of twenty satrapies, though some of these were subdivided during the later empire. As for the satraps, they were all-powerful, omnicompetent, and free from any regular institutionalized system of control.[50] Thus we are invited to envisage the vast empire as divided into its twenty or so provinces, each wholly in the charge of a viceroy, who was backed up by (in some cases) Persian garrison commanders, Persian fief-holders, and Persian military colonies, the mix differing in different parts of the empire. There was, in short, a Persian internal colonization throughout the empire and this provided its ruling stratum, implanted amidst the pre-imperial local power-holders whom it left undisturbed, but utilized for its own purposes and under its control.

Most of our information about satraps relates to the western satrapies, particularly those of Anatolia; about those in the north-east, that is, the Iranian part of the empire (the 'upper' satrapies) we know almost nothing, and they may have differed from the 'lower' ones in important respects since they remain resolutely loyal to Darius III as he retreated before Alexander. From what we know, however, it seems that satraps were members of the

[47] Cook, *Persian Empire*, 242 n. 1.

[48] Cf. A. Toynbee, *A Study of History*, 10 vols. (OUP, Oxford, 1934–54), vii. 580–689.

[49] Meyer, 'Persia'; also R. Ghirshman, *Iran* (Penguin, Harmondsworth, 1954), 144–5.

[50] Not the view of Dandamaev and Lukonin, *Culture and Social Institutions*, who believe that central control was powerfully exerted via the 'king's eyes' (p. 111).

royal family or the other Persian nobility. The former were given the richest
satrapies but were replaced from time to time; whereas over time many of
the nobles' satrapies tended to become hereditary (though always liable to a
royal revocation).

But to return to the description given by Herodotus which we cited
earlier: there is much confusion as to whether the satrap was a civil or a
military official, or both. Even if they commanded military forces, they
would come under the control of one of the four or so 'toparchs' who
assumed supreme command of all the forces in their toparchy in emergency.
There are indeed instances where the local garrison commander exercised
independent command, but the overwhelming impression is that the satraps
commanded large forces even in peacetime, and they indubitably did so
when facing foreign invasion. Apart from the regular troops they commanded, they called out the local levies.

The truth is probably that the responsibilities of the satraps shifted over
time; at first, as simply civil governors and then, by the fourth century BC,
also commanding military forces[51] which they could, it would seem (from
the Satraps' Revolt of 366–360), augment at will. As time went on many of
the western satraps took military action 'quite irresponsibly',[52] and hired
large forces of mercenaries for their own purposes. Their military authority
was by no means restricted to their satrapies. On the contrary, they
commanded their forces for the king in the great battles: Achaemines,
satrap of Egypt, at Salamis for instance. For apart from the 10,000 'Imor-
tals',[53] the Great King had no standing army.

Related to the satraps' military activity was, of course, diplomacy and
here again they enjoyed great latitude.[54] Finance is an obscure topic but the
satraps were in full charge. In so far as they had to forward on the king's
fixed tribute but were permitted to keep the remainder to meet their own
local expenditures, they set the gross tax level. Collection was largely
handled by tax-farmers. In respect of their civil responsibilities, to which
we have already alluded, Xenophon says their duties were 'to govern the
people, receive the tribute, pay the militia and attend to any other business
that needs attention'.[55] They were—he continues—to have lands and
houses in their satrapy so that they may have tribute paid to them there'.

A satrap held his own court, modelled on that of the Great King, and
this was attended by the Persian magnates and notables of the satrapy.

[51] Dandamaev and Lukonin, *Culture and Social Institutions*, 101–2.
[52] S. Hornblower, *Mausolus* (Clarendon Press, Oxford, 1982), 146.
[53] See p. 311 below.   [54] Hornblower, *Mausolus*, 146–8; 152.
[55] Xenophon, *Cyropaedia*, viii. vi. 3 f.

These were the Persian 'establishment' which provided the satrap's back-up. They would include the commanders of the big garrisons which were set up in important satrapal centres like Memphis (of mixed peoples and totalling 16,000 mouths) and the lesser garrisons like that of the Jewish mercenaries at Elephantine, and others at Thebes, Abydos, and so forth—all these in Egypt. There was a string of forts along the Jaxartes River in the north-east. Sardis was the great garrison town of Western Anatolia. Here, where the terrain was hospitable and fertile, Persians had been granted huge estates as fiefs which they held in return for bringing forces to the field. They were immensely rich, and they had their own militia, courts, chancelleries, treasuries, police, and a host of scribes, managers, storemen, and book-keepers. They did not reside on these estates themselves; they preferred the attractions of the *paradise* or the distractions of the city.[56] The term *hyparch*, used in an unsystematic way by the Greeks, would have applied to some of these. These notables gathered at the satrap's court, which was served by a chancellery of Aramaic-speaking scribes.

Below this level, there was no uniform infrastructure and no uniform way of collecting the tribute.[57] Existing systems were maintained in full force—in Egypt and Babylonia, the elaborate administrative systems along with the temples. Sidon had its own city king. In the territory west of Euphrates which the Persians called Abarnahara ('beyond the river') they ruled through a miscellany of city princes (e.g. in Phoenicia and Cyprus), priestly rulers, local despots, and tribal sheikhs.[58] In the Ionian cities of western Anatolia, they operated through the oligarchies (whom they sustained). In short, the entire indigenous apparatus was left in place, so that justice, tax assessment and collection, religious practices and institutions continued as they always had, but under Persian supervision and with Persians as judges. The system seems too beautifully simple not to have had any flaws in it, and of course it did have. One relates to how effectively the satraps were able to control their subjects, and another to how effectively the Great King could control his satraps.

That latter control was founded on one principle—fealty. The Great King was the satraps' liege lord. Satraps recognized the king as the supreme authority, and for most of the time and most of the territory that was enough to guarantee their obedience and support. The satraps themselves depended on this same principle of fealty in respect to the hyparchs and fief-holders in their satrapies. The satraps and their notables were in honour bound. If this seems an odd way of securing allegiance, that is only because

[56] Dandamaev and Lukonin, *Culture and Social Institutions*, 134, 141.
[57] Cook, *Persian Empire*, 173.   [58] Ibid. 174–5.

in the late twentieth century West honour is not a primary social value. But in other societies it is, and the principles of political organization in medieval Europe or Japan are unintelligible unless we suspend disbelief concerning chivalry and *bushido*. Some satrapal revolts against the Great King were, paradoxically, actually provoked by this sense of honour. The prime example is the rebellion of Artaxerxes I's great general, the satrap Megabyzus, the man who reconquered Egypt. Megabyzus revolted because when the Great King executed the rebel Inaros and certain Athenian prisoners of war, he had broken Megabyzus' pledged word that they would not be harmed. Another example would be Cyrus, whose motive for rebelling against his brother King Artaxerxes II was that he had been insulted at court.

For all that, satraps could be swayed by base motives also. To prevent this or to limit the damage was, as we said earlier, a matter of man-management, and in this the Great Kings had an arsenal of techniques at their disposal. The first, of course, was their undisputed title to appoint or remove, and a second was a host of spies and informants, from 'king's eyes and ears' (an intelligence network spread throughout the empire) to members of a satrapal court, even the sons of a satrap, or else neighbouring satraps (all rivals), all of whom were well-placed to detect signs of incipient revolt. If a satrap did revolt, however, he was unlikely to get far without the support of his neighbouring satraps, and as most of these were in rivalry, with no common interest in their neighbours' ambitions or objectives, the rebel was isolated. There is only one case, in fact, of a satrap who did succeed against the odds in setting up an independent satrapy: Datames. Appointed commander-in-chief of the expeditionary force to reconquer Egypt, he learned of intrigues against him at the royal court. Taking up arms he fell back on Cappadocia, and because of its rugged terrain was able to hold it. Datames himself was treacherously murdered by a loyalist satrap, but the Cappadocian satrapy was given to his sons who founded their own independent Iranian dynasty there (362 BC).

In fact, nearly all the satrap revolts took place in the Anatolian corner of the empire, and nearly all of these formed part of the general 'satraps' revolt' at the end of Artaxerxes II's reign. Anatolia, for one thing, was 1,600 miles and ninety days' march from the capital at Susa. Secondly, bordering on a hostile Hellas, the satrapies of Asia Minor and the Syrian area were like medieval 'marches'; their satraps needed and were conceded extraordinary military and diplomatic powers to meet the enemy. Thirdly, the military and diplomatic threat from the Greeks extended itself easily to Cyprus (a tributary kingdom) and Egypt, always on the verge of revolt. By this time, the fourth century BC, warfare was becoming professionalized and the supreme professionals were the Greek hoplite infantry. The Persian march-satraps had become used to the game of backing Sparta against Athens or the other way round, so it was a short step to taking Greek mercenaries into their service and setting Greek against Greek in this way too. The Greek troops were for use against the enemy, but they were also available against the royal court itself.

The Satraps' Revolt in the later years of Artaxerxes II illustrates all these points, and it is worth noting that it was the only co-ordinated rebellion in the history of the empire. Its details are highly complicated, but the point is, first, that the three satraps who revolted initially all did so because they felt or knew that the king was about to move them from their satrapies. (The fourth was a loyalist satrap coerced into joining them.) The second point is that the court was able to play on their mutual divisions and rivalries, two of them turning their coats and going over to the king, the other two betrayed and done away with. Other satrapal revolts were very few. They were each highly idiosyncratic, and they were isolated. In the context of the vast scale and long duration of the empire, therefore, the dynasty was quite remarkably successful in keeping the satraps' loyalty.

It was also highly successful in keeping the loyalty of the subject populations. This is not to say that the court did not have to fight internal wars against recalcitrant populations, only that these fall into two categories. The first are the campaigns against tribesmen, the second the campaign against three or four foci of repeated disaffection. As to tribesmen, governments in Iran have tried to deal with them even up to our own day.[59] The Great King's rule was fully effective only in the centres of sedentary and urban civilization: between these were great tracts of mountain and desert inhabited by wild barbarians. It was not worthwhile to tackle these unless it was to secure lines of communication or to stop them preying on the cultivators. The campaigns against them were 'savage wars of peace', the deadly side of the Persian civilizing mission. There was always warfare with the wild mountaineers like the Carduchians (Zagros) the Uxians (Elam), the Cadusians (the Elburz), the Pisidians, the Lycaonians (Taurus), and the Mysians (Olympus); all fruitless. Xenophon's *Anabasis* of 400 BC, which paints a vivid portrait of such savage mountaineers, demonstrates that north of Armenia royal authority was non-existent.

Apart from tribal areas of these kinds, the Persian rulers met resistance in only four places, and in only two of these did it persist. Babylon's revolt of 482 BC was provoked by Xerxes' slight upon its capital-city status. It was

[59] See e.g. V. Cronin, *The Last Migration*, ed. Rupert Hart-Davies (1957), for the struggles of the 100,000-strong Falquani tribe.

reduced, its temples broken, and the golden statute of Bel-Marduk carried off to the smelter-yard. It kept quiet after that. The Phoenician defection and revolt of Sidon was another one-off episode, provoked it seems by the excessive and repeated exactions to finance the Persians' unsuccessful campaigns against Egypt. This revolt broke out in 352 BC, at the very end of what had hitherto been a cordial relationship with the Persians, the Phoenician cities having enjoyed self-rule under their city kings. Only Ionia and Egypt were obdurately rebellious. The Persians do not seem to have treated the Ionian cities harshly at all: they enjoyed self-government, but the democratic parties in them were bound to oppose the Persians since it was they who kept the tyrants or oligarchies in power. Furthermore, no Greek city-state wanted anything less than complete independence. So the population looked across the sea to the free cities on the Greek mainland, particularly newly democratic Athens. Hence the Ionian revolt of 498 BC. The Persians suppressed it harshly but their subsequent political settlement was both wise and generous. The democratic factions were permitted to take over, and Persian interference with their internal affairs was almost non-existent. But by then the Ionian cities had become the *casus belli* between Persia and Greece.

Egypt was, of course, a complete culture in itself, and that culture, founded on its historic xenophobia and its all-pervasive temple-religion, was still intact. Indeed, under the Saïte dynasty (664–525 BC) it was enjoying a powerful cultural revival. Herodotus' account of the crimes of Cambyses against the Egyptian cults is a fable. In fact, Cambyses took the full titulary of a pharaoh and honoured the goddess Neith of Sais. The stories Herodotus tells us emanated from hostile priestly circles.[60] Darius was solicitous over Egypt: he endowed and restored temples and codified Egyptian law for the first time. The tax burden was comparatively light for so rich a land, and in some sense Darius requited it by pursuing irrigation projects and, above all, by cutting a canal to the Red Sea. The Persian defeat at Marathon in 490 BC marked a turning-point. Egypt revolted in the mid–480s, and when Xerxes suppressed the rebellion he treated Egypt as a conquered province, never visited it, and excluded Egyptians from the administration—to no avail. Revolts broke out not long after his death in 465, repressed only in 454; and again, on the death of Darius II in 404, after which the country was independent until reconquered by Artaxerxes III Ochus in 343. Ochus treated it harshly, carrying off the temple treasures and other booty, removing sacred books, and pulling down city walls. Even so, the news of his death provoked yet another rising (337). Darius III sup-

---

[60] Culyer Young, 'Persian Empire'.

pressed this in 335. Thus Egypt was still part of the empire when it fell to Alexander.

Ionia and Egypt, then, were the only two areas where Persian rule was resented, not just acutely but persistently. There is no evidence of such persistent unrest elsewhere, and in the east the Iranian lands were loyal to the last. Except in Babylonia, taxation was not unduly oppressive. There was no religious persecution. The destruction of E-sagila at Babylon and the plunder of the temples in Egypt were directed at centres and symbols of political rebellion; but the priesthoods, far from being proscribed, lived to celebrate Alexander the Great as their deliverer. Politically, the diverse populations lived much as before—the Ionians with their democracies, the Egyptians with their (Persian) pharaoh, the Phoenicians with their city kings, the Jews with their 'Men of the Great Assembly'. The local laws, customs, and social structures were respected. Unlike the Assyrians and the Romans, the Persians conducted war with great humanity. Conquered kings were dealt with honourably and cities were spared except for the gravest of offences and rebellions like those of Miletus and Sidon. All the inhabitants of the Empire served in its military forces. The garrisons were multi-ethnic.

The Persians left no literature, their art was thoroughly derivative, they were not in the least intellectual, and they were not religious fanatics. It was precisely these negative qualities that enabled them to rule the diverse peoples of the empire in such a relaxed and tolerant fashion. Their positive qualities were their acute sense of dignity, their pride of origin, and their code of fidelity to their king. These were what gave them the confidence to let their subjects lead their own lives, and enough coherence as a ruling class to prevent them breaking away. They also gave them a certain sense of empire. In this particularly do they differ from the murderously exploitative Assyrians. Perhaps Edward Meyer was over-sentimental when he wrote: 'Side by side with these wars we can read, even in the scanty tradition at our disposal, a consistent effort to further the great civilising mission imposed on the Empire.'[61] His list of their contributions must command respect. In Herat, Darius established a great water-basin, Scylax traced the course of the Oxus and navigated the Indian Ocean, a Red Sea canal was completed, ports were established on the Persian coast. And for over 200 years all the peoples in the interior—not the western marches, admittedly, but that vast interior—enjoyed peace. They were protected from one another, and from the savage robber bands of mountain tribesmen and desert nomads.

[61] Meyer, 'Persia'.

6. THE WEAKNESSES OF THE PERSIAN IMPERIAL SYSTEM

The great strengths of the system were the coherence of the Persian ruling aristocracy around their kings and the wide latitude they left to their subjects. In Meyer's opinion, however, the empire reached a turning-point after the Greeks defeated it, 490–466, when it began to degenerate. From those defeats onwards, he maintained, it was reduced to 'immobility and stagnation',[62] and this process was assisted by the deterioration, as a consequence of civilization and world dominion, of 'the ruling race'. 'The influence of the harem, the eunuchs and similar court officials made appalling progress and men of energy began to find the temptations of power stronger than patriotism and devotion to the King.'[63] The examples he gives are the Satraps' Revolt[64] and the murders of Xerxes and Artaxerxes III. Meyer also alleges a 'degeneration of the royal line'. As a consequence, 'the Empire never again undertook an important enterprise but neglected more and more its civilising mission'.[65]

But the Satraps' Revolt can be viewed as atypical,[66] and much too much can be made of the sometimes quite horrific intrigues, murders, and repulsive revenges (especially at the hands of the sadistic royal women) that occupied the Persian court. For what is striking about the assassinations of Persian monarchs is how *frequent* they are, but also, paradoxically, how long most kings reigned. There may well be a connection between the two. Xerxes would have been about 60 when Artabanus murdered him— that would have meant that the heir-apparent, Artaxerxes I, must have been waiting for about thirty years or more to succeed—and Artaxerxes III would have been about the same age when Bagoas poisoned him and put Arses and then Darius III on the throne. Persian monarchs enjoyed singularly long reigns. Leaving out the fratricidal episode of Xerxes II and Sogdianus, the average length of reign, 522–337, is thirty years. This must be among the highest, if not itself the highest, for any of the dynasties mentioned in this history. Despite the impression of perpetual intrigue and turmoil in the court, the throne was remarkably secure and this must have imparted a like stability to a system of which the throne was the lynchpin.

My own impression is—contrary to Meyer's—not that the institutions of the empire were in decay but that they had not evolved. Yet they were perfectly adequate to the needs of the empire, for there are no signs at all of internal collapse in its terminal years except in one fateful respect. Though

---

[62] Meyer, 'Persia'.   [63] Ibid.   [64] See p. 307 above.   [65] Meyer, 'Persia'.
[66] See p. 307 above.

the civil institutions still served their purpose, military techniques were obsolete. The empire did not decay or break up: it was assassinated.

Under Darius the Persian army consisted of a permanent palatine force, the 10,000 'Immortals', and components from the various ethnic groups of the empire, which were brought together at certain collecting-points as the need arose. The host, once gathered, was embattled in units of ten, building up into the thousand, commanded by the *chiliarch*, and the ten-thousand, led by the *myriarch*. The Immortals were all Persian and 1,000 of them formed the royal bodyguard. All carried bow and spear. They were protected by a highly effective leather corselet with iron fish-scales. They bore a wicker shield and could set this up as a protection from which they shot their arrows. Their heads, however, were not protected. The cavalry were horsed infantry, armed with spear and bow; but many of these wore iron helmets. Contingents of other peoples carried their own distinctive weapons. The army was not designed for hand-to-hand tactics. Its technique was to overwhelm the enemy with arrows, and follow up with cavalry. For these reasons, relatively few of the rank and file wore mail, and their shields were light ones, made of hide. Yet, generalled by Cyrus, Cambyses, and Darius they beat everybody—the Medes who were armed like themselves, the Lydians, who were cavalry lancers, and the Assyrians and Egyptians, who were heavy infantry.

Yet at this very time those kings to the west of Persis and Media who could afford it were hiring troops of a completely different kind. From the mid-seventh century Psammetichus I of Egypt was hiring 'bronze men' from Caria and Ionia. They were to be the mainstay of the Saïte dynasty. Croesus of Lydia might never have been conquered by Cyrus had he not sent his Greek mercenaries away for the winter. Again, Greek contingents fought in the neo-Babylonian armies. These Greek troops were recognized as masters of the battlefield. They were the hoplites: armoured infantry, using the thrusting spear and a light round shield, close-combat troops who stood their ground in thin phalanx formation and charged the enemy in line. By the fifth century they were superior to all other armies and among them the Spartan phalanx was supreme. But in battle they did not use cavalry as cavalry nor did they use archers.

The rival types of soldier clashed at Marathon and the Athenian hoplites won, but then the Persians had not used their cavalry. Xerxes' invasions of Greece provided a better test. At Plataea the Persians used their cavalry, and had increased the size of their heavy infantry component; whether they had superiority in numbers is dubitable and the mounted archers inflicted terrible casualties on the hoplites. But they made the mistake of not allowing their enemy to run away and were decisively beaten. In this battle the basic weaknesses of the Persian formation stood revealed. Essentially, they were three. First there was no co-ordination between using bow and using spear; once the enemy had closed in, they had no side-arm with which to fight back. Next, the hoplite was far more heavily armoured and therefore more proof against missile weapons and more protected in close combat. Thirdly, the Persians used their cavalry as horsed infantry and in too small numbers to protect their infantry against the hoplite charge.

A century-and-a-half later the Persian—or rather, the Iranian—component (the vast bulk, in short) of the Great King's field army was still not significantly different. But the Greek military had evolved much further and in the fourth century—especially after the cessation of hostilities in 404— Greece was spawning whole troops of highly disciplined soldiers for hire. For during the interminable Greek wars the cities had had to abandon their citizen armies and enlist professionals. It was the only way to match the Spartans. So, by now, war had ceased to be amateur and part-time. A science of 'stratagems' had grown up, with professional *condottieri* as its practitioners. As the fourth century wore on ways were found of protecting the hoplite phalanx with lightly armed peltasts, to defend its flanks with cavalry, and to attack and wheel in oblique formations.

Wherever the satraps of Anatolia and Abanaharna turned to confront the enemies of Persia—in Ionia, in Cyprus, or in Egypt—it was Greek soldiers who opposed them: mercenaries perhaps, or a force hired out by Greek city-states for a consideration and a share of the spoils. But they themselves did not re-equip and retrain their native forces in the Greek manner. On the contrary, they retained them and took the same easy way out that the French kings did between the fifteenth and seventeenth centuries when up against Swiss and German pikemen: if you can't beat them—hire them! So from the end of the fifth century the satraps used their revenues to hire Greeks. With the end of the fighting in Greece in 404, Cyrus, envious brother to Artaxerxes II, recruited mercenaries under Clearchus the Spartan: ostensibly to suppress rebel tribesmen, in reality to seize his brother's throne. At Cunaxa (401) Cyrus was killed but his army had won the day and from that moment the Great King himself began to take Greek mercenaries into service. He used them in 386 against King Evagoras in Cyprus. Diodorus even alleges that his motive in again enforcing peace in Greece was to create a market in mercenaries so that he could hire them to reconquer Egypt.[67] From this time on until the accession of Artaxerxes II, the satraps of Abanaharna and Anatolia built up Greek armies which, as we noted, they were to turn against the Great King in the Satraps' Revolt. Artaxerxes III

[67] Diodorus Siculus, *Library of History*, xv. 38.

Ochus—a ferocious man—disarmed them (the one satrap who resisted his order to dismiss the mercenaries and rebelled met his death) and forthwith accumulated his own Greek mercenaries to reconquer the Levant.[68] Sidon was taken, a Cypriot revolt quelled, and Egypt was at last assaulted. Nectanebo II of Egypt had an army of 100,000: 60,000 Egyptians, 20,000 Libyans, and 20,000 Greeks,[69] but Artaxerxes had 34,000 Greeks,[70] and with them his two generals took Egypt in a lightning assault.

When Alexander invaded Asia Minor in 334 the Persian cavalry was no different from what it had ever been, so that it was more lightly armoured than the new Macedonian cavalry, though its infantry was somewhat more heavily armoured than before. The royal guards still, it seems, used bow and spear. But the core of the Persian army consisted of 50,000 Greek mercenaries![71]

Here—not in the civil institutions—lay the fatal flaw in the Persian Empire: a formerly martial conqueror had lost confidence in its fighting ability to such an extent that it had to hire its enemy to fight its enemy. Xenophon said it all when he wrote, some sixty years before this time: 'Since the Persians themselves recognize the parlous state of their own forces, they give up: and no one makes war without Greeks any more—either when they fight one another, or when Greeks make war on them. They have decided to use Greeks even in order to fight Greeks!'[72] The supreme irony is that these Greek mercenaries were incapable of saving the empire. This was not because they defected. They were Greeks who hated Macedonians.[73] It was simply that, at Issus, they were given no room to manoeuvre and were located so as to run the risk of being cut to pieces.[74] For, although the ultimate cause of the empire's fall was military sclerosis, the proximate cause was personal. Darius III was, as Arrian justly wrote, 'the feeblest and most incompetent' of soldiers whereas Alexander, his dedicated enemy, was the greatest general of all time.

And yet, for all that, his conquest of the empire was no easy ride. Granted that Darius was perhaps a military nincompoop, that his armies were tactically no match for the Macedonians, and that he faced a military genius: he met Alexander in battle twice and was trying to collect a third army in Bactria when he was stabbed and left to die by Bessus. The conquest

[68] Cook, *Persian Empire*, 223.   [69] Ibid. 224.
[70] N. G. L. Hammond, *A History of Greece to 332 BC*, 2nd edn. (OUP, Oxford, 1967), 667.
[71] Cook, *Persian Empire*, 226. See also Hammond, *History of Greece*, app. 8 for further and detailed particulars on Greek mercenaries in Persian service.
[72] Xenophon, *Cyropaedia*, viii. 26.
[73] Arrian, *The Campaigns of Alexander*, trans. A. de Selincourt, notes by J. R. Hamilton (Penguin, Harmondsworth, 1971), 119.   [74] Ibid.

took Alexander three years. Compare Astyages' conquest of Nineveh—he met subsequent resistance only at Harran, and that was not very serious. Compare, next, Cyrus' conquest of Media (no subsequent resistance at all) and then of Croesus of Lydia (limited resistance from some Greek cities only). Yet Alexander was forced to fight battle after battle, down the coast of Asia Minor, then at the Issus, then at Gaugamela, then against Bessus and the Iranian satraps who offered resistance in the far east. This suggests that the empire was far more coherent than these earlier ones and the reasons, I surmise, lay in the family relationships of the satrapal and ruling stratum and its self-consciousness as the élite class of the empire. This cohesion had lasted over 200 years. During that time it was seriously challenged only twice: when Darius challenged the pseudo-Bardiya for the throne and (less seriously) in the Satraps' Revolt. In both cases the result was the restoration of central rule and the coherence of the empire. Yet once Alexander was dead the entire state broke apart and nobody was able to reunite it in its entirety ever again.

7. RETROSPECT AND PROSPECT

Historians—other than ancient Greeks—have a good word for the Persian Empire. We have already cited the views of Edward Meyer, three-quarters of a century ago. A modern scholar seconds him.

The Persian Empire, compared with what preceded it, was a miracle. It brought peace, both from outside attack and from the sort of raiding for which the Mysians were notorious . . . it brought justice . . . [witness the] famously just Royal Judges . . . it brought prosperity for the Persians devoted themselves . . . to the improvement of agriculture. The Persians were the great gardeners of antiquity . . . maintaining carefully the ancient canals of Babylon, which impeded the Ten Thousand, and making important improvements in irrigation throughout the Empire. Likewise with communications. The great roads they built were for the movement of armies, but they served the purposes of peace as well. The Suez Canal was built by Darius I purely for trade, the whole empire from India to the Aegean was to be linked by sea as well as by land. All in all Persia was one of the chief civilizing forces of history and the Greeks in calling them 'barbarians' as they called all who did not speak Greek, have greatly misled posterity . . .[75]

As a political entity, too, the Persian Empire broke with past patterns. Like its Egyptian, Assyrian, and Babylonian predecessors it was a Palace-type of government. But it was of a different kind. Those previous systems

[75] G. Cawkwell, *Xenophon: The Persian Expedition* (Penguin, Harmondsworth, 1972), 32–3.

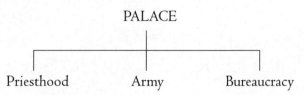

Fig. 2.1.1. Palace-type government

had consisted basically of the palace or court, working through and being sustained by a priesthood and a bureaucracy (see Fig. 2.1.1).

The Persian empire had no priesthood. The palace bureaucracy was numerous, organized and strong, but local self-administration was very highly developed. It had what the others did not possess in any developed degree: a spirited territorial aristocracy of lineage. It was through them, not through the bureaucracy or a priesthood, that the palace governed (see Fig. 2.1.2).

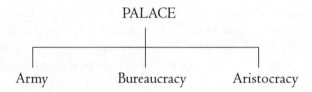

Fig. 2.1.2. Persian Palace-type government

For all that, it stands in the preceding line of absolute monarchies and it found itself confronted by a system of government totally, radically, different. The Persian Empire stands in an evolutionary line from previous Middle Eastern regimes, all of them monarchies, all absolute, all conducted from a palace. The Greek polity it encountered, stood this on its head. It was republican and democratic. It was a Forum-type of government. In Athens this quite revolutionary brand of polity attained the most extreme form in all history. We stand here at a revolutionary break with *all* political patterns so far encountered.

2

The First Republics—The Greeks

With the Greeks we enter a new world. It is impossible to exaggerate the originality of this astounding people. As Peter Levi has it: 'The history of mankind had a crisis in the fifth century BC, an explosion of light which affected everything and still does so today. Europe is the result, and Greece is the key.'[1] No less than anything else, perhaps more so, the Greeks affected the practice and the theory of government. What they worked here was a revolution. From the beginning of recorded history in Sumeria and Egypt—for some two-and-a-half thousands of years—every constituted state had been a monarchy: not only in the known world of the Middle East and eastern Mediterranean, but in the worlds of India and distant China too. These monarchs had all been absolute, and godlike too, except for the Jewish kingdom where God ruled the kings. Suddenly there was government without kings or god. Instead, there were man-made, custom-built republics of citizens. These Greek polities speak to us in a modern idiom and it was the Greeks who coined such terms as monarchy, autocracy, tyranny, despotism, aristocracy, and oligarchy, as well as democracy.

The Greek revolution in the theory and practice of governing was far more *salient* than the one effected by the Jews. The latters' innovation—the notion of supernaturally ordained law and hence limited monarchy—was an implication of their revolutionary theology, a by-blow of it, so to speak. Not so with the Greeks. They addressed the form of government directly. More, they were completely self-conscious of this. As a corollary, their polities became wholly contrived instruments to achieve consciously expressed goals, and indeed were often deliberately reshaped. This, in short, is the very beginning of 'the state as a work of art'.[2] And what they contrived was in the most literal sense antithetical to all that had gone so far. That had been the Palace-type of polity. In that, as we have been seeing, decisions emanated from the closed precinct of the palace, where an autocratic monarch orchestrated the heads of his bureaucracy and standing army, his chief priests, and his noblemen. The people, on whom this narrow

---

[1] P. Levi, *Atlas of the Greek World* (OUP, Oxford, 1980), 10.

[2] G. W. F. Hegel, *Lectures on the Philosophy of History*, trans. J. Sibree (Bell and Daldy, London, 1872), ii. 2, ch. 3.

circle imposed its commands, were so many subjects. The classical Greek *polis* stood all this on its head. Gone were kings, armies, bureaucrats, and priests. The decisions were no longer imposed on the people from the closed palace. They were made by the citizens in the open *agora*. The polity was no more the Palace type; it was the *Forum* type. It remains of this type even when circumscribed by its big men, that is, as an oligarchy, just as the Persian monarchy remained a Palace-type polity, even though circumscribed by its territorial nobility. The 'descending' authority of the Palace polity had been supplanted by the 'ascending' authority of the Forum type.

In one other respect too, the new Greek forum polity was antithetical to most (but by no means all) of the preceding polities. Specifically, it was antithetical to the large country-states like Egypt and those states we have described as empires. One common element among all such was that they were *large*. By contrast, the Greek *polis* was not just small. It was tiny. Athens (admittedly not the largest, but the most perfected—and stable—example of the Forum type, measured only some 33 miles by 33 miles![3] The Greek word *polis* is often translated as 'city-state'. As such, by size and population it falls into the same class as the Sumerian cities, but by form of government it stands at the very opposite pole. What defined the *polis* and marks its complete originality is that it was—as Aristotle himself defined it—an association of citizens. Indeed, perhaps it is this—the status of *citizen* —that is *really* the invention: for it implies the right, in some or many respects, to *participate* in the goods and/or processes of the state. An association of such persons constitutes the *polis*, and it was the nature of the rights attaching to citizenship that determined the small size of the *polis*, not the other way about.[4]

In one respect, however, these Greek *poleis* did resemble their Sumerian counterparts: they were perpetually at war with one another. As in Mesopotamia, some cities—Sparta, Athens, Thebes—attempted to dominate the rest. Again like the Sumerian cities, the Greek cities were too feeble to resist powerful military attack. This was their fatal flaw. Yet belatedly, and after repeated defeats or foreign occupations, some of the Greek *poleis* responded with a second great political innovation: the *Confederation*.

The rest of this chapter revolves around two themes: the common features of the *polis* as such, and the special features of Athens. These two themes relate respectively to *Republic* and to *Democracy*. The third theme—the *Confederation* as embodied in the Aetolian and the Achaean Leagues of the third and second centuries—will be picked up later.

---

[3] It will be remembered that its exact contemporary, the Persian Empire, embraced 2,500,000 sq. mls or 1,581 × 1,581 miles square! [4] See pp. 334 ff. below.

1. THE DEVELOPMENT OF GREEK SOCIETY

CHRONOLOGY

*c.*3500–3000 BC	Beginnings of early MINOAN (pre-palatial) culture in Crete
*c.*2200–1950	Construction of first Minoan palaces
*c.*2000–1600	MIDDLE HELLADIC AGE; gradual southward migration of the 'Greeks'
*c.*1600–1100	MYCENAEAN AGE (= Late Helladic Age)
	(i) 1600–1400 early period
	(ii) 1400–1200 palace period
	(iii) 1200–1100 post-palatial period
*c.*1520	Eruption of Thera
*c.*1450	Destruction of most of the Minoan palaces (by causes unknown). Mycenaeans take over Knossos and much of Crete
*c.*1375	Destruction of the palace at Knossos
*c.*1250–1200	Destruction of Troy VIIa
*c.*1250–1150	Reports of Sea Peoples in Levant and Egypt
*c.*1200–1100	Repeated destructions at Mycenae and elsewhere
*c.*1100–1000	Descent of the Dorians, Ionians, Aeolians into Greek peninsula and islands
*c.*1050	Beginnings of IRON AGE
*c.*900	The GEOMETRIC AGE
*c.*776	Inauguration of the Olympic Games
*c.*800–750	Adaptation of Phoenician ALPHABET
*c.*750–600	Homer and Hesiod. GOLDEN AGE of COLONIZATION
*c.*700	Beginning of HOPLITE tactics
683/2	First yearly archon at Athens
625	COINAGE of a sort attested in Ionia
600–480	The ARCHAIC AGE: rise of Sparta and Athens, science and philosophy in Ionia; Sappho, Anakreon; beginnings of chattel slavery
594/3	Solon, archon at Athens
546–528/7	Peisistratus' tyranny at Athens
528–527	Death of Peisistratus; rule of Hippias
510	Expulsion of Hippias from Athens
508–507	Reforms of Cleisthenes at Athens
493	Themistocles archon at Athens
490	Beginning of the Persian wars. Marathon
*c.*485–425	Herodotus
483	Discovery of new silver lodes at Laurion
480	Battles of Artemisium, Thermopylae, Salamis
479	Plataea
479–400	The CLASSICAL AGE. Thucydides, Aeschylus, Sophocles, Euripides, Pheidias, Socrates

461–446	First Peloponnesian War
427–347	Plato
431–404	Second Peloponnesian War
406	Athenian sea victory at Arginusae
405	Spartan sea victory over Athens at Aegospotami
404	Athens surrenders to Sparta: Lysander
404	Tyranny of the 'Thirty' set up in Athens
403	Democracy restored at Athens
399	Condemnation and death of Socrates
384	Birth of Aristotle
378–371	Athens and Thebes versus Sparta
371	Epaminondas of Thebes defeats Spartans at Leuctra
	End of Spartan hegemony
367	Plato at Syracuse
362	Mantineia. Death of Epaminondas
359	Accession of Philip of Macedon
354	Demosthenes' first public speech
347	Death of Plato. Aristotle leaves Athens
338	Philip of Macedon defeats Athens and Thebes at Chaeronia.
	Macedonian hegemony
336	Philip of Macedon murdered. Accession of Alexander
334	Alexander invades Persia

Greek-speaking tribesmen settled in Thessaly c.2500 BC. Their language was Indo-European, like that of the Aryan invaders of north India and Iran. It seems as if their tribal structure and their gods were similar also. These barbarian newcomers moved slowly southward for some hundreds of years, until the most southerly were near enough to Crete to be irradiated by the Minoan civilization. The so-called *Helladic Age* commencing around 1600–1530 BC ushers in the civilization we call Mycenaean. Warrior-priest kings ruled it from their palaces: their great cities, storehouses of fabulous goldwork and arsenals of bronze weapons, were Mycenae and Pylos. The dramatic and unexplained collapse of Minoan power culminated around 1450 in the Mycenaean take-over of Knossos. The great event of this heyday of Mycenaean culture was the seizure of Troy as commemorated in Homer's *Iliad* and *Odyssey*—if it ever occurred; a claim greeted by much trenchant scepticism nowadays.[5] At all events, after 1250–1200 (the timing suggested for the fall of Troy) some terrible disaster struck the Mycenaeans. It is associated with that migration of the Sea Peoples which, it will be remembered, destroyed the Hittite Empire and was turned back only with great

[5] Cf. M. I. Finley, *Studies in Ancient Society* (Routledge and Kegan Paul, London, 1974; paperback edn. 1978) and *Aspects of Antiquity* (rev. edn., Penguin, Harmondsworth, 1977), 31 42.

difficulty from the shores of Egypt. Between 1200 and 1100 Mycenae was repeatedly sacked and the civilization named after it was entirely destroyed. So began the *Dark Age* which was to last some 300 years.

Into the desolated human and political landscape moved new groups of Greek-speakers, called after their dialects: the Dorians, the Ionians, and the Aeolians. They occupied the entire Greek peninsula and the islands and they settled on the coast of Asia Minor. It was from the east that around 900 BC they received influences which were to result in the economic and cultural renaissance. The so-called *Geometric Age* (after the prevailing style of pottery decoration) lasted till the beginning of the sixth century. Population greatly increased and led to vast waves of colonization, to the Black Sea and southern Asia Minor, and westwards to Sicily and Italy as well as to Cyrene (in Libya) and Naukratis (Egypt). Together with the mainland, these Greek settlements constituted a Greek civilization far larger and wider than the mainland itself. It comprised (but not exclusively so[6]) hundreds of tiny foundations. These were fiercely independent but nevertheless recognized themselves as parts of one people, one culture. They came together in certain places of worship, and 776 is the conventional date for the inauguration of the Olympic Games. These settlements are the origin of the *polis*, the characteristic political form of independent Hellas, and its evolution starts at this point: first from kingship to aristocracy, then—very frequently—into tyranny,[7] and thence back to oligarchy or forward into democracy. The Greeks had, meanwhile, picked up the Phoenician alphabet and ingeniously adapted it to convey the sounds of Greek (c.800). Now Hellas initiated one of its many eternal glories, literature. Homer was set down c.700; likewise Hesiod.

The latter part of the Archaic Age (c.600–480) witnesses the consolidation of the militaristic state of Sparta, the rise of its great rival Athens, and the anti-aristocratic reaction in the shape of tyrannies. It sees the birth of science and philosophy among the Ionian cities of Asia Minor, the outbursts of lyric poetry from Sappho of Lesbos and Anakreon. The theme of the first 'History', by Herodotus (485–425), was the revolt of the Ionian cities against their Persian overlords, the involvement of Athens, the Persian invasion of the mainland, and the Greek triumphs at Marathon (490), Salamis (480), and Plataea (479). With this Greece has come of age and the fifth century is the great age of *Classical* Greece. It registers the supreme genius of the Greek imagination in prose (Thucydides), in drama (Aeschylus, Sophocles, and Euripides), in architecture (the Parthenon), in sculpture (Pheidias), and the beginnings of a new kind of philosophical inquiry by

---

[6] Cf. p. 334 below.   [7] See p. 332 ff. below.

Socrates. Politically, it saw the apogee of *polis*-democracy in Athens: but equally the nemesis of the ideal of city-state *autonomia* in the destructive rivalry of Sparta and Athens. The first Peloponnesian war ran from 460 to 446: the second from 431 to 404. It ended with the total defeat of Athens and the end of its pretensions to hegemony.

The *fourth century* saw no cessation of the interstate rivalries: first Sparta had hegemony (404–371) then Thebes. Athens renewed herself, however, and played a powerful part in the ever-shifting alliances. But prosperity declined on the mainland. A disillusion with democracy followed Athens's defeat: even there, her restored democracy was more professionalized than previously. Elsewhere democracies were mostly supplanted by some form of oligarchy, largely owing to Athens's inability to support local democratic factions by her armed forces. The disillusion was reflected in the political works of Plato (427–347) and Aristotle (384–322), but in them Greek philosophy had reached its veritable zenith. As has been well said, the entire history of western philosophy is a footnote to the works of these two men.

The never-ending strife between the cities worked only to the advantage of bigger and predatory powers. The immediate gainer was Persia, whose gold and diplomacy had sedulously fostered the wars and whose reward (after 387) was the re-acquisition of the Ionian cities. The ultimate gainer was the northern kingdom of Macedonia, reorganized into a most formidable military power by Philip II (359–336). The Greek cities, headed by Athens, recognized her as a threat to their liberties. In 338 the cities suffered a decisive defeat at Chaeronia and were fettered to the Macedonian war-machine. Under Alexander of Macedon the combined forces invaded and conquered the immense Persian Empire (334–323). So commenced the *Hellenistic Age*: the large-scale resumption of eastwards colonization now that Asia was under Greek rule, and the subsequent spread of the Greek language, culture, and city-state we call the Hellenistic civilization. But in the mainland the later dynasties of Macedonia still strove to reassert their hegemony. It was in response to this threat that some cities formed leagues that were more centralized and durable than any previous ones. They effected this by the device of confederation, and embodied it in the Aetolian and the Achaean Leagues. By now (from 200) both they and Macedonia were overshadowed by a new military power: the Roman Republic. She defeated Macedonia at Pydna (168) and turned it into a province (148). Two years later Rome defeated the Achaean League and the sack and destruction of Corinth, 146 BC, marks the conventional date for the extinction of independent Greece.

2. THE COUNTRY AND THE PEOPLE

The mainland of Greece is ridged with mountains interpenetrated by sea. The craggy promontories of its heavily indented coastline are in easy viewing-distance of equally craggy islands from which, in their turn, still more islands are visible; so that to east or west they formed so many stepping stones to Asia Minor and the Levant, or to Italy and Sicily. The land, where cultivable, is rich. Alas, there is not a great deal of it. Three-quarters of mainland Greece is mountain and only one-fifth is cultivable. Nor, apart from some lodes of silver, was the land rich in other resources. Greece was very, very poor, and so were the ancient Greeks: a point it is vitally necessary to remember, always.

The country through which the Greek tribesmen descended and which they proceeded to settle (except in the extreme north where Thessaly and Macedonia were open enough for horse-breeding) consisted of a multitude of small, sharply separated regions where mountain and sea, interlocking, created isolated pockets of arable. There is never a plain that is not soon confined by the sea or the mountains. So, from the first, the incomers split up into numerous political units, each intent on keeping what it had conquered for itself, so that for any unit to expand was arduous, if possible at all. This generated acute internal tensions, which in turn generated a powerful drive to find and occupy further land-resources—in short, to colonize—either because of the pressure of a growing population on local resources or because of political strife (often triggered by this same pressure), or in order to trade. As always in Antiquity, water-borne transportation was usually quicker than land-borne and was always vastly cheaper: and so, with the islands providing a land-bridge, the Greeks took to the water. Maritime cities developed. Their subsistence came from the farms around them, but their riches came from trade. Thus, by its great fifth century BC Greece was the trading centre of the western hemisphere—and by Greece we do not mean just the peninsula, but hundreds of cities that stretched all the way from Marseilles to Anatolia.

By that time the economy had responded to three great innovations. One was the adaptation to Greek use of the Phoenician *alphabet* c.800. By 500 it is reckoned the average male citizen of Athens could read and write, and literacy was widespread outside Athens also, and not confined to any particular social class or group. Popular literacy in the absence of any established priestly caste or sacred book conduced to the peculiar—and major—innovation of Greek culture, namely, 'formal rationality' in its mode of thought. The already fairly open nature of government also assisted.[8]

[8] Cf. O. Murray, *Early Greece* (Fontana, London, 1980), 96–9.

The second innovation was the introduction of *coinage*, and this can now be dated to about 625–600 BC. Fully formed from the start, it had been copied from Lydia, via the Greek cities on that coastline. In Greek tradition it was introduced into Aegina in 585, Corinth in 570, and a little later into Athens: and the reason seems to be that it greatly simplified accounting[9] as well as trading.

The third innovation was *chattel* slavery. This was radical. The ancient world had always known slaves and likewise many other forms of dependent labour—serfs, sharecroppers, bond-slaves (i.e. formerly freemen working out their debt by service to a master). Greece knew such forms in the *helots* of Sparta who were that land's autochtonous inhabitants, now brought to a position of serfdom. But in the sixth century the people of Chios began to acquire barbarian slaves paid for by purchase. The uniqueness of this kind of dependence was two fold: sociologically, in that the labourer suffered not only total loss of control over his labour, but over his person and personality as well; and juridically, in that he was a 'non-person', a mere commodity, whose total lack of all rights was in absolute contradiction to the *eleutheria*, the *freedom*, which characterized a citizen.

Chattel slavery spread rapidly and widely from the sixth century onwards. For Marx it became (in his words) 'the dominant mode of production', and the Graeco-Roman economy the 'slave mode of production'. But what do these phrases mean? It is everywhere agreed that the vast bulk of work in the Greek world was always carried out by free peasants, by more or less dependent tenants, and by artisans. 'Dominant mode' seems to mean that 'slaves dominated and virtually monopolized large-scale production in both the countryside and the urban sector',[10] and so 'provided the bulk of the immediate income from property'. By extension,[11] the phrase can be made to mean 'the main way in which the dominant propertied classes of the ancient world derived their surplus, whether or not the great share in total production was due to unfree labour'.[12]

At all events, it was a massive phenomenon. Its exact magnitude cannot be known. Finley has argued that the proportion of slaves to freemen might have been as high as 3:1 or 4:1 in peak periods of the fifth and fourth centuries; Andrewes that the ratio in Athens was more like 2:1.[13] The

[9] Cf. O. Murray, *Early Greece* (Fontana, London, 1980), 225–6.
[10] M. I. Finley, *Politics in the Ancient World* (CUP, Cambridge, 1983), 82.
[11] G. E. M. de Sainte Croix, *The Class Struggle in the Ancient Greek World* (Duckworth, London, 1981; paperback edn. 1982), *passim.*
[12] de Sainte Croix, *Class Struggle*, 52. I am not sure that this does not boil down to saying that slavery was the 'dominant mode' (of production) because it was the main source of wealth to 'the dominant class'! Quite a different position from Marx and rather circular.
[13] S. Andrewes, *Enlightened Despotism: Readings, Problems and Perspectives in History* (Longman's, London, 1967), 135—not so different from Finley's estimate for the city. Finley, *Politics*, 80.

institution did not just increase the wealth of the Greek cities; it also made possible a class which was leisured enough to participate in the government of the cities. Realizing the potential of 'citizenship' and of a 'forum' polity required the existence of a subclass of slaves to provide for the (relatively) toil-free citizenry. This was particularly true, *a fortiori*, where the *polis* was a democracy (as Athens was). An enormous controversy rages, therefore, as to whether 'democracy' is an appropriate term where some two-thirds of the population are commodities, owned by their masters. Finley's answer is that this controversy is unhistorical, a 'game of awarding credits and demerits according to an historian's own value-system'.[14] Ste Croix is even more specific: 'even though we may regard slavery, *sub specie aeternitatis*, as an irredeemably evil feature of any human society, we must not allow the fact of its existence under Greek democracy to degrade that democracy in our own eyes, *when we judge it by even the highest standards of its day*, for Greek states could not dispense with slavery under any other constitutional form either and virtually no objection was ever raised in antiquity to slavery as an institution'.[15]

A *polis* consisted of its citizens, the *metics*, and the slaves, who outnumbered the citizens by two or three to one. Some of them were state-slaves: as, for example (in Athens), the doomed wretches who toiled their lives away in the sunless caves of the Laurion silver-mines or, at the opposite extreme, the 300 Scythian slaves who comprised the city's police force. *Metics* were free foreigners: they did not form part of the 'governing body', that is, they were not citizens, but they had rights at Athenian law and, furthermore, they could be pressed into the city defence. Most *metics* were traders. As to the citizens, some were the 'well-born' and usually rich; and there were other land- and property-owners also. Together these formed the 'rich' minority, as against the majoritarian 'poor'. The tension between these two classes was the driving force in the cities' domestic politics.

Greek culture is so rich and multi-faceted and so determinative for Europe that all one can do is to pick out the chief elements that bear on political behaviour. The first is the sense of common Greek identity, despite the extensive political fragmentation: 'Our common brotherhood . . . our common language, the altar and sacrifices of which we all partake, the common character which we bear.'[16] As to the first—just as the Jews distinguished themselves from the *goyim*—'the nations'—so Greeks distinguished themselves from the *barbaroi* or uncivilized: all the people who

---

[14] Finley, *Politics*, 9.   [15] de Sainte Croix, *Class Struggle*, 284.   [16] Herodotus, viii. 144.

'couldn't speak proper' but could only 'bar-bar'. Plutarch recounts how Themistocles had the innocent interpreter to the Persian envoy put to death by a special decree of the people because this unfortunate 'had dared to make use of the Greek language to transmit the commands of a barbarian', and he was much admired for doing this.[17]

Religion was not so exclusive a matter as the Greek language. The Greeks imported some of their deities—Adonis for one—and found no difficulty in identifying foreign deities with their own—so that the Egyptian Amon could be regarded as Zeus-Ammon. Yet the Greeks all recognized the same pantheon and the point about the common sacrifice is valid. Pan-Greek games were held in honour of the gods—for example, the Olympics for Zeus, the Pythian for Apollo, the Panathenaic for Athene. Furthermore, all Greeks recognized the authority of the oracles, notably those at Delphi and at Dodona.

The 'common character' that Herodotus speaks of is in a sense all the things and many more that these pages are about. But for all that, the Greeks were singular in some striking respects which made them look with amazement and contempt at other peoples. Take, for example, male nudity. In the Orient—as the Bible clearly shows—to expose a man's genitals was to inflict on him a great indignity, but for him to do so himself was the greatest shame. Yet the Greeks gloried in nudity in the gymnasium. Greek athleticism, likewise, is unparalleled in the Orient. The Greeks not only practised homosexuality but made a great point of it, yet Herodotus tells us that the Persians practised it only after learning it from the Greeks.[18] They perceived their food habits and ritual practices as quite different—and, of course, superior. A fragment from the fourth-century satirical playwright Anaxandrides has a character addressing an Egyptian thus: 'I couldn't bear to be your ally: our manner and customs are so utterly different. You worship a cow: I sacrifice it to the gods. You don't eat pork: I love it. You worship a bitch; I beat her when she eats my choicest food. Our priests are whole: you castrate them. If you see a cat in trouble, you mourn: I'd be glad to kill and skin it.'[19]

In political matters, though, the forces making for self-division and *stasis* were stronger than common bonds. It is tempting to explain the intense competitiveness of the Greeks—as Ehrenberg does, for instance—by force of circumstances: 'the close packing of states inside the Greek world and of men inside the states was the essential cause of the universal urge towards

---

[17] Plutarch, 'Themistocles', *Lives*, trans. Dryden (Dent, London, 1948), 6. Later Themistocles defected to Persia and made a point of learning Persian! Ibid. 29.

[18] Herodotus, i. 135.   [19] Quoted, Olmstead, *History of Assyria*, 418.

the *Agon*, the passion to compete with your neighbour.'[20] Certainly, city fought with city over tiny strips of land in disputes that could last over centuries. But such reductionism may be a bit facile. Whether by nurture or possibly by nature, the Greek *homo politicus* had some very unpleasant characteristics. As Hornblower has pointed out, the reason for the divisions between the states—and we should add, inside the states also—was not just economic contention but a nasty character-trait: *phthonos*, a word which combines the senses of jealousy, envy, grudge, malice.[21] The entire culture was intensely competitive. The sublime side of this comes out in the great athletic, musical, or dramatic competitions, whereas the nastier side and the more destructive stands out in the rivalry, bickering, and betrayals among politicians. Nor were Greeks always too proud to decline a bribe. I find it hard to resist the conclusion that the Greek culture was suffused by three very un-civic vices: cupidity, competitiveness, and covetousness (the last—which is the sin against the Tenth Commandment—being a good translation of *phthonos*). The character of many of the political leaders is tainted: by greed and corruption (notably among Spartan kings and generals); by vaulting ambition (Themistocles); by treachery to their native city (Alcibiades). Between personal ambitiousness and rivalry, and impetuous mass opinion, it is unsurprising how many dangerous or stupid or positively wicked decisions were taken. What is more, whereas Assyrian or Persian atrocities can be ascribed to the unpleasantness of their rulers, among the Greeks it is to the ordinary citizens that we must debit the desire for conquest, for expansion, for tribute, for the execution of opponents and the enslavement of their women and children. Competitive, acquisitive, envious, violent, quarrelsome, greedy, quick, intelligent, ingenious—the Greeks had all the defects of their qualities. They were troublesome subjects, fractious citizens, and arrogant and exacting masters.

In the hands of an Aeschylus Greek religion could speak of the penalties for immorality and of the inexorable justice of the gods; but by and large Greek religion reflected all-too-human attitudes, it did not correct them. The gods were *powers*, just as Egyptian or Mesopotamian gods were powers, and among them 'some, the oldest of them all—square heads that leer and lust and lizard shapes that crawl'. By contrast, the Olympian deities, the familiar Zeus and Hera, Apollo, Poseidon, Aphrodite and Artemis, *et al.* 'humanized' the divinities. All this means is that they represented the powers of nature in the form of larger, enormously powerful, and immortal beings in human shape. It was as well to reverence these gods, to placate them, and

[20] V. Ehrenberg, *The Greek State*, 2nd edn. (Methuen, London, 1974), 7.
[21] S. Hornblower, *The Greek World, 479–323 BC* (Methuen, London, 1983), 14.

above all to fear them. All three acts were performed by ritual and sacrifice. With one important difference—the absence of an organized priestly hierarchy—Greek religion was just as Archaic as the Mesopotamian and Egyptian religions were.[22] Here religious actions take the form of a cult, communication between gods and man is established by worship and especially sacrifice. Myth and ritual surround the cult. There is no congregation, the worshippers are transient and stand outside the officiants. The religion systematizes and rationalizes the cosmic order, but it is a this-worldly religion and Greek religion is especially marked in this respect. Beyond the grave there are only the pale, gibbering ghosts. Nor can the gods save from the grave, for death is the province of *Moira*, Destiny, which constrains even the gods.

The political importance of religion was immense in that, first, no great enterprise might be undertaken without the appropriate rituals and auspicious omens. The Spartans failed the Athenians because they were still performing the rites of the new moon and Alcibiades was recalled from Sicily because he was accused of the terrifying mutilation of the Herms (busts of Hermes set up in public places throughout Athens). In the second place, each city had its own protective deity and its entire public was indissolubly tied in with its cult. No less than sixty days in the year were set aside in Athens for the festivals of one deity or another. No Greek community was not a religious community. *All* social groups, whether family or class, *phratrae*, *phylae* (tribe), and *polis* were also religious unions, with their own cults in which every member took part.[23]

The Olympian gods were, it can be agreed, incapable of wickedness, but only because they were 'devoid of any ethical quality whatsoever. Man could and did turn to the Gods for help in his activities but he could not turn to them for moral guidance: that was not in their power.'[24] And these Olympian gods were not the only ones. The old 'lizard shapes' still commanded worship. So too did Dionysus (a latecomer to the pantheon) whose dark rites the women celebrated by secret and ecstatic orgies. For all that the 'Olympian religion' is held to have 'humanized the Gods'[25] and driven out mystery rites and human sacrifices, these continued to persist. The 'myths of Greece and Rome', never-endingly popular in the nurseries of the West, give a wholly misleading impression of Greek religion, which had a particularly sinister and nasty side. Plutarch relates how, just before the sea-fight at Salamis, the Greeks took three noble Persian captives, nephews

[22] See pp. 23, 141 above.   [23] Ehrenberg, *Greek State*, 17.   [24] Finley, *Studies*, 137, 138.
[25] Ibid. 135.

to King Xerxes, and sacrificed them to '"Dionysus the Eater of Flesh"; for if this were done, it would bring deliverance and victory to the Greeks'.[26]

Now in this very same passage, Plutarch criticizes their action in these words: 'The people . . . were ready to find salvation in the miraculous rather than in *a rational course of action*.' Since the gods were 'devoid of any ethical quality whatsoever', only men could supply this. Hence, for instance, the criticism of the Olympians in Plato and Aristotle, and especially in the later schools of the Cynics, the Epicureans, and the Stoics. Beyond cultic and ritual bonding, the religion was personally unsatisfying. By making gods more-than-life-size humans, the Greeks made the divine amenable to human measurement. (Contrast the Book of Job.) This form of religion induced the thinking Greek into something that Egyptians, Sumerians, Babylonians, Assyrians, and Jews were incapable of: applying rational and indeed secular calculation to nature and to man himself.

The Greeks were the pioneers of rational thought. Their first thinkers' interest was nature, *physis*; in Thales, Anaximander, Anaxamines the approach is not genetic but analytic. The 'beginning' (*arche*) is not a commencement in time, it is the logical first principle. They applied similarly analytic—and critical—thought to the gods. Xenophanes pointed out how each people had made its gods in their own image: instead, he postulated a supreme abstract deity, omniscient and omnipotent. Later thinkers turned from nature to man himself, but, in the same tradition, what they sought was a rational theory of human nature. 'From then on, man was no longer regarded as a mere part of the universe: he became its centre. Man, said Protagoras, is the measure of all things.'[27] Nowhere is this more apposite than for the political form of the city. Some indeed have seen in 'Greek political institutions with their application of rational principles in politics, free discussion, and the development of the concept of law' the veritable origin of this way of thinking.[28]

This abstract theorizing thought originated in Miletus. Significantly, Miletus was a *colony*, one of the very first to be founded in the tenth century BC. It was itself a great colonizer, founding Cyzicus and Abydos on the Euxine and participating in the founding of Naukratis (in Egypt). Why is this relevant? Because nothing political could be more deliberate, more custom-built, then the founding of a colony. The mother-city made a decision to colonize. It appointed a leader, the *oikistes*. The foundation of Cyrene by Thera[29] shows the metropolis conscripting citizens to make up

[26] Plutarch, 'Themistocles', 13.
[27] E. Cassirer, *The Myth of the State* (Yale UP, New Haven, Conn., 1946), 56.
[28] Murray, *Early Greece*, 233–6.   [29] As described by Herodotus, iv. 156–9.

the minimum numbers of men required to defend the colony. Thereafter a fragmentary decree of a Doric settlement in Corfu shows the further course of events. It *stipulates* that the first colonists are to wall their city. They are to allocate each man a house and plot inside the walls and a specified area of land outside them. It also lays down the entitlement of later settlers. Thereafter the colony had to fend for itself, led, for the term of his life, by its *oikistes*.[30]

It is no long step from all this to that other Greek device, settling *stasis* in a city by calling on individuals to give new laws: so Draco (*c.*621) and notably Solon (?638–559) in Athens and the legendary Lycurgus (?9th century) in Sparta. After these the modelling and remodelling of city constitutions—as, for instance, in Cleisthenes' reform in Athens (*c.*508/7) become the commonplace of the *polis*'s constitutional history. Hitherto (the Jewish kingdom is an exception) states had just evolved. Now they were being consciously constructed. In the former it was natural that authority should be 'traditional'. In the latter nothing was less obvious, and every change was questioned and its legitimacy challenged. The *polis* was an artefact and man was its measurer. When Hegel talks of Greek democracy, he is wrong only in restricting his remark to this rather than the numerous other variants of '*polis* constitution'. 'It [the *polis*] is not Patriarchal—does not rest on a still unreflecting, underdeveloped confidence—but implies laws, with the confidence of their being founded on an equitable and moral basis, and the recognition of these laws as positive.'[31]

To all I have said so far I add three brief notes. The first is Greek *power*. As Greek warfare moved in the seventh century from cavalry to hoplite (armoured infantry), their warriors became militarily superior to all and any rivals in the known world. Furthermore, their interminable internecine warfare generated continued improvements on the original model. They were formidable and unconquerable, and in the end, through the development of the Macedonian phalanx and the genius of Alexander, broke the Persian Empire and allowed Greek emigrants to sweep through Asia as far as Bactria and the borders of India. Secondly, the Greeks, as I have noted before, are not just the mainlanders. They were the great dynamic force—as well as the great military force—throughout the eastern basin of the Mediterranean.[32] Finally, and again to pick up a point mentioned earlier, they were arrogantly self-conscious and self-confident of their culture and

[30] Cf. L. M. Jeffrey, *Archaic Greece: The City-States, c.700–800 BC* (London, 1976), 52–5.
[31] Hegel, *Lectures*, 261 (sec. 2, ch. 3) and the title of the section in which the passage appears encapsulates the thrust of the entire preceding argument: 'The State as a Work of Art'.
[32] It is reckoned that in the 5th cent. there were 4 million Greeks on the mainland and another 4 million overseas.

quite sure of its superiority to any other they encountered. Not that they hated these (except the aloof and disdainful Jews); they simply despised them. When they overran Asia, their language and their manners took over the cities. In their rays, the native cuneiform and the once great cults wilted and finally died, and in Egypt the sentence was no more than postponed. The Greeks brought about the death of the Archaic world of Middle Eastern civilization.

3. THE FORMATION OF THE *POLIS*

The basic political structure of the Greek tribes consisted of three components. They were present in Homer and they remain the same throughout Greek history: what alters are their respective powers, and the criteria for their membership. These three components are, first, the executive head. In Homer he is the *basileus*, which we translate as 'king'. The second component is a narrow council of elders, in Homer, the *gerontes*. The third is the meeting of all the warriors, the *agora*. In the earliest times the king took counsel with his *gerontes* and their decisions were put to the *agora*, which listened to the elders debating the matter, but did not itself participate.[33] This 'Heroic Age' arrangement was to undergo the most variegated developments.

The polities the invaders established were of two main types. The *ethnos*, usually translated as 'tribal state', had no urban centre and states of this kind generally lay in the north and west, areas which the Mycenaeans had not settled. (But there were some, too, in the central region, e.g. Locris, Aetolia, and Elis.) In such states the population lived in widely dispersed homesteads or open villages (*komae*, *demoi*). In some, notably Macedonia, kingship persisted, but Thessaly, in contrast, was divided into four 'quarters' (*tetrades*), each ruled by a great family, which in times of emergency came together to elect a war-leader, the *tagos*. Again, Epirus had fourteen tribal subdivisions. But in east Locris the early settlements came together into a *sympoliteia*, which was ruled by the so-called 'Hundred Households', while its Assembly went under the name of 'The Thousand'.

The normal type of political unit, whose numbers ran into hundreds, was the *polis*. It emerges as the characteristic form in, perhaps, the eighth century BC, coincident with an economic revolution (as arable farming supplanted stock-rearing and a great population explosion occurred) and with the disappearance of kingship. Its origins and the particulars of its emergence are shrouded in obscurity. It is clear that neither fortification, nor urbaniza-

---

[33] Murray, *Early Greece*, 58–9.

tion were necessary or sufficient conditions for its advent and recent opinion veers towards the conjecture that the presence of a cult centre provided the stimulus.[34] A *polis* had five basic characteristics, which were: sovereign independence, political unity, identification with a cult, a surrounding rural area forming an extension of its identity, and—with the rare exceptions noticed below—the absence of monarchy. To put this another way, they were republics. This last characteristic was the pre-condition for that attribute which observers from Plato and Aristotle onwards regarded as the singularity that marked the *polis* off from all antecedent political formations; and that is, momentously, *citizenship*.

Certainly monarchy did persist in some areas—in Macedonia, for instance, and also in some places in the south, of which only the Spartan kingship was to survive into the fourth century, and even then with a highly circumscribed role. Everywhere else it was extinguished, or rather it was smothered by 'lateral extension'; the collateral branches of the royal line demanded and wrested a share of the king's authority and in this way the king's military, priestly, and judicial functions were prised away and distributed among the various lineages.

Concomitantly, piecemeal change took place in the relationship between and the characteristic membership of the three primeval branches of Greek government, the executive power, the Council, and the Assembly. To summarize the developments: officers, often elective and annual, were positioned beside the king and in the end supplanted him altogether. But these officers—magistrates, as they came to be regarded and called—were nominated and/or appointed by the aristocratic oligarchy which comprised the Council. (Parenthetically, ambitious and wealthy men who were not 'well-born' were not slow to work their way into this aristocratic circle.) But at the same time as the Council acquired this importance, the Assembly also became more important than before, because oligarchs who failed to get their way in the Council (the *boulē*) would take the matter to the Assembly where they would organize their followers to vote for them. In this way the Assembly itself could develop into yet another political arena. The foregoing synopsis is very crude, to be sure; but its very crudity serves to bring out how a self-generating process had set in, involving some ('the Few'), or more—or even 'the Many'—in public decision-making.

Each of these early *poleis* developed its institutions in its own peculiar way and time-span, giving rise to a bemusing diversity. What generated the rapid turnover in political forms in these cities was the running struggle over the resources of the city waged by its various classes or sectors. Their relative

[34] A. Snodgrass, *Archaic Greece* (Dent, London, 1980), 36–8.

power-status changed according to changing circumstances. Certainly in the seventh and early part of the sixth centuries the population explosion to which we have referred brought severe pressure on the limited land resources and, inevitably, the sufferers turned against the privileged status of those whose landholdings had enabled them to amass riches and enjoy an aristocratic life-style. But this economic conflict was compounded by a change in the relative power-ratings, which itself was due to a slow revolution in the Greek art of warfare.

For, from *c.*750, body-armour became heavier, while warriors began to complete their armoury with the closed metal helmet, the bronze corselet and greaves, and the round shield. These men, armed with long thrusting spears and swords, are the *hoplites,* the soldiery which was to dominate the eastern Mediterranean for the next three to four hundred years, as indeed we saw vividly in the last chapter on the Persian Empire. The completed war-gear of the hoplite soldier is not attested before 675 and their characteristic formation, which was a shield wall-cum-spear phalanx, appears about 650. This military development initiated a profound shift in the societal power relationships, since as the role of the infantryman became dominant that of the cavalry faded. The cavalry were the *hippeis,* and effectively, the aristocracy. The hoplites, on the other hand, were those who could buy the new armour, which was so expensive that only the top third of the citizenry could afford it, and this consisted chiefly of independent peasant farmers with a moderate amount of land. This class became more powerful as the aristocracy waned. Such at least is the hypothesis and it is not new. It will be found in Aristotle, writing in the fourth century.[35]

In many places—but not all, and one must not over-simplify the coincidence of this military evolution with popular detestation of the aristocracy—this occasioned the appearance of a new form of the republican polity, the *tyranny.* In some states like Corinth, and for that matter Athens and Sparta (which are dealt with specifically below), the aristocracy closed its ranks and consciously adapted itself to the changed conditions, often inviting in a 'lawgiver' for that purpose.[36] But where, whether for lack of this or for other reasons, the social tension was not eased, power was sometimes snatched forcibly from the oligarchy by some individual. In the beginning, such a regime could be called either *monarchia* (which, of course, simply means 'one-man rule') or rule by a *tyrannos,* which we translate as 'tyrant'. (This is not a Greek word; it seems to have come from Lydia.) For centuries 'tyrant' and 'tyranny' have connoted bad, oppres-

[35] Aristotle, *Politics,* 1321A. See also, paras 1289B, 10, 11.
[36] Hammond, *History of Greece,* 144–5.

sive rule, but this was not the original sense at all. (Later I shall suggest a hypothesis as to why the word acquired its pejorative meaning.) Most tyrannies exhibited some or all of the following characteristics: irregular seizure/or exercise of power, personal rule, autocratic rule, armed intimidation, pomp and ceremony, but also populist policies. Tyranny reached its heyday in the sixth century BC when, to mention some of the best-known, we find tyrants ruling in Athens, Ephesus, Samos, Naxos, and so forth.

However, on inspection cases like this show that the tyrannies emerged for other reasons than just the collision of an oppressed peasantry and the landowning oligarchs. For instance, it could be occasioned by the effort of excluded but equally wealthy landowners to break into the closed aristocratic circle or by ethnic rivalries. In one particular case (Thrasybulus of Miletus) it was the consequence of a military emergency. So, we must qualify the 'hoplite hypothesis' by admitting that there is little *direct* evidence to support it, and also point out that many tyrannies emerged before the hoplite format became common.

The accomplishment of the tyrants is also problematical. Some won good opinions from even the highly critical Aristotle, notably Peisistratus of Athens, whose rule, he reported, was spoken of as a 'Golden Age'. The contrast 'kings good, tyrants bad' was not established till the fourth century BC, up to when the word 'king' was the more often used for old traditional forms of one-man rule and 'tyrant' for autocracies. It was Plato and Aristotle who invented the sharp antithesis: to wit, unlike monarchy, tyranny was an illicit, wicked, and despotic form of rule.

Personally, I suspect that the abrupt change of meaning resulted from two things. First, during the lifetimes of those two philosophers tyranny had recrudesced and done so in a form which did indeed conform to the character they now attributed to it: for example, with Dionysius of Sicily (430–367), Jason of Pherae (d. 369), Clearchos of Heraclea (d. 353). Secondly, both Plato (in *The Statesman*) and Aristotle (in *The Politics*) were trying, *inter alia*, to systematize the studying of politics, and this entails (not just for them but for any political scientist) reducing the wildly various forms of rule to a few manageable categories. As is well known, Plato ended up with six: three basic forms according to the number of the rulers (the One, the Few, and the Many), each of which could appear in a benign and also a malign form. For Plato the distinction between these two characteristics depended on whether or not the rulers kept within the law; whereas for Aristotle it turned on whether they ruled in the public interest or their own. Now when one constructs a typology one has, obviously, to label the types. Here, then, the problem was to find a dyslogistic name for one-man rule. Monarchy was traditional, of long-standing. Tyrants were in most cases usurpers. Tyranny could therefore be *stipulated* as to be its contradictory. In brief, I suggest that both 'monarchy' and 'tyranny' as found in these two authors are their stipulative definitions created for taxonomic purposes. It is obvious that Aristotle was embarrassed by this choice of terms, for he had to admit that some tyrants had merits, that some kings were indistinguishable from tyrants and *vice versa*, and that by following certain recommended courses of action tyrants can become positively king-like and benign.[37]

By the time Hellas had reached its great Classical Age, the fifth century, that primordial, tripartite, tribal form of the Greek polity had prodigiously diversified. The several hundred separate and sovereign political units all varied, and along many different dimensions. In some, like Athens, all the land was citizen land whereas in others, like Sparta, some of it belonged to the surrounding people, the so called *perioikoi*, who were compelled to military service. Their area varied widely, too. Sparta measured 3,300 sq. miles, Athens 1,000, Corinth 340, Sicyon 140, and Delos a puny two ! Some states, for all that they functioned as political units, contained within them a number of individual *poleis*, for example; the federal state of Boeotia had ten, later swelling to seventeen inside its 1,250 sq. miles. The size of population also varied widely but, as already noted, citizens were universally in the minority, the greater part of the population consisting of the citizens' families, the *metics* and their families, and slaves or other dependants such as the Spartan helots and *perioikoi*.

In every single one of these political units the major organs of government were descended from those three primeval components of the remote tribal polity: the king/magistrates, the Council, and the Assembly. The political diversity of these states lay in the respective powers of these organs and who was entitled to a place in them. And this brings us back to our very starting-point—*citizenship*—for, to reiterate, it is the status of citizen as opposed to mere subject that constitutes the revolutionary break between the *polis* and all previous political formations. The *polis*, says Aristotle, 'is the sum total of its citizens'.[38] So, to understand the variety of *polis* regimes it is necessary—as Aristotle himself expressly foreshadows—to look at the status of citizenship. In my view, at its very root lies the notion of *having a share*—of some kind or another, yes, but a share nevertheless—in the state.

Some have tried to bring home the nature of the *polis* to our own very different age by likening it to a joint-stock company of shareholders. This parallel unfortunately suggests something very arid, distant, and impersonal. It is best to think of it as a co-operative. In Britain you can be a member of a retail co-op by simply purchasing goods at a co-op store and receiving

---

[37] Aristotle, *Politics*, 1314–15.   [38] Ibid. 1275a.

credit-stamps by way of a dividend. This would stand for citizens with *passive* rights. On the other hand, in an Israeli *kibbutz*—which is likewise a co-operative—the member does much more 'sharing'; he shares in goods, labour, and in its government and administration; indeed, his entire life is bound up in the collectivity. Furthermore, a co-operative of this kind is exclusive, for its property and income belong to the members; so that to throw membership open to all and sundry would be just the same as giving all their possessions away. Hence membership is closely guarded, and if a newcomer wants to come in he must buy the equivalent of a share. The *polis* worked exactly on this principle and the two absolute prerequisites for a very long time (and certainly in the fifth century) were *descent* and the *possession of land*. Both of these tended to go together since the first settlers, having conquered the land, divided it up into family plots. Holding land was not just a prerequisite of citizenship, it was widely regarded as the right of one who qualified as citizen by descent. This is why cities took steps to prevent the expropriation of smallholdings by the richer landlords. Having a stake in the country was the most basic and also passive way in which a citizen could 'share', but this status could be highly positive if the state acquired a windfall, like the silver from the Laurion mines which the Athenian citizenry were going to divide among themselves until Themistocles persuaded them to build a fleet instead. And just as citizenship implied a share in rights, so, too, it involved shouldering duties: defending the state, obeying its laws, being loyal to its cults, and, possibly, holding certain offices.

Monarchy and tyranny, by their nature, narrowed the rights of citizens, possibly to just their land-entitlement; from that point on the nature of the regime was a function of the numbers of citizens enjoying *active* rights and notably those of participating in decision-making, and holding office. Since, in Greek thinking, 'the polis is a body of citizens adequate in numbers for achieving a self-sufficient existence',[39] the reason why Plato and Aristotle categorized states in terms of the proportion of the citizenry who enjoyed those active rights of participation—the One, the Few, the Many—follows naturally. But this has to be further qualified by the differing structures of the various *poleis*: for, clearly, the right to vote or hold office in the council would be highly significant where this had strong powers, but not in a state where, for instance, the assembly told it what to do.

In the earliest forms of restricted citizen participation, that is, in the *oligarchies*, a property qualification constituted the basis for full citizenship (in the sense of the previous paragraphs). Later, in some cities, all sources of

[39] Aristotle, *Politics*, 1275b.

wealth were put on an equality with land, and citizen rights and duties were gradated according to one's riches. This is what Aristotle in the *Ethics* calls a timocracy[40] (and what the French, in the nineteenth century, called a *démocratie censitaire*). In some cities, again, the qualification for full citizenship was one's ability to equip oneself as a hoplite (e.g. in Opuntian Locris). The differences between the rights of citizens with one set of qualifications and citizens with others were precisely what was at issue in the intense and widespread civil strife in the fifth century; and the movement to equalize those qualifications was, also, the movement to democracy.

4. SPARTA

Sparta was the largest Greek state, three times the area of her arch-rival, Athens. She was the most martial, and her protracted duel with Athens in the fifth century proved her to be the strongest. Thucydides ascribes to Pericles the view that Sparta was the very antithesis of Athens, and so she has appeared throughout history.

The Athenian polity is incomparably more innovative than Sparta's. Indeed, it represents a revolutionary mutation, even in terms of the general Greek understanding of citizenship, which is in itself a revolution; because in Athens the implications of citizen status were pushed to the utmost limits compatible with the existence of a sub-class of non-citizens, slaves in particular. In the context of the history of government Sparta is one of the freaks, the curiosities. Even among the Greek states it was unique. But for all that, it created a deep, lasting—and strange as it may seem to the present generation—favourable impression on later Europeans. So it necessitates at least a brief description.

Spartan government, like all the rest, was organized around the old, tribal threefold principle but with this peculiarity that here, unlike most of the other states, the monarchy survived and not only that, it was a *double* monarchy, a very strange arrangement for anywhere in the world. Also, having conquered the land and carved it up into family plots (*kleros*, pl. *kleroi*), the victorious Greek tribesmen reduced the natives to serfs tied to their new farms, on which they had to work for the benefit of their dispossessors. These were the *helots*. Like the monarchy, this institution was not unique, for similar outcomes occurred in Thessaly and Crete. When, by *c*.700, the Spartans had conquered neighbouring Messenia, they did not turn all non-Spartiates into serfs. They spared some hundred

[40] Aristotle, *Nicomachaean Ethics*, trans. D. Ross (The World's Classics; OUP, London, 1966), 1160 a.31.

communities (overwhelmingly east of Mt. Taygetus) on the condition that they would become subject-allies who were bound to fight alongside the Spartans wherever and whenever they were called on. These subjects were the *perioikoi*, and they retained their own local government systems and way of life. They were subjects of but not citizens of Sparta. Here again, in the institution of *perioikoi*, Sparta was not unique, for once again we find a similar arrangement in Thessaly. 'Sparta' is really a misnomer. Sparta was the name of the capital, but the Spartan hoplites went to war with a *lambda*, or L, for Lacedaemon, on their shields.

The third step in this evolution was what made Sparta unique. The Spartiate conquerors were a tiny minority, some 2 per cent of the conquered population.[41] From the sixth century certainly, if not before (where legend obscures our view), the Spartiates organized themselves with one single aim: acting as an army of occupation so as to hold down their helots while living off them. It is how they did this, that is, the qualifications and training for citizenship and its duties, that catalysed the three primeval components of the governmental system into something unique.

The citizen body, the Spartiates, lived at the capital as absentee landlords on the income from their *kleroi*. They did not do a stroke of manual work nor did they engage in commerce or the crafts, which they left to the *perioikoi*. They were just soldiers—and citizens. Deformed or sickly sons were exposed at birth. On reaching the age of 7 a boy, still living at home, was entered in a 'herd' (or 'troop'), in which he attended classes for games and physical training, under the supervision of an older boy (who had the right and duty to beat him for misconduct—as, for that matter, did any male citizens who took exception to his conduct). And (so Plutarch says in his 'Lycurgus') if a boy complained to his father that he had been whipped by another father, he must expect a second beating from his own parent.

At 12 the boys left home and remained in junior barracks till the age of 18. They learned reading and writing, the national songs and dances, and the poetry of their native poet Tyrtaeus. They were organized into packs, the doughtiest being appointed as pack-leader, and these themselves were commanded by the *eirens*—25-year-olds—who in turn came under the authority of a magistrate, the *paidonomos*. These children wore nothing underneath their tunics even in the harshest winter; they were half-starved but encouraged to thieve food wherever they could, and were punished only if they were caught. They were expected to take adult male lovers,[42] and

---

[41] V. Ehrenberg, *From Solon to Socrates*, 2nd edn. (Methuen, London, 1973), 31.

[42] The precise relationship is controversial—see K. J. Dover, *Greek Homosexuality* (Random House, New York, 1980), 185–9.

they were endlessly questioned at mealtime by their officers, where an inadequate reply brought down instant punishment. Iron discipline and total obedience to superiors was inculcated by flogging. Fighting-bouts were encouraged and the boys put through paramilitary drill and mimic battles. At 18, when this stage ceased, they went on to two years of intensive military training in hoplite warfare. At this stage too they might be enrolled in the *krypteia*, the secret bands who foraged in the countryside and (in some accounts) had the special mission of terrorizing the helots.

Though a boy might successfully complete all the stages of this training (*agoge*) he was not yet a full citizen. He had still to be admitted into a *syssition*, which was a company—mess—of fifteen men. Membership of a *syssition* was a prerequisite of citizenship and a prerequisite of this mess-membership was a monthly subscription of foodstuffs. This, of course, came from his family lands (*kleros*) and its helots. (The secular decline in the number of full Spartiates, otherwise inexplicable, is sometimes ascribed to individuals' inability to pay these monthly dues; itself a result, it is surmised, of various developments tending towards the loss, reduction in size, or alienation of the *kleros*). Here in the mess all talk was soldier-talk, and here too the young men consumed the notorious Spartan broth of pigmeat stewed in pigs' blood, which the rest of Greece found so revolting. These men lived in their *syssitia* away from home (albeit permitted to marry) until the age of 30.

Men were liable to military service from admission to the *syssitia* at the age of 21 until the age of 60. Relieved of all material cares by their helots—and wives—they devoted themselves to hunting, drilling, and their citizen duties. Plutarch tells an instructive story about this: a Spartan visitor in Athens was told of an Athenian citizen who had been fined for living in idleness, whereupon he asked to see 'this man who was condemned for living like a freeman'.[43]

The end-result of all this education was the Spartan phalanx, never beaten over 150 years, until the fateful Battle of Leuctra in 371 BC. On campaign, the Spartans in their scarlet cloaks marched in step to the sound of a pipe, since this was essential to keep file and rank, which were the prerequisites of phalanx and column formations. Battle-order was highly systematized, uniquely so in Greece, it seems. The basic formations were platoons of thirty men, which were grouped into companies, then into battalions, and then into regiments. Each unit had its own officers and, it seems, deputy-officers too. Embattled, the army formed a line eight ranks deep with levelled spears, each man sheltering under the shield of his right-

---

[43] Plutarch, 'Lycurgus' (*Lives*).

hand neighbour. Discipline, steadfastness, and valour on the field were backed by the certainty of lifelong disgrace for any who fled away.[44]

The Spartans called themselves the *homoioi* ('equals'). From this writers, both ancient and modern, have assumed that the plots of land—the *kleroi*—were all of equal size and all Spartiates equal in wealth. This is certainly not true. There were very wealthy Spartiates who could afford to build houses and very poor ones who had to drop out of the *syssitia* because they could not pay their dues. Indeed, the more the political system is re-examined, the more it seems as though there was an ancient and comparatively wealthy aristocracy behind it. *Homoioi* means simply 'of (roughly) equal political standing'.

Everywhere else in Greece (excluding Epirus and Macedonia) the executive power, as we have seen, had passed out of the hands of the kings, who were replaced by magistrates. Sparta was not only unique in that she retained the kingship and what is more, had two kings reigning in tandem; she had also introduced elected magistrates, the five *ephors*. Together the kings and *ephors* constituted the executive power, working to and with a council (*gerousia*) and the Assembly.

The kings belonged to two different and ancient families. Nobody knows how or why this curious arrangement arose. The two kings retained certain priestly functions and they also kept certain judicial powers, but their really significant function was to lead the army on campaign. Such a power carried with it some influence on foreign policy too. Once in the field, their authority was unlimited—but they were always accompanied by two *ephors*—as representing, one supposes, the domestic political scene. Herodotus relates (v. 75) an occasion when the two kings quarrelled on a campaign against Athens, bringing it to a fruitless close. From that time only one king commanded a military expedition. There was bound to be friction between the kings and the duly chosen *ephors*, whatever the latters' formal powers to check or control the kings (and these are problematical), but an energetic and masterful king could exert great influence.

The board of five *ephors* had wide and important powers. They mobilized the army and arranged the order of calling-up the age-cohorts. They alone could convene the Council. They heard most civil cases. They supervised the educational system. They controlled all the lesser magistrates. They received foreign ambassadors and were responsible for transmitting orders to the commanders in the field. In brief, they were the chief executives of the state.

---

[44] It should be noted that the Spartiate hoplites were supported in mixed formation by the *peroikoi* and by a large force of helots who handled their baggage and supplies and acted as batmen.

They were chosen in a manner Aristotle called 'childish',[45] by and from the Assembly of all the *homoioi*, the Spartiates, for a term of only one year, and they did not necessarily act in unison. They were meant to be ordinary representatives of the Spartan *demos*. There is more than a suspicion that they were manipulable—even bribeable—by elements in the Council, the *gerousia*.[46]

This consisted of only twenty-eight members and the two kings *ex officio*. It was prestigious and powerful. Nothing could come to the Assembly until the *gerousia* had discussed it and it alone had the right of initiative. Also, it formed the court for capital offences. Its prestige derived from its membership and mode of election. You were ineligible until the age of 60 and membership was considered the highest honour the state could extend. Once elected, the councillor retained his seat for life. The mode of this election was singular. Judges were appointed and shut away, while the candidates silently filed through the Assembly. As each one appeared, the Assembly gave a shout and the judges estimated the loudness of each cheer, not knowing, of course, for whom it had been cast. Those who got the loudest applause were declared elected.[47] It was commonly supposed that *any* Spartiate over 60 was eligible for election, but Aristotle seems to say that any might serve but nobody was obliged to,[48] and this is yet another pointer to the existence, among the 'equals', of a crypto-oligarchy of wealthy men, highly influential in the Assembly.[49]

Finally, the Assembly itself may have comprised all male citizens over 30, as in Athens. It elected the *ephors*, the *gerousia*, and the subordinate magistrates. Also, as the legislative body, it had to vote on the measures the *gerousia* put to it. The procedure is problematical. It seems as if it was the Ephorate that introduced business. The real questions are two. First, could the full Assembly debate the matter or simply listen to the kings, *ephors*, and Council-members before it was called on to vote for or against? Second, if it 'voted the wrong way', could the authorities and the Council take the matter back and make a second and definitive decision?

To the first, we can answer that, as at Rome later, only certain people were *ex officio* able to speak, but a magistrate could call on whomever he deemed suitable to express an opinion. As to the second, the Council certainly did take back business, and would not permit the Assembly to amend decrees. All in all, this Assembly was far weaker than in the democratic states.

[45] *Politics*, 1271A, 10.
[46] J. V. A. Fine, *The Ancient Greeks: A Critical History* (Harvard UP, Cambridge, Mass., 1983), 149 n.
[47] Plutarch, 'Lycurgus', 26.   [48] *Politics*, 1271A, 10 ff.   [49] Cf. Fine, *Ancient Greeks*, 150–1.

5. THE ATHENIAN DEMOCRACY

Athenian democracy was quite out of the ordinary. Nothing like it had existed before,[50] and little like it has ever existed since. To start by tracing its history would be long on explication but too short on drama. The sheer audacity of the Athenian experiment requires one to cut out all preamble and plunge straight in.

5.1. *The Economy and its Classes*

Attica, with Athens as its capital, was only some 1,000 sq. miles in extent. This is tiny by today's standards.[51] Interestingly, in view of the colony's latter-day commercial importance, it is just the same size as Hong Kong (including the New Territories). Estimates of its population vary between 215,000–300,000 for 432 BC. Citizens and their families might have numbered 110,000–80,000, *metics* (free resident foreigners) and their families 40,000–25,000, and the slaves 110,000–80,000. The citizens themselves numbered only 45,000–30,000.[52] Until the fifth century its economy was mostly cereal farming. As the city became a great trading centre, it imported its grain from the Black Sea. In 403 three-quarters of the citizens owned some land, the biggest holdings running to some seventy-five acres. The Greek victory over the Persians (490–479) transferred commercial and industrial primacy from the Asia Minor towns to the east coast of Greece; and as Corinth lost importance and Aegina was subdued, Athens rose to first place as a commercial and industrial centre. It was very much helped by two decisions of state: first, to build a fleet with the windfall from the Laurion silver-mines, and next to make Piraeus and not Phaleron Bay its trading port (485). Athens thereupon became the greatest trading centre in the Aegean area. Other factors also contributed to this pre-eminence. Unlike the Spartans and Thebans, Athenians did not despise manual work (*banausos*). In the former towns it was forbidden, and public office was closed to those performing it, but Athens positively encouraged it. Furthermore, Athens was the city where private property was best protected and defended; which did nothing to prevent *metics* from rising high in commerce and finance; which regularized its weights and measures and

---

[50] Not quite true, of course—Chios was Greece's first democracy (6th cent. BC). But for size of state, completeness, and durability, Athenian democracy was far pre-eminent.

[51] In 1979, 153 out of a total of 188 states were 1,000 sq. mls. or more (81%). Of the remaining 35, the largest is Reunion. The smallest are Monaco (0.5 sq. mls.) and Vatican City (0.1089 sq.mls.).

[52] Ehrenberg, *Greek State*, 31. Others, notably Finley, put the number of slaves at about 60,000 and the total population at some 200,000 by the close of the 5th cent.

Table 2.2.1. *Census Classes in Athens, 480–430* BC

	480 BC	430 BC
1–3 Classes	10,000	22,000
Thetes	20,000	20,000

Source: Ellul, *Histoire des Institutions*, 82–3.

was more monetarized than the other cities. All this was guaranteed by its naval supremacy and, for the short duration of the Athenian Empire, by tributes and aids from its allies.[53]

The city was more emporium than industrial centre. She was the leading exporter of vases in Greece: she also exported oil, wine, and silver (from the state mines at Laurion), importing ship-timber, fish, and grain. In return, her industry was based on extracting minerals—copper, silver, and clay—and contained many small-scale workshops. Indeed, the biggest known enterprise is a shield-factory employing 120 slaves. The average workshop had only ten to thirty workmen. There was a wide social distance between the craftsmen—citizens—and the workmen, who usually were slaves. Many *metics* were craftsmen, and if they worked alongside citizens in the same shop they were paid identically—one drachma a day. (A family of four could live off 280 drachmas a year.)[54]

Athenian society had been graded into four census classes (reportedly by Solon the Lawgiver in 594). They were based on the amount of grain or oil a man's land produced. Those whose land produced 500 measures or more were the *pentekosiomedimnoi*. Those of 500–300 measures were styled *hippeis*—'knights'. Those of 300–200 were called *zeugitai* (literally 'yoked together')—the hoplite yeomanry, in fact. The rest were *thetes*—'labourers'. The numbers in each class altered during the century as the status of the *thetes* improved by higher wages, public works, and the creation of military colonies in Greece (*cleruchies*). As the Table 2.2.1 shows, many moved into the higher categories.

Though all these were equally citizens, in other respects they were by no means equal. The ancient and wealthy lineages still played an active, one might even say a dominant, political role. By virtue of their wealth, they shouldered the most onerous 'liturgies' (unpaid compulsory services to the community) and they dispensed gifts liberally at the popular festivals, plays, and concerts which informed the open-air communal life of Athens. They produced the leaders of the democratic party and, till 404 and the defeat by Sparta, were masters of the republic. But they also produced the leaders of

[53] J. Ellul, *Histoire des Institutions*, vol. 1 (Presses Universitaires de France, 1955), 73.
[54] Ibid. 76.

the opposing oligarchic party. Its members met in their clubs, elaborating programmes hostile to 'advanced' ideas. They were doctrinaires and leaned towards Sparta. They were to achieve a short-lived supremacy in the aftermath of the city's defeat. The yeomen, the *zeugitai*, however, were highly independent and individualistic—traditionalists in many respects, but also democrats. Working on their farms they did not often attend the Assembly and visited the city only at festivals. The political strength of the democrats resided not so much in them as in the commercial and artisan elements. Finally, the sailors—risen to great prominence as the city became the great naval power—were the most radical of all the classes. They were heavily state-dependent and therefore always ready to back democratic chiefs in promoting egalitarian measures on the one hand, and in imperialist ventures on the other.

5.2. *The Territorial Structure*

Athens was a unitary state. By *c.*700 BC, the scattered settlements had been brought together and fused into a general 'sympolity' with the city of Athens. Consequently, all the citizens were members of one single political community. Despite the (to us) trivial size of the Attica peninsula, particularism persisted. It is vividly revealed, for instance, in Herodotus' account of Peisistratus: the three rival parties are respectively the 'beyond the Mountain' (i.e. the east), the Plain, and the Coast. Localism was even more deep-rooted. The population lived in settlements called *demes* (from *demos* meaning people, like the Spanish use of *pueblo* for a village settlement) which had always had their own cults and community self-government. Cleisthenes (507) had Attica divided into three Ridings (*trittyes*): the City itself, Inland, and the Coast. Each Riding contained so many *demes*. Most were ancient settlements but some, particularly in the city, were probably new and artificial creations. The Ridings were nothing but geographical circumscriptions, but the *demes* were centres of thriving political activity. Each had its own Assembly (*agora*), headman (*demarch*), and other officials, including a treasurer. It celebrated its own cults at its local shrines. It owned public lands which it rented out for income. Yet the *demes* were importantly linked to central government, as we shall see in more detail. They were the units where citizenship was registered, and also for nominating candidates for certain offices. Hence they were so many springboards into public life.[55]

[55] Cf. Finley, *Politics*, 44–7.

5.3. *The Citizenry*

The body of citizens had been given a highly peculiar structure determinative of the form of government, which is itself wholly unintelligible unless the nature of this structuring is grasped. Up to the end of the sixth century BC Athenians were grouped in four Ionian 'tribes'. How far these were still based on a real as opposed to a new fictitious kinship principle we cannot say.

All this was changed by Cleisthenes. On the existing system Cleisthenes superimposed a new one which, intentionally or not, 'mixed up' the citizenry and provided a wholly new basis for citizen participation.

First, as we have mentioned, Attica was divided into three Ridings, each comprising a number of *demes*. Criss-crossing the three Ridings and their *demes*, ten divisions, called *phylae* (misleadingly translated as 'tribes') were established, each named after an Athenian hero; so that every 'tribe' was a cross-section of three Ridings—that is, it would contain men from the City, the Coast, and the Plain alike.

These *phylae* were given a real corporate identity, each with its own shrine and eponymous hero, its property and rent-rolls, its own officers and its Assembly. Henceforth the *locus* for determining citizenship was no longer the *phratry* but the *deme*. All permanent residents of a *deme* at the time of this reform were inscribed in *deme* registers and became members and citizens of that *deme*. Their sons, at the age of 18, were presented to the *deme* Assembly for inclusion on its rolls as an adult citizen. Membership was hereditary: wherever in Attica he moved, a citizen remained a member of his original *deme*.

The arrangement became *determinant* because, in the first place, the *deme* registers provided the information for raising troops and obtaining candidates for the various offices of the state. Secondly, it was in and by the ten 'tribes', that regular quotas of men were provided for the army, the Council, the boards of magistrates, and the law courts. The operation of every single organ of state presupposed this tenfold sectionalization of the citizen body.[56]

The hereditary nature of citizenship needs to be stressed. Naturalization was possible but in the fifth century it was very difficult and rare.

5.4. *The Structure of Government* (*c.431* BC)

Athens was the first and archetypal 'direct' democracy: that is to say, the citizens took decisions in their own persons, not by electing persons to take them. However, it went beyond what this simplistic definition suggests.

---

[56] See, for instance, p. 345 below, concerning the Assembly, and p. 347 concerning the Council.

Nowadays, the executive branch usually consists of political heads and a permanent bureaucracy. The former are the outcome of election, either directly, as with an American president, or indirectly, as with a British prime minister and his cabinet. But the Athenians thought that election was not democratic enough, except for a very limited range of posts which demanded special skills. Instead, the magistracies were filled by casting lots (*sortition*). Furthermore, there was no bureaucracy to speak of, merely a few slaves attached to a specialized magistrate. Even the judiciary was selected by lot annually (with minor qualification to be noted below). The guiding principle of the political system was that, with the rarest exceptions, all posts, whether executive, legislative, or judicial, should be open, by rotation, to the entire citizen body for a one-year term, and that all their actions should be subject to scrutiny in the last or even in the first resort by as many of the citizen body as could be assembled together in person.[57] This was the *demokratia*, a term which, significantly, does not seem to have come into general use until after the time of Cleisthenes.[58]

Athens, of course, possessed the three usual organs of government—the magistrates, the Council (*boulê*), and Assembly (*ekklesia*), but in her case it is wise to recognize the lawcourts as a fourth organ, constituted independently of the others.

5.4.1. THE ASSEMBLY (*EKKLESIA*)

The Assembly consisted of all citizens, although it is uncertain how many participated. The most assiduous were generally artisans and traders. At the beginning of the fifth century it may have met ten times a year, at its end sometimes as often as forty.[59] The agenda was published four days in advance but it could be modified and there were provisions for emergency sessions. The *ekklesia* had originally met on the *agora* (market-place), situated at this time on the hill called the Pnyx.

Enter now the *phylae*, the ten 'tribes of Cleisthenes'. The Athenian political year was divided into ten and for each one of these time-units one of the ten tribes provided the personnel who organized and presided over meetings of the Council (of 500 members, fifty from each tribe),[60] and the Assembly. So that, inside the year, all ten *phylae* would have served. These presiding personnel were called the *prytaneis*, and every day they cast lots to appoint the chairman who served for that day alone. Thus the convoking of

---

[57] Nobody could serve as a member of the Council more than twice. So, assuming every councillor served twice and had a political life of, say, twenty years, that would have made a limit of 5,000 participants. If only a half of them served twice the limit would be 7,500. The Pnyx, where the Assembly met, held 6,000.   [58] Fine, *Ancient Greeks*, 208.

[59] Ibid. 408.   [60] See p. 347 below.

the Assembly rotated regularly through the ten tribes, and inside these the chairmanship rotated too, but on a daily basis.

Proposals were put to the Assembly by the Council, but any citizen could propose amendments. A citizen might himself also propose a new law or decree, but only with the assent of the Assembly which then remitted the proposal to the Council. But this would hardly be undertaken lightly, for it was open to any citizen to oppose the measure as 'illegal' by initiating a lawsuit called the *graphe paranomon*. In that event, the issue went to one of the courts (the *dikasteries*) which, we must say in anticipation, consisted of up to 1,000 citizens, all chosen by lot. They might find against the measure and inflict a heavy fine or occasionally death on the original proposer. Once passed, the laws were immutable, though they might need supplementation or clarification.

In the Assembly, once all had spoken on a proposition, a vote was taken by show of hands except for certain special matters, such as ostracism (the banishment of a citizen[61]). If a 'snap vote' was suspected or if the presiding officer believed that the mood of the Assembly had changed, he could allow a second vote.

The powers of the Assembly were extensive. It had the final word on war and peace, alliances, the size of the armed forces, finance, currency, and customs duties. It elected all those magistrates who were not appointed by lot (this included the most important ones, and notably the generals) and controlled *all* magistrates, who had to appear ten times a year to report to it, and receive votes of confidence or no confidence as the case might be. It could depose generals at any time, as it deposed Pericles.[62] Its legislative competence we have already mentioned. The Assembly also had jurisdiction over offences allegedly against the state. Miltiades was tried by the Assembly in 489 for having 'deceived the people' (he had failed to bring back the Persian gold he had promised to seize for them), and was accused of correspondence with the enemy. The most usual modes of proceeding in such cases were by the *eisangelia* and the *probole*. The former is the equivalent of our 'impeachment'. The accuser made his charge in the Assembly, which acted like an American Grand Jury and voted on whether there was a prima facie case. If 'yes', it went to the Council which recommended whether the case should be tried in a popular court (*dikastery*) or by the Assembly itself, which could impose any penalty it saw fit in cases of conviction. In the *probole*, or 'procedure', a citizen could introduce a presentment against an

---

[61] See pp. 356–7 below.
[62] Thucydides, *The History of Peloponnesian War*, 2.59, says it was because the populace blamed him for their sufferings in the war.

individual whose activities were, according to him, prejudicial to the state's interests. The Assembly heard the charge and the rebuttal and voted whether it backed the charge or not. If it did, the accuser was then free to bring an action in a court.

No quorum was required for exercising its powers, except in three cases. These were *ostracism*; a vote of an *adeia* (i.e. a decree permitting an individual to move the repeal of a law); and the conferment of citizenship. For all these at least 6,000 citizens had to be present.

5.4.2. THE COUNCIL (*BOULÉ*)

The Council was the *arche*, that is, the 'government' or the 'administration'. Unquestionably subordinate to the sovereignty of the Assembly, it was the essential organ of executive power and was, consequently able to act as the pivot of the democracy. From Cleisthenes' time (*c*.507), it consisted of 500 members serving for one year and only re-eligible once. There were selected by lot fifty men aged not less than 30 years from each one of the ten tribes. The candidates' names were drawn from the *deme* registers and there was an effort to have the *demes* represented in accordance with their population.

Candidates were relatively few because the responsibilities were very onerous, the expenses heavy, and the daily stipend (not introduced, anyway, till 461) was only half the daily wage of a labourer. Consequently, few poor citizens served on the *boulé*.[63] It met every day, as convened by its 'steering committees',[64] which drew up the agenda. Its sessions were public and, if so permitted by the steering committee (or the Assembly), any citizen could intervene in its deliberations.

The 'presiding committees' were the *prytaneis* described above, the fifty men from each of the ten tribes who assumed control in turn for one-tenth of the year, so as to regulate the proceedings and act in the name of the entire body. The foreman (*epistates*), appointed for one day was the president of the Athenian Republic, for he held the keys of the temples (the repositories of the state's funds and archives), he presided over the *boulé* and, if the Assembly were meeting, presided over that body also. A citizen could hold this post only once in his lifetime.

The first reason for the importance, I would say the pre-eminence, of the *boulé* is that it had very tight control over the agenda of the Assembly. The latter could discuss nothing that had not already been discussed in the Council and formulated by it as a *probouleuma*—a 'resolution'. The Assembly could and frequently did propose amendments, but the still widespread notion that the Assembly was an impulsive mob is quite false. The Assembly

---

[63] Cf. Fine, *Ancient Greeks*, 400–1. [64] See following page.

unquestionably made some disastrous decisions and a number of cruel and also capricious ones; but it was an arena where the subjects of debate and the rules of procedure were tightly controlled. There was nothing haphazard about that at all.

The second reason for its importance was that it was the only body that could co-ordinate and control a multitude of ten-man boards, all of equal standing and mutually independent, which carried on the day-to-day admin-istration.[65] According to how we wish to classify these, they numbered between fifteen and twenty, no less,[66] for the arsenals, for religious cere-monies, finance, audit, military logistics, and much else besides. It was the Council, too, that ran day-to-day foreign affairs, although subordinate to the Assembly.

The Council had certain judicial functions, too. It could not imprison a man or inflict the death penalty, but it did have jurisdiction over all complaints against public officials, criminal offences against public order, and the *eisangelia*, already noticed. But one of its most important and commonly used judicial powers was its *challenge* or scrutiny power, the *dokimasia*; that is, its authority to challenge claims to citizenship, to candi-dature for the archonship and the Council itself, and of entitlement to public assistance.

5.4.3. THE ADMINISTRATION

The Magistracies

The magistrates were the executive agents of the Council and Assembly; and the principal preoccupation of the constitution's architects seems to have been to prevent them becoming an oligarchy. Every citizen aged 30 was entitled to become a magistrate. To secure equality of access to all ten tribes, the term of office was one year, and re-election (with exceptions noted below) was forbidden. Most magistracies therefore were commissions of ten members, one member per tribe. Each commission was elected independently of the others and acted collectively. But the term 'elections' here connotes two quite different ways of proceeding to an appointment: election by *lot* (sortition) or elections by *vote*. In the former, the original slate of names was drawn up by the tribe or the *deme*. The list usually comprised only those who volunteered. This was so in the most important case, the panel of names from which the Council members were to be chosen by lot;[67] also, as will be seen, there was sometimes an element of manipulation

---

[65] Compare the *collegio* at Venice, in Ch. 7 of Bk. III below, pp. 1003–5.
[66] Aristotle, *The Constitution of Athens* (Hafner Press, New Yale 1174), 47–61.
[67] Hornblower, *Greek World*, 119.

in selecting by lot. The other mode was vote by either the Council or the Assembly.

Once the magistrates were designated, the *boulé* subjected them to the *dokimasia*, a challenge to their credentials, and after 'accusation' and then 'rebuttal' the names were put to the vote.

'Magistrates' as used here comprises three categories of officials: the 'political', the *archons*; the administrator, the *epimeletes*; and the subordinate staff, the *hyperetes*, freedman or slaves who manned the offices as clerks, secretaries, or archivists.

The *archons* were relics of the executive power of early Archaic times. Now they represented the 'dignified' rather than the efficient part of the constitution. In the old days only the first census-class of citizens were eligible, but the property qualification was reduced progressively through the fifth century. By the time we are speaking of, the *archons* and their secretaries (one for each tribe, as usual) were chosen by lot from a preliminary list which had itself been drawn up by lot.[68] One *archon* was called the *archon basileus*—the 'king archon'—a relic of the primeval monarchy and evidence of how it disappeared, as its functions were 'put into commission' as described above (p. 331). He presided over that ancient council named the Areopagus whose originally wide judicial powers had now shrunk to a few religious ones. He presided over sacrifices, and concerned himself in all lawsuits relating to priests, holy ground, impiety, or sacrilege. The *archon eponym*, as the title suggests, had the year named after him, for he controlled the calendars. He also acted as a kind of state's attorney in suits concerning family-law and the protection of property. The *archon polemarch* retained the vital function of field-marshal until the onset of the Persian wars *c*.490, but was by now left with nothing but the religious aspects of warfare: its holy sacrifices and rituals. The six remaining *archons* were the *thesmothetes*, that is, the guardians of Legislation. They drew the Council's attention every year to defects in the laws and were responsible for the administrative side of dispensing justice— for instance, fixing the hours of court sessions and designating the chairmen and counsel. It was the *thesmothetes* who had jurisdiction over most of the political suits, such as appeals against decrees of the Council or against the 'challenge to credentials' (the *dokimasia*), and in cases alleging corruption and malfeasance of judges. Their jurisdiction stretched to some civil actions too, such as cases of adultery, assault, and false witness.

The *epimeletes*, appointed by lot or election but mostly by the former method, included *all* judicial offices of whatever kind, the financial officers,

[68] On the complex matter of the secretaries, see P. J. Rhodes, *The Athenian Boulé* (OUP, Oxford, 1972), 134–41.

who included the 'Treasurers of Athene' (the largest of the state treasuries) and regulatory officers (appointed by lot) such as the market-inspectors, comptrollers of weights and measures, and the commissioners of wheat sales.

Elections proper (as opposed to the random choice by lot) was reserved for those offices which required specialized technical qualification, or where probity and competence was of the essence. Thus, during the period of the empire (masquerading as the Delian League), the treasurers of the League Chest were elected, not chosen by lot. So were the heads of technical services—such as water supply, architecture, naval engineering, walls and fortifications. A large number of the officiants of cults and festivals, like the Mysteries and the Panathenaean Games, were elected too. Most importantly, all military commanders were elected; this was a matter of highest political importance.[69]

The Services

Taxation and Public Finance

Athenians did not at all like paying direct taxes and except for the war tax, the *eisphora*, which was only levied in grave emergencies, they never did. The state revenue came from a variety of sources: from the Laurion silver-mines, from direct taxes on *metics* and freedmen, and from customs duties and market polls. These usually sufficed, for peacetime expenses were very slight. It was spent on the cult, public works, and a few maritime and military projects, in that order. Then follow such items as the (meagre) stipends and expenses of the officials. At first these were only paid to the Council and the lawcourt juries (*dykasteries*), but in the fourth century they were paid to all who came to the Assembly. Later still, money was paid out for public assistance and pensions.

The *eisphora* was a levy on capital in excess of a specified limit. It seems (in the teeth of much controversy[70]) that all those liable to it paid the same fixed proportion of their capital, whatever its size. Perhaps 6,000 persons were liable.[71] It did not raise a great deal of money.[72]

An important reason for the very low level of taxation and expenditure was the system of 'liturgies'. In our day the word has acquired an exclusively ecclesiastical connotation. It comes from the Greek *leitourgia*, compounded of the roots for 'people' and 'that which works'. In its broadest sense, any public work or duty discharged at private expense is a *liturgy*, a definition

---

[69] See p. 352 below.
[70] Cf. A. H. M. Jones, *Athenian Democracy* (OUP, Oxford, 1960; repr. 1969), 23–8.
[71] Ibid. 28.   [72] Ibid. 29.

which would include military service or forced labour. In this context, it means public duties which the richest discharged for the state at their own expense. In Athens the principal liturgies were matters like raising a choir or troops of runners in each of the ten tribes but also, and by far the most onerous, the upkeep and maintenance of the fleet in time of war.[73]

The money was collected by two ten-man commissions, selected by lot, one member from each 'tribe'. The *poletai* constituted a Commission for Public Contracts. It was they, for instance, who leased out the state's mines to concessionaires or auctioned off forfeited property. But more importantly, it was they who, in the presence of the Council, farmed out the tax-collection in an auction. This done (and a list of the tax-farmers and their payments deposited with the Council), they gave the public clerk the lists of which tax-farmers were to pay their instalments, and when. As the tax-farmers duly came to pay up, the clerk took their list from their pigeonhole and handed it over to the second board, the ten *apodectai* or receivers-general. (These too were chosen, one from each tribe, by lot.) As the sums were paid, so they crossed the entry off the list. The *apodectai* then allocated the receipts to the spending departments, a mechanical process because the laws had appropriated income to specific purposes, for example, the market-inspectors, temple-repairers, and the like. Each of these separate funds had its own treasurer. All this was handled by quite humble citizens, and for all the complexity of petty imprest funds in the spending departments it worked quite effectively, and, as far as one can judge, without corruption. It was, of course, conspicuously visible. Its chief defect was the rigidity of the appropriations because, when money ran out, changes could only be effected by special decree. But a system of supposedly self-balancing funds is really quite common in the history of taxation. Great Britain was using it right up to the close of the eighteenth century until William Pitt instituted the Consolidated Fund.

Any surpluses were stored in the temples, of which the Temple of Athene was the most important. When the city was at its last gasp, the Assembly by special decree borrowed from it—repaying it later with interest.

The Army and Navy

Athens was at war for fifty-six of the years between the battles of Salamis (480) and Aegospotami (405). Whence came the capability for such a protracted effort?

First of all, there were the compulsory contributions, first given willingly and then grudgingly, from its allies in the Delian League which Athens

---

[73] See p. 353 below.

controlled and effectively turned into its empire. This empire kept the sea-lanes safe for commerce and Athens became the very centre of Mediterranean trade, which brought in much wealth. Again as a result of empire, Athens was able to ease her local land shortage by planting *cleruchies* (military cantonments) in various places in Greece. Then there were her own natural resources like the silver mines of Laurion and the taxation and liturgies already mentioned. Furthermore, war was made to pay for war by exactions, forced levies, and the booty (including stores) from captured cities. But Athens' chief resource was its own citizenry. Its army and navy were *militia* forces which cost little more than subsistence stipends on active service.

The armed forces were organized on four basic principles. First, leaving aside the oarsmen who were largely mercenary, they were made up of citizens (and some *metics*). Next, all these were expected to provide their own military equipment. Third, the high-ranking officers were elected and closely accountable to the Assembly, Council, and the courts. Finally the navy, not the army, was the first and last line of defence; for by the end of the century Athens could only feed its population on imports of grain from the Black Sea area. When the fleet was lost at Aegospotami, the city had to surrender out of sheer starvation.

The army was mobilized along two lines: first, by *phylae*, that is, the ten tribes, so forming the basis for *phylae* military commands, and second, according to the old Solonian census classes.[74] The cavalry was enrolled by the ten-man Commission of Enrolment (*katalogeis*), elected by show of hands in the Assembly. The roll contained the names of the *hippeis*, the 'knights', the second census class of men wealthy enough to provide their own mounts. As their names were read out in the Council they could disqualify themselves on physical or on pecuniary grounds and the Council could likewise reject men it thought unsuitable. The cavalry passed under the control of two commanders, the *hipparchs*, elected at large by open vote in Assembly from the whole body of citizens. Each commanded five of the ten tribal squadrons, each of which, in turn, fought under its own elected *phylarchs* or 'tribal' captains. The heavy infantry, the hoplites, were enrolled from the third census class of *zeugitai*, the substantial yeoman-farmers. Both army and navy came under the High Command which consisted of ten *strategoi* or generals. These were elected, *at large* (i.e. not 'tribally'), from *all* the citizenry by vote of the Assembly and, unlike any other officials, they were re-eligible. On the other hand, their tenure was reviewed and could be terminated each month. Towards the close of the fifth century, for special expeditions, the assembly sometimes appointed one of the ten as supremo.

[74] See p. 342 above.

Below the board of *strategoi* came the ten tribal *taxiarchs*, leading their respective tribal formation and elected by open vote. The *taxiarchs* themselves appointed their junior officers—the *lochagi*—as captains of companies.

As to the fleet, its construction and maintenance were administered by commissions controlled by the Council. The master-shipwrights were elected by vote of the Assembly, and the ships, their tackle, and sheds fell under the inspection of the Council. The principle of supplying one's own equipment applied to the top census classes, the *pentakosiomedimnos* and the *hippeis*. These had to serve in rotation for one year apiece, as *trierarchs*, 'trireme-masters'; during this term the *trierarch* was responsible for maintaining and repairing his trireme; recruiting, feeding, and training its crew; and for actually commanding it at sea.

But what of the lowest census-class, the *thetes*? These to some extent provided the oarsmen, together with mercenary non-Athenians. The *thetes* also served as light infantry. Of not much account in the earlier part of the century, they became more important towards its close and became politically significant also, for it was they who helped turn back the superior forces of the 'Thirty Tyrants' after they took the city over from the democracy in the aftermath of the surrender of 404.

These methods raised impressively large armies and navies. The largest land-force is likely to have been that mentioned by Pericles for 431. By that date the population—and the hoplite class, too—had greatly increased compared with the beginning of the fifth century. The figures are 13,000 hoplites in the field army and another 16,000 men, which included the youths (*ephebes*) and older men, plus *metics*, who were manning the fortifications. (Thereafter the totals fall, as the plague, casualties, and the general impoverishment of the city took their toll.[75] In the Fourth Century a maximum of 5,000 hoplites could be mobilized in a time of crisis.) This can be compared with, say, early England: some 6,000–8,000 Saxons at the Battle of Hastings, 27,000 men in Henry VIII's French campaign of 1513.[76] The fleets were large, too—they fluctuated around a norm of about 200 ships.

The land forces were as good as those of any other city-states, except, of course, for Sparta's formidable professionals; though the cavalry, mostly made up of aristocratic youths, was slack and undisciplined according to Xenophon, a good professional judge. The navy, on the other hand, was very efficient.[77] Perhaps the weakest spot in Athens's arrangements lay in the vulnerability of defeated commanders to popular resentment. The

---

[75] Jones, *Athenian Democracy*, 161–80.

[76] At Crécy (1346) Edward III deployed 20,000 men. At Agincourt (1415) there were 6,000 to 7,000 Englishmen against 23,000 Frenchmen. Gustavus Adolphus's army in the Thirty Years War (seventeenth century) was only 20,000.　　　　[77] Cf. Jones, *Athenian Democracy*, 99–100.

Assembly was prone to react by dismissal, even by punishment, *pour encourager les autres*. This resentment was often—I would say, usually—whipped up by self-interested politicians. The recall of Alcibiades from Sicily to face charges of desecrating the Herms[78] is one such case. Unquestionably the worst was the disgraceful judicial murder of the six surviving commanders from the (victorious) sea-action at Arginusae.[79]

The forces were of supreme political importance, and first in this was the panel of the ten *strategoi*, the generals. In the fifth century—but not in the fourth—they were not elected for military skills but for general political pre-eminence, so that the list includes the best-known politicians of the time and in practice they were wealthy and/or of aristocratic birth. Pericles was a general for most of his political life. (He commenced his political career in *c*.465, but from 443 was continuously general until his death). It seems too as if generals had a power to summon the Assembly and perhaps to prevent its being summoned. They had direct access to it. More influentially, they could and often did sit in on the Council. Lastly, on sea or land expeditions they enjoyed the most extended discretion.[80] Given that Athens was almost permanently at war, the generals were necessarily the most significant individual officers in the entire city.

The fact that the army and navy were citizen-forces is also of great political significance. The thirty 'Tyrants' of 404 intended to consolidate their power by restricting 'active' citizenship to 3,000 citizens of the cavalry and hoplite class, and what success they managed to obtain was only due to tricking the rest of the hoplites in the city into disarming. Even so, more and more of those citizens who had kept their arms deserted to the democrat exiles at Phyle while the *thetes* in Piraeus were manufacturing arms for themselves. In the face of such armed resistance by one half of the citizens against the half they claimed to command, the government of the Thirty broke down and the democracy was restored.[81]

5.4.4. THE JUDICIAL INSTITUTIONS

Of all the ways a citizen could participate in affairs, the most accessible was as a juror in the popular courts. This gives Athenian democracy a democratic extension far beyond the most ultra-radical demands of our contemporary extreme left. However, this was not the only method of adjudicating

[78] See p. 327 above.
[79] Xenophon, *Hellenica* ('A History of My Times'), trans. R. Warner, with introduction and notes by G. Cawkwell (Penguin, Harmondsworth, 1981), i. 6, 7 *passim*.
[80] Hornblower, *Greek World*, 121–2.
[81] The entire story is marvellously recounted in Mary Renault's fine historical novel, *The Last of the Wine* (London, 1966).

and it is as well to begin with some general principles. The pre-eminent one is that here, except for sixth-century Judah perhaps—and our information on that is very slender indeed—we find for the first time a distinction between administrative and judicial personnel. Hitherto, in Egypt and Assyria or Persia justice was meted out—usually on appeal for traditional justice by 'elders' in the first instance—by such officials as nomarchs, governors, or satraps. The distinction between the deliberative, the executive, and judicial 'powers' is of course recognized explicitly by Aristotle.[82] This is yet another of those revolutionary 'firsts' that we encounter among the Greeks. A second distinctive feature is that all suits were initiated by a private party, even for crimes against the state, for instance, so that all cases became a *lis inter partes*. The third is the *ephesis*, that is, the appeal against a judicial or executive decision or action. The fourth and least important is the existence of a circuit of judges for minor civil suits.

Owing to the pressure on the popular courts, *deme* courts were established 453/2 BC. Three men from each tribe were appointed by lot to serve for one year. They heard private suits up to 10 drachmae. For larger sums, there were ten groups of arbitrators. If the litigators refused their award, they could then appeal to the popular courts. All the evidence, in writing, was supplied to this court and the court then made its own award which was definitive.

Actions in Athens were either private (*dikai*) or public (*graphai*). In either event, the suits were launched by private persons: those who chose to launch the public action were encouraged by a share of the fine if the action proved successful, but over time this was counterbalanced by penalties in the event of an acquittal. By what we nowadays would regard as a bizarre inversion, homicide cases were private not public suits. Here the tradition of blood-feud underlay the procedure: homicide was considered a religious crime and the survivals of the religious courts took jurisdiction of it, notably the Areopagus.[83] The procedure was exceedingly complicated and has no place here; the point is that only members of the victim's family could initiate proceedings.

There were two components of the judicial system, the magistracies and the courts. The former 'processed' and administered an action, according to their specialized jurisdiction. Thus the *archon basileus*[84] took cognizance of certain homicides and religious crimes, the generals of military crimes, the 'Eleven' (gaolers) of thieves, the special panels of commerce and economic matters for suits relating to these.

[82] *Politics*, IV, 14–16.
[83] Cf. the parallels in the *sharia* of Islam (see below; Bk. III, Pt. I, Ch. 2, p. 691).
[84] See p. 349 above.

The courts' duty was solely to judge on the issue put to them by 'their' magistrate. All cases not sent to special courts came before the largest court, the *heliaea*.[85] All citizens over 30 were entitled—but not obliged—to participate. From lists drawn up in each *deme*, 600 names per tribe were selected by lot so that 6,000 citizen were empanelled every year and paid two or three obols a day (equal to half the daily pay of a labourer) each day they acted as juror. These citizens were then organized into *dykasteries* or juries, of either 200 (for private suits) or 500 (for public suits), and these juries sat every day in the year except for the sixty festival days. The procedure went, roughly speaking, along these lines: the plaintiff, supported by two witnesses, filed his complaint to the magistrate. The latter set a day for an *anakrisis*, a preliminary hearing, which decided if there was a case to answer. If there was, a day was set by the six *thesmothetes* for the full hearing, and a court and jury was 'booked'. On the appointed day the magistrate who had drawn up the case chaired the proceedings. The verdict was decided by a majority.

Such was the very remarkable system of administering justice. Three ancillary notes require to be appended here on *ephesis*, the penalties for homicide, and the process of ostracism.

Ephesis comes from a root which means 'to refer', and therefore may be translated, in this context, as 'referral' or even as 'appeal'. The reason for mentioning it here is because it throws light on the Greek notion of personal *eleutheria* or freedom, the central intent and driving motive force of the entire *polis* concept. A citizen, precisely because he was a citizen and not a subject, stood in a sort of contractual relationship to organs of the state, so that he must himself accept the validity of its action against him. Such actions might be decisions by his *deme*, or even of 'the Eleven' (gaol commissioners) or of a magistrate. The proscribed citizen could block the execution of such decisions by the *ephesis*. His *ephesis*, however, could itself be challenged—but only by the private suit of another citizen. In that case, the appellant had to bring the suit before the popular court. Only this could make a sovereign decision.[86]

Ostracism was not, strictly speaking, a judicial matter. It was a procedure for the temporary banishing of any citizen. It was introduced, allegedly, by Cleisthenes in 507, following hard upon the expulsion of the Peisistratid tyrants and designed, no doubt, to nip in the bud anybody suspected of aspiring to a tyranny himself. Once a regular procedure was introduced, it obviously lent itself to factional strife whereby one set of politicians could engineer the expulsion of their rivals. The most notorious case concerns

---

[85] See H. M. Hansen, *The Athenian Democracy in the Age of Demosthenes* (Blackwell, Oxford, 1991), 191.
[86] Ellul, *Histoire des Institutions*, i. 128.

Aristides 'the just'. Plutarch tells us that some illiterate asked a man to write the name 'Aristides' on his ballot (the *ostrakon*). The man he asked was Aristides himself. He did as requested but ventured to ask 'why?' and received the reply that the voter was sick and tired of hearing Aristides being called 'the Just'. This story trivializes the institution, for the procedure was in fact highly deliberate. In every sixth 'month' (*prytany*) the Assembly had to decide whether to introduce any ostracism. If it said 'yes' the actual vote on the ostracism was postponed to the next *prytany* so that there was a whole month for electioneering for and against the citizens put up for banishment. The actual vote was cast on a potsherd—the *ostrakon*—with the name of the man to be banished written on it. To cast these *ostraka*, the ten tribes went into the now enclosed *agora* by their respective ten entrances. If the total cast was less than 6,000 no ostracism could take place. If the quorum was reached the man named by a plurality had to leave Athens for ten years. Just because a procedure is sometimes abused does not entail that it is a bad procedure. Given the history of *stasis* in the *polis* and the cruelty, even savagery, with which victorious factions treated their opponents, one may well conclude that the banishment of highly controversial faction leaders exerted a calming influence. But in any event it was not often used, and after 415 faded out of existence altogether.

Punishments are an indication of a state's political sophistication. In Athens these included dishonourable banishment with confiscation of goods, a range of forfeitures and fines, and, for the most serious crimes, the death penalty. The fatal drink of hemlock, used in the case of Socrates, has become a byword but it represents a very considerable softening in capital punishment. For most of the fifth century the modes of execution were quite singularly barbarous—the *barathron* (the death pit into which the condemned were thrown) and the *apotympanismos*.[87] The latter persisted even after the introduction of poisoning by hemlock.

5.5. *The Process of Government*

Although the first teachers of rhetoric were Syracusans, it is no accident that the new academic discipline called 'rhetoric' was perfected in democratic Athens. Indeed, Isocrates (436–338) quite explicitly described it as 'an instrument of practical politics'.[88] For rhetoric, in the tradition of Isocrates

[87] '[T]he criminal was fastened by means of five cramp irons to a wooden plank which was then set upright in the ground. It is uncertain whether the victim was left to die in agony after possibly days of exposure, or whether death was hastened by gradually tightening the iron collar.' J. V. A. Fine, *The Ancient Greeks* (Harvard UP, 1983), 420.

[88] E. B. Castle, *Ancient Education and Today* (Penguin, Harmondsworth, 1961), 57.

and Aristotle, is the necessary concomitant of Forum-style government and it decayed (just as Quintillian was expounding it in its most elaborated form) as Forum-type government was itself withering under the Roman autocracy. Few things are more striking than the contrast between Athenian and Roman republicanism and the Chinese political culture in respect of rhetoric. China's increasingly bureaucratic culture relied entirely on the written document. Its education system corresponded to and was centred exclusively on reading and writing and never on the art of speaking. It did not have to be, because the mandarins had nobody to court or to persuade except the emperor. Up to a point, this is true of all the bureaucratic-cum-palace regimes we have or shall have encountered. Palace systems are document/command systems. Forum systems are speech/persuasion ones.

The Greek *polis* is the first Forum-type polity in history and that is precisely why it speaks to us in our own political idiom. Consider for a moment the way Palace and Forum systems differ—and are bound to—in their respective 'styles'. In the extreme, purest form of Palace system the political process takes place inside the tiny arena of the court. The actors are the narrow circle of courtiers-officials-priests. Their activity consists of acquiring access to the king/prince/emperor—the autocrat: bringing persuasion to bear on him, or pressure to bear on him, or replacing him, in that order. In the Forum type of government the arena is unbounded. In its purest form, as in Athens, it is the *demos* itself. The actors here have to court, not a monarch, but this *demos*. They do so in two ways. First, they must manipulate and/or structure the composition of the political organ (which in this case is the decisional audience that emanates from the *demos*). Second, when facing this audience they must manipulate and/or structure its opinion.

'But'—it may be retorted—'this assumes that in Athens there are leaders and led, actors and people being acted on. And we have been told explicitly that this is a system of haphazard arrangement, where office and decision-making went at random, and everybody took turns.'

Without a doubt, the object of the Athenian system was that all posts should, as far as possible, rotate throughout the entire citizen body. This assumed that every citizen was equally qualified to fill any post. But as we have seen, the Athenians reluctantly recognized that this was not true for all posts. Some, like generalships or master-shipwrights, demanded special skills. These posts were therefore filled by election which, to the Athenians, was an 'aristocratic' mode of selection. Yet even here, except for the generals who were re-eligible, no posts could be held for more than a year. These principles were carried out faithfully. There were 500 councillors changing annually and appointed by lot; some 1,400 magistrates at home or overseas, mostly changing annually and appointed by lot; and the 6,000 'jurymen' of the courts, similarly selected by lot, although re-eligible. And all were subject to the mass meeting of the Assembly.

Yet this system carried on without major modifications for some 200 years and in the end it did not break down but was destroyed from the outside. It would be contrary to all experience of political systems to assume that such durability is likely where every office and every decision is decided *ad hoc* by, so to speak, the flip of a coin or the vagaries of a huge open-air crowd—of varying composition—sitting in judgement as the Assembly. So there must have been some kind of pre-structuring in the appointment and decision-making processes. Two elements of such structuring were quite certainly *not* present: there was neither bureaucracy nor political parties. To say what elements *were* present is difficult and somewhat problematical, because the Athenian system is far more opaque to the historian than that of Republican Rome. Here one has to work by scraps of information, filled out by the imagination. But something may be gleaned about it by proceeding along the lines already suggested and looking at the manipulation/ structuring of, first, the *demes*, then the audience (i.e. the Assembly), and finally, its opinion.

First, then, the selection of councillors was not entirely random. Citizens were not *obliged* to offer themselves as candidates, and as the duties were onerous only the better-off volunteered. Consequently, in some *demes* at any rate, there were but few on whom the lot could fall. So, wealthy full-time politicians—Cleon, Demosthenes—could be accused of fixing things so as to secure a Council seat in years critical for foreign policy (427 and 346 respectively). Presumably they did so by influencing dependants or even bribing them *not* to volunteer for the Council, or by getting one faction to refrain from putting forward candidates one year in return for the like favour in the following years, or by acting as a stand-in candidate in a *deme* other than their own,[89] where no native candidates were willing to come forward.

The final decision lay, as we know, with the Assembly. Perhaps 6,000 citizens or so attended it in the fifth century. They would not always be the same people, and politicians had no sure way of securing the audience they wanted. But the effects of a changing membership and the way a politician could take advantage of it is exemplified by certain events in 411. Antiphon and Peisander conspired to terrorize the Council, and then proceeded to try to force an oligarchical constitution through the Assembly. They succeeded partly because the fleet—with its fervently democratic sailors—was absent

[89] Hornblower, *Greek World*, 119; Jones, *Athenian Democracy*, 106.

in Samos, and partly by convening the Assembly at Colonus, outside the city walls, where citizens were afraid to go for fear of enemy attack. But such blatant manipulation was rare: by and large, attendance at the Assembly was unpredictable. Since manipulation of the attendance was impossible, enormous importance attached to the ways and means of manipulating its *vote*. We may be sure that there was much canvassing and lobbying, but no explicit evidence survives.[90] We do know, however, how the politicians made use of cliques and took advantage of procedure. Plutarch tells us how the leader of the aristocratic party, Thucydides (not the historian), opposed Pericles in the Assembly 'by separating and grouping (the aristocratic members) in a single body' instead of allowing them to be dispersed throughout the crowd,[91] and Demosthenes complained of the same thing in the fourth century.[92]

As for procedural tricks, these are a matter of course in any assembly-type body. Procedures are designed to *protect* an assembly from being rushed or pushed into decision, but they can be turned around to produce just this effect. An example comes from the Assembly's debate on the fate of the six generals accused of abandoning the survivors of the (victorious) sea-fight at Arginusae (406).[93] The generals were accused by Theramenes and Euryptolemos spoke in their defence, and the matter was debated and then adjourned to the Assembly's next meeting. Here, a certain Callixenus introduced a motion on behalf of the Council that the matter be voted on without further debate. Thereupon Euryptolemos and his supporters intervened with a summons against Callixenus for putting forward an illegal proposal.[94] This enraged the majority, and the opponents of the generals took advantage of this by proposing that unless Euryptolemos and his friends withdrew the summons the Assembly should judge them on the same vote as it did the generals. Since the furious Assembly would clearly have done so, Euryptolemos withdrew the summons. The way was now clear for the presiding officer, the *epistates*, to put the Council's motion. It happened that on that day the *epistates* was none other than Socrates, the philosopher. Socrates said he would do nothing contrary to the law and refused to put the motion. Callixenus then insisted that if the *epistates* would not put it to the vote, the entire *prytany* (the fifty-man presidency for their month) must do so and—since they were scared stiff—that is what members of the presidency did.[95] But the affair was still not over, for Europtylemus now moved an amendment to the Council's motion to the

---

[90] Finley, *Politics*, 83.   [91] Plutarch, 'Pericles', xi 2.   [92] Jones, *Athenian Democracy*, 131.
[93] See p. 354 above.   [94] Cf. p. 346 above.
[95] This version is not held universally. Cf. the note at I. vii. 5 in Xenophon, *Hellenica*.

effect that each general should be tried separately. He earned the first vote but an enemy of the generals then lodged a point of order. The vote was taken again, and this time the Council's original resolution was carried.[96]

This is an exceptional case where the Assembly overrode some of its own procedural rules. Generally, the politicians had to act within them in such cases, so their task was to manipulate opinion. Those who did this became known as *demagogues* ('people-leaders'), a term of abuse today. The so-called demagogues were in practice politicians who devoted their whole time to mastering the information necessary to the decisions the Assembly would have to make. Often this was highly technical; for instance,[97] the complicated decree altering the assessment of tribute from the subject-states. It has to be assumed—we have no direct evidence—that such men as Cleon had 'unofficial unpaid entourages' which 'devilled' for them. At all events, that they did possess superior information and a *tacte des choses possibles* is clearly presupposed by the measures they introduced, how they expounded them, and how they were received. And the same is true for those speaking on the other side of the question.[98] They have been described as 'a class of semi-professional politicians, at first consisting of the gentry, later partly of the gentry and partly of poor men of rhetorical talent. They were the people who held the elective offices, were chosen as envoys to foreign states, proposed motions in the council and the assembly and prosecuted (and defended) in political trials. In the fourth century they are clearly recognized as a class, distinct from the mass of ordinary citizens . . .'[99] The conclusion reached by modern scholars is that demagogues did not, as the pejorative use of the term insinuates, *mislead* the *demos* but, as the literal meaning of the word conveys, led it. The Assembly took for granted that these politicians and their opponents were both grounding their opposing views on the same basic facts; and that they had been considering these facts and how to respond to them well in advance of the debate. The Assembly, then, was informed in this way, and the power of the politicians resided partly in their recognized mastery of the issues, and partly in the rhetorical skill by which they put their own solutions across. In Finley's words, the 'demagogues' were 'structural to the system'.[100]

The Athenian political system, then, was not tightly articulated through organized parties and pressure groups, bureaucrats, and ministers. But it was not so entirely random and haphazard as it tried to make itself out to be. In

[96] Xenophon, *Hellenica*, I. vii.   [97] Finley, *Politics*, 76.
[98] Cf. Hornblower, *Greek World*, 124–5.   [99] Jones, *Athenian Democracy*, 130.
[100] Finley, *Studies*, 21.

the country of the blind the one-eyed man is king, and such were the semi-professional politicians of Athens.

5.6. *Appraisal*

'A pure democracy—by which I mean a society consisting of a small number of citizens, who assemble and administer the government in person, can admit no cure for the mischiefs of faction ... Hence it is that such democracies have ever been found incompatible with personal security or the rights of property; and have, in general been as short in their lives as they have been violent in their deaths.' So Madison in no. 10 of *The Federalist Papers.*

This opinion—and worse—prevailed for over 2000 years after the destruction of the Greek democracies by Macedonia in 322 BC. The term 'democracy' itself, after being devalued so that it could even be used to describe the Roman Principate,[101] sank still lower, becoming synonymous with 'mob violence, riot', and even insurrection in Byzantine writers from the fifth century onwards.[102] Not until the nineteenth century did the term become respectable again, and then (as a *representative* form of government) it had acquired a different connotation. But in so far as Greek democracy is concerned, Madison's views only began to be qualified in the nineteenth century.[103] To a large extent, they are still held today. However valid they may be for Greek democracy 'in general'—about which we really have only scraps of information—Madison's views quoted above strike me, as far as Athens is concerned, as demonstrably false. Not merely false: they are *contre-vérités.*

Some modern critics attack Athens for not going far enough along the democratic road, others for going too far, and some do both. The first is a 'left-wing' critique, the second a 'right-wing' one, and the last is a 'liberal' one.

The most obvious and frequent criticism that Athens was not democratic enough relates to its slave population. Some argue that because slaves formed a majority of the population and the citizenry a minority, Athens cannot qualify as a democracy at all.[104] In so far as this argument is not simply semantic, the answer is that all Greek city-states possessed slaves, and so did the Roman Republic, and so (in some shape of servitude or other) did all the antecedent forms of state so far considered. But in the matter of

---

[101] de Sainte Croix, *Class Struggle*, 323.   [102] Ibid. 326.
[103] Cf. H. Sidgwick, *The Development of the European Polity*, 1st edn. (Macmillan, London, 1903), ch vii.
[104] e.g. B. Holden, *The Nature of Democracy* (Nelson, London, 1974), 14; 16 and sources cited.

the freemen, such states were open to giving *isonomia* and citizen participation to all of them or to a number of them or to none at all; and Athens chose to extend participation to its free citizens on a scale exceeding all the Graeco-Roman polities.[105]

A weaker form of this argument is that only slave labour made citizen participation possible. This is quite true. As Aristotle said, the only alternative to slavery would be *automata* (today we would say robots or machinery). But it is not to be assumed from this that Athenian society divided into the idle-rich citizenry and the toiling slaves: that—as Jones sarcastically put it—'the average Athenian, in the intervals between listening to a play of Sophocles and serving as a magistrate, Councillor or Juror, lounged in the market place discussing politics and philosophy, while slaves toiled to support him'.[106] Plato and Aristotle, of course, despised manual work, but not so the Athenians. The Assembly was full of working-men; perhaps less than a quarter of freemen owned a domestic slave and very few farmers owned slaves at all—they were too poor. Slaves were used on a large scale only in mining and industry and most of them belonged to the 1,200 richest families, and then, in smaller numbers, to the next 3,000.[107] Another, but related, criticism along these lines substitutes 'empire' for slavery: that democracy was made possible only by the tribute, the *cleruchies*, the trading advantages *et al.* that the empire brought with it. To this only the briefest answer is required. The democracy continued through 403–322 despite the disappearance of the empire.

The criticisms that Athens 'went too far' in its democracy are more various. The first run along Madison's lines: Athenian democracy was mob rule, mass rule, hasty, rash, a scene of ignorant masses throwing up their 'sweaty nightcaps' under the spell of mob-orators. Aristotle berates it for not being a 'rule of law'. Of course, it is true that the Assembly could act like a mob when overcome by very deep emotion, and the trial of the six generals is a case in point. But to take this and the trial and death-sentence of Socrates as characteristic is like taking the trial and execution of Sacco and Vanzetti as typical of American democracy. What strikes a student of constitutions with wonder and admiration is the meticulousness of the Athenian constitution's procedural safeguards. Let me run over these again in summary. First, for all that magistracies were open to all, specialized ones were filled by election and not by lot; all were subjected to the *dokimasia*, which could at least weed out shady characters; all had to submit their accounts to the *logistai* and receive a vote of confidence from the Council every month; at the end of their annual term their accounts were scrutinized

---

[105] See p. 344 ff. above.   [106] Jones, *Athenian Democracy*, 11   [107] Ibid. 11–18.

by the audit commission (chosen by lot, for impartiality); any citizens could lodge complaints against them for alleged misconduct during their term of office and these complaints were investigated by the ten-man commission of *euthynoi* appointed by lot from the Council and a prima-facie case sent the accused magistrates to the courts for trial. The councillors were not immune either. The Council could depose any member it accused of malfeasance and, if he appealed, could hold a formal trial. Furthermore it had to justify its administration to the Assembly at the expiry of its term. If it was unsatisfactory it did not receive the golden crown.

As for the Assembly itself, ignorance can hardly be ascribed to it. The bulk of its members would have served turns as jurymen, as magistrates, as councillors, or as soldiers and sailors. And the procedural rules were designed to—and seem to have succeeded in—preventing hasty and ill-considered legislation. 'Snap' resolutions were precluded by the normal rule that all matters had to appear on the agenda four days before a meeting; new proposals from the floor had to go back to the *boulé* before being voted on; there was provision for a second vote if it was thought the first was (for various reasons) 'unsafe' (this is how the people of Mytilene were spared in 427); and the *graphe paranomon*[108] was devised to prevent politicians putting forward reckless (hence 'unconstitutional') proposals in the Assembly. These procedural rules were designed to secure orderly and deliberate debate. To argue from certain tumultuous assemblies in periods of high tension to 'mob rule' is to forget the boos, cheers, and howls in the British House of Commons or the not-infrequent occasions when its Speaker has to suspend the sitting.

A second line of criticism, made much of by Aristotle, Isocrates, and the pseudo-Xenophon, is that the democracy 'soaked the rich'. This is usually maintained by contrasting the expense of *liturgia* and the *eisphora* (war-tax) and cavalry- and hoplite-service which fell exclusively on the better off, with the payments made to councillors, magistrates, then jurors and, in the fourth century, even assemblymen. The criticism is particularly associated, too, with the fourth century's Theoric fund. This fund was the accumulated surplus of income over expenditure for one year, and a convention grew up of distributing it to citizens on certain festival days at the rate of two obols a head.

In fact, the balance of financial advantage/disadvantage is not as neat as this formulation assumes. For instance, the war-tax, because it was not progressive, hit the farmers far more heavily than the really rich; hoplite service could take a man from his farm for an indefinite period, and so forth.[109] In any case, if averaged as a proportion of capital, the war-tax was

---

[108] See p. 346 above.   [109] Jones, *Athenian Democracy*, 29–33.

very light by our standards—Jones thinks the equivalent of income tax at 2 per cent to 2.5 per cent.[110] However, it was not the absolute burden of tax that provoked outcry. Athens is one of the few states where taxation is not a critical or indeed the critical issue. What the rich could not abide was that it was spent on paying nobodies to become somebodies: that is, to allow common folk the *per diem* allowance that enabled them to sit as magistrates and councillors and to attend the Assembly. The democracy was indeed entrenching itself in this way, of course: but it was also making legal-constitutional rights actual. It only partly succeeded—as we noted, there were few volunteers for the Council—because the pay represented a sacri-fice, not a reward. Another prong to this kind of argument indicts the lawcourts as agents of confiscation. But there is no evidence of this at all, while the evidence that the law of debt heavily favoured the creditor, and also that poorer citizens could be too scared to litigate with a very wealthy man, suggests the charge is unfounded.[111] And one positive fact is of the greatest importance in this respect: throughout Greece the revolutionary demand, and the outcome which really terrified the wealthy, was 'cancella-tion of debts and redistribution of the land', and yet for all the so-called 'radical' democracy of fourth-century Athens, neither was ever even contemplated there.

A third line of criticism alleges ruin through incompetent and misleading mob-orators—the demagogues—Cleon being the prime target. That the Assembly was a reasonably well-informed body has already been shown, and a defence has been made of 'demagogues' also. But the critics are really paraphrasing—or generalizing from—Thucydides' views on the Pelopon-nesian War. To challenge those views is to take on Thucydides, and alas we do not have an alternative history of these events! But take three simple examples. The critics, following Thucydides, allege that Athens's imperia-listic policy made her allies hate her (the inference being that her fall was moral retribution). The answer is simply that the Athenians had enemies in every one of her allied or subject states—the oligarchs; but by the very same token they had friends too—the democrats. Again, Thucydides ascribes the disastrous Sicilian expedition to the democracy, which is fair enough; but he does not ascribe to this same democracy the successful thirty years' resis-tance to a Sparta that had reckoned on a military walkover when it commenced hostilities in 431. To turn to the third example, the critics berate the democracy for incompetent foreign policy, but nothing whatso-ever could equal the incompetence of Sparta after she won the war in 404; so incompetent that within a few years she lost her newly acquired naval

---

[110] Jones, *Athenian Democracy*, 29.   [111] Cf. Finley, *Politics*, 85 7.

hegemony and effectively handed it back to the Athens she had just defeated!

If those critics who say the Athenian democracy did not go far enough can be described as left-wing and 'progressive', and those who say it went too far as right-wing or 'reactionary', there is a third school of critics who may fairly be described as 'liberal'. For them the Athenian democracy is flawed from the outset by an irredeemable defect in design. This flaw, this defect, is that—to formulate it in a number of different ways—it drew no distinction between 'state' and 'society', it allowed unlimited scope to its government and did not absolutely exclude certain areas from any political intervention, it brought the sanctions of law and coercion into what ought to be private life. The great example they cite is, of course, the trial and death of Socrates on a charge of 'corrupting the youth' and 'not believing in the gods'. Carry the Athenian ideal into today, those critics urge, and you have a totalitarian system. This view derives from such various sources as the liberal Constant's speech on 'Liberty in the ancient and modern world' and the historic 'Cité Antique' of Fustel de Coulanges. The argument is that the city had total command over the way you lived your life, and your only consolation was that you possessed in yourself a minute part of its sovereignty. There were no 'inalienable rights of man', no natural rights.

But this is wildly unhistorical, and the practice was not significantly inferior to political behaviour today. It is unhistorical because, of course, it does not relate to any of the precedent state formations where there was no concept of citizenship at all, and equally no notion of procedural or juridical defence against the action of state officials. Nor, for that matter, does it relate to great historical polities after the Greeks like the Caliphate or the Ottoman Empire, to say nothing of imperial China. Instead, it relates the Athenian polity to the democracies of the twentieth century. This, of course, is to pay it the most enormous compliment—that an invention of 2,000 years ago can be exhumed and made to bear comparison to today! For the Greeks were not concerned with their *polis* having too much power over their citizenry, but too little. For them the greater that power the better. They criticized Athens precisely because, as a result of *isonomia* (equality of laws, or legal equalization), the city's power was less hierarchical than elsewhere.[112]

The criticism is equally faulty if one moves away from analytical distinctions and looks at practical outcomes. We, nowadays, make in our minds a distinction between 'things that are Caesar's and things that are not' which the Greeks did not make. We give practical effect to that

---

[112] Cf. Finley, *Politics*, 93–4.

distinction by embodying a list of the things that are not Caesar's in entrenched Bills of Rights in written constitutions (when we do so at all!—Britain's parliament is as sovereign *in law*, institutionally, as the Greek *polis*). But just as Athenian law could be invoked to enforce popular morality and customs (as in the Socrates case), so in countries today which are protected by Bills of Rights popular morality and prejudice can overwhelm the protection of the legal provisions. In the United States the McCarthy era and its persecution of individuals because of their unpopular opinions was fuelled by public indignation and followed its course despite the Bill of Rights. By the same token, a tolerant public opinion can protect private behaviour and opinions even in the absence of an entrenched Bill of Rights, as for instance in Britain. And in any case, as John Stuart Mill realized, there is a tyranny of public opinion invading any political form that may be adopted—and he suffered from it personally. Certainly, the analytical distinction between the *polis* and the liberal state is valid but, on the ground, it does not seem to me that Athens was, in respect of human rights, one whit inferior to the practices of the western democracies, and arguably it was better.

Consider, then, that between 479 and 338 BC this state was at war for two years out of every three and never enjoyed more than ten consecutive years of peace. Yet, despite that, and for all its lack of natural resources apart from the silver mines, it was the greatest of all the Greek states in the half-century between the Persian defeat and the Peloponnesian War: it created an empire; it held its own against the greatest military power in Greece—Sparta—for thirty years. Even then, in less than ten years after its crushing defeat in 404 it rose again to be a first-class power and only crumbled when Macedonia overwhelmed it along with all the other cities. Domestically, too, it was the most successful of all the Greek states. 'The democracy', said Madison, was 'as short in its life as it was violent in its death.' False! The Athenian democracy was stable except for the attempted coup of 411 and the Spartan-backed oligarchy of 404–3; and it lasted from 510 to 322, when Macedon extinguished it. This amounts to 188 years: how old are our oldest democracies, defining these as states with universal manhood suffrage? It was equitable. Whenever before, and how many times since, has there been a state where the better off tended to bear the chief brunt of warfare and the poorer received some pittance, albeit meagre, simply in their capacity of citizens? And where, before or since, was the direction and the day-to-day administration of the state rotated among all citizens, without distinction between the office to be held and the wealth or status of citizens?

This polity is extraordinary. It was a miracle of ingenuity and design, one of the most successful, perhaps the most successful, of political artefacts in the entire history of government. Unhappily, in common with all the other (and more poorly designed) city-states of Greece, it suffered from one ineradicable flaw: it had to be small in respect to both population and territory. It was not and still is not possible to operate government by rotation of office on a large scale. So the *polis* was doomed politically if it expanded and doomed to conquest if it did not. It had to succumb and it did, and the circumstances which permitted it to take root and flourish were never destined to come again.[113]

[113] But compare it with the Italian city-states, and notably Venice; yet Venice was an oligarchy and more like Sparta than Athens! Bk. III, Ch. 7, pp. 993 ff.

3
The End of the *Polis*

For all its enormous gusto, the classical *polis* had a fatal flaw. It could not extend itself, only replicate itself elsewhere in the form of colonies. If it extended, its citizens could not meet together as the Assembly, and if it did not, it fell prey to big consolidated monarchies. There was, one might surmise, a third alternative—confederation—and that was indeed attempted, but the resulting formations failed both tests. They were forced to abandon rule by the Assemblies (in practice, if not in theory) and they were still too weak to preserve their independence. This is not the whole story. Internal development also worked against *demokratia*. Between external attack and internal decay, the *polis* as a special form of state disappeared.

How this happened requires some knowledge of the events subsequent to Alexander's victory over Persia. That conquest heralded the Hellenistic Age, which conventionally ends with Octavian's defeat of Cleopatra at Actium, 31 BC. It has enormous importance for the history of civilization, but nothing like as much for the history of government; effectively, it amounted to giving a somewhat new thrust to absolute monarchy in Asia and Egypt.

Despite political fragmentation, the area of the former Persian Empire formed a vast cosmopolis ruled by Greeks, policed largely by Greek mercenaries and Macedonians, and studded with newly founded or reconstituted cities which formed an archipelago of Greek islands where the gymnasium and the theatre, the dining club and the market-place, were the centre of civic life, and the Greek *koine* (associations for collective action) reigned supreme, in a sea of dependent cultivators still speaking their native tongues. These cities were all endowed with the political apparatus of the *polis*—its magistrates, Council, and Assembly—but all were dependent on the will of the monarch and everywhere the wealthy were in control. The monarchies had started life as so many military dictatorships, the spoils of a successful general, devoid of legitimacy and reliant on a mercenary army and the self-interest of the Greek-Macedonian city-dwellers whose ruling status over and economic exploitation of the natives depended on them. Those kings were absolute, and as they established themselves they obtained a sort of traditional authority among the native population, immemorially accustomed to absolutism; while the Greek ruling stratum began, as is usual in such circumstances, to accommodate its glib casuistry to its *dolce vita* and to invent a suitable ideology for it, that is, a farrago of fawning *apologia* in which the monarch is represented (and 'proved' to be) 'living law', or even more, a saviour (*soter*) and 'divine', the object of cult and worship like other gods and (in Asia) with his own high priest. (In Egypt the Ptolemies had, as far as the native population was concerned, slipped into the place of the divine pharaoh.)[1] If one were to summarize the novel features in Hellenistic monarchy they would come down to these: a hereditary Greek bureaucracy (the 'friends'), a military basis in a mercenary army, an absolutism justified by the king being law incarnate, with a perfected 'divine' status and more efficient, expert, and hence ruthless economic exploitation of the native population than the previous rulers had been capable of. For the rest, they went about the immemorial Greek business of making war upon their neighbours, somewhat mitigated in the third/second centuries by several novelties in resolving inter-city disputes by arbitration.

Fascinating it is, but the history of the Hellenistic world, with its bewildering reversals of alliances and endless wars, is far too long for even a synopsis. From our point of view it embraces four main themes: the economic and political decline of the Greek independent city-states; the breakup of Alexander's Macedonian-Persian empire into three successor empires, which later became further fragmented into kingdoms in Asia Minor and Iran; the concomitant rise of the leagues and of Macedonia in mainland Greece; and their final swallowing up by Rome. All that can be offered here is a brief chronological list of the main events. (Some of these will be picked up further in what follows.)

CHRONOLOGY

The End of the Polis, *and the Formation and Destruction of the Leagues,* c.380–164 BC

380–320 BC	DECLINE OF THE POLIS
	Differentiation and specialization of magistrates' duties. Supplementation of the citizen armies by mercenaries. Revival of tyrannies, founded on mercenary troops
300–200	Mainland economy in full decline
261	Athens's Laurion silver-mines exhausted, end of silver currency, slave revolts in Athens
250	Only 800 Spartiate full citizens remain in Sparta, 262–241 Agis IV, 241–222 Cleomenes III try to redistribute land and recreate a neo-Spartan citizenry

---

[1] A. R. Burn, *The Living Past of Greece* (Herbert Press, London, 1981), 351.

321–248	BREAKUP OF ALEXANDER'S EMPIRE
323	Death of Alexander
321–283	His successors divide the Empire into three:
	(a) Antigonids in Macedonia
	(b) Ptolemies in Egypt
	(c) Seleucids in Asia
	Three-cornered wars for possession of Greece and Aegean
*c.*280	The Seleucid provinces in parts of Asia Minor become independent kingdoms, e.g. Armenia, Cappadocia, Pontus, Bithynia, Pergamon
250	Bactria independent
248	Parthian Empire in Media and Fars. Seleucid Empire reduced to Syria and western Asia Minor

447–146	THE LEAGUES
447–386	First *Boeotian League*
379–338	Second *Boeotian League*
367–189	*Aetolian League*
367	Foundation of Aetolian League
280–279	Smashes Gaul invasion. Military heyday
197	Ally of Rome, defeating Macedonia at Cynoscephalae
189	A Roman protectorate
381–146	*Achaean League*
381	Collapse of first Achaean League
251	Aratos joins the League. Reforms
213	Death of Aratos
146	Conquered by Rome. The sack of Corinth

338–146	THE END OF INDEPENDENT GREECE
338	Macedonia crushes Athens at Chaeronea
322	On death of Alexander Athens revolts; defeated. Macedonians occupy city, impose an oligarchy
266	Athens and Sparta defeated by Macedonia. Second Macedonian occupation of Athens, which ceases to be a power
222	Cleomenes III of Sparta defeated by Achaean League and Macedon
196	Rome defeats Macedonia at Cynoscephalae
189	Rome defeats Aetolian League, reduces it to vassal status
146	Rome defeats Achaean League. Sack of Corinth. Macedonia and Greece become a Roman province

1. LEAGUES AND CONFEDERACIES

The sovereign *polis* ruled by its active citizens was, as the last chapter showed, a revolutionary innovation in the history of government. But some scholars have claimed two more political 'firsts' for the Greeks— 'federalism' and 'representative government'.[2]

Analytically a clear distinction exists between a bonding of individual states and a state composed of parts which are themselves states or are organized like them. The former is a bonding of 'simple' states, the latter a 'composite state'. Ancient Greece knew several types of the former. The most ancient are the *amphictyonies* (unions of 'dwellers around'). Their primary aim was the religious one of providing festivals and sacrifices at a central shrine. Such *amphictyonies* include the Boeotian at Onchestos, the Pan-Ionian in Asia Minor, the one at Delos, and *par excellence*, the one at Delphi, which is also the best documented.

Another such kind of league was the *symmachy*; an alliance for war and foreign policy designed to last permanently or, at least, for a long time. From the sixth century symmachies arose which were dominated by one particular member-state and these are usually styled 'Leagues' in our (English-language) histories of Greece: for example, the Peloponnesian League dominated by Sparta and the First ('Delian') and the Second Athenian Leagues which were prominent in the Peloponnesian War and immediately afterward. They relied on treaties between a hegemonic state and the others drawn up for an unlimited time but terminable upon notice. Effectively they were military alliances for defence and offence. There was no common citizenship but over time the hegemon became supreme and the other members lost their autonomy, so that the League turned into a form of empire. There was no common Assembly but sometimes, as in Sparta's Peloponnesian League and Athens's Leagues, there was a Council.

But elsewhere and at other times there existed in Greece, side by side with the sovereign *poleis*, a class of composite states—what in the second century BC was being described as a *sympoliteia* (so, 'sympolities'). How far these were what we nowadays call *federal* states—and hence how far the Greeks were again innovators—will be the question addressed after describing the more prominent of these polities, to wit, the Boeotian, the Aetolian, and the Achaean 'Leagues'. And the very first point to notice is that all such, not just

[2] Cf. in particular the pioneer study of E. A. Freeman, *History of Federal Government from the Foundation of the Achaian League to the Disruption of the United States*, vol. 1, *General Introduction: History of the Greek Federations* (Macmillan, London, 1863) and then J. A. O. Larsen, *Representative Government in Greek and Roman History* (University of California Press, Berkeley, 1955) and *Greek Federal States* (Clarendon Press, Oxford, 1961; repr. 1967, 1968).

the ones named, originate in backward, tribal, or lately tribal conditions, in the polities called *ethne*, and not between fully established sovereign *poleis*. The Boeotian sympolity, in its first form, seems to date from 447 BC, and was dissolved in 386. Boeotia was a bucolic region of yeoman-farmers, and apart from the rivals Thebes and Orchomenos, its cities were very small. Here there was a clear distinction between two sets of authorities: those of the cities and those of Boeotia as a whole. The cities controlled their own domestic affairs, but for state-wide purposes—chiefly warfare— all Boeotia was divided into eleven constituencies. The cities 'controlled' the representation of a number of these constituencies (or even just a fraction of one) according (one surmises) to their populations. Thus Thebes initially controlled two—later three; Orchomenos, two; others perhaps only one-third part. Each constituency sent one official (significantly called a *boeotarch*) to the state-wide Council, along with sixty councillors, so that Boeotia as a whole was ruled—irrespective of specific services only, of course—by eleven such executives and 660 councillors. This is a very large Council (though we can remember that the Athenian *boulé* numbered 500). Perhaps for this reason, there was no popular Assembly. This all-Boeotian Council operated on the same plan as the city governments. It was divided into *four*, each presiding for one quarter of the year, and this body held final and complete authority on the matters within its competence, which were principally foreign affairs and war. Each constituency was expected to supply 100 cavalry and 1,000 hoplites to the army and likewise, when required, equal contributions to the central treasury. The eleven units also sent men in equal numbers to make up the panels of judges and jurors for an all-Boeotian judiciary. This composite state proved successful for sixty years but fell apart in 386 through the intense rivalry of its cities compounded by the internal struggles between their rival democratic and oligarchic factions. The reformed League, in 379, was dominated by Thebes. Dissolved in 338, when it was reformed for the third time it was to give equal weight to all its components. But, mysteriously, its energies were spent. Such reputation as it acquired was one of excessive wining and dining.

The Aetolian and Achaean Leagues were much more important, both militarily and politically. The former was the older, but both attained international importance at roughly the same time, between c.290 and 250 BC, after which, sometimes in alliance but usually in deadly rivalry, they swayed the destinies of central and southern Greece.

The mountain country of Aetolia was one of the *ethnos* states of Greece inhabited by tribes and sub-tribes who at mid-fifth century were described by Thucydides in Freeman's colourful paraphrase as

The most backward portion of the Hellenic race; their language was difficult to understand, and their greatest tribe, the Eurytanes, were said to retain the barbarous habit of eating raw meat. Above all, they still lived in detached and unfortified villages. . . . we may distinguish the Aetolian League, as a union of districts and cantons, from the Achaian League which was so essentially an union of cities.[3]

Its people had an evil reputation among their fellow Greeks. Freeman (devoted as he was to the rival Achaea) describes them variously as 'an assemblage of robbers and pirates, the common enemies of Greece and of mankind',[4] or 'an assemblage of mountain hordes, brave, united among themselves and patriotic in a narrow sense, but rude, boastful, rapacious and utterly reckless of the rights of others'.[5] These Aetolians always displayed massive tribal solidarity against their enemies and were ferocious soldiers. Their greatest hour struck in 280–279, when a horde of barbaric Gauls smashed their way through a weakened Macedonia and threatened Delphi. They had not reckoned on tribesmen as savage as they were! 'The whole barbaric host was destroyed or took refuge in Asia . . .'.[6]

By this date the institutions of the League were well defined. The state consisted of its 'cities' (such as they were) and, unusually, of cantons intermediate between them and the central government. It is probable—but not certain—that these cantons each had their own *boulé* headed by its *boularch*.[7] It existed for one purpose only: war. The League had not one power base but two: one at Thermos but the other at Delphi, and this gave it control of the whole Delphic amphictyony. The hundreds of documents preserved at Delphi show how, through such control, the League absorbed much of central Greece. Now, these absorbed states did not become constituents of the League but its subject territory, somewhat like the take-over of the *contada* by the Italian cities in the thirteenth and fourteenth centuries AD.

Leaving the *contada*, then, as subject territory to the League proper; its cities enjoyed complete independence in everything unrelated to this. The all-Aetolian Assembly of male citizens met twice a year and it is pretty clear that this was, simply, the army itself: a general mobilization, in fact. This Assembly took the final decision on peace or war and it also elected the chief magistrates: the generals, cavalry commander, and a secretary of state (later there were two). These officers carried out their duties in conjunction with the Council—or *synedrion*—which effectively represented the citizenry between the six-monthly meetings of the Assembly. To this Council each constituent city nominated councillors in proportion to its population. As

[3] Freeman, *History of the Greek Federations*, 326.   [4] Ibid. 323.   [5] Ibid. 325.
[6] Ibid. 228.   [7] Larsen, *Greek Federal States*, 197.

it was probably a thousand-strong, it established a committee of *apocleti* ('select-men') who deliberated in secret. The general and the other officials would consult it whenever they were concerned about exceeding their proper authority. In the Assembly, the voting went by heads, not by cities. When war-funds were required, however, it was the cities who collected and paid them in.[8]

The Aetolian League conducted itself as a prime military power, some-times for and sometimes against Macedonia. In 197 BC it helped the Roman interventionists to their decisive defeat of Macedonia at Cynoscephalae but then, dissatisfied with their treatment, turned on them (the Achaean League taking the Romans' part). Their forces failed to hold Thermopylae and so brought on the defeat of their chief ally, Antiochus of Syria, by Rome. In 189 BC the Romans forced a treaty on them which restricted the League to Aetolian territory alone and took control of its foreign relations. Most importantly, it lost control of Delphi and through this the most important focus of propaganda throughout the Greek world. Its independence was effectively at an end.

The origins of the Achaean League are obscure. It seems to have emerged in the fourth century BC as a *symmachy* to protect its original twelve cities from pirates—probably Aetolians—from across the Corinthian gulf. It fell apart after the death of Alexander (323) and its history really dates from its reconstitution in 280 when four of the original members reunited and were soon joined by another six. These towns were tiny. The history of the League as an important power only begins with Aratos, a well-known man who made himself tyrant of Sicyon and then, for self-protection, took it into the Achaean League in 257. From then to the end of his life Aratos effectively ruled the League. Its constitution provided for an annually elected *strategos*, eligible for re-election only after one year: but Aratos was elected *strategos* in every alternate year and in the intervening years was usually able to name his successor. He died in 213 BC, so his 'reign' lasted thirty-eight years.

The accession of Sicyon—no mean city—was only a beginning. Corinth, Megara, Troizen, and Epidaurus soon joined and the League's territory stretched from the Ionian to the Aegean and embraced the vital Corinthian peninsula.

As in Aetolia, the principal function of the League government was diplomacy and defence. The cities ran other affairs on their own and through their own institutions. As before, this League government consisted of the Assembly, the Council, and the magistrates. There can be no doubt

---

[8] Larsen, *Greek Federal States*, 212.

that the Assembly was comparatively weak and the magistracy very powerful, nor that it was filled by the wealthy and patrician families. Distances
alone made it hard for the poorer citizens to take off the time necessary to
attend Assemblies, while the absence of stipends for the magistracy reinforced the natural tendency for office to reside with the better off. Freeman
denies the League the character of an oligarchy and prefers to call it an
aristocracy, but the narrowness and the élite character of the ruling group is
only emphasized by his distinction: 'birth, wealth and official position'
counted.[9]

The Assembly seems, at least up to 217–200, to have met twice a year. It
elected the magistrates. However, after this date, so we are told, a decree laid
down that 'the many' were not to be summoned to the Assembly except
when issues relating to alliances and war were on the agenda. In such cases
the meeting went on for three days and the Council and magistrates met
jointly with the Assemblymen. If there were no Assembly meetings in a
given year, who then elected the magistrates? It 'seems'[10] that the Council
did so, but there is no direct evidence for this.

The Assembly was open to all citizens aged 30 and over. Voting was by
cities, not by heads. Some say that their votes were weighted according to
their population (so, Larsen), others that all cities were equal.[11] Its debates
and decisions were influenced very powerfully by the magistrates and the
Council. This was made up of city delegations proportionate to population
and voting too was by cities. Its importance was very great, since it had to
act as a surrogate for the Assembly except for the rare and brief occasions
when this came together. This is precisely why Larsen claims that the
League was effectively a 'representative' system of government.[12]

The magistrates were the most influential single element of the system.
Their tenure was annual but, unlike Athens, there was no way to remove
them until their terms expired. The most important magistrate was the
strategos, for he was commander-in-chief and, effectively, the director of the
League's foreign policy. The *strategos* initiated business in the Council and
Assembly, undertook ambassadorial negotiations, and took charge of all
League business up to the point where it was placed before the Assembly (or
Council as the case might be). Assisting him was a *hipparch* (the cavalry
commander) and a *hypostrategos*, that is, second-in-command. The *demiourgoi*
acted as so many ministers, presiding over both the Council and the
Assembly and responsible for putting forward government resolutions and

[9] Freeman, *History of the Greek Federations*, 264.
[10] Larsen, *Greek Federal States*, 220.
[11] Freeman, *History of the Greek Federations*, and cf. Larsen, *Greek Federal States*, 270.
[12] See pp. 380–1 below.

conducting diplomatic and civil business. Together, certain other elected officials, the chief officers, and the *demiourgoi* formed a closed council, the *synarchia*, which acted as the 'cabinet' of the League government.

Finally, a League judiciary took cognizance of cases arising out of League legislation. A common citizenship was extended throughout the League, in the sense of *isopoliteia*—any citizen of any constituent city could acquire citizen rights, for example, intermarriages or owning property, when he moved to another city. League laws (as against city legislation) included wartax, the minting of coins, and military service. The courts had jurisdiction over these laws and related matters like treason.

All matters other than defence, foreign affairs, and those just listed, were handled by the cities through their own magistrates and in their own way. The cities assessed their wartax, collected it, and paid it in. It was they who were told to levy contingents for the League army. There can be no doubt that the Achaean citizen was subject to two different sets of authorities: one in so far as he was a citizen of Achaea and the other as a citizen of a particular city; the first covering one particular list of matters and the second another and different list; the former uniform throughout the land, the latter particular to the individual city. Many regard these features as necessary and sufficient to connote a federation and a federal form of government. Is this so? And, relatedly, is Larsen correct in calling the Achaean League (*not* the Aetolian) a 'representative' form of government (as opposed to the 'direct' democracy of, say, Athens)? These questions can only be answered after a definition of these two terms.

It might be remarked at the outset that the Greeks referred to all such Leagues as *koina*, and *koinon* is a very general term: it connotes any associations of persons—from a state down to two or three persons—practising a common act or engaged in a particular pursuit. They did not differentiate further. They did not possess the concepts of what we call 'federal' and 'federalism'. In contrast to *koine*, these are not terms of art but highly technical ones. Although some political scientists differ on detail, they do broadly agree on what they mean. The most distinguished scholar of the Greek 'Leagues' entitled his book *Greek Federal States*, though he qualified that expression in the individual chapters by calling them 'confederacies'.[13] Larsen defines a federal state as simply one where 'there is a local citizenship in the smaller communities as well as a joint or federal citizenship and in which the citizens are under the jurisdiction of both the federal and local authorities'.[14] But this would equally apply to unitary states (states in which final authority rests in one central body or set of bodies), since most of

---

[13] Larsen, *Greek Federal States*. [14] Ibid., p. xv.

them divide powers between themselves and a number of elected local bodies, and give these a very free hand.

As I understand the term—and certainly as I shall use it in the remainder of this book—'federalism' is a juristic concept. Its characteristics are these:

1. the duties of government generally are divided between two sets of bodies, one exercising its functions over the entire territory, the others exercising their functions inside their own local borders;
2. juridically, these governing bodies are of equal status, in that neither may lawfully invade the other's jurisdiction nor override or veto its operations, nor abolish it, without its own consent;
3. each formulates and executes its decisions through its own organs neither of which—unless by mutual free agreement—may invade or obstruct or override those of the other.

Certain corollaries follow. If we enlarge on (3) above, it carries the implication that the central government acts *directly* on the population of the state *through its own agencies* with no reference to the governments of the constituent regional authorities. Within its own limited range of duties it can act as freely as if these simply did not exist. This is what Hamilton in the *Federalist Papers*, no. 9, called 'consolidation' of the state, and it is by this particularity that the 1787 constitution of the USA made all previous definitions of federalism (which were based on earlier composite states) obsolete.

By contrast there are composite states where the central government represents only the governments of the constituent members, its actions are entrusted to them, and its power resides solely in telling them what to do, for example, to raise troops, levy taxes. Composite governments of this kind are *not* federal but *confederate* states; if you prefer the word, *confederacies*.[15]

How then should we describe the Boeotian, Aetolian, and Achaean Leagues? All possessed the split-level government necessary to qualify as candidates for federalism. As to the second necessary condition, that the central and the local governments be of co-equal status, and that neither might invade the jurisdiction of the other or abolish it, such evidence as we have suggests that this too was fulfilled, in practice at any rate. Nothing leads us to believe that the central authorities as much as thought of suppressing the cities, and reciprocally the furthest that dissenting cities

---

[15] So much for the *juridical* relationship in federal (or confederate) states; but law and practice may diverge. For a unitary state may in practice concede more power to its regional units than a federal constitution concedes to its components. Here we have shifted from the consideration of federalism, a juridical term, to *decentralization*—which is *experiential*: quite a different matter. Centralization or decentralization is measurable, and what it measures is how much *discretion* the central authority allows to its local authorities.

went against the central authority was to try to secede. The critical condition is the third—whether the central authority acted *directly* on the entire
body of citizens through its own agents. To this might be coupled, too, the
question of the scope of the central government's authority. In the first
Boeotian League,[16] the 'pan-Boeotian' (central) government lay in the
Council and magistrates, and these were appointed to represent each of
the eleven constituencies, that is, the local constituent bodies; the judges too
were appointed to represent each of them, and, finally, it was these constituencies who levied the military contingents. This suggests that it was a
confederate and not a federal type of state. This tentative conclusion is about
as far as our rather slender information will allow.

The Aetolian League, however, presents a more difficult case because we
do not know how voting proceeded in the Council. Was it by cities or by
heads? We do know three things, however: the *cities* levied the necessary
taxation (in proportion to their population) and forwarded it to the central
authority; they retained enough control over their warriors to go off on
freebooting expeditions without central consent,[17] and they minted their
own coins, though possibly under some central supervision.[18] There was *no
central machinery of administration* bearing directly on all citizens, only that of
the cities. On the other hand the Assembly voted by heads and not by cities,
the host was led by the *strategos* of the entire community, and the magistrates
conducted diplomacy. What was the sovereign body, effectively? The central
government's powers were confined exclusively to war and diplomacy and
what was the Assembly but the host, the people-in-arms? We have here a
group of small or even tiny settlements all running their affairs in their
traditional fashion, but uniting under common leadership and taking counsel together for purposes of making war and peace. This has more in
common with early *ethnos* states like the Macedonian kingdom or the
kingdom of Epirus than with anything so sophisticated as 'federalism'
implies.

On the Achaean League, where the evidence is more abundant, the verdict
seems to me to be quite clear. The Assembly voted by cities, not heads. So
did the Council. The cities minted their own coins, they provided the
contingents, and they levied and forwarded the wartaxes. The League is
manifestly a confederation.

So, did the Greeks invent 'federalism?' As we have said, they had no
specific term for this concept: they could use the term *koinon* as we have
already explained, and failing that, *sympoliteia*, best translated in this context

---

[16] See p. 373 above.   [17] Freeman, *History of the Greek Federations*.
[18] Larsen, *Greek Federal States*.

as 'composite state'. Unless there is a corpus of political literature that has not come down to us, it seems that they did not develop any explicatory theory relating to this class of states. Now, while it is true that the fact often precedes the concept, it is equally true that concepts arise once people become self-conscious of what they are doing or creating. On the hypothesis that the Greeks had nothing to say on the subject, rather than that their thought has not survived, the fact that the Greeks were not thus conscious suggests to me that their composite states were too unadvanced for them to dwell on their particularity. They did *not invent* federalism—that had to wait for 2,000 years. They did invent confederacy—but in a fit of absence of mind.

I turn now to the second claim—that they also invented 'representative government'. As far as concerns these three confederations the concept only applies, in any strict sense, to Boeotia which had no primary Assembly of the whole people, so that its Council *was* the governing body. But of Achaea, where the Assembly met, even if infrequently, or Aetolia, where it met only twice a year, Larsen, the great proponent of this notion that the Greeks and Romans (and not Teutonic barbarians as commonly maintained) 'invented' representative government, can only say that these are 'essentially' representative.[19] However, Larsen also prays in aid the Thessalian confederacy after 194 BC, and the short-lived Macedonian republics set up by the Romans in 167 BC, none of which had primary Assemblies.[20]

Larsen's examples suggest prima facie that he conceives republics as falling into two classes. There are those with Assemblies and Councils and those with only Councils. The former are direct governments and the latter representative governments. This definition of 'representative government' is not very helpful because it begs the question of who, when, and through what methods of selection people are to be regarded as 'representative'. All he says is: 'Representative government . . . is simply government in which the ultimate decisions on important questions are made by representatives acting for their constituents having authority to make such decisions according to their own judgement.'[21]

But the notion of 'representative' is much richer than this. A Council may be representative in the sense that it reflects the social profile of its electorate, but unrepresentative in that it does not reflect their opinions; or reflects their opinions but not their interests as objectively defined. There is an essential difference between these Greek experiments in 'representative

---

[19] Larsen, *Representative Government*, 86. For the concept of 'Representation' see Bk. III, Pt. 3, Ch. 9 below.   [20] Larsen, *Greek Federal States*, 102–3.

[21] Larsen, *Representative Government*, 1.

government' which, I would suggest, is more properly designated as something like 'delegated' or 'vicarious' government, and the medieval notion from which—apart from Larsen—everybody has believed our modern theory and practice of representation to have been derived. For what we can fairly surmise is that the councillors sat in the Council rather as ambassadors do at the UN or the EU Council of Ministers—to watch over and to assert the interests of their respective countries.

This is not at all the notion which underlay medieval representation, namely, that the representative reflects the entirety of his community and that the council of such representatives represents the entire 'community of the realm'. The sense is well picked up in the medieval English expression for assenting to jury trial *ponit se super patriam*: the freemen of the jury are assumed to be the *patria* in microcosm. The representatives are not, to quote Burke, 'a Congress of rival ambassadors from discrete and hostile interests, which interests each must maintain as an agent and advocate against other agents as advocates, but the deliberative assembly of *one* nation, with *one* interest, that of the whole'.[22] The mere fact that, as far as we know, the 'representatives' on the Achaean Council voted as *cities* and not by heads negates any belief that this notion was extant in Antiquity.

The reason for these flickers of vicarious government, which Larsen has so painstakingly recovered from Greek history is, to my mind, quite simply stated. It may be remarked that the institutions he speaks of appear, when at all (which is not very often) on one or other of two occasions. First, they may appear at a point where the primeval kingly or subsequent oligarchic rulership was being somewhat broadened to include wider classes, but before an Assembly of the whole citizen body had been given a final voice; something like Athens between, say, Solon and Cleisthenes. *Or*, they appear in just the reverse situation, that is, when, as in later Greece, the wealthy and well born restricted the jurisdiction and frequency of Assembly meetings in order to consolidate their own power. In the confederations we have been discussing the sheer physical difficulty of holding frequent Assemblies acted as an alternative reason (as in Boeotia) or as an additional and reinforcing one (as in Aetolia and Achaea). Larsen has seized upon a frozen moment in time, half-way along the road from oligarchy to democracy, or half-way on the road back from democracy to oligarchy, to claim that the Greeks had invented a principled institution; whereas all they had done was to hit on an expedient.

[22] Burke, 'Letter to the Electors of Bristol' (1774).

2. THE END OF *DEMOKRATIA*

It is easy to account for the extinction of the *autonomia*—the sovereign independence of the *polis*—but less so for the disappearance of their *demokratia*. The *poleis* lost independence because they were too militarily weak to assert it against the Hellenistic monarchies or the Roman Republic. Beaten twice, in the Lamian (322 BC) and the Chremonidean (262) wars, Athens could no longer assert herself. The Spartan revival under Cleomenes III (227–222) and Nabis (207–192) was suppressed by the Achaean–Macedonian alliance, then by the Achaean–Roman alliance. The Aetolian League was subdued by Rome in 189 BC, and the Achaean in 147–6 when Corinth was destroyed. As for the Hellenistic kingdoms in Asia, though the kings lavishly and oftentimes proclaimed *autonomia* for their cities, it meant 'always, that the city is not the absolute master of its foreign policy'.[23]

The *demokratia* is another matter. The sovereignty of the Assembly was virtually extinct by the end of the second century AD but that is, after all, four centuries later than the general extinction of the cities' independence. Such scattered evidence as survives suggests it died hard, Athenian democracy in particular. After defeating Athens in 322, the Macedonians turned the democracy into an oligarchy.[24] In 318 this citizen body was somewhat extended but between 307 and 261 the government changed hands and the constitution was altered no less than seven times; on three occasions the city had risen only to be suppressed again. The cycle only ended when, in 86 BC, Sulla sacked Athens. In brief, the democracy was extinguished by foreign military occupation and its support for the local oligarchs. It is tempting to generalize from this to explain the fate of the democracy all through the Greek cities of the mainland but this would be mistaken, for the Hellenistic dynasts and the Roman Republic often found that support for the local democratic faction served their interests better than the oligarchy did. For their part, the latter often saw their self-interest in opposing Rome and asserting their independence.[25] There can be no doubt that in some of the Greek cities in Asia the Assemblies were still flourishing in Cicero's time. In his *Pro Flacco* oration (59 BC) he excoriates them for voting by show of hands, for their rashness and tumult, for being composed of 'dregs of the state', and the like.[26]

The fatal change came with the Roman Principate, because henceforward Rome was universally dominant and no longer had to court democratic factions in the interest of her foreign policy. She could now impose herself.

---

[23] de Sainte Croix, *Class Struggle*, 303, quoting Bikerman.   [24] See p. 367 above.
[25] Briscoe, in Finley, *Studies*, 53–73.   [26] de Sainte Croix, *Class Struggle*, 310.

Rome's rulers had always been an oligarchy and the sentiments of her ruling classes did not change under the Principate. As we know, the cities had always harboured oligarchic factions anxious to destroy the democracy and successful in doing so with foreign support; just as the support of Athens had enabled democratic factions to seize and retain power in the fifth century BC. Now Rome leaned heavily in the oligarch's interest, and bit by bit the democracy was stifled.

I say 'bit by bit' because the process consisted of a change here, tinkering there, until, over time, a complete revolution had come about and what used to be a democracy was now an oligarchy: a city-government wholly in the hands of a Council of extremely wealthy local property owners, the 'Curial' class[27] who, in collusion with the metropolitan authority at Rome, formed the governing class of the later Roman Empire.[28] Of these piecemeal changes, four main types can be distinguished. The most self-explanatory one is pressure, discreet or sometimes brutal, exerted on the magistrates or the Council to manipulate the Assemblies. A second one was, effectively, a kind of mass bribery: the wealthy candidates for office—magistracies or councillorships—bought popularity by liturgies, for example, lavish endowments for baths, gymnasia, choral performances and the like. Sainte Croix quotes Aristotle (*Politics*) to suggest that the linking of liturgies to magistracies was a deliberately planned policy to subvert the democracy.[29] But elsewhere in the *Politics* Aristotle actually advises democrats to prevent the rich 'from undertaking expensive and yet useless public services' like choruses or torch-races if they want to preserve the democracy,[30] so it is not necessary to suppose a deliberate plot.

Another invidious set of changes concerned magistrates. In some cases a property qualification was introduced. In others, magistracies might be held for long terms, or even for life. In some, councils were re-formed on the pattern of the Roman Senate—that is, the Council was composed of ex-magistrates and office-holders.

Finally, the popular lawcourts (or juries)—the *dikasteries*—withered away. The steps by which this occurred are not easy to trace; but they are related to the creeping extension of Roman law and with it of Roman courts side-by-side with the local ones.

Any one of these changes would be apt to restrict a democracy, but taken together and over time they entirely changed its character. Simultaneously, the Roman Peace had emptied life of its most dramatic issues: peace or war, tyranny or republic were no longer debated locally but decided elsewhere.

---

[27] Cf. the senatorial class of the Roman Republic, pp. 427–8 below.   [28] Cf. below.
[29] de Sainte Croix, *Class Struggle*, 305   [30] *Politics*, 1309A

So, by the end of the second century AD, in most of the Greek cities of the Roman Empire Assemblies no longer met, or if they did, had no great role to play.

As the *practice* of democracy sank out of existence, however, the claim to *being* a democracy soared into the limelight. One of those semantic shifts had occurred by which a word or term which originally had a specific—and portentous—signification was now made more and more widely applicable. Such semantic shifts obscure—often deliberately—the shift in practice that has occurred. For instance, today 'democracy' is universally held up to be desirable, indispensable, imperative. Hence no regime would dare to call itself anything else. So we have seen a row of military dictators calling their regimes respectively 'presidential democracy', 'basic democracy', 'guided democracy', 'organic democracy', 'selective democracy', or 'neo-democracy'.[31] In identical fashion did the stranglers of ancient democracy behave. As we have already mentioned, by the third and second century BC, *demokratia* was applied to any republican form however oligarchical; by the end of the first century BC it was used to designate the highly oligarchical Republic of Rome; and by the second century AD it is actually used to designate the rule of the Roman Emperor![32] Glorified in word, it had become emptied in content; the two processes marched in tandem.

---

[31] S. E. Finer, *Patrons, Clients and the State in the Work of Pareto and at the Present Day* (Proceedings of the Accademia dei Lincei, no. 9; Rome, 1975), 220–1.

[32] de Sainte Croix, *Class Struggle*, 322–3.

4

The Roman Republic

*I*t must seem redundant, perhaps impertinent even, to seek to justify a place for Rome in a general history of government. Western Europe is the heir to Rome. Rome was the carrier of the culture of the Hellenic world which she incorporated: of Christianity and of Roman law which have shaped western values up to our day; the planter of a civilization of cities, disseminator of the Romance family of languages, author of a literature including political history that, along with the Greek and the Hebrew, provided European scholars, writers, and statesmen with a common stock of historical experience and models until the nineteenth century . . . and so we could go on, recalling the Romans' feats in engineering, in road-building, in monumental architecture, and the like.

To praise Rome as the progenitor of the West is, of course, not the same thing as praising the Roman Empire in itself. What we have inherited is what we have selected, which means what we have not chosen to discard. And in appraising the Roman Empire in itself scholars are far from unanimous. Herder and Hegel, Marx and Weber, Toynbee and Spengler in their different ways and for different reasons have all been antipathetic.

This chapter, however, is not concerned with the empire but with the Republic, and it is not self-evident that this deserves a separate place in the history of government, apart from the reason that it preceded and gave birth to the Empire, which is true but trivial. There are in fact four good reasons at least for treating it in its own right. First, the durability of this form of government, from 509 to 27 BC or (preferably, as will be argued below) to 82 BC; next, its success in homogenizing very disparate linguistic, ethnic, and cultural societies in Italy and forming something from them highly akin to what we would think of today as a national community; thirdly, a terrible dynamic which enabled it to conquer the Mediterranean world and most of Western Europe; but, finally, because the form of government, the polity, under which (Polybius said 'by which') all those things were achieved, was singular and made an innovation.

In certain and quite fundamental respects the Roman Republic does indeed present analogies with the Greek *polis*. It was (until it became something more) a city-state. That is to say it was an *urbs*, a physical city. It was also a community of citizens in the sense already described

Fig. 2.4.1 Roman Forum-type polity

for the Greek *poleis*.[1] It even possessed an analogous tripartite set of organs—magistrates, Council, and popular Assembly(ies)—so that it, like most of the *poleis*, rested to some degree on a *popular* basis. Hence it too belongs, as they belong, to that type of government I have styled the Forum type.[2] But unlike democratic Athens, where the nobility were ultimately extruded, Roman political processes were a dialectical interchange between an aristocracy of service in which heredity played a large part and the populace, carried on without a professional priesthood, without a professional bureaucracy, and without a professional army. The diagram of this governmental type[3] can be expressed simply as in Figure 2.4.1.

This Roman state never would be or ever aspired to being a *democracy*. It was a *res publica*, corresponding to what the Greeks would have called a *politeia*. The peculiarity of Roman political life lies precisely in that the ruling aristocracy[4] was saddled, irrevocably, with popular assemblies whose attributes included legislation and electing the magistrates. For the greater part of its existence, then, the central political process in the Republic was the one by which the nobility tried to lead, court, or manipulate the

---

[1] See pp. 317, 324, 335 above.   [2] See p. 43 ff. above.   [3] See Cf. pp. 54–5 above.
[4] This, and the term 'nobility', which I use synonymously in the text, need defining. Scholars differ on this matter. R. Syme, *Roman Revolution* (OUP, Oxford, 1939; paperback edn. 1960) confines 'noble' to 'men whose ancestors in the direct male line had held the consulship or magistracies of an earlier period equal or higher in dignity'. P. A. Brunt, *The Fall of the Roman Republic and Related Essays* (Clarendon Press, Oxford, 1988), 5, would extend this to include the descendants of praetors and *curule aediles*. K. Hopkins, (*Death and Renewal*, Sociological Studies in Roman History, 2 (CUP, Cambridge, 1983), 32, specifically rejects the term 'nobility': it reminds him too much of the attributes of the nobility of post-feudal Europe, notably in that it implied inherited right or a prediction of guaranteed success. He also widens the rest of the definition by defining 'aristocracy and aristocratic' as 'several upper layers of Roman society including (a) the political élite made up of high officers of state and leading senators, (b) lesser senators, and (c) a body of wealthy citizens but at any one time not engaged in élite politics'. It is best to think of 'aristocrats' in terms of their possession of landed wealth and the fact that 'their claims to civil and military office were often based on the status and deeds of their ancestors' (a definition I owe to Fergus Millar, the Camden Professor of Ancient History, University of Oxford).

Assemblies. Successful till 133 BC, the process began to break down and finally collapsed.

Rome was a *civitas*, from *civis*, a citizen, and meaning therefore a community of citizens. Two comments ought to be made. These citizens are participants, sharers, in the privileges and equally the obligations of the *civitas*, just as in the Greek cities. For instance, when subsidized grain rations were provided in 133 BC, they were available to all citizens, rich as well as poor, in their equal capacity of citizenship.

But although citizens enjoyed a standard juridical status their material condition was highly unequal. From earliest times, under the kings, a narrow group of families stood above the rest in status. They were aristocrats by virtue of their wealth and large estates. Though membership changed over time, this aristocracy as such was to persist until the collapse of the Republic in the second half of the first century BC. Furthermore its collapse and that of the Republic are the two sides of the same coin: the Republic was ruled by the aristocracy and the aristocracy was what made it a Republic. Rome was an *oligarchy* of aristocratic families competing for the major magistracies (the consulship and praetorship) and operating on the principle of 'Buggins's turn'—a certain *de facto* rotation between them, dependent on their attractiveness to the popular Assembly which elected them. As for this latter, it took for granted that the candidates should be this aristocrat or another. Wholly unlike Athenians, Romans deferred to rank and wealth, and willingly accepted the role of subordinates and retainers.

Rome was an oligarchy, then, but of a special kind, where 'membership of the governing body depends on a property qualification' and which Aristotle calls *timocracy*.[5] The juridical equality and the material inequality of citizens were reconciled through the *census*, which divided the citizen body into classes according to how much property they owned. All rights and obligations flowed from this classification and the Republic's stability and social cohesion down to 133 BC derived from this. Except in direst emergency only the propertied served as soldiers or (when necessary) paid a *tributum* to support the *res publica* (never required after 167 BC). *Proletarii* and other propertyless persons were exempt. In return, these persons—who made up the great majority of the population—had limited voting power in that popular Assembly (the *comitia centuriata*) which elected the consuls and the praetors, while among the propertied classes themselves the upper two (the minority of the relatively rich) could, if united, outvote all the rest. In the Assembly that passed legislation (the *comitia tributa*), however, there

---

[5] Aristotle, *Nicomachaean Ethics*, 1160; *timema* is the Greek word for 'property qualification'.

were no such property distinctions. This censitary allocation of rights and obligations was eroded during the second century BC and the traditional (and logical) balance of political power decayed along with it.

Concomitantly, the relationship between *urbs* and *civitas* was also eroded. The Romans were far more liberal in granting citizenship than any Greek city and the number of Roman citizens became much too large for them ever to be able to meet all together and most citizens lived too far from the city, moreover, to make them particularly care to do so. As this distancing took place, *civitas Romana* became less and less a cosy local community and increasingly an abstract juridical entity, a corporation of privileged males, including many living far beyond the city walls, ultimately all over Italy.

What is true for Italy after 89 BC (when citizenship was granted to the Italians) is true, *a fortiori*, for the Roman provinces. By the close of the Republic, Rome had reached something very near its utmost limit of territorial conquest. This vast area of 1,600,000 square miles[6] consisted of so many provinces. Each was administered, policed, and judged by a Roman magistrate—a pro-consul or a pro-praetor—but the choice of these governors, redress for grievances they had caused, and the final decision of policy affecting the province, were all made by political processes in and at the city of Rome. The inhabitants of a province—unless fortuitously they were Roman citizens—had no say in the matter at all. They were being governed through the institutions of a city-state.

While all such particulars serve to delineate certain idiosyncrasies in the Roman version of city-state, they are marginal compared to the original and important departure the Romans made from previous polities, and this was the nature of their constitution. Hitherto, in the ancient empires of Egypt, Mesopotamia, or Persia, in the monarchy of ancient Israel, and also in the Athenian democracy, the authority to take a final decision lay with some individual organ or person. But the Roman Republican constitution threw up one device after another as time moved on, to *prevent* supreme power resting in the hands of one man or body of men. What the Romans did was to invent, *avant la lettre*, the device of *checks and balances*. This is what I propose now to explain.[7]

1. THE COUNTRY AND THE PEOPLE

When Prince Metternich said that Italy was 'a mere geographical expression', his remark correctly reflected 1,300 years of political disunity there.

---

[6] E. Gibbon, *The Decline and Fall of The Roman Empire* (David Campbell, London, 1993–4), ch. 1.

[7] See Section 4.1 below in this chapter, and Bk. III, Ch. 7, 'The Republican Alternative'.

Since geography did not prevent disunity, then it cannot be the explanation for Rome's success in unifying the country, especially when we consider the terrain in the early centuries after Rome was founded (traditionally, in 753 BC). Romans were Latins and Latins were a minority people. Rome was just one of many such Latin cities and by no means the largest or most civilized. On the contrary. Civilization in Italy resided in the Greek cities of the south, notably Tarentum and Syracuse, and in the Etruscan cities of present-day Tuscany whose sway, at that time, reached as far north as the Po valley and as far south as Capua, indeed for a time, Rome itself. It was from them that the city learned the basic civilized skills: the alphabet, architecture, and military organization. But there were many other peoples in Italy besides. These peoples had diverse histories and cultures and their languages were different; Etruscan was not even Indo-European. Furthermore, from the fifth century a new people (but speaking an Indo-European language) moved across the eastern Alps into the Po valley pushing the Etruscans before them. They were those Celts whom the Romans called Gauls, and by the fourth century they were in complete possession of the plain of Lombardy ('Cisalpine Gaul').

Originally an unwalled township (or perhaps two twin townships) built of wood and thatch, Rome commanded the Tiber traffic down to the sea, and the route between the Etruscan cities in the north and their vassal territories in Campania to the south. It lay in a fertile plain along with numerous other Latin townships. Together they formed what Greeks would have called an *amphictyony* (a league for worship at a common shrine) and also, it seems, a military *symmachy*.[8] This was the *Latin League*. However, this plain was girdled by covetous and aggressive mountain tribes.

Rome was quite small. Two-and-a-half centuries after its traditional founding date, in 509 BC, its territory would still fit into a square measuring a mere sixteen miles on each side (though it was able to field an army of 4,000 men). Although its territory and citizen body expanded greatly in the next three centuries, as it incorporated conquered lands and populations, the direction of the *civitas* always vested in its aristocratic class, made up of the original patricians and also the wealthiest 'plebeians'.[9] This continuity is what explains what 'Roman' came to mean. It ceased to be an ethnic designation. It was more a status and a state of mind—*Romanitas*.[10] 'Roman' became dissociated from a specific ethnic group and came to connote

[8] See above, p. 372.
[9] 'Plebeian' did not mean low class, but simply anyone who was not by birth a 'patrician'.
[10] Not an ancient term.

citizens of the *civitas* irrespective of their ethnic origin and, at the same time, a specific way of life. What I now say about the 'Romans' (up to the middle of the second century, when matters began to change) is to be understood in this context.

The earliest Romans were rough, homespun farmers. Not till the earlier third century BC were true coins minted at Rome—silver imitations of the Greek ones, designed for trade with the Greek cities of the *mezzogiorno*.[11] At that date, too, the city was still no larger than present-day Oxford (between 100,000 and 150,000 inhabitants).

From the earliest beginnings Roman society was unequal and authoritarian. It was dominated by noble clans—the *gentes*—each comprising many families, and the family was to some extent a microcosm of the early *civitas*, in as much as the father (the *paterfamilias*) held the power of life and death over all his household—even his sons. While the vast majority of the citizens were smallholders—yeoman farmers—the *gentes* were wealthy and powerful landowners and from the outset they controlled followings of retainers. Some of these were true clients (*clientes*), but this term is used in many twentieth-century texts to extend to all manner of followers. To the citizens of classical Greece this was the absolute contradiction of individual *eleutheria*, but the acceptance of personal dependency as normal and indeed as right and proper runs through all Roman social and political life, and is central to understanding it.

As in most, if not indeed all, Indo-European tribal societies, and specifically like the Greek, the primeval Roman polity consisted of a *rex*, a Council of Elders, and the Assembly of warriors. Even when the *rex* was replaced by two elected magistrates, the consuls (in 509 BC), and the Council was named the Senate, or *patres conscripti* (the heads of noble clans and families), and the Assembly of warriors developed into the various *comitia*, the primeval threefold structure persisted and, like the Greek, Roman constitutional history turns on the changing forces, powers, and interrelationships of the three organs. The great difference between the Greek and the Roman experience stems from that popular acceptance of dependency among the Romans we have just been alluding to. The original Patriciate slowly and very grudgingly came to share its authority, and along with the wealthy commoners form a new patrician–plebeian *nobilitas*, no less arrogant than before. And there, till about 134 BC, the matter stopped: the populace certainly demanded that limits should be put on the arbitrary use of the nobility's authority, but never demanded (as in Athens) to exercise the

[11] D. Dudley, *Roman Society* (Penguin, Harmondsworth, 1975), 43.

initiative in policy. However, their votes were required in all matters, including legislation, peace and war, and the founding of colonies.

Patriarchal, authoritarian, unequal, and oligarchical, Roman society was also intensely militaristic (in one scholar's view even more so than Sparta).[12] Up to the First Punic War (264–240 BC) the Romans fought on Italian soil, partly in self-defence against the surrounding hill tribes, partly out of land-hunger. It would be hard to find more than one or two single years in the entire span going back to the foundation of the Republic in 509 BC when an army was not campaigning somewhere or other. In these wars every able-bodied citizen between the ages of 17 and 60 was liable to be called up to fight under the consuls they had elected in the *comitia centuriata* which was, in principle, the stand-to of the city-in-arms. Once in the field, they accepted an iron discipline under the unchallengeable authority of the consul (his *imperium*) to mete out the death penalty. The Roman *populus*, even when war-weariness set in in the mid-second century, never objected in principle: its grievances related to fair treatment in respect to the levy, discharge, and the like. Except on two or three occasions, war itself was never voted down in the *comitia centuriata*, which had the last say on this matter.[13]

We of today would call the Romans intensely *superstitious*, though they would have used the term 'religious'. Their earliest ideas of the supernatural saw nature as so many *numina*: forces which were embodied in stones, streams, or trees, or alternatively in processes such as the germination of grain. Their original deities were either insubstantial or natural objects, and it was from the Etruscans that they are said to have learned to think of and portray them in human shape, notably in their triad of Jupiter, Juno, and Minerva. Much later (in the third and second centuries BC) they assimilated this triad and their other gods to the Greek pantheon. Lacking a mythology of their own, they adapted the legends about those Greek gods. These *numina*—or gods—were awesome powers, and *religio* in its secondary and technical sense consisted in placating them by ritual prayer and sacrifice. To this the Romans superadded something they had borrowed from Etruscan religion—the belief that by reciting the correct spells and formulae it was possible to divine the way the gods would react by way of omens and auguries. Developed Roman religion became, above all else, a network of elaborate spells, incantations, rituals, and sacrifices, each to be performed with perfect exactitude (and repeated over and over again, if necessary), if they were to be effective. So arose a civic *ius divinum* (divine law) stipulating

---

[12] M. Crawford, *The Roman Republic* (Fontana/Collins, London, 1978), 52; K. Hopkins, *Conquerors and Slaves* (CUP, Cambridge, 1978), ch. 1.   [13] Below, for the occasions, pp. 415–16.

what must be done or avoided. It consisted simply of cult acts and an elaborate religious calendar with no moral element whatsoever. The priests (*flamines*) of Jupiter, Juno, and Minerva go back to ancient times. Both the individual 'priestly' offices such as *rex sacrorum* and Jupiter's priest (the *flamen dialis*) and membership of the priestly 'colleges' (e.g. augurs, *pontifices*) were monopolized by prominent public figures; in short, by the same ruling oligarchy that held all the magistracies, filled the Senate, and commanded the armies. Given an extremely superstitious population, and a religious code which prescribed some ritual for practically every public act, this cultic monopoly immensely enhanced the power of the ruling class.

Since religion did not prescribe morality, what did? The answer is tradition: what the Romans called the *mos maiorum*, the 'customs of our forefathers'.

The great majority of the early Romans were farmers. Amongst the earliest names, many reflect this agricultural ambience: Piso, from 'grind' (corn); Fabius, Lentulus, Cicero, deriving from the words for 'bean', 'lentil', 'chick-pea'. Their virtues were the bucolic ones. Emotional excesses, wearing one's heart upon one's sleeve, were frowned on. Not for them the Greek flights of fancy. They were stubborn, narrow, and rather unsympathetic characters. In their military role the atmosphere of camp and *agger* and, in the civilian, the nature of the Roman *familia*, reinforced their qualities of honesty, thrift, endurance, and above all, discipline and obedience. Among them the values that were most esteemed were *gravitas*, *pietas*, and *simplicitas* (or *frugalitas*). *Gravitas* signifies sobriety, judiciousness, prudence; *pietas*—an untranslatable term—means dutifulness, acting rightly or properly; *simplicitas* signified a plain frugal way of living.

The common people's ready acceptance of authority is one reason why they made such good soldiers. Involved as they were in the life of the city chiefly through their military service, but also through the popular assemblies, they felt an intensely close community with their fellows. Not for nothing had they adopted the name of *Quirites*, a word deriving from *co-viri* and hence 'companions' (just as the Welsh tribesmen called themselves *Cymri*, i.e. 'the comrades'). It was this sense of solidarity which over a very long period blunted the social conflicts of rich and poor, patrician and plebeian, and enabled them to be resolved, not without friction to be sure, but without the bloodshed and proscription so common to the Greek cities. The ruling class was arrogant, prideful, and ambitious to a degree, but it too embraced *gravitas*, *pietas*, and *simplicitas* and to a large extent lived up to these ideals and set an example to the commonalty. But these same nobles had another code as well; the code that dictated not how one should behave but the ends for which their lives were to be lived. And these were *competitive*

ideals: *virtus*—manliness, guts, spunk; *gloria*—glory; *honor*—unpaid public
office; and *fama*—a great reputation and name. These objectives, though
noble in themselves, contained the seeds of faction and, like the dragons'
teeth that Jason sowed, they came in the end to sprout armed men.

2. CHRONOLOGY

Our interest must be confined to the two matters of Rome's constitutional
evolution and her territorial expansion. The two processes went on simultaneously and interacted, but for purposes of exposition the two chronologies will be dealt with separately.

2.1. *Constitutional Developments*

A tiny city of eight miles by six, Rome began life under the rule of its king,
who was advised by a Council of Elders (*patres* or 'fathers'), and where the
decisions on war and peace were voted in the Assembly of warriors. It
evolved into a republic where the former royal functions and duties—
religious, judicial, military—were exercised by a number of separate magistracies, the Council of *patres* had become a Senate made up of ex-magistrates
with a life-tenure, and there was more than the one primordial kind of
popular Assembly. In the earliest period the magistracies—and the membership of the Senate—may have been in the hands of a narrow clique of
ancient families, the patricians, but a great social struggle was waged as to
who might belong to this exclusive circle. Under the kings it was perhaps a
group of fifty heads of great clans. Their exclusivity was subsequently
challenged by the wealthiest of the commoners (*plebeians, plebs*) who used
the grievances of the poorer commonalty to further their ambitions. The
struggle between patricians and plebeians is known as the struggle of the
Orders. Having broken into the Patriciate, the wealthier plebeians fused
with it as an enlarged oligarchy while the poorer plebeians reacted by
forcing the creation of an office (the Tribunate) that would circumscribe
the absolute power entrusted to the (elected) magistrates. The form taken
by the struggle of the Orders was quite unlike the sanguinary contests in the
Greek cities. Its characteristic was the 'secession' of the plebeians: these
formed the warrior host and, effectively, they staged a sit-down strike, by
withdrawing from their magistrates and commanders (or threatening to do
so) until their demands were met.

2.2 *Territorial Expansion*

CHRONOLOGY

A. *Traditional Dates*

753 BC	Traditional date of founding of the city (*ab urbe conditum*, AUC)
578–535	Servius Tullius
535–509	Tarquinius Superbus
509	The aristocracy *expel* Tarquin. The Republic (*res publica*)
	Senate: 300 *patres conscripti*
	Assembly: *comitia centuriata*
	Two *consuls* co-wielding ex-royal *imperium*
494	First secession of the plebs. Patricians concede them the right, in the *concilium plebis*, to elect representative *tribunes*, empowered to interdict *imperium* in city limits, and lend *auxilium* to aggrieved citizens
445	Intermarriage of patricians and plebeians permitted
434?	Introduction of the census and its classes. Consuls' tasks now almost entirely military
336	One of the consulships thrown open to plebeians
312	Appointments to Senate entrusted to censors
287	Final secession of the plebs. The *Lex Hortensia* gives resolutions of the *plebis concilium* the force of law without Senate approval. Hence, *plebiscitum* ('plebiscite')

B. *Territorial Expansion*

pre-509	Rome member of Latin League of cities
509	Expulsion of the Tarquins, establishment of independence
496	Victory over Latin League at Lake Regillus
494	*Foedus Cassianum*. Rome now leads the League: shares booty with members in their common wars
418	Completion of conquest of encircling hill tribes: Sabines, Volsci, Aequi
396	Conquest of Veii
340	Rome breaks up the Latin League: each city tied exclusively to Rome, forbidden treaty relationships with any others
294	Completion of conquest of Appenine tribes: Roman territory stretches across central Italy from sea to sea
275	Victory at Beneventum over Pyrrhus of Epirus, incorporation of southern Italy

This Roman organization of Italy (save for the Po valley, still dominated by the Celtic Gaul tribesmen), was quite unlike any of the Greek Leagues or *symmachies*. It comprised a network of cities, all politically isolated from one another but each in direct—and subordinate—relationship with Rome. Rome did not give them what Greeks would have called *isopoliteia*, but granted different citizenship-ratings to their respective inhabitants on a graded scale: full-citizen, citizen without the vote, or just 'ally' (*socius*). She had complete control over their manpower (the Allies could muster some 600,000 men to the Romans' 270,000).

270	Subjugation of Bruttium, Calabria completed
261–241	First Punic (Carthaginian) War
241	Rome victorious, incorporates Sicily
238	Seizes Corsica and Sardinia from Carthage
229	First Illyrian war against pirates
225	Gauls confederate and invade Roman Italy. Beaten off
219	Second Illyrian war against pirates, protectorate over east coast of the Adriatic
219	Second Punic war. Hannibal invades, sweeping victories
202	Hannibal's final defeat at Zama. Carthage cedes Spain to Rome
200	Conquest of the Gauls and Po valley completed
168	Macedonia conquered and split into four states. Aetolian League subjugated
146	Third Punic war. Destruction and razing of Carthage
146	Final defeat of Macedonia and the Achaean League. Corinth sacked. Greece and Macedonia become Roman provinces

3. THE CONSTITUTION OF THE MIDDLE REPUBLIC

Rome was now mistress of virtually all the Mediterranean seaboard. The sea had become *Mare Nostrum*, a Roman lake. Mommsen, commenting on this moment, says:

To the later generations who survived the storms of revolution, the period after the Hannibalic war appeared the golden age of Rome, and Cato seemed the model of the Roman statesman . . . During no epoch did the Roman constitution remain formally so stable as in the period from the Sicilian to the Third Macedonian War and for a generation beyond it; but the stability of the constitution was here, as everywhere, not a sign of the health of the state, but a token of incipient sickness and the harbinger of revolution.[14]

For the wars, the conquests, and the spoils were so immense—and so sudden (all more or less within a lifetime)—that they wrought a traumatic change in the conditions that had generated and sustained the ancient Roman constitution. Thereupon the once solid foundation turned to quicksand and the various parts of the edifice poised on it lost their carefully contrived balance and fell apart in ruins.

[14] T. Mommsen, *The History of Rome*, trans. W. P. Dickson, 4 vols. (London, 1911), ii. 340.

Rome was governed through its magistrates, its Council, and its popular Assembl[ies]. The magistrates were elected by the Assembly for a year only (except for the censors, who were elected every five years for an eighteen-month term), and decided on peace and war and passed legislation, while the Senate was a purely consultative body. This, however, is only the beginning of the affair. This simple outline was enormously complicated by four factors. They were, first, the right of superior or equal magistrates to veto one another's actions; the existence of more than one popular Assembly; the latters' inability to act except on the initiative of a magistrate; and finally, the existence of certain officers, the tribunes, who acted as a kind of wild card in their right to bring all public business to a stop, on the one hand, and to initiate legislation, on the other. In the Athenian constitution there was, in the last resort, a clear line of authority: magistrates rotate annually either by lot or by vote, the Council prepares matters for the Assembly, and the Assembly debates and decides. It is a monistic constitution. The Roman constitution is decidedly not monistic. To execute any act of government, a number of magistrates or other organs must concur. It is a collegiate type of government, and of that special type where any component of the college can cancel the action of the others. It is, in brief, the first case in this history of a government of 'checks and balances'. The completest example of this kind in the contemporary world is the government of the United States, though divided up on quite different principles and far less complicated than the Roman. But this American Constitution was enacted all of a piece on rational principles (which have been set out with clarity in the *Federalist Papers*), whereas the Roman constitution was a patchwork that had evolved piecemeal over many centuries as a consequence of social convulsions. Every time a political crisis had to be met some new device was incorporated into the existing constitution to head it off. The Roman Republic 'invented' checks and balances unwittingly, never on the basis of a defined and acknowledged principle. In so far as they discerned *any* principle underlying their system of government, it was another and quite different one—the 'mixed constitution'. Polybius (*Histories*, Book VI) followed by Cicero (*De Republica; De Legibus*) saw the spirit and the strength of the Roman constitution deriving from its admixture of a monarchical element (the consuls), an aristocratic one (the Senate), and a popular one (the *comitia*, or popular assemblies). Supposedly, it benefited from the virtues associated with each individual element while suffering none of their vices. This model was to be carried forward into European history.[15]

---

[15] For this, see Bk. III, Ch. 7, Pt. 6: 'The Legacy of the Medieval Republics'.

3.1. *The Formal Constitution, 134 BC*

What follows is a summary of the strict law of the constitution. Even in outline it is highly confusing. The essential thing is to grasp how self-stultifying it was. The best way to make the point seems to be to proceed in two stages. The first will be the merest outline of the way the various organs of government related to one another; the second will be little more than a sequence of notes giving further and better particulars about the various organs.

The Roman Republic described itself as the *Magistratus, Senatus, Populusque Romanus*, the Magistrates, Senate, and People of Rome (SPQR). It comprised, first: twenty-two high magistracies, to wit, two censors, two consuls, six to eight praetors, eight quaestors, and four aediles. Very briefly—and broadly—the censors made up the lists of the citizenry, the consuls led the armies, the praetors organized justice, the quaestors were treasurers, and the aediles the curators of the streets, buildings, and markets of the city. In addition, there were ten officers who were not strictly speaking magistrates, but the tribunes of the people. Their peculiar powers will be outlined below. The Republic also possessed three different popular assemblies. Finally, it possessed a Senate.

In strict law the Senate was an advisory body. It consisted of ex-magistrates, nominated for life by the two censors. It met only when a magistrate (a consul or, by now, a praetor)[16] convened it, spoke only to the matter he put to it, and issued its opinions as a *Senatus consultum*. For my *present* (i.e. formal) purposes, therefore, it is a supernumerary body and we can turn away from it to the organs that possessed positive—and nega-tive—*powers*. In an over-tidy and highly simplified delineation, we can conceive of the constitution as consisting of two systems, or, better, a system and an anti-system, for the one was designed to check and control the other. And each of these two systems itself consisted of two counter-checking authorities, a popular assembly on the one hand and on the other a set of elected officers. To complicate the model further, these officers, if of superior or equal rank, could veto one another. The first system comprised the twenty-two elected magistrates and *two* popular assemblies—the *comitia centuriata* and the *comitia tributa*. The second and 'anti-system' comprised the ten elected tribunes and the *concilium plebis*.

Let us first sketch out the former system and begin with its popular assemblies. Each was made up of the identical full body of citizens but they

---

[16] And also a Tribunal.

were organized for voting purposes in quite different ways. The *comitia centuriata* was originally simply the citizen-army, and so it was organized into voting units called 'centuries', which were themselves stratified into five census classes according to wealth; and their voting power was weighted proportionately. The *comitia tributa* was made up of exactly the same individuals, but they were organized for voting purposes into thirty-five artificial 'tribes', which were in effect constituencies of equal voting weight, so that it was more democratic than the *centuriata*. Broadly speaking, the *centuriata* elected the magistrates who would rule the Republic for the next year; what legislative powers it possessed were residual. The *tributa*, on the other hand decided on peace and war and passed laws. These sweeping and conclusive powers suggest that Rome must have been a democracy—until one considers the constraints within which they had to operate. For they lacked all power to initiate. They could meet only if summoned by the appropriate magistrate. They could vote only on the matter he put before them and then without debate or amendment, answering simply *Yes* or *No*.[17] And, in matters of legislation, though this was not constitutionally necessary, they were normally expected to have the prior assent of the Senate.

Once they had elected the magistrates, the citizens were in their power. These magistrates form the antithetical pole in the system, standing as they do against the powers of the Assemblies. Two of the colleges of magistrates, the quaestors and aediles, were recognized by the Romans as junior or inferior magistracies. But one cannot overestimate the authority and power of the senior magistracies, namely, the two consuls and the six praetors (and even more so, those of dictators—but this office lapsed after 202 BC). For, whereas quaestors and aediles possessed full power to implement and execute the powers inside their sphere of competence, just as one might expect of any executive official, the consuls and praetors also possessed the *imperium*. This was, in its original conception, the very plenitude of executive power: it carried with it not just the power to exercise jurisdiction and to enforce it (*coercitio*), but also the power of life and death over citizens.

This sweeping *imperium*, then, at first blush suggests that the (hypothetical) 'democracy' of the popular assemblies was no more than a licence to be tyrannized over once they had elected consuls and praetors. Again, this was not the way of it. To begin with, the magistrates (censors alone excepted) served for one year only and could then face charges. More importantly, a citizen condemned on a capital charge could appeal from the magistrate's order of execution to the popular assemblies as long as the

---

[17] But issues might well have been aired publicly in a *contio*, see below, pp. 420–1.

offence had taken place within the city limits (*domi*). His appeal was enforceable, via the action of another magistrate applying what was called the *provocatio ad populum*, an appeal to the people. (By 134 BC it seems as though this was applicable only to high political charges, ordinary criminal cases being handled, with due process of law, in the courts.) But the most effective of all the restraints on the *imperium* lay in the power of any superior magistrate to veto actions of a more junior magistrate (e.g. consul over quaestor over aediles) and *also* to veto any proposed action of his coequal colleagues, so that one consul could (and not infrequently did) cancel the proposed action of the other.

Taken all together, the organs and arrangements outlined added up to a complete constitution. It was, however, further complicated by being joined up with another system of institutions. This might fairly be described, in view of its origins and its objectives, as a 'counter-constitution'. It was the outcome of the struggle between the patrician lineages which had dominated public life since 509 BC, and the plebeians whom they excluded from office and who suffered on this account. This new set of organs and arrangements was conceived and continued to develop, up to the Hortensian Law of 287 BC, as a check and indeed as an alternative to the original patrician constitution. And inside it we again find two organs in juxtaposition and tension—officers on the one hand, a popular Assembly on the other.

This popular Assembly was the *concilium plebis*. It was organized for voting purposes identically to the *comitia tributa*, that is to say into the thirty-five 'tribal' constituencies. The only differences in composition were these. It could be convened and was presided over only by those magistrates it had the right to elect—tribunes or aediles—and it excluded citizens of patrician descent. These were very few in number at any time and became less and less significant politically as time went by. So, in effect, the *concilium plebis* was a replica of the *comitia tributa* except that it was convenable only by its 'own' officers. However, it did not have the same powers as the *comitia tributa* or the *centuriata*. *Qua concilium plebs*, it lacked any judicial powers (whereas the *comita tributa* could hear cases and impose fines), nor could it vote on peace and war. On the other hand the *concilium plebis* could vote a resolution into law irrespective of the Senate. A resolution of this kind was termed a *plebis scitum*, and its binding quality over the entire community was definitively acknowledged in the Hortensian Law. The *plebis scitum*, the product of tribune and *concilium plebis*, was the first of the two ways in which this 'anti-constitution' linked up with the patrician constitution.

The second way lay via the powers of the senior of the two groups of magistracies it elected: the tribunes of the plebs. By this date they numbered ten. Their principal power can be visualized as the very antithesis of the sweeping scope of the *imperium*. For, just as this was the very plenitude of executive power, so the tribunes possessed the very plenitude of what we might think of as a countervailing or anti-power. They could veto and so bring to a halt any or every action of any or every agency—magistrates', Senates', or Assemblies'—in the Republic.[18] If they wished they could, and on several occasions did, halt the raising of the army. But here again, a striking symmetry with the *imperium* came into play. The *imperium* of the consuls and praetors was checked, as we saw, by the ability of any one such magistrate to veto the actions of a colleague. Similarly the 'anti-*imperium*' of the tribunes was checked by the ability of any one of the ten tribunes to veto the veto of his colleague!

Uncluttered by detail as it is, the preceding sketch offers no more than guide-lines—perhaps over-firm ones—to the Republic's constitution. These guide-lines can now be supplemented—and complicated—by some detail.

3.1.1 THE MAGISTRACIES

The Censors

The censors, of whom there were two at any time, were unusual in two respects. To begin with, they were elected every *five* years (not annually like all other magistrates), though they had to get through their duties in their initial eighteen-month period. Secondly, although they did not possess the *imperium* they were the most prestigious magistrates of all. Only ex-consuls were eligible, and to become a censor was the climax of the political career (the *cursus honorum*, which will be set out later). Of all the magistrates who might take the auguries (the *auspices*) he was the foremost; he wore the purple stripe in his toga; and unlike any other magistrates, he was buried in the full purple that had once distinguished the kings.

The two censors did not explicitly possess the right to veto one another. Implicitly they did, however, since 'the Censorship', like, say, the humbler Aedileship or any other magistracy in Rome, was regarded as a single and indivisible jurisdiction held concurrently by a number of incumbents, each of whom could exercise it in the name of the others unless they dissented. To act at all, the censors had to act jointly.

As their name suggests, the primary function of the censors was to take the census of the citizen body. Today's usage must not fool us. This was not

---

[18] With two exceptions: (1) dictator, but as we observed this office was in abeyance after 202 BC, i.e. at the time we are considering; and (2) the censors. But censors did not possess *imperium*.

just a simple business of counting. It was highly political, for the censors alone decided who was slave and who free, who had citizen rights and who not. Next, as we have seen, Roman citizens were divided (as in Athens, see above) into census classes defined by wealth each of which had different voting weight in the *centuriata*, and it was the censors who assigned citizens to a particular census class. Most other citizen roles also depended on these census classes. In this way, the censors had it in their power to block political careers, and this is why they alone, post-312 BC, drew up the list of which ex-magistrates (or others) were to be appointed as senators, left out those who were not, and could also exclude some who had been enrolled previously. Such selection and occasional de-selection implied some prior power to disqualify ex-magistrates from the Senate, in brief, the power to disqualify undesirables. Failure in their public duties, shady private morals, abuse of magisterial power were all duly noted by them as supervisors of morals (from which our current usage of *censure* and *censorious* derives). It is easy to see, therefore, how the simple primordial power to count, and register or not-register, could expand into one affecting the life-chances of every single inhabitant, and why proud ex-magistrates could only endure such a scrutiny of their private morals when it was conducted by individuals deemed to be of a higher status than themselves.

Finally, the censors could not be held to account for the way they exercised these functions. The only check on arbitrary decisions lay in there being two censors who had to agree. Thus, in making up the list of new senators (the *lectio*), one censor could strike off the names proposed by the other and vice versa, so no single individual could pack the Senate on his own.

It is a sign of the incoherent nature of the Republican executive that, as the burdens of state became too great for the number of magistrates at any one time, the difficulty was surmounted either by increasing the number of individuals holding a magistracy or by creating subordinate magistracies (e.g. praetors) or by prolongation of a magistracy (e.g. proconsuls, pro-praetors) or, finally by shifting certain duties around from over-burdened magistracies to those with more time to spare, even if such reapportioned duties were unrelated to the normal work of those magistracies. It was in this last way that the censors were made responsible for the administration of public property. As in Athens, Rome did this by farming it to contractors making competitive bids, and the censors were the magistrates who conducted the auctions. However, in these respects the censors seem to have come under the supervision and control of the Senate; on one attested occasion, even the popular Assembly. But whether this was strict law or simply convention is not known.[19]

The Consuls

The Consulship, the highest of the Offices with *imperium*, was the greatest magistracy in the Republic, even if the Censorship was the more prestigious; the years were dated by the consuls' names. If we forgot that the powers of all the magistracies could be blocked by any equal or superior magistrates, we could be forgiven for thinking that the consuls were, for a year, kings of Rome. Indeed, the Consulship had been introduced precisely in order to fill the functions of the kings, the Tarquins, who had been expelled and replaced by annually elected officers. It was the consuls who convoked the Senate, consulted it, issued its decrees—or their own—in the form of *edicts*, and who convoked the *comitia centuriata* and the *comitia tributa*. They represented the Republic to foreign heads of state. Although they had abandoned jurisdiction in financial affairs and many areas of their criminal jurisdiction were passing to specially appointed bodies, in wartime—and war was almost perpetual—they were the commanders-in-chief. As such they possessed the *imperium* in its narrower sense—effectively, the power of summary jurisdiction and capital punishment. Hence a distinction was drawn between the consular *imperium* inside the city limits and outside it. Inside, it was whittled down bit by bit, as we have seen, by the 'appeal to the People' and by the tribunes' veto-power, for example. But outside the city it applied in its plenitude. Wherever the consul walked beyond the city limits, he was, so to speak, a martial-law administrator.

In practice, both consuls were often in the field at the same time. If both were commanding in the same theatre of war (the *provincia*), the command alternated from day to day, but by now there was nearly always more than one army in the field and one consul commanded the legions in one theatre and his colleague did the like elsewhere. Between 264 and 146 BC the most common arrangement was for one consul to have Italy as his *provincia* and the other a foreign theatre like Greece or Macedon. It is important to stress that the Senate had the power to decide which the two *provincia* for the year would be, and that the consuls were then appointed to these two spheres by the primitive device of casting lots.

The Consulship could be checked in other ways than those already mentioned. Consuls could face charges before the Assemblies after their

---

[19] Cf. A. H. J. Greenidge, *Roman Public Life* (Macmillan, London, 1930), 231 and esp. n. 3 citing Polybius, Livy, and Appian.

annual terms had expired; and ten years had to elapse before an ex-consul was re-eligible. But it was the supreme prize in political life and the family and descendants of a consul became *nobilis*—noble—by that fact.

The Praetors

Praetors were introduced as auxiliary to the consuls. Inferior in rank, they too held the *imperium* and in Rome they took over the consuls' judicial functions. When the consuls were absent from the city they could, if the Senate permitted, carry out such consular duties as calling up the levy and the like. As holders of the *imperium* they could, where necessary, command armies too. Their specialized functions lay in the field of the civil law. Originally there were two praetors but others were appointed as Rome's territories expanded, so that by 134 BC there were six. Like the consuls, the praetors cast lots for which *provincia* each should take over; two of the *provinciae* (spheres of operations) were in Rome, the others in Italy and overseas (the 'Provinces'). The two who acted in the city—and they were forbidden by law to be absent for more than ten days—were respectively the *urban* and the *aliens'* praetors (*praetor urbanus, praetor peregrinus*), the former concerned with citizens, the latter with all cases involving foreigners. These praetors administered the judicial processes and through their *imperium* could enforce decisions by ordering anybody concerned in the case to contract an obligation, for instance, or deem some action they had per-formed as null and non-existent. But they not only administered the legal processes—they also made the law. The *peregrinus* did this by issuing *formulae*. A formula was a conditional sentence such as, 'if the accused has done such and such then condemn him to the following penalty, but, if not, acquit him—'. The judge (*iudex*), by his determination, changed this conditional sentence into a categorical one. The *praetor urbanus*, on taking office, issued an *edict* which glossed the written law: thus he might lay down that 'in the following circumstances I will compel payment: or I will demand an oath'. In principle, these edicts ran only for the praetor's annual term, but each new incumbent received his predecessor's edicts and made only slight modifications. It was by successive layers of such edicts that Roman jurisprudence was built up. The majority of the praetors of each year, however, spent it commanding armies and governing *provinciae*.

The Aediles

There were two pairs of aediles. They both formed part of the same college of magistrates and had identical functions, but were elected by different popular assemblies and had different legal status. The first were called plebeian aediles, and the latter curule aediles; strictly speaking, the former were not magistrates (and hence were ineligible for appointment to the Senate). The two plebeian aediles were the subordinates of the tribunes of the plebs, and like them were elected as part of the plebeian counter-constitution, in the *concilium plebis*. They had to be of plebeian extraction. The curule aediles were created later as a patrician riposte. They belonged in alternate years to the plebeian and the patrician Orders respectively and they were elected by the *comitia tributa*. As such they were magistrates, not just officers, and consequently eligible for appointment to the Senate. All this goes back to the centuries-long struggle of the patrician nobility to retain their grip on the state against the plebeian intruders, and is of no further consequence, for by this time the functions and powers of these four officers were the same. Briefly: they took care of the material needs of the city. They looked after the safety, repair, and cleanliness of the streets and buildings, controlled the water supply, supervised the markets and fixed prices, and saw to it that the city was supplied with corn. They were also responsible for seeing that the various games were provided. In practice, this came to mean that they subsidized or even provided them at their own expense. So the curule aedileship was an excellent post (though highly expensive) for distributing patronage and winning popularity in the election to the higher-ranking quaestorship.

The Quaestor

There were now eight quaestors, delegates of those magistrates with *imperium*. Their chief duties were now financial. They held the keys of the Treasury and kept the state papers and archives. They collected the revenue from the *publicani* who farmed the taxes and public lands, and conducted sales of public goods such as public lands or war booty.

Outside the city, a quaestor with chiefly financial responsibility was assigned to each consul or praetor who took up a military command, later to the pro-consuls or pro-praetors also.

The Tribunes of the Plebs

Tribunes had now acquired both negative and positive powers. The first gave them the right and indeed the duty of offering *auxilium*—assistance—to any plebeian aggrieved by the act of a magistrate and suspending the same by his veto—his *intercessio*. His word *intercedo* nullified a magistrate's action. This power was valid only inside the city limits, but tribunes were forbidden ever to stay a night outside the walls, and their door had to be open night and day. To back up his word *intercedo*, the tribune possessed the enforcement power (*coercitio*), and could impose it on the very consuls themselves. The consuls could not retaliate, since the person of the tribune was sacrosanct. So tribunes had all the powers of arrest, imprisonment, fines, flogging, and death at their disposal. It flowed from this that the Tribunate developed a jurisdiction, the right to refer a magistrates' offence to the *concilium plebis*. This right was called the *ius agendi cum plebe*. Its practical effect was that the tribunes' right to convoke the *concilium* was unqualified. When it was convoked, no one might interrupt them and thereupon they could fine the offender or demand penalties. As time went by, the tribunes' right to veto extended beyond acts of the magistracy (apart from the censors) to resolutions brought before the Senate or the popular assemblies.

This sweeping negative power was subject to only one check—the counter-veto by another tribune. At the beginning the tribunes numbered only two. By now there were ten. The chances of a magistrate or the senators 'persuading' one of these ten to veto his colleague's original veto were correspondingly much higher.

The *ius agendi cum plebe*—the right to act with the plebs—had a positive as well as a negative aspect and this also had widened over time. The tribune had the right to put resolutions to the *concilium*. However, as the *concilium* was not the *populus* but a mere part of it, these must have had no legal force, so what their effective status was is obscure. But in 287 BC (as already stated), these resolutions of the plebs—the *plebis scita*—were given the full force of law on a par with those of the *comitia*. This power was checked, like the *comitia*'s, by the *concilium*'s lack of the initiative. It could meet only if the tribunes summoned it, could deal only with the resolutions they put to it, and was not permitted to amend or debate but simply to answer *Yes* or *No*. This further enhanced the authority of the tribunes as against that of the plebs.

Though inferior to the magistrates in status—they lacked the *imperium*, the right to take auspices, or to wear the purple stripe of the true magistrate—the power of the tribunes went on to expand still further. For, although not entitled as such to sit as senators, they won the right to attend and put resolutions to the Senate, and by 216 BC even the right to convoke it and to preside. This huge extension of the tribunes' authority was accompanied, however, by a *real* shrinkage of their power and perhaps was made possible for this very reason; for the Tribunate had come to form part of the ruling Senatorial order. But this belongs to the later sections on how the purely formal constitution, as described here, worked in practice.

The Magistrates and Other High Officers—*Generalia*

Clearly the principle of mutual veto is a leading principle of this constitution. It was intended to prevent the concentration of powers into the hands of a single man—the *leitmotiv* of the Republican tradition of Roman historiography.[20]

Yet with a characteristic want of political imagination, the Romans could think of no way to prevent such a concentration of power except to multiply officers and empower them to veto one another. Nowadays the same result can be and is achieved by other self-cancelling devices—increasing the powers of a popular assembly *vis-à-vis* the executive, for instance. In Rome, the only device to check absolute power was to subject it to equal but opposite absolute power in other hands. There was, therefore, no *gradation* of the magistracies' powers, and no flexible response to them. It was an all-or-nothing solution.

One mode of checking absolutism was the principle of annual tenure. This caused practical difficulties as the wars went wider and wider and Rome began to acquire dependent territories. It was met by the practice of extending the tenure of a magistracy: this was the *prorogatio imperii*. The practice began in 326 BC when the *imperium* of the commander who was then besieging Neapolis was prolonged, and then it grew to be a regular practice. By the third century BC custom ordained that extensions should be at the sole discretion of the Senate. By this means the consuls and the praetors could find themselves still exercising *imperium* after the end of their year-long term, in the capacity of pro-consuls and pro-praetors.

A third noteworthy characteristic of the magistracies (and Tribunate) is that they were *honorary*. Holders received expense allowances, to be sure, and in overseas administration these were remarkably generous. A related feature of their honorary nature is that the magistrates, and so on, were administrators, one might even say ministers, but not 'civil servants'. *There was no bureaucracy*: it is essential to note this. Continuity—a feature of bureaucracies—was provided elsewhere, by the Senate, in practice. As for execution and implementation of the magistrates' orders, each of them had a salaried staff of various lictors, scribes, messengers, and heralds. They were not numerous. At this stage, to be sure, the demands on the state were small. Matters like public works, taxation, and handling public property were, as we have noted, contracted out to private individuals by competitive tender.

Finally, the various offices were by now ranged in a status hierarchy. This was the *cursus honorum* and it prescribed the age and pre-conditions for

---

[20] See p. 396 above.

running for any specific public office. It was codified by law in 180 BC. The *cursus* started at age 17, when military service began. The richer citizens, those belonging to the cavalry class (*equites* or 'knights') had to serve ten years before seeking election to the Quaestorship (all others served in the infantry and had to do sixteen years service). The minimum age for the Curule (i.e. magisterial) Aedileship was 36 (34 if you were born patrician); 39 for the Praetorship (37 for the patrician); and 42 for the Consulship (40 for the patrician). It was not necessary to have held the Curule Aedileship or the Tribuneship of the Plebs in this *cursus*, but they were rarely omitted because they gave great opportunities for acquiring popularity: the Aedileship through financing the games and the Tribuneship by taking up popular discontents. The *cursus* ended with the Censorship: and to this only ex-consuls were eligible.

While the *cursus* was confined to the offices listed, it should never be forgotten that other, lesser officials also were elected every year: notably twenty-four military tribunes and twenty-six minor magistracies such as mint-masters and minor judges. The reason for mentioning this is to emphasize how extravagantly competitive the quest for office was among the Roman political élite, and the corollary of this, that the outcome of these elections depended on the *populus* in its *comitia*.

It is reckoned that some eighty offices were up for election every year. To become consul it was necessary to win at least three and possibly five elections spread over fifteen years.[21] It can be deduced, also, that the number of candidates must have exceeded the total of elections required, so that there were losers as well as winners in the race. We know about the winners—but what of the losers? We do not even know how many candidates entered themselves for election. Our evidence confines itself to the winners. It has been proved that many sons of the consular families did not go into politics at all, and many of the men who did were grandsons or related in other ways to one of the great families who formed the inner corps of the Roman political élite.[22] These observations have an important bearing on a crucial matter—to be discussed below—in so far as they demonstrate that, for better or worse, by one method or another, the *comitia* were the arbiters of Roman aristocratic status and power, and secondly, in that they erode the notion that Rome was, *de facto*, ruled by a homogeneous élite (aristocracy or nobility) controlling the masses through a network of patronage relationships.[23]

---

[21] Hopkins, *Death and Renewal*, 113.   [22] Ibid., ch. 2.

[23] F. Millar, 'Political Power in Mid-Republican Rome: *Curia* or *Comitia*?' *Journal of Roman Studies*, 79 (1989), 142.

3.1.2. THE SENATE

As this body's work and *modus operandi* is to be described later on, few words
will be offered here. The Senate by now was 'a self-existent, automatically
constituted body, independent of the magistrates'.[24] Its 300 members, drawn
from the ex-curule magistrates and from men who had done well as lesser
magistrates or in the higher ranks of the army, were nominated, as we have
seen, by the two censors. Senators were appointed for life. They could meet
only if convened by a consul—or, failing him a praetor—or, if the consuls
were absent—by a tribune. A successful resolution was termed a *senatus
consultum*. It had no *legal* validity at all. Yet as will become very clear indeed,
the Senate was in fact the central steering authority of the Republic; but this
was through usage, conventions, and the force of things. In law it was a mere
advisory body. 'It possessed no sphere of its own in which it could act
unassisted by magistrates and people. It could control but it could not usurp
the sovereign powers of the people; it elected no magistrates: it possessed no
legislative authority; it could not declare war or make peace . . .'[25]

3.1.3. THE POPULAR ASSEMBLIES

By this time there were three popular Assemblies, any one of which could
pass laws. They were the *comitia centuriata*, the *comitia tributa*, and the *concilium
plebis*.[26]

The *Comitia Centuriata*

This was convened by the consuls or the praetors. It embraced the entire
citizen body. Its legislative powers, exercised as a *Yes* or *No* vote on proposals
put to it, included declaration of war, treaties of peace or alliance, confirmation of the authority of the censors, and general legislation. Furthermore it elected the consuls, praetors, and censors. Its power to try capital
crimes, however, was in course of being transferred to regular courts—the
quaestiones.

This Assembly originated in the stand-to of the citizen army. In its
primitive form this was organized on the basis of Rome's original three
tribes. Each provided 1,000 infantry and 100 cavalry. This organization was
swept away, traditionally by King Servius Tullius (578–535 BC), and replaced
by a system based on the 'century' as the recruiting unit. The centuries

---

[24] *Encyclopaedia Britannica*, 11th edn. (1910–11), s.v. 'Senate' by A. M. Clay.
[25] Greenidge, *Roman Public Life*, 273.
[26] There was indeed even a fourth, the *comitia curiata*, but its functions were obsolescent by this
time.

were ranked according to the weaponry they disposed of, for as in all citizen armies of the time, the citizen soldier provided his own arms and equipment. The cavalry were ranked first and then came five descending classes of landowners, the last being very poor indeed. Outside these classes altogether were those who owned nothing but their offspring, their *proles*—hence 'proletarians'. The *fabri*—skilled artisans and the like—also formed a group.

The *comitia centuriata* was, then, the 'Assembly of the centuries'. In conformity with its distant military origins, it was summoned by the trumpet, met in the Field of Mars outside the walls, and all stood upright during the proceedings. *Qua* popular Assembly, each century cast a block vote *but* the higher the census class, the more centuries or voting units it contained. The precise details of the divisions of the *centuriata* are very uncertain, but it is believed that the *equites* disposed of eighteen centuries, and their next in line, the Class 1 citizens, are thought to have disposed of seventy, so that together they commanded eighty-eight centuries out of a total of 183, virtually guaranteeing victory to the wealthier classes, and it never lost this social bias.

The *Comitia Tributa*

The *comitia tributa* derives from the word *tribus* (tribe) and it was the 'Tribal' Assembly. These tribes were not based on kinship and lineage any more than those of Cleisthenes in Athens.[27] In 471 BC there had been twenty-one tribes altogether, four 'urban' and seventeen 'rural' ones. They were based on geographical location and all occupied areas in or around the city, close enough to come in and vote. At this stage Rome resembled the classic type of nuclear city-state. From 387 more *tribus* were created bit by bit, always in even numbers. They were formed from Roman occupation of conquered land or the incorporation of existing non-Roman populations. By 241, when this process came to a stop, the final total of thirty-five *tribus* had been created. After that, newly incorporated populations were allocated in communal groups to one or another of these thirty-five *tribus* and, in this process, their geographical coherence was lost and they became notional constituencies. Exactly how, why, and when this Assembly came into being is not known but it could be that it was easier to assemble the *populus* by 'tribes' than by the 183 centuries (just imagine the complication!), and that the Assembly began as an easy alternative way of convening the citizenry for matters not important

[27] See p. 344 above.

enough to warrant convening the centuries. Thus, for instance, the magistrates they elected were the lesser ones, not possessing the *imperium*, they never
had a jurisdiction in capital offences against the state, and so forth.

Now this Assembly was in existence at the time the rebellious plebeians
'seceded'[28] and established their own Assembly, the *concilium plebis*. It too was
convened by 'tribes'. So, in composition—but not in powers—it was
identical with the *comitia tributa* except that it excluded the patricians,
obviously fractionally few in number. As the power of the tribunes waxed,
so did that of the *concilium plebis*. It reached its maximum strength with the
Lex Hortensia of 287 BC.[29] This itself testified to the fact that for practical
purposes it was as representative of the citizenry as the *comitia tributa*.
Henceforth the two are distinguishable only by the formalities. If summoned by a tribune it was the *concilium plebis*, if by a consul the *comitia tributa*,
and the powers it discharged were apportioned accordingly.

The *comitia tributa/concilium plebis* thus became enormously influential,
electing as it did the powerful tribunes and possessing the authority to
legislate. It was, on the surface, more egalitarian than the *comitia centuriata*,
since all its *tribus* had an equal vote, unlike the Census *classes* in the *centuriata*,
but for hundreds of years this equality had been illusory since relatively rich
rural tribes made up of big landowners and their dependents could and did
easily swamp the miserable four votes of the city's poor population. However, this situation was completely reversed once Rome had extended
citizenship throughout Italy and expanded overseas. There were more
country voters, yes—but 'distance, social status and economic resources
must have exerted a fundamental influence in determining which persons
out of the vast number with theoretical voting rights actually came to vote.
It could not be claimed, therefore, that the system created, or even allowed,
an equal opportunity to vote for all citizens.'[30] Also, by this time the new
riches that poured into Rome had led the greater landowners to buy out the
peasant farmers who, dispossessed, moved into the city. But there they seem
to have continued to remain members of their original rural tribes, for this
was based on birthplace and did not change as one moved. These dispossessed farmers, being on the spot, were in an excellent position to vote. So
also were the increasing number of manumitted slaves who, as freedmen,
were entitled to vote. And the four 'urban' tribes were, almost by definition,
made up of the poor and very poor. Thus a city 'proletariat' was formed,

---

[28] See p. 393 above.   [29] See p. 399 above.
[30] F. Millar, 'The Political Character of the Classical Roman Republic, 200–151 BC', *Journal of Roman Studies*, 74 (1984), 17.

with great voting strength in the *comitia tributa/concilium plebis*, which became in fact a representative body of the city's poor.

4. ROMAN CITIZENS AND THE ROMAN 'CONFEDERACY'

In the preceding pages I have several times talked of Roman *citizens*. When Rome was a tiny area, citizenship is readily understandable on the exact analogy of any Greek *polis*. But in 270 BC, when Rome had subordinated all Italy south of the Po valley, how did the city stand in relation to it and how did its citizenry stand? Though a minority among the general Italian population, only Romans, no matter where they lived, could participate in the political processes described *and* moreover they could do so only in the city of Rome. These citizens collectively were the *civitas*: and it was they, acting collectively as the *civitas*, that ruled all other Italians, who—by implication—were, in 270 BC, non-citizens. This must now be explained.

One way to do this is by adopting a very bold simplification, which has the merits of being nearly right, but also of having great explanatory power.[31] In the first phase of Rome's expansion she was land-hungry, manpower-hungry, and concerned to build a defensive ring against the Gauls in the north and the Samnites in the south-east. What most conformed to these aims was outright annexation of territory, whose inhabitants willy-nilly became Roman citizens and part of whose lands became Roman public domain. Overlapping this went the foundation of colonies, each of some 300 Romans, to form garrisons, especially on the sea coast. And then, overlapping both, went a policy of founding still other colonies in the joint names both of Rome and the Latin League; these were the colonies of the *Latin name*, the *nomen Latinum*. When Rome dissolved the League in 338 BC she continued to found such 'Latin' colonies and later she was to found also some purely Roman ones, larger than the conventional 300 men. The effect was to create a strong *glacis* between Rome and her hostile neighbours in the north and in the south. When Rome subdued these, much later, she may have planted Latin colonies there—as she did in Cremona and Placentia, for instance—but for the most part she enforced on the subject tribes and peoples her treaties of alliance: they became *socii*.

This great network which the Roman citizenry commanded characteristically lacked an official name. We nowadays call it a *confederation*—but only by

[31] C. Nicolet, *Rome et la conquête du monde méditerranéen*, vol. 1, *Les structures de l'Italie Romaine*, 2nd edn. (Presses Universitaires de France, 1979).

default. Later texts speak of it as 'the Romans, Latins, and Italian Allies'.[32] Though it is clumsy, it is revealing. These were indeed its three components.

To turn first to the Roman citizens, these were of two kinds originally. The first category consisted of full Roman citizens, that is, *optimo iure*. Such were the inhabitants of the annexed areas. In other areas, usually surrounding the former, the inhabitants were granted Roman citizen rights, except the vote and eligibility to hold public office; they do not seem to have served in the legions but, if not, would have provided military contingents and paid taxes like full citizens. These were *cives sine suffragio*. Where their towns already possessed magistrates and a civil constitution, that is, where it was a *res publica*, it was known as a *municipium*, and this model was later to be common in the overseas territories of Rome. In contrast, tribal systems were not *municipia*, but simply *oppida* ('towns'). By the close of our period in 134 BC, however, all these 'half-citizens' had received full citizen rights and their anomalous status had lapsed.

Now we can consider the colonies. In the early and exclusively Roman colonies of 300 men apiece, the colonists continued to be Roman citizens, but after 338 Rome founded 'Latin colonies' whose colonists received a kind of half-citizenship, for they enjoyed the rights to intermarry with Roman citizens, bequeath property, and enter into contracts with Roman citizens and even acquire citizenship, if they chose to reside in Rome. Moreover, from the early second century they enjoyed the protection of *provocatio*.[33] If present in Rome at the relevant mement, *Latini* could also vote, but in only one of its thirty-five 'tribes', chosen by lot. For the rest, they followed their own local laws and only adopted those parts of the Roman civil law they found acceptable. They had to provide military contingents and pay taxes to Rome. These colonies were the *nomen Latinum*, and they were big, of some 6,000 men. They outnumbered purely Roman ones: in 190 BC there were thirty-five of them as against eighteen purely Roman colonies. They must have contained some 431,000 people since, in 225 BC, we know that they were expected to provide 100,000 troops.[34] The colonies proved absolutely faithful in the war against Hannibal and at some unknown time a number of their inhabitants acquired a way to obtain Roman citizenship without residing in Rome, in that any who attained a magistracy in the colony became entitled to citizenship. This policy of extending citizenship to local magistrates was to be extended to the *municipia* of the overseas empire of the Republic and largely explains its success: for by this process there was

---

[32] Nicolet, *Rome et la conquête du monde*, 270.   [33] See p. 398 above.
[34] Nicolet, *Rome et la conquête du monde*, 277–80.

formed an empire-wide network of local oligarchies, all possessing Roman citizenship and so both tied in to Rome and receiving its support.

Finally, outside the central zone there were few Roman or Latin colonies, except, significantly, in the conquered land of Cisalpine Gaul and one or two key areas in the south. Outside these, the people were not citizens or half-citizens but allies (*socii*). They were completely autonomous except that they were obliged, under treaty, to provide massive regular and perpetual assistance to Rome on demand, and to serve under Roman generals. True, they received some share in the booty and did not pay any tribute in cash or in kind to Rome; but in the mid-second century these allies provided between 53 per cent and 59 per cent of the Republic's armed forces. The relationship of Rome and the allies constituted, in fact, a *symmachy* not dissimilar from some Greek Leagues. The way this *symmachy* was tied into the annexed areas and the colonies passed through Rome. All roads led to and from Rome; in the peninsula all relationships did likewise. The citizenry of the *civitas* could and did command the military manpower of most of Italy.

4.1. *Conventions of the Working Constitution*

As it stood, the constitution we have just described was self-defeating. There were three popular Assemblies each having the right to pass binding laws, and twenty annual officers (two consuls, eight praetors, and ten tribunes) each empowered, on the one hand to pilot bills through the Assembly, and on the other to veto the resolutions of their colleagues and juniors. Yet Roman government worked. Indeed, it worked so well that Polybius, writing *c*.150 BC, thought it was the principal reason why 'almost the whole world fell under [its] rule'.[35] It worked, as the British Constitution does today, very differently from what constitutional law propounded, and by the same device: unwritten rules to supplement and/ or circumvent its formal provisions.

Most of these conventions concern the role of the one organ we have merely mentioned. In law the Senate was the council that advised the magistrates, but conventions turned it into the body that directed them. In the Early, but particularly in the Middle Republic, it became the central organ of the state.[36]

The Senate had always possessed authority as a body of ex-magistrates

---

[35] Mommsen, *History of Rome*, 340.

[36] But this centrality is challenged by Millar, 'The Political Character'; id., 'Political Power', as explained below, pp. 417–18, 471.

facing the batch of newly elected magistrates serving only for one year. Where else could these novices seek advice, except from their seniors who had been through all this before? Appointed as it was by the censors, the Senate, *qua* corporate body, was independent of the active magistrates. True, it could only meet when summoned by a magistrate, but as there were sixteen eligible magistrates no problem seems ever to have arisen. The convening magistrate acted as the Senate's president for that session and this gave him the right to propose his own motion(s). No individual senator could himself initiate a discussion. He could only speak when the presiding magistrate called him and asked for his *sententia*. Admittedly, once on his feet he could speak on any topic; this is how Cato is said to have worked in the unrelated proposition *Carthago delenda est*. In so far as senators were called to put their resolutions, its non-curule members were marginalized because the floor went to the consuls, praetors, and tribunes in that rank order, just as the voting did, so that there also the non-curule members found themselves at the tail-end of business.

We mentioned earlier the Senate resolution, called a *senatus consultum*, the *advice* of the Senate, which possessed *auctoritas* (i.e. persuasive force), but could not become operative unless a magistrate embodied it in a decree. And here was the revolutionary convention: magistrates hastened to do just this! It was from this basic convention that the paramountcy of the Senate now flowed. In practice, some magistrates did defy this convention and acted independently of the Senate, which in turn could persuade a compliant magistrate—usually a tribune, and there were ten of these—to veto the rebel magistrate's action. In 167 BC, for instance, the *praetor peregrinus*, without consulting the Senate or informing the consuls, proposed to ask the *centuriata* to vote against war on Rhodes; but his action was vetoed by two of his fellow-tribunes.

Alongside its power over domestic issues, the Senate intervened in administrative policy, and subordinated the magistrates in respect of war, diplomacy and finance to its wishes. It was never formally denied that the *comitia* must have the last word on a peace-treaty, but in practice the Senate monitored the negotiations and the final role of the *comitia* became a formality. Other powers assumed by the Senate in respect to foreign affairs gave it a parenthetic hold over magistrates, in that it was responsible for designating the military commands (*provinciae*). This was a matter of capital importance, for while some *provinciae* could bring in neither glory nor spoils, others promised great opportunities and rich prizes. True, the Senate did not decide who should take which *provincia*—the candidates cast lots for that—but it did decide whether or not to prolong the tenure of consuls and praetors, so that they became pro-consuls and pro-praetors. Furthermore, its undisputed authority to control public finance enabled it to be lavish or mean in allocating the magistrate's expenses for his campaign and other duties.

Never was the Senate's dominance of the magistracy more prominent and more successful than when it assumed command during the war with Hannibal. Page after page of Livy shows it masterminding diplomacy, deciding strategy, and determining the size of the levy. And its successful conclusion of that terrible war unquestionably vindicated and legitimized what Mommsen does not hesitate to call its 'usurpations'.

Now while the Senate became the body that directed the magistracy, what of the *comitia*? The *comitia centuriata* did, after all, elect the senior magistrates. What guarantee did the Senate have that these were suitably docile? And again, the tribunes were elected by the *concilium plebis*, the 'counter-constitutional' structure itself. Why did it not challenge the Senate *and* the regular magistrates?

As a matter of fact, the Assembly—and the tribunes—did run loose from the Senate on a number of occasions. C. Flaminius, tribune in 232 BC, bypassed a hostile Senate to carry a law which gave citizens parcels of the public land that had been confiscated from a Gallic tribe in the Po valley. He also supported a law, introduced by a tribune, to prohibit senators and their sons from owning large merchant ships, so preventing them from engaging in commerce. In 217 BC, when Hannibal was marching into Umbria, the *comitia centuriata* elected Flaminius to the Consulship in the teeth of Senate opposition. In the event his legion was destroyed and he himself killed at Lake Trasimene. But the *comitia centuriata*—which, *par excellence*, reflected the emotions of the army—was still bitterly opposed to the Senate which supported Q. Fabius Maximus and his 'Fabian' policy of wearing Hannibal down by refusing battle. They wanted a forward policy and in 216 elected C. Terentius Varro Consul. Another loser: he led the legions to total disaster at Cannae. (On the other hand, they chose a winner when in 211 they elected the youth Scipio Africanus to command in Spain, where his father had been defeated and slain.)

The *centuriata* also demonstrated in the opposite sense, *against* war, when, after the defeat of Hannibal (201), the Senate wanted to take them into a fresh war with Macedon. A tribune, Quintus Baebius, following what Livy described as the 'traditional course of attacking the Senators', persuaded the *comitia* to reject the war. The august Senate demanded that the consuls convene a new Assembly and retake the vote, which it did, voting this time in favour of the war.[37] More successfully, at the close of the Middle

---

[37] Livy, xxi 6

Republic, when the plebs were sick and tired of war, the tribunes, lending *auxilium* to the reluctant conscripts, actually brought the levy to a halt on three separate occasions.[38]

On the whole, though, both tribunes and *comitia* were quiescent. The former had effectively been incorporated into the Senatorial class—they could now, as we have already noted, convene Senate sessions, attend it, and put resolutions to it—and this itself may partly explain the quiescence of the *comitia tributa/concilium plebis*. It would accord with Pareto's theory of the 'circulation of élites', whereby the political class enfeebles the masses by creaming off their leaders. Another reason was that the citizens' perennial land-hunger had been alleviated by the creation of very large numbers of smallholdings. (It was when this resettlement programme ceased after 170 BC, while the wars continued, that trouble began to build again.)[39] Note that other laws favouring the plebs were passed, notably those softening the penal code; by 130 BC capital punishment for Roman citizens had virtually disappeared and citizens could 'appeal to the People' (*provocatio*) against a penalty of flogging.

But the Assemblies' choice in elections was curtailed. During the crisis of the war against Hannibal, the annual change of consuls—the generals—was suspended and re-election permitted, just as, later, the Senate slyly usurped the Assemblies' right to prolong magistracies by prorogation.[40] But after the war the ten-year interval for consulship was strictly enforced again and in 180 BC the *cursus honorum* was made statutory.[41] (These measures reflect the permanent characteristic of oligarchy, the principle of equality among the oligarchs, or 'Buggins's turn'.) Obviously, then, measures of this kind limited the Assemblies' power to elect.

How is it that this handful of very rich, very distinguished, very aristocratic men who constituted the Senate could and did find themselves, for the greatest part, in harmony with the very differently constituted *comitia*? Different answers are on offer. The conventional one, first advanced in Gelzer's *The Roman Nobility* in 1912,[42] and receiving its most polished and persuasive form in Ronald Syme's *Roman Revolution* of 1939,[43] maintains that the senators, an inner core representative of a wider circle of very rich and prestigious and closely interconnected families, controlled the voting in the

---

[38] 151 BC; 149 BC; 138 BC.
[39] P. A. Brunt, *Social Conflicts in the Roman Republics* (Chatto and Windus, London, 1971), 63–4.
[40] See p. 406 above.
[41] M. Cary and H. H. Scullard, *A History of Rome*, 3rd edn. (Macmillan, London, 1979), 181.
[42] M. Gelzer, *The Roman Nobility* (Blackwell, Oxford, 1969).
[43] Syme, *The Roman Revolution* (OUP, Oxford, 1939).

comitia by its throngs of followers. This is contradicted by recent research which admits the harmony between Senate and the *comitia* and puts it down to adventitious factors. A third view goes much further. It sees the *comitia* counterbalancing the Senate in home affairs, not dominated by it, at least in connection with citizens' rights and the terms and conditions to be set on elected magistrates. Finally, and compatible with this, it is argued that the reason for the harmony that prevailed until about 170 BC, when the land shortage was beginning to surface again, was that both Senate and *comitia* had succeeded in getting what each wanted to their mutual satisfaction.[44]

4.2. *The Political Process in the Middle Republic*

Behind the Republican process of government was oligarchy. From its foundation, the city had been ruled from the top down. This did not alter when aristocrats replaced the kings, nor when the plebeians forced their way into the aristocratic circle. The new aristocratic–plebeian *nobilitas* left the popular assemblies weaker than before by taking their leadership into the 'aristocratic embrace'. This new nobility was highly exclusive. The expectation, the ambition, the purpose of its members was to attain high office, so that they formed the core of the political class of the Roman élite. Thus, for instance, with few exceptions the Consulship between 200 and 134 BC rotated among only twenty-five families.

4.2.1. THE CONVENTIONAL THEORY: CLIENTSHIP AND MANIPULATION

Their rivalry was intense. Striving for *virtus, auctoritas, honor, gloria,* and *fama,* noble families controlled great followings which permeated society by utilizing the distinctively Roman institution of *clientelism.* This was very ancient indeed. In the strict sense of *cliens* it was akin to a father–son relationship, hence the very term *patronus* (from *pater,* a father). The client bore the *genus* name of his patron and his client relationship descended from father to son. The patron was obliged to help his client in court and to give him a preferential place in attendance. In return, the client had to assume certain *obsequia:* services of military, judicial, even financial kinds. One way of recruiting clients was by manumitting slaves, but this only became significant when slavery became so very widespread from the second century on. In

----

[44] These two (highly unorthodox) positions are the ones taken by Millar in 'The Political Character' and id. 'Political Power'.

other cases it was the would-be client who made the move by 'commendation' (as in the European Middle Ages).

The proponents of the 'conventional' theory seem to have assumed that the nature of the *cliens* relationship in the ancient days was still alive and vibrant in the Middle Republic. Hence, that the nobility counted on its throngs of clients for voting support in the *comitia*. To summarize: in Gelzer's words,

> the entire Roman people, both the ruling circle and the mass of voters whom they ruled, was, as a society, permeated by multifarious relationships based on *fides* and on personal connections, the principle forms of which were *patrocinium* in the courts and over communities, together with political friendship and financial obligation . . . The most powerful man was he who by virtue of his clients and friends could mobilize the greatest number of voters.[45]

4.2.2. THE CRITIQUE OF THE CONVENTIONAL THEORY

It is common ground that the nobles, or aristocracy—whichever term one cares to use—filled the high offices of state; but Hopkins has shown that it was not, as often claimed, 'a stable hereditary nobility stretching back for many generations into antiquity'.[46] The conclusion drawn is that in the second century BC the aristocratic and wealthy political élite which 'ruled the roost' consisted of a small inner core which had fairly high rates of succession, and 'a broader band of the politically successful, drawn from the same social class of rich land-owners, but with lower rates of succession. Many members of this outer band of senators were the sole representatives of their families to enter politics for generations.'[47] Moreover, while this ruling aristocracy was 'internally stratified and marked off by landed wealth, style of consumption and social esteem . . . it was permeable to outsiders' comprising 'the descendants of consuls, of senators, knights and some successful outsiders'.[48]

---

[45] Quoted, Brunt, *Fall of the Roman Republic*, 385

[46] For instance, 250–249 BC, 30% of all consuls had no direct consular ancestor in the last three generations and only 32% had a consular son. Praetors' chances were even less—sons and grandsons of consuls made up only 40% of the total number of consuls.

[47] Hopkins, *Death and Renewal*, 117.

[48] Ibid. 44–5. But this is an exceedingly limited social range surely? Elsewhere (p. 32) Hopkins permits himself the extreme expression that 'the Roman senate was *wide open to outsiders*'—which he then qualifies away by defining 'outsiders' as merely 'those who were not themselves the sons of senators'. The fact is that, because Hopkins chooses to extend his definition of 'nobility' or 'aristocracy', it must necessarily follow that the directly hereditary element forms a smaller proportion of the 'élite' and the 'non-hereditary' elements a much larger one than in the findings of his predecessors who have defined 'nobility' more restrictively. See n. 4 above.

Secondly, the notion that such nobles' influence over the *comitia* was based on their clienteles extended by alliances with other similarly placed nobles (*factio* and *amicitia*) has also been discredited. Excluding freemen, provincial and foreign communities, and individuals whom one had represented in the courts, there are only fifty allusions to *clientes* in 1,000 pages of Cicero and Sallust.[49]

Even the attested 'true' *clientes* did not necessarily observe the supposedly hereditary force of their obligations, nor was such clientship confined to nobles but could extend to senators of much lower *nobilis* status. Nor did a client necessarily have only one patron. He might have several at the same time (which was why client loyalties divided in the civil wars). That the electoral process was far from mechanical is made strikingly clear from the *Commentariolum Petitionis*, a tract which purports to tell Cicero how to win an election. Cicero had no *clientes* except in his native Arpinum, and the author therefore advises him that he must canvass. He had claims of gratitude on various tax-farmers, most *equites*, on *municipia* and *collegia* and sodalities. All these must be canvassed and courted and so must senators, consulars, nobles of any degree, and everybody who has any influence in their home-towns or regions. Admittedly Cicero was a 'new man' with no aristocratic forbears and, we might surmise, had to make exceptional efforts to win; but even conceding that, the impression we glean is one of canvassing individuals, not using some bloc of client votes to overwhelm the *populus* in its *comitia*.

The nature and the political significance of the *amicitiae* and *factiones* are also highly disputable. We shall have more to say about this when we deal with 'parties' in the Late Republic. It does not follow that because two men are related by marriage they and/or their allies will remain long united in public life. The individual often felt he had duties to himself as well as his obligations to kinsmen, and indeed, as Brunt justly points out (for his principle is valid throughout political history), 'Aristocratic ambition was in fact itself an obstacle to the formation of a party consisting of the adherents of some outstanding individual . . .The ambition of every individual demanded that the success of others should be limited.'[50]

The great attractiveness of the 'conventional' theory was its simplicity: the harmony of the Senate and the Assemblies was due to senatorial domination mediated through blocs of client voters and in alliances with other, similar, blocs. But if this was not the way harmony was established, what *was* the way?

[49] Brunt, *Fall of the Roman Republic*, 391–2.
[50] Ibid. 43. Cf. S. E. Finer, *Comparative Government* (Allen Lane, London, 1970), 443–9.

4.2.3. THE REAPPRAISAL OF THE *COMITIA*

The conventional theory assumes that the *comitia* were dominated, that they had at best an arbitral role, and though the *populus* could and did on very rare occasions defy the Senate, it was only when it was 'thoroughly aroused, had resolute leadership and could command a majority in one of the assemblies'.[51] The *centuriata*, biased in favour of the rich as it was, unsurprisingly elected men of the wealthy landowning class, yet defied the entire united Senate in electing the mere *eques*, Marius, certainly well outside the narrow aristocratic band (107 BC).

The conventional manipulation theory is strongest on the election of magistrates because these were made in the *centuriata*, the rich man's club. How well does it hold in the matter of legislation? Here we should look to the *tributa/concilium plebis*, where the Hortensian Law had made a *plebis scitum* binding on the entire population. It is argued that the *populus*, whether through *leges* or *plebis scita*, did in fact establish citizen rights and defined the actions of magistrates or the terms on which they could hold office. But how did the *comitia* achieve this, bereft as they were of legislative initiative, unable even to convene except by command of a magistrate, and permitted only to say yea or nay to a proposition without hearing any debate on it, let alone participating in one? In reply, Millar stresses something that receives scant attention in textbooks: the informal meeting of the *populus* that could and usually did take place before the matter was voted upon in the formal *comitia*.

The meeting in question is the *contio*, and it generally preceded the formal meetings of the *comitia* at which the *leges* were passed. Summoned by a magistrate, the *populus* assembled, and after solemn rites heard him speak to the matter before it. As in the *comitia*, the assembled *populus* had no right to intervene in debate but were enabled to judge the pros and cons of a proposal, in that the convening magistrate could call on any citizen to speak. Thus a limited amount of debate among politicians gave the *populus* some inkling of what they were to be voting about when a resolution came formally before the *comitia*. Not merely that: the *contio* was often the only platform from which a politician out of office could press his views. Speakers ascended the rostrum and it was there that oratory was critical: critical to convince the populace but also critical, in the sense that it gave a man a reputation for oratory in a culture which valued it highly and therefore made him that much more eligible for election if he stood as a candidate.

---

[51] Brunt, *Fall of the Roman Republic*, 26.

By means of the *contio*, we may well surmise, the senators acquired a sense of public attitudes and by the same token the *populus* was able to convey its sentiments to the Senate. It is perfectly plausible, then, that this dialectic could lead to a harmonized condition. But in that case why did it break down in the Late Republic, or even earlier, with the land laws of the Gracchi brothers in 133 BC? Millar would answer that 'the first half of the second century [was] not the period of untroubled control of the "people" by the élite, but that in which popular rights had become well established and popular demands for victories, booty and land were quite easily met'.[52]

So much for the four theories on offer. If we consequently reject the 'senatorial domination of the *comitia*' view, how came it that these bodies kept in tune with one another, as they undoubtedly did? I find no difficulty at all in the *populus* always electing aristocrats. Just as it used (justly) to be said that 'All England loves a Lord', so all Rome loved an aristocrat, of whose virtues they were reminded by funeral games and the like. Wealth was another credential. Office was unpaid and carried the additional obligation to provide shows and games, and later corn-doles, to humour the *populus*. It was also required in order to bribe the electorate. We know of a large number of laws passed to suppress bribery, all of which, until 55 BC, proved unsuccessful. Intimidation could also have been used; in the Late Republic it certainly was. And a great importance attached to sheer oratory, just as in the Greek *poleis*.

Rome was *not* a democracy. To its very close it was always ruled by aristocrats elected by the *populus*, which was blatantly unrepresentative of the Roman citizenship as a whole. The curious structuring of the *comitia*, the dispersal of citizens throughout Italy, the concentration of the poor and ne'er-do-wells among the urban *tribus* and the impoverished rural refugees— all these factors skewed the Republic well away from democracy. Roman government was an aristocracy tempered by temporary incursions of unre-presentative assemblies.

Yet, in the eyes of the population, this system was *legitimate*, because it was not a simple oligarchy, not an unqualified rule of the few, but a heavily qualified one: a *timocracy*. It was a carefully devised system by which not only rights but corresponding civic obligations also were graded in accordance with property qualification. Power *and* responsibilities flowed from the *class* into which the censors allocated you. Thus the very onerous duty of military service (*on the average* a citizen spent seven years in the field at this time, and some, in Spain for instance, served for longer) was normally confined to the propertied citizens, and the *proletarii* and others were only called up in the

[52] Millar, 'Political Power', 145.

direst emergency. Similarly, only the propertied paid the war tax (*tributum*). 'The rich, noble and powerful were expected to supply the main military and fiscal effort, and to play the chief part in forming and executing political decisions: those to whom fortune had been unkind were relieved of these various duties and responsibilities.'[53] There is nothing very surprising in this; despite the contrary experience in Athens, the notion that political decisions should be taken only by those with a 'stake in society' runs throughout European history (at least). It was taken for granted in the Middle Ages, it formed the major theme in Cromwell's and Ireton's contribution to the Putney Debates in England, it provided the rationale of the *censitaire* constitutions of France during and after the Revolution, and survived in various shapes and forms in Britain and most European states until the late nineteenth century, in some cases (e.g. Prussia) even later.

The Middle Republic closed when a collision occurred between the Senate and the Assembly, the oligarchy and the *populus*, that went far beyond any similar conflicts in the past. This collision exposed the contrast between what the *law* of the constitution clearly permitted—the sovereignty of a *plebis scitum*—and the *conventions* that had constrained it. It plunged the Republic into one deep constitutional crisis after another until it collapsed.

The basic course of this crisis is plain. Owing to far-reaching and abrupt social economic and intellectual changes in the later second century, the old timocratic balance of powers and responsibilities had broken down and correspondingly a gap began to widen between the perceived grievances of the *populus* and the self-interest of the oligarchy. The 'pre-established harmony' between the two had vanished. The ruling oligarchy was stuck, so to speak, with theoretically sovereign popular assemblies. It could not abolish them—even Augustus did not do that—so, somehow, it had to 'manage' them and, as we shall now see, it did this by a gamut of methods that ranged from persuasion and bribery at one end (both well established even in the Middle Republic) to intimidation and, ultimately, violence. From being a legitimate timocracy, the Late Republic became what, in modern times, has been called a 'façade-democracy'.

By façade-democracy I mean a system where liberal-democratic institutions, processes, and safeguards[54] are established by law but are in practice so manipulated or violated by a historic oligarchy as to stay in office. The

---

[53] Nicolet, *World of the Citizen*, 385.

[54] 'Liberal-democracy' is quite obviously an anachronism, but I let it stand, to serve *mutatis mutandis* for the corpus of checks and balances and liberties and rights, etc., we have so far described; and partly, too, to suggest that what happened in the Republic is an analogue of what has often occurred— and still does—in the modern world.

structure of the government is usually collegiate but for a time it may be superseded by an individual autocratic ruler using similar methods to perpetuate himself. Historically, this type of rule is associated with the social status and economic predominance of a traditional class and is the device by which they made the legal code of civil liberties and popular suffrage serve to perpetuate their own traditional power.[55]

5. WHY THE REPUBLIC COLLAPSED

The collapse of the Republic is instructive about its nature. What happened was that the structure of society that had underpinned the working constitution was swept away and radically transformed by a flood of changes in the course of the second century BC. The resulting incongruity between the old constitution and the new social realities led to collisions between the letter of constitutional law and the conventions which had circumvented it: marked by—for instance—the tribunes' assertion of their own and the *concilium plebis*'s rights against the Senate's insistence on its traditional dominance. As each side strained the law and/or conventions of the constitution to meet its own convenience, marginal illegalities led to grosser ones, force was brought in where manipulation and chicanery failed, and the Republic entered on an irreversible descent into civil war.

5.1. *Social and Economic Changes*

After the defeat of Carthage, Spain, Macedon, and Greece, it was the turn of parts of Africa and then Asia to become Provinces ruled by Roman governors. Empire brought wealth to Rome on an enormous scale. The public treasury was receiving 50 million denarii in tribute from the Provinces in 74 BC and 135 million by 62 BC: enough to maintain 400,000 and 1,100,000 soldiers a year, respectively. Generals and their troops carried off vast booty.[56] Above all, hordes of captives were sold to Roman citizens as slaves. One estimate puts the minimum number of prisoners-of-war taken between 202 and 52 BC at 516,130, excluding the million which, Plutarch and Appian allege, were seized in the Gallic wars.[57] By the close of the Republic in 28 BC there were some 3 million slaves to 4 million free persons in Italy.[58]

Another source of wealth derived from the extravagantly large 'expense'

[55] Finer, *Comparative Government*, 441.   [56] Crawford, *The Roman Republic*, 78–9.
[57] Nicolet, *Rome et la conquête*, 210–11.
[58] P. A. Brunt, *Social Conflicts in the Roman Republic*, corrected edn. (Chatto and Windus, London, 1982), 18.

allowances to governors and the like in these new Provinces. In *one* year as governor of Cilicia, Cicero *saved* 550,000 denarii, equivalent to the yearly wages of 4,600 soldiers. Yet another was the profit margin made by the tax-farmer in the provinces. These were the companies of *publicani*, a rapidly rising group within the class of *equites* who themselves were, more and more, the well-to-do magistrates of the Italian *municipia*, duly enfranchised as Roman citizens. (These publicans—and indeed the *equites* as a whole— were to play an increasingly significant political role in the political contests of the Republic.)

This gigantic plunder made the rich richer and the poor penniless. The rich occupied more and more public domain land above the permitted maximum of 320 acres and, since the poorer peasants had used it as common land, the enclosures made their smallholdings non-viable and drove them off the land altogether. Many small-holders were absorbed into *latifundia* in Sicily, and other parts of southern Italy. Furthermore, slave-labour took over from free labour, further undermining the free peasants who had often relied on casual day-labour on big estates. What economic pressure did not accomplish, interminable warfare might; for now a farmer, especially if unlucky enough to be posted to Spain, might serve for seven years or many more in the field, and return to find his farm in ruin or even in the hands of an unscrupulous magnate. In short, the Roman ruling class 'robbed their subjects abroad so that they could better rob their fellow-countrymen'.[59]

This radicalized the poor and corrupted the rich. We have described the *mos maiorum*—the 'old ways'—the virtues that sustained the Republic through the Punic wars. The Roman annexation of Greece and subsequent adoption of Greek culture and manners undermined these values. Cash currency from the loot of empire did the rest and had the same effect on them as Persian gold had had on the Spartiates. Cupidity and corruption went hand in hand. They were to demonstrate themselves in the illegal extortions of provincial governors, in the venality of individual senators, in the increasing use of bribery in electoral contests. Sallust paints this depressing picture of the *urbs venalis*—'The City for sale and ready to offer itself to the highest bidder'—and whatever may be inaccurate in its detail, his general analysis is only too amply confirmed.

The lure of easy, instant wealth raised the stakes in the always feverish competition for office. To be a consul and so command the army that could sack towns, seize booty, capture slaves, and then return for a public triumph,

[59] Brunt, *Social Conflicts in the Roman Republic*, 40.

became obsessive; so did getting one's Consulate prolonged, so as to go as pro-consul to govern a province, and come back (as Pompey did) with estates worth 50 million. Sallust ascribed the collapse of the Republic to the nobility's 'avarice and ambition', and he was right. So, the second effect of the wars of conquest and the new wealth was to corrupt the old Roman ideal of *simplicitas* (frugality) and to raise the stakes in the competitive struggle for sovereign commands to frenetic levels. This generated a further cycle of competition and cupidity, for money was increasingly used to 'seed' the Assemblies that elected you to office, or to put on lavish games as aedile, for instance, so as to prepare the way for election to higher office. All this expenditure (often financed) had to be recouped, so the struggle to attain the Consulship became ever more urgent.

The interminable wars precipitated another set of political changes. Citizen manpower began to run dry. It will be recalled that, except in the direst emergency (*tumultus*), only the propertied citizens in the census classes called the *assidui* were drafted. As their numbers declined throughout the second century the property qualification was continually lowered to permit the conscription of even the poorest *assidui* (not to speak of under-age youngsters). In 107 BC the consul Marius threw the ranks open to the propertyless—the *proletarii*—and though he enrolled only 5,000 of them, the proportion continued to rise until a propertied citizen army, the essential balance-weight in the timocratic structure, gave way to one consisting of poor and very poor volunteers serving for the chance of booty.[60] But this was uncertain and insufficient for the toils of military service, and beyond that there was no provision for service gratuities or smallholdings on demobilization. These troops, therefore, looked to their generals for some such reward, just as they traditionally looked to them for their share of booty. So the troops transferred their allegiance from the *res publica* to the successful general who led them. Though Marius was not successful in recompensing his ex-servicemen with land, Sulla, Pompey, and Caesar were. In this way the soldiers became dependants of their patrons, the generals, and no longer a corps of yeomen-farmers with 'a stake in the country' and participant-actors in the civic processes of the Republic.

The never-ending wars which generated these changes were one of the causes of a changed sentiment among the Italian allied states which came to a head in 91 BC. Their share of the booty was always less than the Roman troops', nor, unlike them, could they appeal (*provocatio*) against a capital

---

[60] Though these were never numerous enough to dispense with conscription, bitterly resented though this was, especially in the Civil Wars.

sentence. Nor were military grievances the only ones. After 133, when some Roman citizens began to receive smallholdings and subsidized corn, the gap between their material advantages and those of the non-citizens became very wide. At the beginning of the second century, during the Hannibalic wars, the Italian allies had been indifferent to the suggestion that they become citizens. Now they were keen and, finally, demanding. When the Senate refused and their Roman champion (M. Livius Drusus) was found inexplicably murdered, they rose in revolt (91–88) in what is misleadingly translated as the Social War (the War of the Allies—the *socii*).

Such, in barest outline, are some of the more momentous changes that occurred in Roman society from the victory over Hannibal (202) until the first century BC.

5.2. *The Distortion of the Governmental Structure*

The senatorial class, far richer than most Romans, and whose traditional *auctoritas* made them the custodians of the security, wealth, and morals of the Republic, were the *beati possidentes*. As a class, nothing could inspire it with the wish to do any more than preserve the existing state of affairs. But this was not true of individual families. Hitherto, if 'new men' were elected to Consulship it was[61] because the oligarchy allowed them to be so. The only other path to office and fame was to break ranks and go in the teeth of senatorial opposition to the sources of elections, in short, to make a direct appeal to the Assemblies. Ambition drove individual noblemen to do precisely that; and the impoverishment and uprooting of the poorer citizens presented them with the opportunity.

It will be recalled that it was by pure convention that the legislative proposals put to the *comitia* required the prior assent of the Senate, although by the Lex Hortensia this was not strictly required for laws enacted in the *concilium plebis*. These conventions were generally honoured up to 133 BC,[62] but by then the social composition of the Assemblies had altered.

The Assemblies met in Rome and citizens had to cast their votes there in person. Not even in Caesar's day (*c*.50 BC) did Rome contain more than 15 per cent of all Roman citizens, so that the greater Rome's territory and the more extended her citizenship (not the same thing), the less socially representative the Assemblies became, since distance precluded any but a tiny minority attending. Rome itself was a city of the poor. The very, very rich lived away from it. Consequently, the *centuriata* that elected the consuls

---

[61] Until Marius in 102 BC.   [62] See p. 432 below.

and praetors was dominated by well-to-do Italians from out of town, and it was their votes the nobility had to court. But the *concilium plebis* which elected tribunes and made (most) laws was quite differently composed, for *its* voting units were the thirty-five 'tribes', and their elements became scattered in various places throughout Italy as new citizens were created and allocated, some to one tribe and some to another. (This development became highly pronounced after the enfranchisement of all Italians after 89 BC.) The numerical influence of these outlying citizens in the *Concilium Plebis* diminished as their distance from Rome increased (that is, unless rival politicians made extraordinary and very expensive efforts to bring them there). The consequence was that the thirty-one rural tribes were, in absolute numbers, poorly represented. But, to offset this, the citizen population of Rome had multiplied, partly by numerous manumissions of slaves and partly by the uprooted and landless-peasant citizens who flocked to Rome as fellahin in Egypt or peasants in Brazil flock into Cairo or Rio today. Thus the city population now consisted partly of the very poor original city-dwellers, registered in the four urban tribes; needy, greedy and vociferous, they were venal and a ready reservoir of dependants for the nobility. Then there were the freedmen who were, of course, clients of their former masters. And then there were those immigrant and proletarianized peasants mentioned above, who, however, seem still to have been registered as belonging to their original rural tribes. As they were on the spot, they could and did attend the Assembly and therefore were usually *decisive* for the way the rural tribes voted. In short, the tribal Assembly (or the *concilium plebis*) was now dominated by the propertyless and rootless and a ready prey for aristocratic demagogy or manipulation. With the nobility becoming fantastically wealthy at the expense of the poor, who became poorer still, it was now possible for individual aristocrats to make a revived Tribunate of the Plebs a springboard for their ambition.

Let us start by introducing the five political actors. The first—the nobility and Senatorial class—supplied the contenders for office. It is essential to grasp that these were mainly fellow-aristocrats. In Lilian Rose Taylor's simple reduction: 'A set of nobles who called themselves "the Good" (*boni*) men' gained control of the Senate and prevented other nobles and senatorials from obtaining the endorsement of the Senate for their measures. The defeated men turned with the aid of tribunes to the tribal Assembly.[63] With the particularly notable exception of Marius, the defeated

---

[63] L. R. Taylor, *Party Politics in the Age of Caesar* (University of California Press, Berkeley and Los Angeles, 1961), 13.

politicians were also usually nobles, but (apart from the Gracchi) tended to come from relatively obscure families and were trying to break into the circle of grandees. Except for the Gracchi, who were genuine reformers, all the contenders on either side—as Sallust says, 'pro sua quisque potentia certabant'—were all out for themselves; but the prizes they struggled for were now nothing less than the bottomless spoils of empire.

The second set of actors are the knights (*equites*). They were to play an alleviating role, sometimes supporting the oligarchy and sometimes their renegade opponents. Often as wealthy as some senators but preferring *otium* and riches to politics, this Order was essential to the politically ambitious in two ways. First, because as we have already said, they preponderated in the *centuriata* which elected consuls and praetors; secondly because their Order embraced Rome's financial class. This had the ready cash needed (as we shall see) to prime the political pump for aspirants to high offices, and many of the senators were their 'partners, allies and advocates'.[64]

The third and fourth sets of actors comprised the impoverished and landless peasantry, over-represented, as we have seen already, in the *concilium plebis/comitia tributa* and the urban lumpenproletariat. The latter's vote, confined as it was to a mere four tribes out of thirty-five, was not significant, but on the street it was a different story. For these ruffians, alongside citizens who came in from the country to fight as well as vote, formed the Roman 'mob', ready for gang-fights, riots, even lynchings in a city without a police force.[65] Finally, late on the scene (say *c.*80 BC) appeared the fifth set of actors: the personal army, as of Sulla, Pompey, and Caesar.

The opposing 'followings' called themselves the *optimates* and the *populares*. Nowadays, these are sometimes called factions, sometimes 'parties'. The latter term is completely misleading, since it inevitably suggests our present-day political parties which are continuing corporate organizations. Here, however, we have congeries of individual families and communities temporarily grouped behind an individual politician. They were discontinuous, fluid, and above all, *personalist*. The terms obviously echo Greek ones. *Optimates* translates into Greek as *aristoi*, 'the best', and *populares* (from *populus* or people) echoes *demos*. But *populares* does not translate as 'democrats', but as 'populist', that is, those persons or measures appealing—ambivalently—to reliance on the popular Assemblies rather than on the Senate, and/or to popular preoccupations. To do down Senate opposition entailed going over its head to the Assemblies and winning them over by promises of (notably), agrarian laws, subsidized corn, extension of the suffrage, and the like. Their

[64] Syme, *Roman Revolution*, 14.
[65] See the excellent analysis of Brunt ('The Roman Mob') in Finley, *Studies*, ch. 4.

opponents, the *optimates*, stood for the *status quo*. A beleaguered garrison, they were the more coherent and fixed grouping. They stood for strict control on public funds, the defence of property rights (no matter how acquired), strict enforcement of the laws on debt, and the restriction of the franchise However, so as not to lose influence in the Assemblies, they were quite capable of proposing measures that outbid the *populares*.

The man who wanted public office would build a following from his immediate household to begin with, then from as many households of his *gens* as he could win over, and then from alliances (*amicitiae*) with other families, often sealed by marriage compacts. These families were not 'nuclear' (the number of voting individuals in these would be negligible), but the entire *oikos*, that is, all its many dependants, such as freedmen and personal clients. Indeed, family, *gens*, *amicitiae*, have all to be regarded as nuclei of groups of dependants and the art of building a following was to collect as many personal or allied *clientelae* as possible. Clients in the strict sense of the word—those that owed *fides*[66]—included those who toiled up the hills of Rome to their patron's house every morning to offer him their *salutatio*; those (the most respectable) who then went on to the Forum with him; and others, more numerous, who followed him around as he solicited votes. Nearly all the last were from the urban plebs, many of them very poor, so it was not uncommon for a patron to rent out his clients to help a friend's campaign or to provide him with street-gangs. Collecting such 'rent-a-crowds' was the easier in the late Republic in as much as many urban poor were already enrolled in *collegia*: guilds which acted as burial societies or as cult or trade, or neighbourhood associations. Catiline, for example, made use of such *collegia* in 64 BC to terrorize his opponents (as a result of which the Senate disbanded numbers of them).[67] However, whereas individual clients—in the strict sense—were few, and nothing like as dedicated as was once thought,[68] *clientelae* consisting of whole communities are better attested, so that a nobleman's *clientela* could include entire towns or indeed regions which felt obligated to him or his family because of favours received, for instance, the concession of Roman citizenship. But once we use the term 'client' in its looser sense, as many modern authors do, the category would consist not only of clients *strictu senso* but would include freedmen, dependent tenantry, household retainers, and private armies. Together with the clients proper, these made up the 'following' of the aspiring politician. Then, more sinister and life-threatening, at a later date—the process is well

---

[66] As defined earlier at pp. 417–19 above.   [67] Taylor, *Party Politics*, pp. 43–4.
[68] See pp. 418–19 above.

marked by Sulla's time (*c.*90 BC)—a commander's army became his *clientela*. The oath to the consul which soldiers took for their year of service was now being administered for the entire length of their service, and in return these men looked to their commander for rewards such as smallholdings when they were discharged. Sulla, Pompey, and Caesar all honoured their important pledge. The armies, of course, enormously enlarged the number of a politician's dependants and they could be sent to Rome to vote; but they could also go there as armed bands.

So by the first century some *clientelae* in the broad sense of this word were very large. Those of Caesar and Pompey were so big that each could raise a private army from among them. Pompey's *clientela* is instructive. From his father (a consul) he inherited a band of ex-servicemen who had been richly rewarded; he also inherited his father's huge estates in Picenum (on the Adriatic), where droves of hereditary clients dwelt. Among other of his train there were Italians whom he had conciliated in the Social War,[69] and Gauls from the Po valley where he had bestowed Latin rights on certain towns, and also Spaniards to whom he had extended the citizenship. Later he was to add even 'barbarian' clients from among the peoples he had subdued in the east.[70]

By the eighties the situation was as Syme describes it:

The Roman constitution was a screen and a sham. Of the forces that lay behind or beyond it, next to the noble families the knights were the most important. Through alliances with groups of financiers, through patronage exercised in the law-courts and ties of personal allegiance contracted in every walk of life, the political dynast might win influence not merely in Rome but in the country-towns of Italy and in regions not directly concerned with Roman political life. Whether he held authority from the State or not, he could thus raise an army on his own initiative and resources.

The soldiers, now recruited from the poorest classes in Italy, were ceasing to feel allegiance to the State; military service was for livelihood, or from constraint, not a natural and normal part of a citizen's duty. The necessities of a world-empire and the ambition of generals led to the creation of extraordinary commands in the provinces. The general had to be a politician, for his legionaries were a host of clients, looking to their leader for spoils in war and estates in Italy when their campaigns were over. But not veterans only were attached to his cause—from his provincial commands the dynast won to his allegiance and personal following (*clientela*) towns and whole regions, provinces and nations, kings and tetrarchs.

---

[69] See p. 433 below.   [70] Taylor, *Party Politics*, 44–6, 48.

Such were the resources which ambition required to win power in Rome and direct the policy of the imperial Republic as consul or one of the *principes*.[71]

The senatorials and their *populares* rivals used every possible device to gain control of the state. Given the preposterous composition of the Assemblies, manipulation was the rule from the earliest times. In electoral contests great attention was paid to drawing the attention of the multitude to the antiquity and prestigiously august lineage of the candidate's family, and to this end, when a notable of the family died, the candidate for office would display the busts of his ancestors at the funeral and mount the rostrum to deliver a funeral eulogy, and often paint the lily by laying on costly funeral games. These grew in scale and expense so that, whereas in 264 BC three pairs of gladiators were employed, they might be using sixty pairs by the year 183. And spectacles of this sort were not confined to funeral occasions; on the contrary, a general might be voted a triumph, and for this he would put on games and shows lasting several days.[72]

Both in disputes over proposed legislation as well as electoral contests, bribery was used on a massive scale. As we have already noted, legislation proved powerless to check its course and in the Late Republic it attained monstrous proportions. By then it was an organized system which worked through the *collegia* and the *sodalitates*. These had tribal *divisores* to distribute the bribes and *sequestres* to hold the money, while the members were brigaded and enrolled in *decuries*.[73]

When legislative proposals were to be presented, the texts were placarded all over the city. It was most likely that a magistrate would call a *contio* where he could explain the purport of the measure, and could call up any citizen to speak to it. Even if he declined to call an opponent, it was very likely indeed that some other magistrate—and we have seen how many of them there were—would call his own *contio* at which the opposing point of view would be put.

But this was only a first hurdle. The opponents of a measure could and did resort to an arsenal of procedural tricks to delay or shut off discussion. A compliant magistrate could veto the proposal. Or he might delay convening the *comitia* till a time when the bill's supporters would be elsewhere—getting in the harvest, for instance. Or he could convene one in great haste to catch the proponents by surprise. No better source of delay existed than Roman official religion. It was a religion of auguries, *nefas* days, eclipses and other unnatural events, and so forth. So, holders of the priestly offices could

[71] Syme, *Roman Revolution*, 15.   [72] Cary and Scullard, *History of Rome*, 178.
[73] Brunt, *Fall of the Roman Republic*, 425 ff.

postpone elections or legislative votes, for instance, by declaring the omens unpropitious. When trickery failed, intimidation and violence crept in: first in isolated acts directed at individual politicians, then intimidation by armed bands and finally by the legions, and wholesale proscriptions of the opposing faction.

The simple fact is that after *c*.133 the gap between what the *concilium plebis* demanded and the Senate was prepared to concede became unbridgeable. A well-ordered constitution where the rules were clear and precise might have permitted the peaceful—or as we would say 'political'—solution of the conflict. But, as we saw, the rules were neither clear nor precise and the incongruous, self-cancelling institutions of the Republic could (and did) work only when side-stepped by understandings unknown to and indeed repugnant to the strict law. The moment rogue noblemen, desirous of effecting change through the *comitia* (the *populares*) and those who resisted change via the Senate (the *optimates*) chose not to observe these conventions, the Constitution was impotent to resolve political differences. Law was invoked, pull-devil, pull-baker, and so was precedent. Both were infringed; then both were broken; until, after violations of ever-increasing scope and severity, the constitution, finally, was abrogated.

5.3. *Descent into the Maelstrom*

The collapse of the Republican constitution began in 133 BC when Tiberius Gracchus was elected tribune. By then an acute land shortage had arisen among the peasant farmers, and it was Tiberius' intention to ease it through enforcing the laws relating to the occupation and/or ownership of the public domain lands. These had been largely—and illegally—cornered by the wealthiest landowners, who took in more than the legal maximum. By enforcing the letter of the law Tiberius must necessarily bring about the dispossession of these landlords. They, using the Senate as their instrument, refused. This was the *fons et origo malorum*.

Not only did the senatorial nobility reject land-reform; they were not solicitous about the price of grain, either, and cheap corn was becoming a necessity for the starveling *lazzaroni* who now made up most of Rome's population. Tiberius' brother Gaius (tribune 123 and 122) introduced subsidies for corn, but the Senate subsequently reduced them by limiting the number of recipients and/or raising the price. Sulla finally abolished them altogether, only for the distribution to be revived after him, and made entirely free by a law of 58 BC. The armies were another victim of the Senate's stinginess. They were fast becoming a mercenary force manned by *proletarii*, men with no stake in the country and simply there to make money. But their pay was very low, nor was there any provision for discharged veterans; yet, here again, the Senate did nothing. The troops had to rely on their generals to promote their interests and in their turn the generals relied on these troops to enforce their will on the Senate. Again, it was the Senate which, in rebuffing the *socii*'s requests for Roman citizenship, sowed the seeds of the terrible and bloody 'Social War' (99–88).

The situation has been admirably summarized by Brunt:

. . . the great conflicts of the late Republic resulted from divergencies of interest and sentiment between the senatorial nobility at large on the one hand, and (at various times) the Italian allies, the Equites, the urban plebs, and the peasantry, on the other; it was also because the senate had failed to win the hearts of the mass of the rural population that the soldiery, mainly recruited from that population, displayed so little loyalty to the government, and were ready to obey the treasonable commands of generals, to whom they were attached not as clients to patrons but rather as mercenaries to *condottieri*, and to whom they looked for rehabilitation as peasant farmers . . .[74]

The leaders of the opposition to the Senate were fellow aristocrats, many of them, indeed, senators. They put themselves at the head of all these alienated forces in Roman society and, since they could make no headway in the Senate, worked through the *comitia*. Thereafter, again in Brunt's words, 'the senate succumbed to force which it had been the first to employ. Tiberius Gracchus was lynched, his followers persecuted with a travesty of justice. His brother offered a pretext for armed suppression; there was no clear justification for the massacre of his adherents.'[75]

Collisions between the two sides, *optimates* and *populares*, Senate and *comitia*, became more frequent and more frenzied, and as this happened, the constitution was unravelled. It was breached in three overlapping ways. The first consisted of unilateral and opposing interpretations put on it by the senators on the one hand and the tribunes on the other, which set them on a collision course. The second was the piecemeal abandonment of the restraints on the powers of any one single magistrate or tribune, such as, for instance, collegiality and annuality. The third was the initially occasional resort to brawling, which then escalated into the more sustained use of violence to get laws carried, and finally erupted into full-scale civil war and mass executions, and the scrapping of the ancient constitution by Sulla.

The entire story is one of 'parliamentary' ruses and artifices, swindles,

---

[74] Brunt, *Fall of the Roman Republic*, 386.   [75] Ibid. 78.

bribery and corruption, soon followed by and intermingled with assassinations, riots, and pitched battles. Only in the minute detail provided by the Roman historians from Polybius, Sallust, and Appian can one obtain a real sense of the progressive degeneration of the political process. But to write in this detail would be, effectively, to write the history of the Republic's last hundred years, which is manifestly impossible here. What follows is simply the barest chronology of the main events, with special attention to the breaches of law and conventions, as signalled by the use of italics.

CHRONOLOGY

133 BC   Tiberius Gracchus tribune. Re-enacts law restricting amount of public land a private individual may exploit. Strictly legal under the Hortensian Law, 287, but *unprecedented defiance of Senate*. Senators respond by getting another tribune to veto the act. Gracchus gets the *concilium* to depose that tribune—*wholly unprecedented, not necessarily unconstitutional*. The law passes. Gets *comitia* to enact another law by which the state treasury of Pergamon, now bequeathed to Rome, is appropriated to agrarian reform. Senate protests that *this infringes their conventional right to determine foreign policy and its financing*. Tiberius retaliates by *unprecedented step (possibly breaching the Lex Villia, 180) of seeking a second term as tribune*. Clash between his followers and those of the senators. *Tiberius is killed*

123   Gaius Gracchus (brother to Tiberius) tribune. Pursues further radical anti-aristocratic measures

122   Gaius elected tribune for second term: thus *the principle of annuality of offices definitively breached*. Proposes citizenship for the Latins and Latin status for Italian *socii*, but this is highly unpopular with plebs and defeated

121   Gaius presents himself for re-election for third term, but fails. Protests against repeal of some of his legislation. *Armed clash* leads the consul (Opimius) to persuade Senate to issue a so-called *senatus consultum ultimum. Unprecedented*. It declares that the state is in danger and tells the magistrates to see that 'the republic take no harm'. Consul Opimius pursues Gracchus, *armed struggle, Gracchus is slain, and 3,000 of his followers judicially murdered*

119   Marius (not a *nobilis*) elected tribune

118–108   Roman armies repeatedly defeated in Africa and against Celts in Gaul and Po valley

107   *Defying senatorial opposition the comitia elected Marius consul for 107. The comitia overrules the allocation of provinces to entrust the provincia of the war in Africa to him*

105	*Marius elected for second term in breach of the ten-year limit on re-eligibility. Thenceforward re-elected each year until*
100	Sixth Consulate of Marius. His political ally, *Saturninus*, a demagogue, *resorts to force*. Senate issues another *senatus consultus ultimum*, ordering Marius to crush him. Marius does so, fails to prevent Saturninus and his supporters' *massacre*
91	Drusus tribune. Plans an agrarian reform which involves granting citizenship to the Italian allies. *Senate declares the law illegal because carried against auguries, hence null and void.* When Drusus is found murdered the allies revolt, hence:
91–88	The 'Social War'. Vast destruction. 250,000 men under arms. By 88 allies defeated militarily—but politically they are victorious, and they do receive Roman citizenship
88	Sulla consul, with Eastern command against Mithridates. Marius is induced to lend support to a tribune (Sulpicius) in return for the vote of the *comitia tributa* giving him the Eastern Command. *Sulla* retorts by suspending all public business by using the emergency decree of *iustitium, but Sulpicius revokes it. Sulla* flees to his army, and *marches on Rome.* Marius flees
86	While Sulla is fighting in the east, the fellow consul at Rome, *Cinna*, joins forces with *Marius*, seizes Rome, and they *have themselves elected consuls and initiate five-day reign of terror.* But Marius dies of pleurisy
83	Sulla returns, is joined by refugees from the terror, and also by Cn. Pompeius, who raises a private army of 3,000 men from Picenum
82	*Sulla retakes Rome, institutes an even worse reign of terror: the Proscription—a list of those to be murdered*
79	Having abandoned the old constitution and promulgated new contitutional laws (below), Sulla retires from office

5.4. 82–79 BC. *The End of the Ancient Constitution*

Sulla was to retire from office, and die shortly afterwards in 79 BC, having, he thought, finally settled the constitutional issue. In fact he had not, and civil warfare was to continue, on an ever-widening scale, until 31 BC when Octavian (the future Augustus) became undisputed master of the Roman world. This is when, conventionally, the Republic came to its end. The years between are those in which Sulla's lieutenant Pompey rose to mastery and imposed an order on the Middle East while Caesar, Sulla's lieutenant, in his turn conquered Gaul. Then came the rupture between them, the great civil wars from one end of the empire to the other, and Caesar's victory; his assassination by the *optimates* who renew the civil war against his political heirs (his adoptive nephew Octavian and Mark Antony), and the latters' annihilation of the *optimates*. Then the final civil war erupted, between Octavian and Mark Antony, ending in the definitive victory of Octavian.

For all that, it is with Sulla that the Republican constitution as I have described it came to its end, and the terrible convulsions outlined above were but its death-agonies.

In the first place, Sulla's forces were no longer the Republic's armies but personal ones, men who followed him for booty and reward. All the armies of the contenders in the subsequent civil wars were of this kind. Thus, no matter what their formal authority, the Senate and the Assemblies were henceforth dependants.

Secondly, Sulla differed from Marius in the way he treated his defeated opponents. Sulla's proscriptions were systematic and on an altogether vaster scale. He was 'the first Roman to make a formal list of those he condemned to death, to offer prizes to assassins and rewards to informers and threaten with punishment those who concealed the proscribed'. Sulla sentenced forty senators and 1,600 knights to death; later he added more senators and these, taken unawares in the city, were butchered where they stood. Subservient lawcourts condemned his opponents outside the city, throughout all Italy. Not only did Sulla punish individuals there, but entire communities! With the confiscations and sequestrations he imposed, he settled his discharged soldiers in military colonies, thus repaying their client status and also garrisoning the peninsula.[76] Such systematic proscriptions and confiscations were also to become the rule from now on. Thus, the effort to reconcile the opposition within the framework of the constitutional order which the Republic had made with success since the Struggle of the Orders was now abandoned for a policy of simply annihilating them.

Thirdly, the leaders of a victorious faction acquired for themselves tenures of authority unknown in previous history. We have seen how the Tribunate, for instance, had come to be granted two years in a row, and how Marius, for instance, was elected consul seven times; but these breaches of law and convention at least respected the principle of annuality, in that the incumbent had to re-submit to election at the end of his annual term. Sulla established a deadly precedent when, by vote of the *comitia centuriata* he was appointed *dictator legibus scribendis et republicae constituendae*—'dictator for making the laws and reconstitution of the Republic'. This resembled the ancient office of dictator in that it made Sulla the supreme magistrate, but whereas

---

[76] Appian, quoted in N. Lewis and M. Reinhold, *Roman Civilization*, Sourcebook, vol. 1, *The Republic*, vol. 2, *The Empire* (Harper, New York, 1966), 269–71.

the traditional dictatorship lasted for only six months, Sulla's dictatorship was for an unlimited term. Later Pompey, in 67 BC, was granted an extraordinary commission to take action against pirates. It gave him an *imperium infinitum*, that is, geographically unlimited powers, including making alliances and concluding peace at his pleasure, and this was conferred on him for three years. Caesar's command in Gaul was granted for five years in the first instance and when, later, in 49 BC he emerged as sole victor in the civil wars, he was proclaimed dictator for life.

But the most interesting feature of 'Sulla's reconstitution' of the Republic was that in fact it rejected its root principle—checks and balances via the counterposing of the 'monarchical' power of the consul, with the 'democratic' powers of the *comitiae* and the 'aristocratic' powers of the Senate. In the Middle Republic, as we have seen, the incongruous parts had worked harmoniously, but once one part moved into the (temporary) grip of the anti-Senatorial opposition the necessary co-ordination could be obtained only by more and more manipulation and corruption, then coercion, and finally open, armed, and bloody conflict. We do not have Sulla's own explanation of his reforms but we can, I think, infer it. In my view Sulla decided that the only way to make the institutions work together now was to do away with checks and balances altogether and place final authority in one organ, and for Sulla this was to be the Senate, to which all others were to be subordinated.

The tribunes and the *comitia* were diminished. No laws could be passed in the *comitia* without the previous sanction of the Senate. The *comitia tributa* could no longer give magistrates extraordinary commands. The tribunes were enfeebled: their plebiscites were no longer to be valid law unless so sanctioned by the Senate and they lost their right to veto the acts of the consuls and the *senatus consulta*. Not only this: the office, hitherto sought after as a means of gaining popularity in the race for the Consulate, was stripped of this attraction by prohibiting a tribune's moving on to another magistracy.

The power of the regular magistracy was also lessened. The Censorship was not abolished but it lost its right to select and de-select the senators. The allocation of duties to consuls and praetors was once more confided to the Senate, and it seems as if Sulla envisaged that the consuls should continue to receive a *provincia* (by lot) but not go out to it until the following year—hence as *proconsules*—while the praetors stayed at home during their year of election but received a provincial *provincia* the following year by similar use of the lot. Also, the importance of an individual magistracy was diminished by raising the number of praetors to eight and of quaestors to twenty and again by reverting to the strict application of the *cursus honorum*, and once more prohibiting re-election to the Consulship until a longer interval had elapsed.

The Senate, its hitherto 'conventional' status now made statutory in the new law of the constitution, thus became its centre-piece, an effectively sovereign body. Another 300 newcomers were added from among the knights (which must have meant a considerable influx of Italians). Recruitment was taken away from the censors in so far as all ex-quaestors (twenty in number) were to become senators. And the Senate's powers were further strengthened when Sulla gave it the exclusive rights to man the juries in the seven permanent courts which by now had largely taken over criminal jurisdiction from the *comitia centuriata*.

In his perception that the checks-and-balances principle could no longer serve and must be replaced by concentrating authority in one supreme organ, Sulla was undoubtedly correct. Where he erred was in confiding this authority to the Senate, for he himself had set the precedents and the example for subverting it. They were the ones I have outlined above: the personal army, the maintaining of such an army by plundering the political opposition, and the conferment of unlimited powers (*imperium infinitum*) for unlimited periods. The supreme authority that Sulla desiderated could no longer lie in the Senate, only in the man who commanded the legions. The entire subsequent torment of the Republic was to be a commentary on this.

6. AN APPRAISAL

The Republic can be pragmatically justified on three counts. First, it endured from 509 to 133 BC with great stability and with little but a few bones broken; its internal conflicts, at one time very severe, were resolved peacefully. This suggests that the oligarchy was not merely obeyed but, by and large, respected. The fact that so many Roman farmers could serve for years in the armies despite their obviously growing war-weariness and hatred for conscription also suggests that there was a genuine civic bond between them, that the *civitas* was in some sense a real community and not a joint-stock company, and that the balance of power and responsibility which give leadership to the wealthy lineages was acceptable. One can exaggerate what Mommsen could call the 'usurpations' of the Senate at the expense of the People. There was some rational basis for the spread of powers and responsibilities, and till 133 BC this broadly corresponded to popular perceptions. Nor should one underestimate the powerful sentiments of civic patriotism and the (objectively inordinate) fear of foreign attack in making for civic cohesion. A second justification lies in its making of something akin to an Italian nation. From a patchwork of a multitude of communities of very diverse languages, cultures, and stages of civilization, the city of Rome finally forged a largely homogeneous society, with a common citizenship, a common language, a common law, and common way of life and outlook. The third justification is that it was through armies of free citizens, not driven slaves or mercenaries, and through non-professional noblemen serving as generals in rotation every year that Rome conquered the known world. This again attests qualities of endurance, stubbornness, and self-discipline and, above all, voluntarism in the character of the Republic. Though the exact nature of these may elude us, they must have been present.

More than any polity so far looked at except the Assyrians, the Republic was shot through and through with militarism. It is unlikely that there are more than perhaps ten individual years over its entire span when Roman armies were not waging war somewhere or another, and in few previous societies was military glory so central an ambition to members of the ruling class. And discipline in the field was of the harshest kind. The *imperator* could sentence his men to death without appeal and when, late in the second century, appeal was by law finally conceded to Roman citizen soldiers (not allied troops, note) it was evaded by pointing a finger at the condemned, who thereupon had to run the gauntlet through his comrades and was clubbed to death. Defeated units of the army were treated similarly: they were paraded, one in every ten men was selected at random, and forthwith put to death. Conscription was relentless, especially as manpower ran low, so that men could be retained in the ranks without leave for seven or twice times seven years at a stretch.

If the Roman soldiers suffered in this way, the enemy suffered worse. Treachery, massacre, extortion, and looting was the commonplace of Roman wars, notably in the reduction of the Spanish tribes. It is very hard for the reader not to feel more sympathy for Viriathus in Spain or Vercingetorix in Gaul than for the legions.

Again, like the Assyrians but unlike the Persians, the Republic (not the *empire*) gave the conquered next to nothing in return. (The *empire*, as we shall see, is a *very* different story.) Whatever their original motivation, these campaigns were gigantic wars of plunder. It is quite true that all previous states had plundered likewise, but the predatoriness of Rome surpasses all of them by its immensity. The Roman armies slew, carried off booty, exacted vast indemnities, and reduced hundreds of thousands to slavery, but at this Republican stage in Rome's history all they gave in return was a succession of venal and avaricious pro-consuls out to make

their fortune in all the many ways open to a Roman commander exercising the *imperium*.

The Romans are also charged with cruelty. They were indeed cruel but
not, I think, more so than the other peoples of that time. The Romans
crucified thousands of the slaves who had been defeated and captured in the
Spartacus revolt, but the Carthaginians also crucified *en masse*, just as the
Assyrians impaled *en masse*. The entire ancient world was inured to cruelty in
a way we find repellent.

But, finally, I come back to the main fact of this chapter: the Republican
constitution and its political processes. The first was bad; the second in its
final phases, lethal.

The Republican constitution was preposterous. Stripped down to the
legal provisions only, this constitution was unworkable. Yet it did work and
until 133 BC, to be just, it worked very well, but in spite of itself, not because
of it. It worked because of unwritten conventions that its provisions should,
effectively, be side-stepped. This is a great compliment to the men—both
populus and *nobilitas*—who had to accept the conventions. But it is no
compliment to the constitution as such.

After 133 and even worse after 82 BC, it is no longer possible to praise
the men who operated it. On the contrary, the practice of politics in
Rome was thoroughly degenerate. We must not be hoodwinked here by
prating about 'majesty', 'Empire', 'Hellenic civilization', hot baths, drai-
nage, public buildings,[77] and the like—we are talking here about government, not a grandeur, or a culture and anyway, these terms apply to the
Empire, not the Republic. Nor must we be diverted from this by the
tragic elements in the demise of the Republic. Sallust, Appian, Plutarch,
Cicero, Caesar, Lucan, among others have revealed to us the characters
and the motives of the actors in this vast tragedy. They have provided the
theme for Shakespeare and Racine and Corneille. And there is no doubt
that such figures as Sulla, Pompey, Mark Antony, and Caesar were larger
than life, particularly Caesar, one of history's great statesmen. But if you
strip the personalities away—if you forget that what was at stake was the
'wide arch of the ranged Empire', if in fact you put away the drama and
look at nothing but the political process itself—you will find no more
sophistication, disinterestedness, or nobility than in a Latin-American
banana republic. Call the country the Freedonian Republic; set the
time in the mid-nineteenth century; imagine Sulla, Pompey, Caesar as

---

[77] They were made of wood and bricks at this time, anyway. Nor are we in the Augustan Age.

generals García Lopez, Pedro Podrilla, and Jaime Villegas and you will find clientelist factions, personalist parties, private armies, and military struggle for the presidency that parallel at every point the collapsing Republic.

5
The Formation of the Chinese State

*A*ll this while, since and before the second millennium, 3,500 miles eastward of the furthest confines of Iran, in the basin of the Yellow River, a wholly self-sufficient civilization and polity had been evolving in total independence of the Mediterranean world.[1] China was a comparative late-comer to organized political life: the Shang dynasty (and they themselves are as shadowy as their empire was primitive) began their career when the political systems of Sumeria and Egypt were already some 1,500 years old. But this was only the precursor of a polity that was to march ahead of all others in the world in terms of its art and crafts, its grandeur, wealth, extent, and populousness, and its duration and self-sufficient completeness until the era of the French Revolution.

This polity is completely foreign to anything in the Western tradition since the Greeks. Indeed, it is antithetical. This polity, the prevalent belief systems, and the social structure all came to support one another as never since the high days of Mesopotamian and Egyptian government and emphatically as never in the West. Hence the stability and duration of the Chinese social and political system and the restlessness and lability of the West. Where the latter reposed on freely acting and personally responsible individuals, China reposed on collectivities, where all were responsible for the misdeeds of one another. Where the former conceived of citizens, the Chinese state knew only subjects. The Western tradition embodied the notion of human equality before the law and in the sight of God, and so forth. The Chinese state started from the exactly opposite viewpoint. It postulated, *ab initio*, that the young deferred to the old, women to men, men to their fathers, fathers to their ancestors, all to the emperor.

Its ideal was an organic society where all these unequals were induced to cohere into a harmonious whole. It brought this about through a meticulous set of day-to-day rituals and observances which defined precisely who behaved towards what manner of person on such or such an occasion for what particular purpose. The central concept in this web of worldly rituals

---

[1] I would not exclude, however, the possibility of some technical linkages, mediated through central Asia. It seems unlikely, for instance, that the chariot was invented twice over.

was filial piety; the respect due to parents. This was the source and the justification for the exaggerated and at times grotesque Chinese obsession with tradition and precedent. It was equally the justification for fidelity to the paternal but absolute rule of the emperor. China was regarded as *Kuo-chia*, a 'family state': in short, a family writ large. Nor were these the only ways in which Chinese society inverted the values of the West. In Greece, it was the triumphant athlete whom his native city turned out to cheer; in China it was the scholar who had just passed the civil service examinations. It was for victory in war the Romans celebrated their triumphs; in China the soldier was despised. The fourfold classification of vocations— a ladder of social esteem—put merchants at the bottom, artisans just above them and farmers in the second rank, but reserved the top place for the scholar. And this was not an idle obeisance. On the contrary, the governance of the state came to be entrusted to some 15,000 prize-fellows, as it were, the pick of the nation's graduates in classical literature. Nobody in the entire society compared with them in prestige, power, and wealth. Unlike the West, only at rare and brief intervals was China ruled by an aristocracy of blood; ideally it was ruled by a service aristocracy of literary talent.

Another significant way in which Chinese society differed from the West concerns religion. Like Greece or Rome, it was not priest-ridden; and it resembles Rome quite considerably in its meticulous observance of placatory rituals. But religiously it differs entirely from Christian Europe and Moslem Asia. China knew and tolerated a number of persuasions, notably the Taoist and the Buddhist, but its *official* belief system was nothing like salvationist Christianity or Islam. It was a this-worldly ethical code, but one so engaging and, ultimately, so pervasive that although it was not a religion in the western sense it certainly played the same political and cultural roles as Christianity or for that matter Islam did, and do. This code—Confucianism—justified and at the same time prescribed that very social and political order we have been outlining. Moreover, though it started as a wisdom rather than a philosophy, it came to elaborate a metaphysic and a cosmology which ended up by synthesizing the ethics of the individual, the conduct of public affairs, and the social/economic contours of society into an all-embracing philosophy. The state and man were seen as the counterpart of the natural order, as part of a cosmic harmony between man and nature. The way this came about was called precisely that—'the way' or Tao. Balance and harmony of the two contradictory and yet complementary forces of *Yin* (earth) and *Yang* (heaven) pervaded everything sublunary, and the state and the law codes must be constructed and operated to reflect the balance of these two cosmic forces.

In all this there are indeed analogies with some of the positions taken up by various western philosophers, but in China they are asserted, not demonstrated by the rationalistic, logic-based analytical mode of Greek and subsequent western thought. Again, this is as alien to the western tradition as anything we have mentioned so far, as alien as Chinese music, or architecture, or indeed the character, the constructions, and the syntax (or rather the lack of syntax) of the written language of China.

The full maturity of this culture was not attained till the Ch'ing in the early eighteenth century AD. It is clearly apparent under the Sung in the eleventh century. Its archetypal lines are firmly established under the Han, 206 BC–220 AD, after which in a sense all subsequent history is development and elaboration. But most of the constituents of the Han tradition itself were established in the long period between the earliest and tribal condition of the Chinese people and the famous unification of the seven Chinese kingdoms in 221 BC by the king of Ch'in: whence the name we give the subsequent state, nation, and civilization—*China*.[2] In this chapter we attempt a summary of the main developments in this constitutive period.

I. CHRONOLOGY

Chinese civilization, like the Egyptian and Mesopotamian, used generally to be considered as having begun in the basin of a great river. This is the Huang Ho or Yellow River. As a glance at a map will show, this flows through what we nowadays regard as North China, and it was from there that the huge expanse of modern China was civilized—and Sinicized, too, as we shall see. The most obvious reason for the Yellow River basin being the first locus of civilization lies in its soil. This is *loess*, a sedimentary deposit of fine grains. It is *yellow* in colour—hence Yellow River, hence too the legendary 'Yellow Emperor' of China, hence yellow as an imperial colour subsequently. In the Yellow River basin the deposits are from 10 to 30 metres thick! It is the richest of all soils in the world.

The traditional Chinese histories tell of great kings who lived fabulously long lives and introduced the arts of cultivation and irrigation. They were succeeded by dynasties of which the oldest is the Hsia, followed by the Shang, or (as sometimes expressed) the Shang-yin, and then by the Chou. Even by the legendary chronology, Chinese civilization would not date back

---

[2] This seems firmly established at last. See *Cambridge. History of China* [hereafter *CHC*], vol. I (CUP, Cambridge, 1986), 20 n. 23.

to the time before *c.*2500 BC. Even the Shang were considered legendary, until the early twentieth-century discovery of inscriptions on shells, bones, and tombs identified as those of the Shang kings vindicated the historians' king-lists of that dynasty. After 841 BC we have exact dates for Chinese events. Up to then, there are somewhat differing chronologies. So the traditional dates for the Shang are 1766–1122 BC; others put it as 1558–1031 or 1523–1027.

The Shang culture reposed on a population of farmers whose tools and way of living were still of the stone age. The contrast between the common folk and their rulers is apparent from the semi-troglodyte dwellings of the former and the raised pavilions of the latter.[3]

Chinese history begins with the Shang in three senses: they possessed a script, they cast in bronze, and they built and inhabited towns. A word is desirable about all three, particularly the script. The towns excavated—at the sites near Cheng-Chou and An-yang—centre on a ceremonial complex comprising the palaces, temple-quarters, and accommodation for troops and craftsmen. On the site of Cheng-Chou a massive wall of stamped earth, about a mile on each side, attests one perennial feature of Chinese civilization down to the present day: namely, forced labour. This wall would have taken 10,000 men, working 330 days a year, no less than eighteen years to build.[4] It seems that these towns were the centres for the indispensable rituals on which agricultural life depended, inhabited by the military and the rulers, with the common folk living in villages outside. Here is a second feature that was to be perennial: the town is a military and administrative centre. There is little possibility, therefore, of its developing a commune-life like the Graeco-Roman or medieval European cities.

The most staggering finds at An-yang are its now famous ritual vessels in bronze. Their shapes and decorations are distinctively Chinese, but what has caused wonder is their extremely advanced technique. It was way ahead of contemporary work in the Middle East. The vessels were worked by an entirely different technique from that practised in the Middle Eastern and classical world, that is, the *cire-perdue* ('lost-wax') method of casting. The Shang cast their molten metal in earthenware moulds and then joined the cast pieces together with seams and lugs.

The bronze sacrificial vessels, however, do not exhaust the metal artefacts

---

[3] Supported on a platform of pounded mud, these pavilions are identical to those being raised in the 1930s.

[4] P. Wheatley, *The Pivot of the Four Quarters* (Edinburgh UP, Edinburgh, 1971), 76.

of the Shang. For they used the bronze for their armament of spears, arrow-tips, and above all, for the accoutrements of their distinctive weapon—the chariot. As we have already observed, this seems most unlikely to have been invented twice over, both in Anatolia and in China. Innovations in arma-ment notoriously spread much more rapidly than other technologies. It was the possession of this advanced weaponry that enabled the Shang to invade and subjugate the neolithic farmer folk of the Yellow River Basin and establish themselves, inside their towns, as the ruling tribe.

This invasion by 'Chinese', and their subsequent domination, interpene-tration, and, in the end, sinicization of the indigenous peoples is the way the Chinese nation was formed. The Chou, the Ch'in, the Han, the T'ang, Sung, and Ming did essentially the same thing in their own time: the nucleus of the Sinicized people, that is, those using Chinese as their language (*inter alia*), grew larger and larger with each accretion, until the southern borders of present-day China were reached in the fifteenth and sixteenth centuries and the entire country, south of the Yangtse, was overlaid by Chinese civilization. In short, the indigenous peoples living in the territory we call China were *colonized*—over centuries—by the people we call 'Chinese'. The Shang were the first wave, the Chou the next.

So, what is 'Chinese'? A good question. Who were the 'original' Chinese is *the* trick question for Sinologists. I unhesitatingly follow David Hawkes in 'calling Chinese only those who have spoken a language identifiable as Chinese'.[5] And the first *literate* culture of this kind is the Shang. Thousands and thousands of 'oracle'-bones form part of the royal archives found at An-yang. These bones carry the original question on one side and the inter-mediaries' answer to it on the other, and they use some 3,000 characters or ideograms, of which about one half can be identified.

The Chinese script is uniquely Chinese and it is of overwhelming cultural but also political significance for China. *It is much more important than the spoken language*, or rather languages, of that nation. Why is this so? Because, even today, although the regions of China speak similar or cognate tongues, they do *not* speak an identical one. A Cantonese finds a Northerner unintelligi-ble. Similar words are often pronounced very differently, and sometimes the words used are completely different. Thus the word for 'three' in the northern 'Mandarin' tongue is *san* and in Cantonese it is *sam*. But the Mandarin for 'two' is *erh* while it is *yi* in Cantonese; for 'five' Mandarin uses *wu*, Cantonese *ng*; and so forth. But the written characters, though

---

[5] D. Hawkes, *The Songs of the South: Poems by Qu Yuan and Other Poets* (Penguin, Harmondsworth, 1985), 16.

pronounced differently, carry identical connotations: so that, in the ancient phrase, both Northerners and Cantonese can 'speak with the brush'. In this way they can each *read* a text and understand it in an identical way.

The Chinese script is very wonderful, very complicated, very archaic. It is as though Egyptian hieroglyphs were still being used to write Coptic today. It consists of individual ideograms. This system has necessitated a very large number of characters. To read a newspaper one might get by with about 2,000. To communicate fairly well in mundane matters would need some 3,000. An academic or official needs 6,000–7,000 *at least*, and each has to be learned individually.

Hence the political importance of this script. First, it acted as a common medium of communication between cognate but diverse tongues—therefore as a great nation-building instrument. Next, it helped to channel the art of persuasion from *rhetoric* in the Graeco-Roman oratorical sense, to the written document: and this, coupled with the fact that Chinese statesmen were authoritarians and bureaucrats, made Chinese civilization supremely the culture of the book and not the orator. Finally, it takes so long to acquire and makes mass-literacy drives so difficult to mount (even if the will is not lacking, as historically it certainly was in China's past), that it perpetuated a chasm between a literate ruling class and the illiterate masses.[6]

The Shang kingdom could never have been large, since the histories speak of continual wars with the indigenous tribesmen who lived around and among the Shang. It was probably no more than a series of strong-points, colonies, planted among the aborigines but articulated and given direction by a tribal structure at whose head stood the *wang* or king. That structure is what Kirchoff has called the 'conical clan'. It ranks families in terms of the birth order of their founders: offshoots from the main lineage, then offshoots (in birth order) from these secondary lineages, and so forth. The head of the grand lineage was the *wang*, a theocratic and absolute monarch, whose authority derived from the exclusivity of his communion with his ancestors, the gods of the entire tribe. The outlying Shang settlements were ruled by the cadet lines of this grand lineage and, by the nature of the tribal convention, ranked lower and therefore acted as subordinates.

[6] It is indeed possible to get high rates of literacy by long childhood study and compulsory school education: so, Hong Kong had achieved 77% literacy by 1971, whereas mainland People's Republic of China had only achieved 65% over a decade later (*UNESCO Yearbook*, 1990).

1.1. *The Chou*

In 1122 BC, according to tradition (but in all probability *c*.1045 BC), the Shang dynasty was overthrown by another tribe, the Chou. The Chou lived in the west, in what was later called 'the land between the passes', where the Yellow River makes a right-angled turn from the north and the area of the Ordos. The Chou kings ruled through their own collateral or cadet lineages, alongside Shang noblemen who had made their peace and, in some cases, native tribesmen who accepted subject status. The underlying structure, however, as with the Shang, was the 'conical class' hierarchy of families.

The Chou continued to use the same script as the Shang. They were sufficiently different from the Shang, however, to initiate certain changes that were to be significant later. For one thing they seem to have been more aggressive and successful warriors and so they extended the area of Chinese colonization westwards from their capital (near the modern Hsi-an) into Kansu and eastward from their western capital (near Lo-yang) towards Peking. The pattern was the same, however. They established walled towns from which they controlled their satellite village communities and held down the native tribesmen. These cities were entrusted to their rulers—usually a scion of the tribe—by an investiture ceremony not unlike a medieval European feudal baron taking seisin from his lord. (This is one of the particulars which has led many scholars to describe this as a 'feudal' system.)[7] These rulers similarly entrusted their own kinsmen or retainers to rule lesser areas and in this way the colonization went on by a kind of 'swarming process'. In the end, the entire territory may be envisaged as an archipelago of over 1,700 Chou strong-points with castles and garrisons in a sea of potentially hostile villagers and alien tribesmen—something like the Normans in England, Wales, and Ireland. As time went on the natives became assimilated, intermarried, acculturated, and so the 'Chinese nation' swelled by accretion.

The Chou dynasty and its tribal affiliates were able to control the kingdom partly because their chariots and bronze weapons made them militarily superior and, next, because they shared a common interest in establishing a united front against the natives. As in any polyarchic decentralized system such as the Chou kingdom certainly was (whether we call it 'feudal' or not), the individual vassals were regulated by the king, who disposed of two means of doing this. The first was his military superiority.[8]

---

[7] See pp. 864 ff.
[8] H. G. Creel, *The Origins of Statecraft in Ancient China*, vol. 1, *The Western Chou Empire* (University of Chicago Press, Chicago, 1970), 306–7.

Secondly, like his Shang predecessors, he was the fountain of authority in the Chou tribe. The Shang had worshipped a supreme deity—a highly abstract *numen*—called Ti. The Chou worshipped, instead, a *numen* called T'ien which also translates as 'Heaven'. To justify their overthrow of the (after all) sacred king of the Shang, they appealed to what they called the 'mandate of T'ien', the 'mandate of Heaven'. T'ien had punished the Shang for their sins by removing their mandate to rule and instead had invested the virtuous Chou. The mandate, then, was *conditional* on virtuous rule. This doctrine was a rod in pickle for all future rulers. The proof that Heaven had withdrawn its mandate was the overthrow of a ruler. So, rebellion was justified—provided it succeeded: a curiously simplistic piece of circular thinking.[9] For the moment, however, it served to strengthen the new dynasty where the king was known as T'ien Tzu, the 'Son of Heaven'. As such he communicated with the great T'ien, and consulted and sacrificed to his own ancestors, who were the gods of the entire tribe. On him alone, therefore, the luck and prosperity of the entire tribe depended. His sacral and ritual role was central for he was the human collaborator with Heaven in regulating the natural order. Granet[10] has left us a remarkable picture of the exaggeratedly elaborate ritual of the king making his progress through the Nine Rooms of the Ming T'ang (Hall of Distinction) in his palace grounds, which led him to face all points of the compass in turn, in order to make the seasons function properly. His worship of Heaven was, of course, part of the cult of his ancestors, since they too had been Sons of Heaven, so that 'the dynastic cult of Heaven was a sublimation of the cult of the royal ancestors'.[11] It fed directly into the cult of Earth and the harvest, and in this way it related very directly to the ruler's illiterate peasant subjects. It was the king who drew up the calendar: the peasantry could keep no reckoning of months and days and on this depended when to plant, when to sow, to reap—vital facts which otherwise they found highly confusing.

Now the peasants had an intense and emotional attachment to the soil. They thought of Earth as their Mother and their Nurse and the container of all life. When they buried their dead, their substance entered the domestic soil. Hence their cult of the family dead and of the domestic hearth.[12] These peasant beliefs were all of a piece with the ancestor cult of

---

[9] Such circularity was to become commonplace. See e.g. Bk. III, Ch. 1, 'The Byzantine Empire', below. We have already observed it in Egypt (Bk. I, Ch. 2 and 3).

[10] M. Granet, *The Religion of the Chinese People*, trans., ed., and introduction by M. Freedman (Blackwell, Oxford, 1975), 68.   [11] As Granet puts it, ibid. 69.

[12] Ibid. 50–3.

their king, but this went far wider and framed and validated the entire Chou political order. Ancestor worship spanned grandfather to grandson. It was obligatory to have a son, so that he might serve his grandfather. The number of generations over which a departed soul was active corresponded to one's social status: and this status was in the gift of the monarch! He could permit the high-ranking families to serve the ancestors for eight generations back, but the lower-ranking for only four! In this way the purported 'feudal' hierarchy of the Chou was inextricably combined in a uniquely Chinese way with the kinship status-order of the 'conical clan', and both with the deepest religious outlooks of both rulers and ruled.

The king was, therefore, regarded with supreme awe. He was pivot of his subjects' relationship with nature, and it was from this that his power to order and regulate the diverse 'ramages' of the Chou kinship and hence their political authority derived. How seriously this ritual role was taken can be inferred from a simple fact. In 771 BC a troop of barbarians swooped on the western capital, defeated the royal armies, and destroyed the city. The noblemen called out their own troops and installed a successor as king in Lo-yang. The king was at their mercy yet they maintained him and his successors as the one and only *wang* of Chou for another three centuries—because his ritual role was indispensable.

1.2. The 'Spring and Autumn' Period (722–481 BC)

What occurred, according to his traditional sources, was recounted by Ssu-ma Ch'ien, 'the Grand Historian' (*c.*145–*c.*86 BC): the barons (or seigneurs) 'came to an understanding . . . to give the power to the ex-heir presumptive . . . I-Kyu, who became King P'ing—*so that he could take responsibility for the sacrifices of the chou*'.[13] This ritual position was almost all he now possessed, for the nobles endowed him with only the very small domain of Chou. Military power rested with the nobility, who immediately began to make war on one another. Well over one thousand states were involved in literally unremitting warfare,[14] with the larger armies numbering some 10,000. China is not noted for admiring the art of war, but this period is exceptional. The chariotry, which in earlier times had been manned by commoners, now became the preserve of young aristocrats. It was a sort of Homeric age, and

[13] Ssu-ma Ch'ien, *Records of the Grand Historian of China*, trans. from the *Shi Chi* by Burton Watson (Columbia UP, New York, 1961), i. 285.
[14] C.-Y. Hsu, *Ancient China in Transition: An Analysis of Social Mobility, 722–222 BC* (Stanford University Press, Stanford, 1965), 62–3.

the feats of the warriors were extolled as heroic. Chivalry, never met with in Chinese warfare before or since, could be carried to extreme lengths.[15]

This age is known as the *Ch'un Ch'iu* or 'Spring and Autumn' period, after the (very laconic) Annals of the small kingdom of Lu (in Shantung) which cover the years 722–481 BC. In these two-and-a-half centuries, the area of colonization continually expanded and the number of belligerent mini-states contracted as the most powerful annexed the weakest; the nobility killed one another off or were shouldered aside by new families who were abler or luckier commanders; and the blood-tie between the ramages of the 'conical class' thinned as each cadet ramage threw off its own ramages, more and more distant from the Grand Lineage of the Chou. Yet all these independent Chou princes still looked to the monarch as the head of the polity: as the Son of Heaven he alone could sacrifice to heaven, which none of them were entitled to worship personally, so that he remained the visible symbol, the primal source of legitimacy, the vital pivot of the indispensable rituals of the Chou family-connection.

One of these states was Ch'i, located in the Shantung Peninsula. In the early sixth century BC its ruler rallied many of the other states round himself to withstand barbarians pressing in from the north and south. Continuing to recognize the Chou monarch as suzerain, he took the title of *pa*, 'overlord' or 'hegemon'. As such, he convened interstate meetings, settled disputes, and led campaigns against the barbarians. The position was so useful, indeed indispensable, that it soon became institutionalized; the meetings became regular and what had begun as voluntary contributions became compulsory tribute. Consequently, the largest states fought one another for the position of *pa*. For a long time it was held by the prince of the huge state of Ch'in, but this was counterbalanced by the oldest of all these monarchies, the kingdom of Ch'u, which lay *south* of the Yangtse, far removed from the epicentre of Chinese colonization. Half-a-dozen minor states and seven big ones emerged from warfare. The survival of these states did not bring about a peace, but simply generated a new and fiercer phase in the struggle, which Chinese historians call the *Chan-kuo*, the 'Warring States' (481–221 BC).

Prior to the period of warfare, the beginnings of Chinese literature—the *Book of Odes* and *The Book of Documents*, for instance—appear, and along with this the birth of political and moral philosophy. *Confucius* (b. 551 BC)—of whom more later—was a teacher like Plato in that he wandered from

---

[15] For examples, see D. Bloodworth, *The Chinese Looking-Glass* (Secker and Warburg, London, 1967), 35.

princely court to princely court, peddling his recipes for good government, with equal unsuccess. The more obscure, perhaps even legendary Lao Tzu also lived in this period (though precisely when is a mystery), and he is—reportedly—the founder of the persuasion that was to rival Confucianism, *Taoism*. Thus two of the formative philosophies of the mature China (the third is Buddhism, which made its way into China from at least AD 100) originated at this time.

A second great change was to complete the assimilation of the non-Chinese enclaves in the Yellow River Basin, so that there was now a homogeneous Chinese culture-nation north of the Yangtse. The third capital change was the transformation of the social structure.

These 'warring states' continued to rest, as ever, on the backs of the peasantry, but the top, aristocratic echelons were in liquidation. Ancient noble lines died out, or were killed out, or were chased out by upstarts in command of the armed forces. Yet the need and opportunity for literate and educated individuals to administer the court rituals, manage estates, and conduct correspondence multiplied, and was satisfied from that stratum that we used to call 'gentle' or 'gentlefolk', that is, the 'well-born' but humbler scions of noble families: the kind of persons once addressed by the courtesy title of 'esquire' in England. These were the *shih*.

The final change to be noted was the sequence of moves toward the self-contained, rationally constructed centralized state. It is marked by local experiments with systematic taxation in the sixth century BC, specialized court officials, the introduction (fifth century) of the 'county' or 'prefecture' (*hsien*), a local government area directly ruled by a salaried official of the central government. In the fourth and third centuries BC these trends were symbolized by the way one prince after another adopted the title *wang* (king). It was part of Chou state religion that under T'ien there could be but one *wang*. By calling themselves *wang* these princes were implicitly rejecting even the residual ritual authority of the Chou monarch. Instead they got their court scholars to concoct genealogical trees which showed them as in fact coevals of the Chou Grand Lineage or as descendants of local gods in their own right.

The distinction drawn between the 'Spring and Autumn' period and the 'Warring States' is contrived, for it depends on the traditional ascription of the *Annals of Spring and Autumn* to Confucius. Singularly enough, though, the later period does have a different 'feel'. This is because the tempo of change accelerated, while the delinquescence of ancient Chou state religion left the way open to the most unconscionable extremes of statecraft.

1.3. *The Warring States, 481–221 BC*

Rule by aristocrats, articulated by the allocation of benefices and sub-benefices to cadet lineages, became totally defunct. The new polity was a centralized, iron-fisted autocracy. The old states had observed the conventions of an often quaint chivalry. The new ones thought only of advantage. The age of statecraft had arrived.

The motive force in this transformation of the state was military competition but associated now with two interconnected phenomena: the mass-production of iron artefacts and a revolution in the conduct of warfare. Ironworking arose in China in the sixth century BC, long after the Middle East and Greece, but when it did arrive Chinese technology advanced far beyond Europe's—to a stage, indeed, that Europe would not equal till the Middle Ages. The Chinese experience with ceramics had accustomed them to firing at high temperatures. Now they invented the double-action bellows, giving a continuous blast and ensuring higher temperatures still. Consequently the Chinese *cast* iron, and produced cast-iron ploughshares and the like. While such tools were still scarce *c.*400 BC, new iron-mines were exploited, foundries sprang up, and with them merchants who transported their products in river-boats. The rulers took direct control of all these processes in order to expand their military potential. So arose a kind of cameralism, akin to and prompted by the same motives as in the German states in seventeenth century.

The ancient aristocratic role of the chariotry melted away just as it had in seventh- and sixth-century Greece. The new armies may have been composed of infantry armed with iron swords and the newly invented crossbow, and with horses no longer yoked to chariots but ridden into battle as a genuine cavalry in imitation of the nomads of the northern steppe. As the princes mobilized their economic resources so the armies grew in size. It is possible that princes promoted the spread of independent peasant farming in order to multiply sources of recruits, which further eroded the economic and political status of the traditional landowning aristocracy. The great families of antiquity were ruined. Their family cults disappeared and their place at court was taken by the *shih*, as the servitors, administrators, and *literati* of a sovereign who daily grew more self-sufficient and autocratic as the former aristocratic restraints on his military and political power fell away. By the end of the Warring States period, they were all autocracies in which the power of the sovereign was absolute. His power rested on his military might. He acted directly on his subjects, no longer through traditional conventions administered by the local nobleman, but through savage law codes administered by his own officials. The population owed him service both in the field and for public works. Peasant labour gangs built dykes and embankments and huge walls along the frontier to protect the state from invasion.

Despite differences between the Warring States, law was emerging as the command of the sovereign. It was becoming public, and purportedly impartial; no longer an aristocratic secret to be dispensed at discretion and with due regard to degree. It established a social ranking order which determined the duties of each rank in the service of the sovereign and his political plans. Conditions like these were met with to the full in the western marcher-kingdom of Ch'in and came in later and less completely in the other states.

Such reforms in the various Warring States reflect rational statecraft. In Ch'in they reflected—or were themselves a reflection of—Legalist theory, of which more later. 'State institution—civil and military officers, a system of rewards and punishments meted out in accordance with rules that excluded any injustice or favouritism, honorific ranks granted for services rendered, collective responsibility and the obligatory denunciation of crimes within the family group . . .',[16] such were the institutions of Ch'in. Since Ch'in was to conquer all the other states, the establishment there of the centralized state was, as Gernet rightly points out, as decisive for China as the establishment of the *polis* was for Greece and the West in general.[17] Both set the pattern of the future.

2. CONTINUITIES IN PRE-CH'IN CHINA

We have seen the Chinese state develop from a tribal structure to an aristocratic feudalistic one and finally to the centralized autocracy epitomized in Ch'in. Sweeping and profound as these changes were, a number of basic characteristics of the social order outlasted all of them. Indeed, it would be truer to say that each successive state-form utilized these characteristics as its foundation-stones. Foremost is the primacy of the collectivity over the individual. Of such collectivities the family was and always remained the most important, and of all the institutions that safeguarded it, ancestor worship was paramount. Family, class, village imposed themselves on individuality, and set the pattern for political relationships. The cult of the ancestors involved and implied paternalism and patriarchy. The latter was no less the rule in early Rome, but in that case it dissolved and new laws regulated it away. In China, by contrast, new laws were (subsequently)

---

[16] J. Gernet, *A History of Chinese Civilization*, trans. J. Foster (CUP, Cambridge, 1982), 81–2.
[17] Ibid. 80.

introduced in order to perpetuate this ancestor worship. Their long exposure to the shared family and clan relationship predisposed the Chinese to
other, but artificially created, collective activity: the tithing system, for
instance, by which groups of families were collectively responsible for one
another's actions,[18] and the forced-labour gangs for building dikes or walls
or highways.

One other implication is that no individual was free in the Greek sense of
eleutheria, that is, absolute self-determination. Not only was he restrained by
his family clan or peers: subjected from childhood to his elders, his rearing
accustomed him to authoritarianism and absolutism. It accustomed him,
likewise, to inequality of status: from the hierarchy of family relationships to
the hierarchy in the wider society. The family, moreover, was a network of
duties, not rights. For even its patriarch had his duties—towards the
ancestors.

Throughout all the changes in the form of the state, therefore, certain
characteristics continued to prevail. These characteristics are wholly antithetical to those of the Greek and Roman republics (although not of
monarchical Sparta[19]). Collective and mutual responsibility, not individualism; authoritarianism, paternalism, and absolutism, not self-determination; inequality and hierarchy, not equality before the law; subjects not
citizens, duties not rights.

These characteristics were never more clearly embodied than in the state
of Ch'in where they were articulated in a political philosophy known as
Legalism. Yet these same characteristics are also the building-blocks of a
completely antithetical political philosophy—that of Confucius. This
apparent paradox itself underlines the fact that they were so deeply
embedded in Chinese culture that they serve as elements in all public policy.
This, again, explains how in subsequent ages the practical business of
governing China, nominally Confucianist, combined with Legalism in
practice. Legalism and Confucianism proved central to the theory and
practice of the Chinese state for more than 2,000 years to come. Both arose
in this period of decaying aristocratic government and emergent centralization, and represent rival responses to these trends. The period *c*.500–*c*.250 BC
was marked by the rise of the so-called 'Hundred Schools'. This was the
first great creative period of Chinese political thought. We cannot properly

---

[18] The best example of this is the *pao-chia*, first introduced in 4th cent. BC. As the *CHC* says, this
basic idea was 'repeatedly carried out in imperial times and even as late as republican China' (i. 37).
This is too modest. In variant form it is found today, under Communism.
[19] See above, Bk. II, Ch. 2, Sec. 4.

understand the development of the Chinese state without first glancing at these rival philosophies.

3. CONFUCIANISM AND LEGALISM

The Spring and Autumn and Warring States periods stimulated political theorizing and, equally, permitted it as never before. The old order was in full retreat, a new one not yet born. Instead there was nothing but usurpation and barbarity: 'When Nao Ch'ih took power in Ch'i, he bound King Min by his joints and suspended him from a beam in the ancestral temple. There the king hung all night and died the next day. When Li Tui took charge of Chao he slowly starved the ex-King until one hundred days later he was dead.'[20] Although this is from a work of fiction, it conveys a sense of the brutality of the times.

Between the sunset of one order and the dawn of a new one, only three positions were logically open. One was to reject the world and action altogether, and this was taken up by the Taoists. From the second century AD onwards Taoism was to become a very important strain of popular religion, while its theologians were in later times to be influential with a number of emperors, yet it never presented a coherent political credo or programme. The two other pertinent attitudes at this time were either to turn back to the past or to reject it. The Confucianists followed the first and the Confucianist model was a sentimentalized and quite unhistorical version of a legendary Golden Age and of the earliest Chou kings Wen and Wu, and especially (for Confucius) the Duke of Chou who acted as regent for his nephew (1042–1036 BC). In contrast, the Legalist model was the brutal centralized absolutist state that was just emerging.[21]

3.1. *Confucius and Confucianism*

'Confucianism' was to expand far beyond the teachings of Confucius himself and to receive its best-known canonical form no less than 1,500

---

[20] Lu Hsiang, *Chan Kuo Tse* (trans J. I. Crump, Chinese Materials Centre, San Francisco, 1979), 108.

[21] There is a fourth school of thought, that of Mo Tzu (479–438 BC). It is a doctrine of universal love and pacifism—defended for the practical benefits these will bring, hence utilitarian. But the Mohist school disappeared after the 3rd cent. BC, and so will not be discussed further. (See W.-T. Chan, *A Source Book in Chinese Philosophy* (Princeton UP, Princeton, 1963), 211–31, for excerpts and commentary.)

years after his death in the Sung dynasty commentary of Chu Hsi (1130–
1200). In this pre-Ch'in period three authors apart from Confucius himself
made contributions to his way of thought—Mencius, Hsün Tzu, and Tsou
Yen.

Confucius (Kung Fu-tzu, or 'Master Kung'), 551–479 BC, was a typical
shih: the impoverished surplus scion of an impoverished minor noble family.
He came from the ancient state of Lu, where much of the old political
tradition still survived. He seems to have been the first private teacher
recorded in Chinese history. At the age of 50 he quitted Lu and travelled
through several princely courts to proffer advice to their rulers in the hope
of finding one at least who would adopt his policies. The advice was
unsolicited, unwelcome, and in vain, and after ten years of absence he
returned to Lu, dying aged 73.

His authorship is still highly controversial. Just as Solomon was credited
with the Song of Songs and Ecclesiastes, so Confucius was credited with
anything likely—the *Book of Changes* (*I ching*) for instance. An authentic
record of his thought and action is contained in the *Lungyü* or *Analects*, an
unsystematic collection compiled by his disciples. It is indeed possible that
he wrote the 'Spring and Autumn Annals' (the *Ch'un Ch'iu*) since they are
records of his native land, but they are no more than an arid chronology. He
is also credited, however, with either writing or editing other works. While
such claims remain subject to controversy, the *Book of Odes* (the *Shih ching*) and
the *Book of Documents* (the *Shu ching*) contain materials going back to the most
ancient times, and it was from those times that Confucius drew his
inspiration.

Mencius (Meng-tzu, *c.*371–289 BC) is known as 'the Second Sage'. His
Meng-tzu, which came to rank along with Confucius's own canon, is akin to
the *Analects* in format but three times its length.

Hsün Ch'ing's teachings (between 335 and 238 BC) are collected in his
Hsün-tzu. Finally, there is Tsou Yen (305–240 BC). While not a Confucianist,
Tsou Yen is the systematizer of *Yin-Yang* and the Five Agents doctrine which
Han Confucianists were to incorporate into their teaching under the Han.

It is not easy to determine the respective contributions of Confucius and
his followers. The problem is greatest of all in respect of Confucius himself.
If the *Analects* is taken as the core of Confucius's own position, it would
seem that the contribution of Mencius was to make the welfare of the
people the dominant concern of the ruler, and to stress how conditional on
this was the Mandate of Heaven. Mencius seems to maintain, also, that the
scholar-officials' duty was to the Confucian 'way' and not unconditional
service to the ruler. Hsün-tzu dwelt on the role in the political process of
the Rites (the *li*, or social institutions, meaning also the 'proprieties'). Tsou

Yen, as we have noted, brought the Five Agents and *Yin-Yang* doctrines into conformity with a basically Confucianist position. It was a synthesis of such elements that the Confucianists upheld in the Han Empire.

As to Confucius as a person, disagreement is quite violent. The Ch'ing dynasty (post-1644) raised a commemorative temple to his memory in every subprefecture of the state, where he was worshipped as some sort of demigod. Some modern scholars, like Creel, portray him as benign and profound, even in some sense a 'democrat'; but the Chinese communists see him as the propagator of a brazenly overt inegalitarian ideology of the landowning ruling classes. He has been regarded as an arch intriguer at the various princely courts he visited, striving to come into power. Others view him as a sentimentalist, an impractical and hopeless traditionalist, a prig whose recorded remarks are mostly commonplace when they are not pious exhortations. It is unquestionable that the methodology and the doctrine of Confucius founded an ideology which became synonymous with Chinese culture; some see this as China's glory; others, however, see it as China's curse.

Confucius's aim was *restoration*, in particular the rescue of what he claimed were the pious standards of the aristocratic feudalistic government under the early Chou. Hence his collection of the *Odes*, hence too his *Spring and Autumn Annals*, whose method (if it can be dignified by that name) was to present an interpretation of events and draw from them the maxims of proper government. For the right standards, aims, and processes, said Confucius, 'I follow Chou'. The notion that all events might have to change with changing times and problems was repugnant, indeed, alien to him. Man and his problems were timeless. Confucius observed the early Chou and the Sage Kings as one might, through a glass screen, observe the silent movement of heroes of the past, all bathed in golden light. For all that, Confucius was a child of his own time and, one might argue, before his time: a man who appealed to the authority of the past to legitimize certain notions that for his day were rather radical.

What were the essentials of his Golden Age of government? It is difficult to summarize Confucian doctrine without doing violence to elements that some may think vital, and here I concentrate on four particular aspects only: the notion of a common humanity, the importance of education in achieving this, the priority of family relationships over all others, and the way all these relate to the wider community and the state.

Although most men are not 'fully human', any man, whatever his station, can be. To be 'fully human' is to be one of nature's gentlemen: 'gentleman' is one way we can translate the term *Chün-tzu* which technically meant 'lordling', a scion of the aristocratic class. Anyone behaving as a true *Chün-tzu* was the 'superior man'. All others were petty, mean men. Neither the spirits nor Heaven were relevant to this fully human condition: it was realizable only by self-knowledge, self-control, and self-enforcement. The essence of behaving like the 'superior man' was to practice—and do so with complete sincerity—what is called *jen*. *Jen* is benevolence or what the New Testament calls *caritas*, and amounts to treating others with the same consideration as you give to yourself and co-operating with others in this sense.

This carries an important corollary: it is, that men achieve their humanity by being educated, not coerced. Over time this justified—one might almost say led to—the characteristic feature claimed though not necessarily practised by all subsequent Chinese governments: government by merit, as measured in educational achievement, as against the rule of a landed aristocracy. Such government by merit was embodied in the paradigm of the 'scholar-official' and free mobility in or out of the governing class was (in principle, at least) guaranteed by the examination system.

The family is not only the basic and primordial institution but the supreme one. Family duties and responsibilities are laid down by nature. There is nothing contractual about them. Simply by virtue of birth, the father obeys his ancestors and reports to them. The son owes a supreme duty of obedient and loving service to his father, the wife defers to her husband, the younger brother to elder brother, the younger friend to older friend (as though among brothers), and the entire family obeys the ruler, as though he were its own father. These are the 'five relations'. They assume inequality and perpetuate it. The older have greater rights than the younger, males have more rights than females, higher ranks have more rights than lower ones.

The relationship between the family and the ruler, however, contains a formidable ambivalence: in the event of piety to one's father clashing with one's duty to the ruler, which should prevail? Where did the family unit fit in the wider community? Confucius, and more particularly Mencius, were intensely concerned with government. Did they not seek all their lives to tell princes how to behave? Confucius's own answer might be summed up in two phrases: 'Tis love, tis love that makes the world go round' and 'Men, not measures'. Government should be one of good men and not of laws. The supreme and indeed the only duties of the ruler were, first, to be completely benevolent (virtuous) and secondly, to choose benevolent (virtuous) ministers. Having done this, he has brought good government about and has nothing left to do, except sit on his throne in the 'none-ado posture' with folded arms. As ruler, so state: its role was minimal. It should support the honest food-producing peasant (and not the despised parasitic merchant) by light taxation. There should be no state enterprises and no wars except strictly for defence. In this minimal state (so one version of Confucianism has it) filial piety is superior even to the ruler's laws. For, in principle, there should be no need of laws; education should suffice. But—says one famous Confucian story—when a son once reported to the authorities that his father had stolen a sheep (and therefore become liable to the death penalty) the ruler had the son executed for a breach of filial piety—and he was right.[22]

The notion of the family as prototype also determined Confucius's views on the ideal state structure. The early Chou state he idealized was not just a feudalistic but a *familial* form of contractual government.

It was not a purely political institution. The state resembled an enlarged household; the ruler reigned, but he did not rule. Ministers were not important because they held their offices: they were important and held their offices because they were kin to the ruler or because they were heads of important families . . . Since the monarchy was always hereditary, rulers could maintain some control within the ruling house and obviate discussion. But a factor that was inherent in the family relationships and that led to the breakdown of the feudal system was that the sovereignty of rulers was not all that absolute. The respect accorded to the head of the family was personal, not institutional; nobles, brothers, and other close relatives were far from being ruled by the ruler's command since they actually shared his power. A person was not considered to be separable from his assistants who were members of his own family.[23]

But in certain cases the new absolutist and centralized states of the late Spring and Autumn and especially the Warring States period were run by usurpers, serviced by officials, and governed through public codes of law with savage criminal sanctions. In harking back to Chou, the Confucianists were rejecting the new state. This is why they became victims of the First Emperor (Shih Huang-ti) of the Ch'in Empire, and this was why, when the Ch'in dynasty was overthrown and the empire passed to the Han, the Confucianists sought to oppose the reconstitution of a centralized empire and demanded instead that the emperor should divide it on family lines with the provinces assigned as so many appanages to the royal princes. The primacy of the private family; running the state as a family concern; a weak decentralized state; a state where the ruler did little or nothing but choose men of benevolence as ministers and leave everything to them: all these

---

[22] A real law case of such a kind is actually reported during the reign of the Empress Wu some thousand years later. A filial son assassinated the two judges who had (in his opinion, corruptly) condemned his father to death. One half of the court argued that he should be pardoned for being a filial son, the other half that he must be executed for murder and for defiance of the basic order of the state. At one time—by way of a compromise—it was suggested that he be executed and then receive a posthumous award. (This did not carry!)   [23] Hsu, *Ancient China*, 79–80.

notions ran into one another and might be said to form the paradigm of the
Confucianist state.

One more matter remains, however: why a state at all? Well, as Madison
said in the *Federalist Papers*, 'if men were angels, no government would be
necessary', but since they were not, government had to be tolerated.[24] So
with Confucius. Since he was quite clear that the truly 'superior' men were
very much a minority, it follows that the 'mean' men made up the vast
majority. Sometimes he speaks as though these mean men will abandon
their evil ways as soon as they have a holy, virtuous ruler. More often, he
says that the way to govern them is by education into virtue and not penal
sanction. But at the end of the day he has to recognize that where example
and instruction fail, force must be used. So we find the famous phrase in the
Li chi, the *Book of Rites*. (This was one of the books reconstituted after the
First Emperor's alleged destruction of the Confucian texts in 213 BC, so this
compilation was made 300 years after Confucius's death. For all that it
probably contains genuine Confucian material.) In it occur these lines:
'The Rites (*li*) do not extend down to the common people. The punishments (*hsing*) are not applied upwards as far as the Great Officers.'[25] The
Rites (*li*) in this context means 'social control'—enforcements by the
accepted canons of what is proper and what is improper behaviour. *Hsing*
means punishments, including that of bodily mutilation. Confucius's ideal
society was one thing; in practice it was a two-class society: the rites for the
aristocracy, punishments for the poor.

It will be noticed through all this that, first, there is never a glimmer of a
notion of political or social equality, and secondly, not a glimmer of the
notion of democracy or popular control of government. When Creel and
others find 'democracy' in Confucius, they find it in his assertion that all
men are capable of becoming 'superior men' and that they share a common
humanity—'all men are brothers'. This is to assert a duty of caring for all
and of opening the career to virtue. It enjoins universal benevolence, but
under the rule of a benevolently paternalistic sovereign. It is *not* democracy.

One hundred and fifty years after Confucius, Mencius expanded and
emphasized certain elements in this synthesis and these became very prominent in the Neo-Confucian revival of the twelfth century AD, so much so
that the *Meng-tzu* was elevated to the status of one of the 'Four Books'
which, with the Five Classics, became the set curriculum in the civil service

---

[24] J. Madison, *The Federalist Papers* (Penguin Classics, Harmondsworth, 1987), no. 51.
[25] *Li Chi* (The Book of Rites or 'Records of Rituals': being the fourth of the so-called Five
Confucian Classics), ch. 1 and cf. K.-C. Hsiao, *A History of Chinese Political Thought*, vol. 1, *From the
Beginnings to the 6th Century AD*, trans. F. W. N. Mote (Princeton UP, Princeton, 1979), 397–408

examinations. Mencius makes 'the people' his centre-piece. Their welfare—
by 'nourishment' and by education—is the very purpose of the state and its
rulers are to be judged by how well they measure up to the task. Ideally,
government must be of the people, for the people: but, emphatically,
Mencius never for a moment hints that it can ever be *by* the people. Very
much the reverse. 'Those who labor with their minds govern others: those
who labor with their strength are governed by others'; 'if there were no
'superior men' there would be none to rule the rude men. If there were no
rude men, there would be none to provide the sustenance of the superior
men.'[26] Nor did a dissatisfied populace have the right to rebel. They could
and they would and they should withdraw love from their ruler and decline
to die for his officials; but they must patiently wait for 'him who is
appointed by Heaven' to appear before the tyrant could be punished.[27]
(Here again, the argument takes refuge in the circular reasoning of the
Mandate of Heaven theory. The rebel who succeeds is Heaven's agent. This
legitimates obedience to him after he has seized power. But in itself it gives
no indication, in advance, as to whether a rebel is or is not Heaven's agent
and hence does not justify the people in supporting the rebel).[28]

   If such was the relationship of the people to the ruler, how did the
officials and ministers stand towards him? Confucius had maintained that
the ruler was the teacher of his people. But Mencius goes a long step
further: the official or minister was the teacher of the ruler. Officials were
the (virtuous) servants of the people and emphatically not just private
retainers of the monarch. Their duty was to act righteously (according to
Confucian ideas of propriety and morality) and this duty was absolute. In
one passage Mencius distinguishes officials who are kinfolk of the monarch
from those who are not and prescribes the action each should take 'if the
prince has great faults'. Both groups are enjoined to remonstrate: but the
kinsmen should go further and dethrone him, while the rest should finally
quit his service.[29] Mencius championed the right of an official to refuse his
services. Citing the usual precedents from antiquity, he told his disciples
that the condition for an official accepting and continuing in office was that
he must be able to practice the Way, and duly observe the Rites (the *li*).[30]
Indeed, at some points, Mencius maintains that the supreme goal of the
individual is to cultivate his virtue, and that serving the sovereign is simply
incidental to this. These views of the proper relationship of official to ruler

[26] Quoted from the *Meng-tzu*, in Hsiao, *Chinese Political Thought*, 161, n. 47.
[27] Ibid. 161.   [28] But see pp. 465 below for 'signs and portents'.
[29] Hsiao, *Chinese Political Thought*, 162.   [30] Ibid., n. 51.

were to become enormously influential in the period of the empire. They legitimized the ambition of officialdom to reduce the monarchy to little more than a ritual role. This effort and the reaction of the more wilful monarchs to it are, as we shall see, the leitmotiv of the political process under the empire.[31]

We have noted how the *li*—the Rites—are, for Confucius, the moral norms to which the 'superior man' must conform, and at the same time the moral sanctions—'proprieties'—which make him conform. It was Hsün-tzu who elaborated the role of the *li* and made them so prominent in the Confucian persuasion.

The purpose of the *li,* according to Hsün-tzu, is to ordain and establish rank and degree in the unequal society. Noble and humble have their rankings, elder and younger maintain their disparity, the richer and the poorer and persons of greater and lesser importance all have what is appropriate to them. True, this rank position is not to be attained arbitrarily, by noble descent alone, for instance. The unrighteous must not be ennobled, the incompetent not given office, the worthless must not be rewarded, the innocent must not be punished. The nobleman who fails to observe the *li* should be a commoner and the commoner, if able and conformable to the *li* should be a Great Officer. But, this done, the institutions based on the *li* establish the gradations of inequality in society and the duties owed by one person to another, in line with the principles of *Li chi.*[32] The Master said: 'It is by the rules of ceremony that what is doubtful is displayed, and what is minute is distinguished, so that they may serve as *dykes for the people* [my italics]. Thus it is that there are the grades of the noble and the mean, the distinctions of dress, the different places at court: and so the people [are taught to] give way to one another.'[33] Thus the *li* regulate society: and Hsün-tzu is emphatic that this is and must be unequal because 'two noblemen cannot serve one another, nor two commoners direct one another'. By the same token only one ruler can be supreme since he is the very pinnacle of inequality. Finally, he is the 'essential agency for controlling the allotments and assignments in society'.[34]

Tsou Yen's thought is of quite a different nature. He is a Confucianist only in the sense that, like Confucius, 'all [his doctrines] rested on the virtues of benevolence, the proper relations between ruler and servitor of superior and inferior; and among the six relationships'.[35] What he did was

---

[31] See esp. J. R. Levinson, *Confucian China and its Modern Fate: A Trilogy* (University of California Press, Los Angeles, 1964), esp. pt. II.   [32] *Li Chi,* 553.
[33] Quoted, Hsiao, *Chinese Political Thought,* 189, n. 98.
[34] Quoted, ibid. 192.   [35] Ibid. 62.

to graft this system on to an existing philosophy of history and of the natural order. According to this, sometimes known as the scheme of the Five Phases, one era overcomes and displaces its predecessor according to a cycle, wherein Wood succeeds Earth, Metal succeeds Wood, Fire consumes Wood, and Water quenches Fire. Each of the Five Elements has its own characteristic, to which a specific colour, time, and set of activities correspond. One dynasty succeeds another in rotation according to this cosmic drive. But this drive itself is powered by the basic force of the universe, which is the interaction of *Yin* and *Yang*. This, the interaction and interpenetration of the two opposite and equal forces, Male and Female, Heaven and Earth, explains the harmony of the Universe and it governs all subliminal things. Man and Nature interact and whatever that ruler ordains must be in harmony with the Celestial. If not, Heaven will send signs and portents in the shape of wonders and natural disasters. This tied in with the Confucian doctrine, expressed in the chapter of the *Li chi* known as the 'Doctrine of the Mean' and would become adopted as one of the Four Books in the eleventh century AD: 'When a nation or family is about to perish, there are sure to be unlucky omens.'[36] A common law governed both man and Nature: and the nature of Nature is harmony.

These theories proved of the utmost assistance in buttressing Confucius's own extremely humanistic morality with cosmological mysticism, the study of portents and the avoidance of taboos. From the time of the Ch'in Empire—which possibly adopted the Five Agents philosophy, seeing itself as the age of Water and choosing Black for its uniforms and banners—these beliefs are continually found among the arguments by which the Confucians tried to reason with or remonstrate with the emperors.

All the philosophers mentioned above (except Chu Hsi), lived during the later Spring and Autumn and/or the Warring States periods. But their immediate impact on thought and behaviour may have been negligible. Just as it took some 500 years from Gautama's death for Buddhism to make its entry into China and another 500 or so to become influential there, so perhaps with the teachings of Confucius and his disciples.

We have introduced these thinkers at this stage, the period when they lived and taught. However, it is essential to note that their influence was not felt till much later, and furthermore, that the predominant elements in this very composite canon varied with century and dynasty. The most important of such variations will be introduced where appropriate in the chapters on the T'ang and the Ming. For the moment, as we are about to discuss the

---

[36] Quoted Chan, *A Source Book*, 246.

Ch'in and Han empires, that is, the period 221 BC–AD 220, we must bear in mind at least the following.

First: it was in 213 BC that Shih Huang-ti ordered the notorious 'Burning of the (Confucian) Books'. This decree testifies to the influence of Confucian thought but also to how long this had taken to develop, since some 250 years had passed since Confucius died. About one hundred years later, however, in 136 BC, the Han emperor Wu-ti (himself anti-Confucian) decreed Confucianism the official creed of the empire and in 124 BC established an Academy of Confucian lore. But the doctrine was locked in a fierce struggle with crypto-Legalist practice,[37] and it only began to prevail at the close of the Former Han period and only became the fully accepted as well as official doctrine under the Later Han.

During this period, moreover, the doctrine of the Five Phases, along with the significance attached to signs and portents which were logically independent of Confucius's own thought (even alien to it), were melded into the corpus of Confucianism thought. This strand became highly influential from the closing decades of the Former Han period onwards, since it served as a powerful political catalyst. We pointed out earlier that the Mandate of Heaven formula was circular in that the proof of the Mandate was that the emperor continued to reign, while his dispossession proved that it had been withdrawn.[38] The Five Phases theory and the importance attached to signs and wonders provided, however, an *objective* test of the withdrawal of the Mandate. The portentous or disastrous events were so many indications that Heaven was displeased. Consequently the Confucianist advisers to the emperors, especially in the Later Han, were able to use them to threaten and warn the emperor to follow their advice lest the Mandate be withdrawn. By the same token, however, the doctrine, once it had gripped the popular imagination, accustomed the masses to the notion of a change of dynasty, and so fuelled the great millenarian movements that began to spread throughout the empire *c.* AD 140 and led, finally, to the abdication of the Han.[39]

In the great 400-year Time of Disunity after the fall of the Han, Confucianism's creativity declined, while Buddhism and Taoism were active and innovative. During this period, and indeed until the T'ang, Confucianism was no longer the hegemonic ideology. But though Taoism and Buddhism were prominent among both the masses and the cultural élite, Confucianism persisted. By now its ethics were part of the very fabric of

---

[37] See below.   [38] See p. 449 above.
[39] This point has been put with great force and clarity by B. J. Monsvelt Beck, in his analysis of the 'Fall of the Han' in vol. I. of the *CHC*. See esp. 357–62.

Chinese society, its Classics remained the basis of all literate culture, and above all, Confucian values prevailed in officialdom and in the way it was recruited. Under the Sung, however, Confucianism, systematized in a new commentary on Mencius by Chu Hsi (1190 AD), made a triumphant recovery as neo-Confucianism, and Chu Hsi's version became canonical. With the Ch'ing, in the seventeenth century, after yet further reassessment, a form of Confucianism became the supreme and all-pervasive creed of the entire society. It was a wholly Confucianized China that the West confronted—and ultimately corroded—in the nineteenth century.

So, at different times and under different dynasties some of the components of Confucianism predominated over others. But its central cluster of policy stances never altered. It stood for one supreme ruler, a meritocratic service nobility, an unequal society, a patriarchal and paternalistic social structure, a weak night-watchman state, a preference (tempered by expediency) for social control and indoctrination by the *li* over laws and coercion, as well as for pacificism and anti-expansionism; and, supremely, for the primacy of filial piety and the family over all other moral and institutional considerations, loyalty to the emperor himself being its highest embodiment.

3.2. *Legalism*

Legalism is associated with three men. Shang Yang (the Lord Shang, *c*.385–338 BC) was a wandering scholar who became chief minister in the state of Ch'in. Li Ssu (*c*.280–208 BC) was a chief minister of Ch'in some eight years later, and Han Fei (*c*.280–233 BC), fellow student of Li Ssu, was an official of the state of Han. Li Ssu left a work which is a succinct philosophical exposition of the ideas known as Legalist. They run completely counter to Confucianism. Their model is not the family-feudalistic state of the early Chou but the emergent absolutism of the Warring States. They are forward-looking, practical, and ruthless. Legalism, unlike thoroughgoing Confucianism, was capable of being translated into practice and so it was in the Kingdom of Ch'in and in the short-lived Ch'in Empire. As a philosophy it was extinguished along with that empire, but as an influence in practice it survived and informed the entire Imperial era of the Chinese state. To my mind, at any rate, it is quite impossible not to see Legalistic assumptions in the Han code and especially the T'ang code.[40] Indeed, the very notion of a

----

[40] Below, p. 516 and Bk. III, Ch. 3.

public code with fixed penalties for the various types of offences is un-Confucian.

Legalism is the most radical, unmystical, and clear-cut of all the Chinese philosophies. It is wholly antipathetic and antipodal to Confucianism. Its critique of that persuasion is—to my mind—determined, incisive, superbly ironical, and devastating. Because Legalism rests on parsimonious ethical assumptions and proceeds from them with a relentless logic, it speaks to the Western mind much more cogently than all other Chinese philosophies. Because, too, it rigidly extrudes personal private ethics, and indeed all ethical considerations, from what concerns governance and makes *raison d'état* its unique principle, it inevitably invites comparison with Machiavelli's *Prince*. In bold terms, the Legalists viewed the mass of humanity as irrevocably stupid and base and susceptible only to the carrot and the stick. Theirs is a philosophy of power vested in an absolute monarch who rules by severe punishments, through iron codes of law which apply to high and low alike, without any exceptions save the ruler himself, since he alone makes the law and therefore only he is dispensed from it.

The Legalists had no use at all for the past. Present problems demanded present answers. As to the sage kings Yao and Shun, so continually prayed in evidence by the Confucians, what sure knowledge had we of them, who lived 3,000 years before? Anybody professing such sure knowledge was either a fool or a knave. As for virtue and human kindness—there was not enough of it to go round to prevent disorder. The 'superior man' was too rare a beast to have an entire system of government to fit him. 'Government', wrote Han Fei, 'is not for only one man.'[41] As for family and filial obedience being the paradigm, nay, the microcosm of orderly government, what nonsense! As if all children are orderly! So, since they are not, why should the entire populace be?

On the contrary, what the people submit to is not example and education but the application of force. A sovereign does not draw his capacity for ruling from his benevolence, but from the authority of his position and his application of power (*shih*). His servitors owe him absolute obedience. He governs through laws (*fa*) and statecraft (*shu*). The laws are to be public, applicable to everybody both high and low, and backed by savage penalties. Han Fei would have rewarded the compliant but not so Lord Shang, who relied solely on punishment. Whereas the laws were to be public, statecraft was to be shrouded away inside in the mind of the prince: it consists of the

[41] Chan, *A Source Book*, 254.

way he selects the most efficient ministers and officials, how he keeps surveillance over and inspires fear and obedience in them.

As to the substance of the laws, these are directed solely at the benefit of the state as a whole. The individual and his conscience is as nothing compared to this, and indeed, personal scruples and political needs are actually incompatible. Ethics has nothing whatsoever to do with politics, which is the realm of expediency and is dedicated to the strengths, resources, and domestic tranquillity of the state as a whole. There is little room left for any private life; indeed on one reading, there is none at all, since even the recluse is to be executed for no better reason than that he does not co-operate with the ruler. In the interests of the state, all life may be regi-mented. State cameralism must be adopted to expand the national resources, agriculture must be actively fostered; the entire population—men, women, children, and the aged—must be mobilized into military and paramilitary organizations, and all dissent squashed. Philosophy and literature are not just impractical but pernicious: they undermine respect for the laws. They must go. The laws and the laws alone are to guide the people in right and wrong.

This is all quite clear, quite logical, and, most people would probably think today, quite horrible. However, if we are to believe accounts of their later opponents, it was largely put into actual practice in the Kingdom of Ch'in and in the Ch'in Empire, as we shall shortly see. But to conclude this brief exposition of Legalism we can do no better than to quote Han Fei's ironical parody of the Confucianists:

To perform a private favor for an old friend is called being faithful in friendship. Using public funds to make gifts to the poor is called being benevolent. To disdain income but preserve one's personal standards is called being a superior man. To subvert the laws in order to protect one's family is called having principles. Not to support the officials in order to favor a crony is called displaying a knightly sense of justice. To detach oneself from mundane interests and foresake one's responsi-bilities towards superiors is called being highminded. To take up disputes and disobey the ordinances is called showing unswerving spirit. To pass out favors and gain a mass following is called winning the people . . . One who rushes into dangers and is a martyr to honor is a person who would die rather than lose virtue, yet the world will demean him as a fellow whose calculations have gone awry. One of simple learning who obeys commands is a person who will observe all the laws, yet the world will demean him as a simple-minded fellow. One who toils to eat is a person who will be productive, yet the world will demean him as a fellow of no skills. One who is generous and pure-minded is a person of upright goodness, yet the world will demean him as a mindlessly foolish fellow. One who seriously accepts orders and meticulously deals with public affairs is one who will respect his superiors, yet the world will demean him as a cowardly fellow. One who resists robbers and stops evil-doers is one who will uphold the instructions received from above, yet the world will demean him as a flattering trouble maker.[42]

4. CH'IN

The state of Ch'in was a latecomer to the Chinese comity. Indeed, not till after 361 BC was it invited to the congress of state rulers that met under the leadership of the hegemon. Not till about that time did its court introduce 'Chinese' customs and ceremonial observances. Its music (an art much cultivated in the 'true' Chinese states and one of the Six Disciplines learnt by the *shih* class) consisted, so we are told, of 'Beating on earthen jugs, knocking on jars, plucking the *cheng*, striking on thigh-bones while singing and crying wu! wu!' Ch'in was to the Chinese states what Macedonia was to the Greek ones: a rude, semi-barbarous, warlike marcher state, holding the frontier against the western barbarians. The country lay in what the Chinese called 'the land between the passes': the fertile valley in the angle the Wei River makes as it flows into the Yellow River. This land was the ancestral home of the Chou people, and the base from which they overthrew the Shang. It was there the Chou established their first capitals in the west. After the sack of the last one by the barbarians in 771 BC, the remnants of the Chou dynasty fled eastwards to the eastern capital of Lo-yang, and the Ch'in would in time move in behind them. Its role in the Spring and Autumn struggles was marginal. Half-barbarian and founded in the tribal homelands of the aboriginal non-Chinese, Ch'in's social and political structure was simplistic by comparison with the strictly Chinese states. In those, the familial-feudalistic traces remained, the princes held court in the old ceremonial ways and the aristocratic lineages still counted for something. Such lineages were of much less significance in Ch'in, while its monarchy was one of the very few dynasties to survive the turbulence of the Spring and Autumn period. It was less sophisticated and very martial.

Its strength was transformed by the arrival from the east in the middle of the third century BC of the frustrated official Shang Yang, the Legalist statesman we have already mentioned. Shang Yang struck up a close relationship with the prince, Duke Hsiao (361–338 BC); he became his chief minister and carried out a series of revolutionary changes which turned this Chinese 'Macedonia' into a Chinese 'Sparta'. Here, all the tenets of the Legalist school were given practical expression. They are outlined in

---

[42] Quoted Hsiao, *Chinese Political Thought*, 387–8.

the biography left by the historian Ssu-ma Ch'ien in his great *Shih Chi* ('Historical Records').

4.1. *Law*

The laws were promulgated and applied to everybody without exception save for the duke alone, since he was their author. It was even applied to the crown prince (or rather, by proxy, to his tutor, since it was thought impracticable to execute the heir to the throne). The penalties were extreme.[43] To reinforce internal order, Shang Yang instituted a tithing system,[44] the population was organized into fivefold or tenfold family groups to control one another and share one another's punishments. A member who failed to denounce a culprit was sawn in half. Whoever *did* denounce received a reward equal to that given for decapitating an enemy.

4.2. *The Merit Aristocracy*

Shang Yang instituted a series of eighteen orders of honour which were conferred on certain select members of the population in proportion to services rendered to the state, either by way of exploit of arms or production in the fields. Accompanying the orders were privileges such as landed rights of various types, mitigation of sentences passed on convicted criminals, and possibly, exemption from statutory service as a conscript. The lineages were effectively dispossessed and a purely service aristocracy took its place. The old feudalistic benefices, where a seigneur ruled a dependent peasantry, were abolished. Instead the country was divided into so many *hsien* (counties), each governed by a direct nominee of the duke. The former benefice-holder thus lost control of the peasantry, who were henceforth subject to the state and its officials alone. More generally, this supersession of the feudality is the counterpart of the creation of the centralized bureaucratized state. Such a state was more able than the feudalistic ones to collect revenues and raise armies. In such a way did Ch'in grow stronger than its rivals.

4.3. *The Army*

The entire population was at the disposal of the ruler. It was organized for military purposes into three categories: the able-bodied males, who were the

---

[43] For a selection (based on Hulsewé, *Remnants*), see *CHC*, i. 58.

[44] Cf. in Anglo-Saxon and Norman times in England, when groups of ten heads of families were banded together and held responsible for one another's good behaviour.

fighting forces proper; the able-bodied women, who dug or built defences and carried supplies; and the aged and very young, who looked after the cattle and horses and gathered food. The fighting contingents had discarded the chariot. They consisted of infantry-spearmen and crossbowmen, and platoons of mounted lancers and archers. Cowards and deserters were summarily executed. A price in gold was paid to the soldier for every enemy head he brought in. If prisoners were taken we do not hear about them. What we do hear about are the numbers of enemy decapitated in battle. The figures given are not credible. Ssu-ma Ch'ien, tells us, for instance, that in the campaigns of 331, 318, and 312 BC, some 80,000 enemy were decapitated each time, and goes on to say that the number slain in the victorious campaign against the states of Han and Wei in 293 BC was no less than 240,000![45] But though these figures must be highly inflated, they leave a clear impression of unremitting ferocity and executions on a grand scale.

4.4. The Economy

With the abolition of seigneurial rights over the peasantry came the imposition of state land taxes and unpaid conscript labour services. Shang Yang split up the traditional extended family living under one roof by imposing double taxation on households with two or more sons. Trading and other secondary occupations were actively discouraged; Ssu-ma Ch'ien says even that their practicitoners were reduced to slave status. All attention was concentrated on tilling and weaving and those who excelled in them were exempted from forced labour. Farmers were given incentives to reclaim wasteland and the shortage of manpower was met by encouraging immigration from the neighbouring states. Later, two vast public works were carried out: a huge irrigation scheme near Ch'eng-tu and the Cheng-kuo canal which connects the Ching and Lo rivers north of the Wei. These undertakings made central Shensi perhaps the richest granary of China.

4.5. The Expansion of Ch'in

In 316 BC and shortly afterwards Ch'in occupied the lands now known as Ssu-ch'uan but made no impression eastwards. In 247 the 13-year-old Prince Cheng ascended the throne as king—the title that had been adopted for Ch'in's head in 325—and this is the man whom history knows as 'The First

---

[45] Ssu-ma Ch'ien, *The Shi Chi*, trans. Chavannes (1897), ii. 69, 71, 74, 82. Bodde has rejected those figures in a valuable statistical appendix 3 to his chapter on Ch'in in *CHC*, i. 98–102.

Emperor'. He is the unifier of China and his short, barbarous, but prodigiously energetic reign irrevocably shaped the entire subsequent history of the Chinese state. His reign was decisive, and irreversible.

Between 230 and 221 King Cheng annexed every one of the Chinese states in turn. 'The six kings' (says Ssu-ma Ch'ien) 'were subjected to all the penalties befitting their crimes.'(!) The triumphant Cheng invented a totally new title for himself. It was 'First Sovereign Emperor' or *Shih Huang-ti*.

It was open to him to organize his new dominion in the traditional way, that is to say, by parcelling it out as appanages to his kinsfolk, as the Chou dynasty had done before him. This was precisely what the Confucianists wanted him to do. Instead, he treated the conquered territories as his predecessors had treated Ch'in. He divided them into thirty-six military commanderies (*chün*), subdivided into *hsien* or counties, each one of the commanderies being run by a triumvirate of officials directly appointed by and responsible to himself. In a rapid series of far-reaching measures, he standardized the script and the currency. Shang Yang had previously standardized the system of weights and measures, which was now adopted empire-wide.

The new empire was old Ch'in writ large—very large indeed. And it was governed throughout in the strictest tradition of Legalism. Thus the frame of the Chinese Empire was constructed by a process and in a fashion entirely different from that of Rome, and with a social structure, a tradition, and a cast of mind entirely antithetical. The descriptions of the Roman and the Ch'in-Han empires can take off only from this startling contrast.

6

The Han Empire

*A*lthough the Warring States followed a similar pattern of government, they each had different identities. Their administrative arrangements varied, they had their own currency and their own legal codes, and although all spoke versions of Chinese that were more or less related, each had developed its own variant of the script. All these differences were swept away forever when Cheng, the king of Ch'in, completed his conquest of these states in 221 BC.

No single man ever, in the entire 3,000 years of Chinese history, performed so historic a task as he did nor left so great and so indelible a mark on the character of government at any time or in any place in the world. Although he reigned a mere eleven years as emperor, the changes he wrought in China's institutions were determinative. Shih Huang-ti was a barbarous and cruel megalomaniac of cyclonic energies who forged his newly conquered dominions into one community in the image of his own kingdom of Ch'in writ large, and all the successor empires built upon and adapted its basic institutional structures. Furthermore, the political model he established—of the unique, tightly unified, centrally directed *chung kuo*, that is, the world-central kingdom—has inspired every generation of patriotic Chinese down to this day. It is no wonder that the Maoist historians in the Republic make a hero of Shih Huang-ti. For them he is the prototype of the ruthless, anti-aristocratic, anti-Confucian innovator they recognized in Mao.

1.1. *The Achievements of the Ch'in Empire*

Cheng's royal title (which he invented) significantly combined *Huang* and *Ti*, older words for sovereigns of mythical antiquity, which carried intimations of the sacred—hence *Huang-ti*, which we translate as 'emperor'. (*Shih* simply means 'first ever'.)

Cheng rebuffed Confucianist pleas to revert to the ancient, supposedly Chou style of familial-feudalism and did the exact opposite, levelling and standardizing everywhere. Henceforth there was one imperial script, one penal code, one currency, and standard weights and measures that even determined the width of roads, of which 4,250 miles were constructed.[1] Huge armies were hurled in every direction until the empire stretched from Korea to Kunming, and from Hainan into Mongolia. Shih Huang-ti repaired and lengthened the pre-existent rammed-earth walls he found there to create the 1,500-mile-long Great Wall[2] which (in its Ming form extant today) is the most impressive monumental construction I have ever seen.

Although serfdom and the seigneurial class gradually disappeared during the Warring States period, the Ch'in Empire standardized the changes. The peasants received freehold and free alienability of their plots, but had to pay taxes in cash and kind and above all had to perform one month's forced labour per year, so that although serfdom was abolished, dependency was certainly not. The point was, however, that this was now direct dependency on the emperor, with no intermediation through the seigneurial class. The ruling houses of the separate states and their relatives, 120,000 families (totalling some half-a-million individuals, quite apart from perhaps an even greater number of their servants and other dependants) were forcibly deported to the frontier regions.[3]

So also were vast numbers of the general population, while gigantic building projects absorbed huge cohorts of forced labourers, many of them convicts under the harsh penal code. It is estimated that some 300,000 men were employed in building the Great Wall. Ssu-ma Ch'ien tells us that the new Ho Pang palace at the capital (Ch'ang-an) which was big enough to seat 10,000 men, was constructed by 100,000 convicts who had already suffered the penalty of castration. And Ssu-ma's estimate of 700,000 men used in building the emperor's tomb seems reasonable, for its enclosure has been found to be large enough to cover the area of the city of Cambridge.

The literati were silenced at almost the beginning of the emperor's reign. The Confucianists among them were horrified by the uprooting of the seigneurial class, the contemptuous rejection of their ideal 'Chou' order, the massive conscriptions, the aggressive military expansionism, and the harshness of the penal code, all of them completely antithetical to their principles. Enraged when a Confucian scholar remonstrated with him at an imperial banquet, in 213 BC, the emperor ordained that the annals of all the individual kingdoms except Ch'in were to be destroyed and that every-

---

[1] Gibbon estimated the total road-length in the Roman Empire from the wall of Antoninus to Jerusalem as 3,740 miles.

[2] Loewe, *CHC*, i. 62–3, suggests that the Ch'in Wall (in packed earth and brick-faced, not stone like the present Ming Wall) was somewhat shorter than the 10,000 *li* (1500 miles) traditionally ascribed.   [3] Lewis, *Sparta and Persia*, ch. 2.

body except officials and court 'scholars of vast learning' must take their copies of the Confucian Classics to the authorities to be burned under heavy penalty of being branded and sent to forced labour. Furthermore, anyone unwise enough to go on discussing Confucius's 'History' and 'Odes', and indeed all those who 'used antiquity to denigrate the present', were liable to execution. The only books to be spared were 'useful' ones on farming, medicine, and divination. Those who 'wished to study laws and orders' were advised to turn to the officials for instruction. And—so the story has come down—the emperor, seized by an excess of sudden rage, had 460 Confucianists buried alive![4]

1.2. *The Fall of Ch'in, the Instauration of the Han*

Within a few months of the First Emperor's death in 210 BC widespread popular uprisings broke out in rebellion against the perpetual corvées, deportations, campaigns, and the extreme harshness of the penal system. For their part the intellectuals were shocked and revolted by the persecutions, while the ancient nobility were angry at the mass deportation of their best families.

It was in keeping that the rebellion began when a commoner, who was in charge of a convict gang on its way to the frontier, realized that he would be executed for not reaching his destination in time. Proclaiming himself 'King of Ch'u' he was immediately joined by thousands of soldiers and other types of conscripts. Though he was soon defeated and executed, the nobility had taken over the leadership with Hs'iang Yü, a scion of the noble house of an ancient kingdom, Ch'u, as their commander. When Hsiang quarrelled with his chief lieutenant Liu Pang, the two fought it out amid widespreading anarchy until in 202 BC Liu crushed his rival. He took the imperial title under the throne-name of Kao Tsu, which signifies 'High Progenitor', and named his dynasty 'Han'.

1.3. *From Ch'in to Han, 206 BC*

Liu Pang was a roughneck of such brutishness that once (it is reported) he pissed into the ceremonial hat of a court scholar in order to show his contempt for learning. But he was of daemonic energy and the dynasty he founded lasted with only a brief interruption for some 400 years. Only in

---

[4] Ssu-ma Ch'ien, *Shih Chih*, 171–4; 180–1. While recent scholarship accepts the authenticity of the book-burning, there is some doubt about the burying alive. Loewe suggests that they were put to death, not buried alive, *CHC*, i. 71–2, and again, 95–6 (where Loewe presents certain fictional elements in the account).

one significant respect did he depart from the laws and institutions of the Ch'in Empire. Because Liu had to reward his captains, he parcelled the eastern half of the empire into fiefs and appanages for them and for his sons. But in practice their government was carried out through his own imperial officials there, and these territories continued to be divided into the *hsien* and the *chün* under the same Ch'in administrative tripartism, like the rest of the empire.[5] Similarly the population remained subject to cash tax contributions and forced labour, the Legalist system of rewards and punishments gradated according to the twenty-four ranks of dignity was continued, as were the former policies of population transfers, rampaging and ever-victorious expansionism, and gigantic public works. In 192 BC nearly 150,000 male and female conscripts were set to building the new capital, Ch'ang-an; in 132 100,000 soldiers were drafted to repair dykes on the Yellow River; in 102 soldiers and conscript labourers extended the Great Wall to its westernmost extension in Yu Men Kuan (western Kansu); the Yellow River and the Wei were connected by a ninety-mile canal and so forth.

Not all these features were to be perpetuated—the minor kingdoms and the appanages, for instance, were gradually reduced—but the general tenor of Ch'in government was. Thus Shih Huang-ti's revolution in government was institutionalized and persisted throughout the entire imperial period, up and into the twentieth century. Its enduring characteristics were:

- face-to-face administration by the authorities of the population, not through intermediaries;
- bureaucracy;
- centralization;
- 'nested' areas of local administration, one inside another, their scope and discretionary functions lessening from the top echelons downwards;
- economic paternalistic statism, as in e.g. the creation of an economic infrastructure of roads, canals, walls, etc. by public command and forced labour;
- cultural standardization, homogenization, and Sinicization of the entire population, and thus, the creation of a culture-nation;
- the entrenchment of the two-class yet multi-ranked hierarchical society.

Anything more unlike the Confucianists' ideal feudalistic and decentralized night-watchman state would be hard to imagine. Yet in the event, as will be

---

[5] The autonomy of a third unit, *kuo* (kingdom), was gradually whittled away, until it became similar in practice to *chün*.

seen, Confucianism came to easy terms with what was essentially a Legalist political structure.

1.4. *The Han Empire*

CHRONOLOGY

A. *The Former Han: 202 BC–AD 9*

202–195 BC	KAO TSU (Liu Pang). New capital at Chang-an (Sian)
191–187	Softening of penal code. Revocation of anti-merchant laws
195–188	HUI-TI
188–180	Empress LÜ
180	Death of Empress Lü, extermination of her family
180–157	WEN-TI
167	Mutilation disappears from penal code
157–141	CHING-TI
154	Revolt of the Seven Princes. Suppressed
141–87	WU-TI
136	Appointment of the Doctors of the Five Classics
124	The Academy founded for training civil servants in the Confucian Classics
121–119	Crushing of the Hsiung-nu
111–110	Subjugation of Yüeh (from Chekiang to Tonkin) rounds out frontiers of modern 'China proper'
110	Wu-ti conducts the sacrifice to Heaven
102	Western conquests as far as Ferghana
99	Popular insurrections in the eastern regions
51	Palace conference on the interpretation of the Classics
46	Recruitment of specialists in *yin-yang* and portents
41	Academy student numbers raised to 1,000
14	Peasant revolts
8	Academy student numbers raised to 3,000
3	Millenarian cult of *Queen Mother of the West* in Shantung
AD 1–8	WANG MANG regent for child-emperors
2	First census: 57,671,400 individuals
9	Wang Mang assumes emperorship, founds Hsin dynasty

B. *The Hsin*

9–23	Radical reforms of land system, usury, etc. Abolition of noble rank
11	Yellow River floods
17	Peasant revolts
22	The Red Eyebrows insurrection. Rebellions of the old imperial nobility
23	Wang Mang killed in his palace

C. The Later (or Eastern) Han

25–57	KUANG WU-TI. Suppresses Red Eyebrows, eliminates rivals. New capital at Loyang. Restores imperial power in central Asia, regains Annam and Tonkin
58–75	MING-TI
82	Empress Tou alters the succession, and with her family, reigns as empress dowager. The imperial frontiers contract
105–21	Empress TENG rules as dowager for two infant sons
c.140	Law and order begins to break down. Sporadic millenarian revolts. Fiscal crisis deepens
135	The court eunuchs successfully resist officials' plot
157	Census: 56,486,856 individuals
175	Enlargement of the power of the eunuchs
184	The Yellow Turban revolts: 300,000 in arms. Loyang sacked by the rebels
189	The massacre of the eunuchs by YÜAN SHAO
190	Beginnings of the rise of war-lord TS'AO TS'AO
190–220	HSIEN-TI, last Han emperor—a pawn, in custody of successive war-lords
208	The Battle of the Red Cliff: Ts'ao Ts'ao beaten by his two rivals
220	Abdication of HSIEN TI in favour of TS'AO P'EI son of Ts'ao Ts'ao, the emperor of Wei
221	LIU PEI, last scion of the Han proclaims empire of Shu in Szechuan
222	Warlord SUN CH'ÜAN proclaims himself emperor of Wu
220–64	*The Three Kingdoms: the beginning of four centuries of disunity*

2. THE GOVERNMENTAL SYSTEM: AN OVERVIEW

The Han and the Roman empires were not merely contemporaneous but much the same in area, population, and in their overwhelmingly agrarian basis. In the first century BC the 'Eighteen Provinces', or what we call 'China Proper', amounted to about 1.5 million square miles, much as Gibbon ascribes to the Roman Empire. The population of the latter is broadly estimated as 50 to 60 million.[6] China's population, according to the census of AD 2, was 57,671,400 (taxable) persons—hence, somewhat larger than this figure.[7]

At the highest level of generality, in either state the ultimate source of decision-making was a single individual, who was absolute and ruled *directly* through his own officials. (Whatever local autonomy might exist, as in the Roman Empire's city councils, for instance, was a concession by the imperial

---

[6] M. I. Finley, *Ancient Sicily to the Arab Conquest (A History of Sicily)* (Chatto & Windus, London, 1968), 30.　　　[7] Gernet, *A History of Chinese Civilization*, 68.

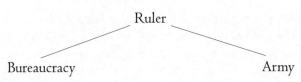

FIG. 2.6.1. Polity of the Chinese Empire

autocracy, which could and did supervise and control it.) Neither state assigned any independent role whatsoever to the populace, in neither did there exist an autonomous organized priesthood or even a priestly caste, and in neither did an ascriptive aristocracy of birth have any assigned constitutional role. Indeed, there was no such aristocracy, though there certainly was a privileged upper stratum. Thus both states belong to the broad class of 'Palace' regime, wholly untrammelled by a countervailing priesthood and with an uneasy relationship to the wealthier stratum of the population.

At this point, however, the differences must be underlined.

In terms of our basic classification the Chinese Empire can be conceived as shown in Fig. 2.6.1, that is, it is quintessentially a Palace regime and the Court is the sole arena of the political process. But it is a Palace regime with a very idiosyncratic character. In the first place, this bureaucracy was an integral part of the landowning classes—indeed, a facet of this class's activities. It also came, in a short time, to act as the functional equivalent of the Church in medieval Europe; for though it was not a religion, the Confucianist persuasion fulfilled the same social functions as the Church in Europe without fulfilling the same salvationist function to individuals. Thus the Chinese bureaucracy simultaneously assumed the roles of part of the territorial aristocracy and a church. The second idiosyncratic feature is that the army was wholly and often humiliatingly subordinate to the civil power. Only when this broke down did it have any political input. It was not a case of *inter arma silent leges* but the reverse—*inter leges silent arma*.

2.1. *The Governmental Structure in Outline*

Han government was much more bureaucratized than Rome's. There was no imperial bureaucracy at all in Rome and the provinces in the year o. Even in the fourth and fifth centuries AD its numbers are estimated at some 30,000, whereas in China, in 2 BC the established posts totalled 130,285.[8] Furthermore, the imperial territory was quartered, re-quartered and re-re-quartered into areas which fitted into one another like so many Chinese boxes, very

---

[8] H. Bielenstein, *The Bureaucracy of Han Times* (CUP, Cambridge, 1980), 156.

unlike the untidy arrangements in the early Roman Principate and much more systematic than the arrangements brought in by Diocletian.

Figure 2.6.2 shows the formal structure. Its apex is the Son of Heaven. He is the pivot of Earth, Man, and Heaven, the fount of honour, and the final and unchallengeable source of all authority. The diagram shows him assisted by the 'Three Excellencies'. In practice there were only two by the end of the first century BC, as the commander-in-chief's office, always intermittent and *ad hoc*, was finally extinguished. The chancellor at this date was the superior of the imperial counsellor, and was the emperor's chief minister, controlling all that passed in nine central ministries. Their titles reflect their original household origins, but by now the grand coachman was responsible, *inter alia*, for cavalry remounts, the herald for diplomatic embassies in the imperial court, and the minister for agriculture was the main treasurer of the empire.

The country was divided into commanderies (*chün*) headed by grand administrators and these in their turn into the *hsien* (prefectures, counties) headed by prefects (*hsien-ling*). They and their junior officials were part of the established bureaucracy and appointed by the central government. The prefects in the *hsien* had the same all-round competence as their seniors, the grand commandants, and at each lower level the officials replicated this same all-round jurisdiction but on an increasingly minor scale and with a lessening degree of sophistication. So, the prefectures were subdivided into districts, administered by a 'Thrice-Venerable' and three officials, and these districts in turn into communes (*t'ing*) run by 'Fathers' (or 'Chiefs') and these in their turn into the hamlets (*li*), under their headmen. From the district officials downwards, all appointments were made by the grand commandants and prefects and not the central government, nor do they count as established civil servants; in brief, they must not be counted among the 130,000-odd officially enumerated bureaucrats. Finally, at the very base, in the hamlets, families were bonded into groups of five or ten, in which every individual was criminally responsible for the behaviour of his fellows.

3. THE EMPEROR

The 2,000 years of Imperial China witnessed a perpetual see-saw between the power of the emperor to pursue his own policy through his own personal instrumentalities, and the power of either his relatives and/or the palace officials and the central bureaucracy to pursue their own. At times the emperor is the active ruler, at others it is his entourage or officialdom that rules. The power of officialdom was at the weakest on the advent of a new dynasty as an outcome of civil war, at its strongest as government again

THE SON OF
HEAVEN

CHANCELLOR	COUNSELLOR	COMMANDER-IN-CHIEF

The *San Kung* or 'Three Excellencies'

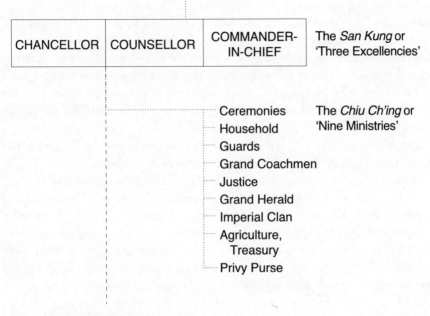

Ceremonies
Household
Guards
Grand Coachmen
Justice
Grand Herald
Imperial Clan
Agriculture, Treasury
Privy Purse

The *Chiu Ch'ing* or 'Nine Ministries'

COMMANDERIES [CHUN]
AD 9 = 103 (Grand Administrators)

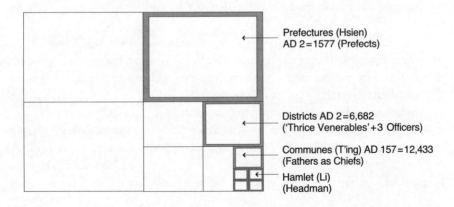

Prefectures (Hsien)
AD 2 = 1577 (Prefects)

Districts AD 2 = 6,682
('Thrice Venerables' + 3 Officers)

Communes (T'ing) AD 157 = 12,433
(Fathers as Chiefs)

Hamlet (Li)
(Headman)

FIG. 2.6.2. The administrative system under Ch'in and Former Han.

settled into routine. It was immensely assisted in asserting itself by two developments. First, officialdom was organically related to the great land-owning family clans that rapidly developed after Ch'in freed the peasantry and established the service nobility; for the most part the higher bureaucracy came from these great clans. Secondly, throughout the first century of Han rule this bureaucracy became more and more Confucianist in training and outlook, and its conversion was completed by the end of the dynasty's second century. This Confucian ideology de-emphasized the active and above all the military role of an emperor to the point, in theory, of limiting it to the little more than state rituals, appointments, and the display of 'virtue'.

Consequently, the emperorship that resulted was very different indeed from that of Rome. First, the Chinese emperorship, whatever else it might be, was irreducibly *ritualistic*: *yin-yang* and the perfect harmony of Earth, Man, and Heaven turned exclusively upon the emperor's actions. The enormous importance of this role is out of all proportion to that of the Roman emperor in respect to the state cults. Secondly, a Roman emperor—and here the exceptions like Nerva and Pertinax accentuate the general rule—was above all a war-leader as the very title *imperator* attests, let alone the careers of the emperors. In China, to the contrary, the civilians dominated the generals and military institutions and disparaged them. Finally, a Roman emperor was supposed to be *active*, to govern, not simply to reign. An emperor like Tiberius was censured because he left Rome for what were taken to be idle pleasures in Capri; but, as we have seen, the ideal Chinese emperor would play a quiescent, ritualistic role, and leave affairs of state to his ministers.

'Only in a few rare instances', Loewe maintains, 'can it be shown that a Han Emperor was personally responsible for initiating policies for guiding the destinies of the dynasty.'[9] 'Once a dynasty had been founded, the role of the emperor in strictly political terms was strictly limited . . . but the enthronement of infants demonstrates [that] . . . an incumbent of the throne was essential for the maintenance of government.' And it was essential because, as Loewe points out, all *authority* derived from him. A perfect example comes from Ssu-ma Ch'ien's account of how Liu Pang, the founder of the Former Han, came to be proclaimed emperor. He says that

[9] Loewe conspicuously declines to include Wu-ti (*CHC*, i. 152–3), but cf. H. H. Dubs (trans. and ed.), *Pan Ku: The History of the Former Han Dynasty*, 3 vols. (Baltimore, 1938–55), *contra*. I am unconvinced by Loewe's method of demonstration in the face of the unequivocal portrayal of an extremely forceful and overbearing character given by Ssu-ma Ch'ien and, surely, illustrated, *inter alia*, by his destruction of chancellors who crossed him. It seems hardly likely that such would be required if he was to be the purely reactive kind of ruler Loewe suggests.

after Liu and his officers had won the civil war and the way to the throne was open, 'various nobles and generals urged him to take the Imperial title for this reason: to those [of us] who have achieved merit, he [Liu Pang] has accordingly parcelled out land and enfeoffed them as kings and marquises. If our king does not assume the supreme title then all our titles will be called in doubt.'[10] But the skill of officialdom lay in doing their own thing behind the cover of the emperor's legitimacy, and this is why they tried to manipulate the succession. 'Ideally', Loewe goes on, 'the Emperor must be persuaded to play a passive rather than an active role; he should rule by force of title rather than exercise of personality; his existence was necessary in formal terms but his personal influence could be negligible in practice.'[11] For these reasons, it is not possible to present the Han emperor except in the context of the court and the bureaucracy: notably in his relationship to the great clans and their rivalries, to the nascent bureaucracy and its interrelatedness with these same landed families.

3.1. *The Imperial Succession*

The succession was hereditary. In principle the emperor could nominate any of his sons as heir-apparent; in practice this was complicated by the fact of his having an enormous harem. It was for the emperor to designate any one of his women as his empress and it was usually understood that it would be one of her sons who would be appointed crown prince; but this simple rule broke down because, just as the emperor could create one of his women as empress, so he could demote her and create another empress in her place. Another source of uncertainty occurred where the emperor died without leaving any sons at all; then, sometimes, the senior officials met and decided, while at other times interested parties at court would fabricate an alleged 'last will and testament' of the late emperor in favour of a particular candidate. A third area of uncertainty could open if the heir or heirs were minors. In such an event their mother—the empress-dowager—was empowered to issue edicts in the crown prince's name. Ideally, this would be a formality on the recommendation of senior officials, but Chinese history is full of strong-willed empress-dowagers who played their own game or that of their families. At its most benign, they merely influenced events through the filial piety that the young prince owed his mother, but some empress-dowagers went far beyond this. Twice in the history of the Han an empress-dowager used her position to do away with the heirs and install one

[10] Ssu-ma Ch'ien, *Records of the Grand Historian*, ii. 106.   [11] Loewe, *CHC*, i. 53.

of her own relatives on the throne. (In the T'ang dynasty the Empress-Dowager Wu actually became emperor![12])

The imprecise rules of succession encouraged the growth of factions among the great court clans and was a major source of instability at the very heart of the empire. In Rome the matter was usually decided in the camp, in China, in the court, often in the harem. Here is another example of the difference between the prevailing values of Rome and China: in the first case the predominant value of what the Chinese called *wu*—'war'—and in the second of what they called *wen*, 'civility' or 'culture'.

3.2. *The Ritual Role of the Emperor*

Whatever else he might be, a Chinese emperor was a kind of priest-king or nothing. We have already noted the sacral function of the Shang emperors and how, under the Chou, the office of emperor persisted in the house of Chou long after all political power had escaped him because he was necessary to carry out the essential rituals.

In the Han this sacred role carried on, but had been modified and redefined under the influence of the school of an extremely influential sage named Tung Chung-Shu (*c*.179–*c*.104 BC).[13] Tung laid great stress on two related currents of thought we have mentioned earlier,[14] that is to say the doctrine of the Five (in his case Three) Phases that the Cosmos engendered through the balance of *Yin* (earth) and *Yang* (heaven). Any imbalance in the two forces was expressed in signs, portents, and natural disasters, and the emperor was the human whose task it was, by right living and prudence, to make sure the balance was maintained. Signs and portents were a warning that he was failing in his duty.[15]

So the emperor, the Son of Heaven, was sacred because he alone could offer to Heaven the supreme sacrifices and maintain the harmony between the terrestrial order and the cosmos. 'He was', says Granet, 'simultaneously the author of every misdeed, the emissary of every expiation, the beneficiary of every pardon, the source of all potency.'[16] Under the influence of Tung, the great Emperor Wu-ti inaugurated the sacred sacrifices to the Triad of the Great One (Tai-i), the Earth Queen, and the Heavenly Father, and the subsidiary sacrifice at the Altar of the Five (sacred) Emperors. It was Wu-ti also who performed the portentous solemn ceremonies at the Great Moun-

---

[12] Cf. the reign of Queen Hatshepsut, in Egypt, at Bk. I, Ch. 3, above.

[13] It is he who is credited with getting Emperor Wu-Ti to make Confucianism the official state doctrine, in 136 BC. He was professor at the Academy, and twice a chief minister.

[14] Bk. II, Ch. 5, p. 458 above. [15] For Tung, see, e.g. Chan, *A Source Book*, 271–88.

[16] Quoted in Wheatley, *The Pivot*, 117.

tain—Tai Shan—at whose base he erected the vast open-air Hall of the Spirits.[17]

3.3. *The Solitary Emperor*

The Former Han made their capital at Ch'ang-an, near the modern Sian (for which reason they are sometimes called 'the Western Han') whereas the Later Han made their capital in Loyang (to the east). Though irregular in layout, Ch'ang-an possessed the characteristics common to all the various capital cities in China's history. The city was surrounded by a moat and massive walls, pierced by the canonical twelve gates (*men*), each leading to a broad thoroughfare that intersected the city. The northern part was the popular city, with its private dwellings and markets. It was enclosed by strong walls. Southward, and beyond them lay the walls of a number of palace complexes which formed the 'Whitehall' area. Still further to the south lay the walled palace of the empress-dowager, and only in the far south-west corner did one find the enormous square perimeter walls of the imperial complex itself, the Weiyang Palace. This contained many pavilions: for libraries, the empress, the harem, and the Hall of Ancestors. It also contained the palace of the emperor himself.

This Weiyang Palace was the 'Inner Court', the *nei-ting*, and that administrative complex to its north-east was the 'Outer Court', or *wai-ting*, and this is the significant point. For in that Weiyang Palace the emperor was the one, the solitary, the unique full male. He spent his life surrounded by no one but women and eunuchs. He was cut off from even his courtiers, and rare indeed were any male visitors: a few important ministers, relatives of his empress, a small number of personal friends. The emperor certainly made many public appearances—at the regular dawn audiences, the sacrifices, and the occasional court conferences—but otherwise he was a recluse. The business of government was being transacted remote from his presence at the other end of the city: so that the great ministers, like the chancellor or imperial counsellor, had to cross from their own offices and seek access to the Weiyang Palace in order to confer with the emperor. When, as was to happen, the emperor developed his personal policies in opposition to his officials, and when the historians describe this as the conflict between the Inner Court and the Outer Court, we have to envisage this physical isolation of the solitary emperor from the ministerial buildings where policies were being made in his name.

[17] Cf. Ssu-ma Ch'ien, *Records of the Grand Historian*, ii. 13–69, the Treaties on the Feng and Shan Sacrifices.

3.4. *The Great Families*

The Ch'in emancipation of the peasantry from their seigneurs entailed their right to buy and sell their land. In the primarily agrarian economies of the past this is usually followed by a process in which land comes to be increasingly concentrated and the free peasantry either dispossessed or constrained to new types of dependency on the wealthier landowners as the pressures of taxation, bad harvests, flood, or similar disasters force the marginal peasant proprietors to borrow against their harvests and finally to give up the farm altogether. We have seen this process at work in Greece and in the Roman Republic. It was to recur many times in Chinese history, which in this respect displays an alternation between the destruction of the wealthy landlord class in civil war, and particularly barbarian invasion, to the advantage of a newly free peasant economy, and then the steady erosion of the latter as land concentrations increased once more for the reasons we have mentioned.

This process of concentration began almost immediately after the Ch'in conquest of the other Chinese states but received a new impetus when Liu Pang (Kao Tsu) became the first Han emperor. He had to reward his relatives and comrades-in-arms and did so by conferring benefices which carried no grant of jurisdiction, but simply the tax receipts of so many villages. His great ministers were (largely) paid in the same way. Some of the new merchants, iron-founders or salt-producers who made fortunes despite official hostility, hastened to invest in the secure and far more respectable market for land. In this way, great landlord families began to flourish in the Former Han and became even wealthier and more politically intrusive in the Later Han, since it was due to them that the Liu family were able to win back the Han throne from the usurper Wang Mang.

I shall not follow those eminent Sinologists like Gernet and Eberhard who call this stratum 'the gentry'. This term has a specific connotation in English social history and to use it in the Chinese context (until perhaps the later Ch'ing) would be confusing. They are best called the Great Families or even the Families. In the Chinese tradition they were, first and foremost, great clans composed of several collateral lines which implanted themselves in different localities, just as the banyan tree of China puts down boughs in the ground which then grow into new trees. At this time all these collateral lines owed unflinching support to one another. These families were now sending the brightest of their sons to the local capital to acquire the education without which they could not enter the most prestigious of all occupations in China—and the most self-serving—to wit, officialdom. They were trained in the Confucian Classics, gained admittance to the central and local civil service, and once implanted helped their clansmen to obtain posts as well. If—as often happened—an official was stripped of his office he fell back on the landed members of his clan, and alternatively, if it was the landed branch that was in difficulties the official used his political influence to help it. (The histories of the Han Empire do not record any cases of a family losing both its lands and its official positions simultaneously.)

Thus these clans were at one and the same time extended families, rich landowners, Confucianist literati, and civil servants. Although those branches that resided in the cities often led an elegantly civilized life as poets, painters, scholars, and philosophers, 'their normal main activity . . . was *politics*, i.e. the effort to enter the provincial or central administration, civil or military'.[18] This met an equally eager response from the government. The founding emperor (Kao Tsu) found himself short of officials and ordered the Commandery administrators to nominate candidates on a merit basis and send them to the capital for appointment or rejection (196 BC). Wu-ti (140–87 BC) greatly extended and systematized this recruitment process and defined 'merit' in terms of knowledge of the Confucian Classics. So arose a synthesis of political ambition, family connection, landed wealth, and Confucianist ideology. A cycle established itself as the successful candidates in the capital showed favouritism for their clansmen in the qualifying tests, while back in the countryside the Commandery administrators were themselves frequently members of these Great Families, and nominated the candidates from their clan. Outside this, candidates had to rely on these Families for nomination.

3.5. *The Empresses' Relatives*

There was a more risky but potentially shorter and far more rewarding route to high office than entrance into the line bureaucracy, and it lay through membership of the clan of the empress. We have already noted the influence wielded by the empress, and, particularly an empress-dowager.[19] Now it was unusual for the Han emperors to put their close relatives in high ministerial positions.[20] But no such constraint applied to relatives of the empress.

The Families, therefore, aspired to become related to the Imperial House.

---

[18] W. Eberhard, *Conquerors and Rulers: Social Forces in Medieval China* (Brill, Leiden, 1952), 15.

[19] See pp. 483–4 above.

[20] Cf. Y.-C. Wang, 'An Outline of the External Government of the Former Han Dynasty', *Harvard Journal of Asiatic Studies*, 12 (1949), 161, who says the only post they were allowed to hold was that of director of the Imperial Clan, and Bielenstein, *Bureaucracy*, 204, 7. *contra*. But Bielenstein cites only seven such cases up to AD 169!

In the worst case, families would present the emperor with a beauty for his harem, but as this numbered some 6,000 women under the Former Han (3,000 under the Later Han),[21] the chance that the emperor might even touch her was remote. However, if she entertained him for just one night it did constitute some claim, while if she bore a male child her status rose dramatically since an emperor had the power to depose the reigning empress and replace her with another woman, whose child would then be in line for the throne.

But in many cases such elaborate planning and waiting was not necessary. A Family could attain its ambition at one lucky stroke if an emperor chose one of its women as his empress, for no sooner was she enthroned than she expected, her clan expected, and the emperor and his court all expected that she would have as many ministerial posts as possible filled by her relatives. So arose the notorious tradition of the *wai-ch'i*—'the outer Relations'. It led directly to the domination of the court and the emperor by a faction: to the struggle between the relatives of the present and the relatives of the former empress, that is, the dowager-empress (the emperor's mother), both factions being challenged by other Families, whose daughters at court had a chance of winning the imperial favour.

3.6. *The Bureaucracy*

Details of the size, recruitment, and organization of the civil service have their place later. The only intention here is to show how rapidly it grew in numbers, differentiation, and in a common ideology. In 2 BC it had reached over 130,000 established posts. It was ruled by a traditionally Chinese passion for symmetry and classification:[22] even the imperial women of the harem were graded into eighteen ranks whose (nominal) salaries corresponded to the eighteen grades of the career civil service.[23] The reality was much less orderly, since the structuration was affected by notions of collegiate rather than single-seated authority and of duplication and overlapping rather than clear lines of command. The elaboration of ministries, divisions, and bureaux was vastly complex.

Higher appointments were mostly made by recommendation of the principal ministers and these ministers made the lesser appointments on

[21] But cf. Loewe, *contra*, who states that the harem in mid-2nd cent. numbered 6,000 and that of the Former Han, 3,000. *CHC*, i. 259. But in either case, the point stands. What, in these circumstances, is a mere 3,000?   [22] Bielenstein, *Bureaucracy*.
[23] Thus, for the Former Han, Kuang Wu-Ti reduced the ranks to only three, but some reappeared in later reigns. (*CHC*, i. 259).

their own authority. Although the Han is credited with the beginnings of the examination system, very few officials were recruited by this route.

They all came from the same social background, the Families to whom they owed their nomination and/or appointment. Additionally, within fifty or so years of the dynasty's foundation they began to come under the influence of Confucian views of the tutelary relationship officials bore to the Son of Heaven.[24] Confucianism had remained under a cloud—the bans on its literature were still in force and we saw how contemptuously Liu Pang treated one Confucian sage.[25] But under Hui-ti the persecution was lifted and the scholars reconstituted the Five Classics which Shih Huang-ti had ordered destroyed, partly out of memory and partly by finding (or purporting to find) hidden copies that had escaped. In 136 BC Wu-Ti banned all other kinds of philosophers from the Board of Erudites that advised the court and so made Confucianism the official persuasion, and in 124 he founded the Academy (University) run by Confucianists for fifty scholars. Although these were enlisted to compete for official posts, few posts were in fact filled this way. But the institution grew so that by the end of the first century BC it had 3,000 students. By that time the Confucianists at court had first confronted the Legalists, then got the upper hand over them. In the Later Han Confucianism was quite triumphant and the University swelled to 30,000 students.

We have already noted T'ung Chung Shu's view that an emperor was to be a perfect moral leader, whose sole political task was to select 'wise and virtuous men' and let them get on with governing. 'In consequence, no one will have seen the ruler do anything: but a successful administration will have been achieved.'[26] In practice the Han ministers did not go as far as that. But they did take the line that they were the natural counsellors of the emperor and bound to stick up for the Confucian virtues even in the face of his displeasure; that in practical terms they prepared the alternatives for the emperor to choose among (emperors themselves did not take initiatives); and finally, that all was to be done by consultation: in small interministerial conferences, in the great court conference where the gravest policies were concerned, and in dialogue between the emperor and his great ministers—particularly, at this time, the chancellor. The chancellor was seen as speaking for the entire imperial service.

---

[24] See Bk. II, Ch. 5, above, *re* Mencius, at p. 462, on the notion that the official was the educator of the monarch. [25] See pp. 474–5, above.

[26] Quoted in Wang, 'An Outline', 163.

4. THE POLITICAL PROCESS AT THE IMPERIAL COURT

4.1. *An Excursus on Administrative and Constitutional Evolution*[27]

On the surface, the events at court recounted by the ancient Chinese historians in great detail (especially Ssu-ma Ch'ien and Pan Ku) are a tangle of conflicts and conspiracies involving the Great Families, empresses and empresses-dowager, eunuchs, generals, and concubines; but on examination two interlocking themes detach themselves. They are the struggle for dominance between the Great Families and the emperor's efforts to resist the line-bureaucracy. The Han Empire is the first of the great Palace polities described so far where we have enough detail to discern the dynamics of the struggles at court, and it exhibits tendencies which we find repeated *mutatis mutandis* in similar polities and indeed in any polities, including those in medieval Europe, where one man is, nominally, the supreme source of policy. It is therefore a paradigm case, and this is the occasion and the excuse for this excursus.

In one-man (monocratic) regimes, administrative and constitutional developments similar to Han China's often proceed like the building of a coral-reef. Coral is a living organism, a polyp. This polyp buds. The bud is at first attached to the original polyp, but, as it develops into a new polyp, so the old one dies—but it leaves its skeleton behind. Thus, over generations, the living elements flourish, but among wider and wider circles of skeletons.

In the palace polities, even including (quite appropriately, as I shall show) the American Presidential system and the medieval English monarchy, this 'coral reef' analogy is expressible in two 'laws'. The first is the *Law of Proximity*. It states that the more decisive the personal will of the ruler in the polity, the more influential are those who have the closest and most continuous access to him. They will be more influential still if they can have *exclusive* access, and many therefore try to achieve this. Hence the claim among the medieval English baronage, for example, to be the king's 'natural counsellors'.

Rulers, however, prefer to choose their advisers, not to be forced to accept them. They often react, therefore, by relieving their 'natural' or 'official' advisers of executive authority and falling back on more intimate advisers of their own choosing. Often a conflict opens between the outer ring of 'natural' and 'official' advisers and the new, inner group. Sometimes the former are able to take over or control these inner posts, so that the ruler finds himself facing the same constraints as before. In that case he

---

[27] This argument was originally intended for the Conceptual Prologue, [eds.].

often reacts as previously—by creating a new, personal centre of advice and execution.

This process leads to the second set of developments, summed up as the *Law of Inflated Titles*. The titles borne by those of the intimate circle (e.g. privy councillor) become prestigious, so that more and more crowd in to form part of this circle. But this is consequently no longer intimate! The ruler transfers his trust elsewhere, to a closer, more intimate individual or circle, for the reasons we have expressed in the Law of Proximity. He wants to make policy himself. Thus the formerly intimate posts become more numerous. They still carry their prestigious titles but wield less and less influence. They become honorific—and empty. Very often, indeed in most cases, the more splendid the title the less its functional importance, while at the same time, the really functional offices are bearing very humble titles: in the Persian Empire the cupbearer, for instance; in late medieval England the king's secretary. Then these humble titles themelves become prestigious and the object of competition—and the process begins, *da capo*.

4.2. *The Former Han Dynasty and the Creation of the 'Inner Court'*

The chancellors and their deputies, the imperial counsellors, acted as supervisors of the entire bureaucracy and represented its view to the emperor and, up to the accession of Wu-ti in 140 BC, emperors collaborated with rather than commanded these high officials. Wu-ti was different: hot-tempered, hasty and aggressive, and intent on having his own way. That way was a complete reversal of the policies pursued so far, both abroad and at home. Against the pacificism and non-interventionist domestic policies espoused by previous administrations and his current advisers, Wu-ti ended the tribute that had kept the Hsiung-nu quiet and reconquered and colonized China's deep south. To pay for these costly campaigns he was driven not only to raise taxes but to follow cameralist policies like those of the Ch'in in order to expand the tax-base, notably by making the production of iron and salt into state monopolies.

In addition to dissenting from the emperor's policies, certain chancellors and imperial counsellors were also caught up in the feuding between the Great 'Outer Relations' Families. For one or the other reason, Wu-ti directly confronted recalcitrant senior ministers; six were executed or forced to commit suicide and few of the others remained long in their posts.

These senior ministers and their officials worked in the Outer Court, away from the palace. It was there that 'memorials' to the throne were received and processed, and finally responded to by draft rescripts which were then presented to the emperor for his consideration. It so happened that inside the emperor's own palace complex there existed a minor office (called the 'Masters of Writing') and, in order to bypass the officials of the Outer Court, Wu-ti expanded and reorganized it as his personal Secretariat. He divided it into four bureaux: for 'Quests' (effectively foreign affairs); for Civil Affairs (memorials presented by individuals); for superintending the Commandery administrators; and the so-called 'Bureau of Regular Attendants'. This office conducted all correspondence with the offices of the chancellor and the imperial secretary. By the end of Wu-ti's long reign it had come to handle all the memorials presented by ministers, *and* to prepare the emperor's rescripts and decrees in response to them, which obviously involved discussion between its staff and the emperor.

In the Regency that followed on Wu-ti's death (87 BC) the regent (Marshal Huo Kang) continued to use the Masters of Writing Office as his personal Secretariat, but by this time the office was actually controlling and directing the offices of the chancellor and imperial counsellor. It was staffed by top-rate officials, since they had to know 9,000 characters (today 60,000 characters exist, but only about 10,000 are used) and six different kinds of scripts. Pan Ku's great history, the *Han Shu*, represents a general as saying in 46 BC: 'the office of the Masters of Writing is the foundation of all the offices. It is the key organ of the state.'[28] But this development did not abash the 'Outer Relations' in the least. Hitherto they had filled the chancellorship and the other high appointments. Since these were now controlled by the Masters of Writing Office, they took successful steps to control this office itself. The convention grew up that a high officer entitled regent and marshal (just like Huo Kang), should *ex officio* control the Masters of Writings Office, which gave him control of all the other appointments. And the individual who filled that post was of course the representative of the then-dominant clan.

Foiled in making the Inner Court his personal instrument of control, the emperor reacted by placing his confidence in an even more intimate location and in a class of personal servants who owed fidelity to himself alone. He turned to his private apartments and to those who staffed them—the eunuchs.

Eunuchs were to play a very active role in Chinese central government up to the very end of the empire. Consequently, their origin and characteristics require some detailed discussion, more than is usually accorded them in the standard works on Chinese government and history. I shall defer that discussion for the moment, since all that needs saying here is that, of all the humans in the palace, these were likely to be the most subservient, the

---

[28] Quoted in Wang, 'An Outline', 170.

most faithful, and, because of their proximity to the emperor, the most intimate, since no men were permitted (save on occasional missions) inside the palace, let alone the emperor's domestic quarters.[29] Wu-ti found it more comfortable to work there in privacy than at the office of the Masters of Writing and arranged for a number of eunuchs to act as go-betweens. One group consisted of so-called 'Palace Writers' and the other, of internuncios, or messengers, and the two groups were both headed by a very senior eunuch entitled 'prefect of the Palace Writers'. It was not long before this intimate staff of go-betweens was itself directing the Masters of Writing Office, and by mid-century an emperor preferred its advice to that of his minister for that office.

By this time, two important and related developments had occurred among the career-bureaucracy. First, the Masters of Writing Office had developed its own bureaucratic routines. Secondly, the Confucianist reaction against the 'modernist' views of Wu-ti's time[30] had prevailed. The bureaucracy was now well established, routinized, solidary, and in its higher ranks at any rate, Confucianist.

Emperor and the bureaucracy clashed head-on in Yüan-ti's reign (48–33 BC). The *Han Shu* recounts that he turned to his eunuch prefect of the Palace Writers, Shih Hsien, and 'entrusted him with the government affairs. All affairs, whether large or small, were reported through Shih Hsien for the Emperor's decision.'[31] The minister for the Masters of Writing Office, Hsiao Wang-ti, a distinguished career bureaucrat and outstanding scholar, remonstrated and lost his life as a result. But his cause triumphed. The next emperor, Ch'eng-ti (32–7 BC), was dominated by his strongly Confucianist mother, the empress-dowager, who persuaded him to abolish the post of prefect of the Palace Writers and disband the bureau.

4.3. *The Later Han: Triumph and Downfall of the Eunuch Secretariat*

There followed the sanguinary intermezzo of the Wang Mang regime and then the very same story we have recounted began *da capo*, but with the principal protagonists all more numerous, better organized, and hence more powerful.

Ascending the throne in AD 25, Liu Hsiu re-established the Han dynasty. Under this (the 'Later' Han), the frame of government remained as before and so did the main actors, but with changed emphases. First, let us

---

[29] See pp. 494–5 below.
[30] Cf. M. Loewe, 'The Campaigns of the Han Wu-Ti', in F. A. Kiermann and J. K. Fairbank (eds.), *Chinese Ways in Warfare* (Harvard UP, 1974).
[31] Quoted in Chü, *Han Social Structure* (University of Washington Press, Seattle, 1972), 431.

consider the landed families. Liu Hsiu's helpers were largely from the southern part of the Yellow River basin, a semi-colonial area of vast estates which they ruled like a plantocracy, in huge haciendas. Here as many as three generations lived together, sometimes one hundred strong. They owned large numbers of slaves. Their resident farmers were their dependants (*k'e* or 'guests') and they maintained bodyguards (*pu ch'ü*). Such families could put a thousand men in the field. The new emperor (Liu Hsiu) who himself had been one of them, was typical: his vast domain near Nanyang was girdled with walls pierced by gates enclosing its own market and guarded by his private militia. These families continued to provide the recruits to the imperial civil service at central and local level and were more involved in court politics than even in the Former Han because, unlike the Former Han emperors, these Later Han chose their empresses exclusively (with one amazing exception)[32] from these extremely wealthy families. Thus the 'Outer Relations' were even more powerful factions than before and their struggles to control the emperor and the court even more desperate.

Also stronger was the Confucian establishment. Its orthodox status was now beyond challenge and this was reflected (as well as reinforced) by the growth of the University, whose student-numbers expanded until by the end of the dynasty they had reached 3,000. In a state where literacy was so very restricted and where scholarship was regarded as incomparably the most prestigious of all occupations, the University was tantamount to 'public opinion', and by reason of the close affinities between students and the filial respect they tendered to their teachers (as they still do in China) they came to be a formidable pressure group.

But the palace eunuchs also became a hierarchical and organized corps; and by the end of the dynasty they were the key agency in central government. So let us pause for a moment and ask why and how eunuchs could become so important.

The first thing to notice is that they were very numerous, and although many served outside the Imperial Palace (outside the 'Yellow Gates') they were the only males who served *inside* it. By far the largest number were domestic menials. Another group serviced the 'Lateral Courts'—the harem—but these lay outside the Palace itself, though inside the imperial compound. If, as most authors suggest, the initial reason for employing eunuchs was to staff the harem, this would not have necessitated staffing the emperor's own palace with them. The objection is reinforced by the Later Han emperors' creation of an Inner Palace guard consisting entirely of eunuchs (the 'Extra Retinue of the Attendants at the Palace Gates'). The

[32] The Empress Ho, wife to the Emperor Ling-Ti (d. 189) was descended from a line of butchers.

'Attendants at the Palace Gates' themselves were the emperors' personal servants who were always in attendance. Finally there was a tiny group which numbered a mere four at first and never rose to more than twenty. These were called 'Regular Palace Attendants' and it is they alone who were the highly political corps that handled affairs of state. By the end of the Han the total number of eunuchs was altogether about 2,000, and by that time they formed an organized structure under the authority of the 'Regular Palace Attendants' as their leaders and spokesmen.

The reason the Chinese emperors made such extensive use of eunuchs seem to me to be twofold. The first is effectively ritualistic. The emperor was so much above other men that it would desecrate his sanctity to have them with him in his palace; but eunuchs were, so to speak, subhuman, another and totally abject species. The other reason is that they had no family connections, no professional status or dignity, and were wholly dependent on the emperor for any kind of career or advancement.[33] In this respect the judgement of the emperor was rarely misplaced, for with very few exceptions the eunuchs were unswervingly and self-sacrificingly loyal to their masters. It is true that many were lavishly rewarded for such loyalty, but that was not the motive for it.

Finally, we must not take the historical Chinese accounts of eunuchs at their face value. These works are without exception written by Confucianists for Confucianists, to whom these eunuch upstarts were the principal enemy. Eunuchs uniformly appear in those histories as rapacious (certainly no more so than ministers were); vicious (ditto); illiterate (obviously false as far as the élite political few were concerned); pusillanimous and unwarlike (in fact they supplied many generals and admirals). The prejudice against them is comprehensible enough. They were *parvenus* of no family and no classical education, but they had supplanted those who had both, the great landlords and the Confucianist scholar officials.

The first two emperors, war-minded and vigorous, brooked no interference. Until *c.* AD 75 neither the great clans nor the eunuchs exercised independent influence, which is understandable enough since two warrior emperors were in command. Kuang Wu-ti's secretariat at the office of the 'Regular Palace Attendants' only numbered four persons.

The Great Families—'Consort Families' (*wai-ch'i*)—only resumed their control of the court in the reign of Chang-ti and Ho-ti (AD 75 onwards). Then over a space of some fifty years (88–144) one great Consort Family after another—Tou, Teng, Liang—succeeded in getting control of both the

---

[33] Cf. our reference to why the Persians used eunuchs in Xenophon, *Cyropaedia*, I. viii. 540, quoted by us at pp. 300–1.

Inner and the Outer Courts. The prize was, of course, prodigious—the command of the pomp and wealth of a vast empire—but the penalties were even more dire. The Chinese convention of collective responsibility for guilt extended to the clans, and nowhere more ruthlessly than to the Consort Families. Their rivals did not stop at expelling them from power but exterminated their entire clan to the third or fifth degree of relationship, while the remainder were degraded to slavery.

The histories show how much some emperors resented their power-lessness.[34] It reflected a sweeping social development: the increasing over-concentration of wealth in the hands of the Great Families and especially of the Consort clans.

At this stage, the eunuch establishment must not be seen as antithetical to the great Consort Families or the line-bureaucracy, but simply as the emperor's auxiliaries, and in an inter-clan struggle they were apt to be as divided as the clans. But to an emperor who wanted to assert his independence they were the only possible resource. Ho-ti (AD 88–106) got rid of the Tou family by calling on one of his eunuch 'Regular Attendants' (Cheng Chu) to organize a coup against them. More dramatic was the plot of Huan-ti (146–68), 'who had felt oppressed and afraid for a long time' by the overmighty Liang family who had ruled for twenty-seven years.[35] I have already said that princes, kings, and emperors in all countries and all times fell back on more and more intimate advisers to help them exercise personal rule, retreating even into the bedchamber (the *cubiculum* of the Later Roman Empire); but few things could illustrate this more forcibly than arranging a plot in the private bathroom! For this is where the emperor called in four of the eunuch 'Regular Attendants' and another personal eunuch to swear a blood-oath to him, upon which he issued his edict for the arrest and execution of the entire Liang clan, which was duly carried out.[36]

The lavish rewards and the titles of nobility which the emperor showered on his faithful eunuchs mightily vexed the now ascendent Tou family, blood-kin of the empress-dowager, who had in fact nominated Ling-ti (an in-law of the Tou family) for the throne; but—and this was new—it inflamed the 3,000 students in the University. Under the name of 'Partisans' they spear-headed an alliance between the Tou and the Confucianist officials. When Ling-ti succeeded (168–89) as the nominee of Empress-Dowager Tou Wu, a member of her Tou clan *ordered* him to arrest his top eunuch officials and so win back supreme power. But, the message having been intercepted, the top seventeen eunuchs took a blood-oath to execute him. By forging imperial

---

[34] Hou Han-shu, quoted in Chü, *Han Social Structure*, 476.
[35] Hou Han-shu, quoted ibid.   [36] See ibid. 476–80.

edicts they rallied the household troops and won over the Northern Garrison (which policed the capital). The entire Tou clan was extinguished—kinsmen, relatives by marriage, retainers—all of them. One hundred of the Confucianist 'Partisans' were executed and 700 others dismissed. Thus, for the rest of his reign Ling-ti was absolute and ruled through his eunuchs.

Unfortunately, when he died in 189, leaving only two infants to succeed, the empire was engulfed in a vast and murderous peasant uprising (the Yellow Turbans) and the armies to crush it were under the command of the late emperor's brother-in-law (the usual Consort Family conjuncture) who saw the opportunity to seize power for himself. To defend her son's succession the empress-dowager relied on the faithful eunuchs, while the brother-in-law set this succession aside in favour of his own nephew (again not unusual), and threatened the eunuchs with extinction. They retaliated by killing him, but by now the capital was teeming with provincial troops levied to suppress the Yellow Turbans. One of the ruffian generals in charge of a troop entered the Palace and massacred all its 2,000 eunuchs, leaving the empress-dowager defenceless. She was promptly murdered by another such general, who installed a puppet emperor and tried to rule through him. His more successful rival war-lords preferred to rule through the child-emperor, and fought with one another to serve his person. In 220 this child-emperor was compelled to make a formal abdication. So ended the Han dynasty, a victim of Confucianist and Great Family resistance to the emperor with his private eunuch staff, at a moment when the empire was convulsed with popular revolt.

The foregoing account has presented the fall of the dynasty in 'Court' terms, to make the simple point that there was a power vacuum at the centre at the very time the population was in revolt. Was this coincidence fortuitous? It is arguable that peasant rebellions like the Yellow Turbans were a reflection of the over-concentration of wealth among the few, and indeed, arguable that throughout Chinese history the fall of dynasties was due to this top-heavy accumulation of wealth and the refusal of the great landowners to accept any reforms that would limit it in favour of the peasantry. The fall of the Former and the Later Han, the early and the terminal T'ang, the Yuan, and the Ming—to go no further—were all accompanied by peasant rebellions, all the more potent because of their millenarian character, their organization into quasi-churches and, often, their leadership by secret societies. But this itself is not a full explanation, because the top-heavy accumulation of wealth was a *constant*, and there were many more peasant uprisings than there were destruction of dynasties. To explain the latter one must take account of the adventitious factors which were the

TABLE 2.6.1. *Local administrative areas, c. AD 140–53*

Name of Unit	Numbers	Average area (sq. miles)		Average population
Chün, and the Kingdoms	99	15,551	(123^*123)	606,000
Hsien	1,179	1,271	(35^*35)	47,169
Hsiang	3,611	407	(20^*20)	16,300
T'ing	12,443	120	(11^*11)	4,821

Source: Bielenstein, *Bureaucracy*, 90–109.

proximate causes of the dynasty's collapse. One such factor was a natural disaster such as famine and—on several occasions—the flooding of the lower Yangtse basin. But the other factor was the one described above: a power vacuum at the top. Emperors who were powerful fought off and defeated popular rebellions; it is the *conjuncture* of the power-vacuum and the peasant rebellion that together provide the explanation.

5. THE TERRITORIAL FRAMEWORK

There is a striking difference between the territorial or provincial arrangements in the Han and the Roman Empire, at least up to Diocletian's reorganization, which gave the Han a more symmetrical and hierarchical pattern. China's chief differences from Rome lie in its system's mathematical uniformity and symmetry, the relatively high numbers of appointed officials, their ubiquitousness and intrusiveness, and the absence of any self-government. Another striking difference is the Chinese reliance on the written word rather than spot inspection and face-to-face interviews; yet unlike the Roman case almost *no* documentary evidence of the Han period has survived to illuminate the actual practice of government. So we have to rely on anecdotal references in the histories.[37]

To the system of local areas[38] already outlined, it is worth adding information on their relative sizes and populations, for we have a substantial body of data relating to AD 140–53. I have assumed the area of the empire to be 'China proper', which is roughly 1.5 million square miles, and its population at about 60 million people (see Table 2.6.1).

Before embarking on the main account, one anomaly must be introduced and explained, the existence of 'kingdoms' (*wang-kuo*). The title of 'king'

[37] However see n. 74 below and A. F. P. Hulsewé, *Remnants of Ch'in Law: An Annotated Translation of the Ch'in Legal and Administrative Rules of the Third century BC, Discovered in Yün-Meng Prefecture, Hu-Pei Province, in 1975* (Brill, Leiden, 1985).   [38] See pp. 479–80 above.

could only be held by members of the royal family and all the royal sons were so ennobled (except for the heir-apparent) and received benefices which numbered between eight and twenty-five, depending on the number of royal sons and their descendants. At the outset, each king set up his own administration on the same pattern as the imperial one, and appointed his own officials with the significant exception of the chief minister, the chancellor, who was appointed by the emperor. The kings and their ministers, however, were all bound to observe the 'laws of Han'. A good deal of friction and petty rebellion culminated in the full-scale uprising known as 'the Revolt of the Seven Kingdoms'. After it was crushed (in 154 BC) the central government appointed all the local officials and reduced the number and status of the king's ministers, so that very soon there was no difference in administration between these kingdoms and the commanderies (i.e. the *chün*). This ended any compromise there might have been with 'feudalistic' elements in the state and consolidated its centralized character. It was this that enabled Wu-ti, the activist and conqueror, to carry out his formidable exploits.

The commanderies (*chün*) were governed by 'administrators' (*shou*) who were civil servants on local secondment, and were shifted around at frequent intervals. They were very senior, rating 2,000 *shih*.[39] They combined both civil and military responsibilities and were responsible for everything that passed in their areas. They were responsible for tax collection and for the population- and land-registration on which this was based; for the suppression of bandits; for mobilizing the militia (but only on imperial authorization and only inside their commandery) and for training it; for criminal cases—here they had to review the verdicts; for public works and corvée duty: and perhaps (according to locality), for providing horses for the cavalry, for granaries, and markets, and so forth. Basically, the commandery was, of course, supervisory, not directly administrative; the administrator was obliged to make a twice-yearly tour of the prefectures (*hsien*). To do all these things his establishment ran into hundreds.[40] His own personal staff included assistants for accounts, for records, and for his Privy Purse, and a military commandant (until this post was abolished under the Later Han). The line-bureaucracy consisted of a number of divisions: for 'merit' (i.e. nomination of candidates for the imperial civil service), for general administrative purposes, for banditry, for criminal cases, and for 'investigation'. This last division was a team of five regional investigators who checked on the work of the lower units.

---

[39] See below, p. 508 and p. 519 ff. for the ranking order.
[40] For the capital *chün* of Honan the total was 892 but this was completely exceptional.

One somewhat puzzling aspect of the administrators' work concerns their relationship to the central government. Administrators did not dispose of enough resources to raise troops and rebel, and in any case they were appointed, rotated, or dismissed too quickly for them to have much chance. But, throughout, the central government's knowledge of their activities seems flawed. At the very outset of the dynasty the only check on them seem to have been irregular descents by *ad hoc* inspecting secretaries. From 106 BC the central government sent out regular inspectors (later called *mu* or 'shepherds') with small staffs to help them. There were thirteen, each covering a 'Province', and their duty was to examine all aspects of the commandery administration and to come to the capital to present an annual report to the imperial counsellor. But these inspectors only ranked 600 *shih*—far below an administrator, who ranked 2,000 *shih*—and must therefore have been comparatively young. The Later Han upgraded the inspectors to 2,000 *shih* status, but they were no longer itinerant; instead they were resident in the province's capital town and there remained, transmitting their reports *in writing*. This reliance on the written document rather than face-to-face encounters will be met with again and again in Chinese history. As we are in a position to demonstrate how misleading and ineffectual it was as an instrument of control in the Ming dynasty, we need not believe it was any more effectual under the Han. For it must always be borne in mind that, whereas many Roman emperors tended to move around their empire, most Chinese emperors were home-bound, and indeed many never went outside the Palace enclosure.

Prefectures—between ten and twelve of them in each commandery[41]— survive to this day as the currently basic local government unit of China. The bigger ones (over 10,000 people) were governed by prefects (*ling*) the lesser by a chief (*chang*). The list of its duties is the same as that in the commandery: law and order and criminal cases; the tax and land registers; the organization of corvée labour and execution of public works; the supervision of the daily work round; and, of course, tax collection. The prefecture was organized like the commandery, but on a smaller scale: staff officers (including two commandants to act against bandits), then divisional heads in charge of 'merit' (nominations), litigation, markets, and so forth. Their personnel were of low official rank (salaries measured in *tou*,[42] not in *shih*). The prefect (or chief) was expected to make two tours of inspection a year through the prefecture. His staff, too, was very numerous—the Loyang prefecture employed nearly 800 lesser officials—but as it was the prefecture

---

[41] But see my caveat on 'lacunae' at p. 504 below.
[42] A *tou* was only one-tenth of a *shih*.

of the imperial capital, this was exceptional. All the same, the average prefecture must have employed at least 400 or 500 staff on the average.

The average *hsiang* (district) covered about one-third the area of a prefecture. Their officials were appointed by the prefect or the administrator. 'Moral leadership'—but no executive duties—was provided by a 'thrice Venerable', but the work was done by the 'Petty Official with Rank', the bailiff, and the patrol leader. The first-named two were responsible for collecting the taxes, organizing the corvée, and dispensing justice. The patrol leader was, effectively, the police chief.

The *hsiang*, as we have seen, were divided into so many communes (*t'ing*), run by a chief (*chang*) or father (*fu*). Their principal task was to maintain law and order and man the postal stations, to which end they resided (as in the Roman Empire) in a building that combined the functions of inn and police-station. On the hamlets (the *li*) we have no detailed information except that they were represented by their headmen and were largely left to their own devices.

The impression one gets—and perhaps is meant to get—is one of a highly bureaucratized and centralized system, arranged with 'Benthamite' symmetry ('always call the same thing by the same name and with the same function') and leaving no scope for local flexibility. That is almost certainly not how it was in practice. It was highly bureaucratized compared to Rome. The discrepancy is entirely due to the localities. For the Chinese chancellor's office in 117 BC employed 382 men (of whom 262 were clerks).[43] Since this was the largest of all the departments, then, even if all the other ten ministries had been of this size, the central administrators would have accounted for only 4,202 of the 130,285.[44] Furthermore, the number of Han officials was greatly in excess of the official figure of 130,285, for these comprise only the ones 'with rank' (i.e. 'established'). That very large numbers were employed in the localities can be inferred as follows. We are told that the capital commandery of Honan employed 892 officials, and its capital *prefecture* of Loyang, 796. Both were outsize. So, suppose we make the conservative assumption that the average *commandery* and the average *prefecture* employed half these numbers (Assumption A) or a third of these numbers (Assumption B). Then in AD 140–33, when there were 99 *chün* and 1,179 *hsien*, the total of all civil servants would be:

---

[43] Bielenstein, *Bureaucracy*, 9, n. 22.

[44] Cf. A. H. M. Jones's (*Later Roman Empire*) estimate of 5,000 in the Palatine offices of the Later Roman Empire.

	Commandery		Prefecture		Total Staff
Assumption A:	44,154	+	469,242	=	513,396
B:	29,436	+	312,828	=	342,264

These calculations do not add up to the official 130,285 because the specification of who was and who was not 'established' is too inexact. They do demonstrate—and that is their purpose here—that on Assumption A, for instance, the *hsien* accounted for ten times more officials than the *commanderies*, and the latter some eleven times the numbers at the capital.

Comparison with the Roman civil bureaucracy is so hazardous it might be called 'fortuitous'. To begin with, the two empires might have defined an 'established post' differently and probably did. Secondly, the Chinese polity had few slaves—it is reckoned they formed only 1 per cent of the population—so that nearly all the menial posts in the Roman service might well have been filled by slaves and therefore not enumerated, whereas they would have been in China. Thirdly, the Roman army performed certain tasks the civil service was called on to do in China.[45]

As we have almost no independent documentary evidence, we have no means of knowing how the Chinese localities were governed in practice, and, above all, how far they could depart from the central government's directions. An informed guess would suggest much more flexibility in the modes of operation than otherwise. The commandery would quite certainly have to reach the government targets for taxes, corvée labour, and the suppression of banditry; these, after all, were either reached or they were not, and this was plainly visible. But modalities and practices were not. At the interface of central and local government one can virtually guarantee considerable accommodation between the interests of the local landlords and the directives of the administrators and prefects. Certainly this is what happened in later dynasties. And Han histories rather bear this out: they contain numerous accounts of complaisant officials—who accommodate the local landowners—and others, the 'harsh officials', who come in and suddenly take vigorous action and sow panic among them. Administrators and prefects would not dare defy the order of the central government but they could administer them more or less determinedly, from one place to another. Biographical entries in the various histories, and local inscriptions with biographical details support this and supply yet one more example of the ubiquitous presence of local 'notables' as the indispensable intermediaries

[45] Finally, Jones's (ibid.) estimate of Roman officialdom does not include the staffs (many of them slaves) of the decurion councils who administered the Roman localities.

between the government's local officials and the administered population.[46] 'For the bulk of the population, local élites were the only significant wielders of power.'[47] These local élites, the *shih* class of educated, cultivated gentlemen, comprised the heads of the Great Families at its apex, and, at its base, the humbler country squire who 'ate plainly, had a slow carriage, served in the commandery (*chün*) as an officer or a clerk, looked after the family tomb and was praised as a good man by the community'.[48] The same families went on producing civil servants to serve in the *hsien*, the *chün*, or the capital, for generation after generation, during which time they continued to maintain a set social distance between themselves according to which of these echelons they served. By and large those serving the *hsien* did not often rise into the *chün* level, but at the *chün* level it was not at all uncommon for a gifted (or favoured) individual to be promoted to serve in the capital.[49]

These local élites formed a great network of kinship and patron–client relationships, which two were linked together and in their turn affected the conduct of government at both the local and the central level. Kinship accounted for a large part of the local appointments: magistrates, prefects, and administrators each had the duty and the right to appoint their own agents, while the administrator of course was the official who nominated candidates for service in the capital. As the role of the 'Outer Relations' expanded under the Later Han, the right to make appointments became linked with these clans' struggles at court. The Family in temporary control there would, naturally, nominate its kinfolk to the administratorships, and through this disposed of the enormous volume of patronage which served as the foundation of their power in the palace and throughout the land. One consequence was that when they were overturned by their rivals not just they but their protégés and nominees were turned out also.

But kinsmen alone were not numerous enough for a clan to be able to overpower its rivals. A further source of support was needed, and was found in clienteles; hence the clan competition to recruit clients. In China the client relationship arose in one of two ways. One, which hardly concerns us yet, was the relationship of the pupil to his former teacher—and this lingers in China to this very day. But the other, which is relevant here, was the fidelity an

---

[46] See above, 'Conceptual Prologue', *re* 'Notables and "Despotism"', pp. 66–70. This entry demonstrates that in all pre-industrial societies without exception, the prime function of 'centralization' or 'bureaucratization' is architectonic. It does not and cannot supersede local élites—far from it—but makes them cohere in a set framework. This was true, as we have seen, of Rome and will be shown to be true of the Caliphate and of course, the feudal *regna* of Western Europe—and for that matter of their 'absolutist', 'centralized' successors till at least the end of the 19th cent. It is equally true of the great Asian regimes such as the Ottoman Empire, the Mogul Empire, and (in an idiosyncratic way) of Tokugawa Japan. [47] *CHC*, i. 637.

[48] Ibid. 638, quoting from the *Hou Han Shu*. [49] Ibid. 638–9.

individual owed to the superior who had nominated or promoted him to office. The clans came to compete so hard to further their court ambitions that the potential clients became selective about to whom they should adhere.[50]

So, at the local level, the Great Families courted the lesser *shih* who filled the clerkships and so forth in the *hsien* or prefectural offices. Not only that. The central government tried to circumvent this dependency by moving the administrators and prefects around from one area to another at frequent intervals, but this simply exchanged one problem for another since they came as strangers and were therefore dependent on the junior staff in post, who were permanencies and natives of the locality.

Nor must one forget the fact that the administration was very patchy. So far we have assumed *averages*, but the distribution of officials throughout the empire was most uneven. Like most pre-industrial agrarian empires its boundaries incorporated vast deserted areas and others where the government's writ ceased to run. In the Yellow River valley, closely governed for centuries and densely populated, the governmental penetration was intense. But in the north-west and south-west, for example, the local government units were more extensive, the populations scattered, the official headquarters isolated from the central ministries, and the officials too few to cover the ground.[51]

As the Great Families expanded their followings of kinsmen 'guests' and clients, and turned their estates into great walled haciendas, they took over the central government's moral leadership of local society. The agricultural situation in some localities which led to the dispossession of peasants and the creation of 'drifters',[52] bred 'banditry', as the multiplication of government mud-brick forts, and the walled and guarded haciendas attest. By about AD 140 the government was failing to maintain order in the localities. With the Yellow Turban revolt there ensued a three-cornered contest between the rebels, the local Great Families, and the imperial centre, but the power vacuum at the palace eliminated the last-named, leaving rival Great Families to fight among themselves and with the rebels too, since these threatened their very existence.[53]

6. THE CENTRAL ADMINISTRATION

6.1. *The Palace*

We have already mentioned that the emperor lived, the only true male, in a palace inside the Inner Court which was inside the Outer Court which was inside the city. We can omit the attendants in charge of the harem which

---

[50] For all of this, see *CHC*.   [51] Ibid. 471.   [52] See p. 523 below.
[53] Cf. *CHC*, i. 620–7.

adjoined the Palace in the Inner Court and concentrate on the Imperial Palace itself. One large group of attendants came under the control of the superintendent of the Imperial Household. He was served by a commandant of the Guards, in command of five units. They were the 'Gentlemen', composed of the candidates for civil service posts nominated by the ministers and grand administrators, who had previously served as guardsmen at the Inner Palace doors. There were also two other troops of 'Gentlemen'—those expecting no further promotion, and those who formed two troops of cavalry, each about a thousand strong. The superintendent also administered the groups called 'Palace Grandees', 'Grand Palace Grandees', and 'Gentlemen Consultants', the last-named to answer the emperor's questions and to deputize for him at ceremonials, such as funerals. Finally, he controlled the staff of *internuncios* (seventy in the Former, thirty in the Later Han); they ran the emperor's highly dignified errands, and hence were chosen, it is reported, for 'beautiful beards and loud voices'.[54]

Outside the Inner Court (i.e. in the compound of the Outer Court) there were still more guardsmen, also under the command of the commandant mentioned above. These were conscript soldiers and guarded the Seven Gates to the Palace compound. They used a system of tallies; even an authorized visitor had to leave his half-tally in the guardroom once he was permitted to proceed, so that so long as it remained uncollected it was known straightaway that the visitor was still inside the Inner Court.

A third group of staff was made up of the domestics. They were administered by the emperor's privy treasurer from the Outer Court. They included staff for the harem, the gardens and grounds, and workshops, as well as bands, orchestras, and the like, and also the grand physician, the provisioner, and the wardrobe master. They included, too, that Masters of Writing Office which, as we have seen, was upgraded by Wu-ti into a secretariat that came to be the key office in central administration.

Finally, there were the eunuchs who overlapped all the foregoing. We have noted at length the critical political role they came to play in the Later Han and I stressed that those who did so were a very small, select band out of some 2,000 eunuchs. One group were simply domestic menials. Another staffed the Lateral Courts which housed the harem. A third is highly significant—nothing less than a eunuch bodyguard. They were called the 'Attendants at the Yellow Gates' (these gates were the ones of the Imperial Palace itself). The prefect of the attendants was duty-bound to see that wherever the emperor went, inside the Palace or outside, he was always

---

[54] Bielenstein, *Bureaucracy*, 26.

accompanied by three eunuch guards. Apart from these guardsmen, there was another corps called the 'Extra Retinue of the Attendants of the Yellow Gates': this was the emperor's personal bodyguard and the only one that protected him *inside* his own Palace, and it rode on either side of him whenever he made excursions.

Only when all these groups are counted do we come to the politically sensitive group of imperial advisers of whom we have already written—the 'Regular Palace Attendants', who as we saw controlled and spoke for the entire 2,000-strong eunuch establishment.

6.2. *The 'Three Excellencies'*

The 'Three Excellencies' (*San Kung*) are often called 'the Cabinet' by western writers. This is misleading in the extreme. Chancellor and imperial counsellor were only a duumvirate in the Former Han and both posts were demoted and later abolished under the Later Han.

In the the first century of the Former Han, however, the chancellor was a truly formidable figure. The chancellor prepared the state budget, kept the accounts, maps, and census registers of the population and of land-holdings. He was responsible for the garrisons' grain supplies and for military preparedness generally. He supervised the local officials by scrutinizing their annual reports and kept a register in which every official's performance was graded, and candidates for vacancies were recommended. Indeed, one of his subordinates was specifically assigned to report to him all illegalities committed by officials: hence his designation as the 'Director of Uprightness'. The chancellor had quite immense patronage in civil service matters. Not merely could he recommend candidates for the higher echelons but he himself, individually, appointed to all posts of 600 *shih* rank and below.[55]

The imperial counsellor assisted the chancellor in all these duties but had special responsibility for the review of judicial decisions and 'expediting' administrative action.[56] Both these officials—the very highest of all in rank—had the important duty of counselling, advising, and conferring with the emperor on policy.

6.3. *The 'Nine Ministries'*

The excellencies ranked 10,000 *shih*, but the ministers ranked only at 2,000 *shih* (like the administrators in the *chün*). We have already mentioned them, but some call for further comment.

[55] Wang, 'An Outline', 143–6.   [56] Ibid. 148–9.

1. THE COMMANDANT OF THE GUARDS headed the (conscript) Imperial Guard of 10,000 men after 145 BC.

2. THE DIRECTOR OF THE IMPERIAL CLAN. Its members had to be provided for according to their degree, by kingships and marquisates. Keeping track of this was one of the director's duties.

3. THE GRAND HERALD. To his original duty of acting as master of ceremony at imperial receptions, he had accumulated responsibility for such barbarian tribesmen as had come over to the empire.

4. THE GRAND COACHMAN (*T'ai Pu*) was much more significant than his so obviously 'household' title suggests. He was now responsible for cavalry remounts. The supply of these was critical to outfacing the Hsiung-nu and Turkic horse-nomads of the north. One source says that the Former Han maintained thirty-six great pastures for grazing 300,000 beasts.[57]

5. THE COMMANDANT OF JUSTICE acted on all cases the administrators failed to settle. Those he himself could not decide he transmitted up to the emperor.

Of the five remaining ministries, we have already touched on (6) the 'Superintendent of the Imperial Household' and (7) 'The Privy Purse'. The 'Minister of Ceremonies' (8) was highly important. He was responsible for the emperor's ceremonies at his ancestors' temples and for his sacrifices to Heaven and to Earth. Also, it was he who recorded portents which (as we have described) provided emperors with a kind of heavenly opinion poll as to how well they were behaving. He identified the auspicious days and furthermore, when the duly nominated candidates for civil service appointments arrived at the capital it was his office that conducted the written examinations. (9) 'The Grand Astrologer' was a vastly learned man. He had to test the candidates for the Masters of Writing Office in their ability to read six different scripts and know 9,000 characters. It was he who drew up the annual and monthly calendar on behalf of the emperor, for whom this remained a central sacred duty.

Finally we come to (10) the 'Minister of Agriculture'. Agriculture, of course, formed the basis of the entire society. This minister was, to begin with, the treasurer. He stored taxes-in-kind in granaries or (if in cash or silk) in the Treasury buildings. Through his own local officers, he administered the Price Equalization and the Price Adjustment and Transportation Services,[58] and until AD 82 (when the service was localized), he was equally responsible for administering the salt and iron monopoly throughout the empire.[59]

[57] Wang, 'An Outline', 159.
[58] Later the second was abolished, however, cf. Bielenstein, *Bureaucracy*, 45–6.
[59] See p. 514 below.

7. THE PERSONNEL OF GOVERNMENT

7.1. *The Civil Service*

The figure of 130,285 civil servants, for 2 BC, does not permit us to estimate how many of these were senior (in later dynasties these numbered around 15,000), and as we saw, fails to embrace the very large number of officials at local level which were not established posts.[60]

7.1.1. GRADING AND SALARIES

The service was gradated into eighteen ranks, each identified by a *notional* salary-in-kind, expressed in terms of *shih* (of grain), which ranged from 10,000 to 100 *shih*.[61] This convention applied to the top sixteen ranks only: the bottom two ranks were designated as (a) officials whose salaries are in terms of *tou*[62] (coins) and (b) the accessory clerks. The total of 130,285 quoted above comprises all these eighteen ranks but none other. Actual salaries were fixed in relation to this ranking, but not in direct proportion. Half was paid in coin and the other half in unhusked rice. Except for the lowest two categories, all these salaries provided a living wage.[63]

7.1.2. RECRUITMENT AND PROMOTION

This civil service differed from the Late Roman in three respects. By the Later Han period it had become imbued with an ideology, Confucianism. Next, owing to the system of training, recruitment, and monitoring, it was more professional. Lastly, it was regarded as the summit of ambition of the private individual, and as the quintessence of legitimate authority. Thus it was solidary, deeply committed, and overweeningly self-confident. The basic qualification was literacy, but better still, knowledge of the Confucian Classics. In the higher appointments candidates were subjected to tests; in the lower appointments the qualifications were taken on trust on the responsibility of the minister who had appointed them. The qualifications obviously raise the question of educational provision. Wu-ti ordered that schools had to be established in the commanderies but it is unlikely that any existed outside the capital towns of the most populous ones. This supposition is reinforced by a decree of AD 3 which ordered schools to be set up in every district (*hsiang*), but it seems unlikely that it was carried out.[64]

In the four centuries of Han rule some 3 million men became officials but

---

[60] See my estimate above, at pp. 501–2.

[61] Some authorities quote these as *piculs*, but Bielenstein asserts that this should not be followed, *Bureaucracy*, 4, n. 2.   [62] A *tou* was one-tenth of 1 *shih*.

[63] Bielenstein, *Bureaucracy*, Ch. 5, *passim*. One *shih* = approximately 20 litres (dry measure): a British bushel = 36.7 litres.   [64] Ibid. 101.

all except 100,000 of them were recruited on the simple nomination of a duly authorized official, to wit, one of the 'Three Excellencies', the 'Nine Ministers', the administrators, or the prefects.[65] Such men filled junior posts and most of them would spend the rest of their lives in the same posts, progressing through seniority. Only the very brightest might hope to secure a recommendation for a higher post from their superior.

To these higher posts the routes of access were different: direct imperial summons (very rare), the *jen* privilege (officials of 2,000 *shih* might after three years' service recommend a close relative, but only as a probationer), and secondment from the University (the most prestigious, but uncommon). The bulk of the recruits came in by recommendation under the system begun by Kao Tsu in 196 BC. Named classes of high officials throughout the empire were to nominate candidates who then took a written examination at the capital. But this failed to produce enough recruits. Hence, in 130 BC Wu-ti ordered all administrators to nominate two candidates a year (so that each year about 200 names went forward). In AD 92 the edict was modified, in that the more populous the commandery the more names it had to put forward. The candidates who passed scrutiny in the capital were posted on a three-year probationary basis to the three corps of 'Gentleman' bodyguards. In AD 132 the qualifications were made much more specific: recommended candidates had to be at least 40 years of age, and were examined by the 'Three Excellencies' and 'Nine Ministers' in the Confucian Classics and/or for drafting ability. (Later the examining was conducted by the Masters of Writing Office.)

Such were the imperfect beginnings of what the T'ang dynasty was to develop, some 500 years later, into the famed competitive examination system. In these early times there was no competitive element, only a qualifying one, and the system did little but provide a vast fund of patronage for the ministers and Great Families. The lack of educational opportunity restricted it to the *shih* class, anyway. It is, of course, absurdly anachronistic to reproach the Han arrangements with social bias. The Chinese system, even in the early phase, did at least demand an educational minimum. The fact that the educational qualifications were literary ones was not as handicapping as it might seem, given the overwhelming agrarian nature of society.

7.1.3. STYLE AND PERFORMANCE

The hermit Wang Fu (AD 90–165) commented that the various ranks of officials were either keeping watch on their subordinates or else anxious about the reaction of their superiors and, consequently, put off making any

---

[65] Bielenstein, *Bureaucracy*, 201.

decision.[66] The service was also highly circumlocutionary. Prefects and district chiefs reported to the administrator in writing, and the administrator reported to the capital in writing. There is barely a mention of central officials being sent on missions to find out for themselves. Again, all communication from the Nine Ministers to the Three Excellencies, and likewise between them and the Masters of Writing, went and returned in written form. So did communication up and down the local-central hierarchy, so that for those living in the localities, government was remote and appeals difficult and slow—a condition not improved by the profusion of contradictory laws. It was conservative, cautious, routine-ridden and it was also corrupt. How far this is true of the lower officials is difficult to determine, though one Ts'ui Shih (AD 110–70?), whose administrative experience stemmed from a tough border area in the north, maintained that the humbler officials, not being paid enough to live on, went in for corrupt deals with the army suppliers.[67] However, as far as ministers and senior officials are concerned, the histories are bursting with anecdotes of corruption. Liang Chi, head of the ruling Liang clan,[68] amassed a private fortune of 3 billion cash—the equivalent of one-half of the tax burden of the entire empire![69] We hear of a minister of agriculture (the state treasurer, it will be recalled) who stole 30 million cash, a grand coachman who made illicit gains of 10 million cash, and so forth.[70] More fundamental, however, was the fact that this higher civil service was a collateral branch of the Great Families and, in accord with this, obstructed all initiatives that ran counter to their interests. This is why they opposed Wang Mang's reform measures, for instance.[71]

7.2. The Army

The Former and the Later Han dynasties began by being highly militaristic but became more and more civilianized, even pacific, once the initial turmoil of civil war was over and the interior was pacified. Victorious troops received donatives (and defeated generals were executed), but emperors did not (with one or two notorious exceptions) take the field in person, and no equivalent of the Roman triumph existed at all, let alone its being the crown of a public career. There was no standing army of any great size (till well on in the Later Han). The suffocating Confucian establishment

---

[66] E. Balazs, *Chinese Civilization and Bureaucracy*, ed. A. F. Wright and trans. H. M. Wright (London, 1964), 203. [67] Ibid. 212.
[68] See p. 496 above.   [69] Chü, *Han Social Structure*, 471, n. 339.
[70] See A. F. P. Hulsewé, *Remnants of Han Law*, vol. I (Brill, Leiden, 1955), for many other examples.
[71] See p. 477 above, AD 9–23 of Chronology.

opposed foreign adventures; the Confucianist historians have no kind words for the martial Emperor Wu.

The only standing forces (till the Later Han) were the various palace guards and the 'Northern Garrison' of some 3,500 men stationed around the capital. The army proper was composed of conscripts who spent one year training and the other in garrison duty in the interior or at the Wall, subject to recall in emergency. Its size is conjectural. It is thought that garrisoning the wall took 10,000 men and an unquantifiable number of support troops. The numbers employed against the Hsiung-nu sometimes reached 100,000, but more common figures for Emperor Wu's campaigns are 50,000–100,000, and the numbers engaged in actual battles are often only about 3,000 or so.[72] These figures may have risen substantially in turbulent periods. The biggest problem in fighting off the Hsiung-nu was logistical, so that one would expect a very large number of support troops and comparatively few fighting units. In peacetime—and there were long spells of peace—the total number of troops under arms in the interior and at the Wall was probably about 50,000 men.

Once the civil wars were over, both in the Former and the Later Han, the army was subordinated to strict civilian control. In the Former Han, the office of 'Grand Commandant' was not regularly filled, and after 87 BC it became an honorific post conferred on the regent.[73] In the Later Han only the first two incumbents were soldiers, their successors all civilians.[74] The office was real enough, however: it exerted general administrative and logistical control over the armed forces in a manner so detailed and bureaucratic as to astonish. This is attested by one of the few pieces of local documentation to survive, in the shape of a hoard of wooden tablets of a northern garrison.[75]

Likewise in the commanderies the (civilian) administrator exercised military functions. In the beginning he had been assisted by a military chief commandant, but this post was abolished under the Later Han in AD 30. As under the Former Han, the administrator had to seek higher permission to levy the militia or operate outside his own area. Only in an extreme emergency did the government appoint a chief commandant, and it discharged him the moment the danger had passed.[76]

There was no regular military profession, though there were established posts for officers commanding the Guards and the Northern Garrison. When a major campaign was mounted the mass of peasant reservists were mobilized and generals were appointed *ad hoc* to command them, to be

[72] Hulsewé, *Remnants*, 94. [73] Cf. above pp. 481 and 506.
[74] Bielenstein, *Bureaucracy*, 12–13.
[75] Cf. M. Loewe, *Records of Han Administration*, 2 vols. (CUP, Cambridge, 1974).
[76] Bielenstein, *Bureaucracy*, 96.

discharged once the emergency was over. A reader of the classic histories certainly finds them thick with persons bearing military titles, but in peacetime practically all of these were honorific. There was no established complement of general officers, just *ad hoc* appointments.

In the Later Han period the conscription system began to break down as more and more free peasants fell into dependency on the great landowners. They became something like the Roman *coloni* and as such were neither conscriptable nor taxable. The dynasty made up the shortfall by volunteers, by levies provided by the landowners, and most importantly, by barbarian auxiliaries. It was with the last-named that the famous general Tou Hsien inflicted the decisive defeat on the Hsiung-nu in AD 89.[77]

For all that it was under civilian control, the Chinese army was formidable. Its organization, equipment, and logistical support was as advanced as the armies of the Late Roman Empire and Byzantium. The men were kitted out with armour and used that great Chinese invention, the heavy (and very accurate) crossbow. It had a large siege-train. By seizing the Kansu corridor and Sinkiang from the nomads, it acquired huge grazing lands to raise mounts for the cavalry army which was indispensable in fighting the horse-nomads of the northern steppes. The difficulty must not be underestimated. The troops could only get at the enemy by advancing into a wilderness, so that all provisions and supplies had to be hauled north on primitive roads. Their primary task was static defence, hence the Wall. They punctuated this with occasional sharp raids deep into enemy territory, the plan being to impoverish the tribesmen by carrying off their cattle until they came to terms. For this task cavalry was essential, which is why the Chinese eagerly recruited the tribesmen as auxiliaries.

Enemy raids did sometimes penetrate Chinese territory. For instance, Ch'iang barbarians irrupted into Kansu in AD 114 and 141, forcing the emperor to evacuate two commanderies; the Hsien-pi raided from southern Manchuria in AD 158, 160, and 166. Yet by and large the northern frontier was not just held but vastly extended. The truly great menace, the Hsiung-nu confederacy, which had struck deep into Chinese territory in the early years of the Former Han, was broken up by the Later Han and the Chinese armies penetrated and held a corridor into the heart of Central Asia.

For all this, the Confucianist ministers, officials, and sages nagged constantly at the policy of armed resistance. They preferred the old dane-geld approach of the Former Han Emperor Wen. Certainly the cost of Wu-ti's wars against the Hsiung-nu exhausted the treasury and impoverished the peasantry,[78] and the trade routes they opened served mostly only for the

---

[77] M. Elvin, *The Pattern of the Chinese Past* (Eyre-Methuen, London, 1973), 33–4.
[78] Cf. Ssu-ma Ch'ien, *Records of the Grand Historian*, ii. 79–106.

importation of luxury products. But the danegeld policy was also costly. The so-called 'gifts' of silk to the barbarians (tribute really) amounted, over the period of first century BC to AD 130 to 30–40 per cent of the public revenue. (If the emperor's private revenue is added to the public revenue, then its proportion of the grand total of tax income falls to about one half the cited figure, i.e. to some 16–20 per cent—still enormous.) Unfortunately for China—and its military policy—this tribute was not an alternative to warfare. Both had to be applied simultaneously.[79]

We may conclude with a brief comparison with Rome. Both empires were successful in containing northern barbarians, but the civil–military relations were quite different. The Roman army was far larger: 300,000 before Diocletian and 600,000 after. It was led by career-officers and, as the route to the imperial diadem, it was central to the political process. In China a figure of 400,000 is the very maximum we hear of as being under arms, and the normal size was more like 100,000; there was no professional corps of staff officers, merely *ad hoc* appointments from senior soldiers of experience; and the entire body was socially disfavoured and completely under the control of scholar-officials.

With one great exception, the only time the Chinese armed forces became politically significant was when a dynasty was faced with popular revolt.[80] To crush a rebellion, emergency armies had to be raised and new colonels and generals appointed. Should this coincide with confusion or even a power vacuum in the capital, these generals and colonels were sucked into court politics as power-brokers. In the extreme cases, such as attended the Ch'in after Shih Huang-Ti's death, or the Former Han during the usurpation of Wang Mang, or the Later Han on the death of Emperor Ling, some of the soldiers could even see the chance to seize power themselves. This accounts for the civil wars that conclude and initiate each great Chinese dynasty. Then, once established and the country pacified, the new dynasty again forces the army off the political stage and puts it back under civilian control.

8. THE STATE IN ACTION

8.1. *Taxation, Monopolies, and Public Works*

The great bulk of revenue came from the peasants. Excises—on carts and boats, for instance—brought in comparatively little. Under Wu-ti, as we shall see, the government raised additional taxes through its monopolies and

---

[79] Gernet, *A History of Chinese Civilization*, 132.
[80] e.g. the revolt of An Lu-Shan under the T'ang, for which see Bk. III, Ch. 3 below.

those on salt and iron continued in the Later Han. Finally, in addition to taxes the common people were subject to one month's unpaid labour service each year.

The two main taxes were a land tax and a poll tax, the former being levied partly in cash and partly in grain, the latter usually in cash. Both depended on a national census and we have already seen that compiling the records of population and of land was a prime duty of the administrators, who collated them from returns from the prefectures and forwarded the results every year to the capital. For tax purposes land was classified into three broad categories according to its estimated yield, and the tax was a norm of one-thirtieth of that yield, but adjusted for circumstances. The poll tax was set at 120 coins (*cash*) per adult and twenty-three for each child over the age of 7. The taxes, in currency or kind, went to the Ministry of Agriculture and were paid out by it. The tax collectors did not constitute a specialized service (as in Rome). The local hierarchy from administrator to prefect was responsible, and at the level of the district (*hsiang*) the man who actually collected the tax was either the 'Petty Official with Rank' or the bailiff (according to its size), and these officials were also responsible for organizing the drafts of corvée labour. The prefects and administrators had to record the amounts collected and forward them to the capital every year.

These taxes did not yield enough to sustain Wu-ti's extensive public works and his wars against the Hsiung-nu, and the government resorted to all kinds of expedients to raise more. It sold honorary rank and confiscated the land of landowners who had evaded payment, and then turned its attention to salt and iron.[81] Private individuals were forbidden to use their own pans to evaporate salt, and to cast their own iron vessels and utensils. Instead, the government itself did both and rented the implements back. Against bitter opposition from the Confucian officials, bureaux were set up all over the empire, conducted by former salt and iron manufacturers. Ssu-ma Chien reports on the immediate effects: lots of new revenue but loud complaints from consumers at the high price and poor quality of the equipment.[82]

The Confucianists also opposed another bureaucratic intervention in the economy, this one being explicitly designed to assist, not to exploit, the common people. It is translated in Watson's edition of Ssu-ma Ch'ien as 'the balanced standard', or the 'ever-abundant granary'. The idea was simply to redistribute grain from areas of surplus to those of shortage. Some

[81] Ssu-ma Ch'ien, *Records of the Grand Historian*, ii. 80–9.
[82] E. Gale, *Discourses on Salt and Iron: A Debate on State Control of Commerce and Industry in Ancient China* (Brill, Leiden, 1931).

twenty bureaux were set up throughout the empire. When they bought cheap grain, the government transported it to the capital and stored it until the Balanced Standard Office had sold it off to the areas where prices were high. Ssu-ma Ch'ien (an independent-minded observer) reported that the central granary was filled within the year, the frontiers had a surplus of grain and silk (the latter was a medium of exchange), and that 'though taxes . . . had not been increased there was now more than enough to cover the expenditure of the Empire'.[83] Despite Confucianist obstruction, the system continued to operate until the end of the dynasty (though its local officials were later transferred to the commandery administrators).

In addition to extractions in cash and kind, the state also extracted labour: every adult owed one month's free labour a year. Here is something not met with on any scale in the Roman Empire, where the most we find is the *angaria* (compulsory help in transportation) and assistance to the postal system. Whereas the Romans had a large population of chattel slaves, China had very few and relied on the corvée for its public works. In the Later Han a minister of works supervised the Bureaux of Command which existed in all the commanderies, and was in charge of conscript labour, convicts, and (by extension), 'transportation'.[84] Still lower down the line, the mobilization of the forced labourers and the supervision of the public works they carried out were the prefect's responsibility and he, in his turn, relied on the district (*hsiang*) officers, petty officials, or bailiffs as the case might be. This reliance on forced labour was (at least) as old as the Spring and Autumn period in the seventh century BC, and is as recent as the Chinese People's Republic today. We have already given examples of the prodigious numbers put to work.[85]

8.2. *Public Order*

The authorities were obsessed with what they called 'banditry'. The histories make it clear that the term included anybody who rebelled. The peasant standard of living suggests that there were always some, and at particular times very many individuals ready to rebel, numbers that tended to swell if or when the exploitation by the Great Families increased.

A command chain for the suppression of banditry reached downwards from the administrator's Bureau of Banditry to the Prefectural Bureau of the same name and its commandant, thence to the patrol leader in the Districts, then to the 'father' who lived in his official inn/police station in every

---

[83] Ssu-ma Ch'ien, *Records of the Grand Historian*, ii. 104.   [84] Bielenstein, *Bureaucracy*, 100.
[85] See p. 474 above.

Commune, right down to the hamlet where, as we have seen, families were bonded in fives or tens, each individual responsible for the conduct of the others.

Scattered evidence suggests that in the second century AD the system was not fully effective; possibly because farmers were so oppressed that they turned bandit, possibly because the administrators lacked trained forces so that the raw levies they raised were easily beaten.[86] One indication, perhaps, is the proliferation of mud-walled strong-points, some built by the government, others by private landlords. These relate also to the nature of the Han judicial system and penal code.

8.3. *Justice and the Penal Code*

Han government was grim and iron-fisted, scarcely less so than the Ch'in which struck the Confucianist historians as the last word in harshness. The Han law-code (if one can call a collection of self-contradictory edicts a code in any meaningful sense) has been lost, but much of its content has been recovered by sifting through the contemporary histories.[87] It is in the tradition of Ch'in, and in one central aspect at least it, together with the Ch'in precedent, set the pattern for the next 2,000 years: the almost entire absence of a civil code or the concept of a *lis inter partes*. A private person who wanted to bring suit against another could do no more than lodge his complaint with the authorities and hope—no more—that they might prosecute. This is the signal difference between Chinese and Islamic law and Roman law. In effect it implicitly denied legal personality to individuals. It was concerned only with administrative and criminal infractions, and consisted of a set of commands and the appropriate penalties for disobeying them. This law has no horizontal citizen-to-citizen dimension, only a vertical, up–down relationship of government-to-subject. Correspondingly there was no private legal profession to conduct the subject's case. Jurisdiction lay with the administrator and the prefect as part of their general administrative duties and it was inquisitorial and summary. As in the T'ang and later dynasties, these magistrates in their *yamen* or courthouse were at once prosecutor, detective, judge, and jury.

It is true that judgements could—in principle at any rate—be appealed. Also, administrators were duty bound to conduct a six-monthly review into the cases of all imprisoned persons in their commandery (a little like the medieval 'gaol-delivery'), and were authorized to lift a death penalty imposed by the prefect and reverse his decisions. The provincial inspectors

<hr>

[86] Quoted, Chü, *Han Social Structure*, p. 33.   [87] Hulsewé, *Remnants*.

or 'shepherds'[88] were authorized to control the administrators, likewise. Specifically, they were to find out whether the administrator had shown due care in doubtful cases; or killed people cruelly; or delivered verdicts on personal impulse; or, alternatively, showed leniency because of pressure from the Great Families.[89] These admonishments certainly tell us that the central government knew how and in what respects justice was perverted; but it is hard to believe that the inspector on a 600-*shih* grade was in a position to fall foul of the administrator on 2,000 *shih*. The apex of the judicial system was the 'Commandant of Justice' at the capital. He settled cases referred him by the administrators (sending the ones that even he could not settle to the emperor): and he also had the duty to review the system of penalties and to regularize and systematize it.[90] The elaborateness of this appeal system might seem more impressive, were it not for the fact that it never applied to 'bandits' or 'rebels', who could be tried and executed summarily on the spot.[91]

Trial procedure was brutal. Here the central fact is that the judge could only convict on a confession. As in many medieval and later states in Europe which had the same rule, this led to all kinds of pressure on the accused, including torture. Court procedure followed a fixed sequence: accusation, imprisonment, and then an interrogation under beating. The interrogator kept notes of the accused's answers. Witnesses, too, were often kept in prison and they too might be subjected to torture. The interrogator's notes were written up in the form of a confession and the accused was invited to confirm it. If he refused to do so, then he was tortured again until he did.

'Code' is hardly the right term for the Han Laws, since they were a chaotic aggregate of contradictory provisions. No less than 409 articles invoked the death penalty, and to gloss them there were 1,882 cases and 13,472 precedents for crimes deserving death. The famous historian Pan Ku, says that 'writings and documents filled tables and cupboards, and the officials in charge were unable to look at them all'.[92] Hence the verdicts varied widely, since officials would apply one set of laws to those they wanted to acquit and another to those they wanted to execute.[93]

Punishment was harsh. The Ch'in had applied the 'Five Punishments' (*wu hsing*): death, castration, amputation of one or two feet, amputation of the nose, and tattooing (as a convict).[94] The Han abolished tattooing and the amputations but substituted flogging. The instrument used was a

---

[88] See p. 500 above.   [89] Hulsewé, *Remnants*, 87–8.   [90] Ibid. 86.
[91] D. Bodde and C. Morris, *Law in Imperial China* (Harvard UP, Cambridge, Mass., 1967), 142. Their reference is to the Ch'ing practice but the contemporary Han histories demonstrate that this was true of the Han also.   [92] Cited Hulsewé, *Remnants*, 338.
[93] Ibid.   [94] Bodde and Morris, *Law in Imperial China*, 76

bamboo baton five feet long and tapering from one inch at the base to half an inch at the top, and the penalty was either 500 or 300 strokes of this baton on the bare buttocks. The victims invariably died, so that all that this humanitarian concern had achieved in place of mutilation was death under torture! These penalties were gradually reduced, however, to a maximum penalty of 200 and a minimum of 100 strokes.[95]

The two other standard punishments, of death and hard labour, remained in force and were applied without mercy. It is said[96] that the thirty-eight-year reign of Henry VIII of England was particularly notorious for its rate of executions—72,000 are said to have suffered death. But on one calculation the Han executed 10,000 persons every year and sentenced 30,000–40,000 to hard labour. Another interpretation would greatly inflate these figures: 50,000 capital sentences every year and 150,000 sentences of hard labour![97]—though one should of course take respective population sizes into account when comparing such figures.

Nor should we think that this terrible harshness was directed only at the common people. Far from it! We are by now familiar with the struggles between the Great Families at court and the historians recount an endless string of accusations and trials followed by the forced suicide of a victim (when the emperor wanted to show clemency) or the most revoltingly painful execution and the extinction of the victims' entire family, or even his entire clan.

8.4. *Dimensions of Subjection*

The Han state was not 'totalitarian'. For one thing, its machinery of government was quite inadequate to make it so. For another it never attempted thought control. 'Wild temples' continued to flourish among the people side by side with the official cults and, even among the literati, teachers and officials never ceased argument and dissent. One very striking feature of the Han state which puts it into the same class as the Roman Empire till Theodosius I—but makes it quite different from medieval Europe, Byzantium, and the Caliphate—was its religious tolerance. During this period (as later, also) Taoism flourished while millenarian cults fermented among the common people.

Nor was Han society uniform. True, it was overwhelmingly a peasant

---

[95] Hulsewé, *Remnants*, 336–7.

[96] *Encyclopaedia Britannica* (11th edn., 1910), s.v. 'Capital Punishment' (W. F. Craies), 279–82.

[97] Hulsewé, *Remnants*, 406–7. On the lower Han estimate, Henry executed 0.05% of the population while China executed only 0.018%. But on the higher estimate China rises to 0.096%—double that for Henry VIII.

mass supporting a wafer-thin stratum of courtiers, officials, and great landowners. Yet despite official disapproval, merchants and industrialists managed to make good. What is conspicuous in comparison with Rome is that the Han Empire's towns were fewer, smaller (Loyang, the capital city, had only 250,000 inhabitants) and above all were the seats of the local official and wholly lacking in self-government.

Yet, though in no sense totalitarian, it was a state in which there was no freedom (in the western sense) but only differing degrees of subjection. Chinese has no equivalent for the Greek *eleutheria*, the Latin *libertas*, the Teutonic freedom. It has only ideograms which translate as 'license' or even depravity. Balazs, who makes this observation, quotes Max Weber approvingly: 'In terms of natural law, no sphere of personal liberty was sanctioned. The very word "liberty" was foreign to the language.' Balazs continues the thought by commenting: 'When they spoke of liberty, it was something negative they had in mind—the idea of letting go, or of letting slide, or of not being bound. And this was only natural for in a despotic strictly hierarchical society, every step towards freedom from ritualistic prescriptions that dominated everyday life was certain to be regarded as a dangerous transgression of the moral code.'[98]

We may query the term 'despotic'; but about the 'strictly hierarchical society' there can be no doubt. The significant thing about this hierarchy is that it is not natural and spontaneous like, perhaps, the deference to 'blue blood' or to wealth or to valour or beauty—to what the popular culture holds as valuable—but is both artificial and official. It is a government-created and government-enforced rank-order of such commitment that everyone in one rank not only defers to those in the rank above, but does so in the most conspicuous and, to western cultures, exaggerated forms. A junior official who has neglected court courtesy makes amends to his superior by coming to his seated presence and falling on his hands and knees. A wealthy landowner in trouble with the prefect, signifies his submissiveness by coming to his *yamen* with bared shoulders, bound arms, and an arrow piercing his left ear. The 'kow-tow' (kneeling, the inferior knocks his head on the ground three times) is the universal greeting to the superior rank. The woman kneels to serve food to a man. The plaintiffs in the *yamen* kow-tow at once to the magistrate: everybody kow-tows to those above them until the emperor is reached and he himself kow-tows to his ancestors and the gods.

Han society was officially gradated into twenty honorary grades. The

[98] Balazs, *Chinese Civilization*, 247, quoting M. Weber, *The Religion of China*, trans. H. H. Gerth, with an Introduction by C. K. Yang (Collier-Macmillan, Glencoe, Ill., 1951), 147.

twentieth and highest grade comprised vassal quondam kings, marquises, princesses, members of the ruling house, or noblemen who had received benefices. The nineteenth grade comprised other noblemen, living off government pensions in the capital. The grades 18–10 were those whose status equalled the Nine Ministers. Grades 9–5 were the *ta-fu* (literally Great/Honourable), that is, the high officials. The bottom four grades were the *shu-jen*, the commoners: in rank order these were the scholars (the shih), the farmers, the artisans, and at the very bottom, the merchants. These ranks carried certain privileges or disabilities. Thus grades 20–9 were exempted from military duty, while merchants were subjected to sumptuary laws.

The greatest of all differences in rank, however, was between those who were government officials and those who were not. The law laid down distinctive dress, ceremonial, and special design of carriages for each different rank, but the social distance between all of them as a class and the common people was enormous. When the official's carriage reached a village, the inhabitants, including the elders, ran off and hid.[99] An official of the lowest rank (100 *shih*) was better off than the farmer with 100 *mou* of land (11.39 acres). The most senior ranks drew even more income if the emperor gave them benefices: for instance, to be ennobled as a marquis entailed an income twice that of the 2,000 *shih* official.[100] (Nearly all these officials invested their surplus in land, as in most agrarian societies; but in China with the added significance we have been stressing, that is, the creation and re-creation of the scholar-official-landlord nexus.)

Not only were the officials prestigious and rich. They were also privileged. They could secure a probationary post in the civil service for their children and junior relatives. They could not be arrested or sentenced or punished by the courts without the prior consent of the emperor. Thus the officials comprised a relatively small, highly organized stratum 'that floated on a sea of isolated peasant communities'. Above it ranked only the imperial clan, great generals (called 'meritorious officials'), and the relatives of the empresses. Below it came all the common people, mostly peasants. As Reischauer points out, we 'already see the old distinction between hereditary aristocrat and commoner transformed into a cleavage between officialdom and the common tax-payer—a division that was to characterize all subsequent Chinese society'.[101]

[99] Chü, *Han Social Structure*, 88.   [100] Ibid. 88–9.
[101] E. O. Reischauer and J. K. Fairbank, *East Asia: The Great Tradition*, vol. 1 (Modern Asia edn.; Houghton Mifflin, Boston, 1960), 96–7.

8.5. *Living Standards*

The standard of living of the peasantry was low and precarious. In times of general shortage or natural disasters, the government and/or the great landlords made their condition worse, the former because it levied taxes and the latter because they levied rents. Yet it is 'impossible' to demonstrate that the government could have done much about it. One-fifth or so of the taxes went on silk gifts as tribute to the northern barbarians, and perhaps as much again to maintaining the army and feeding the labourers on corvée. Military defence and public works were indispensable to the peasantry irrespective of the régime. If all established civil servants had been reduced to the lowest rate of pay (= 100 *shih*), the saving would have equalled the income of only 135,000 peasant families in a population of some 60 million persons.[102] Of course 'structuralist' historians would argue that improvement was conceivable but that it was blocked by the Great Families—and they would cite the Wang Mang reforms and the early T'ang 'equal field' policy as examples. They are bad ones. The former collapsed by their own incoherence as much as by landlord opposition, though there was certainly plenty of that; and as for the T'ang, a later chapter will show that the 'equal field' system applied unevenly and in many localities quite unsuccessfully.

The real enemies of the peasant were natural disasters and extremely poor communications; so that when flood or famine occurred and no help came, entire peasant communities could be reduced to total destitution. The Greek and Roman worlds suffered the same effects and for the same reasons.[103] The local famine and the subsequent food riot was an endemic feature of West European life into the early nineteenth century.[104]

We city-dwellers in a fabulously wealthy West, form no idea of such situations. In basically peasant societies, the peasant lives on what he makes his smallholding produce, and if that fails he will simply starve. If his farm is wiped out he has no insurance. He is on his own, or rather his village community is. What the late Sir Moses Finley said about the Graeco-Roman world has been true of all pre-industrial agrarian societies and is completely applicable to Han China (and indeed to the entire history of that country).

The ancient peasant was always at the margin of safety. Cato gave his chained slaves more bread than the average peasant in Graeco-Roman Egypt could count on as a regular staple. The one normal source of subsidiary income for peasants was

---

[102] For the equivalence, see above, p. 508.

[103] de Sainte Croix, *Class Struggle*, 13–14, 219–21, 313.

[104] C. Tilly (ed.), *The Formation of National States in Western Europe* (Princeton UP, Princeton, 1975), 380 433.

seasonal labour on larger neighbouring estates, especially during the harvest . . .
There is a deep paradox here. The freer the peasant in the political sense, the more
precarious his position. The client of the archaic period or the colonus of the later
Empire may have been variously oppressed, but he was also protected by his patron
from dispossession, from the harsh laws of debt and on the whole, from military
service . . . The genuinely free peasant had no protection against a run of bad
harvests, against compulsory army service, against the endless depredations in civil
and foreign wars.[105]

Only against these comments can we appreciate the peasant condition—and
response—in Han China.

The general population lived on the edge of subsistence. Loewe[106]
calculates the per-capita production of grain at between 21.05/42.1 *shih*,[107]
so that the untaxed income for each member of a family *per diem* was between
3.7 and 7.4 lbs of grain per head. You can certainly live on that but one must
deduct the wherewithal for clothes, religious offerings, and taxes. Furthermore, these figures are averages of big holdings and small ones, good years
and bad years, poor localities and good ones, places suffering famine and
those with surpluses. Once these variances are taken into account, the
margin between survival and utter disaster is a narrow one. The *Han Shu*
of Pan Ku makes many references to famines; there are six where the people
resorted to cannibalism, even.[108] It tells also of the government resettling
destitute peasants after floods. And it frequently points out the contrast
between the farmers' poverty and the wealth of the rich landlords and
predatory merchants.[109]

This is the point at which taxation counted. For the peasant had to pay
land tax and poll tax irrespective of his yield. A bad harvest drove him to
the money-lender at 20 per cent interest—even 100 per cent in extreme
conditions.[110] Or else, he could sell his land and go to work on a large
estate as a tenant-farmer. Or, he could become a bandit.[111] In short, the
same cycle developed that we have noted in Solon's time and in the later
Roman Republic. Taxation tipped the marginal peasant-farmer into debt: he
left the land and the richer landlord, with more staying-power, bought it
from him. This led on the one hand to the declining numbers of the free
peasantry and on the other to the concentration of land into a few hands.
This is what had occurred by the end of the Former Han dynasty. It was

[105] M. I. Finley, *The Ancient Economy*, 2nd edn. (Hogarth Press, London, 1985), 107–8.
[106] Loewe, 'Campaigns of the Han', 82.
[107] A *shih* = roughly 65 lbs. Cf. N. L. Swann, *Food and Money in Ancient China (the Han Shu 24)*,
(Princeton UP, Princeton, 1950), 140, n. 108, for a number of equivalents.
[108] Ibid. 389.   [109] Ibid. 390–1.   [110] Ibid. 392.
[111] Cf. Chü, *Han Social Structure*, 110.

redressed by the death of millions of people in the ensuing civil wars; so many farms were abandoned that there was once more enough to go round to reconstitute the free peasantry. Under the Later Han the entire cycle set in anew, and by the end of the second century AD the land crisis was acute.

The impoverishment of the small peasantry had become a serious problem, driving many of them to migrate south as rootless 'drifters' (p. 504 above). The government tried to stem this by resettlement programmes and up to about AD 140 it sporadically provided grants for the most vulnerable elements in society—the aged and infirm, the widows and widowers, and the childless families—to everyone, in short, who could not count on the customary family-support. It gave massive help to those struck by natural disasters, to which China, especially the Yellow River area was prone. This largess reached its height under Ho-ti (d. AD 106), after which there was an almost never-ending succession of natural disasters which finally drained the Treasury, leaving some areas to general starvation. Yet during all this time agriculture as a whole was prosperous and the Great Families very prosperous indeed. This contrast between prospering Great Families and dispossessed peasantry supplied the context for social revolt.

Here we come to the most conspicuous difference between the Han and the Roman empires—those widespread popular rebellions that were, again and again, to destroy dynasties. Rebellion on the Chinese scale, threatening the dynasty itself, however, did *not* occur in the Roman Empire.[112] The nearest that approaches the Chinese experience is the rebellion of the Bacardae.[113] Why the difference? Because the Chinese peasantry were more oppressed? Or that the Chinese military forces were less effective and committed than the Romans? Or that the Chinese rebels were influenced by millenarian expectations in a way unknown to Roman rebels? The armed spearhead of the Chinese rebel movements turn out to be bandits, that is, marginalized peasants with nothing to lose, and this would be so throughout the next 2,000 years. But there is plenty of evidence of banditry in the Roman Empire—even in Italy, witness the Roman 'Robin Hood', Bulla[114]—yet the rebellions there were localized and, excepting the Bacaudae, ineffectual. Or one might add that the popular rebellions which helped topple dynasties in China were the ones that coincided with a crisis in the dynasty, that is to say, a court conflict that paralysed the central government. But there were many others that failed to topple a dynasty.

There are so many variables here that it would be rash to maintain that the frequent Chinese peasant rebellions prove that the peasantry was more

[112] de Sainte Croix, *Class Struggle*, 474 ff.   [113] See p. 598 below.
[114] AD 206–7, Dio Cassius, quoted in Lewis and Reinhold, *Roman Civilization*, ii. 432

downtrodden and poverty-stricken than the Roman. For all that, the beliefs and actions of the two great revolts that shook the empire in AD 11 and in 184, the Red Eyebrows and Yellow Turbans respectively, do demonstrate the peasants' deep alienation and the persistence among them of a counter-culture. The Red Eyebrows were inspired by popular shamans and shamanesses—Mother Lü, or King Ching of Ch'eng Yang—and they slaughtered all the officials and noblemen on their march to the capital, which they sacked. The Yellow Turbans were inspired by Taoistic dreams of the T'ai Ping—the Supreme Peace—a Golden Age where goods were held in common. In the Yellow River basin, led by a faith-healer (Chang Chueh) and his two brothers, these Yellow Turbans established a religious hierarchy under whose guidance they gathered in vast assemblies similar to Pentecostalist sects today. In Szechuan, the Taoist Celestial Master sect established communities where private property was abolished and women participated in equality with men.

Whether the standard of living was lower than among the Roman smallholders is beyond any secure proof, though we can be sure that 95 per cent of the population of the Han lived on the margin of subsistence all the time—and therefore, at particular times, many fell below it. We can be sure of something else too—the great mass of the rural population was as yet untouched by the arid, this-worldly outlook of Confucianism, and the gap between officialdom and common taxpayer was reflected in the gap between the empire's official creed and the dark forces still worshipped by the villagers. But these forces lay latent and harmless for most of the time. It is significant, so it seems to me, that they only caught hold of the masses when these had been struck by total disasters. In the cases of both Red Eyebrows and the Yellow Turbans, the Yellow River had burst its banks and changed its channel, spewing armies of destitute starving and demoralized millions on the countryside. Yet, the histories recount, there were long periods when the conditions in the countryside were benign and the peasants reckoned as prosperous.

9. AN APPRAISAL

Posterity has provided the Han Empire with a conclusive verdict. That empire set the pattern for all future Chinese government up to and including the present day. As later chapters will show, succeeding dynasties, invaders, or social classes did little more than broaden, perfect and refine, and deepen the institutions that it laid down. The Han was China's prototype empire. To this day the people of what we call China call themselves the people of Han.

The elegant symmetry of the local government divisions, the tidy organization-chart of the central administration, like the flowery names and titles, the universal bowing and kow-towing, should not deceive us. For all the government paperwork flowing up and down the ministries and the localities, the actual delivery of services—taxation, justice, conscription, and the like—was rough and ready. Given the poor state of communications, the overtasking of the bureaucracy relative to its size, the primitiveness of village life, the near-universal illiteracy, this was inevitable. Society was rude, unequal, and regimented; the laws were harsh and the landlords exploitative; and both were facets of one another. It was a two-stratum state, where only the state officials exercised rights and the subjects had nothing but duties.

For all that, the empire was a colossal achievement in state-building. In the very brief space of time between the Ch'in unification and the early years of the Han—let us say, to the reign of Wu-ti—a huge area, some two-thirds the size of today's USA, had been brought from the literally murderous self-division of the Warring States to become a centralized, homogenized culture-state, the incipience indeed of a nation-state. It, remarkably, now possessed uniform institutions, a symmetrical and regular local administration, an elaborate and not inadequate civil bureaucracy, a stable central government, and an army firmly under civilian control.

The usual justification for 'empire' is the Hobbesian one, that it brings peace, and the usual retort is 'pacem appellant, solitudinem faciunt' ('they make a devastation, and call it peace'). In the Chinese case, this gibe might perhaps be applied to the conquest of the northern nomads, possibly even to the inexorable colonization of the south, but it cannot conceivably apply to the Ch'in and Han unification. The Warring States that were conquered were all Chinese. There is no evidence that their people were the worse off or extraordinarily exploited after they came under imperial authority. If Ch'in and Han taxed, conscripted, and made them perform unpaid labour, this was no more than the dukes and kings of the Warring States had made them do. So the cessation of the interminable wars was a genuine and net benefit. As far as China proper is concerned, the new 'empire' is not an empire in the technical sense at all. It is a large, unitary country-state.

Again, though its laws and practices were harsh, the Han Empire was in another respect tolerant; it did not interfere with or prosecute religious opinions. It is quite otherwise for those that followed: the Christian Roman Empire, its succession states in Europe, Byzantium, Sassanid Persia, and the Caliphate. Furthermore, unlike most of the preceding and succeeding empires and states, and notably Rome, the Han Empire despised martial

glory. It was profoundly anti-militaristic. Its virtues were the civil ones—
wen, in Chinese. Taken together, this religious toleration—maybe it was just
indifference—and the exaltation of civility compose a not-ignoble ideal.

Finally, the Ch'in–Han Empire signals a great innovation in the practice
of government. It is a Palace regime, certainly, but one with a remarkable
difference. Only at intervals is it actually ruled by an autocrat. The normal
pattern, which resumes after the creative irruptions of an active and
belligerent emperor like Shih Huang-ti, Liu-Pang, and Wu-ti and their
like, is the pattern of rule by bureaucrats.

Even this, it might be objected, is not really an innovation. The same
might be said of Pharaonic Egypt. The Han innovation is not so much that
the country was ruled, normally, by faceless bureaucrats but that these were
scholars, literati, intelligentsia—whatever the term we choose to apply. The
notion of a state ruled by a perpetual corporation of men of letters which is,
to look at it another way, a bureaucracy indoctrinated in a special ideology,
is something quite new. It is a bureaucracy which functionally doubles for
the role of priests in Christian Europe or imams in the Caliphate. And it
doubles for the nobility also, but, once more, in its own idiosyncratic way:
for here nobility and rank are the *consequence* of being an official, not the
other way round.

In the Han this characteristic was a mere sketch, a beginning. Not until
the T'ang and Sung was the Confucianist bureaucracy reconstituted to
become what we shall then call the Mandarinate. But it was sufficiently
institutionalized by the fall of the Han dynasty to be regarded as quite
indispensable to the successor states in the 400 years of disunity that
followed the Han. Barbarian conquerors learned that it was only through
using it that the Chinese would accept them as legitimate. Three consequences followed. First, the notion of the bureaucratic centralized state
survived; there was no reversion to feudalistic practices. Secondly, in accepting the bureaucracy, the new kings or emperors accepted the tradition of
Confucius, for the rituals all demanded this and by now the tradition of
Confucius was what made the Chinese Chinese—for it comprised the
Chinese odes, Chinese history, Chinese cosmology, and Chinese political
science. The Five Classics were akin to the Bible. Finally, being Confucian,
the tradition kept alive the notion of one all-encompassing Heaven and
hence, only 'One [ruler] under Heaven': in short, the imperial ideal.

In such a way there survived, as a kind of epiphenomenon, the pattern of
a state that was centralized, unitary, bureaucratic, paternalistic, authoritarian, and even despotic: a two-stratum state, of officials *vis-à-vis* taxpayers,
government *vis-à-vis* subjects; a society that was rank-ordered and sanctioned
by rituals and ceremonies. All, till very recently, stemmed from the Han and

the Han built on Ch'in Shih Huang-ti. The entire subsequent course of
Chinese government is nothing but the development of this, and it is not for
nothing that the Maoist historians of Communist China regard as their
grand progenitor none other than—Ch'in Shih Huang-ti.[115]

[115] Y.-N. Li (ed.), *The First Emperor of China* (White Plains, New York, 1975).

7

The Roman Empire: The Principate,

27 BC–AD 284

The end of the Republic and its replacement by 'the Empire' is conventionally ascribed either to 31 BC or to 27 BC. The first date refers to the Battle of Actium by which Octavian, the adopted nephew of Caesar, became the *de facto* ruler of the Roman world, the second to the constitutional settlement in which he came to be addressed as *princeps*, that is, 'First Man in the State'—hence the term 'Principate' to express the nature of the new regime. For two centuries it flourished, but during the third century AD it was badly shaken by barbarian pressure without and civil convulsion within, and after the accession of Diocletian in 284 the apparatus of government was radically altered. This period is sometimes known as the Late Empire or the Dominate.

1. AUGUSTUS CAESAR AND THE PRINCIPATE

We left the Roman Republic at the point where Sulla had replaced the ancient constitution by a new constitutional settlement of his own, but to no avail. There followed even more turmoil: bribery and corruption of the electoral process, pressures, coercion, and intensifying civil wars. The terrible tally of assassinations, proscriptions, insurrections, and wars was bought to an end by a dictatorship, that of Octavian, or, as he was to be known, Augustus. His settlement, in 27 BC, proved to be a successful ground-plan for governing the empire for the next 200 years.

After Actium and the death of Antony and Cleopatra, Octavian was the military master of the world. He was a poor soldier but a political genius, and that genius lay in his decision to constitutionalize his omnipotence and, furthermore, to do it while preserving all the forms and organs of the Republican constitution, and notably the vast self-importance of the Senate. The ancient patrician and noble families had all but killed one another off, and within 200 years there would be only one senatorial family that could trace itself back to the Republic and precious few who could claim senatorial ancestry back to even one or two generations. The elimination of the ancient high nobility and its replacement by equestrian—minor nobility—

families from the Italian country towns, then from the western provinces, then Africa, and finally from the Greek-speaking regions, represent the socio-economic face of Augustus' constitutional revolution and explain why it struck root.

Sulla's constitutional settlement (above, pp. 436–8) had sucked power from the *comitia* and conferred it on the Senate. That of Augustus went on to suck power from the Senate and confer it on himself (and, as it turned out, his successors). This is the essence of the matter. Henceforth, the government of Rome no longer represented a balance of separated powers but their fusion. It would repose in a single individual, where the Senate was reduced to a cipher at the worst, and at the best, but a disunited and timid collection of back-seat drivers. The main provisions of the Augustan 'settlement' are set out below.

SUMMARY OF THE MAIN FEATURES OF THE PRINCIPATE
THE *COMITIA*

| POWERS *LOST* | 1. *Legislative* | initially, exercised only to formalize measures of the *princeps*. Last attested under Nerva (96–8) |
| | 2. *Election* | choice of magistrates, etc. curtailed under Augustus, and abolished by Tiberius |

THE SENATE

Numbers purged and reduced to 600, property qualification raised to 1 million *sesterces*, nomination to its membership effectively dependent on favour of the *princeps*

POWERS *RETAINED*	1. *Foreign Affairs*	(a) advises *princeps* (but only at his request) (b) receives ambassadors
	2. *Judicial*	(a) supreme court for political crimes (b) criminal court for senatorials
	3. *Appointments*	chooses by lot the governors in the provinces designated by *princeps* as senatorial provinces (most of them without armies)
POWERS *LOST*	1. *Foreign Policy*	passed *de facto* to the *princeps*
	2. *Legislation*	its *senatus consulta* given force of law—since only passed on the initiative or with sanction of the *princeps*
	3. *Appointments*	to governorships in the 'imperial provinces' (where most troops were stationed) and Egypt

THE MAGISTRATES

POWERS *LOST*	1. *Consuls*	election by favour of *princeps*, their term reduced to six months and still shorter periods, thus greatly increasing their number
	2. *Praetors*	retain only purely judicial functions
	3. *Lower Magistrates*	their various previous administrative tasks fell to senatorial or equestrian officials appointed by the *princeps*, while there was no room now for the political role of the tribunes

THE *PRINCEPS*

POWERS *GAINED*		
1. Imperium	supreme command of the armies and appointment of governors (mostly ex-consuls or ex-praetors) in imperial provinces	
2. Imperium maius	authority to override all other holders of *imperium*	
3. *Foreign Affairs*	decides peace and war	
4. *Appointments*	(a) *vide imperium* above	
	(b) nomination of candidates for election	
5. *Legislative*	(a) convenes and presides over the Senate	
	(b) promotes legislation in Senate	
	(c) changes laws by edicts, mandata, judicial decisions	
6. *Judicial*	can determine *any* case he chooses, either on appeal or in first instance	
7. *Religious*	*pontifex maximus*	
8. *Oath of Allegiance*	sworn to him by entire population	

2. THE ROMAN EMPIRE TO DIOCLETIAN (284)

CHRONOLOGY

31 BC	Battle of Actium: OCTAVIAN militarily supreme
27	Assumes name of Augustus. New constitutional settlement
AD 9	Arminius defeats Varus at the Teutobergian Forest. The frontier stabilized on the Rhine
14	Tiberius
c.30	Jesus crucified
31	Sejanus' plot; he is executed
37	CALIGULA assassinated
41	Accession of CLAUDIUS after Caligula's assassination
43	Invasion of Britain
54	NERO
61	British revolt under Boudicca
66	Beginnings of the Jewish revolt
68/9	Nero deposed, commits suicide. The Year of the Four Emperors (GALBA, OTHO, VITELLIUS, VESPASIAN)

The Flavians 69–96

69	Vespasian
70	Jewish revolt crushed, destruction of the temple at Jerusalem
79	TITUS
81	DOMITIAN
96	Assassination of Domitian. Nerva

THE ANTONINES

The Golden Age of the empire. Peak of prosperity, political stability, and public spirit. Territorially at its widest extent

98   TRAJAN (adopted son and named successor to Nerva)

117   HADRIAN

132–3   Final revolt of Judaea, Jerusalem razed, depopulation of Judaea: the diaspora

138–61   ANTONINUS PIUS

161–80   MARCUS AURELIUS. The high point of Stoic influence. Pressure by Marcomanni on Upper and the Sarmatians on Lower Danube frontier repelled

180–92   COMMODUS, son to M. Aurelius. Hated by Senate and people of Rome. Assassinated

The Later Roman Empire: 193–284

The Severans: 193–235

192/3   Praetorian interlude: PERTINAX emperor, murdered by Praetorian Guards who auction the throne to highest bidder

      DIDIUS JULIANUS, emperor. Generals Pescennius Niger (Syrian legions), Albinus (Britannia legions), and Septimius Severus (Danube legions) engage in civil war

193   SEPTIMIUS SEVERUS

211   CARACALLA

212   The *Constitutio Antoniana* extends citizenship to virtually all freemen

217   Assassination of Caracalla. MACRINUS

218   ELAGABALUS (Heliogabalus), an adolescent, homosexual, Syrian priest of an obscure Syrian cult, as emperor. Dominated by his mother, Julia Maesa.

222   Elagabalus murdered with connivance of family; accession of his brother, SEVERUS ALEXANDER

227   The refounding of a strong aggressive Persian Empire (the Sassanian) under Ardashir opens severe threat to Eastern frontier

235   Severus Alexander murdered by his troops after Germans defeat them on Rhine

Military Anarchy and Disintegration of the Empire, 235–284

Eighteen 'legitimate' emperors, of whom fourteen are murdered. Barbarian pressure along all frontiers. Difficulties in Persia in the east. Economic and social crisis: the great inflation forces the empire off a cash-currency economy

284   DIOCLETIAN. Commander of the Illyrian legions. Reconstitution of the empire: the DOMINATE

3. THE CHARACTERISTICS OF THE EMPIRE

The million-and-a-half square miles and estimated 56 million inhabitants[1] constituted an empire which was polyglot and poly-ethnic.[2] Its people worshipped all kinds of divinities and it embraced every level of civilization, from the rude, uncultivated tribesmen of Britain whom Agricola was just introducing to warm baths and public market-places (*c*. AD 80), to the sophisticates of the swarming cosmopolitan centres of Rome, Antioch, or Alexandria. It was overwhelmingly agricultural: perhaps as many as nine out of every ten inhabitants cultivated the soil. They did it under diverse conditions: from the slaves in the *latifundia* of southern Italy and Africa, to the exploited and bureaucracy-ridden fellahin of Egypt, through diverse degrees of free smallholding peasantry, particularly in the East. Yet even 10 per cent engaged in commerce and manufacture is no mean leaven in an agricultural society, and was only possible because of the peculiar geography of the empire. Although north-west Europe, the Balkans, and Eastern Anatolia had added a massive hinterland to the earlier conquests in the Mediterranean, this was still the 'Middle Sea'. Sea cargoes were relatively cheap. Moreover, in Egypt, the north, and the north-west, there were eminently navigable rivers such as the Nile and the Danube. This contrasted markedly with all the empires we have encountered so far. The Assyrian, the Persian, and the Chinese were emphatically land-empires.

Structurally, this empire was a constellation of a myriad self-governing cities—10,000 in the east alone—mostly quite small but, as the ruins of Pompeii show us, active, lively, and full of bustle. (The definition and nature of a 'city' we will defer till later.) The empire in this phase was little but a superstructure for co-ordination and control; high policy was indeed made at the top, but the dynamics of workaday affairs came from the cities.[3] Here lies the first and perhaps the most striking difference from the Han Empire. There, the vigorous local self-government on which the Roman Empire was long predicated was totally non-existent.

Sociologically—and politically too—Rome resembled the Han Empire in that society consisted, broadly speaking, of a narrow propertied élite ruling over the wide masses of peasants and labourers, but the *nature* of the Roman ruling stratum was quite different from the Chinese. It reflected the

---

[1] There is no evidence for the size of population. It is conjectural, but adopted by many scholars.

[2] Also, unusually, if not uniquely, it had *two linguae francae*, not one: Latin in the West and Greek in the East.

[3] 'The Roman Empire was like a body whose cells were thousands of autonomous cities', P. Ariès and G. Duby (eds.), *A History of Private Life: From Pagan Rome to Byzantium* (Harvard UP, Cambridge, Mass., 1987), 2.

structural make-up described above, that is, its basis consisted of the myriad self-governing local units. It will be remembered how the early Republic had won the loyalty of the Italian tribes and cities by offering citizenship or (at least) qualified citizen-rights. In the empire, with equal flair, the metropolitan élite (which at this date is effectively the *Italian* élite, consisting of the new-shaped senatorial order and the equestrians) formed links of support with the equestrian order and the far less prestigious 'curial' (local councillor) order in the cities. These acquired Roman citizenship and got political support against the local democratic forces, which were still capable of exerting themselves in a number of cities whose local assemblies were yet alive. The empire did not (or not for long) compartmentalize itself along territorial or ethnic or religious lines. Instead it divided horizontally along a class-status line. Aelius Aristides (AD 117–85), for all that he was a professional eulogist, saw to the root of the matter.

You have divided all the people of the Empire . . . in two classes; the more cultured, better born and more influential everywhere you have declared Roman citizens and even of the same stock; the rest vassals and subjects . . . Under this classification there are many in each city who are no less fellow-citizens of yours [i.e. Roman] than of those of their own stock, though some of them have never seen this city. *You have no need to garrison their citadels; the biggest and most influential men everywhere keep watch over their own native places for you. You have a double hold upon those cities—from right here* [i.e. Rome] *and through the Roman citizens in each.*'[4]

Romanization expanded these local oligarchies and strengthened their authority. Roman civilization was essentially a city civilization, and in its most superficial aspect consisted of the attractions of the Forum, the baths, and circus and theatre: of, too, the Latin tongue (or Greek in the East) for getting on in life, and with it an acquaintance, however superficial, with Graeco-Roman art forms, tags and maxims of the courts (a public spectacle), and with the literature. Romanization spread downwards from the local oligarchies to the wider circle of city-dwellers, and outwards, where it was often superficial and disappeared with the empire; as witness its rapid and total effacement in Britain. But it was substantial enough in its time to create a common pattern of urban life over the whole of this vast area, and a common identity, *Romanitas*,[5] much like (it seems to me) the common pattern one observes throughout the length and breadth of the USA, despite widely different ethnic and religious backgrounds.

In regard to government, however, the Antonine Empire differed antithetically from Han China in four major respects.

---

[4] Quoted in Lewis and Reinhold, *Roman Civilization*, ii. 136. My italics.
[5] Not a classical word.

The first was the role of the army. In Rome (not just under the Principate but through to the very end) the army was the core, the central, the critical institution. It was not merely—and obviously—the warden of the frontiers and the guarantor of internal order, but the greatest of all the avenues of social mobility, the promoter of the local economy in the vicinity of its camps and cantonments, and in some areas[6] the most powerful of all agents of Romanization. Not only this: a Roman politician or official was expected to be, and usually was, a civil official at some times and a military commander at others. To subjugate, so Romans were taught, was their preordained destiny, and the army was its instrument. 'Remember, Romans, these shall be your skills—to rule the nations by your *imperium* and impose the way of peace—to spare the submissive and wear down the proud.'[7] 'It is the gods' will that my Rome shall be the capital of the world: therefore let the Romans cultivate the arts of war and let them know and pass on to their descendants that no human force can resist Roman arms . . .'[8]

'Emperor' is only how we translate *imperator*, which had by now acquired a penumbra of meanings including the troops' acclamation for a victorious general. Augustus took it as his *praenomen*, a precedent his immediate descendants did not dare follow, until Vespasian and all *principes* took it as their title. Far above everything else, an emperor had to be successful in war irrespective of whether he himself took the field. Without the support of the army his reign would be cut short. The army was the ultimately *decisive* political force. The prefect of the Praetorian Guard was the first man to swear allegiance to Tiberius. An officer was one of the plotters in the assassination of Caligula (hitherto, as 'little-boots', the soldiers' favourite). The accession of Claudius was due to them, and it is significant that this very unwarlike character should have headed the army that invaded Britain. Nero was the first of the Julio-Claudians to show no military interest, and he paid the penalty. So it would be for all the (rather few) non-military emperors of later times. For instance, Nerva was quick to adopt the soldier, Trajan, as his successor.

No previous culture, except perhaps the Assyrian and the Ch'in, was so pervasively and intensely militaristic, as Virgil and Livy attest. So does any description of a triumph, where the spoils and the fettered captives were marched along to the hoots of a quarter-million spectators; where the emperor paused in his chariot at the end of the Sacred Way, hard by the Capitoline, to watch his chief captives flung, naked and chained, into the beehive-shaped cesspit of the Mamertine Prison, where they were left to die

---

[6] Not all; for instance, there were no troops in the most highly Romanized parts of Spain.
[7] Virgil, *Aeneid*, vi. 851–3.   [8] Livy, *History*, i.16.

by strangling if they were lucky, but by neglect, cold, and starvation if they were not. What Roman militarism meant is best understood through Josephus' description of the triumph of Vespasian and Titus.

> The war was seen in numerous representations, in separate sections, affording a very vivid picture of its episodes. Here was to be seen a prosperous country being devastated, there whole battalions of the enemy slaughtered: here a party in flight, there others being led into captivity; walls of surpassing size demolished by engines, mighty fortresses overpowered; cities with well-manned defences completely mastered and an army pouring within the ramparts, an area all deluged with blood, the hands of those incapable raised in supplication; temples being set on fire, houses pulled down over their owners' heads; and after general desolation and woe, rivers flowing, not over a cultivated land, supplying drink to man and beast, but across a country still on every side in flames . . .[9]

A second great difference from Han China is Rome's conception of the emperor. Under the Principate he was a very different animal from the Chinese 'Son of Heaven'. Certainly, he was *pontifex maximus*, carried out sacrifices and conducted the rituals to Rome's traditional gods. But he had nothing like the ritualistic significance of his Chinese counterpart, on whom the harmony of Heaven, Earth, and Man was thought to depend. How could a Roman emperor easily pass his entire day, week, and year in rituals as a Chinese emperor could—and was adjured to? The main differences between the two, however, are that in practical terms the Roman emperor was *public*. He appeared in the games, for instance, and many travelled the empire (most usually, on campaign). He was accessible, not secluded from all but his eunuchs, women, family, and top officials. Above all, however, he was *active* and expected to be—active not only in the field but in civil affairs also. He was supreme judge, generalissimo, and maker of imperial policy. An emperor like Tiberius, for instance, was criticized for not venturing outside Rome and inspecting the provinces,[10] and subsequently, when he left the capital for Capri, for 'letting all affairs of state slide'.[11]

The third difference is the almost complete absence of a paid professional bureaucracy[12] in Rome, and even after considerable growth by the reign of Hadrian, it was quite minute in comparison with the 120,000 or so established posts in Han China. In the Roman Empire most of the work that civil servants undertook in China was done by unpaid magistrates and councillors in the cities or by the army (which, when not on campaign,

[9] Quoted in Lewis and Reinhold, *Roman Civilization*, ii. 91.
[10] Suetonius, *The Twelve Caesars*, trans. R. Graves (Penguin, Harmondsworth, 1979) 'Tiberius', para. 38. But except for Hadrian—who traversed the empire—few emperors visited the provinces except on campaign.   [11] Ibid. para. 41.
[12] See below, Sec. 5, 'Provinces' for the 'generalist' character of the higher government officials.

carried out many civilian tasks such as road-building and policing). The menials who actually executed city decisions would not count in any official reckoning of 'officials' (any more than they did in China, for that matter). At provincial level, the governor's 'civil service' was a mere handful of attendants, some of them military personnel, others personal assistants. True, some, like the fiscal procurators, were appointed by and responsible to the central government and were very important. Much of the administration everywhere was in the hands of freemen and slaves of the imperial household. But even when these are counted the total number was small.

The fourth major difference—the increasing elaboration of private law and the continued growth of a specialized legal profession—is partly related to the absence of a paid professional bureaucracy. Admittedly, there is not a lot to choose between Han China and the Roman Empire in the sphere of *repressive* law. 'The criminal system never passed through a stage of strict law, the stage in which exact differentiation and definition is necessary',[13] and the law of treason (*de maiestate*) was arbitrarily expanded beyond all measure. But Roman civil law came to be elaborated in various ways. From the Republic it took over the old code of the Twelve Tables as modified by later statutes and then in the Principate by the *senatus consulta* and the practice of praetors offering new remedies, so elaborating the old law. In a variety of instances, where certain legal principles were held to have failed, the law was consequently modified by imperial edicts, or *senatus consulta*, or by the decisions made in particular cases, and the jurisconsults incorporated these in revised statements of the law. In addition, the determination of ambiguities by these learned professional lawyers was supposedly binding on future judgments. In such ways the civil law burgeoned into a great corpus of reciprocal rights and obligations in respect of persons and family inheritance, ownership and possession, and contracts and delicts, of which *iniuria* was one; a corpus which was so big, so complicated, and withal so much a system of principles abstracted from the detailed rules (not just a collection of discrete rules), that emperors could alter it only marginally. Nothing of this sort existed in Han China, nor would it ever. Indeed, nothing of this sort had ever existed, or would exist for another two millennia anywhere else but in the European West and Islam.[14] We shall return to this vital difference between Roman and other states' law, for it was not just a unique or dead-end innovation which perished along with the Roman state. It was, like the Jewish conception of a law-bound monarch

[13] H. F. Jolowicz and B. Nicholas, *Historical Introduction to the Study of Roman Law*, 3rd edn. (CUP, Cambridge, 1972), 404.

[14] For the *shari'a* and the difference between it and the Roman system of laws, see below, Bk. III, Ch. 2, 'The Empire of the Caliphate'.

and the Greek concept of citizenship, to be progenitive of vast consequences for government in Western Europe.

4. THE CITIES

Earlier, in discussing 'Romanization', I drew a (very loose) analogy with how an American culture has overlaid the original ethnic groups who came to the subcontinent. It is strikingly embodied in the typical layout of every American town—its Main Street, funeral parlour, drug stores, shopping malls, used-car precincts, and so forth. If we had to say today what most evokes or attests Roman civilization in our midst, a few (becoming rarer each year) would specify the literature, a few more might nominate Roman law. Almost everybody would mention the Roman roads, but would equally concede that a road, however well built it may be, does not tell us much about a culture. But the ruins of the Roman towns emphatically do. I think that if the Chinese had built their palaces and temples in stone, the grandeur of the civilization would become blazingly apparent; but they built in wood and the great palaces and public buildings of Chang-an, Kai-feng, Nan-ching, Canton, and other great towns have long since been burned down. The Romans, like the European Middle Ages, built monumentally in durable stone—'quod non imber edax, non aquilo impotens possit diruere aut innumerabilis annorum series et fuga temporum' ('which neither the consuming rain, the powerless north wind, nor the passing years can destroy'). It is no accident that Gibbon should have envisaged his masterpiece while brooding on the ruins of Imperial Rome, and nobody who visits that great city today can turn away unimpressed by their testimony to the wealth, power, and technique that made them possible. But what more truly conveys the sense of the immense vitality and riches of the empire is the spectacle of the selfsame pattern of public baths, forums, shops, aqueducts, and amphitheatres, repeated and over-repeated from any remote end of the empire to the other—in Leptis Magna, in Nîmes and Orange, in Caesarea and Palmyra and countless other once flourishing towns, some large, some like Pompeii, quite small, but no less busy.

Many of these public buildings were the gifts of an emperor, always immeasurably the wealthiest individual in the empire; but the great bulk of them were due to local philanthropy. Wealthy citizen vied with wealthy citizen and city with city in providing public buildings. Others made no less munificent contributions but in a form that the barbarians and time have effaced: cash donations to the city treasuries, trust funds for distributions or, sometimes, for child-assistance and for schooling.

The empire, we have said, was a great holding-company of cities but a *city* is not the same as *town*. For governmental purposes a city signified a self-governing community occupying a tract of territory and almost always possessing an urban centre. In the East, the Romans found the Hellenistic *poleis*, with their assemblies, councils, and annually appointed magistrates. Towns of this kind existed elsewhere too, in Italy itself, in southern Spain (Baetica), and in ex-Punic Africa. Elsewhere, in tribal territory, as, for example, in parts of the West, the Romans organized the tribe on the city-pattern. The town or fortress which had formed the native civic centre tended to become more and more like an Italian city and in the second and third centuries BC the same rules about the duties and responsibilities of councillors and magistrates were made universally applicable, that is, to these as well as the ancient foundations. This was one way in which towns grew up. Others grew up in the vicinity of the legionaries' camps as trading posts, and hence the multitude of towns with names recalling this such as Chester (*castrum*), Cirencester, Worcester, and the like in Britain. On such towns the Romans imposed magistracies/councils on the Roman-Italian rather than the Greek strong-Assembly pattern. Indeed, they exerted all their influence to curb such assemblies. They prescribed property qualifications for election to the local Council (*curia*) and magistracies and much preferred that, instead of elections, local censors should appoint the councillors for life and that these councillors should appoint the magistrates. But this oligarchical alternative was not possible everywhere and, in the earlier part of the Principate, there were still vigorous electoral contests for the magistracy. There are hundreds of campaign fly-sheets in Pompeii, for instance. There, the fruit dealer campaigns for Helvius Vestalis, an individual solicits a vote for Gaius Cuspius Pansa because 'he gets good bread', 'Neighbours' support Lucius Statius Receptus, and so forth.[15]

In city governments, the principal features are the strong local autonomy and the concentration of power in the local rich who commonly came to possess the Roman citizenship.[16] Extant charters bound the councillors and magistrates to act *intra vires*, on pain of some penalty. In the municipality of Salpensa in Spain, for instance, the penalty was 'payment to the citizens of the said municipality [of] 10,000 sesterces, and may be sued or prosecuted by any citizens of the said municipality who has the legal right to do so in accordance with this charter'.[17] It is surely needless to emphasize that a provision of this kind, giving a townsman the legal authority to sue his rulers, was not even thinkable in China at this or any other time, but it was

[15] Quoted in Lewis and Reinhold, *Roman Civilization*, ii. 326–7.
[16] Cf. what Aelius Aristides said about them at p. 533 above.
[17] Quoted in Lewis and Reinhold, *Roman Civilization*, ii. 326–7.

not possible anywhere at all up to recent times except in Rome, Byzantium, and post-Roman Europe. It is imperative to emphasize the *law-bound* nature of Roman government and the persistence of the twin notions of individual *rights* and of *citizenship*. Only in the West were these to persist.

The councillors and magistrates received nothing for their services. Indeed, as we have seen, they were expected to endow their cities. They avidly sought office for glory, no doubt to obtain Roman citizenship also, but this was increasingly becoming a mark of social status rather than of legal privilege since, from Pius Antoninus at least, the distinction between citizen and non-citizen was becoming less important than that between *honestiores* and *humiliores*. The latter were subject to heavier penalties for identical offences. Local worthies were *honestiores*. From AD 212, by a law of Caracalla, virtually all freemen in the empire became citizens, but by then this meant little.

Thus the day-to-day work of governing was not carried out by bureaucrats but freely and as a matter of self-esteem and local patriotism by the wealthy. It was left to them to provide such local services as they chose, such as education, corn supply, water supply, public works, the care of streets and buildings, market regulation, and a civic and rural constabulary. They also provided certain vital services to the central government, for they were responsible for levying recruits, sometimes for repairing the roads and bridges, for maintaining the post-houses on the arterial highways: all of these were unpaid *munera* owed by the general population, but which the city magistrates had to organize and deliver. Above all, they were responsible for guaranteeing and then collecting the direct property and capitation taxes (*tributum*) levied in the province.

5. THE PROVINCES

5.1. *Rome, the Imperial Capital*

Rome, with a million inhabitants, was three times as populous as Alexandria and Antioch, which came next. The policing and the food supply of such large cities nearly always demands an exceptional regime and their streets harbour a political threat to the government. The volatility of the city mobs had not evaporated with the demise of the Republic, so that a constant supply of cheap food was a necessary condition for peace and order. Augustus took very special police precautions. He made an urban prefect (the *praefectus urbi*) responsible for the peace and order of the city, with special troops at his disposal. This official controlled the theatre, the markets, and the guilds. His criminal jurisdiction was so wide that in the third century it had become indefinite and it extended over a hundred miles' radius of the city. He also had a certain civil jurisdiction relevant to maintaining order. The emperor's own personal (Praetorian) guard, about as strong as one-and-a half-legions, was also available to suppress disorder in or near Rome when the emperor was in residence there. Augustus also established a prefect of the Watch of some 9,000 men. Rome was divided into fourteen sections and the Watch were distributed through them to deal with fires, which were a frequent hazard, to keep order, and patrol the streets. A third prefect, of the *annona*, was responsible for the grain supply (not for its free distribution, however, which fell to other officials).

5.2. *Italy*

Just as Rome was an exceptional city, so Italy was exceptional because it was not a province and hence did not pay *tributum*, because by now all Italians were citizens. Troops were only occasionally used to keep or restore order.

5.3. *The Provinces*

The distinction between senatorial and imperial provinces[18] was of small importance. Senatorial provinces were those where there were only a few troops for police duties, such as Baetica (South Spain), Africa, Bithynia. Their governors were all styled proconsuls, chosen by lot from ex-consuls or ex-praetors. They served for one year. Their duties were purely civil and judicial. The *princeps* could and did 'recommend' his own nominees, appoint his own *procurators* for tax-collection, and hear appeals from the governor's court. Furthermore, he could change a province's status from senatorial to imperial (so, with Illyria).

Imperial provinces were mostly those that for one reason or another required a stronger military presence. In general, these provinces were governed by his own legates *pro praetore* and subordinate legates, all of them senatorials, with fiscal procurators. The legate held the *imperium* and wielded military powers as well as civil. Unlike the governors of senatorial provinces, legates' tenure was indefinite: the average was three years, perhaps, but in a few cases it was much longer. This continuity in office was the chief difference the inhabitants would have noticed between the two types of province. (Some provinces were exceptional. Egypt was governed by an equestrian prefect and some smaller provinces were governed by imperial *procurators* from the equestrian order, e.g. Judaea.)

[18] See p. 529 above.

A governor was now salaried. He went out bound by the emperor's special instructions and was forbidden to raise troops, or tax beyond the assessed amount, without the specific authorization of the Senate or the emperor.[19] At the end of his tenure he could be prosecuted for malversation or extortion, but till then he was in complete control. His staff, which as in Republican times was his own personal 'cabinet' which he brought out and took back to Rome, was minute. Since his military forces were limited, it was vital for him to establish contacts with the most important notables and with the city councils. His principal duty, except in frontier provinces, was to keep order, and this involved touring the province on a fixed circuit and holding judicial sessions in the important cities. The governor was often bound by the *lex provinciae* (the constitutional arrangements when it was incorporated[20]), and by his own edict indicating how he meant to proceed in certain kinds of cases. He also had to take into account the local laws and liberties of the various cities. As a result, his time was largely absorbed in handling local challenges to the legal powers of the city magistrates or the very frequent disputes that erupted between some city and its neighbours. Since cities had the right to send embassies directly to the emperor, however, he had to watch his step. Likewise with certain of his other duties. For instance, he was responsible for taxation, but by the second century taxpayers' disputes with the *fiscus* were commonly handled by the imperial procurators. In that century, too, a fair amount of civil and criminal jurisdiction was being appealed, after sentence, to the emperor.

Within these limits, the governor was responsible for everything that passed: order, justice, defence (in an imperial province), the good conduct of minor officials, the highways, and the general well-being of the province. Some notion of the tasks is conveyed in Tacitus' memoir of Agricola, when the latter was governor of Britain. Apart from his active campaigning, Agricola 'corrects' the exactions of grain made by his predecessor, assembles the troops for exercises and training, encourages the construction of towns and the urban culture, and provides for the (Romanized) education of chiefs' sons.

Unlike any non-European state until the nineteenth century, the governor and other officials could be sued (after quitting office). True, he was normally tried by fellow-senators; and senators tended to stick together in such matters.[21] For all that, the ex-governors were forced to make a

[19] Dio Cassius, quoted in Lewis and Reinhold, *Roman Civilization*, ii. 33–4.
[20] See above, as under the Republic. It is uncertain whether there was a *lex provinciae* for every province—probably not.
[21] Cf. the trial of Bassus and Rufus, ex-governor of Bithynia, as reported in Pliny's letters: Pliny, *The Letters of the Younger Pliny*, trans. B. Radice (Penguin, Harmondsworth, 1963), iv. 9.

defence and by no means all of them escaped conviction. From Augustus to Trajan we read of forty trials for maladministration and extortion, but there are gaps in the evidence and after Trajan we have almost none. Obviously there were many more.[22] However, Professor P. A. Brunt has argued that between Augustus and Trajan it was much less easy to bring an offender to trial or secure a conviction than has commonly been supposed.[23] For all that, what strikes me as significant is not that the lady preached badly but that she preached at all; for here we have the Roman extension of the Greek practice whereby the citizens could not merely complain or petition against an official but actually sue him in a court of law. Nowhere does the contrast between the ruler–subject and the ruler–citizen relationship appear to me to be sharper than here: in Rome citizens, and subjects too, had a *right* against officials. And what we have noted here is part of the same presumption we noticed earlier where the citizens of a city could sue their magistrates for abuse of their powers: the *law-boundedness* of Roman society.

In summary, 'the government . . . was far from being a bureaucracy in the modern sense of the word. The ordinary subject, except the inhabitants of the capital, came much less into contact with the officials of the central government than he does in any modern state . . . The imperial officials [were] a mere superstructure added to self-governing communities throughout the Empire.'[24] On the contrary, it was the local magistrates who linked subject and state as judges of first instance for the less serious crimes and civil suits, as the police chiefs, as the agents for tax collection, and as the organizers of *munera* such as we listed earlier.

6. THE EMPEROR

The emperor was the supreme commander of the armed forces by virtue of his *imperium maius*. In addition, he was the head of state, the supreme judge, the chief executive, the high priest (*pontifex maximus*) and, in the provinces, a god. All these attributes flowed from the powers conferred on Augustus by the Senate, but each one became more deeply entrenched and wider in scope as time went by, so that the emperor's absolutism became more conspicuous. The final development in this direction took place with Diocletian's reconstruction of the empire (284), after which the imperial regime is known as the Dominate precisely because the emperor was not styled *princeps* but *dominus* or 'Lord'.

[22] C. Wells, *The Roman Empire* (Fontana, London, 1984), 146–9.
[23] P. A. Brunt, *Roman Imperial Themes* (Clarendon Press, Oxford, 1990), ch. 4.
[24] M. Rostovsteff, *History of the Ancient World*, 2 vols. (Clarendon Press, Oxford, 1928), ii. 259.

To begin with, the laws against *lèse-majesté*—*de maiestate*—which were originally restricted to treasonous attempts against the state and plotting against or resisting its magistrates (which includes the *princeps*, of course)— were abused more and more frequently: by extension of the law to cover mere disrespect of the emperor, by convicting for treason on little or no evidence, and by condemnations without due process of law. The reigns of terror unleashed by Tiberius and, especially, Nero, were pursued under cover of this law. The proofs of guilt required were elastic, the trials were often conducted inside the palace itself, and the arbitrariness was extreme.

For all that, the Roman emperor, at this epoch, was very different from all the emperors we have encountered so far. He was not the incarnation, or the child, or the vicar of the gods but simply a man on whom Senate and people had conferred the powers of an extraordinary magistrate.[25] True, as *pontifex maximus* he nominated and regulated the colleges of priests, but these were lay persons dedicated to the care of the city cults. Again, he himself performed many of the sacrifices and rituals. But these were the traditional propitiatory rites to the tutelary deities and had none of the cosmic significance met with in the Near Eastern, the Egyptian, and the Chinese polities. It *is* true that emperors were worshipped; the Hellenistic monarchs had been worshipped as 'gods' and the Romans took this over from them. From the very beginning of his sole rule Augustus was regarded as a god in the East, usually alongside the 'goddess' Rome, and in 12 BC an official cult was established in Gaul. But it is difficult for us to understand quite what 'a god' meant in these circumstances. It certainly did not mean what we mean: the cult was in no way exclusive, it was not conduct-regulating, and it did not offer salvation. In the West the cult took on a form more consonant with Roman tradition, in that worship was not addressed to the living emperor but to his *genius*, that is, his spirit, and the emperor—or rather some emperors—were 'deified' only after death. I say *some* emperors because it was the Senate—usually on the initiative of the reigning emperor—that conferred this status; furthermore, he became, not *deus* (the word for the high gods) but *divus*—more like 'sanctified' than 'deified'. It was a recognition of gratitude for benefits conferred. But irrespective of its details, nothing in emperor-worship in the West bears any comparison with the sacred and sacral nature of Middle Eastern and Chinese monarchs. The truth is that the Romans were profoundly attached to omens and rituals but lacked religious sentiment in our modern understanding of the word.

The Roman emperor differed, again, in the way he acquired his powers

---

[25] Roman *legal theory* actually has only confirment by the people.

and what kind of powers they were. For they were not innate or inherited but conferred. It was the Senate that gave Augustus his extraordinary powers and gave Domitian and his successors the powers of censor (thus enabling any emperor to pack the Senate at will). What is more, the conferment was made by a formal decree of the Senate followed by the formality of a law in the *comitia*. We have parts of the bronze tablet—the only one of its kind— which contains the last paragraphs of the law of investiture of Vespasian.[26] One clause is especially noteworthy—it confers 'the right and power . . . to transact and do whatever things divine, human, public and private he deems to serve the advantage and overriding interest of the state'.

The emperor was 'absolute'. Augustus and some later emperors had been dispensed by the Senate from certain laws, and this and not the late Renaissance sense was what was meant by *absolute* (i.e. *ab legibus solutus* or dispensed from the laws). In point of fact many emperors averred that they were bound by the laws, and as we shall see, Justinian's Codes are specific in this respect.[27] The later juristic maxim relating to the absolutism of the emperor was a generalization based on the law quoted above, which permitted an emperor to set laws aside, as well as on the fact that some emperors simply ignored the laws and could not be called to account.

At the start, one would not have called the emperor the supreme legislator because, although he could and did get his way, he had to go through the Senate. Yet within a century of Augustus's death the jurists were maintaining he could indeed make laws on his own account. They were hard put to find a satisfactory legal basis for this because, in my view, they had not made the analytical distinction we make today between legislation and judge-made law. For the emperor's lawmaking powers flowed from his position as both chief executive *and* supreme judge. He issued *constitutiones* of three kinds. Like any Republican magistrate before him he issued *edicts* (proclamations) but, as his jurisdiction was indefinite and encompassed all affairs of state, so might his edicts be. He also issued *decreta* (his decisions in actual judicial cases). And, finally, he issued *rescripta* (*epistulae* and *subscriptiones*), his replies to problems put up to him by officials, cities, or private individuals, and such *rescripta* might interpret or change the law. Ulpian's '*Quod principi placuit habet legis vigorem*' is to be understood as saying 'what has been approved by the emperor has the force of law'. We should mention too, in this respect, what we touched on concerning the governors; the emperor issued them with *mandata*—instructions—and these later developed into a standing administrative code.

[26] See Lewis and Reinhold, *Roman Civilization*, ii. 89–91.
[27] See Bk. III, Ch. 1, 'Byzantium'. They maintained they were *legibus allegatus*.

In summary, four things stand out here and make the Roman emperor both similar to and different from the absolute monarchs we have looked at so far. First, for *practical purposes*, the specific powers legally conferred on him made him absolute in our modern sense, that is, a supreme legislator and judge, able to dispense with existing legal restrictions and even despotic in that he could invoke the law of treason (*de maiestate*) to strike down opponents in a completely arbitrary way. Secondly, by comparison, he is a *secular* monarch. Thirdly—and coming back to the persistent theme of Roman government—it is all, even its large sphere of arbitrary discretion, framed and legitimized by *human laws*. Fourthly, he is *imperator*, the active commander-in-chief of the armed forces who take an oath to him and to his heirs. Finally, he is unaccountable, for there were no longer magistrates who wielded powers to equal his, and the *comitia* were defunct.

Just as the Republican constitution was flawed by highly charged omissions and contradictions, so also were the institutions of the Principate. Two were critical. First, there was no regularized rule of succession. Secondly, Augustus' 'Principate' was ambiguous. While some of his successors thought they were monarchs, the Senate thought he should respect their views, objected to his appointing men who were not from the higher orders, and resented unjust or unseemly behaviour like that of Nero, Commodus, and Elagabalus.

6.1. *The Constraints of the Emperorship*

Until Trajan most emperors lived in real or imaginary terror of enemies. Most of the cruelties and arbitrary executions perpetrated by them are ascribable to their fear. Indeed, Suetonius is specific about the intense terrors experienced by Tiberius,[28] Caligula,[29] Claudius,[30] and Nero.[31] But their execution of suspects after trials *intra cubiculum*, and often after none at all, and their punishment of the victims' entire families provoked equal and opposite terrors among prospective victims. Most of these were senators but not a few were military commanders.

In contrast to a reclusive Chinese emperor, the Roman emperor was exposed to a number of forces *outside* his court and family circle: namely, the street, the soldiers, and the Senate.

As to the street, the Roman mob was only politically dangerous in so far as it might encourage or give support to opposition from the other two forces. It never, on its own, either made or deposed an emperor, and in some

---

[28] Suetonius, *The Twelve Caesars*, para. 63.   [29] Ibid., *passim*.
[30] Ibid., 'Claudius', para. 35.   [31] Ibid. 49.

cases (Nero's, for one) it mourned emperors whom those two forces had deposed. But it was an unruly beast and the emperors (unless they went into retreat like Tiberius) had to face it in the streets or at the games. It was an ancient tradition for the audience to roar praise—or insults or execration— at the emperor when he presided over the games. Claudius was pelted and hooted by crowds when the food supply failed on one occasion, and had to get back into the palace by a back door. 'Bread and Circuses' has become trite but is, in fact, exact. Emperors—especially after Claudius learned from his narrow escape—took special measures to ensure the grain supply through the new port at Ostia and special concessions to shippers. Free bread, initiated in the Republic, came to be supplied to no less than a quarter of Rome's population, and market bread was subsidized. The Severi and their successors distributed free oil and Aurelian distributed free bacon. As to the games, even the austere Augustus authorized sixty-six days of games and by the fourth century they numbered no less than 175! And these were in addition to special festive occasions.[32]

It was the army and the Senate who disposed of real political leverage, but in opposite—and unequal—directions because, with one exception, the army (or rather its officers) always won.[33] From Tiberius' day the armies of the Rhine were claiming that it was they and no one else, who chose the *imperator*.[34] During the Year of the Four Emperors (AD 68) one of them struck coins with the motto *consensu exercituum*—'by consensus of the armies'—and this reappeared on the coins of Vespasian, Nerva, and later emperors.[35] And the armies' claim that it was they who chose the emperor had a lot to be said for it. To the armies what we translate as emperor was the *imperator*, their victorious leader. The emperor might be a god to the Eastern people and *princeps* to Roman opinion, but to the soldiers he was their commander-in-chief.

It is quite mistaken to suppose that the army (save in the third century) was forever overthrowing emperors and replacing them with its own candi-dates. On the whole emperors tended to designate successors and if possible give them legal powers and military command in their own lifetime. Furthermore, dynastic sentiment was remarkably deep-rooted and where an emperor had no sons the succession might pass to one he had adopted. Military coups and civil wars generally occurred when an emperor who was killed had designated no one to succeed and avenge him.

[32] M. P. Nilsson, *Imperial Rome* (Schoeken Books, New York, 1926), 246–56.
[33] True to this day. In the last two decades there have been a few instances of NCOs leading revolts, but these have occurred in extremely primitive societies. See Finer, *Comparative Government*, *passim*.   [34] Suetonius, *The Twelve Caesars* 'Tiberius', para. 25.
[35] C. G. Starr, *The Roman Empire, 27 BC–AD 476* (OUP, Oxford, 1982), 44.

In formal terms, however, it was the Senate that gave him his powers, and to them he was the first magistrate, *princeps*. True, once the army had pronounced, there was nothing the senators could do but concur. But the relationship was more subtle and complex than just this. The Senate had quite lost the political initiative to the *princeps*, and from the time of Claudius could not realistically entertain the ancient collegiate alternative to one-man rule; but it did desire to be treated with the respect it thought it deserved and it did not always receive it. Caligula, for instance, made senators run alongside his carriage clad in their heavy togas, and kept them waiting for hours. Nero shocked them by playing the theatre artist and forcing them to attend at his performances. But, for all its abdication of so much authority in favour of the *princeps*, its lack of any military resources, and its unpopularity with the Roman proletariat, the Senate was, alongside the emperor, the very pinnacle of the state. After all, its members were 600 of the wealthiest men in the entire empire, the senatorial order was the highest in a hierarchical society, and individual senators were, as heretofore, magistrates who rose through the *cursus honorum* to become praetors and consuls. Moreover, these offices were more widely rotated now by the system of *suffecti* (a consul served only two months instead of a year, resigning to make way for *consules suffecti* who did likewise), but as such they and they alone became eligible to command the legions and go out as proconsuls and imperial legates to govern the provinces. So they had experience of war and civil affairs, enormous wealth, and not unnaturally, self-respect. From the emperor's point of view they were the only body that could discredit him; more—the only body which could hatch opposition; still more—the only body from which a rival emperor could be selected. (The first non-senatorial emperor was Macrinus in AD 217–18). Finally, as generals and governors, only senators had the real opportunity to supplant him. *Galba*: senator, consul, formerly commander in Upper Germany, imperial governor of Spain; *Otho*: senator, formerly governor of Lusitania: *Vitellius*, senator, consul, commander in Lower Germany; *Vespasian*, senator, consul, formerly proconsul of Africa, governor of Judaea—the career patterns of the four contenders for the emperorship in AD 68 speak for themselves.

Emperors could either court and flatter the Senate or terrify it. Tiberius was most deferential. He called himself the 'Servant of the Senate', referred all business to them for their formal assent, and even accepted being voted down on one or two (minor) matters.[36] But later, angrily suspicious, he turned on them. Claudius was regularly in the Senate and even reproached senators for being inarticulate yes-men, but this did not prevent him, under

---

[36] Suetonius, *The Twelve Caesars*, 'Tiberius', paras 29, 31

the treason law, from executing thirty-five of them.[37] Nero reacted to Piso's conspiracy with a veritable reign of terror.[38] Experience ought to have shown this to be unwise: the four emperors who openly terrorized the Senate—Caligula, Nero, Domitian, and Commodus—all came to bad ends; not so the Antonines, who made it their business to co-operate.

6.2. *The Duties of the Emperor*

An emperor was responsible for everything. If we glance at a biographer like Suetonius or a historian like Tacitus, we find all kinds of decisions attributed to him. But how exactly these were made, and whether they were personally inspired or not, remains curiously opaque. An emperor obviously needed advisers and agents and these (usually senators or *equites*) he summoned *ad hoc* according to the nature of the business.

Some things are certain enough. To begin with, the emperor made all appointments. Next, personal esteem was not necessarily enough; from AD 14 all emperors found it wise to sweeten the troops with donatives. Then again, *qua* head of state and supreme judge, the emperor attracted a large and evergrowing volume of business. Suetonius' artless biographies make it clear how much time an emperor spent on hearing lawsuits; so, too, do Pliny's letters to Trajan. It was this role that occasioned the administrative orders and rulings we mentioned earlier as the *constitutiones*. Because these are responses to requests or to conflicts between individuals or communities, they convey the impression that the emperors were simply reactive (which does not imply that they were passive signatories of the documents brought to them: on the contrary, some certainly read the letters and petitions and dictated the replies. Likewise they were always receiving petitions in person.) The movement of the legions, the decision to annex client kingdoms, to wage campaigns, to make peace and war, to exclude Jews, and the like, were also, nearly all, responses to situations.[39] 'Interstitial' legislation, the major part of changes in the law, was due to some perceived gap or inconsistency. No emperor during the Principate after Augustus thought of making fundamental changes.[40] But for all that, most major decisions were reactive and we know nothing as to *how* they were arrived at; whether, for instance, the emperor initiated them or whether they were premeditated by others in his name. Through what processes did they pass or were they

---

[37] Suetonius, *The Twelve Caesars*, 'Claudius', paras. 12, 29.

[38] Tacitus, *The Annals and the Histories* (Sadler and Brown, Chalfont St Giles, 1966), bk. xv.

[39] Claudius' invasion of Britain is a marked exception.

[40] This was true until Diocletian and Constantine ended the Principate and initiated the new order of the Dominate.

supposed to pass before they became operative? All one can say is that, for the Principate, the almost embryonic character of an imperial bureaucracy suggests at least one pretty firm conclusion: if the emperor wanted to do something, he had no difficulty in having his way.

6.3. *The Imperial 'Civil Service'*

Under the Republic, as we have seen, the magistrate carried out his duties with the assistance of his private *consilium* and his freedmen and slaves. Augustus, as chief magistrate, had an enormous appetite for work and was very good at it, but he too did it through his own household staff and so did Claudius, who was the first emperor to systematize it. How astonishing the contrast with the Han Empire!

For his principal assistants (I shall call them this rather than 'officials') Claudius used freedmen, his former slaves. The three main sections of the administration, then, were: the *a rationibus*, dealing with finance—it was the most important of the sections; *a libellis*—replies to all requests and petitions submitted to the emperor; and *ab epistulis*, the section dealing with administrative correspondence. There were other sections too, but these are ill-attested and may not have been permanent.

Given that these principal officers came from his own household, the likelihood of a collision between them and the emperor was nil, but they were seemingly so influential as to lead Suetonius to write that 'Claudius seemed to be their servant rather than their Emperor'.[41] (One of them—Narcissus—came to possess the largest private fortune in the empire—400 million sesterces!)

These heads of departments in the imperial household in effect converted them into public departments, and they also exercised influence over Claudius' policy which extended beyond their departmental responsibilities. This was true to a lesser extent of freedmen who succeeded them in the next half-century. Their power was resented by senators and others of high social standing partly because of their servile birth. In the second century it became the rule that these departments were entrusted to *equites*. The gradual increase in the number of posts reserved to this order meant that a regular hierarchy came into being with established promotion ladders and posts ranked by special titles, such as *egregii*, *perfectissimi*, and *eminentissimi*, and it became possible too, though unusual, for men to rise in this service without having served in the army. At a lower level a truly civil service was furnished by imperial freedmen and slaves subordinated to the *equites*. But

---

[41] Suetonius, *The Twelve Caesars*, 'Claudius', para 29.

they could seldom exert influence over policy. An exception may be made of those who attended emperors as chamberlains. Like Claudius' chiefs of household departments, they enjoyed the advantage of being close to the imperial person. We find here a faint echo of Han China. Freedmen had the same obligation of loyalty and fidelity in even the smallest things to their imperial patrons as Chinese eunuchs to the Son of Heaven. And just as the Chinese eunuch was despised for his mutilation, so the freedman was despised by the élite for having been a slave. In both cultures envy mingled with snobbery: both kinds of imperial dependants were upstarts who had jumped from ignominy to vast wealth and all but sovereign power. And in both cases the 'law of proximity' had demonstrated itself—for it was by virtue of this that the upstarts had outdistanced the 'natural counsellors' of the ruler.

By the second century we can speak of a regular imperial bureaucracy in the full sense of the word but, as Pliny's letters to Trajan show, the emperor was in full charge and could take advice from whom he chose.

7. THE SERVICES

7.1. *The Army*

The army was the most important and also the most successful of all the imperial institutions. Augustus disbanded and gave land to about half the army at the close of the Civil War and settled its establishment at twenty-eight legions, reduced to twenty-five after the Germans annihilated Varus' three legions in AD 9, and built up again to thirty by the Flavians. In all, they amounted to some 150,000 men. (This was in addition to the twelve cohorts, equal to about two legions, of the Praetorian and urban guards at Rome.) Added to all these were some 150,000 'auxiliaries', recruited from non-citizens. From Augustus' time these units were deployed so as to protect the frontier provinces. Eventually a *limes* studded with temporary or permanent camps and fortresses was created. Hadrian supplemented the auxiliaries with local native levies, the *numeri*, in the usual order of battle.

The upkeep of these 300,000 or more troops constituted by far the greatest single outlay of expenditure in the empire. Augustus seems to have fixed the establishment at the levels I have just cited because he felt the empire could not afford more. By doing so, he effectively predetermined the size of the empire, which he allegedly recommended his successors not to expand; and in fact only Britain, Dacia, and Mesopotamia (i.e. northern Iraq) were to be added, apart from a few frontier rectifications. This number of troops, which had probably risen to some 400,000 in the second century, was really quite small for the task of guarding the long northern and eastern frontiers which enclosed a territory half the size of the United States and a population estimated at 50 to 60 million inhabitants. Nevertheless, it accomplished this task most successfully, since the peoples beyond the frontiers were unable to concert attacks, and, before the fourth century, were not bent on seizing Roman territory. The only major irruptions before the third century were the Sarmatian and Marcomannic invasions at the time of Marcus Aurelius and, once the work of subjugation was complete, the only major rebellions were those of the Jews in the Jewish War, AD 66–73, the diaspora uprisings in Cyprus, Egypt, and Cyrene, AD 115–117, and the Bar Kochba revolt in Judaea, AD 132–5. The Roman armies had to fight very hard to win, but no other provinces joined the Jews, and the Parthians who were the only local power that might have helped them remained quiet. So, with the entire resources of the empire pitted against them, the outcome was inevitable.

The army was also the guarantor of public order. Thus, two legions were stationed in Egypt, where Alexandria was always liable to flare into bloody riots between the Jews and the Greeks, and troops were occasionally called in when fighting broke out between adjacent towns, something that could sometimes occur even in Italy. The troops were used as an anti-riot force. Detachments served at the post-stations on the main highways, and from time to time small parties accompanied the tax collectors; but they were not used to police the towns, although there was pressure on the authorities to allow this.

Since the army was the decisive power in making and sustaining them, the emperors tried to multiply political controls over it. So, for instance, all officers down to centurion rank were commissioned directly by the emperor (though he must have done this on the advice of his generals); the transposable civilian-cum-military *cursus honorum* removed legion commanders from the army and equestrian commanders of *auxilia* after a few years' stint, and the military tribunes[42] after even shorter intervals. Provincial governors could not raise troops on their own account and were discouraged from co-operating with neighbouring governors. Again, soldiers' pay, which is always critical to the morale and loyalty of the troops, was in the hands of an independent procurator, who was not infrequently at loggerheads with the governor. All soldiers took the oath of allegiance to the emperor and as time went by the imperial cult took root in the form of camp shrines containing his statue. In the years following the Four Emperors (AD 68–9) these measures proved effective until after the death of Commodus. Successful

[42] See following page

domestication of the army by the Flavians and Antonines is at once a tribute to the outstanding merit of those emperors and a major reason for the general stability, prosperity, and civilian quality of the early empire.

We have already mentioned that the Roman army was a prime avenue in social mobility and a major agent in Romanization. The key to the first of these lies in the structuring of the officer corps. A centurion was the officer commanding a 'century', a squad of eighty men. Centurions were long-service career officers, usually come up from the ranks, who by virtue of their veteran experience were veritably the backbone of the army. The point is that centurions could, through successive promotions, attain equestrian rank. Officers of field rank (legates and tribunes) were confined to the two aristocratic classes: the officer (legate) commanding a legion was normally senatorial and other high-ranking officers in legions and *auxilia* were equestrians, often from the municipal-magistracy classes. But to be a centurion was open to any Roman citizen; an ordinary soldier could win promotion to a junior centurion post (this would be the *hastatus posterior*) and thence to the highest of such posts (the *pilus prior*) in his cohort. (A cohort consisted of six centuries except for the first cohort which had only five.) From senior centurion in his own cohort, he could win further promotion until he reached the very highest centurion post of all, the *primus pilus*, commanding the first century of the first cohort. This was the most senior of all career posts; it carried vast responsibility as one might expect and it was not only prestigious but highly paid. The *primus pilus* received twice as much as the *primus* of the other cohorts, and these in their turn got twice as much as the junior centurions, who in turn were paid five times as much as the ranker. Apart from his savings and his war booty, a retiring *primus pilus* received a gratuity of 400,000 sesterces, which was enough to qualify him for equestrian status. Roman towns are studded with inscriptions attesting to native sons who had retired from being a *primus pilus* and had settled down to become the big man of the locality. In principle only Roman citizens could join the legions, but this was never true in fact and became less and less so. In 27 BC the legions were mostly Italians but by AD 100 these were rare, though the recruits tended to come from already Romanized provinces. Natives, non-citizens, joined the *auxilia* and this part of the army was a most important agent in Romanization. The raw recruits, often rude tribesmen, came into the almost archetypal Roman ambience—the army camp—and formed part of the quite intense social life (burial clubs, religious sodalities, etc.) of the unit. He came across characteristic Roman institutions—the baths, the *cloacae*, even the amphitheatre—and he had to speak Latin. Then, on his discharge he became a full Roman citizen. It is reckoned that some 5,000 men were discharged every year, so that the cumulative effect was considerable and exponential, since the offspring of these citizens were usually citizens themselves.

The other main way the army served to Romanize was through its permanent camps and fortresses. Crowds of camp-followers trailed the legions on their marches and settled down with them where they dug their camps. There they were joined by the surrounding civil population, since a permanent site of 10,000–20,000 men represented a huge market for primitive rural tribesmen. While these were still on a subsistence natural economy, the troops paid good currency to them for food and drinks, entertainment, and women. Thus settlements called *canabae* (booths) sprang up adjacent to the camps. At the permanent ones the proprietors held the sites on regular five-year leases. In some cases the *canaba* grew so big that on its own it petitioned for and received the charter of a *colonia*, and this is how the towns of York, Mainz, Cologne, and Nijmegen began. Moreover every such camp radiated the Latin language, Roman mores and technical skills, traders and money-lenders into the adjacent countryside. And we must bear in mind, too, that in an imperial province the 'civil government' was in fact a military one. The governor was the local legate, and would use military personnel for discharging his civil responsibilities.

It is certainly true, however, that some provinces were Romananized in quite a different way, through the implantation of Italian colonies. Such, for instance, were southern Gaul, Spain, Africa, Noricum. But this does not significantly detract from the army's importance. Taken all in all—its roles in defence, civil order, politics, social mobility, civilizing and Romanizing— the army is the core institution of the early empire. Its significant success is rivalled perhaps by only one other institution: the law and its judicial arrangements.

7.2. Justice

Other things being equal, the rich and otherwise resourceful benefit from the judicial system more than the deprived. This is true with only a few individual and conspicuous exceptions even in our own day, and it may be taken as a constant over time and place up to the most recent times. It is unhistorical to disparage the Roman administration of justice simply on these grounds or to dismiss Roman private law (which our jurists regard as its crowning glory) on the grounds that it was excessively concerned with private property or irrelevant to most of the population.[43] 'A poor thing,

---

[43] de Sainte Croix, *Class Struggle*, 328. M. S. Anderson, *Peter the Great* (Thames and Hudson, London, 1978), 65 6.

but mine own' it may be, but it insults the intelligence to suggest that the legal guarantee of the poor man's ownership is of no consequence. Whether he could 'cash' his legal right relates to the adequacy of the court system was another matter, and it is there if anywhere that the criticism should be addressed. For instance, the assize courts were too distant for most small owners to seek justice there.

The courts at this time were in a state of transition. In the provinces the governor exercised both criminal jurisdiction over everyone and civil over Roman citizens (where the Roman laws applied) and such non-citizens as chose to use his court; but these two categories of people were converging all through this time until, with the AD 212 Edict of Caracalla, the distinction disappeared. But this still left non-Romans the option of being tried by local law in the local manner, and it has become clear that the use of local law persisted, more than was formerly realized, in Egypt and the Eastern Provinces.[44]

Civil cases that came to the governor were usually decided by *iudices* appointed by the governor who would define the principles by which they were to give judgment. Where he decided cases himself he was assisted by his *consilium*. The court proceeded inquisitorially in criminal matters and with a wide discretion according to the system known as *cognitio*. Here, without doubt, a vicious or corrupt governor could pervert the course of justice. The Flavians and Antonines came out very strongly against this. For instance, though Domitian was loathed by the Senate, Suetonius was yet able to comment: '[He] kept such tight hold on the city magistrates and provincial Governors that the general standard of honesty and justice rose to unprecedented heights—you need only observe how many such personages have been charged with every kind of corruption since his time.'[45] As examples, we may mention Marius Priscus, governor of Africa, who took bribes to sentence innocent persons to punishments and death,[46] or Caecilius Classicus, governor of Baetica, who was convicted out of his private account book that showed how much he had taken in each court case and business deal.[47]

Meanwhile, in the metropolitan territory of Italy itself the jury courts of the Republic (the *quaestiones*) were also giving way to the *cognitio* system. The police jurisdictions of the praetorian prefect and the prefect of the city took

---

[44] W. Kunkel, *An Introduction to Roman Legal and Constitutional History*, trans. J. M. Kelly (Clarendon Press, Oxford, 1966; repr. 1975), 79.

[45] Suetonius, *The Twelve Caesars*, 'Domitian', para. 8. But Professor Brunt, in a private communication, says he does not believe this—that the only department of his administration of which we know anything is the Roman aqueduct, which was corrupt and inefficient although it lay under his (Domitian's) nose, as governor.   [46] Pliny, *Letters*, ii. 11, 12.

[47] Ibid., iii. 9. Note, parenthetically, that citizens in a province were not powerless to strike back.

over many causes hitherto handled by the juries. They were more discretionary than the latter, but much quicker and more knowledgeable. The Senate continued to act as the criminal court for senators. Individuals might also try to have cases heard by the emperor himself, assisted by a learned *consilium*. He could take any cases he chose.

Besides these, there were other courts, administrative tribunals, and ancillary courts like the court of the *annona* and of the *vigiles*, and the fiscal, police, military, and religious tribunals. As yet these were too few to pose a problem of overlapping and competing jurisdictions, which they did in the late empire.

In sophistication, logic, detail, and width of judicial discretion there is a world of difference between what I will call repressive law (crimes, sedition, treason, and the like) and private law. The former is rudimentary, the latter 'the most original product of the Roman mind . . . a thoroughly scientific subject, an elaborately articulated system of principles abstracted from the detailed rules which constitute the raw material of law'.[48] The 'oppression' school of critics of Roman law[49] never cease to dilate on the crudity and harshness of the repressive law (and with good reason, as will be shown). But for all that, it was supposed to conform to certain basic principles of procedure and of legal presumption, just as in the civil law. In so far as a judge applied them, these offered some protection to the accused. How far judges observed them is, of course, another matter and difficult to answer for lack of evidence.

The accused was presumed innocent till found guilty, had the right to meet his accusers face to face, and the opportunity to defend himself against the charge.[50] The onus of proof lay upon the accuser not the accused.[51] Nobody might be convicted on suspicion alone.[52] 'The guilt or punishment of a father can impose no stigma upon the son: for every individual is subjected to treatment in accordance with his own action and no one is made the inheritor of the guilt of another.'[53]

The repressive law is part of the system of government, forming as it does the legal framework for keeping the peace and imposing civil order, and it will therefore be treated under that heading. The substance of the

---

[48] B. Nicholas, *An Introduction to Roman Law* (Clarendon Press, 1962), 1.

[49] e.g. de Sainte Croix, *Class Struggle*; A. H. M. Jones, *The Later Roman Empire*.

[50] Acts 25: 16.

[51] Justinian I, Emperor of the East, *Digesta*, English selections (Penguin Classics, Harmondsworth, 1979), 23.3.2. [52] Ibid. 48.19.2.

[53] Ibid. 48.19.26. Compare these maxims with Han law where, as we saw, the entire family was collectively responsible for the guilt of one of its members and where it was the common practice to flog the accused before hearing his case. See pp. 480, 517 above.

private law is not our strict concern, but its peculiar and highly original nature does prompt some consideration. For one thing, it reflects the notion of the free individual. This was noticeable in the maxim already quoted, that the individual and not his family is alone punishable for an offence. The law was, too, the guarantor and protector of the individual's rights to property or to a certain legal status. However, both of these were vitiated by the gradual insinuation of the distinction between *honestiores* and *humiliores*, which abrogated the Republic's principle of equality before the law (as will be explained below).

The law was to a very large extent quite free-standing, that is, independent of the emperor. This is part of the great paradox of the autocratic empire: that 'Lawyers were concerned with matters which concerned private individuals and in matters involving the state and its interests there was little place for law',[54] 'Rome was governed by Emperors of the most despotic type . . . [just] when private law reached its highest point of technical development . . .'[55] Precisely because the state was *not* involved, the Roman jurists could and did develop private law independently of the emperor. Likewise, when a litigant chose to appeal to the emperor on a point of law, the reply he received had been drafted or suggested by the jurists serving the emperor, and that reply conformed to established law or changed it only marginally. In this way, a huge area of human regulation was extruded from the concern of the ruler and developed independently, in tandem with his contrastingly absolute discretion in 'state matters'. This need not have been so. The government might have undertaken to regulate all such matters administratively or alternatively to have left it all for private individuals to sort out for themselves. China tried to take the former road but ended up with the latter. There, as we saw, the only judicial way an individual could get redress from another was to put the matter to the prefect or administrator and hope he would prosecute—in short, such civil disputes had to be turned into criminal law. In China some matters of private law were always ignored by the magistrates (e.g. contracts), others were given a limited treatment within the penal format (e.g. property, inheritance, marriage), until in the end even these proved too burdensome and the Kang Hsi emperor (1661–1722) declared: 'Law-suits would tend to increase to a frightful amount if people were not afraid of the tribunals and if they felt confident of always finding in them ready and perfect justice . . . I desire therefore that those who have recourse to the tribunals should be

---

[54] P. Stein, *Legal Institutions: The Development of Dispute Settlement* (Butterworth, London, 1984), 107.
[55] Ibid.

treated without any pity and in such a manner that they should be disgusted with law and tremble to appear before a magistrate.'[56]

This coexistence of an autocratic ruler and an extensive regime of private law that was independent of him is not peculiar to Rome. The same principle (the details of the private law were very different, of course) prevailed in ancient Israel. There the Mosaic Law and customary law governed the civil relationships of individuals and the king could not and dared not interfere. Matters of state—war, taxation, police, foreign policy—were by contrast the absolute domain of the monarch.[57] Exactly the same, as we shall see, was to be true in the Caliphate,[58] but it was reached by a very different route.

7.3. Order

It is quite common to find polities in which what are considered purely private affairs are treated with humanity and forbearance (often through conciliation or arbitration procedures), but where anything involving the state's interests are treated with extreme severity; the pre-*perestroika* Soviet Union and the People's Republic of China provide outstanding recent examples. There, penal matters involving the public interest—such as embezzlement and/or theft of state property, currency offences, and the like—are treated with great severity, at times, indeed, savagery. It was like this in the Roman Empire. Slaves apart, a free inhabitant of the empire was safe and sound provided he was not a criminal, not a rioter, not a rebel and, of course, in the worst case, unless he was politically suspect: such a person could be condemned on charges other than *maiestas*. The Roman peace and tolerance extended only so far as men were submissive, and that is the long and short of it.

Let us begin with the most innocuous level, criminal activities, including banditry. Under the Antonines the imperial highways were safe enough, for there were post-stations manned by troops at 25–35 mile intervals. Once away from them, however, lawlessness and violence prevailed, which was only contained by roving military detachments (headed by *beneficiarii consulares*) to reinforce the efforts of the cities.[59]

Criminal trials were subject to the inquisitorial *cognitio* procedure. In this, the criminal sphere, equality before the law did not obtain. Citizens had a higher status than non-citizens and in practice this meant that they were not supposed to be brutalized by the court before proceedings began and had a

[56] Quoted in Stein, *Legal Institutions*, 57.   [57] See above, Bk. I, Ch. 5, 'The Jewish Kingdoms'.
[58] See below, Bk. III, Ch. 2, 'The Empire of the Caliphate'.
[59] Starr, *Roman Empire*, 119

right to appeal to the emperor. The governor was then obligated to report the trial record to the emperor along with the petition of appeal. Furthermore, citizens were punished more mercifully than non-citizens. This distinction between citizens and non-citizens was being overlaid, meanwhile, by a distinction between 'upper class' and 'lower class' individuals, and after AD 212, when citizenship was extended throughout the empire, this distinction became the only operative one: between the *honestiores* and the *humiliores*, the 'better' and the 'lower'. The latter might be tortured in the judicial process, not so the former. Whereas the *humiliores* could be sentenced to the mines, the *honestiores* suffered only banishment. Whereas *humiliores* could be condemned to an atrocious death, the *honestiores* could be offered a speedy execution.

On the whole the ordinary criminal was not liable to the atrocious penalties: the most usual were deportation, the mines, and death. But the authorities took a much more violent view of riot and sedition. Whatever the pretext, nobody must resist authority at all.

'Instigators of sedition and riot or rousers of the people are—according to the nature of their rank—either crucified, thrown to wild beasts or deported to an island.'[60] Hence, as Wells points out, the amphitheatre was

part of this theatre of terror. It was a lesson in pain or death, in the uncertainty of life, in the stratification of society and the arbitrariness of power . . . those who died in the amphitheatre died for the established social order. It was not just entertainment to keep the people quiet though it was that as well . . . more importantly it was a terrifying demonstration of what could happen to those who failed to please their masters, who failed to conform to the established order: slaves, criminals, Christians and not these alone. A spectator who was witty at Domitian's expense was dragged out and thrown to the dogs in the arena.[61] Commodus walked towards the Senators' seats holding in one hand the head of an ostrich which he had just sacrificed and in the other the sacrificial knife.[62]

Worst of all, finally, was the punishment of those who actually rose in revolt. Earlier we described the triumph of Vespasian and Titus over the Jews.[63] Horrible though this is in its gloating satisfaction over burning cities and murderous victories, even that pales besides what the victors inflicted on the defeated in their homeland: some half-a-million killed, 97,000 prisoners sold as slaves or sent to the wild beasts or made to fight one another at Caesarea—and much more.[64]

This was the reverse of the golden medallion of the Antonine Peace.

[60] Paulus, quoted in Lewis and Reinhold, *Roman Civilization*, ii. 548.
[61] Suetonius, *The Twelve Caesars*, 'Domitian', para. 10.   [62] Wells, *Roman Empire*, 277.
[63] See p. 535 above.
[64] Flavius Josephus, *The Jewish War* (Penguin, Harmondsworth, 1959), vi (9.2.3) and viii (3.1).

8. OUTCOMES

8.1. *Material Satisfactions*

'In the cities', wrote Rostovsteff,[65] 'the local magnates competed keenly for the magistracies and performed the most costly liturgies for the community so that the towns were provided with baths, circuses, marketplaces, aqueducts and were remarkable for their planning, cleanliness and excellent sanitation.' In the cities even the poor could share in the civic amenities. But when he comes to the peasantry—some 90 per cent of the population—he can only say that, 'if we have no paeans of joy, we hear also no complaints'.[66] Recent research has only marginally qualified this opinion. The inflow of wealth to Italy diminished in so far as emperors checked the more flagrant extortion. On the other hand the senatorial order owned great estates in the provinces and an increasing rent-roll flowed to them, a flow which was increased as provincials themselves became senators and came to live in Rome. The order was fabulously rich—the wealthiest had fortunes of 100, 200, 300, even 400 million sesterces.[67] The provinces themselves were more prosperous than under the Republic; the buildings, endowments and public games provided by the decurions (the local councillors) show how rich the provincial aristocracy had become owing to the long peace and the decreases in extortion.

Was such prosperity due, as some scholars think, to a generally low level of taxation? Although we have informed guesses about taxation, guesses are what they remain. For one thing they assume the empire's population at 50–60 million but, as we have pointed out, there is no evidence for this. Next: even if one knew the total population, there is no evidence as to the total budget of the empire, and we need both figures to establish the *average* tax burden. Starr has calculated a probable size of the total budget by working from the cost of a legion—which we do know—and then estimating that the cost of the army was 60 per cent of this total budget.[68] But this proportion is itself an estimate based on the work of Tenney Frank, over sixty years ago.[69]

---

[65] Rostovsteff, *History of the Ancient World*, ii. 286.   [66] Ibid. 294.

[67] A. H. M. Jones, *The Roman Economy* (Blackwell, Oxford, 1974), 126. A sestertius of AD 164 would have been worth, perhaps, £1.20 in 1988 prices. I arrive at this by calculating from the price of the 1 lb loaf of bread. This was 0.25 sesterces in Rome; in Oxford in 1988 it cost 30p (Wells, *Roman Empire*, 204).

[68] Starr, *Roman Empire*, 75–8, 84–9. K. Hopkins, 'Taxes and Trade in the Roman Empire, 200 BC/AD 400', *Journal of Roman Studies*, 70 (1980), 101–25, using a different route, reaches the same conclusion—15 sesterces per capita.

[69] Tenney Frank, *An Economic Survey of Ancient Rome*, 6 vols. (Pageant Books, NY, 1933–40; repr. Paterson, 1959)

The truth is that the evidence is very meagre.[70] Also, the levels of taxation—and its modes—varied from one part of the empire to another. Thus, no Italian citizens paid the *tributum*; in Egypt the tenant-farmer paid no tax, but instead 50 per cent of his produce; in Sicily and Sardinia, and very commonly elsewhere, the tax consisted of the tithe—the *decuma*.

The trouble was that all these kinds of taxes had to be wrung from peasants living on the margin of subsistence, with no protection against a run of bad harvests. And a change in the status of the cultivators was occurring, too. Throughout the Antonine period the mass use of slaves in *latifundia* in Italy and Sicily was declining but the transformation of free peasants into the dependent *coloni* on the great estates was only beginning, so that the current trend was towards a free peasantry.[71] Most of these, subsisting on tiny smallholdings, led lives that were 'grim, short and abysmally poverty-stricken'.[72] In the provinces they were hit very hard by the taxation system because this was regressive: the percentage tax was the same for small acreages as for large. Furthermore, agricultural techniques had not advanced—they were far behind China's—so that no more than the old, traditional yields could be squeezed from the soil. These little small-holdings had to support more labour than they needed. Major redistribution of the tax load was not possible given the tiny contribution commerce and manufacture made to the gross national product (a mere 10 per cent?), and the political dominance of the propertied class everywhere. As Finley observes: 'Nothing could be done to raise the productivity of the Empire as a whole or to redistribute the load. For that a complete structural trans-formation would have been required.'[73]

8.2. *Freedom*

The three activities the authorities would never permit were threats to the emperor, any recalcitrance, and impiety to the gods qualified, however, by the fact that all 'ancestral cults' were respected. We have already discussed the first of these restrictions. The importance of the second is not to be minimized. The authorities demanded absolute obedience and, as we have seen, exacted terrible punishment on those who would not conform. The harshness of Roman society cannot be disregarded. It tied up with the

[70] Brunt, *Roman Imperial Themes*, ch. 15, and pp. 531 ff.

[71] Starr, *Roman Empire*, 84. If not with slave labour, the great landowners must have worked their estates with free tenants and their economic condition might not have been better than that of the later *coloni*.   [72] Ibid. 94.

[73] Finley, *The Ancient Economy*, 144.

cognitio procedure which gave the magistrate wide discretion not only in how he handled the case but in charging the accused. The maxim 'nullum crimen sine lege, nulla poena sine lege' was probably as yet unknown.[74] A bloody-minded governor or procurator could act like a despot, particularly if the victim was not a Roman citizen: Verres, the governor of Sicily, stands (by reason of Cicero's denunciations) as the archetypal villain. But, despite the absence of the legal principle quoted above, it is noteworthy that Cicero expected the Roman court to sympathize with the victims.

Under the Principate we hear of ex-governors being condemned for cruelty. A case is cited of a governor who obtained Hadrian's approval for punishing somebody *extra ordinem* for a crime he thought outrageous, and similarly Roman courts would sometimes condemn men for actions which were not specifically banned by the laws but which were deemed to have run counter to their spirit. These instances appear, however, to be exceptions. Why else, for example, did the governor think he had to ask the emperor's approval? Certainly there were evil governors, and at the time of their misbehaviour there was no means of restraining them, but this does not prove that arbitrary 'justice' was not considered an abuse or that it occurred on a great scale.

The *de maiestate* law, originally intended to counter threats to the state, was interpreted and applied in a very broad manner so as to terrify the senatorial and lettered opposition to the emperor and suppress free speech at this high level. But to anticipate unrest and subversion among the common people, other laws were invoked. The civil population was now disarmed. To carry weapons was a criminal offence under the Julian law concerning violence (passed in the Principate of Augustus).[75] By the Julian law on associations, too, all associations (*collegia*) had to be licensed. The great popularity of burial clubs, religious associations, and the craftsmen's guilds earned them immunity, but how suspicious the authorities could be is shown when Trajan forbade Pliny, his governor in Bithynia, to sanction the establishment of a fire brigade of 130 men in Nicomedia. Bithynians, said the emperor, had repeatedly broken the peace, and in any event, 'whatever help we give them and for whatever purpose, men who have gathered together

---

[74] F. Schulz, *Principles of Roman Law* (OUP, Oxford, 1936), 73. 'No crime without law; no punishment without law.'

[75] Brunt, *Roman Imperial Themes*, ch. 11, has collected much scattered evidence together to show that the population did carry arms. But it seems to me that these were largely side-arms such as sword and dagger and club. Again, he points out that pretty well every village must have had its blacksmith, so that arms could be manufactured. But the common people, even if they did carry such arms, were not trained to military discipline; there is not much evidence, at this or later date, of any kind of local militia, with a muster and review and training exercises.

will all the same become a political association before long'.[76] Trajan felt he had no option but to let the citizens of Amisus set up a mutual-benefit society since that city was entitled to maintain its own laws under its original treaty with the empire. 'We cannot prevent them', he wrote, only to add, 'but in cities which are subject to *our* laws, organizations of this nature are to be prohibited.'[77]

'As many enemies as you have slaves', ran a proverb. Not just the authorities, but all wealthy people were terrified of what slaves might do. One story concerns the son of a freedman, now very wealthy, who was so cruel to his slaves that they set on him while he was bathing and beat him to death.[78] Tacitus recounts, too, how—of all people—the prefect of the city was murdered by one of his own slaves, and how, according to a law of the early Principate, the entire slave population of his household was led out in the teeth of violent opposition from the crowd and put to death.[79]

Obedience—this was what counted. But outside that, the authorities seem blind to practically all the other things that have led other governments to disqualify, despoil, rob, deport, imprison, torture, burn, impale, and stab their subjects to death. They did not care what language they spoke, what opinions they expressed (other than seditious ones). They were blind to the colour of their skins and the *ethnos* or race they came from. They did not impose any religious dogma as we would understand the term, either. They expected persons to respect the traditional Roman cults and the cult of the emperor but did not require anyone to perform the latter— merely disqualified them from office if they did not. They permitted the Jews to offer prayers for the emperor rather than to him. Their tolerance of the Jews, whom they loathed, is in many respects remarkable. Jews were very numerous throughout the empire, and over much of this period highly successful proselytizers. Because of their dietary laws, Jews could not entertain or be entertained by gentiles, which set them apart in itself. Yet although the two Jewish uprisings in Judaea were repressed with wholesale massacre and enslavement and the national life was destroyed, and although too the Diaspora revolt of AD 115 brought the destruction of Jewish ascendancy in Alexandria, it was not long before the imperial authorities relaxed anti-Jewish laws outside Judaea (now called Palestine) and reverted to the previous laws of toleration. The reason for this liberal treatment was that it was long-established tradition to allow subject peoples to practise their own faith and Jews came under the protection of this tradition. They

---

[76] Pliny, *Letters*, x. 34. But Professor Brunt thinks Trajan's rulings were due to a special concern to suppress factions in a disturbed province. *Collegia* of fire-fighters were common and encouraged elsewhere (private communication).   [77] Pliny, *Letters*, x. 92–3.
[78] Ibid., iii. 14.   [79] Quoted in Lewis and Reinhold, *Roman Civilization*, ii. 265–6.

were held to be practising the religion of their ancestors, and hence their religion was licit.

Christians were not in this position. On the contrary, to the Romans they had *abandoned* the faith of their ancestors. They were as intolerant of other religions as the Jews, without the excuse, and were, perhaps, more extreme, in so far as they refused even to offer prayers for the emperor. The early persecutions were, it seems, inspired by popular belief that in their secret meetings the Christian indulged in horrible and atrocious practices; but after the Neronic persecutions the authorities' chief objection was the Christians' intolerance of all and every other sect and religion in the empire. It was not the Christian doctrine itself that was suspect. Indeed, to educated pagans it was a vain and ridiculous superstition. Gnostics, who were willing to make empty obeisance to the other gods or the emperor cult, were not persecuted, but the Christians were, because they posed a political threat by offending Rome's tutelary gods and so bringing ill-fortune.[80]

It was just as well for the stability and durability of the empire that its governing class took this kind of view. It was hard put to it to keep the peace in Alexandria or Caesarea where Hellenism and Judaism met in violent conflict. The empire was a multi-racial, multi-cultural, polyglot society where, after the Edict of Caracalla in 212, all were equal in the law's eyes except the *honestiores vis-à-vis* the *humiliores* and the freemen *vis-à-vis* the slaves. If the authorities had taken sides and elevated one ethnic or linguistic or religious community over all others, the empire would soon have split into pieces. Though Italians were disproportionately represented in the higher ranks of government and Latin speakers enjoyed some preference over Greek at the centre, this was because Latin was the language of central government, not in any way the application of some ideology that put one race or nation or language over others. Nor was it crass utilitarianism; it would be wholly unhistorical to maintain that the Roman authorities pursued their toleration policy simply out of fear of splitting the empire. The simple fact is that they were colour-blind to matters which goad modern peoples to madness. For all we have said about the militarism and authoritarianism of Roman government, the mailed fist was the necessary but certainly not the sufficient reason for the empire holding together. 'Empire' in its primary context signifies the particularist domination by one category of people over others (usually ethnic, territorial, or communal groups), and the Republican empire was like this. But sometimes—China and the Caliphate will be seen to be examples of this—such empires change

---

[80] de Sainte Croix, *Class Struggle*; A. N. Sherwin-White, in Finley (ed.), *Studies in Ancient Society*, 210–19; 250–5; 256–62.

into what I have dubbed 'Empire Mark II'. With Caracalla all free subjects
of the empire were citizens and later, under Diocletian, Italy lost its
privileged 'imperial status' and became just one province among many. At
the same time, a common imperial culture had evolved which acted as the
ticket of entry for any who wanted to form part of the ruling élite. By the
end of the Principate the local élites had everywhere come to approve of
Roman rule: it gave them peace and prosperity, secured their dominance
locally, and bit by bit admitted them into the central power. As for the
masses, some two centuries or more had passed since their initial resistance,
and even if memories still persisted they had quite lost their sting. In brief,
the empire was now no longer one of particularist domination. It had
become a way of life.

9. THE ANTONINE AGE: AN APPRAISAL

In Gibbon's famous phrase, the century between the death of Domitian in
AD 96 and the accession of Commodus in AD 180 was the one when, in the
entire history of the world, 'the condition of the human race was most
happy and prosperous'.[81] We may well wish to qualify this in the light of
our present-day values, but there is still a general consensus that in terms of
the values of that time the Antonine period marks the high point of the
Roman Empire. 'A polite and powerful Empire . . . by common consent at
its height both of political and cultural achievement.'[82] 'Beyond all doubt a
brilliant spectacle'[83] . . . 'The creative power of Rome seemed to have
reached its zenith.'[84] Equally, these scholars concur in the reasons that
justify their common judgement. 'The huge area, inside well-developed
frontiers, was a single—and nearly self-sufficient economic unit.'[85] It
enjoyed the 'blessings of the Pax Romana . . . Piracy was extinguished,
the population freed from the fears and burdens of foreign wars.'[86] Again:
'culturally and politically the Empire was a unit', and, via the legal concept
of the civis Romanus, the empire produced a class of subjects whose political
status transcended frontier and race.[87] Rostovsteff adds that 'it was inocu-
lated with Graeco-Roman civilization'; it was a 'higher form of life . . .
regulated by the orderly condition of a civilised state'.[88] It was prosperous;

[81] Gibbon, The Decline and Fall of the Roman Empire, ch. 3.
[82] T. Cornell and J. Matthews, Atlas of the Roman World (Phaidon, Oxford, 1982), 102.
[83] Rostovsteff, History of the Ancient World, ii. 280.   [84] Ibid. 240.
[85] F. W. Walbank, The Awful Revolution: The Decline of the Roman Empire in the West (Liverpool UP,
Liverpool, 1969; repr. 1978), p. 20.   [86] Ibid.
[87] Ibid.   [88] Rostovsteff, History of the Ancient World, ii. 242.

trade and agriculture flourished; and the rich citizens of each city vied with one another in benefactions to their community.

It becomes more and more clear, as we proceed through this history of government, that there are phases in which the state—and this is particularly apparent in large ones whose cohesion presents especial difficulties—strikes a just balance between what it tries to do and what lies in its power. We shall meet such a period in China, in the earlier part of the T'ang dynasty. The Antonine period is the corresponding one for the Roman Empire. It attained a balance between the autocratic dominance of the centre and the vigorous autonomy of the cities, and between the wealth and resources of the state and the activities it chose to pursue.

The chief of these activities was the common defence. The frontiers had been stabilized and fortified, the northern tribes were only just beginning to exert pressure on the Rhine–Danube line, while the resurgence of the Persian state under the Sassanids still lay in the future. Roman manpower, military art, communications networks, and public finance were easily able to match the requirements of the defensive system. There was a similar balance between the strict authoritarian order and personal individualism: for there was freedom of movement, free alienation of property, freedom of occupation, freedom of religion, and apart from seditious and revolutionary talk, freedom of opinion. At the same time, the old predatory concept of empire was dissolving. The concept of a master-people, master-region, master-sect which dominates the 'lesser breeds without the law' had been replaced by one of a Graeco-Romanizing master-*class*, dominating a huge cosmopolis by its wealth and legal privilege, and consisting of the *honestiores* ruling the cities and rural areas around them throughout the empire in alliance with the senatorials at the centre. What was 'Roman' about this class no longer had anything to do with where they came from or of what race they were. They were Roman only in the sense that they carried on the tradition of *Romanitas*: not a natural community of blood, place, kin, language, or religion, but a cultural artefact.

All great things have the defects of their qualities. The 'immeasurable majesty of the Roman peace' is no exception. The empire was a great place for the well-to-do, for city-dwellers, and for quietists. The badly-off were the marginal subsistence farmers in the rural hinterland and the unfree. For all that, the category of beneficiaries and the legal protection they enjoyed was much wider than in any previous large state. (The city-states of Greece, particularly Athens, and the near-theocratic community of Jews are exceptions on account of their small size.) There is no comparison between the size of the Roman beneficiary-class and the corresponding one in the Han Empire, particularly.

One reason the Age of the Antonines appears so golden is because the now-peaceful, civilized, and Romanized inhabitants of those countries were the products of enormous pain and suffering visited on their forebears, not themselves. It spoiled Gibbon's picture of this great golden peace to do anything but ignore the great and barbarous wars the legions fought to dominate Judaea, for instance, or to recognize that here was one case at least in which the Roman peace really did amount to politicide. It is true that the birth of a civilization, like that of a nation, is no immaculate conception, but it is equally pertinent to ask 'Does the worm forgive the plough?'

This Roman kind of peace, moreover, contained self-destructive seeds within itself. It is the peace of *parcere subjectis*—sparing the conquered—and consequently, disarming the population (as far as this was practicable)[89] and confining its defence exclusively to the soldiers. First the Italians, then the more pacified populations of the provinces ceased to enlist, leaving that to the more recently incorporated, ruder inhabitants on the frontiers, and eventually to the barbarians from outside the empire altogether. But though this served the immediate purpose of preventing riot and rebellion, in the long run it robbed the population of any taste or aptitude for defending themselves. When the barbarians broke the armies they were helpless. In a similar way, by putting the full weight of authority behind the very narrow class of notables and suffocating the local assemblies and popular participation in the cities, the Roman peace distanced the mass of common people from their government; if not actively alienated, they became, at least, indifferent. When the time came, not only did they lack the ability to defend the empire but they lacked the will to do so, as well.

This famous phrase, 'the immeasurable majesty of the Roman peace', conveys too a sense of transcendent orderliness that, in fact, did not exist. The Roman Empire did not run like a well-oiled machine. Beyond the great military road network with its frequent military stations, and outside the cities too, there were bandits and footpads; and in rapacity and arbitrariness, tax-collectors and military quartermasters sometimes behaved little differently. We hear of a tax-collector who carries off the family of an absconding taxpayer, tortures them, and even kills them; of soldiers seizing boats and beasts of burdens and supplies without payment.[90] Petty bribery and corruption was a matter of course. A papyrus lists bribes paid by some unknown, which records such items as 2 drachmae and one obol to the military highway-station, 20 drachmae to a guard, 2,200 drachmae for 'the shakedown', 100 drachmae to two police agents, and so forth.[91] Another

[89] See p. 534, above.
[90] Lewis and Reinhold, *Roman Civilization*, ii. 399–402.   [91] Ibid. 402.

such list records the item: 'to the soldier, at his demand—500 drachmaes.'[92]
So, the empire was not altogether secure—but was eighteenth-century
Britain? It was predatory—but as we have seen, its subjects owed it a great
deal in return. There was widespread corruption, but it is only in recent
times—and in the West, at that—that public office has ceased to be
regarded as a legitimate source of private gain. Throughout the modern
world there are entire cities, government agencies, police forces, and so forth
which are seamed and riddled with corruption.

Though the empire did indeed harbour such defects, they were not due to
the incompetence or malice of the Flavians and Antonines—indeed, quite
the reverse. It was due to their sheer inability to direct the detail of so vast
an enterprise. Where they could do so, they gave redress. They did not look
on the population as mere objects of exploitation, but felt a positive duty
towards them according to the very best standards of their times. Pliny's
correspondence with Trajan shows the empire at its best. For instance, Pliny
has a plan to make unwilling town councillors borrow (and hence pay
interest on) the town's surplus funds. The emperor replies, 'to force a loan
on unwilling persons who may perhaps have no means of making use of it
themselves is not in accordance with the justice of our times'.[93] When Pliny
asks how to deal with persons charged with being Christians, Trajan says,
'pamphlets circulated anonymously must play no part in any accusations'.[94]
One last example: the local public prosecutor sues a townsman of Amisus to
recover for the city 40,000 denarii which the town council had voted him.
The prosecutor's case is that the emperor has now forbidden such grants.
But when the case comes before the emperor, he does not automatically take
the side of the public prosecutor. He says that because this grant was made
before his own edict forbidding them, it must stand: and he adds: 'For in
every city the interests of individuals are as much a concern as the state of
public funds.'

[92] Lewis and Reinhold, *Roman Civilization*, ii. 403.   [93] Pliny, *Letters*, x. 33.
[94] Ibid., x. 97.

8

The Later Roman Empire: From Diocletian to Theodoric, 284–526

*I*n 235, when Alexander, the last Severan, was murdered, the empire plunged into crisis. Barbarians in the north and Persians in the east penetrated the frontiers, Roman armies fought their brothers to put short-lived emperors on the throne, and the currency collapsed. The empire that emerged from this ordeal was very different from the Antonines'. The Dominate, conventionally dated from Diocletian in 284, represents the empire adapting to permanent military siege. Its central characteristic was an unremitting and vast bureaucratic effort to mobilize the empire's human and natural resources. These were inadequate and in any case the government lacked the administrative techniques to marshal them. Nevertheless, every check only emboldened it to redouble its bureaucratic interference, and with every such advance the human and natural resources dwindled still further.

By the end of the process the empire was looking more and more like a Hellenistic counterpart of the (now defunct) Han Empire of China. The Roman emperor was exalted into a remote, hieratic figure, sacred and the sole source of laws, at the centre of a palace which itself stood at the centre of a labyrinthine bureaucracy. Increasingly, numerous cities became mere adjuncts of this central power and their councillors its unpaid and unwilling agents; indeed, in some cities local notables came to be unofficially the effective governing body. The somewhat miscellaneous congeries of territorial jurisdictions of former years was reduced to a logical hierarchical order. Freedom of movement and occupation was frozen for large sectors of the population, and after the conversion of Constantine freedom of religion was approaching that condition also.

Society, in which all freemen were now Roman citizens, was re-divided into a hierarchy of wealth and status, unequal before the law, and whose lower class, the *humiliores*, was liable to crueller punishments. Several hundred thousand men of otherwise quite humble social background were exempted from this and counted as the higher, *honestiores*, class: they included, significantly, the bureaucrats and the soldiers. It is very important to note that these two careers, formerly intertwined in the same individual, were now distinct, as they were in China, though in the Western Roman Empire the military were dominant as always. There opened a new distinction, too, caused by adoption of Christianity as the state religion. As an exclusive and uncompromising faith, it was unlike the secular and protean Confucianism of the Han. Its ultimate political effect was to enhance the absolutism of the emperor by investing him with a sacredness akin to Chinese emperors', but at the same time to diminish popular allegiance. Confucianism could be many things to many men. Christianity had to be one thing to all men. But men disputed with the emperor what Christianity consisted of. The empire became racked by a novel cause of self-division: one Christian sect against another.

1. THE LATER EMPIRE AND ITS END

CHRONOLOGY

235	SEVERUS ALEXANDER murdered
235–84	Military anarchy, barbarian invasions, collapse of the currency. Twenty-two emperors and pretenders proclaimed by their respective armies; only two die natural deaths
268–70	CLAUDIUS II (*Gothicus*) repels Goths in Balkans
270–75	AURELIAN (*Restitutor orbis*) defeats German invaders of Balkans and north Italy: Vandals, Goths, Alemanni. Recovers the secessionist provinces of Gaul and Palmyra-Egypt (under ZENOBIA). Fortifies Rome. Withdraws from Dacia
284–305	DIOCLETIAN. Divides empire into western and eastern halves, institutes the 'Tetrarchy'. Reorganization of provincial system, the currency, and the army. Takes MAXIMIAN as co-emperor
305	Abdication of Diocletian and Maximian
306	Proclamation of CONSTANTINE I; contested, civil wars
312	Constantine invades Italy, Battle of the Milvian Bridge, seizes Rome and the entire West
313	Edict of Milan grants toleration to Christians
324	Battle of Adrianople against Licinius secures the eastern half of the empire
324–37	Constantine sole emperor of reunited empire
325	Presides over the Nicaean Council of the Church
330	Dedication of Constantinople as second and eastern capital
337–51	Empire divided between Constantine's sons
351	Battle of Mursa makes CONSTANTIUS sole emperor
361–3	JULIAN THE APOSTATE
379–95	THEODORIUS I forbids pagan worship
395	Co-emperorship of East (ARCADIUS) and West (HONORIUS)

406–7	Vandals and Sueves overrun Gaul (and later Spain)
408	ALARIC the Goth invades Italy
409	Britain separate from Empire
408–50	THEODOSIUS II emperor of the East. The Theodosian Code (437)
410	ALARIC the Goth sacks Rome
418	Visigoths settled in Gaul
439	Vandals, having invaded Africa (429) from Spain, take Carthage
450	ATTILA the Hun invades Gaul
451	AETIUS defeats Attila at the Battle of Chalons
455	Murder of the western emperor, VALENTINIAN III, terminates the line of Theodosius
455–72	Puppet emperors in the West
475	ROMULUS AUGUSTUS emperor of the West
476	ODOACER deposes Romulus, no successor is appointed: hence ZENO the sole emperor, reigning in Constantinople, recognizes Odoacer as a *patricius* and his lieutenant. *The conventional date for the end of the Roman Empire in the West*

2. THE EMPEROR

With the Dominate, the republican trappings which Augustus had wrapped around the *auctoritas* of the emperor were stripped away and the office now appears openly as the autocracy it had always been. There was no change in the principle of succession: to the very end the autocracy was theoretically elective, the choice vesting in the Senate and the army. Either could proclaim an emperor and the act of proclamation constituted a valid title. But whether that individual could make his title effective was a different story. For although the Senate usually accepted the choice of the army, it did not always do so, and in any case there were several armies, each of which might favour a different candidate. In that event the issue was settled by fighting. But the inauguration of the new emperor was not complete (the case of the Emperor Carus, 282–3, is exceptional) until both army (armies) and Senate had consented.

In practice, however, the principle of heredity was indirectly introduced by the emperor designating a co-regent, either from among his sons or, if he had none, from his family, so that the succession tended to present itself as a set of dynasties and it was only in the intervals that the armies and Senate made a claim to elect. The co-regents of the Principate exercised no governmental authority except what the emperor himself chose to confer, but one of Diocletian's most startling innovations was his Tetrarchy. Convinced that the besieged empire could not be defended from a single centre and by a single man, he divided power between himself and three others, in two groups of two: at the head of the empire, two *Augusti* (himself and Maximian) each having a *Caesar* or a junior emperor, to assist him. Each had his own troops and sphere of operation. Diocletian remained *de facto* the senior, and made the supreme decisions. This system foundered in civil war, but from that time down to the end of the Western Empire in 476 the empire was more often as not governed by two and sometimes more sovereign colleagues with equal rights, but differing in seniority. Nor did this preclude any of them from appointing co-regents. Emperors could also designate a successor without making him co-regent.

Also with Diocletian, a hitherto intermittent but persistent glorification of the emperorship became firmly established. The notion of *princeps* vanished and the office was invested instead with all the attributes of the earlier divine monarchies of the Hellenistic East. Diocletian called himself Jovius, implying that he was Jupiter's representative on earth. As the emperor of the *Orbis*, the world, he now has his orb and his sceptre. He is pictured with his head encircled in a halo. He wears a robe of purple silk threaded with gold. He does not mingle but stays aloof in the recesses of his palace. When he does emerge it is in stiff, hieratic style. For he is sacred and so is everything connected with him. His palace is the *sacrum palatium*, his council the *sacrum consistorium*, the government departments (*scrinia*) the *sacra scrinia*. Those ushered into his audience must clasp his knees and kiss the hem of the purple—the *adoratio*. He is no longer called *princeps* but *dominus*: 'Lord' (or 'Master'). The advent of Christianity as the state religion and the conversion of the emperor to Christianity possibly enhanced this very sacredness, for the emperor was now seen as the servant or vice-regent of God who had personally entrusted him with the government of the world.

As before, the emperor was the supreme judge, and the inferior judges judged in his name. He still appointed all the ancient magistrates—consuls, praetors, and so on, though these had become purely honorific—but he likewise appointed all other superior officials, although as a rule he acted at the suggestion of the praetorian prefect.[1] He was the commander-in-chief of the armies and alone decided war and peace. Once the empire had become officially Christian, he was sometimes designated *isapostolos* 'equal to the Apostles' or the thirteenth Apostle, to indicate his responsibility for exterminating paganism and defending the Church.

Whereas the emperor had made laws, but not in strict legislative form,[2] he was now officially recognized as the legislator and made *leges generales* (though in a multiplicity of differing forms) and he alone had the right to interpret the laws. Like Augustus and his successors, he also possessed the

---

[1] See pp. 581–2 below.   [2] See p. 544 above.

power to dispense the laws, even in respect to himself—but (or precisely because of this!) considered himself as bound by the laws—*alligatus legibus*. Though it was honoured in the breach as well in the observance, this admission[3] was a notable contribution to the concept that the empire and its agents were law-bound.[4]

2.1. *Constraints Upon the Emperor*

2.1.1. THE SENATE

The Senate was at perhaps its lowest point of influence, left with mere vestiges of power. Constantine created a Senate at Constantinople, whose importance varied with circumstances and sometimes was no more than a kind of municipal council for that city. Whereas the Western emperor rarely came to Rome, the Eastern emperor was in permanent residence at Constantinople. In the West, Constantine made a great point of admitting officials to its Senate. Many of these new senators, whose number swelled the Senate from its original 600 to some 2,000, were of modest means but that body continued to include a substantial group of fabulously rich senators with huge estates in Africa, Spain, and Gaul. This Western Senate did not recover importance as a governing body, but the richest members of the senatorial *order* (not necessarily senators) climbed up to a near-monopoly of the highest posts in the West. The old equestrian order had disappeared towards the end of the fourth century by the operation of the 'law of inflated titles'; that is to say, the offices that had qualified individuals gradually came to confer senatorial rank, either on appointment or after retirement. In this way high officialdom and senatorial status coincided. Subsequent to the child emperor Honorius, most Western emperors (Anthemius and Majorian being exceptions) were inveterately pious but unwarlike and feeble: the power-vacuum on the military side came to be filled by their barbarian generals and on the civil side by the immensely wealthy landowning senatorial aristocracy. From that point on, they took over the imperial court, monopolized the highest official posts, and exercised a check upon the imperial commanders, notably by making it difficult to draw upon the resources of men and money from the countryside.

---

[3] *Justinian Code* (529 AD), 14, 12, quoted in J. B. Bury, *History of The Later Roman Empire*, 2 vols. (Dover Publications, New York; repr. 1958), 13 and the Edict of 429 (*Justinian Code*) quoted, 13–14.

[4] But, see pp. 595–6 below for the limitations.

2.1.2. THE ARMY AND THE BUREAUCRACY

From Diocletian to Theodosius I, the emperors were all fighting-men and owed their accession—or downfall—to the army. The legions, situated as they were in more or less fixed location along the frontiers were, consequently, distant from the person of the emperor. These frontier forces were now reduced to a screen or 'trip-wire role', backed up by a large and mobile field army in the interior. It has been suggested that this new strategy was conceived less as a rational response to the barbarian threat and more to the emperors' desire to surround themselves with their troops, but it is difficult to argue this. The fact is that the empire was now under much greater pressure than before, as crises occurred in rapid succession at different parts of the frontier, so that mobile troops were essential.

However that may be, it is clear that the precarious relationship between the emperor and the armies continued much as always; but not so his relationship to the civil bureaucracy. This now emerged as a new constraint on the emperor. By Rome's historical standards, it had become very numerous—the estimate is some 30,000 established posts—but the significant point here is that its nerve-centre and apex was in the imperial palace. This is yet another exemplification of the 'law of proximity' (and equally, its associated 'law of inflated titles') that we noticed in the imperial court in China. True (and compare the Chinese emperor's role) 'any Roman Emperor of reasonable ability and strength of character was not only theoretically but actually absolute'.[5] For all that, the 'law of proximity' held: the larger and more routine-ridden the bureaucracy, the more influential was the part of it closest to the person of the emperor, those in and around the palace.

This is shown, first of all, in the evolution of the emperor's *consistory* (which also exemplifies the 'law of inflated titles'). This body was the successor to the, first unofficial then official, *consilium* of the *princeps*. Like the *consilium*, it offered no constitutional check to the ruler. He chose its membership and it discussed only what he chose to put before it. Its subordination was evident in the rule that its members had to stand in the emperor's presence. Up to the death of Constantine it was where important matters were discussed and decisions taken. Its prestige attracted the ambitious, the emperors responded by increasing its numbers, and as it grew larger its business contracted until by the fifth century it was entirely formal and, following the 'law of proximity', its substantive business passed to an inner core. Significantly, this core was styled the *palatium*, or the *proceres*

[5] A. H. M. Jones, *The Decline of the Ancient World* (Longman, London, 1966), 133.

palatii (the 'Palace Notables')—not a collective body any more but simply a cluster of officials from whom the emperor took advice.[6]

The same twin laws ('proximity' and 'inflation of title') were also operative in that as its membership expanded and substantive powers contracted and the title of 'Member of the Sacred Consistory' became highly honorific, its humblest officials rose and rose in influence until they too rose in status. Such was the destiny of the mere stenographers who recorded the consistory proceedings. Their familiarity with its business led emperors to use them on confidential missions, thence to promotion to high posts in the bureaucracy, and thence to high status. Therefore, the competition to enter such a rewarding career attracted upper-class candidates, which raised the status of the office still higher. By 381 the ranking-order of the senior members was the same as that of imperial 'vicars' (governors of huge territorial jurisdictions—see below). The law of inflated titles continued to operate until by mid-fifth century the entire corps was purely decorative, the posts being sinecures that were bought and sold while the actual recording of the proceedings had passed to an originally still humbler class of palace officials called, simply, *agentes in rebus*, 'agents'. Originally they were the official couriers. Traversing the empire as they did, they naturally acquired much information, eagerly consumed by the central government, of a vast territory with slow communications. In this way they turned into licensed spies and informers and from that into confidential agents. (In the very late empire this class followed a regular, complicated, and highly rewarding career pattern: from courier to inspector of the imperial mail, then back to the court to serve as the assistants of the head of the civil service— the *magister officiorum*—see later.) Then, later, they were seconded from this position to the staffs of the prefects and vicars who ran the reorganized territorial subdivisions of the empire (see below), in which post the agent had to countersign all their official orders. They thus became the means through which everything the empire's field agencies did was brought under central inspection and control![7]

The most telling instance of the law of proximity is, however, the emperor's use—*c*.320 onwards if not earlier—of *eunuchs* as his close advisers. We find three important eunuch posts at this time: the 'Grand Chamberlain' (*praepositus sacri cubiculi*), then the 'Superintendent of the Sacred Bedchamber' (*primacerius*), who was his deputy, and then the 'Steward of the Palace Household' (the *castrensis*), who ranked third. It seems as if the individual rose through the ranks by seniority and that all three posts were held by eunuchs.[8] All had substantial staffs.

[6] A. H. M. Jones, *The Decline of the Ancient World* (Longman, London, 1966), 129–30.
[7] Ibid. 205.
[8] K. Hopkins, *Conquerors and Slaves* (CUP, Cambridge, 1978), 175 and n. 12.

The careers of the eunuch Grand Chamberlains Eusebius, Eutropius, Chrysaphius, and Eutherius demonstrate that each was the principal minister of their respective emperor. True, their enormous eminence was exceptional, but as Hopkins points out, 'there were many humbler examples', and he talks of the 'tremendous and sustained influence which court eunuchs were able to bear upon a whole succession of Emperors' and 'their occupation of a regularly increasing number of offices and the high rank which went with them'.[9]

With the Chinese parallel in mind, it is not hard to see why. First, now that the emperor was sacred, remote, inaccessible—the very opposite of a *princeps*—some class of official was required to intermediate between him and those who wanted to communicate with him (but not, though, necessarily a eunuch). Next, now that the imperial civil service was no longer the emperor's private staff composed of his obedient freedman[10] but a very numerous, routine-ridden, and for the most part faceless bureaucracy, emperors also needed some more flexible, and/or personal channel to provide them with information and to convey their commands (again, not necessarily eunuchs). But, thirdly, emperors felt very vulnerable, as indeed they were. Constantius II 'feared his generals and mistrusted his ministers',[11] and that was true, to greater or lesser degree, of all of them. *Eunuchs*, however, could be employed in the firm expectation of an unshakeable fidelity and they were the emperor's own domestics who looked after his private rooms where nobody else would even dare to penetrate. And finally, by virtue of their constant proximity to the emperor, they could receive confidences and dispense advice.

The fact that eunuchs would be ideally suited for these tasks does not, however, tell us how or why there were eunuchs around, since earlier emperors had managed without eunuchs to look after the women's quarters and Domitian, Nerva, Constantine, and Julian all disliked and distrusted them.[12] It would seem that employing them was copied from the Persian empire, and indeed the ages-long tradition of using eunuchs as palace servants in the eastern part of the empire. In fact the eunuchs of the Roman emperors were (with two peculiar exceptions) always barbarian slaves—Persians, Armenians, or from other parts of the Caucasus region.[13]

Precisely because they were slaves, eunuchs, and foreigners and hence totally dependent on the emperor and exposed to the hatred and mockery of everybody else,[14] emperors could permit them to be their intimates of the

---

[9] K. Hopkins, *Conquerors and Slaves* (CUP, Cambridge, 1978), 176, 179.
[10] Cf. p. 549 above.   [11] Gibbon, *Decline and Fall*, ch. 19.   [12] Ibid.
[13] Jones, *The Later Roman Empire*, 567. For further speculation about a Persian connection, see Hopkins, *Conquerors*, 192–3.   [14] Cf. p. 495 above, regarding the Han empire.

bedchamber. So, by their very proximity, the Grand Chamberlains came to control first informal, then formal access to the emperor. People gladly paid them for the privilege of a private audience. Their exceptional position brought on the high-ranking eunuchs the envy, wounded vanity, and malice of contemporary aristocrats, authors, and (later) churchmen. (To all of these sentiments, incidentally, Gibbon faithfully subscribes.) It is easy to see why they were so detested, but they must not at all be seen as their critics picture them. Instead, they should be regarded as instruments by which the sacred emperor, surrounded by potential rivals and served by a huge anonymous bureaucracy, gathered his private information and advice, obtained fore-knowledge of projected plots, and could get his personal missions or commands carried out in complete confidence. Here there exists a *noteworthy contrast* between Rome and China. In the latter, as we saw, the eunuchs were able from time to time effectively to take over from the emperor. In fourth-century Rome the eunuchs did not constitute a quasi-corporation as in China, and were influential only as individuals and through their contact with the emperor. Also, as long as the emperor was an adult and captained his armies, it was always he who was the prime mover.[15] Hopkins has summed up their position:

The tension between an absolutist monarch and the other powers of the state; the seclusion of a sacred emperor behind a highly formalized court ritual; the need of both parties for intermediaries; the exploitation by eunuchs of this channel for the appropriation to themselves of some of the power of controlling the distribution of favours; the non-assimilability of the eunuchs into the aristocracy; the cohesive but non-corporate nature of their corps and the expertise which resulted from the permanence of their positions as compared with the amateurish, rivalrous and individualistic strivings of aristocrats; all these factors in combination and in interaction can account for the increasing power with which the eunuchs were invested and the continuity with which they, as a body, held it.[16]

3. THE NEW TERRITORIAL STRUCTURE

Diocletian completely recast the territorial divisions of the empire. Till his time the old two-tiered structure of provinces and cities had continued to serve, but under increasing difficulties. The army, once the cement of the imperial structure, had become regionalized, and the soldiers were more concerned about their native province than the whole empire; the economic ties between the frontier areas and the central provinces were weaker now,

[15] For an illuminating discussion of the eunuchs see Hopkins, *Conquerors*, ch. 4, 'The Political Power of Eunuchs'.   [16] Ibid. 191.

because the provinces had become self-sufficient in certain of the lines they had previously imported. In reaction the central government was exerting more and more control over the cities. This control—and that of the provinces—could be enhanced by reducing the size of the province—by, so to speak, moving the provincial governor nearer to the cities. (The twenty-eight Provinces of Augustus' day had already multiplied to forty-two by AD 117 and to 119 by the later fourth century.) But military exigencies pointed the opposite way. The Sassanids, who now ruled Persia, aggressively tried to reclaim the boundaries of the ancient Persian Empire, and this threat called for a permanent imperial presence in the East as well as in the West. Diocletian's concept of collegiate government by a Tetrarchy in which he was senior emperor was evolved by reference to this new strategic problem.

Diocletian's completed plan embraced: an emperor and a caesar in each half of the empire, each having his own Praetorian prefect as chief of staff. Each half was then divided into six dioceses, each headed by a deputy of the praetorian prefect (hence his 'vicars' (*vicarii*)), each responsible for the work of the provincial governors within his diocese (roughly four in number). Constantine carried this reorganization further by interposing yet another tier, the *prefecture*, between the emperor and the dioceses. Four (later three or five or even six) dioceses were grouped together under a praetorian prefect. But this is highly simplified. The praetorian prefects were still, probably, accompanying Diocletian and Constantine on their travels. But as the empire was becoming effectively divided into an Eastern and Western half, by the second half of the fourth century the prefects became heads of permanent subvisions of the empire, to wit, Oriens; the prefecture of Italy, Illyricum, and Africa; and finally the prefecture of Britain, Gaul, and Spain. The first of these, Oriens, became the East Roman Empire, but after 395 Illyricum was organized as a second eastern prefecture, though Oriens provided the core of the administration.

The division of the empire laid out in Diocletian's Tetrarchy was made permanent in 330 when Constantine founded Constantinople. He set it up as a shadow Rome, complete with not only its great public buildings but its own demi-imperial Senate. In principle, the joint emperors and their caesars formed a single college, ruling a single empire. Imperial edicts, laws, and constitutions were issued in the name of all, and trade and movement passed freely throughout. In practice, one of these joint emperors was senior to his colleagues. Diocletian and Constantine were certainly as much masters of the empire as any single emperor before them. But the foundation of Constantinople, which flourished from the very start, institutionalized the division in a way nothing else could. When Theodosius I died he divided the empire between his two young sons Honorius (West) and Arcadius (East). The emergence of a Greek senatorial aristocracy meant that thereafter the two halves began to go separate ways. In 438 it was officially enacted that an imperial constitution promulgated by one emperor only applied to the dominions of his colleague if the latter also enacted it. The fact that the Eastern half was Greek-speaking and the West spoke Latin deepened the differences. But this was still to come, in what the future was to prove to be the terminal years of the Western part of the Empire. In the fourth century this was still one single unit.

4. THE CENTRAL ADMINISTRATION

Each half of the empire was governed from where its emperor happened to be. As he was frequently on the move, his household and some 2,500 civil officials moved with him. (On such journeys the box to carry the imperial files was called a *scrinium* so that *scrinia* came, consequently, to be the term for the civil department.)

The civil service had undergone immense changes since the Severan emperors. From about 2,000–3,000, its numbers had increased to between 30,000 and 40,000 for the two halves together, of whom some 2,300 were headquarters staff in each half.[17] With rare exceptions, the military and civil functions were now exercised by different individuals following distinct career patterns.

The soldier-emperors took military organization as their norm, so the civil service, too, had its chains of command, its hierarchy, its graded salary-scales, and its ever-elaborated ladder of honorific titles. At the top, these overlapped with the senatorial order. The entire central administration centred on the emperor and his palace and was consequently called the *comitatus*[18] or the *palatine* officers and offices. Its core was the imperial household, whence radiated various organs, beginning with the consistory, mentioned already. Four great civil departments followed, respectively headed by the *quaestor*, the *magister officiorum*, and the two finance ministers—the *comes sacrorum largitionum* and the *comes rei privatae*, all working down to the various field-officials. Thirdly came the military officials, the *magister militum* commanding household troops at the emperor's side, and other *magistri* in the field (see fig. 2.8.1).

[17] See pp. 585–6 below.
[18] 'Escort, retinue, company': from *comes*, a companion or partner.

The Military Offices		The Civil Offices
The *magister militum* praesantalis	**THE EMPEROR**	Quaestor
		Magister officiorum
Other *magistri militum**		*Comes largitionum*
Comes domesticorum		*Comes rei privatae*

Fig. 2.8.1. The Consistory
* In the fourth century there were two *magistri militum praesentales*—the infantry and the cavalry, then, after Stilicho (d. 408), one *magister militum utriusque militiae.*

4.1. *The Household*

We have already noted that this consisted of two groups—the *cubicularii*, who looked after the emperor's private apartments and the gynaecium, and the *castrenses*, the general domestic staff. It also contained the officers of the *res privata* (privy purse), the wardrobe, and the imperial estates. As we saw, the *praepositus sacri cubiculi* (Grand Chamberlain) and his deputy, the *primicerius*, were personally selected by the ruler and were usually eunuchs. The clerical departments—the *scrinia*—did not culminate in a single office or officer (any more than did their Chinese counterparts) and the consistory, which might have developed into a collegiate cabinet, was too large and on the point of becoming merely formal. For these reasons an emperor needed somebody who, as his personal representative, could see that the multiplex offices would carry out his wishes smoothly and quickly, hence a *magister officiorum.* He would prefer somebody who was not only in constant contact with him but who was so vulnerable—as a self-made person—that he could be entrusted with such enormous power.

The emperor was attended by his personal guards—the *scholae palatinae* (imperial guard) and the *protectores domestici*, an élite corps of officer-cadets commanded by a *comes domesticorum.* From the time of Stilicho there was a single commander-in-chief of all military forces in the West, the *magister militum utriusque militiae praesentalis.*[19]

4.2. *The Consistory*

We have already described this.[20]

[19] This command was instituted by Constantine—until this day, the responsibility lay with the praetorian prefect. [20] Above pp. 573–4.

4.3. *The Ministries*

4.3.1. THE QUAESTOR

Constantine remodelled this ancient office. The quaestor was now the principal legal officer. He drafted legislation, handled petitions, and took decisions on issues which the *scrinia* (ministries) found too intractable. In the fifth century he came to co-operate with the praetorian prefect in handling the personal jurisdiction of the emperor.

4.3.2. THE *PRIMICERIUS NOTARIORUM*

As head of the corps of notaries, he kept the list of precedence (*notitia dignitatum*) of the higher officers, and issued the emperor's codicils that conferred their appointments and the emperor's *sacrae epistolae* which conferred military commissions.

4.3.3. THE *MAGISTER OFFICIORUM* AND THE *SCRINIA*

The *magister officiorum* had very heavy responsibilities, for he was, so to speak, the chief establishment officer of the entire public administration (excepting some very special departments) as well as a good deal more besides. He controlled the personnel of the *scrinia* (i.e. the secretariats serving the *magister* of each *scrinium*); he provided the quaestor with any staff he required; he exercised administrative and disciplinary powers over the imperial guard (the *scholae palatinae*); and he was the administrative head of the imperial couriers, the *agentes in rebus*. He also controlled the two offices concerned with the emperor's timetable and appointments. This gave him control of *access*, and it is not surprising therefore to find him coming to play an important role in foreign affairs.

The three *scrinia* were tiny. Even together, they never employed more than 130 persons or so, even late in the fifth century. These were, however, of high calibre, well educated, and often the sons of civil servants or town councillors (the *decurions*). Each *scrinium* was headed by its *magister*. The *scrinium* called *memoriae* handled rescripts to private citizens, *epistolarum* the rescripts to judges and city or provincial delegations, while *libellorum* was responsible for preparing cases for the imperial high court.

The *agentes in rebus*, already mentioned, had developed into a most important mechanism of centralization. The corps numbered about 1,000 men. From imperial courier, a man could win promotion until he became an assistant to the *magister officiorum* himself. Under Constantius II the most senior were seconded for a year or two to become the heads of the *vicarii* of the dioceses and the praetorian and urban prefects in the provinces. Since no legal order could issue without their counter-signature, by this means the *magister officiorum* obtained regulatory power over the entire territorial administration.

4.3.4. THE TWO FINANCE MINISTRIES

There were two finance ministries, the Privy Purse Office (*res privata*), and the *sacrae largitiones*, the Treasury, which handled all money transactions. (Revenue in kind was the responsibility of the praetorian prefects.)

The emperor's private estate was quite enormous: in some places like Africa and Byzacena his lands formed immense concentrations—making up 18.5 per cent and 13 per cent of the total land area respectively and, of course, a far larger proportion of the cultivable area. The *res privata* worked to its officers in the *dioceses*. Called *rationales*, they controlled the *procuratores*—by now a very ancient office—in the provinces. The *procuratores* administered the estates through a number of *magistri* who in turn had staffs of *tractores* and *exactores* to collect the tenants' rents.

The *sacrae largitiones*' field-staff in the dioceses and provinces was very large.[21] It collected the 10 per cent or so of the Empire's revenue that was paid in coin. There were three main taxes. The *ad valorem* customs duty of 12.5 per cent was farmed out to private contractors. The *Crown Gold*, originally the cities' free gift to the emperor on a few rare occasions, but now an arbitrary exaction every four or five years, was collected by the cities. Finally, the much-hated sales tax on traders (except teachers and doctors), which raised the equivalent of 5 per cent of the land tax (which shows how overwhelmingly agricultural the economy was),[22] was assessed by the praetorian prefects but collected by the tradesmen's guilds. In short, the *largitiones* was a treasury, not a tax-collector. This characteristic is manifested by other of its functions. For one thing, it maintained *thesauri* throughout the empire in which coin and bullion and other precious items were stored. For another, it was responsible for the 'production and control of the currency'.[23]

5. PREFECTURES AND PRAETORIAN PREFECTS

We traced the rise of the office of praetorian prefect in the chapter on the Antonines. That office never ceased to grow during the bad days of the third century, and well before Diocletian's reign the praetorian prefect was the emperor's chief of staff in everything—militarily, judicially, and administratively. His judicial authority was so extensive—and important—that we

---

[21] Jones, *The Later Roman Empire*, 428–9.   [22] Ibid. 163.   [23] Ibid. 428.

find the famous jurist Ulpian holding this military office. He commanded the Praetorian Guard, through his adjutant-general he controlled army recruitment and discipline, and through his quartermaster-general he provided the army with its rations. When, as a consequence of the great inflation, the economy reverted to taxes- and payments-in-kind, he went on to supply rations (in lieu of money wages) to the civil servants also. When the corvée of men and materials was introduced in the fourth century (again as a result of the switch to payments in kind) he, logically, was in charge. He ran the imperial mail (the *cursus publicus*). He came to exercise a general jurisdiction over the provincial governors and could cashier them. He was in effect, a 'grand vizier'. It was logical for Diocletian to assign a praetorian prefect to each member of the Tetrarchy.

Constantine created the post of *magister militia* to command his new mobile field army. How this office came also to be the greatest fiscal agency in the empire happened like this. The office had long been provisioner to the armed forces, and when the currency collapsed in the third century the authorities resorted to collections-in and payments-out (to the armies) *in kind*. Such levies were called *indictiones* and Diocletian regularized the system. So, until Constantine stabilized the currency, most taxes were collected in kind and paid out again in the shape of *annonae* (rations) to the troops and the civil servants; as *capitus* (fodder) for the horses; as assigned men and materials for public works; and as raw materials for the government's arms factories. Since the praetorian prefect had always been the agency-in-post for distributing rations and fodder, he became responsible for what was, logically, only an extension of this function.

Taxes (*tributa*) had always been based on a land tax, to which Constantine added a *capitatio* or poll tax. The amount raised varied from year to year according to need in the following way. First of all the praetorian prefects calculated the global needs of their prefectures in terms of wheat, barley, raw materials, labour, and so forth. This exercise required the military commanders (*magistri militum* and *duces*) to send in returns of their ration-strength and their requirements in respect to craftsmen, labourers, and raw materials for any public works they were undertaking. These operations occupied a large number of highly specialized finance-clerks.[24]

The amount of goods and services calculated in this way represented what had to be raised in tax and by whom. Here a very ingenious theory was applied. By censuses, gradually extending over the whole empire, a cadaster was drawn up of the lands, the crops, and the population. Then, on the basis of estimated land-yields, a territorial area (often called a *iugum* but

---

[24] Jones, *The Later Roman Empire*, 70.

with different names in different places) was delimited on the principle that the extent of each and every *iugum* was determined so as to yield (very roughly) an identical amount of produce. In brief, *iuga* were 'areas of equal yield'. Apportionment then became (in principle) very simple. All the prefects' staff had to do was to divide the global amount they required by the total number of *iuga* (weighted so as also to provide the basis for the poll-tax assessment), and the result was the assessment for each and every *iugum* throughout the prefecture.[25]

But if the principle was simple, the practice was anything but. The collection of the taxes came to this. On 1 September each year the prefects' staff circulated the assessments down to the vicars and the *praesides*, who passed them on to the ultimate units of tax collection, that is, the cities which (we remember) incorporated all the surrounding countryside. The *praesides'* clerks in each province drew up demand notes for each individual taxpayer, which went to the city councils. These had elected boards of officials (*susceptores*) for each of the various levies—for wheat, wine, meat, and labour. These *susceptores* now collected the amounts due from land-owners (villagers appointed their own men to carry out the collection), and were then responsible for transporting them to the state warehouses. If the collectors failed to collect the full amount, the city councillors themselves (the decurions) had to make good the shortfall: and in fact the collectors were often so inefficient that the prefects sent their own agents to organize the levy of arrears by *compulsores* or *canonicarri*. The revenue collected by this elaborate machinery made up *nine-tenths or more* of the public revenue.

6. THE FUNCTIONS OF THE CENTRAL ADMINISTRATION: A SUMMARY

It will by now be obvious from the preceding that the central administration confined itself almost entirely to the care of the palace and the emperor's living-quarters; the armed forces; justice; and taxation. Roads were usually handled by the armies, while the essential services of civilized life—public buildings, schools, fire-watching, street-policing—were still the responsibility of the cities.

The rapid expansion of the bureaucracy attracted the critical attention of contemporaries. It corresponded to two developments in the empire. It represented, first of all, a gigantic effort to mobilize the entire society in a sustained war effort. The threat of military siege was never lifted, and what began in the third century as a set of shifts and expedients became a

[25] Ibid. 454.

regularized system in the fourth and fifth. Indeed, it appeared to the authorities to be even more necessary, and certainly it became more elaborate as the resources of the empire dwindled, although the threat required level funding at the least.

In the second place, it represents an unconscious response to the largely unremarked but in truth very extraordinary change in the social and political character of the empire. Under the Antonines this still retained the heterogeneity of its Republican beginnings. But by now, Romanization and Hellenization, the web of commerce, the fusion of civil law with the *ius gentium*, the inroads of the imperial lawcourts, the flux and reflux of religions: all these and much else were changing it into a sort of country-state rather than an empire in its primary sense. Caracalla's Edict of 212 which granted citizenship to all freemen was, at its least, the symbol of this change. N. P. Ensslin says of Diocletian that his reforms were designed to hold together, via the bureaucracy, 'the heterogeneous elements in an Empire that was of great territorial extent so *as to form a unified state*'.[26] The Western half of the empire was overrun before this transition was completed, but the bureaucratization we have signalled registers that such a transition was in process.

Indeed, as we have remarked before, it is now hard to see why we should call the empire an empire in its primary sense. There was no longer a single capital city, province, tribe, *ethnos*, sect, or any other segment in society that held *imperium* over the rest. Instead, this *oekumene* was overlaid and run by a stratum sharing the same imperial culture. This is what *Romanitas* now meant. To possess this culture was the necessary passport to an active role in society. Islamic culture—and Chinese—serve as parallels.

7. THE CIVIL SERVICE

As in Imperial China, the civil service consisted of two grades: the lower service was called the *militia*, and about its recruitment we know little. The posts of superior grade (governorships and heads of department) were styled *dignitates*, *honores*, or *administrationes*, and their holders received their appointment by the emperor's *codicil*.

With a few exceptions, higher posts were short-term appointments. They were gradated and each grade had its own honorific title. So, the praetorian prefects and the prefects of the two capital cities, along with the chief palatine officials, were the *illustres*, for example, while vicars and the rest of the proconsuls were *spectabiles*. The governors of provinces (*consulares* and

[26] *CAH*, xii. 390 (my italics).

praesides) were *clarissimi*. The lowest rank was that of *perfectissimus*. It was unusual for an individual to make a career by holding successive posts.

The aristocracy (who were effectively the only ones qualified) considered these posts as distinctions to be won, not public service to be given, and they competed fiercely for them. In the West, the numerous very rich members of the senatorial order were so well placed at the end of the fourth century that they monopolized all those high governing posts open to them: at Rome, in Italy, and as proconsuls of Africa and Sicily.[27] Their motive was not riches—for they were prodigiously wealthy—nor was it political influence (though they never scrupled to use this to make sure they held office in the area where their lands lay and took pains to see they benefited[28]) but *honour*—a status that befitted them. The fifth-century emperors shortened the term of office to satisfy the clamorous peer group by making sure of enough honours to go around.[29] Unsurprisingly, apart from the quintessential professional lawyers, none of these higher civil servants had any special qualifications.[30] But the *militia* were held by career officials who spent their lifetime in the service, in which promotion went strictly by seniority alone. Their low salaries were partially augmented by the fees which many of their services carried with them, as well as by 'tips' (*sportulae*); giving such tips was so ubiquitous and ineradicable that in the end it had to be officially recognized and regulated by an official tariff. As remarked earlier, how they were recruited we do not know, except that many came into the service on the basis of a recommendation (*suffragium*) which was later often sold to them for money.

Contemporaneous Han practices form a stark contrast to the Roman ones: their arrangements were still crude by later standards, but there was an effort to secure trustworthy recommendations, there were qualifying examinations, there was a review of performance to justify promotion, and the service was a life-career. In comparison, the Roman arrangements were perfunctory, sloppy, one might even say frivolous.

Though regarded as grotesquely large by such observers as Lactantius, the service was only a quarter the size of the Chinese (for roughly the same order of population). Jones estimates it as 30,000–40,000 persons, as compared with China's 130,285, but any comparison must bear in mind the obligatory service of the city officials in the Roman Empire and the civil functions of the army. Nor can we be sure that in counting established posts in the two services we are comparing like with like. For all that, it is quite

[27] J. Matthews, *Western Aristocracies and the Imperial Court*, AD *364–425* (Clarendon Press, Oxford, 1975). [28] Ibid.
[29] Jones, *The Later Roman Empire*, 355. (The principle of 'Buggins's Turn'.)
[30] Ibid. 388.

certain that headquarters staffs alone were more numerous in China than in Rome.

The quality of the Roman imperial civil service was very low. Action was terribly slow:

an ordinary law suit might take several years. A law issued in Milan might reach Rome in twelve days but delays of three weeks are known, and six week delays are also recorded. Navigation stopped in winter and laws issued in autumn normally only reached Africa in the following spring . . . Long delay came to be expected. A court official might absent himself from his duties for six months before penalties began to be applied. A year's absence was punished with the loss of ten years of seniority, and only after he had stayed away for more than four years could the official be dismissed from the service.[31]

8. THE ARMY

By the end of the fourth century the army had suffered a dramatic and historic change. Not only were its grand strategy, tactics, and command structure completely different: above all else, many of its best fighting troops and its top generals were *foreigners*. The Roman Empire was being defended against invading Huns and Germans by other Huns and Germans and, in the West, ineffectually at that. The Western imperial authorities had lost control of their armed forces, and their survival was only a matter of time.

Of the army's fighting performance we shall speak later, but here we are concerned with its size, structure, and composition. Diocletian had doubled the number of troops to some 450,000 (with auxiliaries), later rising to 600,000, but it was Constantine who effected the great turn in grand strategy. He thinned out the frontier troops (called *limitanei* or *riparii*) and stationed them in permanent locations whose function was simply to delay the enemy until a large mobile field army could come up and confront the enemy. This field army was the *comitatus* and consisted of cavalry *vexillationes*, and infantry elements called *auxilia*. In time the frontier legion (now consisting of only 1,000 men, not the traditional 5,500) became less and less effectual.

The command structure reflected this new strategy. The field army (or armies, for later emperors decided to have more than one) were commanded by *magistri militum*: one such force (the *palatini*) formed the emperor's own entourage. The frontier commanders, each charged with a sector of the

---

[31] Jones, *The Later Roman Empire*, 604–5.

front, were called *dux* (plural *duces* or *comes* 'sometimes translated—mis-leadingly—as 'count').

Severan emperors had long ago made it easier for troopers to obtain commissioned rank and this was now the regular practice. An outstanding soldier would be recommended for enrolment in the *protectores*, a corps of officer cadets. Civilians, however, also received commissions, which is how the *protectores* later became purely ornamental; for, as the corps was the avenue to commissioned rank, the young sons of high military officers and town councillors (decurions) began to secure easy postings; in short 'the law of inflated titles' was taking effect here, just as in the civil service.[32]

Diocletian's expansion of the army ran up against an acute shortage of manpower. Individual recruits were still to be had from the old recruiting grounds of Gaul, Illyria, and Thrace. Under the Antonines the bulk of recruits, other than these, had been the sons of legionaries who were following their father's profession; but these no longer sufficed and, though Diocletian decreed that they were legally obliged to serve, it seems that his edict was never systematically enforced. The authorities therefore introduced conscription. This had always been hated and feared. The population reacted with self-mutilations to make themselves unfit for service, or by deserting while being marched to camp. Moreover, the levy was not carried out as before, when the authorities hand-picked the men. Instead, they now used the tax census to assess lands for so many soldiers. Smallholders were formed into consortia to provide one recruit between them, while the great landlords provided a batch. Obviously they picked out the frailest or most disreputable types, and the quality and tone of the armies declined. At the same time, some taxpayers preferred to commute the military obligation to a money payment with which the authorities hired volunteers but, as will be seen, largely from foreigners.

But none of these modes of recruitment keep pace with the wastage, and the cruellest comment on the empire at this stage is that most of this shortfall was self-inflicted. For the rival war-lords (the would-be emperors) did not hesitate to pit their picked troops against one another, and in these battles the flower of the armies perished. Thousands and thousands of Maxentius' forces were killed when Constantine defeated him at Turin (312), and even more and on both sides in the murderous fight at Rome's Milvian Bridge. Worse still was the campaign of 323 when Constantine was pitted against Licinius in the East: at Adrianople 34,000 soldiers died, and at Chrysopolis only 30,000 of Licinius' 130,000 men escaped.[33] Mursa (351) is

---

[32] Jones, *Decline of the Ancient World*, 225, 227.
[33] J. Burckhardt, *The Age of Constantine the Great*, trans. M. Hadas (first published 1880; 2nd edn., University of California Press, Los Angeles, 1949; paperback edn., Pantheon, London, 1983), 281, 282.

said to have been the bloodiest battle of the entire century: 30,000 soldiers perished on the one side and 24,000 on the other. And while these wars were pursuing their self-destructive course, the enemy was not always idle, inflicting still more losses. The most calamitous of these was the Goths' victory over Valens at Adrianople in 378. The shattered East Roman field army lost 40,000 men—two-thirds of its strength! But if a *notitia dignitatum* is to be believed, the armies in the West were still quite large in the 410s and 420s.

The government made good the losses as fast as it could by bringing *limitanei* back from the frontiers, a device that simply made the field troops inferior and also exposed the frontier. But there was another source of reinforcements in such barbarian tribesmen as were, for one reason or another, on good terms with the empire. This expedient was only too inviting to pursue because, in some measure or other, it was of long standing. Among other expedients, it had been fixed policy to conclude treaties with chieftains outside the *limes*, under which they undertook to respect a province and provide toops to defend it when called upon. These were the *foederati*—the 'federates'. They supplemented the regular units, but became proportionally more important as time went by. After 450 they seem to have become the only troops to matter, though regulars may have survived—in garrisons, for instance. The field army had come to be largely made up, not simply of German recruits, but of *foederati* who were now fighting *not* under Roman commanders and *not* according to Roman drill and discipline, but in their own way and under their own chieftains and kings. And the supreme commanders-in-chief were such men—all Germans—as Bauto, Arbogast, Stilicho. In sum, in a relatively brief time, not more perhaps than a half-century, while the 'Roman' units were being recruited from the least Romanized dregs of the population, the imperial armies were also absorbing bigger and bigger intakes of uncouth and, above all, *non-Roman* tribesmen. One might have thought that in this way the imperial army ceased to fulfil what was arguably its most important historical function: Romanization.[34] Paradoxically, it continued to Romanize more than ever, and this was because the *foederati* learnt Latin and became Christians. What their military service did not inculcate in them was the sense of Roman nationhood and patriotism.

In the event, the armies could not maintain the frontiers. As a diplomatic reply to the barbarian pressure, the government agreed to settle large groups of them inside the empire: for instance, Salian Franks in north-eastern Gaul in 358 and the Visigothic tribes in Moesia and Thrace in 382. These aliens

---

[34] See pp. 534, 552 above.

settled under their own chiefs and formed barbarian enclaves. There were lots of precedents, true; but in the last quarter of the fourth century such intakes were too frequent, too numerous, and too close-knit for the empire to assimilate and Romanize. Many of the frontier provinces had already been infiltrated by the tribesmen before the fatal New Year's Night of 406 when the vast host of Suebi, Vandals, and Alans crossed the frozen Rhine and burst into Gaul. The frontier had been pierced, and thenceforward the infiltration and subsequent dismemberment of the provinces, though piecemeal, continued unremittingly. It took nearly three-quarters of a century for the Western half of the empire to crumble, but crumble it slowly did, and then disintegrated.

9. SERVICES AND PERFORMANCE

When Marcus Aurelius died, Dio Cassius wrote 'our history now plunges from a kingdom of gold to one of iron and rust'.[35] Dio was premature— the baths of Caracalla and of Diocletian show what immense resources the empire could still command. It is the century after Diocletian, the period of so-called 'Imperial Recovery', that is really 'the age of iron and rust'. In that century, human and natural resources dwindled while the military threat grew. The state tried to match the former to the latter by regulating areas hitherto left to individual and local enterprise, and the balance tipped increasingly towards the central government. It failed: but its failures only generated still more regulation of the same kind, and so the balance tipped again. In this way the state sank into a spiral of extraction, diminished resources, increased extraction, increasingly diminished resources, and so on. All this was in order to maintain the armed forces, which in the Western half of the empire ultimately failed to justify the huge drain, so that when the barbarians pierced the frontiers they entered a polity in terminal decline: remote puppet emperors, undisciplined armies, corrupt administration, chaotic courts, an impoverished economy, and a strait-jacketed society.

The elements in this tragedy—the army, administrators, cities, cultivators—all reacted on one another, sometimes as cause, sometimes as effect. It is necessary to discuss them separately before trying to bring them all together again, at the close of this chapter.

[35] Quoted in Lewis and Reinhold, *Roman Civilization*, ii. 419.

9.1. *Army: Strategy, Morale, and Cost*

The Roman army was by far the greatest and most sophisticated fighting force in the West until modern times.[36] Its professional command structure, administration, quartermaster arrangements, and logistical infrastructure were equally unsurpassed, and it is no accident that a great sixteenth-century European commander, Maurice of Nassau, should have carried everywhere the works of the Roman military commentator Vegetius. In the world of that day only the Han armies could compare with it in battle drill, armament, logistical support, and administrative arrangements.

Diocletian's expansion of the army and Constantine's Grand Strategy of *limitanei* as trip-wire troops and the *comitatus* as the mobile strike force, plus the administrative division of the empire so that it faced its enemies to East and West simultaneously, did succeed in holding the frontiers until the Eastern army's disaster at Adrianople (378). But was it really an improvement on, say, Diocletian's elastic defence at the frontiers? It involved thinning and diluting the *limitanei* on the assumption that the mobile *comitatus* could move laterally along the frontier to confront the enemy wherever he was breaking through. This corresponds to some intuited theory of the economy and superiority of 'fighting on internal lines'. The theory would be valid for Rome if the Rhine–Danube line had had a railway running its full length. As it was, the *comitatus* had to march along it on foot at 15 miles per day, while the enemy would have broken through into open, undefended country. Once the *comitatus* caught up with them it could and did (except at Adrianople) inflict sanguinary defeat, but in the meantime the countryside was ravaged, ransacked, and burnt, as Ammianus so vividly describes in his account of Julian's campaign in Gaul. So, everything depended on the speed with which the *comitatus* could engage the enemy. Here the Eastern half of the empire held a decisive geographical advantage over the Western, whose frontier was three times as long. Furthermore, once the Rhine–Danube line was breached the West had no second line of defence, whereas the Eastern Empire could, and for another eight centuries did, safely retire behind the impregnable walls of Constantinople.[37] By contrast, in the West, if forces were concentrated to defend Italy and Rome the enemy could press on in Gaul; and that is precisely what happened in 406/7. In the end, therefore, the Grand Strategy failed to hold the West. But is the comparison with Diocletian's Grand Strategy to

---

[36] Not perhaps till the later 18th cent. do European armies' logistics bear comparison; and they were much, much smaller.   [37] See Bk. III, Ch. 1, 'The Byzantine Empire'.

the point? Did Constantine and his successors have any alternative but the course they adopted?

Usurpations were particularly likely in exposed frontier provinces. Domestically, the armies were still as menacing and troublesome to their emperors, their commanders, and their own countrymen as they had been under the Principate, perhaps more so; it is impossible to judge.[38] But there is graphic evidence that they were unruly, mutinous, and predatory; they stole, looted, and brawled; they neglected their arms and equipment.[39] They resisted discipline. This is why they murdered the Emperor Probus.[40] 'Always savage and bitter towards the civilian', says Ammianus.[41] They mutinied. Julian's hungry troops insulted him as 'Asiatic', 'liar', and 'fool'.[42] They were fickle, as Valentinian found when, having just been acclaimed emperor, he faced his angry soldiers.[43] They were greedy for donatives and this was one potent reason for their making and then unmaking an emperor, or for following one claimant against another.

They also cost a lot of money. Though soldiers' pay was in real terms only two-thirds of its value at the beginning of the third century, the army's paper strength was about double its previous size. Taking this together with the upkeep of some 30,000 civil servants, Jones calculated that the *minimum* increase in taxation (over the level of the early empire) required for these two items alone was 40 per cent. However, all these figures are too high. In calculating the army's size Jones made assumptions about the size of various formations which are certainly too large; hence his total is too large. His estimates of taxation rest on very few documents, and again are almost certainly too large.[44] Nevertheless, the tax base was still almost wholly agricultural; the technology had not significantly improved; and its incidence per capita was greater because, in the West at any rate, less land was being cultivated.

9.2. *The Economy, Taxes,—and Regimentation*

In some areas of the Western Empire the cultivated area shrank by some 10–15 per cent,[45] and the population also declined, possibly because poor peasants could not afford to maintain so many children. Their poverty finds graphic expression in their habit of flocking into the towns in time of famine in the hope of receiving government food supplies.[46] The decay of

---

[38] Jones, *The Later Roman Empire*, 1036.
[39] *Historia Augusta*, quoted in Lewis and Reinhold, *Roman Civilization*, ii. 3.
[40] Ibid. 426.   [41] Ammianus Marcellinus, *Rerum Gestarum Historia*, XIV. x. 4.
[42] Ibid., XVIII. ix. 3, 4.   [43] Ibid., XXVI. 2.
[44] Jones, *Later Roman Empire*, 208–9.   [45] Ibid. 1039.   [46] Ibid. 1043–4.

monumental building in the towns, and indeed their contraction, conforms to this impression of economic blight. The invasion, civil wars, and great epidemics which afflicted the empire contributed to this. But probably the chief reason was over-taxation.

Faced with the need to increase per-capita revenue, governments have historically reacted by tightening the methods of collection, expanding the tax base, and of course, by increasing taxes. The imperial authorities were no exception. But the cumulative effect was to constrict and even strangle liberties enjoyed under the Antonines, and induce institutional sclerosis.

The first area affected was that of tax-collection, and here the prime targets were the cities. The decurions who made up their councils had always been responsible for getting the taxes collected, but by Diocletian's day they were collectively liable for any shortfall. The once high-priced property qualification for decurion had been progressively lowered and in some cities might be a trivial fifteen acres of land. Blenching at the financial consequences of shortfalls in the tax quota, these decurions began to refuse to stand for office, to which the government responded by making it obligatory. The son must fill his father's vacancy and no decurion might move away or take up an exempting profession (including the army) or even sell up his lands! As these measures proved ineffective emperors closed the (exempting) civil service to them and limited the new and burgeoning drone-class (also exempt) of Christian clergymen. Thus, by the end the decurions were a hereditary caste, forbidden to leave their localities without express permission,[47] although some managed to do so with the connivance of their colleagues.

The decurions, for their part, naturally enough connived at their colleagues' (susceptores) extortionate and oppressive methods providing they brought in the required quota. The tale of deceit, illegality, and extortion is, surely, by now wearisomely familiar. The susceptores prevaricated when asked for receipts; issued invalid ones; used false weights; over-assessed; demanded receipts that had been lost—and woe betide the defaulter: 'imprisonment, lashes of leaded whips, weights' and other tortures.[48]

In the treatment of the city councils we can discern the principles underlying all corporatism: formally free individuals are made collectively responsible for delivering goods and services. In China, as we have seen, collective responsibility had been the basic feature of social and political responsibility from prehistoric times.[49] The Late Roman Empire's movement from

---

[47] See excerpts from the Theodosian Code, quoted, Lewis and Reinhold, Roman Civilization, ii. 481. (The enactments mentioned there, it must be noted, were already in force before the Code.) See the long discussion of this matter in Jones, Later Roman Empire, 737 ff.

[48] Theodosian Code quoted Lewis and Reinhold, Roman Civilization, ii. 427.

[49] See p. 455 above.

individual responsibility to corporatism is yet another of the ways in which its government was converging on that of the Han.[50] The second principle of corporatism, which combined very readily with the former, was that of *inherited obligation*: the corporations were made self-perpetuating by compelling sons to follow in their father's occupations. We have already noted the application to the decurionate, and Diocletian's decree that the sons of serving soldiers and veterans must also become soldiers.[51] This principle was increasingly applied to other occupations.

The Roman state had, for a long time, operated certain economic enterprises that were important for the army or for taxes, notably the mint, the mines, and the armament factories, but most trades were organized into traditional guilds (*collegia*) duly authorized by the government. In the general economic decline the authorities, in order to guarantee the survival of essential trades and professions, legislated to forbid their members and their sons from quitting.[52] Because the food supply of Rome was absolutely critical to the empire—as it had been from as far back as the Republic—Constantine turned the *navicularii*, the masters of the grain-ships that took corn to Rome, into a hereditary caste too, while exempting this from all other public duties. In brief, whole groups were, along with their children, legally bound to their vocation and the principle was even extended to fill the lower ranks of the civil service.

One way to raise more money was to improve the tax *base*, and again the corporate-cum-hereditary principles were applied. The problem here was identical with one that dogged successive Chinese dynasties till early modern times. It was that in both countries the great bulk of revenue came from the tax on *land*, not on individuals as such. Therefore, to maintain the revenue it was essential to keep individuals cultivating their land.[53] Already in the third century independent peasants, caught by bad harvests, conscription, the devastations of invaders, the plundering of bandits, and the extortions of the imperial armies were fleeing the land altogether or becoming tenants of neighbouring landlords. So, whereas mass chattel slavery had declined, in the Western Empire (mostly) the colonate system took its place. The *colonus* was, to be brief, a tied tenant. As time went by he more and more approximated to the condition of a serf. He would, usually, be working in a villa akin to a Latin-American hacienda, that is, an enclosed estate worked by peons on a (usually) half–half basis,

---

[50] See p. 503 above.   [51] See p. 587 above.

[52] This measure, however, only applied in the Western Empire.

[53] Chinese dynasties took measures to resettle migrant and/or landless labourers on the land, by all manner of expedients. For *Chinese* ways of tackling the problem see Bk. II, Chs. 5 and 6 above, and Bk. III, Chs. 3 and 4 below.

where the *estanciero* (the *potens* in Late Rome) provided all their requirements while isolating them from the authorities by acting as intermediary and, if necessary, as protector.

When landlords came to argue that they could not keep their estates going without a guaranteed supply of labour (and no farming meant no taxes!), Diocletian enacted that tenant-farmers must remain where they were registered at the time of the census, and by Constantine's day not only they but their children were permanently attached to that place. They had become *adscripticii glebae*, and in 332 a law even allowed landowners to chain up tenants to prevent them absconding. Yet how far these laws were effective is a different matter. In the absence of a detective police, it must have been hard to prove that an individual was an escaped *colonus*, especially since other landlords would have been anxious to retain any escaped *colonus* who came to them—and all this in the absence of identity-papers.

Another expedient for increasing the revenue was to raise the general level of taxation. Whereas in Antonine times the tax burden was light, it was now almost insupportable. And this is to reckon without the *munera*, the obligations to supply goods and services. It had been customary to assist the troops with boats, carts, and beasts of burden, but now the population had to maintain the roads and bridges, grind corn and bake bread for the soldiers, burn lime and provide timber for public works, and so forth. In addition, they owed military service. In brief, the non-exempt *humiliores* class of the population were subject to corvée. Here was another respect in which the practice of the Late Empire was converging on that of China.

9.3. *Enforcement and Evasion*

Yet the more the goverment tried to regulate, the harder it was to enforce the regulation. The reaction to raging inflation in every military regime in today's world is practically the same. Like these, Diocletian issued an edict (301) which fixed maximum prices and wages for the entire empire, under pain of death or exile.[54] It was a dead letter.

The many other regulatory measures described above were rarely if ever as unsuccessful as Diocletian's edict on prices, but neither were they enforced everywhere or to the full. Identical or similar laws had to be repeated over and over, and social and occupational mobility remained considerable despite the restrictions. There were both inherent and factitious reasons for this. All criminal charges had to be laid by private individuals, there were

[54] See excerpts from its extensive text in Lewis and Reinhold, *Roman Civilization*, ii. 463–73.

no detective police, there were no identity-cards, and the quality of administration was poor. Standards had fallen since the Principate. The hyper-
inflation of the third century cut governors' salaries drastically, as it also did
civil servants'. A governorship was regarded as a financial prize, so that
candidates paid money to buy the *suffragia* of the ministers close to the
emperor. And citizens paid bigger *sportulae* to expedite their legal suits. Of
course, as we have already noted, such practices had been usual in the past.
What was new, perhaps, was that with the growth of officialdom appointments had become more impersonal and more bureaucratic and therefore
money became that much more important. Tighter administration meant
more opportunities for extortion by officials from members of the public
who needed the officials' consent for whatever they wished to do.

There were other and more adventitious reasons for the patchiness and
incompleteness of law-enforcement. There is a passage in Gibbon where the
historian lists certain 'favourable circumstances which tended to alleviate
the misery' of Constantine's subjects. One was that 'the sage principles of
Roman jurisprudence preserved a sense of order and equity unknown to the
despotic governments of the East'.[55] Up to a point this is true. It is very
striking indeed, for instance, that the élite of the Roman bureaucracy, truly
well trained and equipped for their tasks, were lawyers. (In the Eastern
Empire, under Justinian, the qualification for entering the service was a legal
training which demanded that the candidate should be able to recite the
Code by heart.)[56] But though the 'sage principles' of jurisprudence were still
in evidence, they were at this particular time in chaotic disarray. Laws and
decrees overlapped and contradicted one another, and likewise the opinions
of the jurisconsults on whose interpretation counsel were wont to rely when
pleading a case. (Such lawyers might confound the court by citing as
authority the work of a jurisconsult so obscure that the judge had never
heard of him.) Furthermore, the growth of regulatory agencies had spawned
a large number of special tribunals.[57] Consequently there were frequent
conflicts of jurisdiction.

The higher courts were excessively slow, the judges were not selected for
their knowledge of the law, their terms of office were brief, and they were
both corruptible and vulnerable to pressure and intimidation. Above all, the
costs—particularly in the supreme court—were prohibitive, for court fees,
counsels' fees, and the expense of long journeys to and from the court were
all extremely high. In inferior courts opponents could bribe and intimidate

---

[55] Gibbon, *Decline and Fall*, ch. 17.   [56] See pp. 649–50 below.
[57] Jolowicz and Nicholas, *Historical Introduction*, 448.

the judges or wear out the plaintiff by frequent appeals, and in these courts too the expenses were very heavy.[58]

In any case, we have already observed that the 'sage principles of Roman jurisprudence' hardly applied to the criminal law, and this was much more important for law-enforcement than civil law. Criminal law was inefficient, unequal, and increasingly brutal. The lower classes (*humiliores*) were as subject to beating and torture (from which Roman citizens were no longer exempt) as they were in Han China, and again (unlike *honestiores*) they were liable to corporal and capital punishments. The latter included degrading and disgraceful forms of punishment such as burning alive or being thrown to the lions. In the fourth and early fifth centuries, capital crimes were multiplied and terrible punishments devised, like mutilating the limbs or gouging out the eyes of convicted criminals. The arrested suspect faced a miserable time. He was cast into prison, where he would starve unless he had relations or friends to feed him. He would have to wait there for months before the governors found time to hear his case, and when this finally came up the court took little care to sift the evidence. When Constantine enacted that judges might not pass a capital sentence unless the witnesses were unanimous and the prisoner confessed, the courts responded by torturing not only the prisoner to get his confession but the witnesses too, so as to secure the concordant evidence![59]

The increasing barbarity of the punishments is not evidence of the effectiveness with which the regulating laws were pursued but the reverse. It was intended to strike terror. It was also a response to evasion. Flight and change of identity was one avenue of escape. Banditry was another. Banditry had always existed, but by the middle of the fourth century it was so extensive in central and south Italy that nobody was permitted to ride horses.[60] There are other evidences of the breakdown of order and security, and indeed of civilized living: parents sold off their children in times of famine, tombs were plundered for their costly marble, the population was once more allowed to bear arms, so that they could fight off brigands. A law of 406 classed deserters with *latrones* (robbers, brigands); provincials were granted full powers to exercise 'public judgement on them' and the praetorian prefects were authorized to execute them.[61] The great post-roads and their *stationes* were falling into disrepair and the animals went uncared for.

The economist Hirschman made a highly original study of competition between firms, which is also applicable to politics in the Late Empire. He

---

[58] Jolowicz and Nicholas, *Historical Introduction*, 432.
[59] Jones, *Later Roman Empire*, 194–5.
[60] S. Dill, *Roman Society in the Last Century of the Western Empire* (Macmillan, London, 1898), 201.
[61] Ibid. 200–1.

analysed the likelihood of consumers staying with a firm's product into the play of three elements. The consumer might *voice* his dissatisfaction with the firm, expecting it to respond. Or he might switch (*exit*) to another firm. Or, despite his dissatisfaction, he might stay with the product out of *loyalty*. Hence the three elements, Exit, Voice, Loyalty.[62]

In the Principate, apart from the Roman plebs, the common people had no recognized channel for 'voice'. But by contrast, in their individual capacity, the richest members of the senatorial order became more influential than ever before—especially at the end of the fourth century and in the fifth—in the Western half of the empire,[63] and those who chose to live in Italy frequented the imperial court. The order, then, glowed in wealth and pride. This class ruled the countryside as *potentes*. In these provinces, their influence with the governors and the courts enabled them to escape taxation, while in Italy and Gaul (as we have observed) they came, in the fifth and last century of the Western Empire, to monopolize the top ministerial positions and act on the imperial court. Their weakness was that they did not command a significant number of armed followers. Nevertheless, while the political *voice* of all other social classes diminished or disappeared, that of the landlord senatorial class became paramount.

The silenced social classes' alternatives were either *exit* or *disloyalty*. 'Exit' in the form of actually leaving the empire was not a serious option. But 'exit' in the sense of 'internal exit'[64] or opting out, *was*. The harassed decurions tried to enter the senatorial order if they were wealthy enough since this was exempt from *munera*. This practice was repeatedly forbidden in the fifth century, and some decurions already in public service were sent back to their cities and their council seats. The poorer tried to move sideways or to a lower status: into the army, as we have seen, or into the Church, which provided a rich haven since the clergy were exempt from decurial duties and charges.[65] The very poorest, with little but smallholdings, tried to become tenants of the great landlords. Cumulatively, the 'exit' of the decurions must have been quite considerable for the Theodosian Code (438) contains no less than 192 enactments 'concerning Decurions'.

The common people 'opted out' in the ways already described: by deserting the army or by turning brigand or, more widespread and far more significant, by becoming the tenant of the local *potens*. Not many

[62] A. O. Hirschman, *Exit, Voice, and Loyalty: Responses to Decline in Firms, Organizations and State* (Harvard UP, Cambridge, Mass. and London, 1970).

[63] This is the half we are particularly concerned with here, as the fate of the Eastern half will be taken up later, in the chapter on the Byzantine Empire.

[64] S. E. Finer, 'State Building, Boundaries and Border Controls', *Social Science Information*, 13 (415), (1974), 79–126.

[65] Jones, *Later Roman Empire*, 925–7.

were ordained into the priesthood, but the Church offered another route of escape—monasticism.

'Voice' being denied and 'exit' harassed and partially contained, the only alternative left was disloyalty. In context, this meant some kind of revolt, and here lies a great mystery: why were peasant revolts endemic in Chinese history but virtually non-existent in the Roman Empire? Sainte Croix[66] has collected together what must be the most comprehensive set of references to popular unrest and uprisings yet made, and it must surely be nearly if not completely exhaustive. Most of the evidence, however, relates to brigandage and bandit-gangs, like the revolt of Maternus in Spain (as early as 186). Maternus persuaded some of his fellow soldiers to desert with him and was joined by more and more in similar plight. They finally fought their way into Italy, apparently with the intention of killing the Emperor Commodus and, it seems, making Maternus emperor instead.[67] This reads like a Roman version of the Chinese revolt against the successor to Shih Huang-ti.[68] Its evolution conforms exactly to the pattern of bandit-led rural uprisings (emphatically *not* of peasant-farmers, but of expropriated ex-farmers and landless labourers) which occurred time and time again in China.[69] So too does the limited political objective: to set up a good emperor in place of the existing one, not to fashion a new social order.

The most serious and protracted popular rebellion in the Western Empire (assuming the Donatist uprising in Africa to be primarily sectarian) was that of the Bacaudae in the area between the Loire and the Seine.[70] The first rising occurred in 286, and was suppressed. Another and endemic set of uprisings began in 407 and went on till mid-century, as did similar ones in Spain, but there is no reason to suppose continuous activity in between 286 and 407. In fact, it seems most unlikely. The Bacaudae were cultivators in revolt against the landlords and aimed at seceding from the empire. Apart from that and their takeover of the *latifundia*, nothing is known of their social programme.

Only these Bacaudae could be rated as a large-scale *peasant* uprising in the Roman Empire (as opposed to banditry). Why so few and so localized compared with China, where they spread far and wide, took on the imperial armies in pitched battles, and penetrated and sacked the capital itself? It could not be because the Roman security forces were more effective: since

---

[66] de Sainte Croix, *Class Struggle*.

[67] E. A. Thompson, 'Peasant Revolts in Late Roman Gaul and Spain', in Finley (ed.), *Studies in Ancient Society*, 306–8.   [68] See Bk. II, Ch. 6, above.

[69] See Eberhard, *Conquerors and Rulers*.

[70] J. Drinkwater, 'Patronage in Ancient Gaul and the Problem of the Bacaudae' in A. M. Wallace-Hadrill (ed.), *Patronage in Ancient Society* (1989), 189–203.

they failed to suppress the Bacaudae, *a fortiori* how would they have fared against empire-wide rebellion? The explanation can only be that the population had less reason for discontent or else less motivation to act upon it. This brings us back to the point where we commenced this inquiry, the issue of *loyalty*. The impression formed by contemporaries and modern scholars alike is that while there was some co-operation with the barbarian invaders, the mass of the empire's population felt neither disloyalty to the empire, nor loyalty either. They were simply passive. The empire did not embody any ideal: its population saw it, simply, as the natural order. It had 'always been there', and they continued to believe, even among all the barbarian invasions, that it always would be. Furthermore, for some 400 years they had been given no military training of even the most primitive kind and had been taught instead to leave their defence to the soldiers. Finally, they had also been told to leave their concerns to the authorities and betters. They had no part to play except to do what they were told. In short, systematically and over centuries, the common people had been militarily, patriotically, and politically *neutered*.

10. CONCLUSION

The fourth century—the age from Diocletian to Theodosius I—is still the age of soldier-emperors, still the age of the empire one and indivisible. It is important not to anticipate the religious supineness of the Western emperors in the next century.

All explanation of government in this age begins with and returns to the armies. It was they who made the emperors and unmade them. They kept the frontier and sustained order in the interior. But they necessitated a fiscal burden so great that it not only spawned a huge civil bureaucracy but led to the suppression of free movement and occupation, a huge rise in taxation, and the imposition of the corvée on the lower class. All this was ruled over by an autocrat whom no sector of the population could control. Government's central objective was to maintain the army. This was what led it to centralize and to regulate cities, lives, and occupations. In trying, it outran its administrative capabilities and overstretched its exactions from a primitive agricultural economy. The Antonine balance was upset and tilted further and further away from city and individual autonomy towards the authority of the central bureaucracy.

Time-scale, distance, the untrained and amateurish quality of its administrators, let alone their greed and insufficient numbers, all conspired to thwart its efforts. Its subjects did not revolt and could not deter. But they could and did contrive to escape. They found loopholes and contrived boltholes. The administrators' tight machinery was discovered to be full of vents and exhaust-pipes.

It did not satisfy, but it managed. 'Though the collection [of taxes] was often slow and incomplete and arrears had periodically to be written off, the bulk of the revenue came in, recruits were levied and the armies were fed and clothed and armed and paid. Order was on the whole maintained and judgements of the courts were executed. Overt defiance of the government was rare and was usually repressed without difficulty if the government acted firmly.'[71] So, after the calamities of the third century, the empire not only survived but revived.

But it harboured terrible and potentially lethal political weaknesses. The worst was that the armies, by reason of their nature and relationship to the civil power, were emperor-makers. But there were many armies proclaiming rival emperors and they bled each other white. By the century's end they were not numerous or skilled enough to keep the frontiers and they were increasingly being recruited from the barbarians. A gap opened between them and the last—and vigorous—custodians of *Romanitas*, which in the West was the revivified senatorial order of opulent landowners, four times as wealthy as the wealthiest under the late Republic.

Herein lay the second weakness. This order did not care for soldiers or soldier-emperors. Historically, it never had. The senatorial nobility of the late empire was completely civilian. The demilitarization of the Roman senatorial class, indeed of the whole Romanized urban educated upper class, was a gradual development of the imperial period completed at the begin-ning of the fourth century. Subsequently these people neither served in the army as officers nor commanded armies as generals. The third weakness was the positive discouragement of all popular involvement in the concerns of government, followed by the destruction of the decurial (town-councillor) class which had acted as the central government's watchdogs and lapdogs throughout the provinces.

In the fourth century the weaknesses were concealed because the emper-ors were still soldier-emperors and the pressure on the frontiers had relaxed. The empire of that day still stood secure. It was no longer the Antonine polity. Instead, in many concurrent ways, it had approached the contours of the empire of the Han. Its ruler was remote, sacral, and absolute. He was served by a large and complicated bureaucracy. The extremities had become mere extensions, branches of the central body. They were ordered into a rational hierarchy of units and subunits. Society was graded into a status hierarchy, mobility and movement were purportedly frozen.

[71] Jones, *The Roman Economy*, 406.

Those three political weaknesses became more apparent in the next, the fifth century, and in the West they proved lethal. Though one can exaggerate the personal responsibility of emperors for the slow collapse, too many of them were no longer war-leaders chosen by the knock-out competition of civil war but pacifistic and pious Christians, young and destined to be the puppets of the foreigners who commanded their foreign troops. (Among the warlike exceptions are the emperors Majorian and Anthemius, both military commanders.) The Roman senatorials of the West took control of the civil power. Out of avaricious self-calculation they never helped to provide Roman recruits for the armies from their estates. This was by unenlightened self-interest. In this way the highest authorities of the Western Roman Empire had relinquished the military power to only half-Romanized barbarian mercenaries and, when these failed to hold the frontiers, the long habituation of the common people to passive obedience left the empire naked to its enemies.

11. AN ASSESSMENT OF THE ROMAN CONTRIBUTION

Polyglot empires had existed before Rome and so had empires studded with autonomous cities, such as the Seleucid. In stumbling from the bankrupt republican form of central government to the Principate and finally to autocracy, Rome was treading a well-worn and easy path. For, as this history of government demonstrates, autocracy is the rule, not the exception. Nor did the Romans invent the notion of a salaried professional bureaucracy: they stumbled into this in their own way, but in any case, as we have seen, the bureaucracy is the very oldest of all governmental devices: the first and most salient feature in the Sumerian city-states and the concomitant of the Pharaonic rule in Egypt. In any case, their administrative techniques slowly foundered in the barbarized German kingdoms of the West and proved less durable than the physical skeleton of their empire—its city foundations like Cologne, Trier, Saragossa, Paris, Lyons, Milan, and the like, and its roads which continued to serve as Western Europe's major highways till modern times. These themselves were far less durable and pervasive than the *lingue populare*, derived from Latin, which survived the German settlement throughout the West (except in Britain) and even—amazingly—in Romania which (as Dacia) had been occupied for only 165 years.

But in other and most important respects Rome made massive original contributions of incalculable importance. The first relates to the very nature of that empire. Like the Persian, it contained a variety of peoples, religions and languages, and was ruled on the comparatively naïve basis of the central government entrusting full military and civil power to its plenipotentiary governors on the post. This was not new: it recalls the Persian satraps. But in two other ways its government was indeed highly original. In the first place, it buttressed itself by—one might almost say it founded its central rule upon—an empire-wide network of local oligarchs, whom it progressively incorporated into the apparatus of imperial government itself. It is an early form of 'consocial' state. States called by this name contain ethnic and/or religious communities which have few relationships with one another, but live peacefully side by side and feel they have their share in the government *via* their own communal leaderships, which strike bargains with the other leaderships, and with them form a central policy-making body.[72] From first to last, from *urbs* to *orbis*, from Italian city-state to world-empire, Rome integrated her *allies* and *federates*, or her *provinces* and *civitates* along these identical lines. She never developed the notion of *representation*, indeed, we never find the barest hint of this concept: that was, paradoxically enough, to be discovered by her barbarian and homespun successors in the West of Europe. Instead, she created and sustained a ruling stratum throughout the empire which took no account of race, nation, language, colour, religion, or culture, but looked only to wealth and local influence.

The second originality of the Roman Empire is its transcendence of the narrowly specific meaning of 'Empire'. At the outset there was the ruling *city*; then the ruling *province* (Italy). From Hadrian's day, Italy began to lose its privileges, a process completed by Diocletian: when every freeman was a citizen (since 212) and no place, province, or people was politically superior to the rest. The empire is so-called only because it is the Roman *imperium*, that is, the Roman sphere of power, or (by the same token) because the autocrat who rules it is called an *imperator*. The common people were in fact beginning to call it *Romania*, and themselves, Romans.

Associated with these peculiarities of the empire is the second of the Roman 'inventions'—the first elaboration of the concept of what subsequently, from the sixteenth century, has been called 'the state'. (It is a word more readily understood on the Continent of Europe and its ex-dependencies than in Britain, the United States, and the British Commonwealth, and this is not surprising since the former are the countries that live by the ex-Roman civil law.) I mean that the Romans evolved, and their constitutional development embodied, the idea of political authority as something abstract and not personal. In the Greek city-states authority was tangible, it was the citizenry: as such it fused the political and the adminstrative and was personalized. In the other great state-form, the empires, authority was magical and mysterious and incarnated in the man who exercised it, who

---

[72] Cf. A. Lijphart, *Democracy in Plural Societies* (Yale UP, Ithaca, Conn., 1977).

was of a different essence than his subjects. Political authority was personal to him and often led to the theoretical claim to own his subjects, their lands, and their chattels. The Romans, however, were the first to conceive of a *res publica*, a nexus of goods, activities, and institutions which belonged *at large*. They conceived of political authority as something abstracted from the person exercising it, and consequently unaffected by changes in the regime or in the incumbents of office. It was not embodied in the city-institutions of Rome. It floated free, extended to the empire. It implied a distinction between the political and the administrative. It was plastic; it was able to accommodate to the accretion of highly diverse territories and their different kinds of constitution. Authority, in short, was not the person who exercised it, nor the form of the regime in which he did so. The *res publica* survived changes of incumbents and regime alike, an abstract, impersonal attribute of the collectivity. This notion was to founder in the Dark Ages and the feudal period and not to resurface again until after the kingship had reasserted itself in the sixteenth century.

The third innovation is one we have dealt with on more than one previous occasion—the ubiquity of law in both the public and the private sector. Cities had their laws, provinces their statutes, the empire had its *constitutiones*. Roman citizens were litigious, lawsuits public spectacles, and the lawyers and advocates a specialized profession. The criminal law, we have seen, gave governors and judges enormous discretion, which was at its most arbitrary in cases of threats to the ruling and social order; but for all that, a suit could now only be initiated on a specific charge. Much criminal and public law might well be defective: but the empire and the emperor were, nevertheless, law-bound.

And this leads us to the fourth innovation—the nature of this law, notably the civil, or private sector of law. It was all to disappear in the West with the barbarian invaders and not to be revived till the Middle Ages, but it was our current modern paradigm of 'law' that was here invented. Roman law differs from all previous types and codes in three ways. First, there is nothing superhuman either in its sources, sanctions, or application to particular cases. It exists in a purely human dimension. Next, it is *rational*. A code of law can be—and all up to this time were—a mere string of individual judicial decisions. The Roman law, when finally elaborated, formed a complete system, derived by formal and logical reasoning; not, for example, from subjective irruptions into morality. It is a set of general principles, plus a juridical technique for applying these to concrete cases in all their singularity. Finally, it is a set of mutually coherent categories. All this was to go under in the West as the barbarian kingdoms implanted themselves; but it did more than merely survive in the East—in Byzantium—for it was there that Justinian brought it all together in his Codes and these formed the basis of the 'reception' of Roman Law in the Middle Ages and the Renaissance period in Western Europe. It was adopted in different stages—the twelfth- and thirteenth-century glossators, the four-teenth- and fifteenth-century commentators—until its general 'Reception' throughout most of Western and Middle Europe in the sixteenth and seventeenth centuries.[73]

We have already dwelt on some of the most significant areas of private law—private property and possession, juridical personality and contract and obligation—elaborated here in a way unmatched elsewhere in the world. It only remains to stress again that this private law creates a juridical world of free-willing and equal individuals. More than that, it presupposes individual action to bring suits to law. The law is not imposed by the state, *it is invoked* by individuals. Finally, and uniquely until the revival of law in Western Europe in the Middle Ages and later, in the Roman Empire this law empowered individuals to bring government agents and agencies, such as the *fisc*, to court and engage them in a *lis inter partes*, invoking the law as of right, not supplicating as a subject asking grace. It is quite true that the individuals who pursued such a course must only be the wealthy and powerful. Common people could not afford to. But collective groups of them could and did. Citizens could sue their councillors, their councillors could sue the government agencies, villages could sue the governor, and so forth. However limited the practical application, the principle of being able to sue the authorities was and would in the future of Europe come to be of overriding importance, and it represents the greatest, most durable, and far-reaching of all the Roman contributions to the history of government; for in an autocracy—and most of the world most of the time has been and is autocratic—in an autocracy, I repeat, the law and *the law alone* stands between the private individual and the forces of oppression.

As the Western Empire slowly foundered, so its notion of the state, its concept of the nature of law, and much of its substantive content sank from sight. Roman practice ceased. There was—save in a few especial areas—no direct transmission of these matters from one generation to another. But there was a transmission, nevertheless. For all the overwhelming physical witness to Rome—its roads and amphitheatres, its city foundations and their aqueducts, markets, and baths—its legacy, like that of the Greek democracy, or its own Republican period, was ideational. Without it neither Europe, nor after Europe the entire world, could ever have been remotely like it is today.

---

[73] See W. S. Holdsworth, *A History of English Law*, vol. 4 (Methuen, London, 1924), 217–28, 240–52, 289–93.

BIBLIOGRAPHY

AMMIANUS MARCELLINUS, *Rerum Gestarum Historia*, 2 vols. (1591); Loeb edn., ed. and trans. J. C. Rolfe, 3 vols. (Heinemann and Harvard UP, 1935).

ANDERSON, M. S., *Peter the Great* (Thames & Hudson, London, 1978).

ANDREWES, S., *Enlightened Despotism: Readings, Problems and Perspectives in History* (Longmans, London, 1967).

ARIÈS, P., and DUBY, G. (eds.), *A History of Private Life: From Pagan Rome to Byzantium* (Harvard UP, Cambridge, Mass., 1987).

ARISTOTLE, *Nicomachaean Ethics*, trans. D. Ross (The World's Classics; OUP, London, 1966).

—— *The Constitution of Athens and related texts*, trans. with a note by K. Von Fritz and E. Kapp (Hafner Press, New York, 1974).

ARRIAN, *The Campaigns of Alexander*, trans. A. de Selincourt, notes by J. R. Hamilton (Penguin, Harmondsworth, 1971).

BALAZS, E., *Chinese Civilization and Bureaucracy*, ed. A. F. Wright and trans. H. M. Wright (New Haven, Conn., 1964).

BARKER, E. (ed. and trans.), *The Politics of Aristotle*, (Clarendon Press, Oxford, 1946).

BIELENSTEIN, H., *The Bureaucracy of Han Times* (CUP, Cambridge, 1980).

BLOODWORTH, D., *The Chinese Looking-Glass* (Secker & Warburg, London, 1967).

BODDE, D., and MORRIS, C., *Law in Imperial China* (Harvard UP, Cambridge, Mass., 1967).

BRISCOE, J. 'Rome and the Class Struggle in the Greek States 200–146 B.C.', in M. I. Finley (ed.), *Studies in Ancient History*, 53–73.

BRUNT, P. A., *Social Conflicts in the Roman Republics* (Chatto & Windus, London, 1971).

—— *Social Conflicts in the Roman Republic* (corrected edn. Chatto & Windus, London, 1982).

—— *The Fall of the Roman Republic and Related Essays* (Clarendon Press, Oxford, 1988).

—— *Roman Imperial Themes* (Clarendon Press, Oxford, 1990).

—— 'The Roman Mob', in M. I. Finley, *Studies in Ancient Society*, 74–102.

BURCKHARDT, J., *The Age of Constantine the Great*, trans. M. Hadas (first published 1880; 2nd edn., University of California Press, Los Angeles, 1949; paperback edn., Pantheon, London, 1983).

BURKE, E., *Letter to the Electors of Bristol* (1774).

BURN, A. R., *The Living Past of Greece* (Herbert Press, London, 1981).

BURY, J. B., *History of The Later Roman Empire from Arcadius to Irene (395 to 800 A.D.)*, 2 vols. (Dover Publications, New York; repr. 1958).

Cambridge History of China, vol. I (CUP, Cambridge, 1986).

Cambridge Ancient History, vol. 12, *The Imperial Crisis and Recovery A.D. 193–324*, ed. S. A. Cook, F. A. Adcock, M. P. Charlesworth, and N. H. Baynes (CUP, Cambridge, 1939).

Cambridge History of Iran, 2 (Cambridge, 1985).

CARY, M., and SCULLARD, H. H., *A History of Rome*, 3rd edn. (Macmillan, London, 1979).

CASSIRER, E., *The Myth of the State* (Yale UP, New Haven, Conn., 1946).

CASTLE, E. B., *Ancient Education and Today* (Penguin, Harmondsworth, 1961).

CAWKWELL, G., *Xenophon: The Persian Expedition* (Penguin, Harmondsworth, 1972).

CHAN, W.-T., *A Source Book in Chinese Philosophy* (Princeton UP, Princeton, 1963).

CHÜ, T., *Han Social Structure* (University of Washington Press, Seattle, 1972).

COOK, J. M., *The Persian Empire* (Dent, London, 1983).

CORNELL, T., and MATTHEWS, J., *Atlas of the Roman World* (Phaidon, Oxford, 1982).

CRAWFORD, M., *The Roman Republic* (Fontana/Collins, London, 1978).

CREEL, H. G., *The Origins of Statecraft in Ancient China*, vol. 1, *The Western Chou Empire* (University of Chicago Press, Chicago, 1970).

CRONIN, V., *The Last Migration*, ed. R. Hart-Davies (London, 1957).

CULYER YOUNG, Jr., T., 'The Persian Empire', *The New Encyclopaedia Britannica*, 15th edn. (1974, reissued 1979), ix. 829–39.

DANDAMAEV, M. A., and LUKONIN, V. G., *The Culture and Social Institutions of Ancient Iran*, trans. P. L. Kohl and D. J. Dadson (CUP, Cambridge, 1989).

DE SAINTE CROIX, G. E. M., *The Class Struggle in the Ancient Greek World* (Duckworth, London, 1981; paperback edn. 1982).

DILL, S., *Roman Society in the Last Century of the Western Empire* (Macmillan, London, 1898).

DIODORUS SICULUS, *Library of History*, trans. C. H. Oldfather (Loeb edn., London, 1935, repr. 1961).

DOVER, K. J., *Greek Homosexuality* (Random House, New York, 1980).

DRINKWATER, J., 'Patronage in Ancient Gaul and the Problem of the Bacaudae', in A. M. Wallace-Hadrill (ed.), *Patronage in Ancient Society* (1989), 189–203.

DUBS, H. H. (trans. and ed.), *Pan Ku: The History of the Former Han Dynasty*, 3 vols. (Baltimore, 1938–55).

DUDLEY, D., *Roman Society* (Penguin, Harmondsworth, 1975).

DVORNIK, F., *Early Christian and Byzantine Political Philosophy: Origins and Background*, 2 vols. (Washington DC, 1966).

EBERHARD, W., *Conquerors and Rulers: Social Forces in Medieval China* (Brill, Leiden, 1952).

EHRENBERG, V., *From Solon to Socrates*, 2nd edn. (Methuen, London, 1973).

—— *The Greek State*, 2nd edn. (Methuen, London, 1974).

ELLUL, J., *Histoire des Institutions*, vol. 1 (Presses Universitaires de France, Paris, 1955).

ELVIN, M., *The Pattern of the Chinese Past* (Eyre-Methuen, London, 1973).

Encyclopaedia Britannica, 11th edn. (1911); 15th edn. (1974).

FINE, J. V. A., *The Ancient Greeks: A Critical History* (Harvard UP, Cambridge, Mass., 1983).

FINER, S. E., *Comparative Government* (Allen Lane, London, 1970).

—— 'State Building, Boundaries and Border Controls', *Social Science Information*, 13 (415), (1974), 79–126.

—— *Patrons, Clients and the State in the Work of Pareto and at the Present Day* (Proceedings of the Accademia dei Lincei, no. 9; Rome, 1975).

FINLEY, M. I., *Ancient Sicily to the Arab Conquest (A History of Sicily)* (Chatto & Windus, London, 1968).

—— *Aspects of Antiquity*, rev. edn. (Penguin, Harmondsworth, 1977).

—— (ed.), *Studies in Ancient Society* (Routledge &; Kegan Paul, London, 1974; paperback edn., 1978).

—— *Politics in the Ancient World* (CUP, Cambridge, 1983).

—— *The Ancient Economy*, 2nd edn. (Hogarth Press, London, 1985).

FRANK, T., *An Economic Survey of Ancient Rome*, 6 vols. (Pageant Books, NY, 1933–40; repr. Paterson, 1959).

FREEMAN, E. A., *History of Federal Government from the Foundation of the Achaian League to the Disruption of the United States*, vol. 1, *General Introduction: History of the Greek Federations* (Macmillan, London, 1863).

GALE, E., *Discourses on Salt and Iron: A Debate on State Control of Commerce and Industry in Ancient China* (Brill, Leiden, 1931).

GELZER, M., *The Roman Nobility* (Blackwell, Oxford, 1969).

GERNET, J., *A History of Chinese Civilization*, trans. J. Foster (CUP, Cambridge, 1982).

GHIRSHMAN, R., *Iran* (Penguin: Harmondsworth, 1954).

GIBBON, E., *The Decline and Fall of the Roman Empire* (David Campbell, London, 1993–4).

GRANET, M., *The Religion of the Chinese People*, trans., ed., and introduction by M. Freedman (Blackwell, Oxford, 1975).

GREENIDGE, A. H. J., *Roman Public Life* (Macmillan, London, 1930).

HAMILTON, A., MADISON, J., JAY, J., *The Federalist Papers* (Penguin Classics, Harmondsworth, 1987).

HAMMOND, N. G. L., *A History of Greece to 332 B.C.*, 2nd edn. (OUP, Oxford, 1967).

HANSEN, H. M., *The Athenian Democracy in the Age of Demosthenes* (Blackwell, Oxford, 1991).

HAWKES, D., *The Songs of the South: Poems by Qu Yuan and Other Poets* (Penguin, Harmondsworth, 1985).

HEGEL, G. W. F., *Lectures on the Philosophy of History*, trans. J. Sibree (Bell & Daldy, London, 1872).

HERODOTUS, *The History*, transl. G. Rawlinson, 2 vols. (Everyman edn.; Dent, London, 1940).

HINZ, W., 'Achämendische Hofverwaltung', *Zeitschrift für Assyriologie*, 61 (1971), 260–311.

HIRSCHMAN, A. O., *Exit, Voice, and Loyalty: Responses to Decline in Firms, Organizations and State* (Harvard UP, Cambridge, Mass. and London, 1970).

HOLDEN, B., *The Nature of Democracy* (Nelson, London, 1974).

HOLDSWORTH, W. S., *A History of English Law*, vol. IV (Methuen, London, 1924).

HOPKINS, K., *Conquerors and Slaves* (CUP, Cambridge, 1978).

—— 'Taxes and Trade in the Roman Empire, 200 BC/AD 400', *Journal of Roman Studies*, 70 (1980), 101–25.

—— *Death and Renewal, Sociological Studies in Roman History*, 2 (CUP, Cambridge, 1983).

HORNBLOWER, S., *Mausolus* (Clarendon Press, Oxford, 1982).

—— *The Greek World*, 479–323 BC (Methuen, London, 1983).

HSIAO, K.-C., *A History of Chinese Political Thought*, vol. 1, *From the Beginnings to the 6th Century AD*, trans. F. W. N. Mote (Princeton UP, Princeton, 1979).

HSU, C.-Y., *Ancient China in Transition: An Analysis of Social Mobility, 722–222 BC* (Stanford UP, Stanford, 1965).

HULSEWÉ, A. F. P., *Remnants of Ch'in Law: An Annotated Translation of the Ch'in Legal and Administrative Rules of the Third century BC, Discovered in Yün-Meng Prefecture, Hu-Pei Province, in 1975* (Brill, Leiden, 1985).

JEFFREY, L. M., *Archaic Greece: The City-States, c.700–800 B.C.* (London, 1976).

JOLOWICZ, H. F,. and NICHOLAS, B., *Historical Introduction to the Study of Roman Law*, 3rd edn. (CUP, Cambridge, 1972).

JONES, A. H. M., *The Decline of the Ancient World* (Longman, London, 1966).

—— *Athenian Democracy* (OUP, Oxford, 1960; repr. 1969).

—— *The Later Roman Empire, 284–602*, 2 vols. (Blackwell, Oxford, 1964; repr. 1973).

—— *The Roman Economy* (Blackwell, Oxford, 1974).

JOSEPHUS, *The Jewish War* (Penguin, Harmondsworth, 1959).

JUSTINIAN, I, *Digesta* ('English Selections', Penguin Classics, Harmondsworth, 1979).

KIERMANN, F. A., and FAIRBANK, J. K. (eds.), *Chinese Ways in Warfare* (Harvard UP, Cambridge, Mass., 1974).

KENT, R. G. (ed.), *Old Persian: Texts* (Yale UP, New Haven, Conn., 1950).

KUNKEL, W., *An Introduction to Roman Legal and Constitutional History*, trans. J. M. Kelly (Clarendon Press, Oxford, 1966; repr. 1975).

LARSEN, J. A. O., *Representative Government in Greek and Roman History* (University of California Press, Berkeley, 1955).

—— *Greek Federal States* (Clarendon Press, Oxford, 1961; repr. 1967, 1968).

LEVI, P., *Atlas of the Greek World* (OUP, Oxford, 1980).

LEVINSON, J. R., *Confucian China and its Modern Fate: A Trilogy* (University of California Press, Los Angeles, 1964).

LEWIS, D. M., *Sparta and Persia* (Brill, Leiden, 1977).

LEWIS, N., and REINHOLD, M., *Roman Civilization, Sourcebook*, vol. 1, *The Republic*, vol. 2, *The Empire* (Harper, New York, 1966).

Li Chi (The Book of Rites or 'Records of Rituals': being the fourth of the so-called Five Confucian Classics).

LI, Y.-N. (ed.), *The First Emperor of China* (White Plains, New York, 1975).

LIJPHART, A., *Democracy in Plural Societies* (Yale UP, Ithaca, Conn., 1977).

LIU HSIANG (attributed to), *'Chan Kuo Ts'e' or 'The Intrigues of the Warring States'*, trans. J. I. Crump, 2nd rev. edn. (Chinese Materials Centre, San Francisco 1979).

LIVY, *History of Rome* (Penguin Classics, Harmondsworth, 1960; repr. 1971).

LOEWE, M., 'The Campaigns of the Han Wu-Ti', in Kiermann and Fairbank (eds.), *Chinese Ways in Warfare*, 67–122.

—— *Records of Han Administration*, 2 vols. (CUP, Cambridge, 1974).

MATTHEWS, J., *Western Aristocracies and the Imperial Court, AD 364–425* (Clarendon Press, Oxford, 1975).

MEYER, E., 'Persian Empire, History of' (in part), *Encyclopaedia Britannica*, 11th edn. (1911), xxi. 202–24.

MILLAR, F., 'The Political Character of the Classical Roman Republic, 200–151 BC', *Journal of Roman Studies*, 74 (1984), 1–19.

—— 'Political Power in Mid-Republican Rome: *Curia* or *Comitia?*': Review Article, *Journal of Roman Studies*, 79 (1989), 138–50.

MOMMSEN, T., *The History of Rome*, trans. W. P. Dickson, 4 vols. (Dent, London, 1911).

MURRAY, O., *Early Greece* (Fontana, London, 1980).

NICHOLAS, B., *An Introduction to Roman Law* (Clarendon Press, Oxford, 1962).

NICOLET, C., *Rome et la conquête du monde mediterranéen*, vol. 1, *Les structures de l'Italie Romaine*, 2nd edn. (Presses Universitaires de France, Paris 1979).

—— *The World of the Citizen in Republican Rome*, trans. P. S. Falla (Batsford Academic & Educational Ltd., London, 1980).

NILSSON, M. P., *Imperial Rome* (Schoeken Books, New York, 1926).

PASCAL, B., *Pensées* (Dent, London, 1932).

PLINY, *The Letters of the Younger Pliny*, trans. B. Radice (Penguin, Harmondsworth, 1963).

PLUTARCH, *Lives*, trans. Dryden (Dent, London, 1948; rev. edn. Everyman, 1973).

OLMSTEAD, A. T., *History of Assyria* (University of Chicago Press, Chicago, 1923; repr. Midway, 1975).

REISCHAUER, E. O., and FAIRBANK, J. K., *East Asia: The Great Tradition*, vol. 1 (Modern Asia Edition; Houghton Mifflin, Boston, 1960).

RENAULT, M., *The Last of the Wine* (Longman, London, 1956).

RHODES, P. J., *The Athenian Boulé* (OUP, Oxford, 1972).

ROSTOVSTEFF, M., *History of the Ancient World*, 2 vols. (Clarendon Press, Oxford, 1928).

SCHULZ, F., *Principles of Roman Law* (OUP, Oxford, 1936).

SHERWIN-WHITE, A. N., 'Why Were the Early Christians Persecuted? An Amendment', in Finley (ed.) *Studies in Ancient Society*, 250–5.

SIDGWICK, H., *The Development of the European Polity*, 1st edn. (Macmillan, London, 1903).

SNODGRASS, A., *Archaic Greece* (Dent, London, 1980).

SSU-MA CH'IEN, *Records of the Grand Historian of China*, trans. from the *Shih Chih* by Burton Watson (Columbia UP, New York, 1961).

—— *The Shih Chih*, trans. Chavannes (1897).

STARR, C. G., *The Roman Empire, 27 BC–AD 476* (OUP, Oxford, 1982).

STEIN, P., *Legal Institutions: The Development of Dispute Settlement* (Butterworth, London, 1984).

SUETONIUS, *The Twelve Caesars*, trans. R. Graves (Penguin, Harmondsworth, 1979).

SYME, R., *The Roman Revolution* (OUP, Oxford, 1939; paperback edn., 1960).

TACITUS, *The Annals and The Histories* (Sadler and Brown, Chalfont St Giles, 1966).

TAYLOR, L. R., *Party Politics in the Age of Caesar* (University of California Press, Berkeley and Los Angeles, 1961).

THOMPSON, E. A., 'Peasant Revolts in Late Roman Gaul and Spain', in Finley (ed.) *Studies in Ancient Society*, 304–20.

THUCYDIDES, *The History of Peloponnesian War*, the Text of Arnold, with his argument (John Henry Parker, Oxford and London, 1850).

TILLY, C. (ed.), *The Formation of National States in Western Europe* (Princeton UP, Princeton, 1975).

TOYNBEE, A., *A Study of History*, 10 vols. (OUP, Oxford, 1934–54), vol. vii.

UNESCO Yearbook, 1990.

VIRGIL, *The Aeneid*, with notes by R. Sowerby (Longman, Harlow, 1984).

WALBANK, F. W., *The Awful Revolution: The Decline of the Roman Empire in the West* (Liverpool UP, Liverpool, 1969; repr. 1978).

WANG, Y-C., 'An Outline of the External Government of the Former Han Dynasty', *Harvard Journal of Asiatic Studies*, 12 (1949), 134–87.

WEBER, M., *The Religion of China*, trans. H. H. Gerth, with an Introduction by C. K. Yang (Collier-Macmillan, Glencoe, Ill., 1951).

WELLS, C., *The Roman Empire* (Fontana, London, 1984).

WHEATLEY, P., *The Pivot of the Four Quarters* (Edinburgh UP, Edinburgh, 1971).

XENOPHON, *Hellenica* ('*A History of My Times*'), transl. R. Warner, with introduction and notes by G. Cawkwell (Penguin, Harmondsworth, 1981).

—— *The Cyropaedia*, trans. W. Miller (Heinemann, London, 1914).